Romantic
Revolutionary

ROBERT A. ROSENSTONE

Romantic Revolutionary

A BIOGRAPHY OF JOHN REED

VINTAGE BOOKS
A DIVISION OF RANDOM HOUSE
NEW YORK

First Vintage Books Edition, December 1981
Copyright © 1975 by Robert A. Rosenstone
All rights reserved under International and Pan-American
Copyright Conventions. Published in the United States by
Random House, Inc., New York, and simultaneously in Canada
by Random House of Canada Limited, Toronto. Originally
published by Alfred A. Knopf, Inc., New York, in
September 1975.

Library of Congress Cataloging in Publication Data
Rosenstone, Robert A.
Romantic revolutionary
Reprint. Originally published: New York: Knopf, 1975.

Bibliography: p.
Includes index.
1. Reed, John, 1887-1920.
2. Socialists—United States—Biography.
I. Title.
HX84.R4R67   1981   070'.92'4 [B]   81-11547
ISBN 0-394-75123-X   AACR2

Manufactured in the United States of America

Front cover photo of John Reed, courtesy of Culver Pictures
Front cover photo of Kremlin, courtesy of The Bettmann Archive, Inc.

For Cheri—

you taught me
love is work is love

Contents

Illustrations

Preface

Since a book speaks for itself, I will not indulge here in elaborate explanations of what is to come, but only share a few thoughts to help guide the reader. Because John Reed was a prolific writer, and a man of strong convictions about artistic, social and political problems, the pages of this work are filled with the development of his attitudes. Without necessarily sharing such ideas, I have tried to explain how—within the context of his experiences—they made sense to him. To avoid interrupting the narrative, I let the ideas emerge from discussions of his work and actions; the careful reader should have no difficulty separating Reed's opinions from my occasional comments upon them.

Believing a biography should capture the tenor and feeling as well as the factual truth of a man's life, I have tried to give a picture of Reed's emotional life, but have not imposed any full-blown psychological theory upon his development. My own understanding of how and why men act is involved here, and this in turn is an amalgam of my own experience and of reading about and reflecting upon the human condition. To the best of my knowledge, I have indulged in no wild guesses or outright fantasies, and his states of mind are all logically inferred from the notes, letters, articles, fiction and poetry produced in any given period.

Some readers may be surprised by my casual use of first names or even nicknames for historical personages. To me they seem an inevitable part of a work which deals with a generation of people who were delightfully informal in their own behavior. After reading their letters and memoirs, I came to believe that the use of surnames alone would violate the spirit of their lives, and I think they would agree. Frankly, it is hard to believe that John Reed would want to be remembered as "Reed" rather than "Jack."

One final note of caution: Readers who expect to learn, in some larger sense, what John Reed's life "means," or what his life says about America as a society, will have to invest their own intellect and imagination in what follows. In the last chapter I do suggest some ideas which occur to me, but this is not an attempt to sum up the entire "meaning" of his thirty-three years. Researching and then writing this work was a deep learning process, one that left me with the conviction that a man's life "is" rather than "means." Of course we do give meaning to the lives of others, hence the interest in biography and history, and also in fiction. Like the novelist who creates a world and its characters, I have attempted to re-create the world of John Reed, and as the novelist embodies his values in that world, so have I embodied my own in this narrative. They are there in my choice of subject, in many of the critical attitudes I obviously share with Reed and his friends, in my approval of people who wish to experiment with life, in my admiration for many of Reed's actions and my dismay that he could not be a more caring human being. But as the novelist knows that readers will impose their own interpretations upon his world, so I expect readers to see Reed and his generation through a lens of their own interests and values. If the act of writing history is a dialogue between the individual and the past, then that of reading history should be the same.

Although my name alone appears as author, and although ultimately I am responsible for its contents, this book is a cooperative enterprise, a result of many individuals who have touched me over the years. Naming them all would be to indulge needlessly in autobiography; so, with a general thank-you to everyone who has provided encouragement, let me specifically cite those who have helped bring this work to fruition.

Most necessary to the researcher is the librarian, and those of the Millikan Library of the California Institute of Technology who have proved themselves indispensable on this project include Elizabeth Dilworth, Sophia Yen, Don MacNamee, Erma Wheatley and Ruth Bowen. While all the librarians of the collections mentioned in the bibliography have been helpful, Carolyn Jakeman and Joseph McCarthy of the Houghton Library, Harvard University; Sarah McCain of the George Arents Research Library, Syracuse University; and Arthur Spencer of the Oregon Historical Society went out of their way to provide aid, suggestions and hospitality. Helping me to work in libraries and collections, I have at times had the assistance of Chuck Slosser, Roger Chretien, William Crowley and Jeffrey Blair, all of whom were capable and diligent.

For financial support my gratitude goes to the Research Committee of the Division of the Humanities and Social Sciences at the California Institute of Technology, which provided an Old Dominion Fund grant that enabled me to devote an entire year to research, paid for my assistants and underwrote journeys to both Portland, Oregon, and the Soviet Union. A grant from the American Philosophical Society helped to cover travel expenses to Cambridge, New York and Washington, D.C.

Information and useful suggestions came from a number of other people working on overlapping topics, including Justin Kaplan, Julia O. Bibbins, William Greene, Virginia Marberry, Lee Lowenfish, Herbert Shapiro, Ronald Steel and Edwin Bingham. Among those people who knew Reed and generously consented to be interviewed either in person or by letter are Carl Binger, Andrew Dasburg, Lesley Miller and Frances Nelson Carroll. Granville Hicks not only gave an afternoon of his time, but encouraged me to go ahead with a project that clearly intruded on ground he had already covered. Through their generosity, the Reed family added immeasurably to this book; I wish to thank Mrs. Pauline Reed for interviews and Helen and John Reed for opening both their family files and their home to me, for their continuing support and interest, and for in no way trying to influence my interpretation of family events.

One of the unique pleasures involved with this project was the opportunity it provided for contact with citizens of the Soviet Union. Historians Victor Malkov and Abel Startsev of the American History Section of the U.S.S.R. Academy of Sciences provided leads, while Boris Gilenson went out of his way to send me materials that appeared in Soviet publications and helped me to secure copies of documents from Professor Alexander A. Soloviev, Chief of Archives at the Institute of Marxism-Leninism in Moscow.* My distant relative Bertram Aranovich not only served in the important role of guide to Moscow, but also stood by to aid in the search for material at the Lenin Library. Galina Moller of Caltech far surpassed

* Previously unused Russian documents are detailed in the Bibliography, pages 411-30.

the normal courtesies due a colleague in her lengthy synopses and translations of materials from Russian.

While many friends and colleagues patiently listened to my continual questions and theories about radicalism, history, social change, art, Bohemia, literature and personality development over the last four years, several undertook the burdensome task of reading the manuscript and making lengthy critiques. For these efforts and for their friendship, I am indebted to Robert A. Huttenback, Daniel J. Kevles, Richard A. Hertz and Louis Breger. While they should not be blamed for any of its mistakes, their comments certainly saved the book from exhibiting even more historical or stylistic blunders than it now contains.

At the conclusion of composition, others take over, but my debts to secretaries long predate the final draft. Margy Robison devoted herself to this project, Joy Hansen and Rita Pierson helped in numerous ways and Edith Taylor's strong dedication, startling skills of speed and accuracy, and ability to keep track of elusive details all were important factors in bringing the work to completion. My deepest thanks also go to Harold Strauss and Ashbel Green of Alfred A. Knopf, who have not only treated me like a human being rather than a commodity, but also shown me that editing can be a creative art.

Finally, there are some gifts both immense and ineffable which underlie my work. In many deep ways, Joseph Boskin has contributed to this book. From my father, with his longings for a son who could be a writer and articulate the dreams that he could never put into words, and from my mother, who always found meaning and romance in history, I received enough love and support to last a lifetime. And from Cheri I learned that when all the words are done, it is the truth of the meanings beyond them that makes life worthwhile.

ROBERT A. ROSENSTONE

Hollywood, California
February 1974

Romantic
Revolutionary

1

The Legend

"Though he is only in his middle twenties and but five years out of Harvard, there is a legend of John Reed. It began, as I remember, when he proved himself to be the most inspired song and cheer leader that the football crowd had had for many days. At first there was nothing to recommend him but his cheek. That was supreme. He would stand up alone before a few thousand undergraduates and demonstrate without a quiver of self-consciousness just how a cheer should be given. If he didn't like the way his instructions were followed he cursed at the crowd, he bullied it, sneered at it. But he always captured it. It was a sensational triumph. . . .

"Even as an undergraduate he betrayed what many people believe to be the central passion of his life, an inordinate desire to be arrested. He spent a brief vacation in Europe and experimented with the jails of England, France and Spain. . . . The next incident took place during the Paterson strike. Reed was in town less than twenty-four hours before the police had him in custody. He capped his arrest by staging the Paterson strike pageant in Madison Square Garden, and then left for Europe to live in a Florentine villa, where he was said to be hobnobbing with the illegitimate son of Oscar Wilde. . . . He made speeches to Italian syndicalists and appointed himself to carry the greetings of the American labor movement to their foreign comrades. He bathed in a fountain designed by Michelangelo. . . . He tried high romance in Provence. One night, so he says, he wrestled with a ghost in a haunted house, and was thrown out of bed. . . .

"By temperament he is not a professional writer or reporter. He is a person who enjoys himself. Revolution, literature, poetry, they are only things which hold him at times, incidents merely of his living. Now and then he finds adventure by imagining it, oftener he transforms his own experience. He is one of those people who treat as serious possibilities such stock fantasies as shipping before the mast, rescuing women, hunting lions, or trying to fly around the world in an aeroplane. He is the only fellow I know who gets himself pursued by men with revolvers, who is always once more just about to ruin himself.

"I can't think of a form of disaster which John Reed hasn't tried and enjoyed. . . . He is many men at once, and those who have tried to bank on some phase of him, to regard him as a writer, a correspondent, a poet, a revolutionist, or a lover, lose him. There is no line between the play of his fancy and his responsibility to fact; he is for the time the person he imagines himself to be. . . ."[1]

WALTER LIPPMANN, 1914

"John Reed was one of those epic characters who arise in times of transition, when laws and traditions have begun to break down under the stress of economic change and when it is necessary for individuals to make new laws for themselves and to rely on their own powers. In the United States, which has, of all countries, least felt the touch of this period of worldwide change, John Reed seemed a romantic figure, a hero out of a fairy tale background. We have as yet no sufficiently heroic tasks for such persons to perform, and we customarily put them in jail when they appear alarmingly upon our scene. . . ."[2]

FLOYD DELL, 1920

"When John Reed came, big and growing, handsome outside and beautiful inside, when that boy came down from Cambridge to New York, it seemed to me that I had never seen anything so near to pure joy. No ray of sunshine, no drop of foam, no young animal, bird or fish, and no star, was as happy as that boy was. If only we could keep him so, we might have a poet at last who would see and sing nothing but joy. Convictions were what I was afraid of. I tried to steer him away from convictions, that he might play; that he might play with life; and see it all, live it all; tell it all; that he might be it all; but all, not any one thing. And why not? A poet is more revolutionary than any radical."[3]

LINCOLN STEFFENS, 1920

"John Reed lived true to himself. He came nearer being honest than any man I have ever known. . . . He was big and brisk and breezy, with the body and mind of a man who could fight, and the temperament of a knight of romance. He . . . dressed carelessly, talked freely, laughed when the joke was on him, worked hard, loafed hard, tried everything once. He was a born non-conformer. . . .

"I recall Jack Reed's fundamental humanity, his spontaneous, un-calculating kindnesses, his generous strong hand. Yet neither generosity nor sympathy seemed to me his dominant characteristic. They were both part of something, some light, that was central in him. It was not the customary 'inner light' conscience. Reed was seldom bothered by ortho-dox conscience. He could be a law unto himself. What moved him was the revolutionary's faith in himself, and the equally revolutionary faith in human dignity and potentiality. There is something unhallowed in such a faith. People resent it. Jack Reed was forever being talked about. . . . He liked friends and their applause, but when they failed to see his light or failed to follow it he went his way blithely, surely, reckless of safety, reputation, comfort, possessions. . . ."[4]

ROBERT HALLOWELL, 1920

"Whom the gods love, die fighting! and the gods, being human in their birth, loved Jack. He was a robustious son of Oregon, a tender son of Tom Paine. He was a poet and cheerleader, a humorist and Bolshevik. He was an author of force; but his true genius . . . was in his life."[5]

EDWIN JUSTUS MAYER, 1923

"Poetry to Reed was not only a matter of writing words but of living life. We were carrying realism so far in those days that it walked us right out of our books. We had a certain scorn of books. Jack Reed did especially. His comradeship with Louise Bryant was based on a joint determination to smash through the hulls of custom and tradition and all polite and proper forms of behavior, and touch at all times and all over the earth the raw current of life. It was a companionship in what philistines call adventure, a kind of gypsy compact. And that will to live, to be themselves in the world, and be real, and be honest, and taste the whole tang of it, was more to them than any writing. It was more to them than any particular practical undertaking, even a revolution. It was as though they had agreed to inscribe at least two audacious, deep, and real lives in the book of time and let the gods call it poetry."[6]

MAX EASTMAN, 1936

"Restless and resistless, he was an idealist who combined boisterous humor and a quiet passion for truth. Others have depicted him as a fighter dedicated to oppose old systems, old morals, old prejudices. But I remember him chiefly as the invincible romantic, the poet-satirist formed into action by the stupidity even more than by the inhumanity of man. . . .

"Dead for more than forty years, Jack remains in my mind as the most vivid figure of the period . . . the exuberant champion of a day to come when it will be possible for poets to challenge and perhaps change the world with their vision."[7]

LOUIS UNTERMEYER, 1965

2

Portland

"Once in a far country, on the shore of the Western Ocean, lived a little boy named Will. Out of the sea he came one stormy night, lashed to a spar, and cast high on the beach below old Hebe Twiller's cottage. Hebe was a sour, silent man, always alone since his wife had died, so therefore the village gossips were utterly amazed when he suddenly adopted the homeless little wanderer. . . .

"The village stood between two high mountain capes, overlooking a sheltered bay where the lazy fishing boats rocked in the long ocean swells. Behind, dense forest stretched away into the far mountains where the sun came every morning, and one could stand in the narrow street and see the far endless blue where the tired sun went down every evening.

"As Will grew older he wandered about in the woods, hearing strange sounds that no one else heard. He used to get up before dawn sometimes and walk with bare, cool feet up the brown road that connected his home with the big busy world. Then he seemed to hear the *woods and earth and sea singing to the sky, and dreamed dreams of cities and palaces, and of the shining knights like those who had once ridden past his door bound for the wars. . . .*

"Once a week the post-rider clattered into town on a great roan horse, carelessly tossing the mail-sacks to the carrier. Will admired him immensely for the regal grace with which he tossed off a foaming mug of the inn-keeper's ale, his brown beard shining with tiny drops. Once he spoke to Will, a cheery 'Hello, my fine young rooster!' and Will questioned him suddenly and eagerly. Was the world big and splendid? Were there lots of fine, strong men like him out there? He waved a vague hand toward the East. The post-rider laughed, evidently pleased. 'Come and see,' he said. 'Some day we'll need you, young rooster, out there!' He spurred his horse. 'Come some day and see!' he shouted back over his shoulder, and vanished behind the trees. Will stood a long time in the road, dreaming after him.

"Spring came and went, and summer burst suddenly upon the fisher-folk. Will was now big and strong. All day he worked at his father's salmon nets. . . . At night he usually came home worn out, and tumbled into his cot at once; but sometimes he lay awake thinking, and the more he thought the more he began to be restless and disgusted with his life. People did not understand him. The other boys worked and ate and slept like young animals, but Will was silent and solitary; his comrades distrusted and often feared him, for the unearthly look in his eyes. 'Crazy Will' they called him. Some of the older folk hinted that he was in league with the devil, for had not Goodwife Muller seen him walking alone on the mountain-trail, talking aloud to thin air? Even old Hebe himself tried to draw out his adopted son, but retreated in disgust at Will's tales. Voices and singing in the woods—maidens laughing in the breakers—absurd! . . .

"Finally the boy determined not to stand it any longer. Out there— in the shining cities—they would understand him. He made up his mind to leave home one night, and so, just before dawn, he slipped from the cottage and took the brown road into the pines. The old music was there, singing in his blood of victories and glory which were to come to him in the East. As he passed the last house Will turned and waved his hand to the old sea, and then the dusk of the pines swallowed him. . . ."[1]

An outcast, an orphan, a stranger lost from some other time, some other place—this feeling about his hometown, his childhood, was so much a part of John Reed that in a prolific career of writing, these few brief paragraphs were the only ones about youth that he ever published. They are enough to explain why there were not more. A dreamer, a child full of wild fantasies, he had always felt different from other youngsters. For years the attitude was half-conscious. It surfaced in a vague discontent, the feeling of being separate and alone, the longing to escape to other worlds. Only at the age of twenty-one, away at college and already following his own road, could he stop to articulate in fiction the loneliness that had shaped him. One brief backward glance was enough. Youth was a period he did not care to relive. Reeking of half-forgotten memories and painful emotions, the short story could only suggest the dimensions of his early alienation.

Like Will, Reed was raised in a community not prepared to understand his dreams. Portland, Oregon, where he was born in 1887, was hardly beyond the frontier stage, yet its leaders were already beginning to proclaim that they had achieved an ideal, a city that was sober, public-spirited and virtuous. In public life, the businessmen who controlled the community upheld the stern and frugal virtues of their New England ancestors. For them work was life and life was work. The poetry they knew was confined to the Bible, music to the plain and simple hymns of Protestant churches, imagination to the opportunities for economic development of the abundant Northwest. Conservative in politics, suspicious of gaiety and color, they were hostile to deviance from traditional norms in behavior or social theory. Their self-image was enunciated in an official history which sang the virtues of the city fathers, "staid residents . . . of a morality, religious conviction and force of character not exceeded by any class in America."[2]

Despite such claims, there was another side to Portland life. The harbor was crowded with sailing vessels that carried Oregon wheat, flour, fruits, salmon and timber to ports in China, England, Australia and India. Near the docks was an area of bars and ramshackle hotels where foreign sailors mingled with a variety of tough frontier types—leathery cowboys just off the range, grizzled miners hoping for a stake, lumberjacks with a fistful of change, prostitutes, cardsharps and con men. Here there was heavy drinking, feverish gambling, brawls and jaunts to opium dens. Intimately connected to the city's economy, such activities were officially deplored as "without purpose, unguided by principle, reckless of money and health, and even destructive to life," and city leaders piously hoped that as men built homes and churches, there would be more restraint of their "appetites."[3]

Nestled in the lush valley of the broad Willamette, with the peaks of Mount Hood, Mount St. Helens and Mount Adams visible in the distance, Portland sprawled across the river. Until the first bridge was built late in the 1880s, ferries joined its two halves, the undeveloped east of shacks and muddy roads and the more important west, already plotted into a no-nonsense gridiron of streets. Close to the western wharves centering on Front Street clustered stores and office buildings. South of downtown, woolen factories and lumber mills blocked access to the water, while north, toward the junction with the Columbia, grain elevators and warehouses dominated the skyline. West of the business district the land rose slowly. Commercial establishments faded into a region of small frame houses, then larger ones set amid many overgrown empty tracts. Around Sixteenth Street began the curlecued wooden mansions of the town fathers, often hidden from sight by elaborate landscaping. Beyond were meadows and small vegetable farms, watered by creeks; then the land climbed sharply into tree-clad hills. At the top of B Street, above groves of ash and willow, on the highest point in town, was a five-acre estate with a mansion known as Cedar Hill, constructed by Henry D. Green, John Reed's grandfather.

A highly successful pioneer capitalist, Green was courtly and elegant, a commanding figure whose life was touched with a kind of romance that would still appeal to the imagination of his grandson when he was a committed radical. At the age of thirty, Reed would write, "All that remains to me of my grandfather is his majestic height, his long slim fingers, and the polished courtesy of his manners." Yet Green had died two years before John's birth, and such comments only reflected the lingering impact of a powerful individual who had seemed to live with taste, gusto and enthusiasm. Reed proudly reported, "He had come around the Horn in a sailing ship when the West Coast was the wild frontier, made his pile and lived with Russian lavishness. Portland was less than thirty years old, a little town carved out of the Oregon forests, with streets deep in mud and the wilderness coming down close around it. Through this my grandfather drove his blooded horses to his smart carriages, imported from the East—and from Europe—with liveried coachmen and footmen on the box!"[4]

This picture of Green's life was not far from the truth. In 1853, at the age of twenty-eight, he cut loose from a community in western New York to seek his fortune. Sailing to Oregon, he entered a partnership with his older brother, John, and another associate in an Astoria mercantile house that competed for Indian fur trade with the Hudson Bay Company post at the mouth of the Columbia River. Soon the brothers had enough capital to transfer their scene of operations to Portland, only a decade old. Shrewd enough both to seize opportunities and to create them, the Greens prospered, their fortunes based largely upon city utilities. Henry married in 1862, fathered four children and personally supervised the design, construction and landscaping of Cedar Hill, the "pride of the city."[5] Even so, the longings for adventure that had driven him West were somehow not fulfilled. A society increasingly structured, safe and status-conscious made him feel uncomfortable. Entertaining in his elegant home, puttering with exotic hothouse plants and riding fiery horses did not fill the void. Outwardly he upheld all common notions of decency and propriety, but in private Green turned increasingly to drink. He had lived the American dream, going West, making a fortune, growing up with the country, helping to spread civilization. The end result was a society where conformity was valued higher than youthful adventurousness. The ironic lesson here somehow carried first to his sons, then to his grandson John. All three descendants would be driven toward a scattered, rootless existence, as if instinctively knowing that the demands of a settled community could trap a man in strong and subtle ways.

When Henry Green died unexpectedly of "congestive chills" on a business trip to New York in 1885, he was eulogized in a lengthy *Oregonian* editorial as "one of the foremost men in our public affairs," and lauded less for riches than for his taste, poise, friendship and charity, for being "a man who rose to wealth without resorting to oppression and one whose courage was equalled by his modesty."[6] He left an estate valued at $330,000, his good reputation as a man of status and probity, his children, the showplace home and his widow, who would consider John Reed "the favorite of all my grandchildren." Also a native of New York, Charlotte Jones Green had come to Oregon with her brother via the Isthmus of Panama in 1859 at the age of twenty-one. During Henry's lifetime, while raising two boys and two girls, she had shown a spirited side in her expansive way of life. Emulating upper-class Eastern relatives, Mrs. Green sent her daughters to a finishing school in New York at a time when good Portland girls stayed home to learn how to bake and sew. She also enjoyed entertaining lavishly at Cedar Hill, and took great pride in her carriage and liveried coachmen, the first such outfit to be seen on Portland's muddy streets.

Charlotte's behavior became more venturesome after her husband's death. In an age that considered women weak, frail and unable to fend for themselves, she undertook voyages to far-off countries like Japan and China and the Biblical lands of the Middle East. At home she refused to act the gloomy role of bereaved widow, stepped up the tempo of entertainment at Cedar Hill and became the town's acknowledged "social queen."[7] Years later her grandson well remembered the boisterous parties: "The lawn terrace below the house was surrounded on three sides by great fir trees, up whose sides ran gas-pipes grown over with bark; on summer evenings canvas was laid on the turf, and people danced, illuminated by flaming jets of gas which seemed to spout from the trees. There was something fantastic in all that. . . ." When it was too cold or damp for dancing outside, the third-floor ballroom was crowded with people eating, drinking and laughing into the early hours of the morning. Shocking to the staid elements of Portland, such parties were even more so because the exuberant Mrs. Green's guest list was broad. At her home bankers and industrialists mixed with shopkeepers and schoolteachers. Yet, no matter how such gatherings might offend the community's sense of decorum and class propriety, nobody was ever known to refuse an invitation to Cedar Hill.

Shortly after Henry Green's death, both his daughters were married, Katherine to an army officer who was soon transferred East, and twenty-two-year-old Margaret to a businessman, C. J. Reed. A well-bred young lady with a good deal of intelligence, Margaret possessed some of the charm of her parents but almost none of their individualism. Finishing school had given her a dilettante's interest in music, books and the "finer things," but it had also strengthened a sense of class; years after he had become a social and political radical she would still be urging John to spend more time getting to know "the better sort" of people, and she would object to his radical friends on the grounds of their ill manners, foreign backgrounds and lack of breeding rather than because of their revolutionary politics. Occasionally she referred to herself as a "rebel," but Margaret's tentative noncomformist streak emerged only in peripheral ways; later in life she was one of the first women in Portland to smoke in public.

Charles Jerome Reed—always known as "C.J."—was in 1886 a comer on the Portland commercial scene. His move to the coast was typical of a later generation than Henry Green's, less an adventurous search for riches than a matter of practical business. Born in 1855 and educated through high school in Auburn, New York, Reed was sent West by D. M. Osborne and Company to supervise the sale of agricultural machinery throughout the entire Northwest. He was outgoing and likable, a man blessed by a quick mind and a quicker wit who was soon embraced by the business establishment. A few years after marrying the popular Margaret Green, he was asked to join the Arlington Club, described in the *Portland Blue Book* as the "most aristocratic" in the town. Twice elected to the organization's board of directors and once to the post of first vice-president, C.J. achieved prominence on the basis of personality rather than position. He specialized in sallies that punctured the sobriety of fellow members and became a center of attention at the daily luncheon table. From there his fame spread until the *Spectator*, the local "society" newspaper, rhapsodized over his talents:

> Humor oozes out of him. Stage humorists copy his walk. . . . Minstrels used to try to imitate his smile. But they failed. His smile is inimitable. When he is stringing a victim Mr. Reed's face wears an expression which Bret Harte borrowed and fastened on the innocent features of his immortal Ah Sin. . . . Neither age nor position nor dignity saves Mr. Reed's friends from his humor.[8]

The wit that made him well-known also made him feared. Famous enough to be taken into San Francisco's Bohemian Club, noted for its ribaldry and hi-jinks from coast to coast, C.J. was resented by many of the same local associates who bragged of his accomplishments. Perhaps they sensed that beneath his humor lurked contempt. Reed longed for the "refinement & higher ideas of an older & more conservative civilization," and he would once write: "I have not in twenty-five years of residence on the Pacific Coast become tolerant of the rawness and crudity of the West. . . ."[9] Never fully at home, he used wit as an acceptable way to express scorn for the pretensions of Portland's business class. It represented the distaste of the cultured man for a society that boasted no higher ideal than the pursuit of wealth.

When John was born on October 22, 1887, less than a year after his parents' marriage, the Reeds were living with Mrs. Green. His earliest view of life was from the grounds of the "lordly, gray mansion with its immense park, its formal gardens, lawns, stables, greenhouses and glass grape-arbor." From here he could look down at a panorama of roofs, green lawns and church spires, with the curving river beyond, and mountain peaks floating in the distance. Being raised at Cedar Hill meant a special kind of life. From the earliest days John was watched over and cared for by nurses, who kept him neat, tidy and out of any mischief. Playmates were confined to his brother, Harry, two years his junior, or to youngsters from those families wealthy enough to live in the exclusive West End. This meant that for years he was sheltered from the town's rougher elements, the tough, profane youngsters from working-class homes who would later fascinate and terrify him. Most important, an atmosphere of glamour suffused the estate, the heritage of his grandfather's exploits—much embroidered—the teams of horses, the fine carriage, the uniformed footmen, the shadowy dances under flaring trees —all these things excited the child's imagination and made it feed "on fantasy."

Margaret Reed's brother Horatio, seventeen years older than John, was a source of fantasy too. A "romantic figure who played at coffee-planting in Central America, [and] mixed in revolutions," Uncle Ray was always off in the far corners of the world. Picture postcards chronicled his travels, and then he would suddenly blow into Portland, "tanned and bearded," and the Green clan would gather at Cedar Hill to hear his latest tales. How much fact they contained and how much fiction nobody ever knew, but to John it hardly mattered: "Once the tale ran that he had helped to lead a revolution that captured Guatemala for a few brief days, and was made Secretary of State; the first thing he did was to appropriate the funds of the National Treasury to give a grand state ball, and then he declared war on the German empire—because he had flunked his German course in college!"

Uncle Ray was a sometime visitor, while one source of romance and mystery was ever present: the Chinese. Most of the servants in Portland were of this nationality, and some stayed with the Greens long enough to become virtual members of the family. Impressed by their exoticism, John always recalled the way they "brought ghosts and superstitions into the house, and the tang of bloody feuds among themselves, strange idols and foods and drink, strange customs and ceremonies . . . they have left me a memory of pig-tails and gongs and fluttering red paper." His favorite was Lee Sing, and his earliest recorded memory was of that cook "ordering my grandmother from the kitchen." A true artist, Lee disdained recipes, yet "seemed to mix and cook things by a sort of divine perception." Years later John's mouth would water at the memory of Lee's feasts: "Such delicious roasts! Such delicate, creamy dressings! Such crisp, cool salads! And flaky pastry that would put Aunt Jemimah to the blush." Despite this culinary skill, Lee himself never touched American food—"a little butter slightly rancid, a few dried vegetables of oily taste, the 'ripe' intestines of fowls, smoked and seasoned, and tea—these were his delicacies."[10]

Viewed from the outside, Reed's early years might seem enviable, even ideal. But the child was not always happy, and in retrospect the good and bad aspects of life were closely intertwined: "The beginning of my remembered life was a turmoil of imaginings—formless perceptions of beauty . . . sensations of fear, of tenderness, of pain." The tenderness came from loving relatives, Charlotte toward a first grandchild, C.J. proud of his eldest son, Margaret doting on the baby of whom she would later say, "I worshipped him always."[11] Beauty and fear were more elusive, deep, private emotions that set him apart from others and sometimes seemed overwhelming. For years he would wrestle with their meaning, struggle to conquer a nameless terror that could arise from nowhere, try desperately to capture and express the beauty in words.

Serious pain arrived when at about the age of six Reed suffered a severe attack in the left kidney that sent him to bed for days. Easing by itself, the illness was recurrent. When doctors could find no suitable treatment, Margaret decided John was a delicate child and began to act as if he were made of porcelain, bundling him off to bed at the slightest sign of illness. One result was a view of himself as sickly: "A great deal of my boyhood was illness and physical weakness, and I was never really well until my sixteenth year." Certainly this chronic condition both fed his fear and made the moments of beauty more precious. Sharp and often unrelenting, kidney pain would be a familiar companion for a good deal of Reed's life. It was a cross that he learned to bear in silence.

Protected from the world and coddled because of his illness, the boy did what might be expected of a youngster with a fertile imagination—he plunged into the world of fictional romance. After Margaret taught him to read, John spent days and weeks with his nose in a book. History was an early passion, the time of romantic knighthood his favorite period. Reveling in tales of "kings strutting about and the armored ranks of men-at-arms clashing forward in closed ranks," he also loved the splendors of the Arabian Nights and devoured the humorous tales of Bill Nye and Mark Twain. Stimulated to create his own fiction, he was soon recounting "fairy stories and tales of giants, witches and dragons" to boys and girls of the neighborhood. Once he invented a monster called "the Hormuz,"* a weird creature who lived in the woods near Portland and ate little children. This tale not only frightened friends, but became so real that his own heart beat faster in terror. All the reading and story-telling had a serious consequence. Knowing it was a fine thing to be able to entertain others and oneself at the same time, Reed by the age of nine had a future profession in mind—he was determined to be a writer.

Long before this decision was made, his world began to expand. While Charlotte Green prepared for her first long journey, the Reeds purchased what John remembered as a "little house" but in reality was a substantial two-and-a-half-story structure in the West End, small only in comparison with Cedar Hill. Depression touched Portland in the wake of the Panic of 1893, and for a period money was in short supply. When D. M. Osborne was bought out by International Harvester, C.J.

* Much might be made of the implications of this monster. Reed's pet name for his mother, one she came to use, was always "Muz." The coupling of this with the sound "Hor" and the activity of eating little children may be psychologically significant.

was briefly out of work. Then he became manager of another agricultural-machinery firm, the locally owned Columbia Implement Company. For a couple of years belts were tightened, but little worry over a diminished income was communicated to the children. Vaguely realizing "we were poor," John was not much affected. Even when C.J. was forced to sell the house and move the family to the Hill, a residence hotel, life seemed bright with "a crowd of gay young people around my gay young father and mother."

Into this household came a combination of laughter and tragedy in the form of affable, fun-loving Henry Green, Margaret's twenty-three-year-old brother. Like Uncle Ray, Hal had inherited his father's taste for pleasure unbalanced by any desire to work. Two years after coming of age, the extravagant young man had already dissipated most of his patrimony, and now was trying to settle down by living with the Reeds and working under C.J. At school in the East, then in Europe, liquor and love had been Hal's chief delights. These tastes resulted in many fascinating, mildly racy stories of sprees and women for a wide-eyed eight-year-old nephew John, then had more serious consequences. Unfulfilled by work, despondent when a woman he loved married another, Hal began to neglect his job and drink heavily. In the midst of a binge on November 15, 1895, he entered the Portland Hotel bar, poured an envelope of cyanide of potash into a glass of water, calmly announced his intention and drank it down at one gulp. His death left the family bewildered and distraught, and called forth stern editorial words in the *Oregonian* against those "who conspicuously failed to inculcate in him manly principle, habits of industry and a wise economy of time and resources."[12]

During the summer of 1898, Margaret took her two young sons East to visit relatives. After spending a month by the seashore in Plymouth, Massachusetts, the Reeds passed through Manhattan en route to the nation's capital. The metropolis was a bundle of negative impressions for John, a combination of "awful summer heat . . . vermin in our boarding-house, and . . . steam-engines on the elevated." Washington was much better, less crowded and dirty, a white city that still buzzed with the excitement of cavalry assaults up Cuban hills and naval victories in the Far East. While the Reeds viewed historical sites, word came that a defeated Spain had agreed to sign a peace protocol, confirming a stunning American victory in a brief, glorious war. Touched by the mood of national triumphs, John sent his father a childish drawing of the battleship *Maine*, whose sinking had triggered the conflict. Briefly he thrived on the martial spirit that gripped America, sent Uncle Ray off to the

Philippines with the Second Oregon and brought him back later with a wonderful new story about how he had been made King of Guam.

Healthy enough for travel, John was finally allowed by his protective mother to enter school. Times might still be hard, but the Reeds were too class-conscious to place their children in the public system, and he was enrolled in the Portland Academy, a six-year-old institution that was already sending graduates off to Eastern colleges. At first Jack—as school-mates called him—was an eager student. Already a good reader, he seized the opportunity to broaden his intellectual horizons and approached classes with a fierce appetite. But soon he ran into the problem that many bright, sensitive minds encounter in formal education—a curriculum set up not to stimulate the imagination, but to confine and channel it and provide youngsters with a patina of knowledge that will make them "good citizens."

In theory the Academy was devoted to the "principles of a scientific, classical and literary education, under Christian influence."[13] Reed found the result deadly: "Why should I have been interested in the stupid education of our time? We take soaring young imaginations consumed with curiosity about the life they see all around and feed them with dead technique: the flawless purity of Washington, Lincoln's hum-drum chivalry, our dull and virtuous history and England's honest glory; Addison's graceful style as an essayist, Goldsmith celebrating the rural clergy of the eighteenth century, Dr. Johnson at his most vapid, and George Elliott's [sic] 'Silas Marner'; Macaulay, and the sonorous oratings of Edmund Burke; and in Latin, Caesar's Gallic guide-book, and Cicero's mouthings about Roman politics."

Nothing was inherently wrong with the subject matter; the real problem was the teaching. Perhaps mathematics and natural science, Latin, Greek, French, German and English, and, above all, history, the doings of Washington, Lincoln, Caesar and Cicero, might have come alive had not teachers been desiccated men and women who showed no sparkle of enthusiasm, no joy in learning, no attempt to make any subject a living explanation of the world. With few exceptions, he came to despise such people "whose chief qualification is that they can plough a dull round of dates, acts, half-truths and rules for style, without questioning, without interpreting, and without seeing how ridiculously unlike the world their teachings are."

Such education was worse than a waste of time. Years later Reed bitterly recalled that "many fine things I have had to force myself to explore again, because school once spoiled them for me." So dreary was formal learning that Jack made little effort to do well. Nobody ever doubted he was intelligent—some teachers said brilliant—but in all his school years he remained an indifferent student. At the Academy, the boredom combined with suppressed anger that school was confining both his body and his mind and emerged in a typical way: Jack became a behavior problem. At one point the brunt of his anger was directed at Miss Addison Jewell, both a civics teacher and the principal. Feared as a stern disciplinarian, she was a perfect representative of the system. As if taking on a challenge, Reed began to torment her. When she assigned work, he neglected to study; when she asked questions, he refused to answer; when she lectured, he was loud and boisterous; when she gave him low grades, he showed no concern. Yet when an outside expert arrived in class to administer a new kind of intelligence test, Jack seized the opportunity to shine, completing the exam swiftly and well. Somehow it was like winning a battle, and his victory reinforced an emerging stubborn, independent streak.

Overt hostility was not characteristic of him. More commonly, Jack withdrew from school, either emotionally or in physical fact—by feigning illness and playing on Margaret's fears he could often manage a day at home. Occasionally, when a class like chemistry was well taught, he temporarily became an avid pupil. Poetry and composition were the only subjects of continuing interest, and in his sixth year they became a passion when Reed encountered a teacher who could touch him. From the first, Hugh Hardman, a Columbia University graduate, recognized Jack's talent for writing. Sensitive to the boy's individualism, he allowed Reed to follow his own inclination in subject matter and style, and was pleased to receive "excellent work" from a pupil who was "original, independent, tenacious of his opinions, respectful in presenting them, and not afraid to disagree."[14]

Classes were hardly the most important part of school. Recognizing the Academy as a separate social world and desiring recognition in it, Jack found himself ill-equipped for success. His thin, frail body, quick mind, love of solitary pleasures like reading and writing, and stubbornness—none of these traits was the sort to make him popular with other boys. From the first day, he was an outsider: "I can still see the school playground full of running and shouting and clamoring boys, and feel as I felt when they stopped here and there to look at me, a new boy, with curious and insolent eyes. . . . At the beginning I didn't mix much." This situation dogged Reed into his teens, as he was torn by two contradictory impulses. Wanting very much to be accepted, he held himself aloof. He was a loner who blamed loneliness on his own shortcomings, the recurrent bouts of illness that kept him in bed, the fact that he "hadn't the strength or fight enough to be good at athletics." Uninterested in the elaborate "codes of honor and conduct" that defined the world of youth, he was capable of transgressing unspoken, sacred rules. In a childish game he might openly exhibit boredom or suddenly pick up and go home, leaving brother Harry to make apologies. Put off by such behavior, other children grew hostile; Reed interpreted their anger as contempt.

Disapproval from others did not cut as deep as self-contempt. This emotion was stoked by the nameless fear long before it had any basis in life experience. When the family first lived in town, he was briefly part of the Fourteenth Street gang, joining other lads "tearing up lawns and making mud-balls . . . running and shouting up the hills to give battle to the Montgomery Street gang." This period of bravery quickly passed. In puberty he turned dreadfully shy and fearful. Much to the amusement of acquaintances, he refused to strip in locker rooms to take showers. His daily walk to the Academy, through Goose Hollow, a working-class district "peopled with brutal Irish boys," became a journey filled with terrors. Worried that youngsters might be "laying" for him, Reed would sneak over the back fence and take widely circuitous routes to school, even if it meant punishment for being late. Avoiding fights, he preferred being called a coward: "My imagination conjured up horrible things that would happen to me if anybody hit me and I simply ran away." Once a boy warned Jack not to publish a joking paragraph about him in the school paper and he abjectly complied. When a Goose Hollow lad demanded a nickel to abstain from punching him, Reed cringed in humiliation, but walked home to obtain the money. Oddly, even Jack realized the largely imaginary nature of his anxiety: "The strange thing was that when I was cornered, and fought, even a licking wasn't a hundredth time as bad as I thought it would be; but I never learned anything from that—the next time I ran away just the same, and suffered the most ghastly pangs of fear." So deep were these wounds that years later, when he had proved his bravery many times, Reed would in an autobiographical sketch twice refer to himself as an "abject physical coward" during his teens. The phrase still hurt so much that he both times crossed it out.

Humiliation was compounded by John Reed's belief that he fell far short of C.J.'s image of a son. Grateful that his father "never said much about it," he was certain that his sickliness, cowardice and lack of skill in sports were a source of great disappointment. This was simply not true. Already something of an insurgent, a supporter of Theodore Roosevelt's attacks on monopoly, the elder Reed looked forward to the day when his son would be more cultured, refined and worldly than the businessmen of Portland. He believed Jack a talented writer and did not disapprove of a literary career as long as one could make a living at it. It was John himself, brimming with shame, who projected his viewpoint onto C.J. Having internalized a vision of the two-fisted he-man from the environment, he held it more strongly as an ideal than his father ever did.

Boredom in school, lack of popularity and abject cowardice—three factors that left Jack with the "impression of [his] boyhood as an unhappy one." It was far from the whole story, for he also experienced love, joy and fulfillment. Many pleasures were solitary—playing alone, reading widely, writing poetry and prose. Characteristically, his best athletic skill was in a nonteam sport, swimming. In the summer he would spend days at Captain Bundy's bathhouse on the Willamette, swimming for hours, practicing difficult back flips and twists from the highest diving platform. He shared a pony with Harry, and often the two boys rode off into the woods, built tree houses, played at Robin Hood or trailed imaginary bears, Indians and outlaws. In good weather C.J. took his sons on outings—down to the ocean, where Astoria fishermen pushed small boats into foggy dawns, or to the Cascade Mountains, where the lads huddled around campfires, listened to cougars and coyotes wail beneath the stars and pretended they were back in the pioneer days of Henry Green. These jaunts provided a view of frontier Oregon—cowboys jogging south from Burns, forest rangers atop bald peaks watching the timber for smoke, Indians on the Siuslaw squatting beside summer lodges, scrub deserts shimmering in summer heat, the stark silence of Crater Lake. Such scenes sank deep, becoming part of the beauty he was trying to capture in the written word.

About the time the Reeds moved to a good-sized house on Stout Street, just before the turn of the century, Jack started to pull out of his shell. He was still not a success at school, but was at least beginning to shine among a small circle of young people whom he did not envy or fear. Inspired by Roman history, he once planned a banquet, arranging couches around a table and inviting friends to recline. Then, with an imperial air, he clapped his hands and ordered, "Ho, slave, bring on the repast!"[15] The slave in this case was a black cook—outraged by the slur, she stormed out of the Reed household. Jack was also the driving force behind a theater set up in the attic of his home, writing and directing plays performed for parents and friends. Once a professional producer attended and was impressed enough to suggest the troupe might make some money in public performances. But the disapproval of Margaret and C.J. squelched fantasies of a career on the stage.

By the age of fifteen, Jack was beginning to enjoy typical boyhood adventures. In the summer of 1903 he and four friends sailed off on a camping trip. Competing for a prize offered by a local newspaper, he wrote an account of the expedition, making it sound as romantic as possible: "We were a tough-looking crowd, Cliff wearing a soft felt sombrero, a blue cotton shirt with an old bandana [*sic*] knotted around his neck, and old trousers, with a revolver in their hind pocket and a murderous looking bowie-knife hanging from his cartridge belt. . . . For equipment we carried a canvas wagon-sheet for a tent, five rolls of blankets, six valises of old duds, and provisions enough to last us about a day. . . ."

Sailing about twelve miles up the Willamette, the boys pitched camp on a narrow island and spent more than a week exploring, shooting rabbits and grouse, swimming and fishing. Ideally they might have lived off the land, but Reed truthfully reported that this proved impossible and twice they had to sail two miles to Oregon City for provisions. Occasionally weather interfered with fun. One morning "the rain began to come down like everything. We immediately went back to the tent and went to bed. There we staid [*sic*] all day, playing cards, reading and, much to our disgust, eating cold meals." A few days later they encountered "a very high wind almost like a gale" that nearly capsized the boat. Thrown against the side of the cockpit in the storm, Jack injured his back. Suffering serious kidney pain, the next day he was also sick to his stomach. When Margaret fortuitously arrived, he was happy that she insisted "I had to go right home."[16]

The following year was John Reed's last at the Portland Academy, as both parents agreed that he would benefit greatly from two years of college-preparatory work in the East. The knowledge that he would soon be leaving helped make the school year more pleasant, but there was an even more important factor—the kidney problem was beginning to ease. Attacks were less frequent and severe, and a special diet and certain sedatives prescribed by a new doctor proved effective. Beginning to throb with the "furious energy" that would ever after drive him, Jack felt physically and mentally sharper, more alert. Much less timid, he romped through a course at dancing school, attended mixed social affairs that lasted into early morning hours and even carried on flirtations with a few young ladies. Soon he began to be known as a fun-loving wit, and then as a daredevil and mischief-maker, a youngster who enjoyed thumbing his nose at the staid elements of Portland. Fascinated like so many middle-class youths by the tough, crude, even vicious elements of society, he led parties of friends to the waterfront area to mingle with sailors, prospectors and railroadmen, wander through streets lined with cheap saloons, gambling joints and opium dens, gaze furtively at women lolling in the doorways of cribs. For other boys this was an escape to dreams of adventure and manly deeds soon to be buried beneath responsibilities. But for Jack the repeated glimpses of waterfront life were like a curtain rising on a world he wanted to make his own.

Literature, a realm that seemed more real than life, was still his first love. Reed served on the editorial board of the school paper and was a perpetual fund of articles, poems and jokes for the *Troubador*, the Academy magazine. Increasingly fascinated by the newspaper world, he hung around local editorial offices, and after being friendly for years with the children of Colonel Charles Erskine Scott Wood, Portland's rebel, free-thinking author, he began to drop in on the older man to discuss the world of books. Yet underneath, concealed by the new socially adept exterior, the sensitive youth who had for so long fallen short of his own image of bravery and social success remained alive.

At the age of sixteen, John Reed seemed unconsciously to know he required a stage other than Portland. Like Will, the character he would later create, Jack felt that in his hometown he would always be misunderstood. In truth, Portland was not the city to embrace the playboy, poet and radical that Reed would become. But his youthful misgivings did not as yet have anything to do with this kind of reality. At home his memories of defeat and humiliation—real and imagined—would always be hauntingly present. To expand and stretch out, Jack felt the need for a place where his past was not known, where he could begin with a clean slate. He did not know that he would always carry his own past, or that the heritage of Portland and family would prove important. Unable to see, much less acknowledge, the positive aspects of his upbringing, Reed in 1904 was anxious to leave home. Like Will, he believed that life, real life, where important things were done and written, would have to begin in the shining cities of the East.

3

Morristown

"*It was very still in the woods; just before morning things seem to pause breathlessly, waiting for some bird-song to startle them again into life, and it came home to Will that he would perhaps never see these trees and mountains again.*

"*There came a rustle of leaves, and suddenly a little thin man leaped out into the road. He was dressed in brown and dark green like a hazel-bush, and when he smiled, it seemed as if the trees bent down and smiled too. . . . 'Oh ho!' cried the little man cheerily. 'Off for the world, eh? Not content to follow your destiny? Well, what are your wares? What have you to sell? How are you going to succeed?'*

"*'What do you mean?' said Will. 'I have dreams and I am strong. . . .'*

"*'Very good,' his questioner smiled, 'but dreams and strength sometimes fail to stay together. Sometimes they wither away in the long fight. . . .'*

"*'Who are you?' asked Will, in great surprise. . . .*

"*'I am the little flame of fire that burns in the hearts of all dreamers. . . . Through me alone you can gain success. . . . Will you listen?'*

" 'Yes, yes,' cried Will intensely; 'tell me how I can win success. Tell me how I can at last be understood. I will listen.'

" 'Oh ho!' the old man pirouetted amazingly on one foot. 'Follow me!' and he plunged into the forest. Behind him Will followed. . . . When they came to an open glade among the trees, the little man stopped. A great black rock loomed out of the ground, half buried in the earth and rising above Will's head. . . . In its shadow bloomed one white wake-robin.

" 'Listen,' said the old man. . . . 'One man in all the world can move this rock or pick this flower. If you are the man, you may choose your destiny. If you pick the flower and wear it near your heart, want can never trouble you, nor discontent. If you lift the rock, you shall have unlimited wealth and power, you shall lead the world to war, you shall have as your wife the most beautiful woman on earth. Choose!'

"During this Will stood silent, his imagination following the thin voice of the old man. He hesitated. Three times he stooped to the flower, and three times he drew slowly back. All at once he lifted his head. Wealth, fame, beauty, victory—were they not the greatest things in the world? 'I choose the rock!' he cried.

" 'Oh ho!' said the old man, a little sadly. 'The greatest and the smallest choice, the best and worst, the most glorious and the most sordid.'

"Will did not understand him. . . ."[1]

Young John Reed never doubted that wealth, fame, beauty and victory were indeed the most important things in the world. But America in the early twentieth century was not a land of kings and knights in splendid armor or one where magic elves lurked in the woods. It was not even a land where fortune awaited on the frontier, as it had for Henry Green less than half a century before. In an increasingly industrial, bureaucratic civilization, the way to the top led not along enchanted forest paths but through the classrooms of formal schools, and Jack was ready to accept this road toward the rewards and excitement the world had to offer.

Conscious of being provincial, Portland's social elite were sending sons to Eastern schools. For Margaret, with her finishing-school education, this meant that Jack and Harry would gain entrance into the best circles and reach the social level of her wealthy relatives. Less interested in status than in cultivation, C.J. went beyond merely wanting them to have the college education he lacked. For his sons, only the best was good enough— that meant Harvard. To smooth the transition and ensure entrance without difficulty, two years at a respectable prep school seemed a minimum. After studying catalogues and seeking advice from friends and relatives, the Reeds selected Morristown, in New Jersey, a school that was distinctly upper-class and run by three Harvard graduates, men who would certainly know how to prepare youngsters for their alma mater.

John arrived at school in mid-September of 1904, a tall and slender young man with an unruly head of brown hair, a broad forehead, intense brown eyes and a snub nose above an irregular mouth and heavy chin. Wandering through the Colonial white frame buildings and onto the athletic fields those first days, he found himself one of sixty students, mostly from Eastern families. Morristown was not at the top of the prep-school hierarchy, but its students were nonetheless snobbish and complacent. Immediately Reed sensed he was walking into a familiar, uncomfortable situation—once again he was an outsider.

This time it was different. A "stranger" among "strange boys," Jack soon found "that they were willing to accept me at my own value."[2] Freed from Portland, in fine health and bursting with vitality, he was ready to make a splash, and Morristown offered a full round of important activities. That fall, on crisp football afternoons, he became involved in a team sport for the first time. His 139 pounds were about average weight, but at five feet ten inches he towered over most other players. Gangly and awkward, what he lacked in experience he made up in enthusiasm. Reed scrapped to a starting position, held it through a season of seven games and played well enough to win this notice in the school paper: "He is a good tackler and runs well with the ball."[3]

Football was immensely important. More than a game, it was glamour and heroism, a first chance to shine among fellows rather than in regions of the mind. Jack loved the cheers, the springiness of turf underfoot, the tension as a whistle blew and a foot thudded the ball into the air, the crunch of bodies when he tackled a runner or slammed into an opposing lineman, the sheer elation as he plunged through a hole in the line. On October 21 he dived into the end zone to score the only touchdown in a Morristown victory. Life could bring no sweeter moment than that.

Never a star player, Reed achieved enough recognition to boost his self-esteem. Then his verbal skills won him a reputation for "breeziness and unconventionality." When boys gathered for nighttime bull sessions, he established himself as the most outspoken, especially on the crucial topic of sex. Bursting with imaginative stories of adventure, he held classmates enthralled: "He would tell us ribald and rather hair-raising tales about his wanderings on the Portland waterfront and in places of ill repute in that city; one never knew how much was true and how much made up to give us a thrill." Truth hardly mattered. Continuously "delightful and entertaining," Jack—like C.J. at the Arlington Club—was a center of attention.[4]

Carrying fantasy into action, Reed became a leader in pranks and daring exploits. When students defied the school curfew, climbed down fire escapes and tramped into the nearby village for an evening, he was always among them. Convincing friends to crash local social affairs and dance with country girls, he led long, moonlit walks that ended with everyone slipping back into the dormitory just at dawn. Soon he was among the "social butterflies" who enjoyed openly flirting with Morristown's young ladies. All this activity reinforced a new self-image: "Busy, happy, with lots of friends, I expanded into self-confidence. So without trying I found myself; and since then I have never been very much afraid of men."

The stage was very different from Portland: "The ordered life of the community interested me; I was impressed by its traditional customs and dignities, school patriotism, and the sense of a long-settled and established civilization, so different from the raw, pretentious west." But rather than adopting Morristown's standards, Jack used the school's conservatism and decorum as a foil for exuberant exploits. With everyone from a similar, sheltered background, Reed in effect took the place of the tough Goose Hollow youngsters he both admired and feared. Boarding school, which "meant more to me than anything in my boyhood," allowed Jack to affect a worldliness beyond his years and experience. The pose worked. As a Westerner he was expected to be different. Playing that difference for all it was worth, he usually retained enough social sense to avoid overstepping boundaries that could have put him outside the realm of acceptability. Like a man on a tightrope, he was daring and careful at the same time.

Boldness that won admiration and envy from fellow students brought mixed reactions from schoolmasters. One was delighted with his energy: "He seemed to bring to Morristown some of the openness of the West— its lack of conventional restraint—a newer point of view and a marked eagerness in all he did."[5] Headmaster Francis Woodman, charged with the duty of keeping the school functioning smoothly, was less pleased: "Jack was a difficult and rather disturbing influence in the school. . . . His powers as a boy were turned too much towards mischief and disorder." Tempering this opinion was the acknowledgment that Reed "possessed real power and I liked and respected him in many ways. . . ."[6]

Staying in the limelight meant continually flouting authority, and Jack was often in trouble. Every report home bore criticisms of his conduct. A concerned C. J. Reed wrote to Woodman more than once apologizing for his son's behavior and supporting the school's disciplinary action. It was easy to blame "boyishness" on Portland: "[I] sent him to you to learn that he could not be heedless and childish always. Also to know that the Western lax ideas were not the right ones." Expecting such faults to "disappear in time," C.J. could not help taking pride in his boy's vitality. His own youth had been "full of breaches of discipline," and he believed that some hell-raising was good for a youngster. Life might be a serious business, but it tasted sweetest to the passionate. Some time later Reed explained to Woodman: "Harry is much more serious and quiet than Jack and consequently will not get as much out of life. . . ."[7]

Permissive and indulgent, C.J. tried to make his son's stay at Morristown as happy as possible. When Jack wanted to start a newspaper or make a special holiday jaunt to New York City or Washington, his father wrote Woodman that he was "willing that Jack should do anything he can that you consider proper and right." At a time when financial affairs were going none too well, he continually wired funds to cover special expenses, explaining, "I do not want Jack to lack anything for a moment." Generosity had limits. After paying some large bills at Manhattan stores, C.J. was forced to ask the headmaster to handle the accounts, for his son seemed to have no sense of the value of money: "As for making a special deposit for Jack to handle himself, I fear that it would be more expensive for me than a valuable experience for him."[8]

Reed finally went too far. Late Victorian society understood boyish pranks, but some canons were held inviolable. Knowing this did not stop Jack, during a social engagement in the spring of 1905, from slipping out of his room to place a chamber pot atop a suit of armor standing between the first and second floors of the main building just as some female guests arrived. The titters of fellows vanished in the horror of young ladies, shocked into silence. Reprisal was swift and severe. Confined to school, Reed lost all privileges, was deprived of his room in the Harvard dormitory and put into the less prestigious Columbia Hall. Stunned by the punishment, he complained that it was too severe, that his action had not been malicious. C.J. was not sympathetic. Worried that the boy might be thrown out of school, he wrote the headmaster that he had urged Jack to "take his punishment like a man & try to reinstate himself in the good opinions of his teachers and the boys of the school." With some severity C.J. added: "I am glad that you do not overlook pranks which are in the least vulgar & I agree with you that Jack's punishment will in the end prove beneficial."[9] Ultimately the incident did no lasting harm; among schoolmates Reed emerged as a bigger hero than ever.

Jack's introspective streak did not vanish but was channeled into writing, and the monthly *Morristonian* printed three short stories and an equal number of his poems over the year. Since this literary magazine provided no space for humor, he promoted the idea of a comic paper, somehow convinced skeptical masters of its worth and then secured financial support. The result was the *Rooster*, a thin bimonthly publication edited and largely written by Reed. Full of bad puns and schoolboy jokes, the magazine was enjoyed by a student audience, which found it brimming with "wit and sarcasm."[10] Teachers who found themselves the butt of thinly veiled sketches worried that the *Rooster* contained material unsuitable to a school paper, but refrained from censorship. Perhaps they preferred to have Jack's wild streak confined to print.

Activities were more important than classes and allowed Reed to ignore his low grades in Greek and algebra and failures in geometry and Latin. He acquired two affectionate nicknames, "Farmer" and "Rooster." He sang in the choir and also joined the pool and bowling clubs. At a student debate on the Presidential election, he endorsed the Democratic candidate, Alton B. Parker, and, in a speech reflecting youthful hyperbole rather than political acumen, "compared the Democratic Party . . . with the old Greek Democracy."[11] He visited the family of classmate Frank Damrosch at Thanksgiving, and spent Christmas vacation with relatives in Washington. During winter he enjoyed new experiences —snowball fights, snowshoeing and ice-skating. The year ended in triumph as Reed won the faculty's prize for the best historical essay and was elected to three positions—vice-president of the Athletic Association Committee, editorial board member of the *Morristonian* and co-editor of the student annual, the *Salmagundi*.

Compared to the excitement of prep school, a summer at home promised to be dull, and on the train journey to Portland Jack wondered how he would spend the next three months. His worry was unfounded. During his absence, C.J. had undertaken a role in government that provided an absorbing new perspective on Portland. From being a local gadfly, the elder Reed had evolved into a crusader, and most of his time and energy was given over to political and legal maneuvering and battles. This meant that father and son spent less time together than both wished, but if Jack was sometimes ignored, he experienced little disappointment. For the activities of C.J. were turning a long-admired father into a full-blown, genuine hero.

Looking back on this period, John Reed described C.J. in worshipful terms: "He was a great fighter, one of the first of the little band of political insurgents who were afterwards, as the Progressive Party, to give expression to the new social conscience of the American middle class. His terrible slashing wit, his fine scorn of stupidity and cowardice and littleness, made him many enemies, who never dared attack him to his face, but fought him secretly, and were glad when he died. As United

States Marshal under Roosevelt, it was he who, with Francis J. Heney and Lincoln Steffens, smashed the Oregon Land Fraud Ring; which was a brave thing to do in Oregon then." Accurate in outline, this recollection exaggerates the roles of both Steffens, who arrived on the scene as a reporter, and C.J., more an aide than a central figure in the government prosecutions. Yet it does catch the spirit of his father's role. In 1905 C.J. was up to his neck in a struggle against corruption that shook Oregon's political and financial structure.

An investigation under Teddy Roosevelt's Secretary of the Interior, Ethan Hitchcock, had turned up evidence of vast land frauds in the Pacific Northwest, where hundreds of thousands of timbered acres had been illegally seized by speculators. The game of land fraud was almost a tradition in America, as a profligate, business-dominated government had for a century been casually divesting itself of millions of acres. Now there was a new spirit in Washington. Patrician and middle-class reformers had become concerned with the health of the nation's citizens, the oppressive conditions of factory life, the mushrooming of gigantic trusts, the spoliation of natural resources and the general state of public morality. By 1905 prosecuting fraud in Oregon was as natural for the reformist Roosevelt administration as initiating antitrust suits against monopolies.

It was also as difficult. A major problem with fraud in Oregon—and, as Steffens had found, throughout the country—was that, far from being confined to shady criminal elements, it was inextricably entwined with the local establishment. Some of the state's most solid, churchgoing citizens and political leaders were involved in illegal land dealings. Federal law specified that to acquire a section of public land, a claimant had to swear that he had occupied and improved it for five years. By systematically falsifying government records and creating bogus settlers, various groups of politicians, officials and businessmen had either seized huge tracts or, because of payoffs, ignored such criminal actions performed by others. When Heney, a tough ex-cowboy from Arizona, arrived as a special prosecutor appointed by Roosevelt, many local officials obstructed his efforts, including United States Marshal Jack Matthews, the state's Republican boss, who refused to cooperate, blocked the impaneling of juries and tampered with judges. An appeal to T.R. brought the removal of Matthews, and then Heney went looking for a man who would ensure that juries were free and fair.

It did not take him long to ask C.J., an acquaintance from the San Francisco Bohemian Club. A stranger to partisan politics, Reed had served for two terms as Jury Commissioner for the United States District Court, a position that brought whiffs of official misdeeds. He was used to mocking the foibles of associates but hesitated now at the prospect of serious political involvement. Two years before, he had left the Columbia Implement Company to become an agent for Manhattan Life Insurance. With livelihood and family welfare dependent upon a good reputation, his internal struggle was between two kinds of duty. Attuned to the winds of Progressivism blowing through America, and knowing that men were putting themselves on the line in the name of honesty and good government, C.J. could not withdraw into the shell of family and career, and the underground stream of contempt for Portland businessmen which had previously surfaced only in humor helped in his decision.

In mid-May Reed took the job. Arriving home a few weeks later, Jack found a determined father going about the marshal's duties, his cynicism replaced by fire and conviction. Touched and proud, the youngster wanted to help in the glorious business of jailing grafters and thieves. He loved to drop in at the marshal's office in the gray stone Post Office building, listen to C.J. and Heney plan strategy and enter the political discussions of Progressives gathered there. Politics was a strange, exciting world and his education in it that summer was a broad one: trusts, conservation, bossism, boodling, party maneuvers—all were aired and analyzed in detail. Never again would he be tempted to compare the working of American politics to the democracy of ancient Greece, or believe that the United States government functioned in the simplistic, mechanical manner that textbooks described.

Political lessons merged into the personal. From Heney and even more from C.J., Jack learned firsthand about courage. In their positions, physical danger was a possibility, but rumors and threats did not deter them. As a Portland resident, the elder Reed braved another kind of force, an ever-mounting social pressure, snubs from old friends and hints that he was a traitor to the community. Undaunted, C.J. never even lost his sense of humor for very long. In the thick of battle, he and Heney would take time out to poke fun at chief detective William J. Burns "for his Hawkshaw makeup and ridiculous melodramatics." The twin examples of courage and wit were invaluable. In future years, when under fire for his own convictions and actions, Jack would emulate his father, withstanding attack with a combination of humor and determination.

Like a peeling onion, each case of fraud exposed new layers of corruption. Dragging on for five years, timber prosecutions resulted in the removal of numerous officials—county clerks, mayors, city attorneys, sheriffs, judges, state senators, United States attorneys, General Land Office representatives, members of Congress and United States Senator John Mitchell, who received a six-month sentence. As investigations continued, even community elements that once had welcomed the exposure grew weary and annoyed at the bad publicity Oregon was receiving. Arguments that the point had long since been made did not influence Reed, an increasing object of ill-concealed hostility at the Arlington Club. He rarely went there for lunch any more, but could take a kind of grim satisfaction in a strange memorial to his more popular days. Hosting Lincoln Steffens a few years later, he pointed out a table surrounded by "the crowd that got the timber and tried to get me." Then he went on: "And there, at the head of the table, that's my place. That's where I sat. That's where I stood them off, for fun for years, and then for months in deadly earnest; but gaily, always gaily. I haven't sat in that place since the day I rose and left it, saying I'd never come back to it and saying I would like to see which one of them would have the nerve to think that he could take and hold and fill my place. . . . I am glad to see that it is vacant yet, my vacant chair."[12]

Important as it became, politics was not the sole source of Jack's summer delight. Stronger and more physically fit than before, mentally alert and bubbling with sharp repartee, he began to cut a swath through Portland society. A good-looking, dapper young man, dressed in a striped single-breasted jacket, a high collar and a wide necktie, often sporting a straw boater, he impressed friends with stories of deeds and misdeeds at Morristown. Many days he passed roaming the grounds of the Pacific Exposition and Oriental Fair, the state's contribution to the Lewis and Clark Centennial. Often he and Harry went down to the Willamette to swim or mounted horses for long rides into sun-dappled forests.

Political excitement, social activity and family warmth did not prevent Jack from growing restless before vacation ended. So continuously were the glories of Morristown on his lips that C.J. began to kid him about loving teachers more than parents. More than once father and son were driven to discuss the lamentable state of his scholarship. Jack promised to concentrate more seriously on studies, and wrote to Woodman in midsummer to explain he would definitely complete his course at Morristown in the coming year. The school, geared to Harvard's entrance requirement, demanded twenty-six academic units for a diploma, and because of two failures Reed had earned a total of only eight. Heading east in early September, he was moving toward a formidable academic challenge.

At school his good resolves quickly vanished. Leadership and notoriety were addictive, and the tedium of classes did not stand a chance. Besides, activities had a funny way of multiplying. In October the *Rooster* was buried by financial liabilities. C.J.'s hopes, as he paid the publication's debts, that this would leave his son more time for studies proved vain. Avoiding football as too time-consuming, Jack managed the team, then went on to the same position with the baseball squad in the spring, simultaneously earning a track letter by competing in relays. Positions on two publications and with the Athletic Association ran through the year, each month after January he was elected to the student-government Committee of Seven and in May he was chosen for the Dance Committee. Supplementing this schedule were trips to cities—Washington to see relatives, Philadelphia to compete with the relay team in the University of Pennsylvania games. One glorious New York weekend he spent with a friend both older and more daring. The classmate picked up a prostitute and entertained her in the hotel room, but an envious Reed could not bring himself to emulate the action.

Again this year he continued to run afoul of authority. Small skirmishes led inevitably to a major conflict in the spring. Details are unknown, but it must have centered on policies of the *Morristonian*, for the faculty advisor removed Reed and Chief Editor Frank Damrosch from the magazine. Feeling wronged, the two boys protested in a self-righteous petition to Woodman. A hearing was granted, and after some time they were restored to the editorial board. Vindicated, the youngsters knew the decision made little difference—unknown to the faculty, they had continued to edit the publication during the suspension.

Of all Reed's activities, certainly literary efforts meant the most. Serving as one of four editors of the *Morristonian* not only provided a chance for judging the works of others, but also taught something about the technical aspects of journalism. Though editorials bewailed the fact that students were not submitting enough manuscripts, he was not bothered, for this meant the pages were wide open to him. Now that he was freed from the *Rooster*, Jack's production soared, and a total of three stories and nine poems were published over eight issues. One of the latter captured a prize as the best literary work of the year.

If much of Reed's time at Morristown can be seen in terms of an explosive energy seeking an outlet in athletics and mischievous deeds, on teams, committees and school publications, this is far from the whole story. The vivid inner world of experience, important since childhood, did not disappear, but grew more intense as the anxieties and longing of puberty arose. Romantic dreams of conquest and victory were enlivened by the faces and bodies of women, tempting, beautiful and distant. Once during a football game a vision of Galahad and the Holy Grail flashed within him, and often his mind's eye transformed flesh-and-blood young ladies into Guinevere and other ethereal heroines. Moved by overwhelming feelings and urges with no specific aim, he attempted to diminish them by forcing emotions into written words.

One potential outlet was poetry, but Reed's work in this form only hinted at what he felt. An index of immature literary skill rather than a measure of emotional depth, this may also have been due to a certain unwillingness to expose himself, a desire to keep the world from seeing that beneath an exterior of growing strength and certainty there lingered a soul still troubled by painful doubts and fears. Like most schoolboy work, his poems were conventional in technique and form, often imitative of the author most recently read. Rarely were they personal. He could describe God's glory and mercy without having any strong belief in Him, and write works on classical themes, praising the bravery of Leonidas and his Spartan warriors, or painting a somber vision of the dead King Arthur. Even love could be impersonal, as in a poet's traditional charge to his own work: "Bridge the vast twilight gulf betwixt us two/And whisper my soul to hers with throbbings low."[13] Steeped in English poetry, Jack liked to relate to the masters. Apologizing to Milton, he penned a playful parody which began: "Oh Daisy, thee I envy, to be sure/Who dost not have to do a stroke of work."[14] More serious was an invocation of Tennyson to help him become a real poet:

> Give to me thine inspiration
> Let thy soul my soul immerse
> Till through sweetest meditation
> I can sing my soul in verse.[15]

Loving descriptions of the West were the closest Reed came to singing himself in verse. Fascinated by the fury and power of storms, he attempted several portraits:

> That wind has stirred the mighty pines
> That cling along Mt. Shasta's side,
> Has hurled the broad Pacific surf
> Against the rocks of Tillamook;
> And o'er the snow-fields of Mt. Hood
> Has caught the bitter cold and roared
> Across the prairies, piling high
> The huge white drifts of swirling snow;
> Has carried on its mighty wings
> The blinding blizzard through the night
> When the gray wolf, wild with hunger, howls
> Alone across the empty plain.[16]

One storm evoked a most personal statement. Standing at midnight on a "high and barren cliff," the narrator sways in a furious gale. Below, breakers beat on the rocky coast, while far out at sea a lone vessel "buffets the storm." Inspired amid rumbling thunder and flashing lightning by the ship's battle against the raging sea, the poet has a sudden insight into his own place in life:

> An atom in the world of might and night,
> I stand alone.[17]

Fiction was a less personal medium than poetry. Attempting that Western genre, the tall tale, he utilized labored exaggeration to achieve rather feeble humor in a story about an American who accidentally becomes a witch doctor for a tribe of South American Indians. More innovative and clever was a short work about a man driven insane by the confused crowds and bustle of a Manhattan department store. Sharing with many young authors a fascination with cataclysmic events, Reed turned often to destruction and ruin. Here he could use his powers of description to best advantage. "The End of the World" was no more than an excuse to paint verbal pictures of earthquakes and tidal waves, volcanoes and fires wreaking havoc across the country. Similar descriptions fill "Atlantis," a tale in which the marble cities of that fabled continent sink into the ocean beneath an angry red moon. A group of Roman legionnaires, blown there by a great storm, are trapped on the dying world and meet their fate with a stoic calm. The final sentence affirms a virtue considered most important by the young author: "Greater even than the story of Atlantis is the tale of how a Roman died as Romans could die in the brave days of old."[18]

Bridging the gap between ancient and modern varieties of courage and heroism is "The Transformation," the story that tells most about Reed in his Morristown years. Billy, the star halfback of a college football team, feels that "once upon a time I lived another existence" and has "vague impressions of having seen deep forests and mountains reaching down to the sea, all untouched by the hand of the white man." During the big game of the season he is knocked out while plunging over the goal line with the ball. Awakening, he finds himself a Tillamook Indian brave, involved in a defensive war against another tribe. At a tribal council he offers to find single-handedly the hiding place of the Tillamooks' enemies. Captured during the search, he struggles and slays one foe before a tomahawk crashes down upon his skull. Once more he awakens, this time in his college room. Opening his eyes to a crowd of anxious faces, Billy is told that his touchdown won the game, and then friends roar out the old college cheer. He smiles and says, "Boys, I'm glad to be back."[19]

Not only does Billy share a name with little Will, who left home seeking fame and fortune, he also shares Will's identity as part of John

Reed. By the summer of 1906 this seemed a much different youngster from the one who had departed Portland less than two years before. No longer shy, reticent or aloof, he appeared aggressive and self-confident, sometimes to the point of caricature, but these new qualities covered rather than replaced the former ones. Nurtured by prep-school successes, a tendency toward action had now taken its place alongside the desire to withdraw into realms of romance. As Billy could remember a former life and enjoy a brief trip there, Reed was content both to cherish dreams and to strive in the real world. At Morristown he learned not only that reality contained numerous roads to excitement and adventure, but that he possessed talent and power enough to capture many of its shining rewards.

4

Harvard

"*Now that I look back, I realize what a 'sorehead' I was. . . . I had some reason for soreness to be sure; for I had just been beaten in a managership competition by an influential man who hadn't done half the work I had, and then, to crown it all, a notice had arrived informing me that I was on probation on account of neglected work. How I hated the Dean and everybody else!*

" '*Well, here I am,' I remarked bitterly to Brodsky, who lived across the hall, 'with not a thing to show for it but this notice and half a year's wasted work.'*

"*Brodsky sagely nodded his shaggy head. 'I knew it was so . . . I tolt you a Mt. Auburn Street fella would get it.'*

"*I was young and grievously disappointed, and for two hours I unburdened my wrongs . . . then I must have stopped, for suddenly in a silence I heard the Mem. clock strike two. Without a word Brodsky stealthily arose and began to put on his coat. . . . 'Where are you going?' I asked. . . . 'To a meeting of a club . . . Want to come along? . . .'*

"Out through the Johnston Gate we went. . . . Brodsky shuffled ahead past the Coop. and thrust open a door in the strange looking building next to it; and we began to mount interminable stairs. At the very top landing . . . Brodsky knocked five times, and with a click the door swung silently in and we entered a pitch-dark room. Behind our backs the door shut mysteriously with an ominous sound, and the room flashed into sudden brilliance. . . . A line of men . . . sat at a long table . . . and drank deeply of greenish liquor. They were of many types—a Chinaman, a negro, two or three men with slavic features, and Merriman, whom I remembered as having been fired from college at the beginning of my Freshman year—but all were distinguished by the same wild look.

"The negro rose from his seat with a terrible look on his face, and thrusting a glass of liquor toward me, bade me 'Drink!' . . . With trembling hands I seized the glass and drained it. The liquid was bitter-sweet, and thick, but not unpleasant to the taste, and as the fumes mounted to my unaccustomed brain, I lost my fear, and over my body crept a delicious glow . . . while these strange men seemed somehow kindred of mine and strangely linked with my fate. Then, as if in a dream, I heard Brodsky saying softly, 'Tell dem about de managership.' In a moment I was talking, explaining my wrongs, and pleading eloquently with fiery denunciation of the Athletic Association, of the college, and of the Dean. I never talked so brilliantly, and when I finished, my audience burst into a fierce cry of approbation.

"Then one after the other rose and recited his grievances against the office, and at each one we became more frenzied in our cries for 'vengeance.'

"Finally the negro stood up and quieted the uproar with a gesture of his powerful arm. 'You are now,' he said to me, 'among the Red Hand, who stand for equal rights and help to abolish despotism. . . . Are you with us?' In a mad rage I shouted 'Yes.' "[1]

The path toward success was not always smooth, and John Reed could become very angry when he stumbled over obstacles. With fiction one outlet for deep feelings, it is significant that his only story set at Harvard, "The Red Hand," was a tale of revenge. Rooted in personal experience, in a sense of private rather than social injustice, the work culminates in an outrageous fantasy when the narrator explodes a bomb in the office of the dean. Such an act of terrorism, beyond the dreams of the wildest campus radical in the early twentieth century, both served the author's emotional needs and indicated the hostility he could feel toward an institution he usually claimed to love. Because it provided great opportunities but simultaneously withheld certain kinds of deeply desired recognition, Harvard was a confusing source of fulfillment and frustration, leaving Reed, at the deepest level, ambivalent toward it for years.

Acknowledged the best university in the country both socially and academically, made more desirable because his parents had urged him to go there, the school was all the more precious because Jack almost did not get in. Failures at Morristown had left him eight points short of a diploma, and then he botched Harvard's own examinations. Scraping by in English with a C, history and French with Ds and chemistry with a pass, he failed both Latin and geometry. Luckily the deficient scores were considered high enough to allow him a second chance, and in the summer of 1906 he worked diligently with a tutor in Portland. While he traveled East with Margaret and Harry in September, Morristown relented and proffered a degree. Receiving the news, C.J. wrote to thank Woodman and explain, "Jack is looking forward to his life at Cambridge with his customary enthusiasm and optimism."[2]

Reed went to Harvard expecting to conquer it as he had Morristown, with humor, daring, ebullience and talent. Success at prep school had whetted an already large appetite for power and prestige. A few days after arriving he accosted freshman Bob Hallowell, an artist, with a proposal that the two of them collaborate on a book about the institution. At first speechless, Hallowell then wondered aloud how two freshmen who knew nothing about Harvard's history and customs could undertake such a project. With a wave of the hand, Jack swept such misgivings aside: "Hell, we'll find out doing the thing."[3]

Such brashness was characteristic; so was the failure of the project to get beyond the talking stage. The gesture was a way of reaching out to another human being at a time when Reed was feeling very much the outsider again. Unlike Morristown, the school was too big and complex to be quickly shaken: "My college class entered over seven hundred strong, and for the first three months it seemed to me, going around to lectures and meetings, as if every one of the seven hundred had friends but me. I was thrilled with the immensity of Harvard, its infinite opportunities, its august history and traditions—but desperately lonely. I didn't know which way to turn, how to meet people. Fellows passed me in the yard, shouting gaily to one another; I saw parties off to Boston Saturday night, whooping and yelling on the back platform of the streetcars, and they passed hilariously singing under my window in the early dawn. . . . The freshmen clubs were forming. And I was out of it all."[4]

There were good reasons for this, and Jack slowly began to understand them. Wandering alone the elm-shaded paths of the spacious Yard between historic brick buildings leafed with ivy, poking into bookshops on Cambridge Street and Massachusetts Avenue, sauntering down Mt. Auburn Street to envy the rich students living in elegant private dormitories of the "Gold Coast" or ambling along the quiet waters of the Charles River, Reed came to realize that as a Westerner, and one who had not attended a prestigious prep school such as Groton, Exeter or Andover, he was basically a nobody. At the top, Harvard was a tight social world dominated by rich Eastern families. Partially open to outsiders, the system would admit only those who conformed closely to its values and waited quietly for the call.

Jack was too impatient. Aching for instant recognition from the world of elite clubs, praying "to be liked, to have friends, to be popular with the crowd," he blundered over countless subtle, unspoken social rules. When classmates didn't invite him to their rooms, or snubbed him in front of members of the best clubs, Reed openly confronted them in a manner most offensive to those who expected reticence and formality. Rejection made him so pushy and aggressive that social leaders recoiled even more. These first impressions were lasting. Years later clubmen would recall Reed as someone who never learned the difference between "cricket and non-cricket."[5] That this was more than simply background became apparent a couple of years later when his brother Harry, a model of decorum, was adopted by Harvard aristocrats as one of their own.

Stymied on the path to social success, Jack poured his considerable energies elsewhere. As usual, studies did not absorb him. Along with the English and German formally required, he elected Latin, French, medieval history and ancient philosophy, none of which proved very stimulating. He learned quickly it was not difficult to pass, and he was free to explore other realms. First he went out for the freshman football team, but was cut in mid-October. Then, in a serious effort to win a place on the freshman crew, Reed spent evenings, weekends and one vacation period in the empty boathouses, plugging away at the rowing machines. The effort was in vain, for in March he was assigned to the second team.

With few social activities as diversions, Reed threw himself into writing. The first publication to welcome his contributions was the *Lampoon*, the bimonthly humor magazine that defended the values of establishment Harvard by poking gentle fun at them. By late October Jack's humorous verses and brief jokes were appearing regularly, and at the end of the year—as he proudly pointed out in a letter to C.J.—his name appeared in the index more times than any other member of the Class of 1910. The *Harvard Monthly* took longer to crack. Its literary heritage included works by George Santayana, Edwin Arlington Robin-

son and William Vaughn Moody. Reed's first efforts were rejected, but
with sympathy, suggestions and words of encouragement. Near the close
of the school year the *Monthly* published his most mature works to date,
the poetic story "Bacchanal" and the sonnet "Guinevere."

Literary recognition was a boost, but as the school year dragged on,
he became gloomy. Like his father, Reed felt something of an outcast,
stranded three thousand miles from love and family. Students he had tried
to befriend were "whirled off and up into prominence, and came to see
me no more." Only one youngster remained close, "a shy, rather
melancholy" New York Jew, Carl Binger, an outsider because of his
religion. Always together, the two lads shared experiences and intimacies
to ward off loneliness, but this made Jack feel worse: "I became irritated
and morbid about it—it seemed I would never be part of the rich splendor
of college life with him around." Knowing that in this social world it
was nice to have a companion, he reluctantly made plans to room with
Binger in the sophomore year.

The summer of 1907 was not a happy time. A subdued Jack rattled
around Portland and spent long hours in his room, quietly reading and
writing. The *Pacific Monthly* accepted a short poem, "October," providing a brief lift, but the basic, troubling problem seemed insoluble. Poised
between acceptance of what seemed to be second-class citizenship and a
fight for recognition, the youngster looked to his father for guidance.
C.J. would soon write to Steffens, "My few friends . . . are entirely wiped
out by my lining up with Heney, and I am today practically alone, much
to my amusement."[6] Yet undeterred, he was continuing as marshal to help
with prosecutions. Some of this courage rubbed off on Jack and mingled
with a natural combativeness. The situation was different but the idea of
struggle similar. Returning to Cambridge, Reed was once again determined to make a name.

For those seeking social success, the second year at Harvard was
crucial, as the complicated club system began to divide the elite from
the ordinary. Many students never understood its workings, but Jack
knew them in detail, realized that the Institute of 1770 would select one
hundred men from his class "who would thereafter regard themselves as
the socially elect." This group would enter sophomore Waiting Clubs,
then fill the ranks of Final Clubs in the junior and senior years. Befitting
an elite, the Final Clubs controlled "all 'popular' college activities." To
the ambitious undergraduate, membership in one could seem "the end of
earthly ambition."[7]

Determined that nothing should interfere with his chances, Reed in
September bluntly informed Carl Binger that they could not live together,

then moved into an apartment with a more acceptable roommate. He refused to recognize his obvious liabilities—open ambition, outspoken attitudes and offensive behavior—and then was insulted and hurt when the elections passed over him. Shame over his treatment of Carl meant he could no longer face a former friend, then helped fuel a growing anger that led to further assaults on the establishment. One was aimed at the *Crimson*, Harvard's daily paper and a principal bulwark of the status quo. Knowing he could write well, Reed sailed into the competition for staff positions, but the editors ignored him. More naked in overt discrimination was the competition for assistant manager of the varsity crew, a position based on the sales of season tickets. Hustling night and day, Jack posted the largest total, but the manager extended the deadline long enough to allow another student time to convince a wealthy father to buy a large block of tickets and win him the job.

Reed was saved from being totally crushed by successes in other realms. Just after the turn of the year, the long hours in the Willamette paid off as both the varsity swimming team and the water-polo team selected him as a member. Boosted by athletic recognition even in such minor sports, he was increasingly honored by the *Monthly* and the *Lampoon*. Because staff members were judged by talent rather than manners, both publications elected him to the editorial board, and the two magazines became the center of his school life. Different in tone and purpose, they helped foster a dichotomy in his writing. Anything that smacked of literature went to the *Monthly*, while works tinged with humor, however strained, appeared in the *Lampoon*. Only once was this division violated. At the *Monthly* initiation, prospective editors were required to recite an original poem. Typical was a solemn work about death by Edward Hunt. Cockily, Reed used the occasion to parody one of the sea verses of editor John Hall Wheelock. The recitation ended lugubriously: "O voiceless, murmurous sea,/Full of salt water and the great sad crabs."[8]

Most of his half-dozen sophomore contributions to the *Monthly* and the occasional pieces printed by the *Harvard Advocate* differed from Morristown efforts only in the maturity of language. Some of his *Lampoon* pieces criticized the Harvard establishment obliquely. One target was the *Crimson*, which always managed to praise the football team, however inept. This led to a parody sports report:

> It is true the backfield is very slow, but this is made up by their exceeding lightness. The line is . . . awkward, but this is offset by the grit with which they lie down in front of our plays.[9]

Aiming higher, Reed generalized the attack to Boston's upper classes, the chief support for the school's social system. In the diction of an Englishman, he described Bessie, a society lass from Back Bay:

> I kissed her once, I kissed her twice
> She was a chawming creatchaw,
> But every time I touched her face
> I froze anothah featchaw.[10]

Made openly, such an attack on the values of a puritanical society would have been unacceptable. But Reed was learning that humor was a fine way of sweetening social criticism.

In the spring of 1908 things were going well. Accepted on two magazines and two athletic squads, Jack found other students becoming more friendly. Increasingly part of a busy circle of writers and editors, he learned a lesson that would often be reaffirmed: "When I am working hard at something I love, friends come without my trying, and stay; and fear goes, and that sense of being lost, which is so horrible." In March he was able to publish a "Spring Lament" which made fun of the sources of his growing reputation:

> The spring is coming. God! Must we endure
> Another flood of that impassioned verse
> That burbles from the *Monthly* so demure,
> Or *Advocate*, so infinitely worse?
>
> Must we sit silent under *Lampy's* slams
> About uncharted oceans in the Yard,
> And must we flunk again those damned exams
> And slyly dodge the office postal card?
> (*The poet is overcome and forcibly removed*)[11]

While Jack was beginning to carve a place for himself in the world of Harvard, a significant ferment began in the student body. Two years after graduation he described it as "the influx of discontent, of revolutionary ideas, of criticism and revolt"[12] into the life of the university. Winds of change blowing through the United States finally began to stir the college campuses. For more than a decade Americans had been responding to the works of radicals and reformers, muckrakers and social critics. While angry Populist farmers had railed against Wall Street and under the leadership of William Jennings Bryan had made a try for the White House, middle-class politicians had moved to curb bossism, pass regulatory social legislation, control the power of trusts and make the cities more livable. Meanwhile, Marxism was gaining a foothold, and under the leadership of Eugene V. Debs the Socialist Party appeared to be growing into a mass movement. New points of view, new actions, new ways of thinking—all were encouraged by the wave of reform. Characteristically, the children of the middle class were more affected than their parents by the changes. With less stake in the old order, their attack on the system could be more radical.

The new spirit struck Harvard with great force. With a long heritage of intellectual insurgency, the school, under the forty-year leadership of Charles W. Eliot, had changed from a provincial college of one thousand students to an internationally recognized university with four thousand students in the college, graduate and professional schools. Boasting a splendid faculty that included William James, Josiah Royce, Barrett Wendell, George Lyman Kittredge, William Ellery Channing and F. W. Taussig, Harvard offered the freest elective program in the country. Professors might complain that students showed little enthusiasm for the banquet of world knowledge spread before them, but there were always a few eager for the feast, young men who belonged to what James called Harvard's tradition of "independent and lonely thinkers." Around 1908 such undergraduates began to concern themselves collectively with social problems. When they did, the school was thrust on the defensive against seekers who disdained the kind of education Harvard offered.

The basic cry was for relevance. Dissatisfied with "dusty and mechanical scholarship," with knowledge that seemed "devoid of life," the insurgents—as Reed called them—began a frontal assault. In the January 1908 *Advocate*, junior Lee Simonson excoriated both students and faculty for their indifference to the problems racking the modern world and the vital forces striving to change it. Judging that undergraduates were full of "the contented, unassertive virtues of middle-age," Simonson denounced professors for showing little connection between their knowledge and current affairs. More serious, the faculty was not "in touch with tomorrow," and he called for teachers to "become constructive and radical, [to] set our faces toward the new dawn and make us look at the light of unrisen suns. . . ." Simonson's charge was echoed by others, and soon many small groups that had gathered in student rooms at night to discuss the writings of Anatole France or Karl Marx, modern drama or current literature, anarchism or the newspaper of the future, emerged into daylight, blinking with surprise to find so many others like themselves. Long-winded and often contentious, they shared an attitude of wanting "to see their theories *applied*—not merely academically discussed —applied to the world, to themselves, to *Harvard*."[13]

The ferment affected the student body long before the faculty. Within four months of Simonson's article three organizations with appeal to the insurgents were formed, and Jack developed close connections with two of them. One was the Cosmopolitan Club, nicknamed the "Cosmos," encouraged by President Eliot as a way of fostering relations between foreign and American students. Such organizations have a way of becoming fatuous, often being little more than an excuse for social affairs where students dress up in native costumes and perform the songs and dances of their homelands. At Harvard the club did have its social side, but under the spur of the radicals—as they were coming to be called —it became a serious forum for discussion and controversy. At Cosmos meetings men of twenty-seven nations debated world peace, syndicalism in France, political executions in Spain and American foreign policy. Introduced to international problems and concerns and stirred by talk of revolution on the part of students from India and China, Jack began to realize "what a fire for Causes was abroad in the outside world."

Closer to his literary concerns was the Dramatic Club, a direct outgrowth of undergraduate restlessness. A couple of years earlier, Professor George Pierce Baker, responding to a demand that students be allowed to write plays rather than do research in the history of theater, had begun a course on "The Technique of the Drama." Not fully satisfied, students agitated for an organization to perform their works. When Baker was doubtful, undergraduates formed a club dedicated to presenting original plays and bringing the school "into vital contact with all that is significant in modern drama."[14] From its inception, Reed was a most enthusiastic supporter and participant.

Most important of the new groups was the Socialist Club, organized by nine undergraduates in March 1908. The preamble to its constitution announced "there is a widespread opinion that the present state of society is fundamentally imperfect, and that a basis for reconstruction must be found."[15] Devoted to considering "Socialism and all other programs of reform which aim at a better organic development of society," the club quickly attracted thirty members and the sometime interest of fifty more, but its influence was larger than its numbers. Soon the inner circle, including Walter Lippmann, permeated the university, stirring up criticism, revolt and discussion. As leaders in publications, debating societies, religious organizations and political clubs, the young radicals made Socialism a continual topic of conversation. Interested in changing the world rather than merely understanding it, club leaders moved to draw up a platform for the Cambridge Socialist Party, then went on to draft legislation that was introduced in the Massachusetts Assembly. They attacked the university for not paying employees living wages and the *Crimson* for not accurately depicting undergraduate life and interests.

After Lippmann, in the pages of the Harvard *Illustrated*, criticized the Department of Economics for treating Marxism as a dry theory rather than "a living thing in our midst," students successfully petitioned the faculty for a class in Socialism.[16] At the same time some professors were moved to include material of a current economic, social and political nature into courses.

During Reed's last two years at college, the Socialist Club was a potent force. Its members filled the pages of publications with charges and countercharges over the meaning of education, helped to resuscitate various campus political clubs and moribund debating societies, then caused the spinoff of a host of new organizations—the Social Politics Club, the Single Tax Club, the Harvard Men's League for Women's Suffrage, the Anarchist Club. Supported by a handful of faculty, scorned or ignored by others, feared by some administrators and openly attacked in alumni journals, the radicals went too far. Eventually some of their programs were vetoed by the Harvard Overseers on the grounds that "the halls of the University shall not be open for persistent or systematic propaganda on contentious questions of contemporaneous social, economic, political or religious interests."[17]

Clamps on radicals came two years after Reed's graduation, about the time he would in a lengthy article laud them as prime movers in the "Harvard Renaissance." Skirting the fact that he had never joined the Socialist Club and only sporadically attended its functions, Jack neglected to explain this apparent lack of interest. Given his drives, the reason is clear. Debates on social questions were alive, interesting, fascinating. But so were football games, beer halls, weekend jaunts to Nantucket, dances and endless editorial conferences. Political and economic issues might be important, but to Jack they were less so than learning how to write poetry, plays and short stories. Besides, one part of Reed knew that all the furor "made no ostensible difference in the look of Harvard Society, and probably the club-men and athletes, who represented us to the world, never even heard of it." If years later he could claim that the "Renaissance" made him realize "there was something going on in the dull outside world more thrilling than college activities," this was mere hindsight. While he was there, Harvard was Jack's world, and no other realm was so interesting or important.

Still, he was affected by the intellectual ferment. Exposed to both national and international questions, he became familiar with new, and often radical, points of view. More important, the "Renaissance" provided a host of new organizations in which to exercise his talents, creating a kind of alternative social order with its own status positions. While the elect moved self-importantly into the Final Clubs, Reed in his junior year was assistant to the Dramatic Club's manager, Hans Von Kaltenborn, soliciting advertisements for the program, writing publicity releases and riding herd on students building sets. At the same time, Cosmos Club meetings occupied at least one night a week. In May 1909 he was elected vice-president of both organizations.

More familiar activities also absorbed his energy. Swimming and water-polo practice was exhausting and exhilarating, and full schedules took Reed to other campuses. He won his letter in March, and the next month the water-polo squad chose him captain. Meanwhile his contributions overflowed the *Monthly* and *Lampoon* onto the pages of the *Illustrated* and the *Advocate*. If editorial duties seemed to consume immense amounts of time, he never begrudged the long hours selecting jokes, cartoons, stories and poems, arguing with other editors over choices, worrying about makeup problems, leaning over the stone in print shops, reading proofs and dashing off last-minute fillers before dragging wearily back to his room.

The *Monthly* and the *Lampoon* were harbingers of adult life and breeding grounds of lasting relationships. One close friend was Robert Hallowell, named chief of the *Lampoon* in January 1909, when Reed was elected to the post of Ibis, the second in command. Another was Eddy Hunt, a gentle poet with enough grit to work through school and still find time to become Drama Club president, Class Poet and Phi Beta Kappa. In a congratulatory note on Eddy's appointment as editor of the *Monthly*, Reed described their kind of friendship as "one of the real things one *gets* from college."[18] Among his other acquaintances were Walter Lippmann, too dry and cerebral at times for Jack's taste, but a writer of mature, dispassionate, incisive editorials; and Alan Seeger, whose single-minded devotion to beauty made Reed's most poetic efforts appear frivolous.

Another source of friends was the newly formed Western Club, an important center for students outside the social whirl. Elected president soon after joining, Jack began to play the role of his father at the Arlington Club, dominating the head table and entertaining listeners with a stream of witticisms. When Lippmann arrived as a luncheon guest one day, Reed leaped to his feet, made a deep, effusive bow and solemnly announced, "Gentlemen, the future President of the United States." More often humor was on a lower level as the Western lads, cut loose from the uncongenial Harvard decorum, shouted aloud, threw food around the table and indulged in elaborate practical jokes. Loving this open spirit, Jack was as boisterous, raucous and noisy as any member. Nowhere else in Cambridge could he so much be himself—nowhere else did he feel so much at home.

Swamped with activities, clubs and teams, Reed as a junior at last found a college teacher who could make him catch fire—Charles Town-send Copeland. One of Harvard's characters, small in stature, prickly in personality, Copey—as everyone called him—was no scholar, and failure to publish had kept him at the low rank of instructor for years. Yet genera-tions of students remembered him as the best teacher they ever encoun-tered. Copeland's method was unique, for he was a man who, in Walter Lippmann's words, "acted on the assumption that teaching is not the handing down of knowledge from a platform to an anonymous mass of note-takers, but that it is the personal encounter of two individuals. . . ."[19] Keeping his composition course small, Copey met students in his own rooms. Each session was a performance. Playing the autocrat, making slightly off-color remarks, delving into topics that had nothing to do with writing, he alternately exhibited anger, irony, rage, horror or sym-pathy when students voiced opinions. No matter what subject was broached, Copeland was on top of it with "something witty to say, . . . something inspiring to teach." A devastating critic of student writing, he went overboard with enthusiasm on finding good work. For a Harvard writer, receiving praise from Copey could seem the pinnacle of achieve-ment.

Reed received a good deal of such praise. A delicate, sickly man who covered infirmities with a sharp tongue, Copeland admired Jack's bare-chested attitudes as much as his prose. Before long, Reed felt himself part of Copey's circle of "privileged individuals" who "stay after hours in his room, who walk across the yard with him, who sit with him on the bench under the elms on spring afternoons. He treats them as brothers; some of them would rather tell their troubles to him than to their families. He is always ready to advise, to comfort, to laugh." When the instructor's words spurred notions of finding adventure and heroism in the modern world, Reed became a true disciple. Aside from C.J., he later recalled only two men "who give me confidence in myself, who make me want to work, and to do nothing unworthy." The first of them was Copeland.

For Copeland's friends, Saturday night was always a special time. About ten o'clock Reed would climb the south stairway of Hollis Hall to Copey's residence for a weekly open house. Entering a room over-flowing with "athletes, editors of college papers, Socialists, atheists, gentle-men, social stars and . . . lesser orbs," he looked for a seat and often had to settle for a small patch of floor. The atmosphere was congenial and warm—the walls lined from floor to ceiling with books, a dim light ema-nating from a coal fire and a single candle on the mantelpiece. Presiding from an armchair, Copey led a conversation in which everybody talked "of the thing nearest his heart" and managed to sound "alert, quick, almost brilliant."[20] A magic time of closeness, such an evening in the shadowy room with voices rambling through philosophic systems, recent books, travels, drinking parties and political movements made life seem rich and beautiful, full of great wonders to see and deeds to do. This was a truer sort of education than all the classes Harvard had to offer.

College life was somehow much more than the sum of textbooks and activities. It was the clean wind on fall mornings when trees flared with color; the thunder of the stadium on football afternoons; walks at night on grassy shores while lights flickered on the waters of the Charles; sudden budding friendships as friends shared intimate thoughts about love and death; predawn cups of coffee with buoyant editors after a magazine was put to bed; a romp through a Colonial cemetery while feeling young and immortal; knee-deep snowdrifts along Massachusetts Avenue and icicles clattering on naked Yard trees after a storm; roisterous weekends in a North Woods cabin; bloody fistfights with Cambridge roughnecks that left collars torn, cheeks bruised and a joyous feeling of manhood; night-long, drunken train rides into the darkness of northern Maine; the sheer fun of trooping through Lexington's streets, rattling windows and shouting, "The British are coming!" College was life, and life was desire, ambition, confusion and pain, the wonderful possibility that all dreams would come true.

One perennial dream of love could sometimes become a reality. Reed was a young man who enjoyed the company of females. Girls often found him too boyish and immature, objected to his rough manners, and thought he acted younger than his classmates. But he was big and brisk and breezy, handsome and unconventional enough to quicken the pulses of some young ladies. One was Miss Amy Stone, his "first love." The evening after meeting her at a dance in January 1909, Reed not only wrote a note to express delight, but included his first poem to a flesh-and-blood woman. It closed with a perfect description of his own feeling, as a "lark with song unfurl'd/Soars up to beat his wings against the sun."[21] When the brief infatuation terminated, there was still that sense of soaring to cherish.

The romance with Amy was all in the mind and the heart. At early-century Harvard, love was one thing, sex distinctly another. Girls were not chaperoned, but there was little question of overt physical relations with the females from Radcliffe or Boston whom students dated. While upperclassmen were expected to drink and smoke—and Jack did both—sexual relations with women were a blot on any reputation. One acquaintance of Reed explained that "men who boasted of their immoral relations with women were not highly regarded at Harvard, and seldom reached prominence."[22] In such an atmosphere, love flourished only as an ideal.

This was no doubt congenial to Jack. If he did lose his virginity during college days, he certainly never bragged of this to close friends.

Because of so many involvements, Reed had little time to spare for Harry, who arrived in Cambridge in 1908. Held together by a strong bond of affection, the two boys were torn apart by divergent interests. Harry was an affable, conventional youngster moving toward the world of elite clubs. Only occasionally did the brothers have a few moments together before each whirled off to an engagement. When Harry slipped onto probation and seemed close to failing out of school, Jack did prevail on Woodman at Morristown to intercede. After the headmaster wrote to the dean, a grateful Reed penned a letter of thanks for helping to keep his brother "among the living."[23]

Soon he was forced to write Woodman on his own behalf. In April, for the first and only time, Reed ran afoul of university authorities. It began at spring vacation when Joe Adams—a delicate lad who disagreed with Jack's opinions but followed him around in an almost worshipful way—and senior Bill Pickering went with Reed to Manhattan. For several days the trio roamed the streets, attended the theater and sloshed through bars. Catching a train to Morristown, they spent an evening leading the students in college songs. Back in the city, Reed came up with the idea of a trip to Bermuda. Adams was delighted, but Pickering, not wishing to jeopardize his graduation, begged off. Scribbling a letter to Hallowell on Tuesday, April 20, Jack claimed to be "all tired out and in need of a rest," enclosed some contributions for the *Lampoon* and asked rhetorically, "Can you make up this number all right?"[24] The next day he and Adams were aboard a steamer, with vacation due to end in three days.

Bright and colorful with sun-splashed houses, swaying palms, white beaches and lively nightclubs, Bermuda was a sheer delight. Touched by a momentary shadow of concern, Reed wrote Dean Byron Hurlbut to explain why the two of them needed more vacation time, then lost himself in hiking, loafing, swimming and dancing. To earn money for hotel bills, he sold several poems to a local newspaper and Adams pounded the piano in a shady resort hotel. When they returned to Cambridge, an entire week of school had passed.

The administration was neither amused nor sympathetic. Reviving "rustication," a form of punishment unused for decades, Harvard sent Adams and Reed to Concord to pursue studies under a local schoolmaster for the remainder of the term. Indignantly Jack complained to Woodman that his grades would suffer in exile, and then added: "I am also the only one who knows how to run the Dramatic Club or to edit the *Lampoon*."[25] The patient headmaster did his best to explain Reed's concern, but Hurlbut remained adamant. Amused at his "illness," the dean pointed out that Jack seemed well enough for activities and asked Woodman to deliver a sermon "on the importance of putting College work ahead of the *Lampoon*, Musical Clubs and all those other avocations which tire one out 'completely' and make a young gentleman ill so that they cannot do any College work." Caustically, Hurlbut added, "It is really time for him to go away from Cambridge and note that although he is away the University does not totter."[26]

Concord was lovely in the spring—the rural world budding into green life, the simple memorial to the embattled farmers, Hawthorne's old manse by the gleaming river, the deep quiet of Walden pond, the dark hillside cemetery where Thoreau and Emerson slept, the Colonial buildings of the tiny village—all helping to carry Reed back to a simpler age. Slowly the anxiety that he would not be missed ebbed away, and when Eddy Hunt met him in Waltham to discuss the next issue of the *Monthly*, Jack was reaffirmed in the belief he was an important force at Harvard. Resigned to rustication, Reed studied, continued to write for the magazines and found time to send the Western Club a regular humorous bulletin. One issue was devoted to a description of an attempt to catch a huge, elusive moth: "In the scrimmage two windows were broken, one electric light globe, and the lid to the slop jar. A large moth was severely injured about the neck and ears. Two old ladies who room below us and are Seventh Day Adventists thought that Christ had come again, and prayed violently all night."[27] Exile might not be agreeable, but it obviously did not dampen his buoyancy.

The summer of 1909 was the last carefree, extended period Reed spent in his hometown. He was already thinking beyond Harvard, and often discussed with an approving C.J. his determination to become a journalist. Having published a short story in the *Pacific Monthly* the preceding year, he took to visiting its editor, Fred Lockley, for chats about literature and life. Looking over his recent work and sensing the strength of his drive, Lockley was encouraging. To both C.J. and the editor Jack spoke of a deeper desire, his hope that journalism was only a first step on the road to a creative life as a poet, playwright and novelist. He began to sketch notes for a novel, the wild story of an Oregon Indian who is really a god lost from heaven, and who somehow becomes mixed up with genies, newspapermen, politicians, musicians, magicians and a Caucasian girl. This uneasy mixture of realism and fantasy began to baffle its creator, and he put it aside. He was young. Novels could wait.

Serious writing was made difficult that summer by the tug of Oregon's beauty and the charms of a young lady, Frances Nelson, considered one of the loveliest coeds at the University of Oregon. Coming from her

home in Albany to be Jack's blind date for a July dance at the Portland
Heights Club, she conquered him with looks, grace, hints of affection for
a Yale man, and a vast knowledge of poetry. Overriding objections, he
dragged Frances away from the dance for a trolley ride up to Council
Crest, overlooking the city. Clouds covered the moon, and the darkness
of the shadowed river valley was pinpointed with flickering lights. Shivering, the two stood close together, and like a holiday rocket, Jack's heart
burst into space with love.

Frances became the center of life. Remaining in Portland, she joined
him for dances at the Waverly Country Club, small dinner parties and
picnics in the country, fascinated by his "alert and intelligent" conversation, the talk of books and poets, the dreams of fame as a writer. After
going home for a few weeks, she returned in early September for a date
to see a visiting opera company, stayed with the Reed family and promised
to come East the following June for Jack's graduation. Less smitten than
he, Frances was both attracted by his unconventional attitudes and a
touch disturbed by the obvious fact that "he liked being different."[28] This
side showed through his flowery letters. Along with mock indignation—
"I don't see why you insist on addressing me as 'Mr. Reed' even if you
are wild and shy (by the way, only *one* of those adjectives is appropriate
to your behavior"—and roundabout professions of affection—"Somehow
I haven't enjoyed a single one of those dances since you left. Understand,
my honesty prevents my saying absolutely that it is your absence that
makes the difference"—went a lot of elaborate fussing over the quality of
the letter paper—"This is the last piece of writing paper in the house. . . .
Don't you hate anyone who's as sloppy in his correspondence as I am?"
Underscoring this consciously unconventional behavior was the proud
announcement that he had bypassed a formal wedding in favor of swimming—"I presume the bride was lovely, but the river was far lovelier
to me"—and some heavy irony about the city—"Portland is still the same
giddy bewildering place that makes people leave New York in the gay
season and come out here for fun."[29]

As Frances spent most of August at home, Jack embarked with three
friends on a two-hundred-mile walking trip down the primitive Oregon
coast, promising, "Every night when we camp on the beach I'll send you
a vibration."[30] The four young men tramped through spruce and pine
forests and along lonely dunes, fished in streams for rainbow trout and
cooked at twilight over open fires while cougars wailed in nearby mountains, then stripped and dashed into phosphorescent breakers, feeling, in
Reed's words, like "pagans . . . and star-worshipers to the bottom of our
souls."[31]

Fired and aching with the uncapturable beauty of it all, Jack for a moment bent toward that flower of contentment. Among friends at Harvard there had been some idle discussion of homesteading in the West, starting a colony where creative men would live close to the rhythm of nature. Back in Portland late in the month, Reed was moved to write Hallowell he would happily "jump in" to such a life and expressed fear the idea would "peter out with you fellows."[32] He was correct, but not only about friends. The rewards Jack sought were not to be found in the West. A letter to Frances just after his return to Cambridge underlined the crucial differences between the two regions: "The change from West to East is a very great one. Out there the strength of body, here the fire of the mind." Forced to choose between the two, he would take the East because "You have no idea how it really thrills you to feel and think as we here feel and think together, how it makes you glad all over. That's something you cannot get out West. . . . Don't *you* often feel that hunger for people to open your heart and mind, and not be laughed at or misunderstood."[33]

Reed's senior schedule bordered on lunacy. Responsible for a regular *Lampoon* column, he began to contribute most of the magazine's editorials. The *Monthly* claimed his duties as a board member as well as a writer. When the Cosmos president failed to return to campus, he was elevated to the post—this meant attendance at Thursday meetings, Monday afternoon tea and monthly entertainments. He presided daily at Western Club luncheons, gave afternoons to the swimming and water-polo teams and managed the Dramatic Club and the Glee, Mandolin and Guitar, and Banjo clubs. A member of the Debating Club, Symposium and Round Table, all devoted to the exchange of ideas, Reed also joined the Memorial Society. With such commitments, it is little wonder that he drowsed in class, or yawned so broadly that an angry professor could snap, "If you must yawn you might at least cover it with your hand, or, in this case, I believe that both hands would be necessary."[34]

At the beginning of the school year Harvard underwent a change of leadership. Retiring after forty years, President Eliot was succeeded by Abbott Lawrence Lowell, a member of an old Brahmin family. Jack hailed the inauguration in the *Lampoon*, but was quickly disappointed in the new leader's policies. As a professor of government, Lowell had led a faculty attack on the elective system, and shortly after taking office he curbed it in favor of student concentration in specific academic areas. Concerned with community and hoping to bridge the gulf between rich and poor, he then announced plans to put all freshmen in a single set of dormitories.

Along with the student radicals, Reed was upset by such moves against individualism. Hardly a theorist, he knew from the relationship with Copey that education was not a matter of requirements—it was more the magic of two individuals coming together in some ineffable manner and winging into uncharted realms. Some men might now graduate "without having learned anything," but this did not disturb him. More important than a minimal culture for all was the fact that freedom allowed the most talented and intellectual students to flourish. Reveling in contrasts, fascinated by a world in which "some men came with allowances of fifteen thousand dollars a year . . , [while] others in the same class starved in attic bed-rooms," Jack loved a Harvard filled with "all sorts of strange characters, of every race and mind, poets, philosophers, cranks of every twist," and feared the stifling attempts of authorities "to weld the student body together, or to enforce any kind of uniformity."

Annoyance at Lowell's system led Jack to a new role, that of critic. Previously his editorials had dealt with such momentous issues as the desirability of extending athletic eligibility or doing away with senior robes. Now he denounced plans for the freshman dorm and defended the "intellectual free lunch counter" of the elective system with the argument that the freedom "found in no other university" was the basis of Harvard's preeminence. Turning serious even in the *Lampoon*, Jack pointed out that the "narrowness of the world is due to the fact that we must specialize to succeed," and he argued that college was not the time for specialization. Uneasy in the role of pundit, he found humor more congenial and suggested a dorm for the faculty: "Freshmen *must* rub off the sharp corners in four years—our preceptors and instructors never do. Living alone, they often develop morose manners, not to speak of repelling and even forbidding exteriors. Their ill-humors are vented on their pupils, when they might well be exhausted on other professors equally quarrelsome."[35]

Closer in spirit now to radical undergraduates, Jack was led to wonder about broader issues. This drew him to Lincoln Steffens. Twice the year before, after campus speeches, the renowned journalist had briefly conversed with Jack and sent C.J. news of his son. Reed had then been frightened of the older man's searching questions on social and political issues. Now he invited Steffens to meet with the *Monthly* editors and became excited by his suggestion that the magazine begin to probe the structure of Harvard. Such social criticism did not enter the *Monthly* until after Reed's graduation, but his admiration for Steffens blossomed. Later in the year Jack gave a rave review to his book *The Upbuilders*, a series of Progressive biographies. Calling it a justification "to men who believe in the beautiful potentialities of our government"—men like

C. J. Reed—he ignored its political implications and saw it through the lens of his own interests: the ultimate of Progressive mentality would be realized when the movement "finally gave birth to a new and splendid national expression in art."[36]

It was a spirited senior year. Reed wrote one play for the *Lampoon* initiation and another for the Cosmopolitan Club, based on the idea of the Tower of Babel workers organizing into a union and going on strike. One Cosmos beer night found him playfully slipping an empty bottle into the pocket of a distinguished visiting scholar, while on another such occasion he pretended to be hypnotized by a fellow student, climbed into a professor's lap and twisted his lengthy whiskers. In a spirit of fun— laced with some hostility—he and Alan Seeger disturbed a formal stand-up supper of the Symposium by harassing a stuffy railroad president with questions about the financing of his companies. During spring vacation he and classmate John Kelley spent a week in Nantucket and stole a sailboat for the return to the mainland.

His humor filled the pages of the *Lampoon*, where he poked fun at professors, students, radicals, clubs, football, suffragettes, marriage, the *Crimson*, Boston society—and himself. Regularly he ridiculed the variety of activities so crucial for his own development. Because after football season there was nothing to occupy students but "a few paltry studies," young men naturally joined organizations to fill up their hours: "It has become so now that any man who goes through college without forming at least three clubs is without any life, and anyone who is not a member of eight or ten is a social outcast."[37]

Another outlet claimed his startling energy in this final year. Harvard's individualism was manifest in a decided lack of "school spirit" and notoriously apathetic football crowds. When pressure to support the team began to mount, Reed's belief that organized sentiment was silly clashed with a love for the game. Without resolving the contradiction, he ran for and won the job of cheerleader just at the time he was disdaining Lowell's plans for regimenting undergraduates. Truthfully, he could not help himself—the chance of showing off was too delicious to bypass. No matter how sullen or reticent the crowd, Jack cursed, bullied, sneered and exhorted until the fans followed his directions. The result was spectacular. Leaping before the grandstands, he exulted in "the supreme blissful sensation of swaying two thousand voices in great crashing choruses."

Shortly after the close of the football season, a new temptation arose. With days and nights jammed, Reed rarely paused to focus on the world of Final Clubs. Partially repelled by their narrow elitism, he could not wholly shake the feeling that the clubs were suffused with glamour, and in describing them, the words "aristocrat," "glittering" and "elegant" always came to his mind. As if he were tied to the world that Cedar Hill represented, something in Jack wanted those words applied to his own life. All the positions, notoriety and honors, all the radical social analysis and all the crude manliness could not wipe away the lingering idea that success with the "better sort" of people was important. So when the aristocrats stretched forth a very tentative hand, he grasped it with alacrity and passion.

December was the time of Senior elections, when students chose officers to preside over graduation-week ceremonies. Traditionally the positions went uncontested to members of the elite, who lived in the private apartments of Mt. Auburn Street. In the class of 1910 the poorer —and supposedly more democratic—students of the Yard dorms decided to contest the offices with their own candidates. Radical students scorned such elections, but not Reed. Soon he was caught in a web of plots, schemes and political intrigue which ended with the aristocrats—in an attempt to broaden support—offering Jack a position on their ticket. He accepted, and went down to defeat with some of the class's chief snobs. Later he would pay homage to this "democratic revolution," but at the time he despised it. Ashamed over having made a fool of himself and no doubt feeling guilty for having betrayed associates who were not in clubs, Reed for a few days lost all sense of proportion. He angrily scrawled a poem that accused his opponents of being "traitors to Nineteen Ten," then tried to convince active friends to resign all their posts in protest against the way Yard men had introduced ward-heel politics into an honor election.[38] This mood slowly ebbed, but the influence of the event lingered. It would be a long time before Jack could admit that in the struggle between social status and conscience he had chosen the world of his mother rather than that of his father; once he did, he would try not to make the same mistake again.

The ambition that pushed Jack into the election soon led to another equivocal move. Hasty Pudding was an elite club chiefly concerned with the production of an annual musical comedy. Sometimes short of talent, it was willing to admit late members to help with the show. Needing a lyricist in 1910, club leaders grudgingly offered Reed membership to fill the slot. Shamelessly, he blotted out the past and accepted. One penalty was having to work with George Martin, writer of the book for a show entitled *Diana's Debut*, a young man with ill-concealed contempt for Jack's origins and past antics. Revenge emerged in lyrics criticizing Boston society. One described a swank social affair: "From the lack of heat / All of Beacon Street / Surely must have been there." More pointed was advice on how to achieve social success:

> Just insist that your aunt was a Cabot
> And your grandmother's real name was Weld.
> Try hard to make rudeness a habit,
> And be careful with whom you're beheld.[39]

There was no time to dwell on the ambivalence of this final college honor. After *Diana's Debut* was performed in April, the year rushed to a close in a flurry of banquets and farewell celebrations, after-dinner speeches, farcical skits and musical shows that occupied Reed as toast-master, writer and performer. In mid-June, seniors in soggy black gowns led proud relatives through the shady Yard. Frances Nelson had begged off, but C.J. and Margaret arrived, and with Harry close at hand, the Reed family trooped around Cambridge to meet other parents, students and professors. On a hot and muggy graduation day, June 24, crowds in the stadium listened to Eddy Hunt recite a moving class poem, heard the singing of T. S. Eliot's ode, drowsed through the speeches of orators promising to seize the challenge of the world. Bored and restless, proud and anxious, Jack looked beyond the crowds to the past. Yesterday he had been a lonely freshman praying for success. Now he was one of the best-known men at the university. No doubt he was a success, but it was diffi-cult to total the sum of four years of experience and effort.

Certainly the least important part of school had been classes. Although he was a supporter of the elective system's broad perspective, Jack's choice of courses had been narrow. Of twenty-three, eighteen came under the heading of language, literature or composition and the others represented excursions into history, art, music and philosophy. College had taught him to read German with a little difficulty, French and Latin with ease. Knowing something about poetry in those two languages, he also had a good grasp of the full body of English literature. Since all the courses in history, philosophy and art had been confined to medieval and ancient periods, his education was wholly grounded in the distant past. If it included little preparation for the modern world, Harvard was not to blame—Reed's curiosity had never led him to elect any course with subject matter more recent than the eighteenth century.

Activity was obviously his realm, the drive for recognition his spur. In a frenzy he had sought positions, joined clubs, tried for teams. A boundless vitality had brought him to the top in many groups, let him touch different worlds and suggested a radical analysis of society. But making a name took precedence over principle. The drive he rationalized most—not only at Harvard but for years afterward—was the need for acceptance by the social elect. Despite this, he never attempted to tone down his personality to fit in with the sedate "club-man" mentality. Many of those who possessed such proper minds would always remember Reed not only as "offensive," but also as a "grand-stand player" and a "publicity seeker."[40] These judgments contained more than a little truth. There is no doubt that Reed was a self-centered young man, one whose egoism could often dull his sensitivity to the needs of others. Capable of being a good friend, warm and giving, he could on occasion be unkind, even ruthless. He was in some ways a man who could be more easily admired than fully trusted.

Action might be central to his personality, but Reed thought himself basically a writer. He was quite prolific, publishing more than twenty poems and nine stories in four years, along with numerous editorials, sketches, columns, jokes and pieces of light verse. Several of his plays had been produced on campus, and unpublished or half-finished works jammed a trunk. All this production did not mean his writing was mature. With so many commitments, he did most of this work in haste; there was never enough time to rewrite and edit. Ideas came in a burst and he seized the easy image without worrying over how derivative it might be. A writer he was, but certainly Jack was not yet an artist.

Writing showed his basic nature clearly—here it was most obvious Reed was a romantic. Though his humor could be timely and topical, almost everything else indicated a longing for a world both fantastic and strange. In a class paper on the eighteenth-century novel, he had written, "Mystery has dwelt in the minds of men since the very beginning," and his own works largely fell into the tradition of romance and horror the essay described. Western landscapes in his poetry included deserts, mountains and forests human in their loneliness and turbulence. Often animals were portrayed with the feelings and motives of men, a sea gull baring "his gleaming armor" to battle a squall, a coyote crying to brothers in a mournful lament "For the day that's dead / And the hunt that's fled / And the terror of things unseen."[41] Love for real women did not prevent poetry from transforming them into creatures disembodied as smoke:

> Now in the east pale sleeping fairies weave
> From dreams, the wan grey gossamer of dawn
> And lay it on your hair; so fair, so fair
> You sleep—and yet, the shadowy dancers leave,
> The swaying phantoms one by one are gone,
> The deathless music fades in breathless air.[42]

More fantastic was Reed's fiction. Even works set in the present were touched with mystery: the "Red Hand" tale with its magic potions and bizarre conspirators; the story of an invasion of modern England turned back by the arrival of King Arthur bearing Excalibur; the lighthouse keeper of "The Singing Gates" drawn to a strange death by a lonesome Indian god; the traveler in "Bacchanal" who sleeps in an ancient Greek temple with a goddess dead two thousand years; the story of the forest ranger asked to become the husband of a mermaid in a mountain pool. Most congenial to his imagination were works set in ancient or wholly mythic realms: the adventures of little Will; the Egyptian high priest of "The Pharaoh," prevented by the goddess Astarte from stopping a revolution; the "Story About Kubac," a decaying kingdom lost in the backwash of time.[43]

Such strange tales suited Jack's talents. Description was his real strength, tone his métier. Mood was the best element in his stories: the solemn Greek valley haunted by memories of hoplites marching to war; the clangor of Thebes as a torch-bearing army storms a temple; the ghostly lighthouse shrouded by fog on a pine-clad headland; the excitement of shadowy Round Table knights sweeping across a plain into battle. This skill at description, like the inability to frame realistic plots, was easily explainable. A portion of Reed was fixated on that period when as a sickly child he first discovered high adventure in the world of books. For all the explosive competitiveness, there lurked within him the frightened little boy who doubted his capacity to cope with the world of men. Overlaid by a strong body and forceful manner, the child emerged in fiction to cry for escape into a magic realm, dangerously overflowing with mystery and yet safe because it was the product of imagination. Part of Jack knew that in the real world failure was possible—that safety lay in withdrawal to an inner life that was more easily controlled—just as another part insisted he continually test himself against reality. In the struggle between the two, Reed's destiny would be determined.

As a twenty-two-year-old graduating senior, Jack did not know this—perhaps he never did. Little given to introspection, he rarely probed the wellsprings of his actions and desires. Only once—in an unpublished essay—did he try to assess the meaning of his Harvard years. Here he divided classmates into three kinds of people: athletes, scholars and activities men. The first, admirable in their "youthful passion for bodily perfection and glory," were alien to the real meaning of Harvard and forced to "occupy the innocuous position of figureheads." Devoted to learning, scholars worked in a tradition dating back three hundred years, but were too narrow and serious, too lacking in "natural desires." With his record, it is hardly surprising Reed found activities men "the realest expression of what Harvard means today." Enthusiastic, delighting in athletics as an experience rather than an end, tasting scholarship "for the mental experience it gives," such men were dreamers, poets, seekers of "what real standards there are by which to judge a man." Equating masculinity with decisive action, he named Theodore Roosevelt as one of the greats in the tradition of men "who make the wheels go round."[44] At the end of his college career, Jack totally identified with such figures.*

In June of 1910, Reed had achieved enough success to face the future confidently. Any and all doubts were momentarily hidden—even from himself. Once he had described college as basically a time for "reading good books, making good friends, keeping young our hearts and bodies, thinking big thoughts and dreaming." It was also a period of preparation for the prizes of a world waiting beyond. In discussions he had always taken a dichotomized view of life after college: "It all comes down to this . . . Happiness and experience, or money and a rut."[45] Whatever the specific road, there was little doubt that John Reed was looking for one labeled experience.

* Admiring Roosevelt, his father's great hero, did not prevent Reed from finding humor in the exaggerations of T.R.'s personality. An unpublished bit of doggerel about the ex-President is illuminating:

> Writer, fighter, peace-inviter
> Brave and fiery speech-reciter
> Arbitrator, legislator
> Up-to-date calumniator
> Early riser, like the Kaiser
> Nature's revolutioniser.

5

Europe

"The first effect of being over here is a pretty full realization of all you ever dreamed of. This is followed by a sort of top-heavy exhilaration, when you want to be arrested, or join the Foreign Legion, or tear off a bizarre party in the Apache district. And then one morning you wake up just five years older than you were the night before. Every bit of self-confidence you got in college leaks out, or at least mine did. I'm just emerging from a period of shakiness and doubt in myself that was pretty morbid for about two weeks. Paris is marvelous; but unless you've a philosophic disposition, unless you're an artist, or unless you're a real bohemian . . . you're bound to get restless and dissatisfied with an existence so deliberate. . . ."[1]

Five months after graduation, when he was living in the Latin Quarter, John Reed's deep feelings momentarily broke through with an honesty rare in his correspondence. Behind were numerous experiences with sailors, hoboes, prostitutes, peasants and police that filled all his youthful fantasies and were generally recounted to friends and family in letters so impersonal in style that they seemed to be stories about someone else. Now life on the Left Bank was a reality as good as any dream. He slept late, took breakfast coffee and croissants at small cafés, poked through the Louvre, the Petit Palais and bookstalls along the Seine's stone quais, loafed in the Tuileries gardens, sat over evening wineglasses at Deux Magots to swap stories with other young Americans, drank his way across the bistros of Montmartre and often danced all night at the Bal Bullier or Maxim's. Artists, writers, professors, expatriates and a number of charming French ladies filled the hours with pleasure, but could not banish those painful moments when Reed sat alone in a small hotel room plastered with bright posters, attempting to write.

Following Copey's advice, he was trying to capture experience in prose, yet, apart from realistic accounts of travels and some *Lampoon*-style humor, he was producing little. Often his mind returned to Harvard. Remembering himself as a substantial figure there, Jack became angry when fellow graduates disparaged Cambridge days, and he confessed, "College always looms tremendous to me."[2] In his new life, totally divorced from college, the future sometimes yawned like an empty chasm. When the work did not go well, there was nothing to hold on to, no role into which he fitted, and then fear rose like a portentous, over-whelming presence.

The best remedy was action. Reed's need to see, touch, taste, feel and do was stronger still than any desire to become an artist, and restlessness pushed him out of the room, sent him off to explore Paris and the sur-rounding countryside. It was easy to write wistfully, "Oh to be a lazy philosopher . . . who can sit on his tail, at friends with the world, and suck the sweetness of things!" But such a role was not for a man who could say, "I've got to hustle, or I'll die of dry rot!"[3] All instincts led away from the desk, and he was fooling both himself and others by proclaiming he had come to France to write. Neither a philosopher nor a real Bohemian, Jack was still a boisterous college boy with a streak of the wild, a youngster who liked to stow away aboard ships, haggle with streetwalkers and sneak past gatekeepers to enter private estates, one who delighted in a life where there were no obligations, no commitments, no deadlines.

Jaunts abroad after graduation were common enough for Harvard men, but, characteristically, Reed's plans were most grandiose. Expecting first to take in western Europe, he planned to sail down the Danube, stop in Constantinople, trek along the south shore of the Black Sea, follow the footsteps of Xenophon's army into Persia, then journey eastward to India and on to San Francisco. While college men made tours in leisurely elegance, Jack was looking forward to hiking across countrysides, scaling mountain ranges, working at odd jobs, sleeping in haymows and barns, sailing on fishing boats and river barges. Appreciating—even craving— luxury liners, hotel rooms and restaurants, Reed nursed an inner fear that such comfort might cut him off from some of life's realities.

This search for a tough life was half of the fantasy that sent him to Europe. It was part of a state of mind suffered by many middle-class artists who found slums more stimulating than everyday life, workers and peasants more romantic than doctors and lawyers. For Reed, who had feared and then emulated the toughness of the Goose Hollow boys, such a search had the very personal meaning of proving his manhood. It lay alongside the fantasy world that had flourished in his stories. Europe meant the possibility of touching the mystery of the remote past, the realm of heroic knights and beautiful damsels. Within Jack were inextricably mixed together the desire to dream amid the ruins of Tuscan castles and to rub shoulders with sailors in Marseilles dives, to listen for the footsteps of goddesses in crumbling Aegean temples and to drink from wineskins with peasants in stubbly Castilian fields. There is no doubt that Reed dwelt in two separate worlds and they in him. Only his strong search for adventure put the two together.

Romantic dreams never obliterated Reed's practical side. The simplest kind of travel took money, and his father—sensing that he was about to be forced out as marshal by the Taft administration—was in poor financial shape. Though C.J. pressed a hundred dollars and a letter of credit on him after graduation, the young man really hoped to earn his own way by selling articles on "strange and unusual places" to magazines or newspaper syndicates.[4] Even the well-connected Lincoln Steffens was unable to procure him a commitment from any publication, sympathetic as he was to Jack's wish to return from travel with reputation enough to launch a successful writing career.

Somehow it did not matter. Europe was calling, and Reed, feeling strong and resourceful, knew he would make out. Years after yearning over the tall-masted vessels sailing out of Portland, he was hoping to ship before the mast. Not wishing to do so alone, he persuaded a wealthy classmate, Waldo Peirce, a burly but lazy sort, to give up reservations on the *Mauretania* and join him. Together they boarded the S.S. *Bostonian* on July 9, with Waldo already grumbling over the venture. His fears were justified. A British vessel carrying 648 steers, the freighter was a wretched hulk with a dank forecastle, an unbearable stench of cattle and unpleasant officers. After a noon meal that featured worms in the soup, Waldo left his wallet and watch on Reed's bunk and dove overboard to make a ten-mile swim back to shore. Nobody saw him go, and when he was found to be missing, nobody except Jack believed anyone would try to swim so far. Because he held Peirce's effects, Reed was, by the end of his first day at sea, scheduled to face murder charges in England.

Unworried by the fate of Waldo—an excellent swimmer—Jack enjoyed the notoriety. Hardened sailors viewed him with a certain amount of respect and deference. Among the dozen students on board, he assumed leadership in trying to make the ship more livable. First they organized a university club and erected a sleeping tent on the poop deck, where they could spend nights on clean straw, far from the foul breath and stale body odors of shipmates. Then, bribing officers, they obtained permission to turn on the saltwater pumps for baths on deck and were allowed to sunbathe. The vile quality of rations presented a bigger problem, and when a deputation—bearing money in hand—was chased out of the galley by an angry head cook, it looked as if the students might really have to "rough it with the rest of the crowd." Fortunately, the second cook was more corruptible, and meat, fruit and cake from the officers' mess helped round out their diet.[5]

The work was arduous. Signed on as a bull-pusher, Reed volunteered to be night watchman, imagining himself a lookout who would sit and ruminate poetically beneath the silence of the stars. In fact, from eight thirty every evening to four in the morning he was below decks, amid the smelly cattle pens. When the ship rolled in heavy swells, he had to plunge among bellowing steers to make sure they did not strangle on neck ropes or trample each other. Before crawling off to sleep, he fed the creatures, and then spent every afternoon hauling bales of hay. Yet it was worth it. With all the work, there was the sea rolling away to every-where, the flat blue summer-afternoon sky, his elation rising as the red sun swam into darkness and the lands of Europe were another day closer.

Getting to know the crew was the best part of the voyage. With few exceptions, he came to like the engineers, stokers, lookouts and common deckhands, all warmhearted and friendly, much more "kindly and sociable than Yankees of that same class." His favorites were the roisterous Irish-men, good talkers, hard drinkers and foulmouthed as the devil. Loving their bawdy anti-English rhymes, Reed learned to spice his conversation with their favorite phrase, "bloody fuckin'." Less to his taste were two "Middle-Western muckers from the University of Illinois." These lads, the only ones not from Ivy League schools, somehow offended the other college men and were expelled from the university club, with Jack telling them "to leave and never come back to our tent." Swearing with common

Irishmen was fine, but he was too full of Harvard to tolerate improper behavior from graduates of state universities.

Eleven quick days gave way to one long night of fear. Locked in irons in a small cabin while an English rain beat monotonously on the deck of the *Bostonian* steaming slowly up the Manchester canal, Jack blamed himself for ever convincing Waldo to board the ship, worried that his strong friend might have met a stronger sea. The next morning, in a dark-paneled, gloomy room, he faced the Board of Trade, a dozen solid Britons with walrus faces. Just as the hearing began, Waldo—who had caught a fast liner—bustled into the room, all smiles and hearty shouts. A few minutes later the young men stormed off through the grimy streets of Manchester to find a pub. Jubilantly Reed scrawled a note to Bob Hallowell: "I am in my element. The unexpected has happened from the start and promises to happen to the end."[6]

England was bully. The day after Jack landed, Waldo caught a train for London, but Reed was determined to make a walking trip. Buying an outfit of homespun, he escaped into the countryside. Steeped in history and literature, Reed was immediately at home with the landscape and people. From the first he loved the dense, tame forests, the green open meadows studded with live oak, the rambling country mansions with manicured hedgerows, the homey thick-walled inns with huge fireplaces, dark taprooms and deep featherbeds. Everywhere he went, people were provincial but friendly, and much "cleaner and happier than our farming and village people. There are *no country muckers*. No matter how poor they are, they are always courteous and never talk dirty or write dirty things on the walls the way our villagers do."[7]

For ten days after leaving Manchester, Jack was on the road, marching long distances through summer cloudbursts, seeing himself half humorously as "an example of American pluck, democracy and independence." The past was everywhere: in medieval Chester, with its Roman bath, twelfth-century walls and soaring Gothic cathedral; in the brown, treeless mountains, where ancient castles crumbled on hilltops; in the charming rose-covered stone villages of Wales; in the wild-haired old man who lived in a turf hut and wanted to teach Reed ancient Welsh; and in the brightly costumed villagers at Chipping Norton who were dancing on the green. Covering vast amounts of ground did not preclude taking time out for mischief. On a damp night when inns were full he slept in a sheltered haystack behind Mrs. Alfred Vanderbilt's Tudor mansion, persuaded a liveried servant to bring him soap, water and a towel in the morning, and sent his formal card in with regrets that he had been unable to stay and see the mistress of the house. At Kenilworth, closed on a

Sunday afternoon, Jack and two fellow students found the Duke of Leicester's private entrance, broke in and climbed all over Mervyn's Tower. On his way to Oxford he invaded the Duke of Marlborough's estate at Blenheim and spent the afternoon swimming in his private lake. Disappointed that Stratford-on-Avon had been "spoiled by Americans, & other tourists," he sneaked into Shakespeare's tomb without paying, and then rushed out ahead of an exasperated attendant.[8]

By the time he reached London, Reed felt himself the experienced traveler, and he had been so frugal that most of his original $100 was intact. Wanting to be fashionable, he shed the homespun and used C.J.'s letter of credit, quickly spending thirty-four pounds on a wardrobe: "I am now completely outfitted, except for a light coat and some pumps and a leather travelling bag. I have a heavy suit & shoes for walking, a light tweed suit for mornings on the back streets, a morning braided cutaway, silk topper, chamois gloves and a silver mounted stick, all for mornings on Piccadilly and Hyde Park, or afternoon calls. Then I have a dazzling dress suit and Tuxedo suit, made by the tailor to the King, & shirts, etc., to match."[9] Apologetic for spending so much, he rationalized in a letter home that it was worthwhile because now he could see, do and profit more from traveling.

Impeccably attired and reunited with Waldo, Jack found London "the greatest city you can imagine." It was also expensive, and he drew heavily on his father's account. Making formal calls on friends and distant relatives, the boys found much of their money going for returning invitations, and treating new acquaintances to meals at famous restaurants—the Trocadero, Simpson's, the Hotel Savoy, the Globe, the London Tavern, the New Mermaid Tavern and Dr. Johnson's old hangout, the Cheshire Cheese. When Waldo left on a golf expedition, Reed found he could live much more cheaply, taking meals at a small chop house where newspaper men congregated, or dining for a shilling on tea, bread and jam under the trees at Hyde Park. Dutifully he covered the sights—the Tower of London, Westminster Abbey, Parliament, Whitehall, the British Museum, the Tate and National galleries. More to his taste were the untouristed regions where the lower classes swarmed in the back streets off Petticoat Lane, Whitechapel and Blackfriars.

In a vague sort of way, Jack had thought of working in London. An introduction from Steffens brought him to Joseph Fels, a wealthy Progressive, who offered a letter to several newspapers. Halfheartedly making the rounds, Reed learned that any reportorial job would be at least several weeks off, and he was anxious to meet friends across the Channel. Enjoying himself too much to settle into a routine, he let a professed self-reliance

collapse. One evening when Fels lectured on the great economic opportunities in England, Jack drowsed over his food. Worried over having
been rude, he penned a thank-you note in which he apologized for a
lack of interest in business: "I am evidently much too callous and un-
matured to worry about economic conditions. They do not bother me
in the least—especially in this country."[10]

The third week in August Reed went to Canterbury, then hiked
ten miles to Dover, determined to cross the Channel "by some fraudulent
game."[11] Disappointed when a day of snooping around the waterfront
turned up no smugglers to join, he somehow convinced Peirce to stow
away on the midnight packet to Calais. In spite of a rough crossing, all
went well until, just in sight of the French harbor, some sailors pulled
them from hiding. Only by quickly producing two dollars each did the
boys escape being handed over to the police. Annoyed at being dragged
into pranks, Waldo suggested they separate, bought a compass and struck
out across the fields, while Jack picked up a map and started down the
coast of Normandy.

Three days and one train ride later, he was in Paris. The city was
still a confused whirl of broad boulevards, heavy traffic, cafés with bright
awnings and attractive girls when, on the second day, he encountered two
Harvard friends, Carl Chadwick and Joe Adams. That evening the three
men, dressed in tuxedos, dancing pumps and fine gloves, and carrying
canes, dined at the chic Café de la Paix, did the rounds of Montmartre—
Moulin Rouge, L'Abbaye, Rat Mort and Café Royale—and finished by
dancing at Maxim's until four a.m. Without going to bed, they climbed
into Chadwick's auto and drove to Grez, where his family lived in a
sprawling mansion covered with roses.

After a good night's sleep, Chadwick took Reed and Adams to St.
Pierre, on the Normandy coast, where a large group of young people were
summering. Amid the most "wonderful crowd of girls," Jack found his
halting textbook French improving rapidly. Center of attention was the
Filon household, with three sisters—Madeleine, Marguerite and Geneviève
—and a number of their friends, all "talented, well-read and up-to-date,"
attractive and beautifully costumed at all times. For a week the men and
women were inseparable, on the courts at the tennis club, in the chill ocean
waters, at an air meet in Le Havre, in casinos playing petit chevaux, driving
to out-of-the-way country restaurants. Everywhere they drank champagne
and wine until the conversation was hilarious and more risqué than any
Reed had ever heard in mixed company.

Stunned and pleased by the experience, he was most impressed by the
freedom of the French girls: "They go without a chaperone everywhere

. . . everybody turns in at the same hotel, or we all sleep together in a haystack by the roadside. Everybody makes jests about the most delicate subjects and everybody roars with laughter." To illustrate, he explained that at first everyone joked that the fair-haired Adams was really Chadwick's mistress in male disguise, because "there are no blond men in France." The question was settled only when the whole crowd trooped down to the ocean to watch Adams bathe naked.

Back at Grez they found Peirce, and Reed received a batch of letters. Some were invitations to visit distant relatives in England, but already that country's luster was dimming. France was infinitely more interesting because "there is so much less prudery and affectation, there is so much gaiety and happiness." From his mother came word that C.J. had announced his candidacy for Congress as a Progressive. Momentarily homesick, Jack wrote a note of support: "It's certainly bully, and I wish I was out there to stump your district for you. If you want me to come home for any reason, just say the word and I'll be there."[12] The mood did not last. An hour after finishing the letter he was in the car with Waldo, Carl and Joe, on the way to Spain.

A cloudless, early September sky smiled as they motored through the chateau country of Touraine, where grapes in the vineyards were ripe to the bursting point, stopped to see the splendors of Blois, then drove through Bordeaux and along a tree-lined highway to the frontier. At the fashionable seaside resort of San Sebastián they took in a bullfight. Preferring the spectacle of sun-drenched arena, bright costumes and martial music to the blood rite, Jack was more impressed by the attendance of the king and his court than by either toreros or bulls. That night his friends lost heavily at the gaming tables, and as their money drained away, so did any desire to see Spain. Wishing to tour the country on foot and alone, he was more pleased than disappointed. When they returned to France, he bought a cheap peasant blouse and corduroy trousers, swung a camera over his shoulder and, not knowing a word of Spanish, started south.

Spain was the land of torrential rains and bleak deserts, the glory of the past and a threadbare present, a gold-encrusted church and a ragged peasantry, ancient universities and deep superstition. In a whirlwind ten days Reed saw much of its landscape, felt many of its jarring dichotomies, was alternately awed, amused, warmed and repelled by its people and customs. South of San Sebastián he hiked along manicured fields and broad rivers spanned by mills, passing sturdy men plowing and women gracefully carrying baskets on their heads. In Tolosa he became part of a drunken fiesta crowd of blue-shirted peasants, dancing and singing in the streets. Vicious rainstorms in the Pyrenees made him give up traveling on foot. Boarding a stuffy, uncomfortable third-class train carriage—a "survival of the Inquisition"—Reed crammed into close quarters with the peasantry for the first of many night rides. Good-natured and boisterous, they plied him with questions, insisted on sharing food and wine, and seemed like "perfect children" in their curiosity about his origins and their ignorance of the outside world.[13]

Under a moonless four-o'clock sky he descended in Burgos and was enveloped by the past. Wandering from the station through dark, muddy streets, he was "filled with the joy of an explorer in a strange land." From far off came the lonesome cry of the *sereño*, the city nightwatch, and then "the mighty history of the place rolled upon me like a flood. Through the dim light the shadow of El Castillo, the gray hill at whose foot the Cid was born, rose against the East. One could imagine a splendid cavalcade of knights come riding down the crooked streets, off to drive the Moor from Toledo." In the morning he followed a religious procession that seemed "most laughable in its solemnity" into the cathedral, where amid the gloomy light beneath the arches, the harmony of choir voices, the shiny splendor of vestments, the hundreds of kneeling people with faith shining in their eyes, he felt "the power of Catholicism in all its naked strength." Retreating into white sunlight, he climbed the cobbled streets, ate a lunch of bread and cheese and dreamed over the Tower of the Crusaders. Present-day superstition broke into his reverie as a noisy crowd of men and children bustled down the street, cursing and yelling after a bent old woman whom they thought to be a witch.

Reality pinched Reed more than once in the next couple of days. Hooking up with a sailor who spoke a few words of English, he shared a room in a Valladolid hotel. Thriftiness made him question the next day's bill and uncover a good-natured plot of landlady and sailor to make him pay for both. Weeks later he was still suffering from the incident—not from the bad faith of his companion but because the lice contracted in sharing a bed were so hardy and difficult to kill. The next day, dozing in the early morning hours at the Medina del Campo railroad station, Jack was grabbed by military police, questioned in Spanish and placed under armed guard. When a French-speaking soldier was found, Reed learned that the king's train was due to pass through and authorities were on the lookout for foreigners and anarchists. After he was roughly searched and found to be carrying no bombs, the soldiers at last believed that he was just an American student traveling for pleasure.

Salamanca seemed the real Spain—full of bright gardens, ancient buildings with arcades of red-brown stone, streets that swarmed with "colour and life." Tattered beggars were everywhere, cripples, blind men, women displaying anemic babies, children with open sores. On corners, in church-yards and around cafés they lay in wait for sympathetic tourists, but Jack —filthy as any of them—with a torn coat, a red sash around his waist and rumpled corduroys, took pride in the fact that he was not approached. In the cathedral, over the tombs of "good knights and virtuous ladies" now carved in stone, he mused upon man's basic impulse toward religion, the feeling that both underlay and transcended any church, "that spirit whose supreme expression is the sunlight and the starlight. . . . How true the instinct of the primevals who worshipped it." Shaking the unaccus-tomed mood, he went off to the university, a mere shell of the center of learning that once housed six thousand students from all over the world. Its classrooms were unimpressive, but he sighed over the patio where Lope de Vega and Calderón and Cervantes had "walked across those very paving stones, under the shadow of those very buildings."

Toledo was the high point of the trip, a city simultaneously regal and pathetic, once the home of the brilliant Spanish court, now a hulk "living for its ruins." But what ruins these were—delicate Moorish palaces, the church where the Christian conquerors had sung their first Te Deum, ancient synagogues with ivory-inlaid roofs, exquisite mosques, the stately home of El Greco, "the most living figure" of all Spanish painters. For two days Reed wandered in a labyrinth of narrow, steep streets and alleys, losing his way among the "prison-like façades," blundering into blank cul-de-sacs, emerging onto unexpected terraces high above the wild gorge of the Tagus River, marveling as the sun painted the buildings with a subtle, shifting palette of earth tones. On Sunday in the cathedral he was pierced by the strange contrasts of the church: a ragged peasant kneeling on the hard floor, tears rolling down his cheeks, while in the sacristy priests smoked and laughed as they changed vestments, then locked faces into "exalted, devout" expressions before returning to the altar.

Madrid was a disappointment, its solid stone buildings, grand boule-vards and open squares more European than Spanish. Weary of traveling, tired of having to struggle to be understood, Jack saw the city with hostile eyes. He recoiled from the teeming streets, and spent hours in the Prado viewing art treasures and in the Palace examining the collection of medieval armor. Vainly searching for color, he drifted through a nightly series of cabarets, finding no joy and life, but only flamenco entertainers who were dull and vulgar compared to the Carmen in his mind. With money running low, he tried a very cheap hotel and quickly fled from a room dirtier than a stable to a bed of leaves in El Retiro park.

Disheveled and grimy as a beggar, Reed could still enjoy himself by playing on the contrast between his appearance and his pocketbook. Already he had done this several times. Stumbling wearily into an elegant hotel where bellhops were dressed "like admirals," he had melted a frosty desk clerk by pulling out a roll of money and tossing down a large tip. In Toledo, when a dubious waiter had questioned his ability to pay for a one-peseta dinner, he had grandly ordered two and had one set on the floor for dogs to eat. Now he dropped into one of Madrid's fine cafés to drink chocolate and write letters home, reveling in the "indignant stares" of the patrons.[14] Thumbing his nose at the pretensions of solid citizens was a good sport, though a limited one. So the next day he bought a third-class railroad ticket, anxious to head back to friends in France.

Paris was "the greatest place in the world." Moving into the Hotel Jacob just off the Boule Miche in late September, Jack—financed by the letter of credit—began to taste a new way of life, one with a deep air of "freedom from every boundary, moral, religious, social." It was a freedom to "loaf all the time, and keep busy doing it," to sit in cafés for hours reading, watch children sailing boats in the ponds of the Luxembourg, go to bed late or not at all, visit a young lady in her room and stay overnight. The city was enjoying an extended Indian summer, with clear, crisp days and the trees in the Bois and the Tuileries a riot of colors. Its boulevards, monuments and fashionable crowds made Paris "the most marvelously beautiful and sensual place you can imagine," what he had "dreamed of unconsciously all my life."[15]

Settled in the Latin Quarter, Waldo Peirce had a net of acquaintances that quickly widened to include Reed. As formal dinner and theater invitations from French and American families arrived, Jack was able to accept them—he wrote his mother—only because of the new wardrobe. Good attire was also necessary for dinners at the home of Professor Schofield of Harvard, on exchange with the Sorbonne, who was treating students to a series of lavish, stiff evenings. He was flattered by the attention, but his craving for excitement was not filled by such social affairs. When he found that Waldo felt much the same, the two became inseparable. Together they liked to stroll down the Boulevard St.-Germain in the early morning hours, "getting a free French lesson by parleying with every whore we see."[16] At night they frequented the distinctly low-class Bal Bullier, often broke into respectable parties dressed in bizarre outfits, brawled in cheap cafés and then bragged endlessly about their exploits.

Wanting the city to fulfill its reputation as a center of love, Reed went on the hunt for female companions. The crowd from St. Pierre was in town, and he called on the Filon sisters, danced and drank champagne at the atelier of a Madame Beaurain and attended a "hilarious affair" that lasted until six on a Sunday morning.[17] One day he and Waldo escorted a wealthy dowager and two lovely daughters to a fair in St. Cloud, and all afternoon in the gardens he flirted with one of the girls and entertained wild fantasies about slipping away to make love to her. Fantasy became a reality with a young French lady. Ignoring the money that changed hands between them, he played at love by bursting into her room to heap armloads of flowers on the bed. Soon his dreams of romance were shattered by Gallic practicality. When one night she happened to ask how Jack earned a living, he became furious at the intrusion of reality, threw on his clothes and stormed out of the room.

Crowded with students, especially from Cambridge, the Latin Quarter had "all the aspects of a small Harvard."[18] Most were clubmen, and though in letters Reed claimed to be avoiding Americans in order to "pound away on the French," he regularly dropped into the seven-o'clock gathering of the sons of Cambridge at Café Deux Magots. Aware of the football season at home, he suggested to Waldo they catch a steamer and turn up at the Yale game because "It would be such a characteristic thing for us to do."[19] He laid bets with Elis on the outcome, attended the annual Yale-Harvard dinner at the Café Voltaire and, when the disappointing news of a tie game was received, went off for an evening of consoling drinks with compatriots.

Harvard men might do for an evening, but they were not good companions. Accepted, even welcomed, by men who had snubbed him in the Yard, Jack was irritated by the Mt. Auburn Street set. Somehow they had managed to transfer their way of life intact across the Atlantic. The sexual mores were different, but aside from that, they lived "as they would in New York, gathering each night for their cocktails before dinner, smoking Philip Morrises, always dressed immaculately."[20] At ease, sure of themselves and their values, self-confident and unquestioning, they increasingly frightened Reed, who was sinking into a turmoil of painful self-doubt as his Paris stay continued.

The trouble was that, for all the cocky exterior, Reed did not know where he was going. Supposed to be a writer, he was turning out little of value. Some humorous stories for the *Lampoon*, travel sketches which were overlong, flabby and packed with clichés, a couple of feeble stories, a few scraps of verse—this was the sum total of the long afternoons trying to write. Worse yet, he was obviously hampered not by lack of material but lack of imagination and will. Other Americans with similar problems seemed better able to cope. Gluyas Williams, his successor as

Ibis on the *Lampoon*, was doggedly sweating away over canvases day and night in an atelier. Peirce, too lazy to work much on painting, seemed to enjoy a life of café lounging. Unable either to force himself to write or to forget about work altogether, Reed could become irritable and bitter.

It was easiest to lay the blame on others, the people who acted as if they knew what they wanted, but there was the nagging thought that to be at odds with the world, "it *must* be my fault." Vacillating between two extremes, Jack "had a fight with Waldo because he said that cheering didn't help the team at all," then broke with Professor Schofield, who presumed to lecture him on his coarse behavior. Soon realizing his adversaries had been right, Reed did not feel apologetic: "If you try to pretend you are wise, you're a goner; somebody'll get you sooner or later. Therefore say your mind on everything, no matter how stupid it seems. If someone talks high philosophy & you think low, out with it, and be despised if necessary." The trouble was, such a philosophy had led him to "shooting off his face" too much, and he resolved to listen more and talk less in the future.[21]

The clubmen, Waldo, Williams and Schofield all touched a sensitive nerve, Reed's role in college. As the pursuit of experience cycled into repetition, his mind drifted to Harvard. Pestering friends for news of Cambridge doings, he wrote the editor detailed critiques of the *Lampoon*, sent advice on the Drama Club and the Symposium, worried over the admission of someone he did not like to Hasty Pudding, cabled congratulations to Copey when he was advanced to assistant professor, and asked Alan Gregg—with seriousness beneath the humor—for information on all "organizations in which I was such a powerful influence, and among which my memory is no doubt venerated." Grappling with the question of just what college experience had meant, he decided it was not a preparation for life in any material way, but more a microcosm, a world of triumphs and defeats that helped make one a man. To Gregg, worrying over the same question, he wrote: "Forget what's coming ahead, and just throw yourself into the present. That constitutes the preparation."[22]

Self-doubt, despair, anger and the impulse to live in the past were moods that vanished mysteriously as they arrived. Usually his letters home rippled with good humor, but slowly his plans changed. In mid-October he decided against journeying around the world, contenting himself with prospects for a springtime trip through Germany, Italy, Austria and Greece. Informing his brother that the decision was due to Waldo's unsuitability as a traveling companion, he added, "It's no damn fun to bum your way alone."[23] More important were family financial problems, and when news came of C.J.'s defeat in the September primary election, Reed had the perfect rationale. With his father now out of work, it seemed "ridiculous for me to stay over here doing nothing but getting a little more education." Even if money were not tight, he confided to his mother, "I think I would rather come home and get busy." A considerate son, Jack was being pushed in this decision more by his own need for achievement than by concern for family problems. Someday he would span the globe, but only "when I've done something worth while myself."[24]*

A decision about the future made life in the present more enjoyable. The clear, blustery days of October, with leaves piling along the quais, gave way to a gray November, with clouds lowering over Montmartre, rain wetting the cobblestone streets and cafés removing tables from sidewalks. Despite the weather, the colorful autumn crowds in the streets were lively, and Reed wandered through them, visiting museums, art galleries and bookstores, lunching on a sweet roll from a boulangerie, writing letters in steamy cafés, dining in cheap restaurants, attending the theater, joking with young ladies at the Taverne Pascal, reading late into the night. By December Paris seemed alternately "cold, bleak, colourful, beautiful, torturing," leading him to savor a kind of sweet homesickness. Appreciating his parents' generosity, he labored through much of the fall on a Christmas present for them—a vellum book, hand-lettered with some of his best poems, and illustrated profusely with painstaking color drawings. Titled *Songs from a Full Heart and an Empty Head*, it was alternately sentimental and playful, dedicated to his mother as "the fruits of a frivolous existence, for which she is responsible."

The frivolous life grew tiresome. During a round of holiday parties that included a bash with the Chadwick family and friends at Grez, Jack suddenly threw over the idea of a spring trip. Shipping most of his clothes, books and half-completed manuscripts home, he headed south in early January looking for sun and romance in the Midi. Soon he found both.

* In later years, after his father's death, Reed felt guilty about all the money he had spent and began to blame himself for many of C.J.'s troubles in life. In the essay "Almost Thirty" he remembered that C.J. lost the Congressional race "by a slim margin, mainly because he came East to see me graduate from college instead of stumping the State." This was simply not true. Replaced as U.S. Marshal on July 13, Reed did not enter the Republican primary until August 14, so late that his platform did not appear in the state-published election pamphlet. Despite the backing of outsiders like Heney, Steffens and Robert La Follette, he ran third in a field of four in the September 24 primary. Judged by the pages of both the *Oregonian*, which opposed him, and the *Oregon Journal*, which backed him, Reed's campaign was much less extensive and vigorous than those of the first two contenders.

Dressed in the ragged Spanish outfit and letting his beard grow, he found the days in Orange "almost warm," marveled at the Roman arch and theater, attended a country-church mass where a slovenly priest "devoured the Blood and Body of Christ with a cannibalist relish, which denoted a lack of breakfast." Avignon, with a cold mistral blowing, was "the most beautiful city I have ever seen," its romantic air weaving a Renaissance spell around him. He hiked along white roads under a clear sky, passed lovely, dark-skinned women and men with Roman faces hunting rabbits, and began to think of publishing a book of travel sketches. The air of the Midi felt charged with energy, and he became excited about the Provençal poets and painters. Finding the Roman arena at Nîmes now a bull ring, with electric lights, water closets and other modern conveniences, Reed was at first disappointed, then realized "it's as it should be to make use of these things in the same spirit as the Romans did."[25]

Marseilles was "bluff and splendid and masculine," uglier than Paris but more "*romantique*." Its sun set behind the Pillars of Hercules, its waters led to "Greece, Asia and Egypt" and in its streets jostled sailors from all over the world, "Copt and Pict, Chinaman and Turk . . . the cultured French . . . the artistic Italian and the barbaric and crude American." Registering in a hotel that housed streetwalkers, Jack joined the crowds of the Cannabière, the great street that ran from the Vieux Port to the Heights, "flanked with splendid cafes and hotels and shops." He dined expensively on bouillabaisse and filet of mountain sheep at Pascal's, one of the city's oldest restaurants, then headed for the part of town described in a guidebook as "dangerous after dark" and stayed until one in the morning "talking with all the motherly old prostitutes, and childish young prostitutes and Lascar sailors." The next day he spent "crashing around the great quais" seeing "thousands of ships, & the great basins, and the miles of coconuts from Africa, and the mountains of peanuts," and hearing "every known language under the sun—some that never existed."[26]

On January 14, Reed journeyed to Toulon to meet Waldo, Harold Taylor, two of the Filon sisters—Madeleine and Marguerite— and Mme. Beaurain for a walking tour of the Riviera. Shaved and dressed a little more respectably in a tweed Norfolk jacket, soft shirt, necktie and corduroy knickers, a pack hoisted on his shoulders, Jack led the way. For nine days they hiked toward Nice, in the mountains and along the beaches, picnicking in the woods, swimming in the chill sea, visiting Roman ruins, staying in charming hotels where the rooms and meals were "cheap as dirt," laughing always and growing together.

With time in Europe drawing to a close, the trip was a magic "dream of joy from beginning to end." Reed's normally acute senses were heightened—never had pine forests smelled so sweet; never had bread, cheese and sausages tasted so delicious; never had the sun painted snowy mountain peaks such subtle shades; never had friends felt so open and close and warm. Soon the closest and warmest was Madeleine, slender, delicate and dark-skinned, "the exact image of a pretty gypsy."[27] Occasionally alone together, they said little, somehow knowing that words could not capture a feeling that swept in on the sea wind and up from the depths of the heart to hang unspoken between them. Then one afternoon, playing a Roman gladiator in the ancient arena of Fréjus, Jack —sword in hand—knelt before Madeleine, who was seated in the crumbling grandstand like an empress. Perhaps when he raised his head and their eyes met, they knew at last. By the time the trip ended in Monte Carlo, Madeleine had consented to become his wife.

It was a fitting conclusion to a trip that had begun with the unexpected. Since Reed had left Paris for the south, knowing he was soon going home, his depressions and worries had ceased. From Marseilles he had written C.J. that, like college and the "general run of womenkind," Europe had been one of those splendid realities that had "surpassed my wildest dreams."[28] Always Jack was happiest when on the move or aiming at a specific goal, and his engagement fitted a recurrent pattern of behavior. If he could not yet write as well as he wished, he could still throw himself into the present and act; if he could not continue a life of indolence in Europe, he could take a little of the Continent home with him. When he left for America he was a man with two definite purposes in life—"to make a million dollars and get married."[29]

6

Manhattan

"In New York I first loved, and I first wrote of the things I saw, with a fierce joy of creation—and knew at last that I could write. There I got my first perceptions of the life of my time. The city and its people were an open book to me; everything had its story, dramatic, full of ironic tragedy and terrible humor. There I first saw that reality transcended all the fine poetic inventions of fastidiousness and medievalism. I was not happy or well long away from New York. . . ."[1]

The long-running desire for a real home, a place to be understood, was at last fulfilled for John Reed at the age of twenty-three in the greatest shining city of the East: Manhattan, glowing with the luster of real life. Unlike Portland, bathed in the romantic haze of virgin forest, full of cowboys and Indians and hard by the western sea; unlike Cambridge, which, for all its fierce status struggles, was a college town bounded by the gentle Charles; unlike England, France or Spain, where poverty was a picturesque backdrop against which an American youth could play—

unlike these, New York City was a daily reality where Jack's struggle for achievement paralleled that of other men. Wealth and squalor, joy and despair, love and hatred, beauty and ugliness, idealism and crassness, fame and obscurity—in the few square miles of Manhattan such ideas became tangible.

Inspired by the vibrant colors of street life, Reed slowly retreated from dreamy visions of mythic realms. Molded by New York, he in turn reshaped the city in his imagination. Describing it became a matter of blending the "real" and "enchanted" aspects, fusing keen observation with poetry: "I wandered about the streets, from the soaring imperial towers of down-town, along the East River docks, smelling of spices and the clipper ships of the past, through the swarming East Side—alien towns within towns—where the smoky flare of miles of clamorous pushcarts made a splendor of shabby streets; coming upon sudden shrill markets, dripping blood and fish-scales in the light of torches, the big Jewish women bawling their wares under the roaring of great bridges, thrilling to the ebb and flow of human tides sweeping to work and back, west and east, south and north." In this mixed response to New York, John Reed the professional writer was born.

His arrival there was natural enough—for an ambitious writer it was in 1911 the only place in America to be. Returning from Europe on a liner rather than a cattle boat, Jack had stopped briefly in Cambridge to see Harry, Copey and friends, then had gone on to Portland, where Margaret and C.J. were delighted and surprised by his appearance. Months of short rations and long hikes had trimmed down a fleshy abdomen, making Reed appear more mature. Although boyish and exuberant in recounting adventures to anyone who would listen, Jack was now an adult, and his father decided to shelter him no longer. When the first flurry of visiting was over, C.J. sat him down to explain the state of family finances.

Conditions were lamentable. With no office to work from, the elder Reed was on the street trying to sell insurance in a town whose businessmen—with few exceptions—thought him a traitor. Earning barely enough to cover daily expenses, C.J. was keeping Harry in a Gold Coast apartment and paying his way through Spee, one of the most exclusive Harvard clubs. As an executor of the Green estate he was sunk in a morass of financial dealings with hostile partners and overly mortgaged property, and at the same time struggling unsuccessfully to keep Charlotte Green from squandering the rest of a shrinking inheritance. Much as he loved Jack, there was no money to stake him. From now on, his eldest son would have to stand alone.

His parents were worried about Jack, but managed a cheerful front to cover dismay over what seemed a "fool engagement."[2] Wanting his son to stay out of debt and young at heart, to have more time to play with life, C.J. asked Steffens to look out for him. "He is a poet, I think; keep him singing. Let him see everything, but don't—don't let him get like me."[3] Margaret was more concerned with the social consequences of the engagement. "The good people of Portland," Jack wrote to Waldo, "seem to attach an opprobrious significance to the adjective 'French' when applied to a girl, and mother has received more condolences than I have congratulations."[4] This straitlaced attitude toward a foreign woman only reinforced what Reed already knew—Portland was no place to linger. By early March he was in New York, living temporarily at the Harvard Club and looking for work in journalism, ready for "any amount of hard labor, short leisure, danger or drudgery, so long as I can do something worth while."[5] Turning to Steffens, he found the man who had once seemed so serious to be warm and understanding. When Reed was unsure about what kind of career to pursue, the older writer calmed fears that poetry and prose would not mix, and stated, "You can do anything you want to" with so much conviction that it seemed true.

Steffens gave more than moral support. Within a few weeks he landed Jack a half-time trial position on the *American*. This was a good place to begin. Six years previously the publication had been taken over by the group of journalists who had helped create the muckraking movement as writers for *McClure's*—Ida Tarbell, Ray Stannard Baker, John Siddall and Steffens. As the tenor of the magazine slowly shifted from criticism to qualified support of the social and political status quo, Steffens had departed. Now the *American*'s pages were open to a diverse array of factual pieces, fiction and short poems. Reed did some editing, corrected proofs, helped with makeup and gave a hand with miscellaneous problems. One of his main tasks was judging manuscripts, and from the first he enjoyed having a chance to "contemptuously reject" works by well-known authors. His great delight was rotten poetry: "I have wreaked my fiendish worst on 'lady' bards, too—a breed which I despise, especially when they attempt to write like Kipling!"[6] Quickly learning both editorial duties and the needs of the commercial marketplace, Reed impressed the editors as an "awake, vivid, companionable and expressive" young man and was retained permanently.[7]

The *American* had only one great drawback—it paid a very modest salary of fifty dollars a month, barely enough to live on. Somehow it did not matter. Even when forced into an occasional odd job, Jack did not resent the lot of a young writer. The reward was not the money, but the excitement of New York. The atmosphere of the city, the environment of editorial offices, professional journalists and writers of all sorts, the hurrying crowds, the dim saloons, the chic stores with glittering displays, the shabby tenements, the continual roar of Broadway traffic and metallic clangor of the El, and the purposeful hustle of the streets cleared away the block suffered in Paris. Suddenly the energy of Harvard days returned, and words that described and created experience began to flow from his pen.

From the first, Jack scattered himself in many directions. Poetry was put aside for odd, late hours. Straight reporting, satire, sketches, short fiction and humorous essays could be sold more quickly. Dusting off some college stories, he tried to rework them, but soon abandoned the idea—somehow rewriting was more difficult than starting afresh. Drawing on the European experience, he made a short story out of Waldo's dive and a rambling travel article out of the "Dash into Spain." After both had collected enough rejection slips, he sold rights in the shipboard tale to popular writer Julian Street for fifty dollars, and was listed as coauthor when the work appeared in the *Saturday Evening Post*. Ideas for stories were easier to conceive than execute. Pulled by the contrary impulses of romance and realism, Reed began many, but completed few. Two accepted by the *Century* were semihumorous O'Henry-type tales about a bumbling Parisian inspector, Monsieur Vidoq. "Showing Mrs. Van," a witty, fashionable picture of poor American students in Paris, was returned often before winding up in the *Smart Set* two years later.

While rejections of fiction were pouring in during the spring of 1911, he turned to subjects closer at hand. At Steffens' suggestion, Jack researched a lengthy study of the New York Fire Department, full of incompetence because of political appointments. Perhaps the day for such exposés was past; certainly the piece was so dull and devoid of enlivening detail that it is not surprising nobody would buy it. Doggedly he reworked the same information into a portrait of the department's Chief Croker, but again there were no takers. In a more personal view, he described misadventures dining at a new American institution, "The Quick Lunch," invented by "some canny Yankee [who] discovered that eating not only cost money, but a lot of time which might be used in making money." Decrying the inhuman speed, clatter and sterility, he zeroed in on the vegetarian variety, where large posters warned against "the moral degeneracy caused by the Porter-house Steak."[8] Evidently other editors were paid well enough to avoid such eateries, for this, too, found no market.

Reed's first published works, undistinguished in style, gloried in individualism. The May 20 editorial section of *Collier's* carried a short, unsigned sketch, "Immigrants," which in best land-of-opportunity tradition described the landing of a boatload of eastern Europeans. Awestruck by the "jagged mountain range" of skyscrapers, they sing and shout and weep with joy, "For this was America, and happiness lay just across the river."[9] In June the *Trend* published a byline work, "The Involuntary Ethics of Big Business." Subtitled "A Fable for Pessimists," it was a lengthy, uninspired defense of capitalism which laboriously sought to prove that the big businessman who seeks only profit will—in spite of himself—create a society full of liberty, justice and beauty.

Work on the magazines and literary efforts absorbed Jack's time as 1911 rolled toward summer, but he was not the sort to lock himself perpetually in a garret. A gregarious type, he needed to drink, laugh and play. Two companions were former Harvard cronies: Walter Lippmann, on the staff of *Everybody's*, and H. V. Kaltenborn, a reporter for the Brooklyn *Eagle*. One day on the street he bumped into Alan Seeger, whose dreaming eyes and pale face bespoke the romantic poet. Borrowing money, Seeger dragged Reed off to dinner at Petitpas, a homey French restaurant on 29th Street. There, expatriate Irish painter John Butler Yeats presided at a nightly table of painters like John Sloan and Robert Henri and young intellectuals like Van Wyck Brooks, all passionately discussing the problems and promise of American art. Such talk was interesting, but Reed was just as happy listening to the gay, drunken chatter at the Working Girls Home, a huge, smoky, double-deck beer hall with murals and elkheads on the walls, crowded by an odd array of pickpockets, con men, gentlemanly gangsters with their overdressed "skirts," and portly Germans.

Masculine pleasures such as beer, cigars and good talk hardly constituted a full social life. New York was a city of attractive women, many interested in a good-looking man with a talent for letters. Avoiding such females, Jack wrote almost nightly to Madeleine, attempting to confine passion to words. Inexplicably, ardor cooled until his fiancée seemed more a sentimental memory than a real woman. Letters from her gave less pleasure than those from Waldo, splashed with vivid pictures of wild artists' balls where naked models and lesbians cavorted. By late spring it was a nightmare to write to her. After analyzing the problem endlessly, he began to wonder openly about calling off the engagement. Friends said flatly, "The pact is sacred," but the experienced Steffens gently insisted that Jack should not marry the girl unless he loved her. Unable to easily slough off mores imbibed from infancy, the gut reaction that an engagement was indeed inviolable, Reed was "appalled at the inevitability of the thing."[10] Ultimately, however, he was not a man to bow to social convention. In June he severed the engagement.

His parents were delighted. C.J. wrote: "You are right to get out of it and be able to lead your own life without care and responsibility at your age."[11] Support came from the raffish Waldo, who looked askance at the institution of marriage. Backing was nice, but the action alone made Jack feel "like a new man, who's had something the matter with his eyes, & is finally cleared up." To Peirce he confessed: "I thought I knew something about women, the universal nature of Love . . . I find that I don't." Never had he realized that the intense love felt in France could fade, or that daily problems might interfere with it. Bringing Madeleine to New York would have been like "making a skyscraper out of the Louvre," and trying to support her on a meager income would be folly. A near-disaster, the experience had proved beneficial: "I've lost my sentimentality; & I guess that's the only way a man can be a real artist." Now he understood an important truth: "A man *does not* meet his pre-destined mate—never. He could love and marry, and be happy with any one of a thousand." As for marriage, one should "Do it quick, without waiting. Slam it through."[12] With this new level of worldliness, Jack quickly opened to the opportunities at hand. By early July the self-imposed vow of chastity taken at his engagement was no more.

In the summer of 1911 John Reed moved to Greenwich Village, joining three friends to take third-floor quarters in the dilapidated brick building at 42 Washington Square South, near the corner of MacDougal Street. Renting for thirty dollars a month, the apartment contained rooms with high ceilings, wide windows, enormous fireplaces and a temperamental water supply that often ran hot in summer and cold in winter. Like many dwellings in this borderline slum, the building was largely occupied by a new kind of tenant—young men and women of vaguely artistic tendencies who preferred the confines of the Village, with its quiet, twisting streets, to the roaring gridiron of the metropolis. Visible through leafy trees were elegant north-side brownstones occupied by wealthy families, but Jack's bedroom looked south and east over the squalid back-yard of an Italian tenement where children squalled, drunken workers beat wives, and colorful washing—"the short and simple flannels of the poor!"—drooped from every window.[13]

His roommates were all Harvard men, Robert Andrews and Alan Osgood, both of the *Lampoon*, and Robert Rogers of the *Monthly*. Andrews, now in the advertising department of Lamont, Corliss and Company, was a flippant sort with a penchant for dalliance, while the

hefty Rogers, a reporter for the Brooklyn *Eagle*, upheld the stiff traditions of his native New England. Something of a dandy, Osgood worked
in a bank and was always ready for late-night excursions to the beaches
of Staten Island, the Bowery or any one of a number of tough working-
class bars where Jack liked to soak up local color. Gaining a reputation
as a lively center, 42 became a kind of way-station for other Harvard
men. Often somebody was camping on the floor—Alan Seeger, who
drifted from a cabin in the New Hampshire woods to Manhattan carrying sheaves of poetry; Joe Adams, now with an investment house in
Chicago; Eddy Hunt, currently an assistant dean in Cambridge; or Jack's
brother, Harry, usually very broke on excursions into the big city.

Days were always hectic. Morning began with the "horrid sound"
of an alarm clock, and a mad scramble from kitchen to bathroom as the
four dressed, crowded each other away from the sink, hastily gulped
coffee and raced to the subway. After eight hours sometimes packed
with story conferences, interviews and last-minute makeup changes, and
sometimes leisurely with long, wine-drenched lunches, Jack returned to
the apartment to enter the nightly debate over dinner. Usually the slim-
ness of pocketbooks governed the choice, and fortunately the area
abounded in small, family-run Italian restaurants—Paglieri's on West
Eleventh, Bertolotti's on Third, Mori's on Bleecker, all of which served
baskets of warm, crusty bread, spicy antipasto, heaps of pasta and plenty
of dago red at prices low enough for the poorest Villager. After dinner,
"the red wine dancing in our feet," the group bounced along sidewalks
where shabby families lounged on stoops, romped past couples on the
benches of the square, laughing and joking aloud. Back at 42, they lit
pipes and cigarettes and, with "windows open to the roaring night," began
to play cards, banter, perhaps even take time to scrawl a lyric poem.

Friends dropped by—the correct, foppish Bob Hallowell, now an
illustrator for the *Century Magazine*; the placid Lippmann, talking of
recent readings in Freud or Marx; Seeger, solemnly discussing aesthetics
in a "bell-like voice"; the sculptor Arthur Lee, preaching "the inspired
word of Modern Art"; the slovenly vagabond poet Harry Kemp, fresh
from an amorous venture and ready to argue about anything; blond,
handsome Harry Reeves, a self-professed Nietzschean freethinker. Intellect and emotion soon clashed over the latest doctrines in art and
politics. By midnight voices were harsh and tired. To refresh themselves,
members of the party adjourned to the basement of the Brevoort Hotel
on Fifth Avenue, or the nearby Lafayette, where, amid elderly French-
men playing chess, noisy Italian musicians and other tables of would-be
poets and artists, voices were renewed by wine or Cointreau and the
conversation continued until waiters began to pile chairs on tables and

sweep the floor. In the early-morning hours Reed and his roommates stumbled under the pseudo-Roman arch, past huddled shapes on the grass of the darkened square. Sunrise was not far off and, young as they were, some sleep was necessary to continue the same pace the next day.

In September, Lincoln Steffens—recently widowed—moved into an apartment on the second floor in response to Jack's urging, and a relationship of master-to-disciple ripened into friendship. The two had much to give each other. Steffens, brown hair combed in bangs over his forehead and eyes twinkling behind round glasses, was a famed journalist who had been everywhere and knew everyone. With paradox the core of his belief, the playful intellectual was slightly weary of life, and Reed's energy and enthusiasm proved tonic. At any hour of the day or night Jack would slam into his room to discuss recent adventures, to talk of the "most wonderful thing in the world," a play, a girl, a restaurant bouncer, a group of bums, a singer in a nightclub. Conversation would meander through a whole range of topics, from politics to marriage, from socialism to literature, as the two men—alternately laughing and serious —traded anecdotes, information, theories and ideas. The older man's influence on Reed was enormous. In talks with him, insight came "like flashes of clear light; it is as if I see him, and myself, and the world, with new eyes. I tell him what I see and think, and it comes back to me beautiful, full of meaning. He does not judge nor advise—he simply makes everything clear." This process occurred with personal as well as intellectual difficulties. When broke, Reed went to him for money. When he had problems writing, or at work, he turned to Steffens, who patiently listened "until I solved them myself in the warmth of his understanding." When he fell in love—a frequent occurrence—Steffens helped with common-sense advice: "You're not in love, or you'd never put it that way: 'Damn it! I'm afraid I'm falling in love again.' You're not, and you weren't before. So look out. When you really fall in love you'll know it. . . . Wait for the real thing. It's worth waiting for. . . ."[14] The successor to Copeland, Steffens was the second man to make Jack want to "do nothing unworthy."

Like Copey, Stef gave one piece of advice over and over: go out and see the world, then write about it. Reed hardly needed prompting. New York was a magic city where "everything was to be found." The Village, with its delicatessens, bookshops, art studios and saloons, its long-haired men and short-haired women, artists, writers, radicals and Bohemians, was the center of his life, a starting point for exploration: "Within a block of my house was all the adventure in the world; within a mile was every foreign country." Soon he knew these lands well, Chinatown, Little Italy, the Syrian quarter, German Village and the Jewish district of the Lower East Side. On foot he went everywhere—to the Bowery, where long lines of tramps huddled before rescue missions and flophouses; to the Fulton Fish Market, "where the red and green and gold sea things glisten in the blue light of the sputtering arcs." He drank in McSorley's and Sharkey's and the dives of the Tenderloin, ate in obscure foreign restaurants, talked with girls who walked the street in "Satan's Circus," Spanish longshoremen on the docks, drunken merchant mariners on shore leave, ragged old men on park benches. From them he learned strange lessons—how to buy cocaine or enter secret gambling dens, where to hire a man to kill an enemy. Sometimes he accepted unusual invitations—to a gangsters' ball or a free Christmas dinner for derelicts given by a Tammany ward boss.

Fascination with the underside of Manhattan did not dim the luster of the city's high life. Drawn to the fashionable crowds and smart stores of Fifth Avenue, Jack loved to splurge on expensive uptown restaurants. Broadway openings and the Metropolitan Opera pulled like a magnet, and he was in the audience for everything from the Ziegfeld *Follies* to Verdi's *Otello*, saw popular plays starring Ethel and John Barrymore and such serious works as *Oedipus Rex*, Strindberg's *The Father* and the Irish Players performing Synge. He attended air meets on Long Island, took the train to Princeton and New Haven for Harvard football games, cheered the Giants against the Athletics in the World Series, viewed exhibitions of contemporary works at the National Arts Club and romped through the tinsel delights of Coney Island. Accompanied by roommates, friends or young ladies, Reed everywhere seemed to have a splendid time.

The excitement of New York did not conceal its problems, the exploitation of man by man so glaring in an urban setting. Ghettos might be picturesque, but Jack sensed that they stunted human development. Solutions to the problems they posed were tied up with theories that would transform the nature of society, with radical ideas aired by friends or enunciated in occasional lectures like one in Carnegie Hall, where Emma Goldman debated Solon Fieldman on the topic of "Socialism vs. Anarchism." Made uneasy by theorizing, Reed retreated to an older idea, the belief that cities were evil because they were out of rhythm with nature. On the other hand, his own experience showed that they throbbed with a life that was "quicker, more passionate."[15] Ambivalence over the issue could not be settled by rational argument, but was expressed in a sometime desire to escape Manhattan. On Saturdays he might dress in old clothes and catch a train to Redding Ridge, hiking eight miles from the station to Ida Tarbell's farm to spend the weekend feeding chickens and lolling beneath the trees. On a Sunday jaunt to Westchester County he discovered a vacant home thirty miles from the city, nestled in an apple orchard on top of a hill, and he raced back to town full of plans to rent it with friends, buy a secondhand car and commute to work. Immediately he wrote Waldo to return and join them because there were "the most lovely great hills to paint."[16]

These plans fizzled—as did others for buying various farms—because, for all the tug of nature, Jack simply could not tear away from the color and excitement of New York, especially at the point where its rewards were beginning to descend. Secure as an editor on the *American*, he was becoming a contributor as well. The November 1911 issue carried two short articles by Reed, a reminiscence of a Cambridge day spent with William James and a feature on Copeland. The next few months saw other pieces on interesting personalities carried by the *American*, along with some poems, while stories and sketches began to appear in other magazines. He was highly regarded enough to be elected in December to the Dutch Treat Club. At weekly luncheon meetings he began to mingle with editors, writers and artists already at the top of their fields, or judged to be on the way by the elite of the magazine world.

Such an idea was reinforced by people far from the New York journalistic scene. Early in the summer of 1911 Copey commended his "progress and prosperity," and a few months later lavishly gave thanks for the article which praised "your aged friend far beyond his deserts."[17] Inviting Jack to address English 12, he urged him to follow through on an idea with which Reed and Osgood had been toying, that of sailing around Cape Horn. Early in 1912, Robert Benchley, a *Lampoon* editor, requested advice on how to begin a career: "Would you advise me to storm the Big City, and from what point is it best approached? I ask you, who have so soon gained the outer ramparts."[18] Often Eddy Hunt asked for information on breaking into the publishing world, and sent along poems to place with a magazine.

His parents were now beginning to lean on Jack for emotional support. Expressing loneliness in many letters, Margaret said, "We are so ambitious for you—far more than you can be for yourself." Critical of some early works and fearful he was writing carelessly, she cautioned: "Do *not* do any cheap work if you can help it."[19] C.J. was always affirmative: "I think and talk of you every day, and love you and am proud of you every hour." While Margaret concentrated on news of people, his father described Oregon politics. Active in the movement to help Roosevelt wrest the Republican nomination away from Taft in 1912, he was delighted to learn Steffens had introduced Jack to T.R.: "He is all man & the greatest American alive today. In his day & time as great as Lincoln." Less happy were business affairs. Lamenting that "I have been cursed with debts all my life," C.J. urged his son to "stay out of debt and save a little." Worries could also be expressed in humor. Complaining that none of the Greens had any sense of money at all, his father described Charlotte on her latest extravagant tour:

> Yesterday came a large photograph of [her] mounted on a camel, holding with a death grip to a Bedouin shiek who looked as if he could cheerfully chop her with a scimitar. . . . In the background stands the Sphinx with a nauseated expression. . . . Surely the long line of Pharaohs were in great luck to have become only a memory before [she] invaded Egypt. If Moses could have subsidized her there would have been eight instead of seven plagues. . . .[20]

All the admiration of family, friends and colleagues had an effect. Reed's flush of success brought to the surface the streak of self-importance exhibited at Harvard. Of course it depended on who was viewing him and in what context. To roommates and close friends he was still the same bouncy young man they had known in the Yard, loud, talkative, often extravagant in language and behavior, but basically a good companion who would lend money and possessions, commiserate in times of trouble and take genuine pleasure in the accomplishments of those he liked. But new acquaintances—and older ones who were not close—often found him hard to take. Some thought him vain, basically interested in the idea of success, in gaining the limelight. Carl Chadwick, back from France and married to Madeleine's sister Geneviève, accused him of being a poseur, a self-conscious romantic acting like "the drinkers of life" only to win attention.[21] Thomas Beer, reading law at Columbia, saw two incompatible sides to Jack. One was the obnoxious young man he invited to the Yale Club, who first tried to be funny and then "piled the exasperatingly vapid on the horror of the expected" as he bored a tableful of men who lived in Paris about his adventures there. Then there was the somber Reed encountered one damp winter day on Riverside Drive. Standing by the Hudson, hands stuffed in the pockets of a loose overcoat, staring moodily at the river, he talked about the Pacific Northwest, described Tacoma and a blind man who grew roses in his backyard, the long Sound shrouded in the soft gray mist of autumn and the ramshackle brothels strung up slopes, the smell of burning cedar bark in Portland. Finding himself moved, Beer concluded that Jack was not a brilliant talker, but a man who "made beauty" while speaking of things he loved.[22]

The loud showoff, the introspective dreamer—these two different sides to Reed had always been there, and the life in New York served to make the split sharper. By early 1912 experience was providing evidence that the desire to be recognized and yet maintain his integrity would come into conflict. Not yet seeing the problem whole, he was facing a fundamental conflict of the artist in a society that defines a man in terms of success—the clash between what he wants to say and the need of the marketplace. And this was compounded by his own doubts, fears and hopes about whether or not he had the talent to be a great writer.

A primary internal battlefield was poetry. After a dry spell Reed had begun to compose again, and by the spring of 1912 several short works had been accepted by the *American* and other publications. But such acceptance did not mean he was a poet. More than once he had been forced to return Eddy Hunt's "wonderful" poems because they were not commercial enough. It was easy to rationalize that Hunt's works were too "literary," but increasingly he knew magazines would print only the most trifling sort of poetry, "short lyrics that will produce dry gripes in the Ladies Ibsen and Culinary Club of Wenatchee, Wash."[23] Certainly it was disturbing when editors said poetry was a declining art and then accepted Jack's work.

He was in a painful period of readjustment, trying to move beyond undergraduate poetry and the nineteenth-century romantic movement. While his mind still naturally ran to lines like "the heavy-eyed moon/ Drowsily sinks on the Dawn's pale breast," a new impulse was stirred by the impact of New York: In "A Hymn to Manhattan" the diction was old, but the subject new:

> O Let some young Timotheus sweep his lyre
> Hymning New York. Lo! Every tower and spire
> Puts on immortal fire.
> This City, which ye scorn
> For her rude sprawling limbs, her strength unshorn—
> Hands blunt from grasping, Titan-like, at Heaven,
> Is a world-wonder, vaulting all the Seven![24]

Firmer language and a strong flavor of romance joined in a description of men building a skyscraper:

> Clamor of unknown tongues, and hiss of arc
> Clashing and blending; screech of wheel on wheel—
> Naked, a giant's back, tight-muscled, stark,
> Glimpse of mighty shoulder, etched in steel.
> And over all, above the highest high,
> A phantom of fair towers in the sky.[25]

Tracking something new, Jack began to experiment with unrhymed blank-verse slices of city life. None was fully satisfying, and the pieces he published were all rhymed and touched either by humor or by a romantic vision of the world.

Much to Reed's dismay, there was no market for his most accomplished poem, "Sangar," a deft mixture of politics and mythology. A tribute to Steffens, the work grew out of his mentor's attempts to settle a bitter quarrel between capital and labor. In late 1911 Stef went to Los Angeles to cover the trial of the McNamara brothers, steelworker organizers accused of exploding a bomb that killed eleven employees of the anti-union Los Angeles *Times*. Despite nationwide support from labor and the intellectual community, the brothers faced almost certain death sentences. Toying with the doctrine of Christian anarchism—in fact, probably the only Christian anarchist in the country—Steffens was convinced the local establishment had nothing to gain from executions. He worked out a deal with the *Times*' publisher, the prosecution and the defense attorney, Clarence Darrow. The terms were simple: rather than maintaining innocence, the brothers would confess to the crime and be given short sentences. After the McNamaras reluctantly agreed, the plan aborted. The admission of guilt destroyed public support for the local labor movement and ruined the candidacy of Job Harriman, a Socialist previously conceded a good chance of winning the 1911 mayoralty election in Los Angeles. Worse yet, one brother was sentenced to fifteen years and the other to life imprisonment. Besieged by the wrath of both labor and intellectuals, Steffens returned to Washington Square in disgrace with many former friends.

Jack greeted him warmly. Following the dispatches from Los Angeles, he had not quite known what to make of such antics, but in argument had passionately defended them. Not very good at political debate and unable to persuade anyone else, he put his admiration into poetry. On Christmas Eve, over a bottle of wine in a restaurant, Reed recited "Sangar" to an appreciative Steffens. A romantic allegory, the work describes a great medieval battle in which the aged knight Sangar—a ferocious killer in youthful wars—leaps into the fray without a weapon and, in the name of Christ, attempts to stop the carnage. For a moment the armies waver, then he is denounced and slain by his hot-blooded son, and as the battle rages the knight goes to his reward:

> Oh, there was joy in Heaven when Sangar came.
> Sweet Mary wept, and bathed and bound his wounds,
> And God the Father healed him of despair,
> And Jesus gripped his hand, and laughed, and laughed. . . .[26]

Well meant and well written, the tribute clearly made the son a symbol of a rising radicalism which muckraker Steffens had helped to foster.

Perhaps there was another level, but neither man was inclined to wonder if the symbol could in any way be personal.

The lack of outlet for "Sangar" only reinforced a belief that narrow-minded editors were not interested in serious poetry. Soon there was similar evidence for fiction. Beginning far more works then he could hope to complete, Jack still tended toward dreamy stories of men in armor or humorous tall tales, but in late 1911 his urban experience began to emerge in prose. Sketches of immigrant children, artists starving in garrets, fashionable and flirtatious young ladies and elegant dandies grew into stories, and some proved most difficult to sell. The best was a short, simple tale of a girl from the low-class Haymarket dance hall who saves money for a European trip, meets a South American nobleman and goes to Rio as his mistress. Overwhelmed by homesickness, she eventually returns to New York and a regular table at the gaudy, raucous night spot, happier among friends and customers than with foreign nobility.

Annoyed that this story, "Where the Heart Is," was collecting rejections, Reed pressed an editor of *Everybody's* for an explanation. He answered with praise, but said that only Flaubert or Maupassant could write delicately enough to have such a work accepted, and continued:

> The magazine is bought by the year. The father of children, counting on its past record of avoiding the treatment of sex problems, allows the magazine to come into the house, and to lie carelessly on the library table. His children can read it, even before he looks it over himself. He counts on us to be the censor of it. And that is the main reason why magazines must be very careful about the points of view they present in their stories. You have been working at the *American*; you ought to know their point of view. You can't override such a proposition.[27]*

---

* Earlier he had received a similar rejection of another story from *Adventure Magazine*. An editor friend had written on September 9, 1911: "You see, Jack, the story is fundamentally immoral, and all proper adventures are highly moral. . . . If you can restrain your lawlessness, or if you must be lawless, you can be conventionally lawless, *Adventure* will be delighted to see some more of your stuff." The problem was shared by most serious writers. Years later James Oppenheim mocked the comments of a muckraking editor in *Mystic Warrior* (New York: Alfred A. Knopf, 1921), 95:

> No matter what you have to say there is a way to say it
> So all the people will understand . . .
> It is simple enough—of course a sacrifice or two . . .
> Don't be too gloomy, and don't be sordid,
> Don't open the stink-pots and the lavatories,
> Don't offend people's moral scruples and religious creeds,
> Keep out of politics, and sex, and socialism,
> Don't be highbrow, don't end up in tragedy—
> In short, uplift the people. . . .

Disagreeing with this viewpoint, Jack did recognize it as the prevailing one in the publishing world. For the time being the story remained in his desk.

Wary of serious poetry and offbeat fiction, magazines seemed an uncongenial market for Reed's newest writings, but one side of him—the reporter—had barely been tested there. He had learned from Stef that reporting could be an art, something which laid truth bare with grace, wit and style. Jack knew that the pieces in the *American*, personality sketches of successful men, were essentially trivial.* Casting about for something more substantial, he found a subject close to his heart—Harvard University. The old ambivalence about the school was not gone. Recently it had appeared in a story portraying an effete and ineffectual clubman now living in New York. Setting off his foppish, vaguely ridiculous behavior is a tough-talking, uncouth newspaperman—obviously a self-portrait—"who wore the most disreputable clothes in public places" and sat for long hours around the Harvard Club with two other "low brows," smoking, drinking and laughing uproariously at vulgar tales.[28]

Pleased with the story, Jack passed it around to friends. When Bob Hallowell not only objected to the portrait of the aristocrat, but went on to protest that out of bitterness he was running "the risk of doing the University" serious harm, Reed exploded with rage. First in person, then in a condescending letter, he scoffed that Harvard was far too great to be harmed by anything he—or anyone—could write. Far from being bitter about snobbery, he found it "picturesque." Only two kinds of people would object to his portrait: "Old Farts, who once laughed at that very thing themselves, or wrote about it in Lampy, or young Farts who take themselves too seriously." The direct slam was then softened: "Don't let my confounded arrogance make you sore. We love each other enough to be able to speak out."[29] Affection was not the problem. However stuffy they were, Hallowell's comments had touched a spot still sensitive. The wounds of college life were taking a long time to heal.

The idea for an article on Harvard arose in February 1912, and blossomed during a class reunion in Boston late the next month, where Jack had gone—supposedly—to sneer at "plutocratic New England Class-mates."[30] Already the *American* editorial board had okayed a piece on "Harvard the Intellectual Center" and now, among alumni, he entered discussions over a recent ruling against any political activity on campus,

---

* The two after Copeland were sketches of "Frederick Muir," LXXIII (April 1912), 678–80, an entomologist for the big sugar planters of Hawaii, and "Joseph E. Ralph," LXXIV (October 1912), 679–81, chief of the Government Bureau of Engraving and Printing.

prompted by the ongoing activities of radicals who insisted on inviting Progressives, Socialists and—what was evidently worse—women suffragettes to the sacrosanct halls. Making the cause of the students his own, Reed soon had a focus. The article would deal with the background and importance of the "Harvard Renaissance," that inchoate movement in politics and the arts. On fire with the idea, he plunged into research, reread student publications of the last few years, interviewed friends and associates, pestered Hunt, Lippmann and a number of current student radicals for articles, documents and opinions on what had been happening since 1908. The work took up all his time, but he was content. "Full of facts and enthusiasm and theories," in April he was sure the story would be "the biggest thing ever done about Harvard."[31] By the end of the month he completed a draft of twenty thousand words and shipped it off to friends for corrections of fact and criticism of interpretation.

"The Harvard Renaissance" was a good article. Overly long and hyperbolic, it was yet well researched and often eloquent in catching the excitement of student body and faculty awakening to the fact that knowledge connects with the world outside college, and in defending the right of free speech and inquiry. Justly placing Lippmann and the Socialist Club at the center of events, it even connected the democratic strivings of Yard against Street in the Class Elections of 1910 to the ferment. Friends and current radicals were equally delighted with the piece, though some thought it contained too much poetic exaggeration. The editors of the *American*, unfortunately, did not share this enthusiasm. Frightened by the implications of such unequivocal support of student radicalism, and by the attack on Harvard as a bulwark of conservative social and business interests, they first asked Reed to trim the work to six thousand words, then decided the tone and content would have to be altered. The cuts he could live with, but not the changes. "Temporarily in despair," at the end of May, Jack reached the conclusion that an untrue piece would be worse than none, and so the work never appeared in print.[32]

An attempt to put his college years in perspective, to reassess what was important and to declare independence from what was not, the article also marked a definite turning point in Reed's view of magazines. Fiction, poetry and journalism—all were being approached timidly. Often Jack had argued with *American* editors over content, and had lain awake at night wishing to see its policies changed. Now he produced a three-page memo to clarify his attitude. Willing as a staff member to abide by current practices, he attacked the so-called "democracy" of content, the attempt to write so that the "simplest person can understand." This was the ruination of the "great literary genius," the artist who could speak to the most intelligent. Calling on Nietzsche, Shaw, Whitman, Emerson, Shelley and Ibsen for backing, and echoing an article by H. G. Wells in the current *Atlantic Monthly*, he argued: "A real artist goes on creating for art's sake whether he achieves publication or not." Writers did not need magazines, and personally he would no longer write expressly for them, "though I sincerely hope that things which I *choose* to write will be considered worthy of publication."[33]

Before he could carry this new policy into action, Reed went to Cambridge for Harry's graduation. Suddenly there came a wire saying C.J. was gravely ill. They rushed to Portland to find their father failing after a heart attack, and on the morning of July 1 he passed away. The swiftness of breakdown and death was unreal. Gone was the vigorous, witty man who had always seemed "more like a wise, kind older friend than a father." Now head of the family, Jack tried to comfort his prostrate, weeping mother, but, torn by painful despair, he plunged into a rainy Oregon night to walk the dark streets alone until morning. Daylight brought the sun, but no relief from inner gloom. Then came the stiffness of the formal funeral, flags flying at half-staff on official buildings and the strange, soft green beauty of the hilly Riverview Cemetery, crowded by a thousand people honoring "a fine, big spirit," quietly laid to rest next to H.D., John and Henry beneath the tall stone marker of the Green family plot.

Despair led to quiet anger and self-recrimination. Wanting to blame the people of Portland for killing C.J. by making him an outcast, Reed settled on a reason closer to home: "My father worried himself to death —that's all. He never let any of us know, but he was harassed into the grave. Money!" An unbearably burdened C.J. had made heroic efforts to let them "live like rich men's sons" at school, and the cost was too high. Proud of the "brave, honorable, stainless life that he led so jauntily," Jack sank into remorse at his own shortsighted selfishness.[34] Guilt feelings spiraled until history was rewritten and Jack assumed blame for many family problems and disappointments, including the election loss of 1910. Convinced that C.J. had "poured out his life" for the family, Jack made a silent vow to justify his death.

So badly tangled were financial affairs that he was forced to linger in Portland for weeks, then months, helping to settle a pitiful estate consisting of a few thousand worthless shares in gold and silver mines, debts totaling many thousands of dollars, and a single tangible item, a gold watch, willed to Jack. Finding the town strangely beautiful—"flowers by the millions, woods and mountains and such air!"—he grew nostalgic for childhood, tramped from the site of a now subdivided Cedar Hill into the sun-splotched pine forest beyond the western ridge of town, remembering two boys and a pony on the track of imaginary Indians and bears. A desire to settle in Portland and take his father's place momentarily overtook him, but such an impulse could not last, for reality said, "There is no one to talk to, and I'd go mad in a year."[35] There was no reason to worry about Margaret because Harry, forced to give up plans for Europe, was remaining in Portland. As days shortened into autumn, Reed became "half dead for New York," and at the end of October he finally boarded a train for the East.[36]

Despite the restlessness, the four months in Portland were important. With few friends to hold his interest, Jack spent days and weeks alone. After a year and a half of running in New York, he had time to ponder the problems and direction of life. More than once he clashed with his mother over his life-style and friends. While insisting she was not a snob, Margaret did not hide her dismay that he was hanging around with so many "would be Bohemians," and he countered that she was interested only in the "narrowest" kind of society people.[37] Such continuing criticisms helped jiggle free dormant questions. When he began to spend long hours at his writing desk that summer and fall, the question of life-style was uppermost. Aside from playing with a children's operetta and composing a serious, restrained poem of homage to C.J., most of his work was an attempt to gain perspective on life in New York.

Not self-consciously a Bohemian, Reed saw himself as merely a young, struggling writer out to taste as much experience as possible. Of course he did not fit into comfortable middle-class patterns, for, as he had written in a poem entitled "Revolt":

> Oh, there is peace in wrong-doing,
>   Joy in the blasphemous thing,
> Sweet is the taste of a prodigal waste,—
>   Lawless the songs that we sing.
> And you, who are holy, have made it,—
>   Have ticketed men and their ways,—
> Have taken the zest from all that was best
>   In these contemptible days![38]

When he began a novel tentatively named *The Bohemians*, it was not at all a story of struggling artists. Centering on a beer hall on Greenwich Avenue, it featured such characters as a young newspaper reporter, a retired sea captain, a streetwalker who quotes Omar Khayyam and a Polish revolutionary. Once again he had trouble making progress in this long literary form. Verse felt more congenial, and while he hunched over a desk, a satire began to take shape. Incorporating some short lyrics produced at 42 Washington Square, writing and rewriting to capture exact meanings, Reed's pen raced ahead. By the time he returned to New York, he had completed a poem of close to fifteen hundred lines.

"The Day in Bohemia, or Life Among the Artists" was the best thing he had ever written. Overflowing with humor, it sang, burbled and bounced through the story of a day in the "life led by the geniuses in Manhattan's 'Quartier Latin,' " none other than John Reed and his friends. Using a variety of styles, cleverly parodying other poets, the work was alternately loving and satirical, both celebrated Bohemia and made fun of it, showed life in Washington Square as amusing, pretentious, colorful, gay, foolish and carefree. Dedicated to Steffens, "the only man who understands my arguments," it begins with an invocation to the poet's muse:

> I would embalm in deathless rhyme
> The great souls of our little time:
> Inglorious Miltons by the score,—
> Mute Wagners,—Rembrandts, ten or more,—
> And Rodins, one to every floor.
> In short, those unknown men of genius
> Who dwell in third floor-rears gangreneous,
> Reft of their rightful heritage
> By a commercial, soulless age.
> Unwept, I might add,—and unsung,
> Insolvent, but entirely young.

Describing the delights of Greenwich Village, the restaurants, hotels, winding streets, tiny squares and charming mews converted into art studios, he then points to the chief attraction of the area:

> Yet we are free who live in Washington Square,
> We dare to think as Uptown wouldn't dare,
> Blazing our nights with arguments uproarious;
> What care we for a dull old world censorious
> When each is sure he'll fashion something glorious?

Depicting the Immortal Four of 42 Washington Square, the work paints a picture of their grimy apartment. The poet's room looks out over the wash of Italian families, described in the style of other poets:

Shelley:
> Like battle-riven pennants fluttering,
> Float on the serene and variable air
> The many-tinted wash. How fair a thing
> Is linen cleansed!

Keats:

> Fire me to sing the vision curious
> Fronting my casement. Woven phantasies
> Yield to caresses of each wanton breeze;
> Here linen mellowed by the lapse of Time
> Woofed in Damascus. From exotic clime
> Bandannas pied, and underclothing bright
> With Tyrian dye-stuffs;

Whitman:

> Undershirts, underdrawers, kimonos, socks, bedclothes, pajamas;
> Pink, red, green, of various tints, shades and colors;
> Some with holes in them, some without holes in them;
> Tattered, faded, patched, the Female's equally with the
>   Male's I sing!

After a scramble to work in the morning, Jack goes through a normal day, arriving at the office late, lunching for three hours with other members of Dutch Treat, playing the purist as he argues with editors of the *American* over poetry. Late in the afternoon he hurries to a dimly lit studio for an "aesthetic tea" hosted by the painter Umbilicus, who has studied the masters in Europe for so long "That neither vision, fire, nor self was left." Then comes a picture of "neo-bohemian dubs" whom the narrator abhors: the poet who writes "one short verse a year"; the painter who believes "artists should be steeped in all the vices"; the nature poet who "never stirs from his steam-heated flat"; the phony peasant girl wearing a $300 "pastoral dress"; the anarchist who "wouldn't feel safe without police"; the rich man who "tries to be Maecenas—and is Midas"; and a dozen curious women "Who would be, and again would never be males." Over tea and sandwiches, the company squabbles about life and art, arousing a scornful reaction:

> Cranks, cranks, cranks, cranks,—
> Blanks, blanks, blanks, blanks,—
> Talk about talking and think about thinking,
> And swallow each other without even blinking.

Escaping, he finds it easier to breathe outdoors. The streets may be crowded and dirty, but there is life in them, and the promise of future greatness in the city:

> This spawning filth, these monuments uncouth
> Are but her wild, ungovernable youth.
> But the skyscrapers, dwarfing earthly things,—
> Ah that is how she sings!

> Wake to the vision shining in the sun!
> Earth's ancient, conquering races rolled in one,
> A world beginning,—AND YET NOTHING DONE!

The day finishes at home among friends, arguing art and politics not as an idle pastime but as a vital, living concern:

> Now with an easy caper of the mind
> We rectify the Errors of Mankind;
> Now with the sharpness of a keen-edged jest,
> Plunge a hot thunder-bolt in Mammon's breast;
> Impatient Youth, in fine creative rage,
> With both hands wrests the quenchless torch from Age;
> Not as the Dilletanti, who explain
> Why they have failed,—excuse, lament, complain,
> Condemn real artists to exalt themselves,
> And credit their misfortunes to the elves;—
> But to the Gods of Strength make offertory,
> And pit our young wits in the race for glory!

"The Day in Bohemia" captured and fixed the joy and excitement Reed had felt as a young, poor, ambitious writer for more than a year in New York. Touching important issues, it took none of them too seriously, for as he looked back from Portland in the fall of 1912, life still seemed a grand game. Sometimes, however, experiences with magazines and his father's death could lead him to pensive moods. In a serious essay on New York he slipped into a former attitude, describing the city as wondrous and magical, full of "palaces more magnificent than Satan built himself in hell." But a new note was the recognition of the social cost: "Never in history have men possessed power or wealth such as a few possess under our democracy." Life was unfair, but democratic too, for men starving in "hall bedrooms nursing a dream" one day might make a killing on the stock market, or sell a popular novel, or marry an heiress the next.[39] Success was a solid metal genie with no heart and a fixed, cold smile—one at the bidding of those who rubbed the proper lamp. Solidly of his culture, Jack could still insist that, despite vast discrepancies between rich and poor, anyone might have access to that lamp.

For all this faith, the trials of his father in Portland and his own observations were leading to the conclusion that something must be wrong with American life. This emerged in notes for possible essays: "We are a conquering, gross, dull Roman race. . . . We have banded together to crush sensitiveness and fineness." The culprit was the drive for success, which made each man "intent upon merely making a little money for himself, without any thought of the . . . incongruity of his plan with the immutable rhythm of nature." Striving for gain resulted not only in an unjust society but also in a people so practical and dependent upon facts that they feared and tried to murder intelligence and imagination. Among topics for essays on the state of society, he listed "Individualism," "Why I hate my government," "The newspapers as disseminators of misunderstanding," "The senility of God," "Labor" and "Radicals."[40]

Despite problems, it was still possible to "paint and write and sing of wonders," for America might be redeemed by poets. When he received a letter in September from Harriet Monroe asking for contributions to *Poetry*, a new magazine of verse starting in Chicago, Jack responded with "Sangar," some other short pieces and a letter that summed up his feelings about the state of writing in America. Commending her for opening *Poetry* to "all forms and all thought," he lamented that commercial magazines "are degrading the quality of poetry in America just as they have begun to degrade the short story." The argument was much the same as that made in his memo to the *American* staff in May, but one belief had sharply changed—no longer did he feel that artists wrote only for the most intelligent:

> The pathetic, mawkishly religious middle class are our enemies. A labor-leader . . . read aloud to me Neihardt's *Man Song* more naturally and beautifully than I have ever heard a verse read. . . . Art must cease, I think, to be for the aesthetic enjoyment of a few highly sensitive minds. It must go back to its original sources.[41]

Four months are not a long time, but in Reed's life they were enough to allow a new set of ideas to sprout tentatively, like tiny blades of grass poking through the earth to seek the sun. The ground had been prepared for a long time—by New York City and life at Washington Square, by commercial success and the failure of serious works that showed magazines to be a bulwark of middle-class values, by meetings with editors, writers, sculptors and radicals, by discussion with Steffens and Lippmann and other friends, by a thousand sights of city life—weary sweatshop girls trudging home and jewel-encrusted women riding in limousines, panhandlers in the Bowery and nightstick-swinging cops walking their beats. In June he had stopped by Lawrence to see the mills where the Industrial Workers of the World had two months before won their first great Eastern strike against the textile kings of Massachusetts. In Portland he had watched men who had reviled his father in life honor him in death. All this led to the beginnings of a critical attitude toward the United States. Most natural to him was the viewpoint of the elite artist, scorning the materialistic values and insipid taste of the American public. Newer was an identification with lower-class workers, men exploited by an unfair economic system. If the stances were different, the enemy in both cases was the same—the middle class, which somehow stifled the impulse and capabilities of people to live more fully.

Instinctively, John Reed in the autumn of 1912 was edging toward a way of putting the two kinds of criticism together. Not a man who systematically thought through such problems, he expressed himself indirectly in a mid-October letter to Bob Andrews. Hoping that his roommate had not abandoned some "socialistic tendencies" exhibited in the spring, Jack offhandedly announced, "I have become an I.W.W. and am now in favor of dynamiting." That this commitment was neither terribly deep nor angry is shown by the letter's postscript: "Here's my Yale game application. Put it in with yours. *Must* go."[42] Of course there was no reason for Reed to forsake football just because his interests—like his father's—had widened to include social problems. Portland, Harvard, the magazines, New York, America and the world might be in the hands of conservative, hypocritical men of no imagination. To oppose them was to live as fully as possible, to love art, youth, heroism and all the glorious activities that made life rich.

7

Greenwich Village

"The broad purpose of The Masses is a social one; to everlastingly attack old systems, old morals, old prejudices—the whole weight of outworn thought that dead men have saddled upon us; and to set up many new ones in their places. So, standing on the common sidewalk, we intend to lunge at spectres,—with a rapier rather than a broad-axe, with frankness rather than innuendo. We intend to be arrogant, impertinent, in bad taste, but not vulgar. We will be bound by no one creed or theory of social reform, but will express them all, providing they be radical. . . . Poems, stories and drawings, rejected by the capitalist press on account of their excellence will find a welcome in this magazine. . . . Sensitive to all new winds that blow, never rigid in a single . . . phase of life, such is our ideal for The Masses. And if we change our minds about it, well—why shouldn't we?"[1]

Two months after returning from Portland to New York, John Reed composed a manifesto that both captured the spirit of a publication he would soon join and expressed an alienation from the values of the New York publishing world. The aim was freedom, the liberation of the individual from old beliefs and oppressive systems, and the means was "social reform" taken in the broadest sense. Starting with the roaming imagination—poetry, humor, fiction and art—such freedom would mysteriously work to alter the realms of morals, politics and economics. Foggy about how this might occur, Jack foresaw vast changes in life, art and society, the commencement of a new age. The movement might be called liberation, rebellion, even revolution—whatever the name, as a process it was bound to be enjoyable.

The ability to fashion, out of his own experience, a manifesto that echoed the concerns of many artists showed that Reed's development had not been unique. And the existence of an audience for a magazine of stormy rebellion like the *Masses* indicated that writers and intellectuals were reflecting significant shifts in some strata of American society. These changes were associated with the realm of Bohemia, described so buoyantly in his lengthy poem. Only Bohemia itself was changing, and when he returned from Oregon in late October 1912, Jack found the Village more alive, frenetic, serious and colorful than ever before, the center of a large, inchoate movement of people out of sympathy with prevailing values, searching for more meaningful ways of living and convinced that American society as a whole needed a thorough renovation.

Nothing new to the Western world, Bohemia had roots deep in the culture, could be traced to the wandering troubadours of the Middle Ages who, like the legendary François Villon, wrote lyrics and brawled in wayside alehouses, and were too scandalous or temperamental to attract the interest of a wealthy patron. Another line ran back to what was in England called Grub Street, the crowded quarter housing an intellectual and artistic proletariat that had been a constant of great capitals since Imperial Rome. As a way of life, Bohemia dated only from the nineteenth century. Rather than an existence followed by necessity, it implied a life-style adopted by choice, a conscious revolt against the seriousness and instrumentality of bourgeois civilization. Often comfortably middle-class, residents of Bohemia imitated the customs of penniless artists, flouted social conventions and proclaimed art more important than industry. Colorful, diverse and sexually free, Bohemia was "Grub Street romanticized, doctrinalized and rendered self-conscious"—it was "Grub Street on parade."[2]

The capital of this realm without boundaries was Paris, its center the steep streets of Montmartre and the old student section of the Quartier Latin. Reed had brushed Bohemia while rambling around that city. His own impulse to practice writing there was common to American artists, for the United States had always seemed barely tolerant of formal culture, let alone any kind of avant-garde. Yet even in the iron age of nineteenth-century America small shoots of artistic dissidence had sprouted, and small versions of Bohemia appeared. Most memorable was the pre-Civil War gathering in Pfaff's basement beer hall, on Broadway just above Bleecker Street, where personalities from the intersecting worlds of journalism and theater met over foaming steins. The star attraction was Walt Whitman, who held court at the same table every night and gave his own admiration to the beautiful Ada Clare, acknowledged Queen of Bohemia. Acclaimed equally for her prose, poetry, acting and notorious love affairs, this Southern-born lady penned the following:

> The Bohemian is by nature, if not by habit, a cosmopolite, with a general sympathy for the fine arts, and for all things above and beyond convention. The Bohemian is not, like the creature of society, a victim of rule and customs; he steps over them all with an easy, graceful, joyous unconsciousness, guided by the principle of good taste and feeling. Above all others, essentially, the Bohemian must not be narrow-minded; if he be, he is degraded back to the position of a mere worldling.[3]

By such a definition any mildly unconventional, vaguely cultured person could think himself a Bohemian, and in late-nineteenth-century America this became the case. The experience of San Francisco was common. In the 1870s a group of newspapermen, finding their homes too small for gatherings, formed the Bohemian Club, a social center where they could mix with writers, artists and denizens of the Barbary Coast. Over the years its character changed until, by the end of the century—when C. J. Reed became a member—the club was a stronghold of businessmen, preferred millionaires to poor artists and required formal dress for dinner. Boston, New Orleans, Philadelphia and Cincinnati were flavored by the same decorous, tepid kind of Bohemian life, and New York was not much more exciting. Manhattan's salons featured evenings as stiff and formal as those of the aristocracy, and central figures like Edmund Clarence Stedman, simultaneously a poet and a Wall Street broker. More spirited was the Dutch Treat Club, whose journalist members confined social deviance to hitting the bottle together one night a week.

By the turn of the century, Bohemia in America was no revolt against the values of bourgeois society, but rather a splash of color on a gray social canvas, a safety valve that allowed some members of a serious business civilization to speak of "culture," express occasional unconventional attitudes and indulge in activities considered risqué by straitlaced maiden aunts. Meanwhile, the seeds of a new Bohemia were taking root, and in the second decade of the century—when Reed moved to Washington Square—they were beginning to bloom. For the first time in the United States a large number of talented, dedicated, fun-loving and serious young men and women were claiming Bohemia as their own. In Greenwich Village their dedication to art met a new spirit of intellectualism spawned by universities, then mixed with the unstable compound of American radicalism. The results were a vigorous subculture, a minor renaissance in the arts and new visions of man and society that would seem fresh more than half a century later.

Precision in dating the advent of the new Bohemia is difficult. So is the attempt to pin down causes. Certainly it was connected to the increasing fragmentation and affluence of American life. Industrialism, urbanism and technology had whirled society into confusion, uprooted people from traditional ways, moved populations off the land, piled men up into polyglot cities, created new modes of work and play and new styles of living, all the while insisting that the old morality and Puritan ethic were still valid. Progressivism had assaulted trusts, promoted conservation, attempted to protect both consumers and workers, and had fixed its eyes on a nobler future in which America would somehow be returned to its presumably Edenic, Jeffersonian roots. And somewhere in the interstices of this lumbering social giant, wrenched free from the traditional ethos, sensitive to the sound of voices at home and abroad preaching strange new doctrines about life—Bergsonism, Pragmatism, Freudianism, Marxism, Anarchism—middle-class young people were beginning to follow the path John Reed had taken, from a faith in the beneficence of the political system to a questioning of its premises, from an acceptance of capitalism to a criticism of materialistic individualism, from a belief in art to a search for new forms to express the twentieth century, from paying lip-service to Victorian morality to an outright defiance of conventional codes.

At first such dissidents felt alienated, alone and more than a little queer. Blaming this on the drabness of the American town, its nosiness and prying, its general suspicion that diversity was deviance, art useless and sex wicked, youngsters from small communities found that urban counterparts were no less estranged from families, no less suffocated by the world. Soon young people from all backgrounds came to feel that all America shared the manners and morals of Main Street. Floyd Dell, a sensitive refugee from Davenport, Iowa, described their collective experience: "Through the long years of their youth [they] felt themselves in a solitary conflict with a hostile environment. There was a boy in Chicago, and a boy in Oshkosh, and a boy in Steubenville, Indiana, and so on—one here and there, and all very lonely and unhappy. . . . They were idealists and lovers of beauty and aspirants towards freedom; and it seemed to them that the whole world was in a gigantic conspiracy to thwart their ideals and trample beauty under foot and make life merely a kind of life imprisonment."[4] Only around 1910, through publications, letters from friends and word of mouth, did this generation find that others like themselves existed. Coming together in Bohemia, were it a move from the provinces to the city or merely one from uptown down to the Village, was a way of ending the alienation. The city itself was a lonely place, but at least it provided regions where they could be close to one another; their flight from home was really a flight to a new community.

Outposts of Bohemia existed in urban areas across the nation, with major centers in San Francisco and St. Louis, while Chicago became an especially vital community after 1910, when writers, dancers and artists took over a series of Jackson Park storefronts, hung gaudy curtains on windows, set up single-burner stoves, scattered pillows on floors and gathered to drink cocktails—still unknown to the bourgeoisie—by the flickering light of candles. Here Floyd Dell argued literature and socialism with George Cram Cook; Arthur Davison Ficke and Witter Bynner wrote Imagist poetry; Sherwood Anderson and Vachel Lindsay read their latest works; the morose, slouching Theodore Dreiser—famed for battles with censors—discussed books with the prim Harriet Monroe; and the crusty, renegade economist Thorstein Veblen critiqued American institutions. Creative as this group was, sooner or later its members felt dwarfed and lured by the growing reputation of New York, and the move of Dell to Greenwich Village in 1913 marked the journey of a talented provincial to the center of civilization.

Located in the shadow of the country's chief financial and cultural institutions, the Village inevitably became the center of American Bohemia, drawing artistic youngsters just as New York sent out a call to ambitious men all over the land. Low rents were one of the attractions, but no more so than the feel of an authentic village, protected by its meandering pattern of roads and lanes from the implacable rush of Manhattan. Here were quiet, twisting streets like Gay, Minetta and Christopher, tiny cul-de-sacs like Milligan Place and Patchin Place, charming mews on MacDougal Alley and the inviting oasis of Washington Square, all surrounded by swarming Italian and Irish ghettos, with raucous bars, homey restaurants and cheap grocery stores where credit was easily available. Tradition was a factor, for the Village boasted a long history of artists and dissenters—here Tom Paine had produced *The Crisis*, Edgar Allan Poe had suffered and drunk himself into obscurity, Stephen Crane and Frank Norris had created American naturalism, and poet John Masefield had labored as a bartender in the Working Girls Home. Already the Village was more than a little self-conscious, for since 1905 the *Bohemian* magazine had been broadcasting the charms of the area, describing the older, genteel Bohemia and unveiling the newer one by publishing works by Louis Untermeyer, George Jean Nathan and Dreiser.

Even before the trip to his father's deathbed, Reed had been living outside reigning social conventions, in what one later resident aptly described as a "homeland of the uprooted where everybody you met came from another town and tried to forget it; where nobody seemed to have parents or a past more distant than last night's swell party."[5] Not a cohesive community, Greenwich Village was a hotbed of circles, clubs and cliques, indifferent to and sometimes suspicious of each other. On hand or soon to arrive was an array of talented people with a bewildering diversity of interests—intellectuals like Lippmann, Max Eastman, Van Wyck Brooks, Randolph Bourne and Waldo Frank; poets Seeger, Harry Kemp, Alfred Kreymborg, Edna St. Vincent Millay and Orrick Johns; feminists Crystal Eastman, Henrietta Rodman, Neith Boyce and Susan Glaspell; old Progressives and journalists like Steffens, Frederic C. Howe and Hutchins Hapgood; radicals Emma Goldman, Alexander Berkman, Bill Haywood, Carlo Tresca, Morris Hillquit and William English Walling; artists John Sloan, George Bellows, Robert Henri, George Luks, Marsden Hartley, Andrew Dasburg and Max Weber; playwright Eugene O'Neill; and birth-control champion Margaret Sanger.

When he returned from Oregon, Reed was just in time to take part in the transformation of the Village. Previously there had been some meeting places and informal clubs—Petitpas, which he had visited with Seeger; the Tuesday-night Crazy Cat Club at Paglieri's, where comic troubador Bobby Edwards strummed a ukulele, sang satirical off-color songs and led dancers in the Turkey Trot; Club A, on Fifth Avenue, a communal residence whose members included novelist Ernest Poole and writer Mary Heaton Vorse; the Photo-Secession Gallery at 291 Fifth Avenue, where photographer Alfred Stieglitz exhibited the latest post-Impressionist paintings from Europe and presided over freewheeling intellectual discussions. Now, in the fall of 1912, the Village began to be transformed into a genuine community, with its own self-conscious events, institutions, organizations and publications.

On two separate occasions groups of drunken Villagers received publicity for declaring independence from the United States and proclaiming the Republic of Washington Square; but, though symbolic, these acts contained more fun than substance. Much more important were the renovated version of the *Masses*, chief mouthpiece for the new Bohemia; the advent of Mabel Dodge's salon, where the various factions and interest groups came face to face; the Armory Show, which drew a neat line between avant-garde and traditionalism in art; and the move of the Liberal Club down from Gramercy Park to provide a permanent, central meeting place for Villagers. With all of these Reed was to have some connection—indeed, with most his tie would be intimate.

After four months of exile, Jack plunged once again into the life of the city. Tramping familiar streets, reveling in the noise, confusion and vibrancy of the metropolis, he felt comfortable and at home, despite the fact that things were changing both at 42 Washington Square and in his circle of friends. On the road to respectability, Bobby Rogers was living on Riverside Drive and preparing to move back to Cambridge for a teaching position at the Massachusetts Institute of Technology. Seeger had departed to write poetry in Paris and Harry Reeves was on the Left Bank living in Reed's old hotel room. Most shocking, the happy-go-lucky Alan Osgood was dead. Remembering a joint fantasy of shipping before the mast for China in imitation of Conrad, Reed was shaken. The life string could be broken for a youngster as well as a middle-aged man like C.J. Living fully was important; finding something to live for even more so.

Jack enjoyed returning to the *American*, its editorial conferences, long lunches, deadlines and office banter. Lonely for close friends, he successfully urged Eddy Hunt to come down from Cambridge on occasional weekends, then managed to secure his friend an editorial post on the magazine. After Hunt moved into 42, the two men were inseparable. One day they ran across another classmate, Robert Edmond Jones, looking hungry and gaunt as he wandered up and down Broadway trying to break into the theater as a designer. Taking him into the apartment, they made a collection from other Harvard men, fed and clothed Jones and helped to arrange contacts in the theatrical world.

As always, literature was on Reed's mind. His first long piece of reportage, a description of Tammany Boss Tim Sullivan's dinner for Bowery bums given on Christmas Day, 1911, appeared in the December *American*. Full of sharp detail, it caught the flavor and feeling of the affair, the crowds of scruffy, ill-clad, hungry derelicts shivering in line before the hall doors open, the boisterous jocularity inside, the savory turkey and heaps of mashed potatoes washed down with beer, the sentimental conversation about the old sod of Ireland, the ultimate pathos as the meal ended and red-eyed, sniffling men shuffled out, bent, worn and homeless.[6] Reed knew it was a controlled and mature work even before friends praised it, but he was plagued by one nagging uncertainty: was this really the sort of writing he wished to do?

Poetry—that was still his first love, and it was pleasant to be drawing some recognition. Seeger was one supporter, and Edwin Arlington Robinson another. A backhanded boost came from William Rose Benét of the *Century*, who liked his work but abhorred the Village life-style enough to write, "What do you want to do among the half-ass poets? You're not one of them."[7] Answering Reed's letter written from Portland, Harriet Monroe termed his poems "a pleasure," and selected "Sangar" for the December number.[8] When it appeared, Jack was surprised by the volume of congratulations and then pleased to have it chosen one of the ten best poems of the magazine's first year.* To an effusive note of praise from Percy MacKaye, he answered: "No one has ever before written me so about anything I ever did. It opens up vast possibilities and stimulates my imagination to conceive a time when I shall be able to tell people a little part of the glorious things I see. Every day of my life I see more of them."[9]

The desire to show people "glorious things" presented a dual problem: how to create valid art and support himself at the same time. Steeped enough in the world of commercial publishing to know that serious poetry paid virtually nothing, Reed needed an income not only for himself but also to help his brother and mother out of current financial difficulties. He carried another burden, one less easily admitted. In Jack the flow of verse was now more a trickle than a brimming river. Perhaps a deep-felt need for success was channeling his creativity into more popular forms, and this was coupled with a lingering doubt about his own depth and abilities. Conscious of the new poetry just surfacing in small publications, the breakthrough into modern verse heralded by the Imagists and the widespread experimentation with new language, forms and subject matter, he felt out of step. He was temperamentally more a romantic than a modern, more an enthusiast than a skeptic, more gushing than hard-boiled. Modern topics and diction did not come easily, and all the accolades did not banish a worry that poetically he was not riding a wave of the future, but was trapped in a stagnating tidal pool.

Not one to share such difficulties easily, Jack wrestled with the problem of literary direction alone, worried endlessly over what forms

---

* Being selected one of eight "honorable mention" poems in the first year of *Poetry* was no mean distinction. First prize went to William Butler Yeats and second to Vachel Lindsay. Among other first-year contributors were Ezra Pound, William Vaughn Moody, Arthur Davison Ficke, Richard Aldington, H.D., Rabindranath Tagore, George Sterling, Amy Lowell and William Carlos Williams.

might suit him best. If some friends noticed him floundering, only Steffens openly mentioned it: "You haven't found your form; your 'lay'; your 'line.'" Then came the advice of master to disciple: "My rule is the only one for you to respect so far. You remember it?—*You may do anything you can in art*."[10] With a solid career under his belt, Stef could say such a thing, but it was difficult for Reed to believe it. Surely some written forms were literature, while others—perhaps journalism—were different from and less than that. Reed had a student's reverential attitude toward the names of famous authors marching through textbooks like survivors of a victorious, decimated army—he always thought of Art and Literature with capital letters.

At the beginning of December a temporary way out of his dilemma appeared. Around the Village, people were talking about the latest issue of the *Masses,* and when a copy fell into Jack's hands, the jolt was electric. He found the fiction, poetry and essays timely, fresh and imaginative, and was struck by the dual wit and seriousness of Art Young's double-page cartoon, which depicted the press as a lavish whorehouse whose services were bought exclusively by big advertisers. Most succinct and gripping was the editorial statement, promising a magazine devoted both to "free and spirited expressions of every kind" and to the cause of Socialism. Here was what he had unconsciously been looking for, a publication that gave voice to all his wide-ranging interests and would attempt to answer unformulated questions about the relationship between radicalism and art.

Reed pulled the story of the dance-hall girl and a couple of other short pieces from a drawer and found out where *Masses* editor Max Eastman lived. On the phone he overrode a reluctant voice and insisted on delivering his work immediately. Barging in on the slender and handsome Eastman, Jack was in such a flurry of excitement that he did not notice the discomfort of his reticent host. Eastman would ever after remember his unfavorable first impression of Reed, who "stood up or moved about the room all through his visit, and kept looking in every direction except that in which he was addressing his words."[11] Sighing with relief when the door finally closed behind Jack, the shy editor wondered just why he had taken on the *Masses* job.

The roads that brought Reed, Eastman and the *Masses* to the same intersection were circuitous. Born in January 1911, the magazine—a cooperative enterprise—was the brain-child of Piet Vlag, a dark-eyed Dutchman who managed the restaurant in the basement of the Socialist Rand School. A laughing, boisterous sort, Vlag energetically rounded up the financial backing and personnel to produce a publication devoted to the interests of working people and to his pet formula for social improve-

ment, the cooperative movement. Despite the talent procured—artists John
Sloan, Art Young, Charles A. Winter and Maurice Becker, and writers
Louis Untermeyer, Mary Heaton Vorse, Ellis O. Jones and Inez Haynes
Gillmore—the *Masses* was a dull publication. The editor's zeal for co-
operatives placed him among the most conservative Socialists, and rather
than showing any lively, radical impulse, the magazine embarked on tepid
campaigns against the "militaristic" Boy Scouts and the rising cost of
living. By the summer of 1912 Vlag was ready to sell out to a radical
women's magazine in Chicago.

Prevented from doing so by the editorial board, whose members felt
the need of an outlet for noncommercial works, the founder left the
Masses in their hands. The editors, however, did not wish to be bothered
with the day-to-day business of running it, and were in a quandary until
Art Young remembered a recent discussion with Max Eastman about the
dullness of the magazine. Eastman was a young Ph.D. in philosophy from
Columbia University who had organized the Men's League for Women's
Suffrage and had recently been converted to Socialism. Previously more
interested in aesthetics than in politics, he was just at the point—much
like Reed—of very much needing "to romanticize New York life and
romanticize the revolution." When he received a note saying, "You are
elected editor of *The Masses*. No pay," he was both skeptical and intrigued.[12] At a meeting of editors one night, he found a warm atmosphere
of drinks and exciting conversation filled "with a sense of universal revolt and regeneration, of just-before-the-dawn-of-a-new-day in American
art and literature and living."[13] Charmed, impressed and more than a little
flattered, Max agreed to edit one issue of the *Masses* and then join the
others in helping to raise money for its continuation.

A cooperative in theory, the magazine became a one-man show. Of
all the editors only Dolly Sloan, the tiny, scrappy, devoted Socialist wife
of the painter, knew anything about the practical side of the publication,
and, overburdened with work, she was ready to defer to Eastman. Before
the first number was out, he was fully in charge of raising money, dealing
with printers, handling correspondence, convening the editors and making final decisions on what would appear. The burden was great, more
than Eastman really wanted, but the position had its satisfactions—helping to clean up typography and create a modern format, printing works
the capitalist press ignored and, above all, changing the editorial policy to
left-wing Socialism, in support of the class struggle. Weighing factors
pro and con, Eastman was annoyed enough by Reed's intrusion to decide
"to bring out one more number and quit."[14]

Reading "Where the Heart Is" changed his mind. Max had sus-

pected that a magazine which could not pay contributors would receive
decent works only from its editors. Now he knew differently. Reed was
obviously "a man writing about a significant phase of American life that
no other magazine would dare to mention unless sanctimoniously, and
writing with unlabored grace—a style both vivid and restrained." For
the first time, "the idea that *The Masses* might be good, that there really
was a creative literature stifled by commercial journalism," took a firm
grip on Eastman, and he dashed off a note to Jack saying, "Your things
are great," promising to print the story in the next issue and asking for
"a brief study, or comment, humorous or dramatic, on some current
matter as often as you can."[15]

The praise brought Reed back. Calmed by acceptance, he was more
direct, and a warmer Max soon found him "kindly and sagacious." Anxious
to join the staff, Jack tentatively offered a manifesto for the masthead.
Eastman read it and was disappointed that Reed either had not read the
editorial page or had not understood what he read. Trained under John
Dewey, thinking himself a "revolutionary experimentalist," Eastman had
stressed the need for a "carefully thought-out program of class struggle"
and was dismayed by Jack's visceral, freewheeling commitment to any
and all kinds of radicalism.[16] Borrowing the idea and impertinent tenor,
along with some of its phraseology, Max composed a manifesto of his own.
The editors voted that it be run permanently about the same time they
elected Reed to the board.

Being an editor of the *Masses* was fun. Reed shared the job of win-
nowing poetry contributions with Louis Untermeyer, who found his new
partner "big-boned, broad-shouldered, handsome, semi-theatrical."[17] The
two men shared a seriousness about poetry, a distrust of any work too
fastidious or hermetic and a grand passion for "unforgettably bad" poems.
Out of the piles of verse that poured into the office they began to compile
an anthology of *The World's Worst Poetry*. Together they howled with
delight on discovering particularly execrable rhymes, and often left notes
for each other calling attention to choice examples of dreadful verse.
Twice a month Untermeyer and Reed took the best works to evening
editorial meetings held in dim, bare studios, where over glasses of beer and
through heavy cigarette smoke, drawings were scanned, poems, essays and
stories were read aloud, and everyone wrangled over what to include in
the next issue. The atmosphere was dreamy, almost unreal, for, as Art
Young recalled, "We were sailing out, so to speak, with no chart but our
untried beliefs and a kind of confidence that any way might be better
than the old way."[18] Debates were often heated, and Reed, in particular,
could become so petulant that he was remembered as "the spoiled child of

The Masses meetings."* Tenacious and unbending in argument, Jack soon regained perspective. After one tiring, dogmatic session, he commented to Untermeyer, "God damn it, Louis, we're a bunch of much-too-serious Samsons. We've forgotten that the only weapon feared by the Philistines is the jawbone of an ass."[19]

Sometimes serious, such meetings were frothy, too, for the editors were a playful bunch united in a desire to shock the bourgeoisie and change the world. Despite the intellectual acumen present, certain problems could never be resolved. When tiny, mustachioed and always-angry Hippolyte Havel, an anarchist, interrupted one meeting by screaming, "Bourgeois! Voting! Voting on poetry! Poetry is something from the soul. You can't vote on poetry!.," many editors knew there was sense in the criticism, but, committed to a cooperative venture, they could think of no other method of selection.[20] Nor could they successfully answer the dilemma posed in a popular Village rhyme:

> They draw nude women for the *Masses*
> Thick, fat, ungainly lasses—
> How does that help the working classes?

Middle-class, committed to revolution in society and art, editors of the magazine believed that liberation of the working class would accompany the downfall of bourgeois morals, for economic exploitation was connected to puritanism in art and society. Even the knowledge that the readers were mainly young men and women involved in or sympathetic to the new Bohemia did not disturb them. Piet Vlag's first number had promised to help free working-class people "whether they want it or not." In the joy of breaking old shackles, Reed and his fellows were not yet bothered by the elitism of this view.

A connection with the *Masses* put Jack at the center of the Village revolt. All the doctrines swirling through Bohemia eventually swept into the Greenwich Avenue office in the form of manuscripts, drawings or excited authors anxious to air pet theories. Marxism, anarchism, syndicalism, revolution, birth control, industrial unionism, free love, cubism,

---

* Capable of recognizing his own petulance, at least later, Reed at the *Masses* trial in 1918, when the government was attempting to prove that the publication's editors had conspired to interfere with the draft, described one memorable editorial meeting: "I brought this poem. I did not tell who wrote the poem, I gave it to somebody to read, and they read the poem out loud, and the meeting voted it down, whereupon I proclaimed my identity and insisted it should go in, even if everybody, all the editors and readers disliked it, I insisted it go in, and it did go in." A copy of this testimony is in the Granville Hicks MSS. For further details on the trial, see Chapter XIX.

futurism, Freudianism, feminism, the new woman, the new poetry, the new theater and direct action—all these were depicted, expounded and discussed in the magazine's pages by a roster of talented young Americans —Amy Lowell, Carl Sandburg, Sherwood Anderson, Susan Glaspell, William Carlos Williams, Harry Kemp, Randolph Bourne, Stuart Davis, Arthur B. Davies, Jo Davidson, George Bellows, Robert Minor, Boardman Robinson, Upton Sinclair and James Oppenheim—with foreign contributions coming from Bertrand Russell, Maxim Gorki, Romain Rolland and Pablo Picasso.

Because of its wide interests and diverse personnel, the magazine was a source of continuing education. Reed's ideas about life, art, literature and politics had greatly altered during eighteen months in the Village, and the *Masses* hastened the process of change. Stimulated by Eastman's editorials, the socialist opinions of Young and Sloan and the anarchist views of Bellows, he began to read radical literature and attend public meetings, generally more interested by the "different human types" than by what they espoused. Theories never touched him as much as people did, and his politics came from the gut rather than the head: "On the whole, ideas alone didn't mean much to me. I had to see. In my rambles about the city I couldn't help but observe the ugliness of poverty and all its train of evil, the cruel inequality between rich people who had too many motor cars and poor people who didn't have enough to eat. It didn't come to me from books that the workers produced all the wealth of the world, which went to those who did not earn it."[21]

Broadening in knowledge of political movements, Jack also had his visual imagination stretched by friendly artists. The forty-two-year-old Sloan, a brilliant conversationalist, was a man of broad vision and deep human understanding, alternately witty and wise, always ready to philosophize with a young colleague. He had worked slowly to Socialism from the shock of viewing city life rather than because of any personal deprivation and no doubt he sensed that Reed was on the same trajectory. Part of the Ash Can School, his paintings were full at once of fascination with and repulsion from New York street life, something like the stories Reed was beginning to produce. Unblinded by his own social realism, Sloan was open-minded and sensitive to the avant-garde, just then changing the old rules of visual art and ushering in a fresh vision of man.

This new world burst on the United States in the international exhibition of modern art that opened at the 25th Street Armory on February 17, 1913. Hung in the enormous former home of the 69th Regiment and organized by artists rather than curators, the sixteen hundred pieces of painting, sculpture and graphics provided a survey of modern

European and American trends, while its most advanced works became a storm center of controversy. Like everyone interested in the world of art, Jack attended more than once. Struggling to enjoy the new depiction of man by the Fauves, like Derain, Dufy and Matisse, and Cubists Picasso, Braque and Léger, he—like all visitors—stopped before Duchamp's "Nude Descending a Staircase" and tried to square his view with the current jokes that it was not a lady but a man, "an explosion in a shingle factory" or a "staircase descending a nude." If his tastes ran more to Impressionists and the Ash Can School, Reed was sensitive to the political implications of the new forms. While Robert Henri and Alfred Stieglitz were calling the exhibit a battle cry of freedom for art, and the pine-tree flag of Massachusetts during the Revolution had been chosen as its symbol, the organs of middle-class America argued against artistic modernism in political terms.* Conservative critics not only termed modernists "immoral" and "decadent," but *The New York Times* called them "cousins to the anarchists in politics." This drew Jack's interest, and he realized that traditional standards in art—like those in society—were a defense against change. If America felt threatened by modernism, then he was all for it. His view was similar to that voiced by old radical Hutchins Hapgood in the *Globe*, who equated experimentation in art with that in society, saw unrest in politics, social conditions and the artistic world not as signs of decay but as the necessary "condition of vital growth."[22]

Threatened by an art exhibit, bourgeois society felt more endangered by the free sexual relations already making the Village notorious. Reed was hardly a theoretician of free love, and he never spoke the simplified Freudian language of freedom from repression so common among Bohemians, or took the detailed interest in Village affairs that so fascinated Floyd Dell. He could appreciate the antics of the well-known young lady who combatted prostitution by giving herself to every man she met, but he still believed in love, if only serially. For all his attractiveness, he was not a man who devoted large amounts of time to women. When interested in a woman, Jack quite naturally expected her to go to bed with him for their mutual pleasure, much as he expected her to be alive to the changing world. Early in 1913 his most constant female companion

* Many people involved in the Armory Show spoke in terms of revolution. Mabel Dodge wrote Gertrude Stein on January 24, 1913, that it would be "the most important public event that has ever come off since the signing of the Declaration of Independence, and it is of the same nature. . . . There will be a riot and a revolution and things will never be quite the same afterwards." See Donald Gallup, ed., *The Flowers of Friendship: Letters Written to Gertrude Stein* (New York: Alfred A. Knopf, 1953), 70–1.

was a lovely, affectionate schoolteacher with whom he sometimes stayed the night. Their arrangement was convenient for both, something more serious than a casual affair, yet far short of a deep, loving commitment.

Such alliances were so much the norm in the Village that Jack never had to face negative judgments of them. Yet the expression of traditional morality could touch off anger. His quarrel was with the whole Progressive mentality that believed in "moral uplift," in legislating or cajoling people out of so-called vices like drinking and promiscuity. When a group of rich, fashionable ladies of the Committee on Amusement and Vacation Resources for Working Girls began to investigate the evil influences of lower-class dance halls and the immoral, ugly and salacious nature of modern steps like the Grizzly Bear, the Turkey Trot and the Tango, Reed launched into a vitriolic article. Asking "What business is it of anyone to quarrel with the working girl's sense of beauty?" he excoriated the pernicious instinct of "well-fed, 'moral' persons" to improve their "social inferiors." Evil was in the eye of the beholder, and if such dances were sometimes sensual, this was only because "the workers are simpler in their attitude towards sex than we of sophisticated society." Vice was socially induced and defined, and neither legislation nor exhortation would change people. Freedom, not restriction, was the cure for anything considered immoral, and Jack was sure such libertarianism would prove the contention that "human nature is essentially good."[23]

Involvement with the *Masses*, art, politics and friends did not solve problems about his direction in writing, nor did it divorce him from the world of commercial publishing. When *The Day in Bohemia* appeared in February—privately printed by Frederick Bursch's small Connecticut press—Jack hawked copies for a dollar and basked in warm praise from all quarters. Julian Street thought it "a little jewel . . . brilliant and altogether delightful" and predicted that someday copies of the limited edition of five hundred would sell for $1000 each.[24] Village people devoured the lilting descriptions of their own existence and began to look to the author as a chief spokesman for their life-style, a fair-haired boy wonder who lived and wrote with an ideal gusto. Around the square, in cafés and restaurants, Jack was pointed to with pride and not a little awe as the "Golden Boy" of the new Bohemia.

Uptown his fame reached a pinnacle when members of Dutch Treat selected Reed to write and direct the club's annual dinner show at Delmonico's. Quickly churning out the book and lyrics, he called rehearsals, hectored actors, refused to let professional humorists change his lines and worried for weeks over every detail of the performance. The result was a rollicking attack on magazines, *Everymagazine, An Immorality Play*, which contrasted high-blown pretensions with the reality of performance, the claim to be free of outside interference with the heavy dependence on advertisers, the self-styled posture as molders of public opinion with the fear of offending popular viewpoints. Because it was fun and satire, Jack could indulge himself by naming names. Old, staid publications like the *Century*, *Scribner's* and *Harper's* were lumped together as fossils— "I'm aristocratic, very, / I'm a live obituary"—while Progressive magazines like the *Outlook* were depicted as hypocritical: "I'm a moderate reformer just because reform's the thing. . . . It's a policy that gathers in the kale."* The finale had all the publications proclaiming their own totally unbiased attitudes while the chorus posed a different view:

> A silly tale I've heard
> That round the town is flying
> That every monthly organ
> Is owned by J. P. Morgan.[25]

When the curtain descended, Reed was applauded, cheered and deafened by congratulations, and he celebrated by drinking himself into lovely oblivion.

Like his new status in the Village, the Dutch Treat success was another sign of personal triumph. Unfortunately, life was more a process of day-to-day affairs, and acclaim could not banish one nagging problem —he was fed up with the *American*. Weary from drudging over manuscripts untouched by the exciting currents lighting Bohemia, he found the labor "inconsequential" and "petty."[26] Not only was desk work a bore, but city life was taking a toll and he worried over his lack of exercise, his increasing taste for liquor and cigarettes, and the roll of flab

---

* Reed did not neglect to bite the hand that fed him. His song on the *American* included:

> Are you next to reading matter, Are you next
> Do you know the way to brighten up your text
> Stick an ad of Bass's ale
> In the middle of a tale
> Or anything at all that isn't sexed.
> It's a little bit confusing I admit
> Is this an advertisement or a poem
> Use Arnold Bennett Soap, try a Baker, there is hope
> Have you a little Ferber in your Home? . . .
> Are you wise to colored pictures, are you wise
> Do you know the way to rest the Reader's eyes
> Into every paragraph
> Slam a colored photograph
> Of anything you want to advertise. . .

padding his midsection. Trying to break the routine, he developed plans for a serious but commercial all-fiction magazine and managed to stir some interest at the Crowell Company. To improve his physical shape, he sought the country, first taking a week-long walking trip with Bobby Jones, then searching once more for a farm. When he found the perfect place, reality stepped in to squelch fantasies of escape—faced with the choice, Jack still was unalterably wedded to Manhattan.

Ambivalence surfaced in moodiness. Subject to sharp alternations of euphoria and despair, Jack was restless in the spring of 1913. Often his mood seemed as gray as the clouds pressing like weights on city towers. Then rays of sunlight would break through and he strode the streets with winged feet, laughed with friends late into the night, talked endlessly of the new world about to be born. Contacts in the Village and on the *Masses* often raised the question of the connection between art and politics, and a concern about relating the two spilled over into social life. Introduced to poet Sara Teasdale in March, Reed so quickly shifted a literary conversation to social issues that he came away feeling like a boor. Penning a note of apology for browbeating her with "social reform," he received a courteous answer full of assurance that she had found the conversation "very interesting."[27] Even so, he worried about becoming too serious.

Writing was always a good way of finding self, and, pleased with his current status, Jack—like any artist—knew it was the next work, not the last, that meant the most. Already the carefree life-style described in *The Day in Bohemia* was partially screened by more serious issues that hovered at the edge of consciousness. Sometimes grappling with them in slice-of-life stories about cops, bums, prostitutes and poor scrubwomen, Reed also fled into romantic verses about the rolling sea and the seasonal flowering of the world. Seeking new means of expression, he tried a genre ignored since Harvard and in April completed a three-act play. His model was the drawing-room comedy, but even this light form became an index of an uneasy state of mind.

Enter Dibble centered on a character who shares many of Reed's characteristics. Revolting against a snobbish Harvard background by becoming a laborer, Dibble simultaneously becomes engaged to a rich man's daughter and organizes a strike at his future father-in-law's construction company. While the resulting complications are occasionally humorous, the work is also a vehicle which allows the hero to declaim passionate speeches about poor working conditions and condemn the hypocrisy of capitalists who protect precious daughters by exploiting other humans. Dibble shares with his creator the role of the intellectual scorning the middle class and committed to the cause of the workers, but he is different from Jack in one important respect: he is actually on the firing line. Here, then, was a deep dilemma, rising silently out of Reed's unconscious. For most of his friends, it was enough to be an artist or a critic working for the cause of freedom. But Reed, whose needs drove him to a medium of action as well as one of words, was beginning to ask himself whether it was enough for a writer to commit only literary talent to the struggle for liberation. Formulating such a question took a long time—answering it would take even longer.

8

Paterson

"*As soon as the dark sets in, young girls begin to pass that Corner—squat figured, hard-faced, 'cheap' girls, like dusty little birds wrapped too tightly in their feathers. They come up Irving Place from Fourteenth Street, turn back toward Union Square on Sixteenth, stroll down Fifteenth (passing the Corner again) to Third Avenue, and so around—always drawn back to the Corner. . . .*

"*The Place has its inevitable Cop. He follows the same general beat as the girls do, but at a slower, more majestic pace. It is his job to pretend that no such thing exists. This he does by keeping the girls perpetually walking—to create the illusion that they're going somewhere. Society allows vice no rest. If women stood still, what would become of us all? When the Cop appears on the Corner, the women who are lingering there scatter like a shoal of fish. . . ˮ.*

"*Standing on that Corner, watching the little comedy, my ears were full of low whisperings and the soft scuff of their feet. They cursed at me or guyed me, according to whether or not they had had any dinner. And then came the Cop.*

*"His ponderous shoulders came rolling out of the gloom of Fifteenth
Street, with the satisfied arrogance of an absolute monarch. Soundlessly
the girls vanished. . . . He stood for a moment, juggling his club and peering suddenly around. . . . Then his eye fell on me.*

" 'Move on!' he ordered, with an imperial jerk of the head.

" 'Why?' I asked.

" 'Never mind why. Because I say so. . . .'

" 'I'm doing nothing,' said I. . . .

*" 'Come on then,' he growled, taking me roughly by the arm. . . .
The Cop and I went up Fifteenth Street, neither of us saying anything.
. . . We entered the dingy respectability of the Night Court. . . .*

*"There was another prisoner before me, a slight, girlish figure that
did not reach the shoulder of the policeman who held her arm. . . .*

" 'Soliciting,' said the hoarse voice of the policeman. . . .

" 'Ten days . . . next case!' . . .

*"The Judge was writing something on a piece of paper. Without
looking up he snapped:*

" 'What's the charge, officer?'

*" 'Resisting an officer,' said the Cop surlily. 'I told him to move on an'
he says he wouldn't—'*

*" 'Hum,' murmured the Judge abstractedly, still writing. 'Wouldn't,
eh? Well, what have you got to say for yourself?'*

"I did not answer.

" 'Won't talk, eh? Well, I guess you get—'

"Then he looked up, nodded, and smiled.

*" 'Hello, Reed!' he said. He venomously regarded the Cop. 'Next
time you pull a friend of mine—' Suggestively, he left the threat un-
finished. Then to me, 'Want to sit up on the Bench for a while?' "[1]*

On the loose, rambling around Manhattan's streets in search of fiction
and adventure, John Reed learned that reality could be symbolic. There
was no need to embroider this kind of incident, or unnecessarily to
freight it with meaning, for it was complete, a brief, stark reminder that
the line separating fiction from fact was hazier than the one dividing
justice and injustice. Reporting such a story hardly ended the matter.
If he could get away with thumbing his nose at a cop, others could not;
if he could climb onto the Bench, others stood before judges unprotected
by reputation or powerful friends. Out of sympathy with such discrimination, he increasingly longed to strip away those elements which
gave shelter from the brute reality faced by other men. Like the cattle
boat or the cross-country marches in Europe, this was part of a desire

to test himself. The difference was that then raw experience had been its own end, and now it was increasingly justified by radical social theories that reinforced an internal sense of justice inherited from his father.

Village radicalism came in many flavors. Not one to select a theory by which to live, Jack accepted them all, casually, yet inevitably, pulled toward action by a slow tide. Then, when radicalism came clothed in magnetic, urgent human flesh, the time was right. It happened one evening in a stuffy Village apartment where he met William D. "Big Bill" Haywood, chief of the Industrial Workers of the World, the massive, battered, uncompromising, one-eyed labor leader who was a current hero in Bohemia. For hours Haywood related what a virtual news blackout had been concealing—that twenty-five thousand silk workers on strike for an eight-hour day in nearby Paterson were being treated by city officials as if they were manning the barricades of revolution. Strikers were being clubbed off the streets and jailed in record numbers, all meeting halls had been closed to the IWW and criticism of the city administration or the police was being met by trials for sedition. Explaining that nationwide publicity seemed essential if workers were to receive much-needed outside support and aid, the labor leader struck a responsive chord—Reed decided he would go to Paterson to help publicize the repression.

Two days later, with Eddy Hunt beside him, Jack arrived there on a chill, slate-gray morning. Beneath low clouds and a misty rain the six a.m. streets of the industrial city astride the murky Passaic River were bleak and deserted. Hands deep in pockets, coat collars turned up against the damp, Reed and Hunt hurried toward the mill district. Turning into a long street, one side lined with the dark, fortress-like mills, the other with dilapidated wooden tenements, they found men and women clustered in windows and doorways "laughing and chatting as if after breakfast on a holiday." In front of the factories fifty people, dripping with rain, tramped in a picket line, and as the day warmed into light, their ranks swelled into the hundreds. Damp and ragged, the men, women and children on the line were in a jovial, wisecracking mood that lasted until police pushed onto the scene, ordered workers to disperse and then shouldered roughly among the pickets as if hoping to start trouble. Good humor quickly vanished, and the strikers regarded their antagonists "with eyes full of hate."[2]

Separating from Eddy for a look around and drenched by a sudden downpour, Jack climbed onto the porch of a frame house for shelter. Immediately a nearby policeman ordered him to move. His refusal enraged the officer, who leaped up the steps, seized his arm and jerked him down to the sidewalk, where another cop closed in. Together they shoved Reed along the pavement.

"Now you get the hell off this street," the first ordered.

"I won't get off this street or any other street. If I'm breaking the law, you arrest me!" Reed retorted.

Not wanting to make an arrest, the officer said so with a great deal of profanity. Retaining his humor, Jack calmly wrote down the policeman's badge number and then asked his name.

"Yes," the angry cop bellowed, "an' I got *your* number! I'll arrest you."

Taking Reed by the arm, he marched up the street, swearing and threatening to beat him with a nightstick. Two other cursing policemen helped hustle Jack into the patrol wagon, which then clanged its way along a cheering, waving picket line to headquarters. Hurled into a filthy four-by-seven-foot cell, he was later in the morning brought into the court of Recorder Carroll, a man with "the intelligent, cruel, merciless face of the ordinary police court magistrate." There was no defense attorney. The charge was read, he was permitted to give his story and then heard "a clever melange of lies" about his lawlessness recited by the officer. Carroll, who had already jailed hundreds of strikers on flimsy evidence, was little inclined to believe or much care about a snoopy reporter. The verdict was swift: "Twenty days."

For all the injustice, Jack did not seem a martyr as he left the courtroom. One reporter described him as "smiling and happy," and attributed this mood to the rare opportunity he would have for picking up "local color" behind bars.[3] As he entered the Passaic County Jail, a large, dank, unsanitary, vermin-ridden building dating from the Civil War, the smile faded. His personal possessions were taken away and he was forced to strip, bathe in a foul, scummy tub and don prison garb: dirty gray trousers, a canvas coat and a faded blue shirt. Thrust into a long, dark corridor lined with cells, where the only ventilation came from one small skylight in a tiny airshaft, he was among ragged and demoralized prisoners —a man with open, syphilitic sores on his legs, a youngster whose mind seemed half gone, a cocaine addict waiting for a fix smuggled in from outside, an inmate with a terrible face who wandered back and forth screaming in a weird, monotonous voice.

Feeling strange, displaced and semihuman, Jack was soon locked into a cell with a large Negro and a swarthy, bearded foreigner who identified himself as Carlo Tresca. He extended a hand and tried to engage the IWW leader in conversation, but Tresca refused to answer questions and drew away. With only two beds in the cell, the Negro deferentially offered to sleep on the floor, but neither of the others would allow this. Through the hours of darkness the three men lounged about saying nothing, a bewildered and frustrated Jack smoking one cigarette after another. Early the next day he ran into Haywood—just arrested—in the prison yard, and when the big man introduced him around, Reed learned the cause of Tresca's hostility. Because he was obviously not a silk worker, the labor leader had thought him a stool pigeon planted by police. Now the Italian heartily embraced him, other strikers eagerly gathered around to meet an editor of a well-known radical magazine and his sense of dislocation melted away.

The courage, warmth and humanity of the strikers—these things made jail worthwhile. Immediately Reed fell in love with these Italians, Lithuanians, Poles and Jews, small, dark, tough, boisterous men who cheered the IWW, incessantly sang union songs and fearlessly denounced their jailers. Many had faces scarred and bruised by billy clubs, or "lined and sunken with the slow starvation of nine weeks' poverty—shadowed with the sight of so much suffering, or the hopeless brutality of the police." Yet all were full of fight and ready to return to the picket lines. From them he heard many stories about the inhumanity of the police— how passive strikers had been beaten, abused and crammed into tiny, unventilated cells to await trials where the sentence was often six months. Admiring Haywood, he of the "massive, rugged face, seamed and scarred like a mountain," a man whose calm voice communicated hope to the men around him, Reed began to feel the silk strike was, more than any individual, the many "gentle, alert, brave men" with whom he shared food and cigarettes. Behind bars his enthusiasm for the cause grew, and he wrote Hunt: "If you saw the strikers in here, you would realize it is a *great strike*."[4]

However warm his union friends, however great the strike, a jail in which cockroach races were a chief form of entertainment was "worse than the cattle boat." The comparison of this new experience with the boat trip was significant. Then Reed had tried to act as hardy as a deckhand, and now he hoped to prove himself tough as the striking workers. As on the voyage, he was unable to fulfill such a role wholly, and this resulted in volatile feelings of pride, shame, confusion, self-consciousness and occasional humility that showed clearly in the many notes datelined "Reading Gaol" that he scribbled to Eddy Hunt. The basic problem was that Reed always enjoyed standing out from the crowd. Proud to report, "I am a Personage in here," he had difficulty in behaving like a common striker. Finding the meals—greasy soup, rotten potatoes, rancid meat—inedible, he had Hunt send in food from nearby restaurants, and for a while he savored the idea of suing the County of Passaic for false conviction and having the policeman demoted for "brutality." He also urged Eddy to "save all the newspaper accounts for my delectation," and carefully preserved a ditty sent by Harry Kemp which equated Reed with many great historical figures "Who spake truth in the face of Power / And languished oft in dungeon cold."[5]

Sometimes Reed became very touchy. Worried about both the reaction of his family and the security of his job on the *American*, he became annoyed when others mentioned such mundane considerations. In sober moods he easily admitted, "I'm neither a hero nor a martyr—the whole business is a joke," and in frank ones said that, despite the discomfort of jail, "My infernal sense of Romance and Humor makes me rather enjoy it." But what he could stipulate was less acceptable coming from others. When Hunt said at visitors' hour one day he was keeping mum about details of the arrest "so you'll have all the fun of telling the story yourself," Jack became so enraged at this simple truth that he devoted several pages of a letter to denouncing his best friend for treating him "like a child." To such petulance Hunt could only respond with humor:

> Your wild young letter . . . leads me to think that Romance and your Sense of Humor have temporarily deserted you. If you intend to come from the confines of jail, clanking your chains and writing of your rights —God help you—and us.[6]

In Cambridge Bobby Rogers read news of the arrest and, without knowing details, wrote that if the judge thought Reed was a danger to the community before, he was a fool for not knowing "how much more of a menace he'll be when he gets out. . . . I see the *American*'s circulation booming. 'Twenty Days in Hell' by Jawn Reed Esq. T'will be pretty reading."[7]

His friends knew Jack well. After four days' confinement Reed was sprung by an IWW attorney, and back at Washington Square he began to write an article for the *Masses*:

> There's a war in Paterson, New Jersey. But it's a curious kind of war. All the violence is the work of one side—the mill owners. Their servants, the police, club unresisting men and women and ride down law-abiding crowds. Their paid mercenaries, the armed detectives, shoot and kill innocent people. Their newspapers, the Paterson Press and the Paterson Call, publish incendiary and crime-inciting appeals to mob violence against the strike leaders. Their tool, Recorder Carroll, deals out heavy sentences to peaceful pickets that the police net gathers up. They control absolutely the police, the press, the courts.

Going on to recount what he had seen and done, Reed's prose flared into the dramatic as it portrayed the plight of the strikers. The burden of the article was that rather than the IWW being "anarchistic," it was the Paterson establishment, masking violence as "law and order," that was acting "contrary to American ideals." Denouncing both the American Federation of Labor and the Socialist Party for not aiding fellow workingmen, he kept his jail mates squarely in focus: "Think of it! Twelve years they have been losing strikes—twelve solid years of disappointments and incalculable suffering. They must not lose again! They cannot lose!"[8]

The article was hard-hitting, vivid and angry, and it showed that Reed had undergone a change, had shifted from being a sympathetic reporter to an involved partisan. A trip begun partly as a kind of lark, little different from the day at Boss Sullivan's dinner for derelicts or jaunts among underworld elements in the Tenderloin, had taken on more serious overtones. Primed for something new by a growing boredom with work on the *American*, the increased radical contacts through the *Masses*, the inability to find a suitable form for his literary impulses, and the desire to escape the rounds of Village life, Jack had found a cause. Without worrying about the problem or even consciously making a decision, his personal involvement was transformed into a commitment. When he emerged from jail Reed knew that something had to be done—by him. The article was a first step, but already he sensed that more weapons than a pen would be necessary to win this fight.

The silk strike in Paterson was an important event, not only for John Reed, but also for the IWW, the labor movement and that increasingly large section of Bohemia interested in social questions. Less than a decade old, the Wobblies were a shaggy product of the frontier, spawned in Western logging camps and grim company mining towns where few middle-class amenities masked naked exploitation and class struggle. The latest in a series of attempts since the Civil War to form unions based on unskilled industrial labor rather than craft organization, the IWW was both militant and class-conscious. Originally the union had drawn the support of Socialists like Eugene V. Debs and Daniel De Leon, but when it proved itself to be against political action—however radical—such backing drifted away. The IWW saw politics as a kind of game, calculated to divert the workingman from his true economic interest. It was far more important to organize workers than voters, to win strikes rather than elections.

The Wobblies won few labor struggles in their first years, but managed to gain national attention largely because of the way America reacted to them. Radical in rhetoric, union leaders believed in the necessity of overthrowing capitalism, and their vocabulary was studded with terms like "general strike," "sabotage" and "propaganda of the deed." However much the IWW's ideology was a strange brew of Marxism, syndicalism and anarchism, Wobbly chiefs knew that workers flourished on immediate gains rather than hopes of a distant utopia. For all the radical talk, the IWW in a strike situation was both responsible and conservative, cautioning workers against any violence and accepting limited goals such as shorter hours and higher pay. Despite this, the press always heard calls for revolution and direct action, and the union's struggles with authorities filled the newspapers. No matter that the violence might be the work of police or company detectives. By 1910 the IWW was fixed in the American mind as anarchistic and revolutionary.

Like the rest of the country, Bohemians saw Wobblies as wild and woolly revolutionaries, only for them this gave the IWW a romantic rather than a frightening aspect. Greenwich Villagers were generally pleased by recent triumphs of the Socialists, with Debs capturing six percent of the Presidential vote in 1912 and party members being elected to hundreds of local offices across the nation. But paradoxically, by contesting and winning elections, Socialists could seem too much part of the system, too attached to the middle-class conventions against which Bohemians were in revolt, and to someone like Reed the Socialist Party was "duller than religion."[9] This could never be said of the IWW. With its bindlestiffs, tramp poets and two-fisted organizers, its noted free-speech fights in Spokane, Fresno and San Diego, its aura of violence and sabotage, its battles with police and vigilantes, the IWW was a dramatic organization that made radicalism a heroic cry for freedom, brave words sung into the barrels of militia rifles. To side with the Wobblies was to fight for justice and smell the excitement of the barricades.

Villagers gave their hearts to the IWW after 1912 when the union successfully invaded the East Coast, organizing the multinational workers of Lawrence, Massachusetts, for a struggle against the largest textile manufacturers in the country. Headlines had etched charismatic leaders into the public mind—Haywood, Tresca, the handsome, mystical poet-organizer Arturo Giovannitti. When the IWW won that strike against the massed power of capital and state, it seemed a turning point in history; the press worried about the rising tide of revolution, while Wobblies and their sympathizers saw the dawn of the new era at hand. And John Reed, stopping by Lawrence to look over the post-strike situation, joined many in believing that the union now "dominated the social and industrial horizon like a portent of the rising of the oppressed."

Paterson was the second major Eastern effort of the union, yet the

IWW could not take credit for starting the strike. Working conditions in the mills were already wretched, with long hours and low pay, when a speedup—making workers tend four looms instead of two—precipitated a spontaneous walkout at the largest mill in February 1913. Only then did the IWW, which had been attempting to organize the town for years, find its efforts paying off. Soon all the largest silk mills in the country were shut down, and the owners—believing in a kind of domino theory of union organization—were determined not to yield an inch, to resist collective bargaining not only for themselves but also, dimly, for other industries that might be threatened. The denunciation of the IWW as un-American from press and pulpit, the behavior of city officials and police and courts all followed from that decision. Wanting another victory, IWW national chiefs hurried to Paterson, only to be arrested. While union numbers jumped rapidly, nonunion members were well represented on strike councils, and Wobbly leaders were content to accept demands of Paterson workers for an eight-hour day and a minimum wage in some job categories. These were hardly revolutionary aims, but they could at least satisfy desires for continued IWW growth and success.

The gulf between the image of the IWW as revolutionary and its actions as sober, responsible and nonviolent was not wholly apparent to well-wishers from Greenwich Village who now flocked to see their working-class heroes in action. After the publicity surrounding Reed's arrest and his sustained efforts to rouse friends to the gravity and importance of the silk strike, Villagers like Walter Lippmann, Max Eastman, Henrietta Rodman, Ernest Poole, Margaret Sanger, Harry Kemp and Leroy Scott made pilgrimages there. Sunday was the best time to go. Free from the necessity of picketing, workers would gather for mass meetings. Because Paterson officials refused to issue permits, thousands of families trekked to neighboring Haledon, a little community with a Socialist mayor. On a hillside meadow owned by a strike sympathizer, fifteen to twenty thousand workers and children lounged on grassy slopes, eating bread and cheese and drinking wine, listening to the speeches of leaders who stood on the balcony of a farmhouse. At first the gathering seemed to some visitors like a Sunday School picnic, but the words spoken gave quite another flavor. Some of the language was violent, with Tresca exhorting fellow Italians, "*Occhio per occhio, dente per dente, sangue per sangue!*" More typical were the words of the popular, red-haired girl orator Elizabeth Gurley Flynn, who preached a doctrine of striking with folded arms and assured the audience that employers feared nothing so much as the violence contained in the mere refusal to work.

Most of the Village emissaries brought word that the outside world looked to the strikers as men and women taking an important step toward industrial democracy. When Reed on his first visit was asked by Haywood to speak, he gazed down at the sea of faces spread over the green hillside and felt at a loss for words. Silently waiting, he felt a curious kind of rhythm swelling in the crowd, connected it to a similar motion he had sensed in jail when strikers had sought to banish troubles in song, then whirled back to an image of Harvard Stadium on a fall afternoon when the team was behind. Overtaken by the old vocation, Jack began to lead the workers in song, first, the "Marseillaise," then the "Internationale." Below him, Italians and Germans, Poles and Greeks and Jews were welded together, and as choruses resounded off the hillside, he was filled by a wave of triumph that made the day of victory seem close at hand.

Speaking, singing, the written word—how did these help families slowly starving in Paterson? Perplexed Villagers searched for a way of making aid more concrete, and sometime before mid-May the idea of the Paterson Pageant was born.* In conception it was simple and unpre-

* The origins of the idea for the pageant are difficult to pin down. Mabel Dodge unequivocally states that the idea was hers and, without giving a precise date, indicates she suggested it on that evening when Haywood first explained the Paterson situation to Villagers. She then has Reed—it was their first meeting—popping up, seizing the idea, announcing, "I'll do it," and then going off to Paterson to get arrested and gather material. Hutchins Hapgood, in his autobiography, follows this story precisely, but he used her work to jog his own memory. Bill Haywood's autobiography says simply, "At a small gathering in the home of a New York friend of mine, it was suggested that it would be an excellent idea to stage the strike in New York City." See Mabel Dodge Luhan, *Movers and Shakers* (New York: Harcourt, Brace, 1936), 188–9; Hutchins Hapgood, *A Victorian in the Modern World* (New York: Harcourt, Brace, 1939), 350; William D. Haywood, *Bill Haywood's Book* (New York: International, 1929), 262.

For all its apparent plausibility, in some ways it is difficult to accept this explanation. Mabel liked to take credit for moving and inspiring people around her, especially the many men in her life. The real problem, however, is that nowhere in the letters of Reed or his close friends is there much indication he went to Paterson to gather material for a pageant. Notes to Hunt indicate that once in jail, he wanted to stay a few days to get the full flavor of the experience. In a humorous, one-page play written on April 30, Hunt has Reed in prison saying, "Don't get me out. I'm gathering material for an epic," but this does not necessarily mean a pageant. Earlier the play indicates that Reed was arrested haphazardly, rather than with the intent of having a jail experience, and in one note to Hunt he insists upon the point: "If you think it was anything that I did wrong which got me jugged, I don't agree with you. If you think I wasn't strictly within my rights, you're crazy. . . . It's a clear case of injustice against a citizen who wasn't even mixed up in the business." Other memoirs (see bibliography for this chapter) also indicate that trips to Paterson on Sundays preceded the idea of a pageant, and yet no such journeys were undertaken before Reed's arrest. The first newspaper account of the proposed

cedented: dramatize the strike by reenacting its main events in Madison Square Garden, using the workers to play themselves. Simultaneously a propaganda vehicle and a money-raising venture, it might also be a way in which the antibourgeois attitudes of the intelligentsia and the anti-capitalist thrust of the proletariat would fuse into a powerful weapon in the war against their common enemy, seen as the complacent, repressed, exploitative middle and upper class.

If Reed did not create the idea of the pageant, there is little doubt his prodigious efforts brought the project to life. Of a six-man executive committee, he was the most committed, the most active, the one who gave direction to what was otherwise a "poor, inefficient, disorganized" crowd of individuals who could agree on nothing but the general idea. Nightly meetings were held at the cramped uptown flat of Margaret Sanger. For days the apartment was crowded with a collection of anarchists, socialists, suffragettes, playwrights, poets, schoolteachers and rich patrons of radical causes, who sat on tables, bookcases, beds and the floor hotly debating each decision. There was Haywood, "his seamed, scarred, bloated . . . face bent down, his huge arm about the shoulders of a slattern girl"; F. Sumner Boyd, a Socialist jailed in Paterson for reading the free-speech clause of the New Jersey state constitution; Alexander Berkman, who had spent fourteen years in jail for the attempted assassination of Henry Frick during the Homestead Strike in 1892; elderly Jessie Ashley, "sweet and old-fashioned in appearance as a Puritan grand-aunt," active in many radical causes; the wealthy Mabel Dodge, interpreter of Gertrude Stein and hostess of the notorious Fifth Avenue salon; novelist Ernest Poole, who had gone directly from Princeton to a settlement house on the Lower East Side in 1907; rowdy Harry Kemp, always on the lookout for the perfect young lady to grace his bed. Debates on problems of money, publicity, arrangements could go on forever, and always in the noise and confusion it was Jack who "jumped into the fray with all four feet and began to bellow" until he convinced them to pull together.[10]

While the committee thrashed out financial and other practical ar-rangements, Reed took charge of writing the scenario and staging the production. Enveloping friends with a mounting enthusiasm, he per-suaded Bobby Jones to design the stage setting, John Sloan to paint scenery and Eddy Hunt to act as a kind of general assistant. The problem of rehearsals—held in a union hall—was formidable, for strikers of dif-

pageant was in the New York *Times*, May 22, 1913. All this evidence at least makes the origins of the pageant somewhat more problematic than Mabel Dodge's memoir indicates.

ferent nationalities had difficulty understanding Jack and each other. He took cues from the players, first asking them to act out how they felt going to work in the morning, marching on a picket line, facing the clubs of police, then had others comment on the performances. Soon the strikers were both actors and critics, suggesting, helping, throwing themselves wholeheartedly into the task. From three hundred the first day, rehearsals swelled to over a thousand. When police closed the union hall as "disorderly," he had to direct on a nearby vacant lot, sometimes in a warm spring rain. Weather, harassment, confusion—none of this squelched a flowering, indefinable spirit that was expressed each day when strikers shouted, "*Musica, musica, musica,*" until Jack led them in song. Responding to their enthusiasm, he produced a revolutionary work by setting the words of an IWW favorite to the melody of "Harvard, Old Harvard."

Hurrying back and forth between Paterson and Manhattan, Reed wore himself down. There was no time to eat properly, no time to change clothing, no time to sleep, no time to take care of all the details of production in the three available weeks. A few days before the performance, financial disaster threatened and the executive committee was forced to vote to give up the project, but sympathetic New York silk workers came up with the necessary funds, and suddenly it was the eve of the pageant with nothing quite ready and the whole burden of possible failure crushing upon Jack. Near to the breaking point, he pushed on. On the afternoon of June 7, twelve hundred silk strikers, led by Tresca and Haywood, marched solemnly from the Hoboken ferry landing to Madison Square Garden, where they fell ravenously on sandwiches and coffee. Then Reed, without a coat, his sleeves pushed up, shouting through a megaphone until he was hoarse, put the amateur performers through the final rehearsal. When it finished late in the day, he collapsed in exhaustion over a makeshift desk in one of the Garden offices.

By eight o'clock Jack was up and "chipper as ever." Already streets around the arena were jammed with people and long lines stretched before the box office, while red electric lights blazed the letters "IWW" ten feet tall from the four sides of Madison Square Tower. Before entering the auditorium, Sheriff Julius Harburger treated reporters to his views of the "treasonable . . . un-American . . . hysterical, unsound doctrines" of the IWW, lamented that a court order prevented him from banning the singing of the "Marseillaise" and vowed: "Just let anybody say one word of disrespect for the flag, and I will stop the show so quickly it will take their breath away."[11] Inside, the vast cavern rocked with noise. Hung with immense red banners, the balconies were packed, and the sounds of shuffling feet and vendors hawking radical pamphlets competed with a brassy IWW band. Finding the lower rows of one- and two-dollar seats filling too slowly, the committee hurriedly decided to sell all remaining tickets for a quarter. At nine o'clock, with some of the fifteen thousand spectators still choking the aisles, Reed gave a signal and the Paterson Pageant began.

The set was spectacular. At one end of the darkened arena was a huge stage and behind it an immense backdrop of menacing silk mills, life-size, with lights blazing through tiers of windows. Down the center of the Garden a wide street bisected the audience, and along it small groups of listless silk workers began to straggle toward the factories. Slowly, dejectedly, they disappeared through the black doors, and for a long while there was no sound, save the harsh, mechanical vibration of looms. Then, suddenly, voices inside the buildings began to shout, "Strike, strike," and laughing, jostling workers poured out of the mills, filled the stage and began to sing the "Internationale." After that, the sounds and lights of the mills were dead, but the performers were vivid and alive as they acted out events they had lived—the mass picketing, the arrival of police, the brutal fights between cops and strikers, the gunshots into a crowd that killed a worker, the funeral procession and burial where each striker dropped a red carnation on the coffin, the May Day parade with flags flying and bands blaring, and the final meeting where they unanimously pledged never to return to work until the demand for an eight-hour day was met.

From the moment the performance began, it was a success. The audience, largely New York workingmen with a sprinkling of Bohemians and middle-class sympathizers, jumped up to join voices in the first singing of the "Internationale," and after that hardly anybody sat down. With the subtle line between actor and spectator breached, the crowd was at one with the strikers, booing the police, roaring in unison revolutionary songs, responding to the words of Tresca, Haywood and Flynn, applauding and shouting approval continuously until the solemn moments of the funeral, when they gazed on raptly while tears ran down many cheeks. Newspaper reporters were impressed by the intense rapport between audience and performers, and the next day's editions were enthusiastic, calling it a "spectacular production," speaking of "a poignant realism that no man . . . will ever forget," or even suggesting that the pageant was the birth of "a new art form."[12] Bohemians could see visions of a revolutionary popular theater with the power to engage the emotions of the masses, while Hutchins Hapgood acclaimed the conception, the performance and the vision: "This kind of thing makes us hope for a real democracy, where self-expression in industry and art among the masses may become a rich reality, spreading a human glow over the whole of humanity."[13]

The glow was there already, in the breasts of the audience, the hearts of striker-performers, the minds of artist-intellectuals like Reed who had opened themselves to a new dimension of reality. It was a human glow, fanned into life by the collective experience, but one which could not survive reality outside the theater. Many men emerged from the Garden renewed in a determination to win the Paterson strike, but there was still a world of police, intransigent millowners, hungry children and unpaid rent bills. Moving, elevating, ennobling, a work of art could not banish a world of exploitation, greed and power.

Reality first returned in the notices of the daily press. Having second thoughts about good reviews written by drama critics, editors began to explain that, however effective the pageant and however justified some of the strikers' grievances, the IWW was an unacceptable, "destructive" organization that promised only hatred, violence and possible anarchy for America.[14] Such a response might be expected from important dailies, but the grim financial report released on June 25 by the executive committee was a more serious blow. Rather than a profit, the pageant showed a deficit of almost $2000. The costs of putting on a one-night performance were heavy, and there had not been enough money to allow renting the Garden for more than a single night. Of fifteen thousand seats, a good many had been sold for twenty-five cents, and a large number had gone free to people who flashed a red IWW membership card at the door. With $10,000 going for rent and other expenses, the deficit was a matter of simple economics.

Since reasons—even good ones—are not edible, this explanation could not help hungry union men. In many ways the pageant had diverted attention from the central issues—hours and wages. With funds running low in Paterson, strikers had pinned unreasonable hopes upon the performance, and those who had seen the response of the audience had even dreamed of vast profits. When the Paterson press seized upon the bad financial news to accuse sponsors of lining their own pockets, there was enough discouragement among weary strikers to allow this idea to make headway. The result was, in Flynn's words, "disastrous to solidarity."[15] In July the workers' front began to crumble and some returned to the mills. A trickle soon became a flood, and by August the strike was at an end with none of the original demands having been met.

By the time the bright hopes of May and June were dashed, John Reed was far away from Paterson, living a very different kind of life. Years later he recognized the full disaster of the aborted strike, and understood that the failure resulted in an irrevocable IWW retreat from the East Coast. Never again did the Wobblies win a strike in that region, and, as Jack accurately stated, after being "smashed" in Paterson, the union "never recovered its old prestige." It is not apparent if he ever fully realized that his activity may have had a negative effect upon the cause, but he eventually did come to understand that the battle of an in-dustrial union to win recognition was too immense a problem to be solved by a theatrical performance. The power of art and all the support of talented Bohemians could not significantly alter the realities of an en-trenched economic order. Carried away in the feverish preparations for the pageant, Reed may have believed momentarily in the power of art to affect history. But close friends who were less involved knew such an effect could be marginal at best. Writing congratulations to him in July, two ex-Harvard radicals suggested as much in saying the IWW "is helping to stir up life more abundantly in the working class, and that is what they need. *Our help won't do any good unless they start the rumpus.*"[16]

Knowing in lucid moments that the pageant was at best peripheral to the grim business of class struggle did not make the strike less im-portant. In Paterson Jack had smelled, tasted and felt the spirit of radicalism and found it good. Falling under the spell of Wobbly leaders, he admired "their understanding of the workers, the boldness of their dream, the way immense crowds of people took fire and came alive under their leadership." The strike was "drama, change, democracy on the march . . . a war of the people," a glorious experience because of hopeful visions it called forth and the contagious feelings of bravery, camaraderie and warmth that emanated from the strikers. A last visit to Paterson on June 17, recounted in a letter to his mother, showed the human, rather than the ideological, to be uppermost:

> When I told them I was going away, ten thousand people asked me not to. Don't tell this around because it sounds ridiculous. But I led the singing again, and when I came down they crowded around me saying, "We have been so lonesome for to sing—you come tomorrow," and "You make the people to be happy." . . . *That's* what I'm doing, Muz.[17]

Reed's commitment was a short-term affair. Notorious in the national press for having been arrested and for staging the pageant, he em-phasized to Margaret that he was not straying from the path of parental values:

> Don't believe the papers that say I am tying up with the I.W.W. or any other limited, little bunch. I am not a Socialist any more than I am an Episcopalian. I know now that my business is to interpret and live life, wherever it may be found—whether in the labor movement or out of it. I haven't ever been patient with cliques any more than Paw was, and I

won't be roped in any more than he was, in some petty gang with a Platform.[18]

Disingenuous in suggesting he thought the IWW was limited, Jack was quite truthful in explaining his vision of his own role, that of a writer on the track of excitement, wherever it was to be found. Radicalism was a splendid arena of movement, drama and emotion, but it was hardly the only one.

Like other Bohemians who went to Paterson, cheered the Wobblies and attended the pageant, John Reed could—unlike the workers—go on in the summer of 1913 to something else that seemed as interesting as the cause of labor. But he could not forget what he had seen and helped bring to the Garden stage, the moving spectacle of fearless men acting out "the wretchedness of their lives and the glory of their revolt." Nor could he forget the enveloping warmth of workers "ennobled by something greater than themselves," who by their love had made him feel noble, too.[19] Other paths might call, but Paterson had planted a seed in his heart.

9

23 Fifth Avenue

"Celia belonged to a race of women who are the world's great lovers. They seem less of the earth than of the spirit of earth. . . . They respire habitually in the thin, high atmosphere that artists sometimes breathe. They see Truth, not in flashes, but as a steady white light; Truth often at variance with the world's ideas. . . . They are as innocent as a swallow in mid-air, for even when they know evil, they cannot understand it. They are always beautiful.

"Such a woman is created for love alone. Although by breeding and delicacy she shrinks from vulgarity, yet she will give herself to a beast among men if she love him. Gladly she will follow him into the brutal places of life, and if he merely says, 'I love you,' she will forgive. . . . Deliciously human, they desire human love above all else. They are brimful of the joy of the world, shifting colors, jewels, robes, the pageant of lights and moving people. They are like chalices filled with unbounded passion and infinite faith in the love of men."[1]

Women in the world of Bohemia might be emancipated, free to develop as full human beings outside the norms of conventional roles, but this did not prevent John Reed from sometimes seeing them as vaguely unreal creatures, startling combinations of passion and innocence. Sexually experienced, affecting an air of general worldliness, he viewed females through a haze compounded of idealization and his own need for affection. The former was in part literary. Under the sway of a romantic vision he could write such a description of a woman rarely—if ever—met in reality. Obviously, here was a personal ideal, a female compounded of earth and heaven, innocence and experience, full of beauty, love and joy, and ready to follow her man anywhere—be a virtual slave—if only he spoke the magic words, "I love you."

Neither a persistent student of women nor an ardent pursuer of them like some Bohemian contemporaries, Reed could both entertain such a fantasy and show flashes of insight into feminine behavior. In fiction he had a certain knack for portraying prostitutes, scrubwomen, shopgirls and early versions of the tough-talking flapper, letting speech patterns give dimension to character. Sometimes in a few words he was able to fix a type, such as in this satire of the subculture's ideal woman: "Figure that will stand a Greenwich Village uniform; thorough comprehension of Matisse; more than a touch of languor; a dash of economic independence; dark hair, dark eyes, dark past."[2] Partly a male ideal, this was also a role that many young village ladies were trying their best to fill.

Reed knew that women were creatures to be loved. In his early New York days—after breaking the engagement—he had fallen in love with such startling regularity that among friends it was something of a joke. Each time his heart caught fire it burned brightly, and for weeks he felt larger, stronger, fuller than before. Obviously, what most men call "infatuation" he called "love," and, boyish poet that he was, Jack sought this emotion as a flower seeks the sun. Like the flower, his quest was not conscious. Love descended swiftly from nowhere and later vanished just as mysteriously. A strange gift from the gods, it was ultimately so unknowable that never once did he attempt to portray its causes and consequences realistically—poetry seemed the only medium that could even suggest the dimensions of love.

No greater proof of love's capricious nature could be given Reed than what occurred in the three weeks before the pageant. Overextended, harassed and tired to the marrow as he raced back and forth between New York and Paterson, Jack was also succumbing to the familiar emotion. The woman was Mabel Dodge, one of the members of the executive committee, and though she returned his growing feeling, both realized there was no time for any real lovemaking until the performance was done. Outsiders noticed the deep glances they exchanged, the unspoken communication that flashed between them. Watching closely, Hutchins Hapgood, Mabel's good friend, well understood the meaning of her expression: "When I saw that look on her face, I knew it was all over for Mabel, for the time being, and also probably all over for Reed."[3]

A powerful woman, Mabel Dodge was eight years older than Jack. The daughter of a rich Buffalo banker, she married at twenty-one, was widowed at twenty-three, and a year later married Edwin Dodge, an independently wealthy Boston architect. Between 1903 and 1912 she and her husband lived in a sumptuous villa at Arcetri, on a hill above Florence, lavishly entertaining expatriates, aristocrats and artists. To them came theatrical titan Gordon Craig, the actress Eleonora Duse and author Gabriele D'Annunzio, while the still-unknown Gertrude Stein was a good friend who remained long enough to write one of the first of her noted character sketches, "A Portrait of Mabel Dodge at the Villa Curonia," which managed to mention neither Mabel nor the villa.

By the time the Dodges returned to America in mid-1912, Edwin and Mabel were becoming estranged. As their lives drifted apart, she came into touch with the powerful currents flowing through Greenwich Village. A longtime rebel herself, Mabel became involved in the creation of the Armory Show, seeing it as a personal way of attacking middle-class life: "*I* was going to dynamite New York and nothing would stop me."[4] Soon acquainted with many artists and radicals, she began to receive visitors in her elegant apartment, its rooms painted the color of eggshells and furnished with delicate Italian antiques, at 23 Fifth Avenue, just across from the Brevoort Hotel. Informal visits grew until Mabel found herself the hostess of what Steffens called "the only successful salon I have ever seen in America."[5]

The time was ripe for such an institution, and Mabel Dodge was the perfect hostess. Wealthy, attractive, knowledgeable and generous, she had a rare facility for being able simultaneously to stimulate and soothe people, to make them think more fluently and wish to express their thoughts. When the casual entertainments were formalized into regular "Evenings" in the late fall of 1912, they became a central institution of the Greenwich Village scene. All Bohemia's factions met under her roof— artists Marsden Hartley, Andrew Dasburg, Max Weber, Charles Demuth and John Marin; intellectuals Lippmann, Steffens, Eastman and Hapgood; anarchists Goldman, Berkman and Hippolyte Havel; writers and poets Carl Van Vechten, Edwin Arlington Robinson and Amy Lowell; IWW's Haywood, Tresca, Arturo Giovannitti and Frank Tannenbaum; Socialists

William English Walling and Morris Hillquit; and various single-taxers, suffragettes, birth-control advocates, politicians and journalists.

The salon was a forum of free speech where everyone had his say to a colorful, variegated crowd, where women in floor-length formal gowns argued with Wobblies in stained denim, or young ladies in bobbed hair and sandals accepted cigarettes from men in starched linen and tails, or a successful editor in a Russian peasant blouse toasted an anarchist wearing a business suit. Debates ranged over a wide spectrum of social, intellectual, artistic and political issues. Occasionally, over the plentiful whiskey, beer and wine, conversation grew "riotous and foolish," but often the talk seemed brilliant and illuminating: "Arguments and discussions floated in the air, were caught and twisted and hauled and tied until the white salon itself was no longer static. There were undercurrents of emotion and sex."[6] Around midnight the doors to the dining room were flung open and everyone rushed for a supper of Virginia ham, white gorgonzola sandwiches, cold turkey, salads and rare, imported liqueurs.

By the time work on the pageant began, Mabel was something of a celebrity, for the fame of the salon had reached beyond Village circles. Despite the fact that friends like Steffens and Lippmann were often there, Reed somehow had never attended, and he first got to know her while planning the performance. Of course he had heard of her wealth, contacts and reputation and understood the social power that emanated from them. Mabel was a self-described headhunter of the famous, one whose maternal instinct often led her to young men. Once Jack took command of the pageant he became the kind of figure she wished to snare. At the basis of their mutual attraction was some kind of desire to explore the glamour and strength that each possessed.

Mabel's attractiveness was more than a matter of money and fame. She was not conventionally pretty, but possessed a unique, full-blown look that drew men, and this was complemented by an individual sense of dress. No matter what the current fashion, Mabel wore long gowns of fine silk and floppy hats that made her seem soft and feminine, a delicate woman with no roots, "a cut flower."[7] Coupled to this was a strong mystical streak. Always "on the trail of the infinite" himself, Hapgood thought her a "God-drunk" soul mate, and her conversation was studded with references to the "spirit of the Universe" flowing through her, making decisions, directing the stream of her life. A lovely rationalization for her own desire to control others, it was this "great force behind the scenes" that—she claimed—both led to beginning the salon and brought her John Reed.[8]

Jack and Mabel were still not free when the pageant was over. Exhausted, he desperately needed a vacation, and this dovetailed nicely with her desire to return to Italy for the summer. For ten days Reed wound up business affairs and prepared to sail. More than once he felt like a deserter, leaving behind the workers still on strike in Paterson. Guilt also dogged him in the form of family obligations, for complications had arisen in connection with C.J.'s estate, and Margaret wanted him home. Writing that he felt "like a brute to run away and leave you and Harry to do all the dirty work," he explained: "I'm really tired for the first time in my life—and I know I can do finer work if I can 'rest for an aeon or two.' "[9]

Jack and Mabel boarded the German steamship *Amerika* at the end of the third week in June, accompanied by her ten-year-old son, John, Miss Galvin—the boy's nurse—and Bobby Jones, off to study theater in Germany. Despite the excitement of departure, the occasion did not seem happy to Reed. Leaving the harbor was "like pulling up roots, or changing my skin snake-like, or something painful of the sort."[10] Since Jones felt much the same, the two men passed the first few days at sea gloomily brooding together.

On the *Amerika* one could at least brood in comfort. Traveling first class, with "flunkeys" all around, Reed found that with its fine restaurants, elevators, gymnasium, glassed-in decks and lack of motion, the ship seemed more like a resort hotel than a vessel. In principle he disliked the "softness and upholstery" of the grande-luxe accommodations and had difficulty hiding antipathy to the "many nasty, rich people with jewels softer than their faces and dogs scarcely less intelligent than they." Yet the old rationale about experience remained intact; despite drawbacks, the voyage was worthwhile as "a new, glamorous sensation." Part of this was the unfamiliar feeling of finding money "absolutely no object." Nervously signing Mabel's name to a large check for the first time, he was told by a steward, "Oh, you're good for any amount, sir!"[11] Never had days on the cattle boat seemed so far away.

Mabel was generous with money but less so with herself. Anxious to consummate his rising passion, Jack was held at arm's length, and this was an "experience" he did not relish. She seemed suddenly conventional, outwardly fussing about the possibility of someone discovering Reed in her cabin, while to herself she gloried in power that came from withholding something precious, in the "high clear excitement of continence, and the tension . . . that came from our canalized vitality." After many refusals, he grew restless and morose. Cursed with foresight that knew from the first that love must end, Mabel burst out one day, "Oh, Reed, darling, we are just at the Threshold and nothing is ever so wonderful

as the Threshold of things, don't you *know* that?"[12] Hardly agreeing, he
retired, baffled, poured frustration into words and produced a poem that he
slipped under her door at midnight:

> Wind smothers the snarling of the great ships,
> And the serene gulls are stronger than turbines;
> Mile upon mile the silent hiss of a stumbling wave breaks unbroken—
> Yet stronger the power of your lips for my lips. . . .

> I cried upon God last night, and God was not where I cried—
> He was slipping and balancing on the thoughtless shifting miles of sea—
> Impersonal he will unchain the appalling sea-gray engines,
> But the speech of your body to my body will not be denied![13]

Poetry worked no better than the spoken word. Not until they were
already settled in the Hôtel des Sts. Pères, with her son and Miss Galvin
on the train for Italy, did Mabel open her bedroom. Seen through her eyes
and words, that first night in Paris was ecstatic. Having held on to
tension for so long, she came to Reed "like a Leyden jar, brimful to the
edge, charged with a high, electrical force." For Mabel, sex meant total
surrender, yet Jack was a lover worth being conquered by, for he made
the rest of the world vanish: "Nothing counted for me but Reed . . . to
lie close to him and to empty myself over and over, flesh against flesh."
When he whispered to her in the night, "I thought your fire was crimson,
but you burn blue in the dark," the conquest was complete—"a mania of
love held me enthralled." Despite the experience of two marriages, it
was about these European days that she would write: "At last I learned
what a honeymoon should be."[14]

If Mabel later remembered little of those Paris days "except that they
were interruptions in the labor of passion," it was not the same for Reed.
Yes, he was in love, and perhaps Mabel—as she claimed—was the most
marvelous bed companion he had known. But, however strong, love did
not mean there was no time reserved for the world of men. The second
morning a loud knock made Jack leap from Mabel's bed and slip into his
adjoining room. At the door was Waldo Peirce—still studying art—who
insisted he come out into the sunny world for breakfast. From the other
room Mabel "heard the two male voices, insouciant and gay, chaffing each
other." As Reed quickly dressed and left, she found that her "heart began
to break a little right then."[15]

It was good to be back in Paris, to stride broad boulevards, taste
once more the sweet indolence of café life, attend ornate productions at
the Opéra and mingle in European artistic circles. One evening Mabel
took Jack and Bobby Jones to 27 Rue de Fleurus to meet Gertrude Stein,

Alice Toklas and Pablo Picasso. Somehow too raw and American for the formal French living room hung with the incongruously wild paintings by Matisse, Picasso, Manet and Cézanne, Jack did not make a hit. His boisterous conversation bored Picasso and offended Stein: "Reed told me about his trip through Spain. He told me he had seen many strange sights there, that he had seen witches chased through the streets of Salamanca. As I had been spending months in Spain and he only weeks, I neither liked his stories nor believed them."[16]

A week in the steamy French capital was enough. Early in July, Mabel, Jack, Bobby and New York Times music critic Carl Van Vechten drove out of the city on a "mad, happy, smouldering junket." They reached the Mediterranean, motored along the Riviera and stopped to play roulette in Monte Carlo. On the eleventh they crossed into Italy, and attended a fishermen's ball in a pavilion on the beach. Relaxed and enjoying himself as they passed Genoa and drove through treacherous mountains to Spezia, Reed found the new land amusing: "This is the most comic-opera country that ever I was in. There's not a thing arranged for convenience's sake. The houses are all painted to represent windows where there are none, marble friezes, groups of statuary, etc. Nobody works. Its glorious hot weather—lots of good food and wine."[17]

Mabel's home in Arcetri was overwhelming, more a castle than a villa, making Reed "feel like the fisherman caught up by the Genie's daughter and carried to her palace on the mountaintop." The Villa Curonia—its contours attributed to Michelangelo and a courtyard to Brunelleschi—perched above the valley of the Arno, on a hillside flowering with gardenias, oleanders and grape arbors and virtually hidden by groves of cypress, myrtle, laurel and plane trees. Furnished with priceless antiques, its rooms were as magnificent as the setting. Most impressive was Jack's enormous bedroom, "hung with strips of crimson damask edged with gold which came from an old church in Venice," crowded with "great fourteenth-century armoires reaching to the ceiling" and opening upon a high terrace with a view of endless, rolling Tuscan hills.[18]

Enchanted with the surroundings, Reed cast aside any idea of writing and drifted along, absorbing impressions like a sponge. He swam in a marble fifteenth-century pool set in an olive grove, and one evening was amused when two priests, swinging censors and chanting, performed an exorcism ceremony to rid the villa of a ghost. Groups of Mabel's friends—among them Paul and Muriel Draper and Artur Rubinstein—arrived, and soon the villa was "full of very smart, clever, hard Londoners . . . a real picture of ultra-modern, ultra-civilized society."[19] Showing him off, Mabel circulated copies of The Day in Bohemia and lauded Reed's role in the pageant until he felt "quite the lion of the occasion."[20] But he was increasingly out of touch with an atmosphere where intrigues blossomed like hothouse flowers among the "very raffiné and effete" guests. Van Vechten quarreled with Jones over the attention of Muriel Draper; Rubinstein and Paul Draper argued over musical interpretations, and Muriel insisted on Artur performing Bach, a composer whom Carl despised. More than once in this "constant ferment" Jack stepped in as a calming influence, "stopping things to make room for life to be lived in."[21]

However strong the emotional storms of companions, they never much affected Reed. The world was too splendid to be fouled by petty jealousies or even real problems. When bad news from Paterson reached him in the form of post-pageant clippings from Eddy Hunt, his mood was dampened only a bit. Expressing regrets, he did confess, "I feel like a coward being off here, with you people stewing and sweating and helping." But his real state of mind was indicated in the next sentence: "I never was so happy in my life."[22] That a small tinge of guilt underlay this mood was shown once during the summer when Jack visited an Italian Socialist Congress. Introduced as an American Socialist and journalist, he went to the podium and drew applause for bringing greetings from the workers of America to their Italian brothers.

Political problems were of momentary concern. As on the first trip to Europe, Jack was again sinking into a dreamy world of historical imagination. Like a prince in a magic tale, every night he climbed down a silken ladder to Mabel's room to make love in a bed with four golden lions at the corners. On motor trips he fell in love with the antique Italian towns—Siena, "the red city on the hills"; Assisi, its three lovely churches "covered with frescoes by Giotto"; San Gimignano, with towers "looking like a medieval New York skyline"; Venice, so "gorgeous" with gilt-encrusted centuries of art that it was almost impossible to either describe or leave.[23] Awed by the beauty, he often murmured, "The things *Men* have done!" and then wistfully added: "But I wish that I could have been here at the *doing* of it or that they were doing it *now*."[24]

Reverence for the works of men did not endear Reed to Mabel. Insanely jealous, she wanted to be the center of his world every moment of the day: "I hated to see him interested in Things. I wasn't, and didn't like to have him even *look* at churches and leave me out of his attention." She accused Jack of being immature, arguing that nothing men had ever done could compare with "the odor of the jasmine in the window or the warmth of the sun." Such sentiments might appeal to the poet, but they dashed helplessly against the lover of great deeds. Despite her cutting words, he remained "sturdily loyal to his own wonder."[25]

The clashes were more portentous than he guessed. Despite her quiet manner and professed reverence for the flow of life, Mabel was most comfortable controlling people. With men this meant that even her successes were failures—those she could bend to her will ultimately did not seem man enough, while the others inevitably tired of the game. No wonder she had wanted to linger at the threshold, for once sealed in flesh, she knew—however obscurely—the dynamics of her personality would soon lead to love's deterioration. Midway in the summer this was already happening. Viewing man-woman relations as a power struggle, she experienced his interest in people and things as assaults on her integrity. Solace came only in the dark when Jack rolled her in his arms: "Every night I recovered him, reconquered him, triumphing over the day's loss."[26]

Boyish, enthusiastic and blinded by love, Reed did not perceive the vicious, complex struggle gripping Mabel. She was actress enough to hide a growing depression, and the overt quarrels over people and places struck him as typical lovers' spats. To counter complaints about "Things," he teasingly professed jealousy of her "everlasting It." So delighted was Mabel—who was short of a sense of humor—that she took seriously the elaborate, farcical, mocking play Jack began to write which featured such characters as God Almighty, Inevitability, Gertrude Stein, the Voice of Hutch Hapgood and a Chorus of Pederasts. Similarly, she misinterpreted a poem, "Florence, Summer of 1913," as Reed's "capitulation" to her view that "the old age of Italian wonder was wearisome." In truth, this work unfavorably compared effete modern artists—his view of the houseguests —to the heroes once born in the "miraculous Tuscan soil," and expressed worry that a living poet might be smothered in their company. Its portrait of Mabel was affectionate and insightful:

> Through the halls of the Medici, queenlier far than they,
> Walks she I love, half peasant, half courtesan,—
> In her right hand a man's death, in her left the life of a man,—
> Beware which you choose, for she changes them day by day;
> Sun and wind in the room of her soul, and all the beasts that prey![27]

Despite growing tensions, the Italian summer floated by like a pleasant dream. While Bobby Jones was busy painting a fresco in a nearby villa and others lounged about in comfort, Jack roamed the countryside, climbing through the stony Apennines, wandering lonely stretches of beach near Pisa with only the seagulls for company, hiking dusty roads through the ancient, terraced farms of the campagna. Tanned, rested and healthy, he and Mabel joined late-August holiday throngs in Siena.

Amid vivid banners and silk costumes of the Middle Ages they watched the running of the famed Palio around the lopsided central plaza, a colorful pageant that Reed thought he would "never forget . . . as long as I live."[28] They returned to the villa to pack for the journey home, and two days before the sailing date of August 30 he awoke with a high fever. It was diagnosed as diphtheria, and their departure had to be postponed.

Mabel, who had been unhappy over Reed's physical and mental meanderings, was quietly pleased. Helpless and totally dependent in bed, belonging fully to her "without any chance to escape," Jack seemed like a baby, and she reveled in a heightened sense of power. This pleasure proved fleeting: "A man completely at a disadvantage, disempowered, and delivered up to us, we find to be no man at all."[29] With the villa now empty of guests, a bored Mabel tried to be kind, consoling and cheerful to her patient, whose forced inaction expressed itself alternatively in dejection and anger.* Both sensed that something was wrong, but the illness could easily be blamed for the frustration that marked their last days in Europe.

Late in September when Jack and Mabel reached America, Greenwich Village was humming with activity. Youngsters from all over the country were landing in Washington Square, battered suitcases in hand and heads stuffed with dreams of artistic glory. Coming to escape a world of regular jobs and confining moral codes, they found the Village friendly and tolerant of extreme behavior—within its ill-drawn boundaries many, like Edwin Justus Mayer, were first "touched with the sensual and spiritual possibilities of freedom."[30] When Floyd Dell arrived from Chicago in October, his first evening was spent in the apartment of "a beautiful girl dancer who kept a pet alligator in her bathtub," but the reptile proved more affectionate than the young lady. Within a few days Dell shed the high collar he had worn as a member of Chicago's artistic set and began to sport a comfortable flannel shirt, for now he was in "a place where one . . . might wear a necktie for a belt without its attracting any attention."[31]

As Bohemia swelled with arrivals, new institutions arose to help keep it cohesive. The most stable of these, the Liberal Club, came to the

---

* One indication of anxiety was a new concern over Paterson. In a letter to Walter Lippmann on September 18, he wrote: "For God's sake, write and tell me whether the Paterson strike is finished or not. No one will write me—and the Globe, which we have taken all summer, never said a word about it. I've written everyone to ask—but they pay no attention." Letter in possession of Ronald Steel, Lippmann's biographer.

Village just about the time Reed returned from Europe. Founded in 1907, the original club—in rooms on respectable Gramercy Park—had been a haven where upper-class reformers, genteel Socialists, wealthy philanthropists and disgruntled Progressives could meet to talk or listen to lectures on sober social questions. Infiltrated by some younger residents of the Village, the organization was now rent with dissension over whether to admit Negroes and whether to allow Emma Goldman to become a member. Added to this struggle was the case of Henrietta Rodman, a militant feminist involved in a battle over her dismissal from a high school teaching position. Miss Rodman—recently married—had been fired for the crime of matrimony, for a School Board regulation barred married women from teaching. Her attempts to overturn the rule were well publicized, and the resulting furor helped split the club into conservative and radical factions. When the former withdrew en masse, Henrietta and friends moved the organization to the Village.

In its new home at 137 MacDougal Street the reorganized club was much more lighthearted, activist, varied and lively. Villagers crowded its two sparsely furnished, high-ceilinged parlors, brightened by avant-garde posters and paintings. One statistical-minded member separated the club into six "interest groups": poets; novelists and story writers; graphic artists; theatrical people; lawyers-newspapermen-publishers; and sociologists, the latter a term to cover all members whose chief interest was social questions.[32] Categories really didn't matter much. Everyone who was anyone sooner or later showed up at the club to lounge about, talk with friends, dance to the latest ragtime numbers performed on an upright piano, play poker, take part in short dramatic productions under Dell's direction or listen to lectures on topics both faddish and weighty: free verse, the Tango, eugenics, the slit skirt, sex hygiene, Richard Strauss, the single tax, anarchism and birth control.

Two adjoining institutions helped fix 137 MacDougal as the chief social center of the Village. In the basement was Polly's Village Restaurant, run by tall, serene Paula Holliday, recently of Evanston, with the assistance of her lover, the volcanic anarchist Hippolyte Havel, who loved to sneer "Bourgeois pigs!" as he slammed trays down before customers. Simple, inexpensive and tasty, the food at Polly's had been drawing crowds even before the club moved in upstairs. When it did, the restaurant not only prospered, but the two establishments imperceptibly merged—card games and conversations which began in one would finish in the other, while the restaurant's plain white walls were soon covered with the overflow from art exhibits upstairs. The other extension of the club was the Washington Square Bookshop, founded by Charles and Albert Boni, located next door at 135 MacDougal. The bookstore wall was soon broken through, allowing traffic to flow from one to the other. Occasionally, timid newcomers to the Village like poet Alfred Kreymborg might venture into the bookstore first and only then be swept into the world of the club next door.

Among recent immigrants and older residents alike, Jack Reed was viewed as a hero who always seemed a little larger than life. At the club or in Polly's he exuded what Hapgood called a "three-dimensional self-confidence." Annoying those who did not know him well, he spouted definite opinions on almost any topic and exhibited a brash virility that fell just short of caricature. Even people put off by Reed's apparent theatricality—the disheveled clothing, the way he hitched up his pants and ran fingers through always tousled hair, his manner of gazing around the room as if to see who was watching—had to admire his solid accomplishments: the lilting *Day in Bohemia* that helped to define their life-style, the short stories in the *Masses*, the electric reporting from Paterson and the triumph of the pageant, already glowing into the realm of legend. Now the Village buzzed with his latest achievement as word spread that Jack was living with the enigmatic, desirable Mabel Dodge.

Moving into the elegant white apartment at 23 Fifth Avenue did not solve the conflict begun in Italy. As before, Mabel rarely went out, but friends like Hapgood, his wife, Neith Boyce, Steffens, Van Vechten, Lippmann and Eddy Hunt came to call, and soon the Evenings were under way again. Mabel invited more and more people in the belief that "my victories would act upon Reed like an aphrodisiac." Instead, the reverse happened, as he proved to be one of the salon's attractions. Such a development reaffirmed her belief in relationships as a kind of struggle. Projecting her own needs, she was convinced that Jack in holding forth was only trying to assert his worthiness: "If I had power, he, then, must have more power."[33] The truth was that Reed was no different than before; the struggle was solely in her mind, for his battles were only with himself and the world.

The real problem between them was simply two incompatible views of life. She reveled in a febrile world of tangled human relationships, passively drawing power from others, while he was a young man concerned about making a mark. Attracted more than a little by his strength and ability to move people, she sometimes longed for a calm home and resented the fact that his active nature made her only part, rather than all, of his world:

> Reed himself was ready for anything! Ready at any moment to pop off into some new enthusiasm. He always seemed to have his lungs too full,

and he would draw in his round chin in an effort to quiet his excited heart. *Always* there seemed some pressure of excitement going on in him. His eyes glowed for nothing, his brown curls rushed back from his high, round forehead in a furious disorder, and the round highlights on his temples gleamed, his eyebrows went further up. . . .[34]

Mabel's annoyance began early each morning. Languishing in bed over breakfast, she watched Jack eat at a little table next to her, the paper propped up before him. While she inwardly fumed over his indifference, Reed's "honey-colored round eyes" were popping over "the news," which if it was not about friends meant nothing to her. When he read items of interest aloud, she felt used "merely as a focus," and grieved that "the world had won him away from me again." Soon the paper was crumpled on the floor and he was gone, leaving Mabel "deserted and miserable." Her dilemma was painful, but nobody knew better than Mabel its basic source: "We can't seem to live with the men who want to sit at home with us, and the men we want to live with can't sit at home with us, and there's no peace to be found either way."[35]

In spite of all the passion the two lovers could give each other at night, the situation could not help but deteriorate. Attempting to keep the relationship stable, Mabel tried to balance her emotions and made a few feeble attempts to enter his world. On one occasion when he wished to undertake a typical exploration of the Lower East Side, she surprised him by agreeing to go along, ordered the car and chauffeur and had them driven through the ghetto streets like tourists on a sightseeing bus. Groaning inwardly in the luxury of the limousine, Jack tried to remain amiable, but it was too difficult. The genie's daughter seemed utterly unable to understand that life was not a spectator sport, but something you plunged into, no matter how deep the waters. The knack of living was all in learning how to swim.

Reed's own actions did not help the situation. He could not see Mabel's lack of interest in the lives of other human beings, and, obtuse as a child, he confided intimacies that only served to drive her away. When he told her one night of a conversation with a strange, lovely prostitute whose magic aura had given him a vision of the world's beauty and mystery, she threw herself on the floor and pretended to faint. Contrite, he swore faithfulness. But this did not stop him from sharing a deep wonder over the maddeningly pure, impersonal allure of another young lady. Enraged and hurt that he persisted in sharing such things, Mabel screamed until he shut up.

Sexual fidelity was hardly the only source of conflict. She was as jealous of time he spent at the Liberal Club, Polly's, the *Masses* office or with male friends as she was of any woman, and objected strenuously to his growing closeness with F. Sumner Boyd. Facing a possible prison term for activities in Paterson, Fred Boyd had been a Socialist since his youth in England. Reed both admired him personally and was fascinated by his informed Marxist analyses of social and economic questions. Bored by lengthy political discussions in her own living room, Mabel harangued Jack for hours about the "mediocrity . . . superficiality . . . [and] unworthiness" of this new friend.[36]

In November the situation degenerated into tears, laments, hysterics and harsh words that resulted in Mabel taking an overdose of veronal. For the first time Jack realized the depth and seriousness of her jealousies, and he began to learn that the other side of love is pain. Confused, shaken and upset, he took the unusual step of confiding in others, telling Hapgood, "Mabel is wonderful, I love her, but she suffocates me, I can't breathe."[37] Friends made comforting noises, but provided no answers. Reed could not understand the source of the difficulty—he loved the woman, she loved him, and yet neither could accept the other. His emotional state became a series of frightening question marks when she made further threats of suicide. By November 21 it was all too much. Informing only Steffens, Jack fled to Boston leaving a note:

> Good-by, my darling. I cannot live with you. You smother me. You crush me. You want to kill my spirit. I love you better than life but I do not want to die in my spirit. I am going away to save myself. Forgive me. I love you—I love you.[38]

Cambridge was a haven from the close-knit world of the Village. Taking Reed in and making him feel at home, playwright Dave Carb—a friend since undergraduate days—proved a good listener and late-night drinking companion. Copey was there, too, and it was a pleasure to walk with him through the Yard or sit in the comfortable room in Hollis discussing great deeds and books. Solid, conservative, quiet with the calm of academe, the red brick buildings of Harvard seemed fixed and eternal, a sharp contrast to Reed's scattered, hectic life.

In this atmosphere Jack had time to ponder the course of his life in recent months. More than the relationship with Mabel was troubling him. Ever since early June he had been drifting, uncommitted to anything meaningful. Exhaustion after the pageant and weakness after the bout of diphtheria were part of the reason, but the illnesses had also served as convenient excuses. In the last two months there had been time to swagger around the Village enjoying notoriety and also to serve temporarily as managing editor of the *Masses*. Both roles had been enjoyable, but temperamentally Jack was not fulfilled either by playing at being important or by helping with the editorial duties of a monthly magazine. Neither involved a commitment that made him feel whole.

Writing was the heart of the matter, and since the pageant he had produced little. Works were still appearing—humorous short stories in the *Smart Set*, a couple of spare, naturalistic vignettes and a one-act play in the *Masses*, brief poems in *Collier's* and the *American*—but all had been completed before Paterson. Out of that experience had come "Sheriff Radcliffe's Hotel," an article muckraking conditions in the Passaic County Jail, hardly much to show for six months in the life of a writer. When he had tried to work, words had remained stuck in the typewriter. An idea for a play based on the life of Bill Haywood had not moved past the outline stage, and a promised one-acter for the Liberal Club Dramatic Group remained unwritten. Here was the real dilemma—for the first time since those frustrating days in Paris, Reed was bereft of subjects. Coupled with the ongoing personal battles, this dry spell had studded the fall months with an unusual number of moody interludes. Even seeing this clearly now, he could think of no easy way out.

Somehow it came back to Paterson, the feeling of the workers and the excitement of the pageant—he still did not know how writing related to that. Complimenting him in mid-June, Bobby Rogers had raised disturbing questions just before Jack sailed:

> And if by the time you get back . . . you have cut out doing the quick-lunch, emotionally effective propaganda dope, such as the Jail story in *The Masses*, I shall be very grateful. You can either do that, or you can try to do literature without strings tied to it. The latter for the sake of art, or the first for the sake of Big Bill. You can't do both, as far as I can see. *The Masses'* story was a dam [*sic*] effective, well-written in a Sunday supp. style, rather hysterical piece of special pleading. Don't mistake me. It gets its effect, gets there with both feet. If there is no strong climax in it, it's because every paragraph is a climax. I merely wondered if that was the sort of thing you wanted to do.[39]

Without necessarily accepting this dichotomy between literature and propaganda, Reed recognized it as a problem, and in November was still wondering what he wanted to write.

Three days after leaving New York he received a reassuring note from Steffens—Mabel was well and temporarily staying with the Hapgoods. Anticipating fear over a possible suicide attempt, his friend advised, "You stay put—don't worry. They [don't] do all they say any more than we do." Two days later another letter reported, "She has listened to reason (Hutch) and she sees it right now. . . . She wants what you want; exactly, she says. . . . I think all will come out right now with you. . . ."[40] Warmed by both the news and the tone, Jack prepared to return. In six months' intimacy with Mabel he had learned more about women than in the first twenty-five years of life. Not only had he discarded the sophomoric idea that the mere words "I love you" were enough to ensure a woman's untrammeled devotion, but he had deeply felt the weird mixture of ecstasy, pain, delight, confusion and anger that men know as love. There was one more thing the affair with Mabel had taught, something he would not easily forget: necessary as love might be to complete a life, by itself love for a woman was not sufficient to bring him happiness.

10

Mexico

"*The Tropa had already ridden on ahead, and I could see them, strung out for half a mile in the black mesquite brush, the tiny red-white-and-green flag bobbing at their head. The mountains had withdrawn somewhere beyond the horizon, and we rode in the midst of a great bowl of desert, rolling up at the edges to meet the furnace-blue of the Mexican sky. . . . A great silence, and a peace beyond anything I ever felt, wrapped me around. It is almost impossible to get objective about the desert; you sink into it—become a part of it. Galloping along, I soon caught up. . . .*

"'*Aye, meester!' they shouted. 'Here comes meester on a horse! Que tal, meester? How goes it? Are you going to fight with us?'*

". . . *Captain Fernando at the head of the column turned and roared 'Come here, meester!' The big man was grinning with delight. 'You shall ride with me,' he shouted, clapping me on the back. 'Drink, now,' and he produced a bottle of* sotol *about half full. . . . 'Drink it,' yelled the chorus as the Tropa crowded up to see. I drank it. A howl of laughter and applause went up. Fernando leaned over and gripped my hand. 'Good for you,* compañero!' *he bellowed, rolling with mirth. . . .* 'Now you are with the men' *(los hombres)."*[1]

Suspended in John Reed's writings are incidents that float delicately between the realms of fact and fiction, with the narrator a character living in a world of romance, enacting a truth more emotional than literal. Details and dialogue altered for the benefit of dramatic structure, the result is an account of events that transcends the world of reportage. It is possible Reed never downed half a bottle of sotol while members of a guerrilla band cheered him on. But there is no doubt the scene contains the core of his reaction to Mexico. There, among the ragged troops of revolutionary armies, Jack underwent many experiences that could be summed up in the glorious feeling that he was truly one of *los hombres.*

This incident, like much of his reporting from Mexico, told as much about Reed as about the revolution. A fusion of self with historical event occurred because his writing reflected a search for meaning and self-definition. The question raised in these paragraphs is central to his whole experience in Mexico; indeed, it had hovered unspoken in his mind for years: how does one become a man? Following the illnesses and nameless fears of childhood, the problem had been masked by the vigor displayed for years at Morristown and Harvard, in Europe, the Village and Paterson. Playing football, working on the cattle boat, hiking the highroads of England, France and Spain, rubbing elbows with gangsters and pimps in Tenderloin bars, facing belligerent policemen, sharing jail with Wobblies and making love to Mabel Dodge—all these were manly activities; yet the writer in him often seemed half a spectator of his own actions, and in circumstances like the cattle boat and the Paterson jail he had failed to share fully the rigorous life of the seamen and inmates. Despite a furious quest for experience, Jack still fell short of the image of two-fisted manliness imbibed as a sickly child in Oregon, where lumbermen, sailors and cowboys had drunk, brawled and whored with a savagery that seemed heroic. The image was mixed up with his father, whose political struggles were full of bravery that had led to an untimely death. For Reed, being a man had something to do with drinking, swearing, fighting, enduring hardship and making the kind of principled stand that might lead to destruction.

Revolutionary Mexico, a land of machine guns and machetes, with more than a little danger from natives who thought any *gringo* should be shot on sight, was a good place for a self-test, and for Jack, American interest in turmoil south of the Rio Grande could not have come at a more opportune moment. In November 1913, rebel leader Francisco

"Pancho" Villa won decisive military victories at Juarez and Chihuahua City and by early December loomed as the giant figure of the revolution. Master of the state of Chihuahua, Villa and his horseback army became sensational news, and correspondents rushed to the border. Editor Carl Hovey of the *Metropolitan*, searching for a good reporter, asked Lincoln Steffens for a recommendation and obtained Reed's name. Only two weeks back in New York, and finding life temporarily sweet again, Jack nonetheless accepted the assignment immediately.

Mabel was appalled. Distraught and tearful, she tried to make him give up the commission, but to abject pleas he answered, "I will take you with me in my heart. But we *must* be free to live our own lives." Reed also obtained an assignment from the New York *World* to supplement his income. The night before his departure was an Evening, and Mexico was discussed at length, with Fred Boyd giving a Marxist view of developments, Steffens dropping clever remarks from a chair in the corner, and a happy Reed, "puffed up and excited, his curls tossed back, standing up and declaiming wildly." When the guests departed, the dark hours in bed were filled with "a welter of tears and love." Clutching Jack, Mabel "wanted to drown him in myself so that he couldn't leave me," but in the morning he rose, dressed, kissed his lover and departed, leaving her sobbing on the pillow.[2]

Mabel impulsively followed a few hours later and caught him in Chicago. Welcoming company for the long train ride to El Paso, Reed spent so much time locked with her in the compartment that he jokingly referred to the trip as a "honeymoon" in a note to Eddy Hunt: "Mabel has already decided that the rebels are part of the great world-movement, whatever that may be, and this when she knows that I'm trying to go there without any prejudices! I think she expects to find General Villa a sort of male Gertrude Stein, or at least a Mexican Stieglitz." When they took breakfast in the Austin station restaurant, "Mabel appeared in a bright orange sweater (she also has a crimson one, and an Alice blue one for the campaign), whereupon two Mexicans become epileptic out of sheer covetousness, and an Indian had hysterics." His good humor included himself: "With me in my bright yellow corduroy suit and Mabel in her orange hat and satin-lined tiger-skin hunting-jacket—with . . . an expense account, and a roll of blankets and 14 different kinds of pills and bandages . . . we shall descend upon El Paso. . . . If I don't get a single note from the front—if I don't set foot over the frontier I'll have material enough for six books."[3]

The border town was a hotbed of intrigue, "the Supreme Lodge of the Ancient Order of Conspirators of the World." Crowded into hotels and restaurants was a variegated crew of Americans and Mexicans, rich men whose estates had been expropriated, representatives of U.S. corporations with interests below the border, mineowners and railroad presidents, confidential agents from the State Department, spies from various revolutionary and governmental factions, salesmen from arms and ammunition companies, prostitutes and con men running a hundred different shady games. Most amusing were the detectives: "They quite out-number the rest of the population . . . and are conspicuous by the elaborateness of their disguises. . . . Whenever a great man leaves the shelter of the hotel, he is shadowed along the street by a detective, who in his turn is shadowed by another, whose every move is watched by a third, and so on. . . . These processions of persons, all going the same way, pretending to look up at the buildings or the sky, seriously impede traffic."[4]

Reed's mind was pulled to Mexico. Deciding the best immediate story possibility was at Ojinaga, which housed remnants of the federal army shattered by Villa at Chihuahua City, he left Mabel and hired a car for a bumpy two-hundred-mile ride to Presidio, a straggling collection of adobes scattered along the desolate Rio Grande sand flats. The town was a miniature El Paso, full of arms salesmen, smugglers, cowpunchers from both sides of the border, Texas Rangers and secret agents. Barred from Mexico by military officials, American journalists lolled about Presidio "and twice a day concocted two-hundred-word stories full of sound and fury." That was not Reed's way. After climbing up on the flat mud roof of the post office to gaze across a mile of low scrub and past the yellow river to the square adobes and jutting church towers of Ojinaga, Jack sent a request to General Mercado, the commanding federal officer, for an interview. An ominous reply came from another general, Orozco, whose staff had intercepted the note:

> Esteemed and Honored Sir: If you set foot inside of Ojinaga, I will stand you sideways against a wall, and with my own hand take great pleasure in shooting furrows in your back.[5]

The words gave Reed pause. Despite his good humor, he "was afraid of death, of mutilation, of a strange land and strange people whose speech and thought I did not know." Yet urging him on was "a terrible curiosity . . . I felt I had to know *how I would act* under fire. . . ."[6] In Presidio, as in the months to come, the desire for experience proved stronger than fear. Wading across the river, Jack climbed up into the town, laconically reporting: "Luckily, I did not meet General Orozco."

He did find Mercado, "a fat, pathetic, worried, undecided little man" who blubbered and blustered a long, involved tale about how the American army was helping Villa win battles. Wandering off through white, rubble-filled streets, Jack saw the cost of warfare: hardly a house had a roof intact, and building walls were riddled and crumbling. Ragged federal soldiers, thin and starved, lived in the ruins and systematically robbed the exhausted refugees who tramped by on their way to the U.S. Disgusted by the spectacle, he joined peons running a gauntlet of American border officials. Wading across the ford, one woman wore a huge poncho which humped up in front as if she were hiding something.

"Hi, there!" shouted a customs man. "What have you got under your shawl?"

Slowly opening the front of her dress, she answered placidly: "I don't know, señor. It may be a girl, or it may be a boy."

Back in El Paso, he was greeted by a bored and fussy Mabel, who announced she was going home. Not unhappy with this decision, he took her across the border into Juárez for a look around on December 21. In the plaza fronting the racetrack came a first glimpse of the revolutionary army, two thousand dark, Indian-looking horsemen, many of them teen-agers, dressed in blue denim or khaki brightened by vivid neckerchiefs. Full of happy spirits, the soldiers "rollicked around like kids . . . shouting and singing and eating peanuts." When a general arrived, they mounted horses, gathered in a ragged formation and, at the sound of a cracked bugle, sprang into action: "Two thousand nondescript, tattered men, on dirty little tough horses, their serapes flying out behind, their mouths one wild yell, simply flung themselves out over the plain. That's how the general reviewed them. They had very little discipline, but . . . what spirit! . . . A great bunch, believe me. And what pageant material!"[7]

By Christmas Day Jack was in Chihuahua City, Villa's headquarters. Set in the middle of a desert, with mountains all around, the town was like a jewel: "Its outskirts are of brown adobe huts, and from there toward the center of the city the color gets brighter until . . . all is white, light red, pink and light blue stone and wash. There are the most astonishing golden yellow and mosque-like white churches." Despite the recent battles, the city functioned as in peacetime; public services were running smoothly and a band played in the plaza each evening. At any hour of the day the streets might fill with armed horsemen, riding to some unknown destination, and at night armed sentries challenged passers at every corner. All this made it "as romantic as can be."[8]

A holiday celebration at the great opera house, with flags flying, bands playing and massed crowds roaring "Viva Villa," provided his first glimpse of the rebel general. Early the next morning Reed was ushered into his office in the huge, ornate governor's palace. Wearing a rumpled brown business suit, Villa sat behind a desk reading letters, dictating answers crisply, conferring with aides and facing delegations of peons. At all times the general's presence was impressive: "He is the most natural human being I ever saw—natural in the sense of being nearest a wild animal." Villa seemed slightly awkward and stiff below the knees when he stood up or moved around, but his hands, arms and trunk moved with the "swiftness and sureness of a coyote." Most of the time his face "looked good natured, almost simple," but the eyes belied this geniality— dark, active, full of energy and brutality, "absolutely hot and steely," they were those of a man who could kill.

After a while, the general turned to Reed. Something about his visitor's big-boned, easygoing nature must have appealed to Villa, for he quickly dubbed him with the affectionate nickname Chatito (pug nose) and promised that Jack could follow him around on daily duties. From then on Reed was welcome in his office and at formal dinners, quiet luncheons prepared by Villa's mistress and even occasional policy-making sessions. Between the two men a feeling grew that was not friendship, but something much warmer than the normal relationship of journalist to official. Exasperated by persistent questions, Villa could on occasion grumble that Reed should be "spanked and sent to the border," but such threats were idle and humorous. Realizing on his part that Villa was a "terrible man," Jack never let this judgment dampen his admiration for the "absolute dictator" of Chihuahua.[9]*

With his open manner and ability to mingle with cutthroats, peons, generals, gamblers and government officials, Reed in one week was able to gather much information about conditions in Mexico. Before crossing the border he had talked to people and read what could be found, but most such information was an unstable alloy of fact, fiction, rumor and speculation. In Chihuahua the sources were similarly biased, but looking participants in the eye, listening to the ring of voices, testing the truth of words against the tenor of the land and people, he was able to evaluate recent events. Naturally his view of the revolution, its causes, leaders and probable outcome, was influenced by preconceptions as much as by things he heard and saw.

Reed sensed rather than knew something that is fundamental for understanding Mexico—in reality the country was undergoing two revolutions simultaneously, one political, the other agrarian. The events

* Some indication of the relationship between Reed and Villa may be seen in a pass the general issued which remains in the JR MSS. It says that not only should civil and military authorities give Reed aid and protection, but that he should be allowed to use both railways and telegraph lines without charge.

of 1910–11 that had led to the resignation and exile of Porfirio Díaz, dictator for thirty-five years, had been caused by supporters of both kinds of revolution; but the man who succeeded to the Presidency, Francisco I. Madero, a strict constitutionalist with little sympathy for social reform, attempted to crush the agrarian revolt of Indians in Morelos, led by Emiliano Zapata. When General Victoriano Huerta, with the advice and complicity of American Ambassador Henry Lane Wilson, overthrew and then executed the President in February 1913, Madero's reputation as a revolutionary was saved. Revolts that broke out all over the country used him as a martyr, and rebel soldiers were proud to be designated Maderistas. But the two revolutionary strands still existed, the agrarian personified by Villa and Zapata, and the political by Venustiano Carranza, governor of the state of Coahuila, who took the title of Commander in Chief of the Constitutionalist Army. Establishing a shadow government first in Hermosillo, then in Nogales, the self-designated First Chief presumed to speak in the name of all Mexico. But many revolutionaries, disgusted with Carranza's conservative view of land reform, hoped to see Villa or Zapata seize the Presidency.

To become a partisan of Villa was to identify with a heroic myth. Without all the facts arranged and neatly categorized, Reed understood enough of the situation to know where his own sympathies lay. Revolution was a word often used in Greenwich Village, even if few people could give a precise idea of what it signified in political and social terms. From his experience, especially in Paterson, Jack was skeptical of constitutional government as a guarantor of liberty. Wobblies might have the vote, but in a showdown with capital, their civil rights were violated by police, courts and private detectives all carrying out the will of wealthy industrialists. With little knowledge of the land starvation felt by the peon or the virtual serfdom in which millions lived, he instinctively felt that no Mexican revolution was worth the name if it was being fought merely for a constitution. Realizing that Carranza was more a politician than an activist, and one who had taken no positive stand on social reform, Reed's heart naturally embraced the Villistas.

To become a partisan of Villa was to identify with a heroic myth. Reckless and romantic, the general was the subject of countless poems and ballads that portrayed a kind of Robin Hood. In all these stories, fact and fiction could not be separated. Born Doroteo Arango, the son of ignorant peons, he had killed a government official at the age of sixteen—supposedly for violating his sister—and had fled to the mountains of Durango to become an outlaw. Twenty years of banditry spread his fame as a desperado whose hatred for rich landowners led to the burning of many haciendas and the distribution of spoils to the poor. An early supporter of Madero, Villa became a captain in his army, was later imprisoned for insubordination and then escaped the country to live in El Paso until April 1913, when with a small band of companions he crossed the border one night to begin his own revolt. Recruiting in the mountains where he had lived as an outlaw, he raised an army that in eight months had cleared Chihuahua of Huerta's federal troops and made northern Mexico the stronghold of revolution.

Villa had proclaimed himself the state's military governor, and was engaged in "the extraordinary experiment . . . of creating a government for 300,000 people out of his head."[10] Uneducated and semiliterate, he displayed a canny peasant intelligence that cut through confining webs of educated sophistries. Though he was surrounded by intellectuals, these men seemed no more than resources to answer his continual questions about traditional educational, judicial, financial and legislative practices. Watching him was like watching Bill Haywood—both men were decisive, forceful and willing to take the consequences of their actions. In a way, government under Villa was what government under the Wobblies might be, a clean, swift, turning of the tables on the exploiters of the people.

The general's chief talent as a ruler, it struck Jack, was the ability to make simple decisions about intricate, complex questions. Faced with a problem of business stagnation and food scarcity due to a lack of circulating currency, he had two million pesos run off the presses, gave them away to soldiers and poor people, declared all other banknotes counterfeit and imprisoned anyone who discriminated against his money. Political enemies were expelled from the country and their holdings confiscated, including the seventeen million acres and numerous business enterprises of the Terrazas family, the virtual overlords of Chihuahua. Out of the expropriated lands Villa gave 62.5 acres to every male citizen of the state and declared these parcels inalienable for a period of ten years. He put soldiers to work running public utilities, and established schools everywhere. Whatever Carranza might plan for the future, Villa was already promoting a social revolution.

Highwayman, military chief, governor, revolutionary—and admirable in Reed's eyes for all these reasons—Villa completed the picture by showing himself a genuine democrat and an intensely human man who drank life with gusto. Dressed in a soiled brown suit, his collar open, a sombrero pushed back on his head, the general joined in dusty, sweaty jobs like kicking recalcitrant mules onto boxcars, joking and roaring obscenities. He was a passionate gambler who put aside problems of state every afternoon to fight his own birds at the cockpit "with the happy enthusiasm of a small boy," and late into the evenings he often played faro. Unlike most Mexican soldiers, Villa neither drank nor smoked. Living openly with a catlike, slender mistress in Chihuahua—while his wife stayed in El Paso—he was reputed to have violated many women. Asked by Reed if this were true, he pulled on his mustache and answered blandly: "I never take the trouble to deny such stories. . . . But tell me; have you ever met a husband, father, or brother of any woman that I have violated?" Pausing for a moment, he added: "Or even a witness?"[11]

Villa did have faults, but they were excused by Jack because of the general's background and his two important unspoiled qualities: imagination and the capacity to dream. Unhampered by a knowledge of traditional military strategy, Villa improvised tactics which Reed—with characteristic exaggeration—described as "Napoleonic" in their genius. Hugely amused by a pamphlet on the Rules of War sent him by American General Hugh L. Scott—"What is the difference between a civilized war and any other kind of war?" he asked—Villa allowed captives to be executed, and never reprimanded his right-hand man, Rudolfo "The Butcher" Fierro, who was known to shoot hundreds of prisoners after battles for the sheer pleasure of killing. This did not unduly disturb Reed, who could accept the idea that revolution was bound to be brutal. More important was Villa's dream of a future when there would be no more army in Mexico and no more dictators supported by guns. The general foresaw a country with colonies composed of veterans of the revolution, where men would alternately work the land, receive military instruction and teach the peons how to repel invaders. Claiming he was too ignorant for the Presidency, Villa wanted to live in such a military colony, working in a saddle factory and raising cattle and corn. His ambition was summed up simply: "It would be fine, I think, to help make Mexico a happy place."[12]

In marked contrast to Villa's activities and dreams was the desire of many people—Mexicans and foreigners alike—to continue their four-century exploitation of the populace. Feeling great distaste for the military bureaucracy and the Catholic church, which exchanged promises of an afterlife for the current blood and sweat of the peons, Reed's greatest antipathy was toward capitalists, especially those from the United States. One day he went out to visit a mining camp owned by an American company. Press credentials earned him a correct, cool welcome from the manager, who climbed with him over hillsides of lead and silver shafts and continually complained about the lazy "*gringo*-haters" who worked there. Visiting some of the miners' hovels, Jack found them "the poorest people I have seen in Mexico, underfed, bare-footed, physically degraded," yet he was treated well and offered coffee. Back in the manager's comfortable house, he learned that company profits were threatened by the "god damned scum that join a revolution just for a chance to murder and steal." Since 1910 miners had been getting "uppish" and talking about wages and working conditions. In his own way the manager liked the country, rather as a buzzard likes carrion: "These damned Mexicans don't deserve it. All we want is peace and a chance to work. We could turn over a pretty piece of change." This would happen if the United States sent in troops to pacify the revolution. Sensing Reed's opposition, the manager said: "If you write anything to discourage intervention, we'll get you."[13]

After a week in Chihuahua City, Reed was itching to join the troops in the field and see more of the country. On the last day of the year he hooked up with a twenty-five-year-old "American in the raw" named Mac—a "boss mechanic" in a Durango mine. Together they drank in the New Year with Tom and Jerry's while the cracked bells of the ancient cathedral called people to midnight mass and sentries all over town fired rifles into the air. A huge man, Mac had worked all over the U.S. and Mexico at everything from railroading to cowpunching, and as the drinking continued he spouted homilies on the immorality of Mexican women, the purity of the American home and the joys of "hunting niggers" in Georgia. If Jack did not demur strongly at such sentiments, it was not because of the liquor. Mac had promised to take Reed south with him.[14]

On New Year's Day they climbed aboard a gutted, bullet-riddled coach attached to a train of freight cars jammed with soldiers. Crowded with men, women, children, dogs and chickens, their car was a noisy, happy oasis as the train labored slowly through desert country. People shared tequila from a leather bottle, gathered around to bet on a cockfight, joined in a rollicking impromptu dance and listened to a blind, aged peasant recite a long revolutionary ballad, while at every station the coach was besieged by vendors of cigarettes, pine nuts, milk, tamales and sweet potatoes. Pulling into Jiménez late in the evening, the two Americans went to the Station Hotel, only to find the door barred. They pounded furiously until an "incredibly ancient" woman peered out a window, then admitted them. An eighty-year-old, New England-born widow, she would not let men into the hotel with women other than their wives, and explained their reception by stating: "There's so many damned drunken generals around today that I've got to keep the door locked."[15]

While Mac lounged in the bar, Reed went out for a look around. On a long, tree-lined street toward the center of town, the spell of Mexico enveloped him. The night was "full of a subtle exotic excitement; guitars twanged, snatches of song and laughter and low voices, and shouts from distant streets, filled the darkness." A troop of horsemen clopped softly past, then came a mule-drawn streetcar full of drunks wildly firing revolvers. Around the brightly lit plaza were ruins of stores, looted in recent fighting, and on the stand a regimental band played a spirited counterrevolutionary song. But neither war nor politics had anything to do with the colorful *paseo* in progress, señoritas promenading around the square in one direction, soldiers strolling the opposite way. The sexes never mingled, but sometimes a man slipped a note into the hand of a girl, and later—Jack imagined—they would meet for a secret rendezvous. Ignoring evidence of a rigidly structured courting system, he believed that "The whole business is the most natural in the world. A girl and man who like each other fly to each other's arms." Such behavior was in stark contrast to that of five young, ragged Americans huddled on a bench beside the plaza. Soldiers-of-fortune recently dismissed from Villa's army, they were full of complaints about the land and the people. After listening for a couple of minutes, Jack abruptly left, disgusted by such "hard, cold misfits in a passionate country."[16]

In the next few days Reed saw a good slice of that country as he and Mac, in a creaky buggy pulled by two mules, rattled southwest toward Durango. Along rivers the land was fertile, cut by irrigation ditches and long stands of ash-gray alamo trees. But most of the countryside was desert surrounded by rocky mountains and spotted by black mesquite, cactus, the charred remains of ranchos burned in the revolution. At night they camped in dense thickets of chaparral, or accepted the hospitality of inhabitants of the solid, square haciendas, where young girls gracefully balanced water jars on their heads, naked babies crawled in the dust and women knelt to grind cornmeal in stone pestles. When they separated in Magistral, a mountain village three days from the nearest railroad line, Reed was deeply enamored of this wild, empty land.

If the Mexican countryside was impressive, the Mexicans were more so. The poorest of them shared meat, chiles, tortillas and cigarettes, and refused payment until Reed learned to make it seem a favor if they would take money to buy liquor to drink his health. In many places politics meant little to the peons, and far from armies Constitutionalists, *pacificos* and Porforistas could be friends. This was due to a spirit deeper than all governments and social systems: "No people who I have seen are so close to nature. . . . They are just like their mud houses, just like their little crops of corn."[17]

Riding for two days with an Arab peddler in a two-wheeled gig,

Jack reached Las Nieves—headquarters of Villa's subordinate, General Tomás Urbina. The general's hacienda was immense, its patio the size of a full city block. Picking his way past a sentry and a swarm of pigs, chickens, goats, peacocks and children, Reed found Urbina seated in a broken wicker armchair. Extending a limp hand, the general said he would go into battle in about ten days, and promised food, liquor, a horse or a woman to keep Jack amused while waiting. Disappointed, Reed spent the next morning photographing the vain general on three different horses, with his mother, his mistress, his children and, finally, with the entire family, armed with swords and revolvers, and on the ground before them their prize possession, a phonograph.

Later in the day the general suddenly burst from his room roaring orders, and in a bustle of confusion the household packed. Led by Urbina on a gray charger, a hundred troopers—named, simply, La Tropa—rode away from Las Nieves, with Jack behind them uncomfortably bumping along the uneven desert track in a dynamite-laden stagecoach. Early in the next afternoon, someone lent Reed a horse and he rode out to join La Tropa. Ragged and picturesque, the men were clad in everything from overalls to tight vaquero trousers, with cartridge belts crossed over chests, high sombreros flapping in the breeze and immense spurs chiming. Immediately dubbed "the meester," he became a part of the group that evening at a hacienda when Captain Fernando took him by the arm and asked, "Will you sleep with the *compañeros*?"[18] Joining them in a storehouse, Reed was welcomed with shouts and cries of laughter. Some of the troopers were softly plucking guitars and singing, the room rumbled with loud snores, was stuffy with smoke and fetid with human breath, and many of the soldiers had fleas that quickly transferred allegiance to his body. None of this mattered much. Rolled in a blanket, Jack slept on the stone floor with the soundness of a man at peace.

The next two weeks were "the most satisfactory" of John Reed's life.[19] Up in the cold gray mornings long before dawn, the members of La Tropa scrunched in their saddles wrapped to the eyes in colorful serapes. During the long days they rode south, across a barren land beneath a sun that "beat down with a fury that made one reel." Mouths parched and lips cracking, they reached muddy rivers and hurled themselves into the water. Sometimes they whooped after coyotes in the brush, and for noon meals slit the throat of a steer, ripped the meat from the carcass and ate it raw, believing this *carne crudo* made them brave. Long after nightfall they stopped in the burned-out ruins of a great hacienda, then spent hours drinking and dancing with local señoritas until it was time to move on. The pace was grueling, almost killing, yet Jack was content.

Reed grew to love these tough, undisciplined, dirty, ex-outlaw saddlemates for much more than their politics. Questions about why they had taken up arms were as likely to be answered, "It is good fighting. You don't have to work in the mines," as with any statement about the struggle for *libertad*. One trooper, on learning there was no current war in the United States, could wonder aloud: "How do you pass the time, then?" Once a tired soldier, volatile with liquor, wanted to shoot Reed for being a *gringo* spy; another time an angry one accused him of cowardice for not carrying a rifle and screamed, "We want no words printed in a book! We want rifles and killing!" No matter. What was important was the acceptance by most of La Tropa: the men who shared drinks and cigarettes, taught him to dance the jota, laughed and clasped him in powerful *abrazos*. What was important was the friendship of Captain Gino Güereca, who asked Jack to be his *compadre*, always slept next to him at night, and brought him to the family rancho with the introduction, "This is my dearly beloved friend . . . and my brother." Such acceptance allowed Reed to write proudly: "I made good with these wild fighting men and with myself."[20]

At La Cadena, a hacienda built on a plateau ten miles from an important mountain pass being held against the federales, La Tropa stopped. The soldiers relaxed for a few days and amused themselves with amateur *corridas*, cockfights and trips to nearby hot springs. Very early one morning Reed awoke to shouts that federal troops had broken through the pass. Rushing to the patio, he found men hurriedly saddling horses, clicking cartridges into rifles and riding in groups out to the desert. There were no horses to spare for a noncombatant, and feeling vaguely unreal, he loaded his camera and looked out over the landscape. For a long time there was nothing to see. Then dust began to rise from the desert floor and soon formed a white cloud, shining in the sun. When some troopers, blood and sweat staining their clothes, rode back into the yard and found the ammunition depleted, fear began to grip the soldiers left behind. Discovering that he had been hearing rifle shots for some time, Jack suddenly could see the battle, hundreds of little black figures riding furiously through the chaparral. Indian cries began to fill the air, a few bullets droned overhead and then a wild huddle of troopers, "all blood and sweat and blackness," rode furiously past in a headlong retreat. Realizing it was a rout, the troops in the yard began to scatter. Following one, Reed clambered down an arroyo and then out onto the desert.

The rest of the day was so unreal it seemed to be happening to someone else. Straight toward the western mountains they raced, Jack falling behind his companion, dropping the camera, shedding his coat, running until he could run no more, his breath coming in painful sobs and cramps gripping his legs. Death was all around. Half a mile ahead three horse-men gunned his companion down. Not far to the rear another fleeing soldier was trampled to death by enemy horses. Somehow Reed was not terribly frightened, for this was "like a page out of Richard Harding Davis," and he kept thinking, "Well, this is certainly an experience. I'm going to have something to write about." Pushing on through the brush, he hid in an arroyo when federal troopers rode past. The sharp rocks cut his boots, drawing blood. Stopping on the top of a ridge, he looked back and found La Cadena a white blur "in the immeasurable reaches of the desert." Painfully staggering on, Reed reached the rancho owned by Güereca's family at noon, drank quarts of water, ate a meal of eggs and cheese and then limped onward. Five hours later, "with stiff legs and bloody feet, a backache and a spinning head," he reached safety at the Hacienda del Pelayo, where kindly peons welcomed him for the night.

At Santo Domingo the next day Reed learned the whole bitter story. Vastly outnumbered, La Tropa had been virtually destroyed and most of his friends—including Güereca—were dead. "Sick to think of so many useless deaths in such a petty fight," he was haunted by memories of companions through a strangely peaceful afternoon while gentle winds rustled the high branches of trees around a courtyard where Indians played handball. At sundown the remains of La Tropa straggled over the hills, "defeated men—on horseback and on foot, wounded and whole, weary, sick, disheartened, reeling and limping. . . ." Surprised to see him, one came alive and shouted, "Why, there's meester! How did you escape?" When Jack answered, "I ran a race with the goats," the trooper laughed, "Scared to death, eh?" but there was little joy in his voice. Weariness and tears were the common denominator of the troops who spread out through the patio, accepted food and drink from the in-habitants and slowly began to recount tales of battle. The knowledge that Güereca and his friends had died bravely could not make up for the absence of the blithe, beautiful, jolly, brave *compañeros* who had made him feel fully a part of their important cause.

Back in Chihuahua City by the first of February, Reed followed Villa to Juárez, then crossed the border and settled into an expensive El Paso hotel. Disdainful of the many correspondents who sat over bottles in the Cactus Club and composed "spirited descriptions of events that are happening, or that ought to be happening," five hundred miles south, he bragged of his own exploits to Carl Hovey, announced he was "the only white man" who had witnessed the battle at La Cadena," and proclaimed, "I have brought most of the authentic scoops out of Mexico this last few weeks."[21] As he began to commit experience to words, Jack found the notes hastily jotted each night in Mexico to be so evocative that few changes were necessary, and he quickly turned out two articles on La Tropa for the *Metropolitan* and a short story for the *Masses* based on the character of Mac. Assailed by doubts after shipping off the first piece, he sent a follow-up letter asking Hovey for help: "You'd better eliminate all my sentimental little editorial quips . . . I think the thing will stand stronger just in raw colors. Please go through it carefully, and where I have slopped over, edit mercilessly."[22]

The worries were unfounded. On February 17 Hovey wired: "Battle article received. Nothing finer could have been written. We are absolutely delighted with your work." Three days later there was a telegram from Eastman, saying simply, " 'Mac—American' is a peach."[23] Elated by the praise, Reed answered the *Metropolitan* editor with the promise of a great exclusive, Villa's life story in the general's own words: "I bought Villa a saddle and a rifle with a gold name plate on it and a Maxim silencer. He is hugely delighted, and will do almost anything for me now. The story is going to be not only exciting to the limit, but the greatest human document you have ever seen. It is a beat on the whole world."[24]

While writing about the past, Reed was also looking ahead. Expecting Villa's next battle to be an assault on Torreón, he would cover it and return "with a great story of the taking and sack of a big city." After that, it would probably take another six months for a strike at Mexico City and he did not want to spend the intervening time "waiting around."[25] Unfortunately, it seemed that the war in Mexico was about to change. As Villa's army became better equipped and drilled and more obedient, the war would become like any other: "The Army of the North is getting respectable—professional. It is not going to be distinctive, nor Mexican. Not like The Tropa." Casting about for something more colorful, he seized on "the only revolt of the People that I knew about which has not let up for three years," that in Morelos led by Emiliano Zapata. Every letter to Hovey was filled with requests that he be sent south to see Zapata, "the great man of the Revolution. . . . He is a radical, absolutely logical and perfectly constant . . . the guy to be reckoned with in any future of Mexico." Best of all, no American journalists were reporting his activities. This would make for an important scoop: "His story, such snatches of it as I have been able to hear, is as marvelous as an Arabian Night. I don't think we can get a true picture of this business if we don't get to know Zapata."[26]

Another aspect of the Mexican picture emerged in El Paso, even more crowded than it had been two months before with arms salesmen, detectives and government agents. This was the danger to the revolution posed by the representatives of American business interests. Minds on profits, extremely legalistic about land titles and deeds, they feared any government that might want to reclaim lands and mines sold off during the Díaz regime. Openly contemptuous of "greasers," they voiced sentiments like this: "Madero . . . was a dreamer. He was a crazy man. He wanted to let the Mexicans govern themselves. . . . Ain't that a hell of an idea for a man to have in Mexico?" Believing such men were working for intervention, Jack worried about debauching a whole people in the name of American civilization, "a process which consists in forcing upon alien races with alien temperaments our own Grand Democratic Institutions: I refer to Trust Government, Unemployment and Wage Slavery." One stereotype proclaimed Mexicans incapable of understanding freedom, but Reed thought they had a broad ideal of liberty. A member of La Tropa had once told him, "Libertad is when I can *do what I want!*" Some might think such a statement "irresponsible," but to him it was a far better definition than the American concept: "Liberty is the right to do what the courts want."[27]

By now wholly committed to the proposition that the Mexican revolution was basically a fight for land, Reed was increasingly suspicious of Carranza, whose own holdings were feudal in size. Vague on the land question, he had contributed "nothing but congratulations" to Villa's conquest of the north. In the sprawling town of Nogales to interview the First Chief, Jack found his negative feelings quickly confirmed. Carranza was hidden by a hierarchy of officials and could be seen by reporters only in the company of his secretary of foreign affairs after all questions had been submitted in writing. When Reed was brought momentarily into Carranza's presence, he found the leader a large, stiff, "slightly senile old man" who nervously gnawed on his mustache and denounced the revolution's enemies in a quavering, high-pitched voice. This view of the First Chief only reaffirmed the belief that Villa and Zapata spoke for the true Mexico, and led Jack to a difficult decision.[28] Loyal to the revolution, he reported the interview for the *World* without dwelling on his negative impressions. They would have to wait until a time when the Mexican situation seemed more settled.*

Returning to Chihuahua, he found the atmosphere hectic with preparations for the advance on Torreón, one of the last major obstacles on the road to Mexico City. Because everyone knew such an attack was

---

*Reed withheld his full view of Carranza for more than six months. It finally appeared as "Carranza—an Impression," *Metropolitan*, XLVIII (September 1914), and was incorporated into *Insurgent Mexico* as Part V.

coming, timing had to be kept secret. Jack now thoroughly enjoyed his growing reputation among the many correspondents now with Villa, one based as much upon amatory exploits in the Village as on his friendship with the general, and he spent evenings drinking at Chee Lee's and playing poker with expense-account pesos at El Cosmopolita, the most fashionable gambling hall in town. Then one Saturday morning he awoke to find telegraph communications severed and some troop trains already gone. In a boxcar fitted with bunks, an icebox, a stove, two barrels of beer and a Chinese cook, Reed and the other journalists attached themselves to one of the long trains for the ride south.

They caught the army in Yermo, a desolate outpost in the middle of a desert with no water for forty miles. Along the single railroad track were ten enormous trains, crammed with artillery pieces, ammunition, food supplies, mules and horses, while nine thousand soldiers and their women camped in the surrounding chaparral, drinking, eating, loving and singing the endless verses of "La Cucaracha." When Villa arrived, his face was drawn into lines of fatigue. Explaining he had stopped off at the wedding of a friend, he grinned wearily. "We started dancing Monday evening, danced all night, all the next day, and last night, too! . . . I am worn out—*rendido!* It was harder work than twenty battles." As the army prepared to move, Jack asked for a horse, and the general became sarcastic: "Why, you correspondents will be wanting an automobile next! *Oiga,* señor reporter, do you know that about a thousand men in my army have no horses?"[29]

When the attack began, Reed left the comfort of the boxcar to follow the troops on foot. For five days he was just behind the front lines as Villa's men stormed through Bermejillo and assaulted the strongly defended Gómez Palacio, a few miles outside Torreón. Carrying a blanket, a camera and a notebook, he lived like a common soldier, always within the sounds of heavy artillery and machine guns, sharing his canteen and cigarettes with the troops, coming under fire from enemy snipers, spending a night of writhing agony caused by poisoned water drunk from an irrigation ditch. He acquired a mule and closely followed the action, saw countless examples of heroism and cowardice, watched men assault entrenched machine guns while comrades fell around them, witnessed panics and retreats, encountered Villa everywhere, shouting, joking and encouraging troops. Seeing men with their limbs shot away and broken, bodies twisted in the violent calm of death, he learned to live with horror. Always hungry, thirsty, exhausted and short of sleep, he talked tirelessly to foot soldiers, artillery captains, *pacíficos* and camp followers and was continually impressed by their mixture of fatality, humor and anger. They were a remarkable people, the Mexicans, in war as in peace, in death as in life.

Reed grew bored with slaughter as the army fought into the streets of Gómez Palacio and a bitter house-to-house struggle began. Against Villa's specific order that news not be reported until the battle was over, he managed to break through censorship on March 25 with a story to the New York *World* on the fall of Torreón. Catching a hospital train to Chihuahua, he hurried on, reached El Paso on the thirtieth and filed another report that said Villa was at last fighting within the city. On April 1 he once more reported the city's fall, this story based on a telegram from Villa to his wife. Jack was still two days early, for only on the third did the last federal troops flee Torreón. News of this great victory quickly obliterated the fact that in scooping the world Reed had anticipated the actual event by a week, and had done some vivid reporting about a battle he had not witnessed.

Even if he had not seen these events firsthand, Jack knew enough of conditions, had watched enough of the battle, to portray its flavor accurately. War was more than a matter of troops marching, guns being fired, officers shouting orders and men seizing specific objectives. It was heavy cannon sunk in the mud of irrigation ditches while soldiers cursed and sweated to get them out, starving peasants begging for food because both armies had picked their fields clean, prisoners being lined against walls and gunned down, soldiers looting stores and then setting fire to them until entire towns rose in pillars of flame. This was the kind of reporting Jack could do on the fall of Torreón, and it was powerful enough to turn what had often been seen as a kind of comic-opera war into a desperate matter of life and death among suffering human beings. More than the facts of individual events, his stories caught the spirit of Villa's most important victory.

Flavorful as were his newspaper reports, they seem cramped and lifeless next to the articles in the *Metropolitan*. While he wandered through shrapnel around Gómez Palacio on March 23, the series on La Tropa was being advertised in newspapers with a drawing of Reed wearing a sombrero, a revolver and a gunbelt, underscored by a hyperbolic text: "Word pictures of war by an American Kipling. . . . What Stephen Crane and Richard Harding Davis did for the Spanish American War in 1898, John Reed, 26 years old, has done for Mexico." Walter Lippmann sent an enthusiastic note to El Paso:

> Your . . . articles are undoubtedly the finest reporting that's ever been done. It's kind of embarrassing to tell a fellow you know that he's a genius. . . . You have perfect eyes, and your power of telling leaves

nothing to be desired. I want to hug you, Jack. If all history had been reported as you are doing this, Lord— I say that with Jack Reed reporting begins. Incidentally . . . the stories are literature.[30]

Reed accepted the acclaim gracefully, for he knew the writing about Mexico was his best. Secure now as a war correspondent, he labored diligently over the material for the next three months, carefully turning out pieces for both the *Metropolitan* and the *Masses*, then gathering the best into a work which summed up his whole experience in the revolution south of the Rio Grande.

Insurgent Mexico is a book for the eye, a vast panorama like one of the great murals of the Mexican painters, full of color, motion and the life-and-death struggle of a people. Its power comes from the close identification of the author with his subject. Friends of Reed realized this, Lippmann by noting that the writing was "alive with Mexico and you," Dave Carb in saying, "It's so much Reed that I suspect it is very little Mexico."[31] Obviously conscious of this approach, Jack told a story not only of Mexico in arms, but also of an American radical's reaction to revolution. Less clearly did he realize that he was writing an important slice of autobiography, a kind of modern picaresque tale of one man's education in an arena of danger, an adventure yarn about how an American poet becomes a man.

In composing the book, the poet was stronger than the journalist, making *Insurgent Mexico* more encompassing than any straight factual account.* Its artistically arranged scenes have a balance, coherence and

---

* At least two writers familiar with Mexico agreed that Reed had managed to capture the flavor and spirit of the revolution. Fellow journalist Gregory Mason of the *Outlook* recalled this in "Reed, Villa and the Village," *Outlook*, CXL (May 6, 1935), 1, 3. Edgcumb Pinchon, co-author of a book on the revolution published about the same time as *Insurgent Mexico*, wrote a letter of fulsome praise for Reed's articles on July 26, 1914, JR Papers. Seeing Jack as a very conscious radical, Pinchon understood his method, writing that "the awakening of the general sympathy with what is human in us all is of at least equal importance with a clear intellectual recognition of the class-struggle. That, I take it, is your position." Reviews of *Insurgent Mexico*, which appeared after the opening of the World War, were mixed, but Reed's fame was already secure. The *Nation*, C (January 21, 1915), 82–3, prissily objected that the work was a "lurid exaggeration . . . and the frenzied manner of the whole composition aims not so much at depicting sober truths as at shocking the reader by disgusting naturalism. . . ." The *Dial*, XLVII (October 16, 1914), 303, took Reed to task for "his peculiarly jaunty manner," but admitted the book "conveys vivid and presumably truthful impressions of Mexican life. . . ." More positively, the *Outlook*, CVIII (October 21, 1914), 440, said, "None of the war correspondents in Mexico has got so close to the Mexicans themselves; he describes them as they are, without idealizing them or concealing their ignorance, brutality,

integrity that daily experience lacks. Skies often turn blood-red after battles, simple peons speak with uncanny folk wisdom, the narrator has sudden flashing insights into the symbolic meanings of complex events— such things occur too often to be taken as a literal transcription of what Reed saw, heard and did. Yet the rearrangement, careful selection and poetic rendering allowed him to create a deep feeling for the texture and quality of a land in the throes of a vast, historic change. As Lippmann later wrote, "The variety of his impressions, the resources and color of his language seemed inexhaustible . . . and Villa's revolution, till then reported only as a nuisance, began to unfold itself into throngs of moving people in a gorgeous panorama of earth and sky."[32]

While the poet played with settings and mood, the dramatist altered character and chronology. Banished from the pages is Mac, and his place on the trip south is taken by a Mexican officer who first tries to shoot Reed, then becomes his blood brother. Obviously the brutish American, with his distaste for "niggers," is hardly a suitable companion for the narrator as revolutionary sympathizer, while the Mexican officer—based on a man met briefly in Jiménez—illustrates the dangers the author faced and his ability to be embraced even by people who hated *gringos*. By shifts in chronology, the story is made more dramatic, and the violence of revolution is bracketed by Jack's adventures. Early on come the baptism into La Tropa and the details of the hardships of life with Urbina's men. The final section finds the narrator loafing in two Durango mountain villages—actually visited before he joined La Tropa—peaceful, sleepy towns drowsing in the sun and the lingering romance of lost Spanish gold mines. Here, beyond the reach of government, peons live without politics in a world where no such word as war or revolution is spoken. After many sections of death and destruction, the book ends on this pacific note, as if the author wants to show that the result of revolution will be gentle people living in harmony with nature and each other.

Central to the book is the portrait of Villa. Earthy, passionate, uneducated and a dreamer, he is the perfect symbol of Reed's Mexico, the vessel of his deep feelings about the land and its people. What Reed liked best was that life in Mexico had all the characteristics of youth: "impetuosity, hot blood, heroism, pose, bombast, cruelty, love, abandon, asceticism, grace, rudeness, warmth."[33] Such characteristics were not only

---

or semi-barbarism. Emphatically his book is dramatic; his frequent use of the dialogue form of narrative gives an effect at times like that of a skilled fiction writer, while the abundance of incident and anecdote makes the book immensely readable. . . . It bears the marks of truthful delineation, and it is remarkably vivid."

Latin, they were those of a preindustrial society now threatened by the strong waves of modern life—"machinery, scientific thought, and political theory"—crashing against the country's shores. One nagging problem was how the color, warmth and romance of the people could be preserved by a modern government, for the ability to live fully and passionately seemed just as important as the need to end exploitation.

Acceptance by the Mexican revolutionaries allowed Reed to become part of something clean and meaningful—as important as his father's battle against the timber interests. Still C.J.'s admirer, he could not help seeing the issues in Mexico as more serious than those of Oregon. Fraud and exploitation might spring from the same impulse, the desire to become rich; but, as he had learned in Paterson, the human consequences of the latter were more devastating. In a way, the situation south of the Rio Grande was Paterson writ across the face of a land, the exploitation of the many by the very few. But here was a situation where no middle-class morality or legacy of constitutional rights existed to buffer extremism. The result was a widespread upheaval that stained a nation with blood and destruction. Life itself was cheap in time of revolution, but having seen men go joyously into battle, having come under fire himself and learned "that bullets are not very terrifying, that the fear of death is not such a great thing," Reed understood that a cause could be more important than life. Begun as a job, the Mexican journey had become a rare experience that served to fuse self-fulfillment and social concerns. Not only had he lived up to his own image of manhood in situations of violence and death, but he also now had a subject worthy of complete literary commitment. His writing was important not only as a means of self-expression, but also because his words might have an effect in the world, might influence America and thereby help his Mexican friends to achieve success. Composed to help both the revolution and himself, *Insurgent Mexico* was a tribute of thanks to the people and country that had helped John Reed to "find himself again."[34]

11

Ludlow

Only the mass . . . the multitude . . .
Only the majestic sweep of people:
The sweeping stream blends everyone.
The brain that thinks, the body that is capable of action, the space animate
*   with form unseen, the object tangible . . . all the expansive breath of*
*   life . . .*
A stretch, unending, of expression . . .
The plain, smooth, merging crush of birth and death.
Nothing separate, nor lost, nor helpless, nor oppressed . . .
But greeted, welcomed, challenged. . . .
Nothing dead:
But life made up of dying. . . .

The great, new day; with white winds washing it,
And wide-spread distances lying open in it:
Walls that hold themselves in readiness to move;
Poles that stalwart stand . . . erect . . .

That stiff in swelling passion stand
And walk, over moist, welcoming, close-molding earth.
Movement upflung! . . .
Daring as the dawn . . .
Surging unrestraint . . .
Things shining, clear, demanding, giving:
Living eagerly with lust for living . . .
Journeying through deaths that bear to new lives . . .

This your Faith . . . your hope . . . your journeying:
This your aching muscles . . . this your strength withheld.
This in your hearts! . . .
And a bursting freedom in your living! . . .
Hear the daring chant of space!
Step with a firm full stride of Faith!
Upset the force of things that are your menace,
By calmly passing through them,
To laws living in your heart.[1]

In the late spring of 1914 everything seemed to come together for John Reed, and his sense of fulfillment was reflected in these groping fragments. Except for some images elicited by his love for Mabel, poetry had been far from mind for a long time, neglected because of journalism, but now his emotions called for a more personal means of expression. The feeling, the form, the diction—all were new. Here there was no rhyme, no traditional meter, no florid rendering of land and seascape, no song of tall buildings piercing sky and clouds, no semifictional "I" strutting heroic boards; here was Jack Reed—pushed off to the third person singular—singing of his own life's journey; the aches, hopes, fears and longings of a young man ready to face and grapple with whatever challenges lie ahead. Perhaps unimpressive as poetry, such fragments are indispensable as an index of Reed's heart.

"Faith," somehow a strange, old-fashioned word for him to use, was central to Reed's post-Mexico mood. It had nothing to do with churches and creeds. Rather, it was the newfound faith in self, in his own manhood. The ability to stand erect, "stiff in swelling passion," was more than a sexual image—it meant that he could succeed fully in the competitive world of men at home and abroad. The long-envisioned "great, new day" seemed at hand; the possibility of merging self with the "majestic sweep of masses" more real than ever because now there was a firm self that would not disappear. All this could not only be experienced—after *Insurgent Mexico* it could also be encompassed by his art.

The Reed who returned to Manhattan in early April found himself a celebrity.* At the salon there was an Evening entirely devoted to his views of Mexico, and, as Mabel recalled, with "eyes shining and curls bobbing back, temples agleam" he sparkled for hours, overshadowing the other normally bright talkers.[2] Publicity in the press had spread his fame far beyond the confines of the Village. Besieged with more lecture invitations than he could accept and interviewed by reporters, he was listened to attentively, often quoted in print and made the object of more than the usual number of inviting glances from women. At first such adulation was pleasant, but Jack soon grew bored. Like an expensive suit of clothes, fame was externally impressive, but it did not fulfill the inner man.

Secure in his new métier, Reed worked on articles about Villa's army while casting about for other stories. The first week back he found time to cover an unemployment demonstration for the *World* and correspond with journalist Robert Dunn concerning the possibility of joining a mountain-climbing expedition to Kamchatka. On April 20 at Ludlow, Colorado, a massacre of striking coal miners by state militia came as a reminder that class warfare was not limited to Mexico. Immediately he and Max Eastman hurried West. In southeast Colorado the two men found tranquil mining communities basking in bright sunlight beneath snowy mountains, but they learned appearances were deceptive. First poking through the charred remains of the workers' colony at Ludlow, burned to the ground by militia, they then climbed through the canyons to visit mine sites and sagging company towns, talked with miners, merchants, railroadmen and workers' wives, and watched as federal troops under President Woodrow Wilson's orders entered the area to disarm both strikers and National Guardsmen. The story of industrial exploitation they uncovered made conditions in Paterson seem almost benevolent. Like areas in Mexico, the soft-coal counties of Las Animas and Huerfano were virtual feudal domains, overlorded by the Colorado Fuel and Iron Company, one of John D. Rockefeller's interests. The corporation owned

* The extent of Reed's fame and influence is difficult to judge precisely. *Metropolitan* advertisements were quoting Rudyard Kipling as having said Reed was the writer who had made him "see" Mexico, but the origin of the statement cannot be found. In "Wilson and Mexico," *Collier's*, LIII (June 13, 1914), 17, the articles about Villa were termed "the best correspondence that has come out of Mexico," even though the magazine disdained his obvious admiration for Villa. After the battle of Torreón, Villa was taken both more seriously and more sympathetically by large segments of the American press, and Reed's reports surely had something to do with this. For a press roundup, see "The Rise of Villa's Star," *Literary Digest*, XLVIII (April 18, 1914), 889, and "Our Debt to Villa," *ibid.* (May 16, 1914), 1166–7.

all houses, schools, saloons, churches and stores; hired all teachers, doctors and ministers; picked all judges, coroners, sheriffs and marshals; and ignored Colorado's safety and wages-and-hours laws. As the governor of the state admitted, within those two counties no constitutional law existed.

Given these conditions, CF&I reactions to the United Mine Workers were predictable, and union organizers who appeared in southern Colorado in the summer of 1913 were treated like revolutionaries, alternatively shot or jailed by local deputies. In September when miners began to demand that CF&I merely abide by Colorado law in the matter of wages, safety regulations and the right to vote in elections, company guards abused workers and management fired them. Late that month eleven thousand miners—ninety percent of the labor force—walked off the job and moved into tent colonies. The largest of these was at Ludlow, which became the focus of company hostility. When detectives in armored cars began to make forays against the camp, armed miners were quick to shoot back. By late October, after some ten men had died, the governor declared martial law and sent in the National Guard, which proved no more neutral than company guards. Not only did the troops protect imported strikebreakers, but through a bitter winter miners and their families were subject to continuous harassment—false arrests, nondelivery of mail, illegal searches of tents—and they fought back with terrorist bombings. By April the two companies patrolling the region consisted of mine guards temporarily drafted into the National Guard, men whose salaries were paid by CF&I, so the massacre was the logical result of company attitudes. With no warning given, machine guns placed on hillsides had blazed into the tent colony, then the militia had moved in to set fire to the encampment. Twenty-six bodies of men, women and children were recovered from the site.

Enraged by the story, Jack went to Denver, where the governor was being denounced by some citizens as an accessory to murder. Immediately it became apparent that no redress would come through the political or judicial system. As with the Paterson strike, much of the local and national press was presenting a distorted picture by focusing attention not on events at Ludlow, but on the subsequent actions of armed bands of angry miners who roamed the countryside burning company property and shooting at mine guards. Both the newspapers and the Colorado legislature were echoing the sentiments of company officials who attributed the violence to "ignorant foreigners" and claimed CF&I actions were preserving a great principle, the right of Americans to "earn a living without a permit" from the UMW.[3] Seeing once more the alliance of government and press with business, Reed did what he could to help, speaking at meetings to gather relief money, and serving on a national committee with Judge Ben Lindsey of Denver, George Creel and Upton Sinclair to win support for the strike. But his real weapon was the pen, and soon he hurried East, stopping for a luncheon in Chicago to deliver an address to a group of newspapermen at Hull House. So impassioned did he become that Jane Addams, his hostess, never forgot the speech, so full of Reed's "vivid understanding of the miners, his ardor, his belief in the underdog."[4]

Life in Manhattan was too hectic for the work at hand. Fulfilling a promise to Headmaster Woodman, he spent one evening at Morristown entertaining the students—who included Mabel's son—with an account of his Mexican adventures. Then he traveled with Mabel to Provincetown, at the tip of Cape Cod, where she had rented a summer house. This quiet fishing village was becoming a refuge from the city for Villagers prosperous enough to get away. Full of friends like the Hapgoods, Susan Glaspell and George Cram Cook, Mary Heaton Vorse and Fred Boyd, the town offered opportunity for both pleasure and work. Jack confined his socializing to evening drinks, took at least one long swim a day and concentrated on writing. Forced to divide attention between the book on Mexico and an article on Colorado, he hired Boyd as an assistant. Fred was especially helpful with "The Colorado War," for, unlike the personal reporting from Paterson, this was a lengthy piece documented from official government reports—what it lacked in firsthand excitement was made up by an implacable array of facts.

New ideas kept bubbling through Reed's head and the problem of American intentions toward Mexico troubled him. In the *Masses*, the *Metropolitan* and *The New York Times* he forcefully denounced the idea of intervention, and to friends said he would rejoin La Tropa to fight any American invasion. But when in late April U.S. troops landed in Veracruz, it was not the intervention he feared. Rather than an American army marching to put down Villa or the Constitutionalists, U.S. marines—on pretext of an insult to the flag—had captured Huerta's chief port and were evidently preventing German arms shipments from reaching the Mexican dictator. To confuse the issue, while both Huerta and Carranza condemned the occupation of Veracruz, Pancho Villa issued a statement welcoming American forces. Then late in May, President Wilson, who had legalistically refused to recognize Huerta because he had come to power in violation of his country's constitution, was quoted in the Saturday Evening Post as favoring a Mexican government that would pursue a program of agrarian reform.

Curious about this new position—which paralleled his own—and hoping to influence the United States toward giving aid to his revolutionary friends, Jack played on his growing reputation to secure high-level interviews. He arrived in Washington in mid-June and called on William Jennings Bryan at home on a steamy Sunday afternoon. The Secretary of State met him in a parlor crowded with Oriental vases, tall oil paintings of obscure rajahs and sultans, expensive haircloth furniture and numerous busts of himself. Wearing a cutaway, half-glasses with a black ribbon dangling and a white bow tie, Bryan had a "noble head" and a fine mane of hair that made him look fully "a statesman." He spoke like a statesman, too, "slowly, impressively, with massive seriousness." A pacifist who believed fervently in mediation, Bryan detested Huerta, backed the policy of nonrecognition and expressed some sympathy for Villa as a reformer. But his general reactions were those of an unworldly citizen of Nebraska, unfamiliar with either foreigners or revolution. Leaning over at one point, the Secretary said: "I must confess to you that there is one thing I cannot understand about the Mexicans. Do you know, when one faction captures a soldier of another faction, they stand him up against a wall and *shoot him down!*"[5] Jack realized Bryan was more familiar with Mexico than with labor conditions in Colorado.

The next afternoon Reed met the President in the Oval Room. Dressed in white flannel, Wilson rose from a desk and shook hands so warmly that Jack was immediately at ease. The immaculate trees and flowers of the mansion's gardens were visible through tall French windows, where curtains swayed in a warm breeze, but when the President began to speak, his ruddy face was so alive it was impossible to look elsewhere. Using no gestures, speaking in a calm, even tone of voice that made everything seem "tremendously important," Wilson exuded quiet power, understanding, authority and sincerity. Scribbling notes, Reed had no time to ask questions or express his own views on the Mexican situation. Only after leaving did he realize the President knew how to utilize a reporter to his own advantage.[6]

For a long time afterward Reed mulled over the unusual character of Wilson. Animated by simple ideals—"Christianity, Liberty, and Fair Play"—he appeared almost naïve, but this was the deceptive simplicity of a powerful and complex mind. Though he exhibited a "deep faith in [the] fundamental political genius" of the country, Wilson was far from blind to the real problems of society. The President understood that "industrial tyranny" and "predatory minorities" plagued the land, but believed all such problems could be solved by traditional political means. The first chief executive in "ten administrations" to be "more interested in principles than in policies," Wilson was probably as good a leader as one could hope for in modern America. But Jack had to question whether this was good enough. With no more faith in the federal soldiers now patrolling Colorado's mining regions than the militia they had replaced, he could not help wondering if even a dedicated, idealistic President could curb the lawlessness of industry.

Reed was delighted with the "extraordinary interview," and hurried to Provincetown to commit it to paper.[7] Spurred by a note from the White House in which Wilson commented, "I want to say how warmly I appreciate your desire to help and your whole spirit in this matter," he focused on an explanation of the President's critical Mexican policy.[8] Wilson started with the traditional American opposition to tyranny and support for people in revolt, and was determined to help the Mexican people choose their own leaders constitutionally. Nonrecognition of Huerta and the occupation of Veracruz became—through some semantic shuffling—not interference in Mexican affairs, but merely an attempt to check an illegal regime. Expressing sympathy for agrarian reform, the President legalistically hoped that the government which emerged from the revolution would not confiscate the great estates, but recognized this as an internal matter to be settled by Mexicans alone. His main purpose was all Jack could wish: "that no one shall take advantage of Mexico— in any way; neither military dictators, citizens of this country, citizens of foreign countries, nor foreign governments."

Because the chief executive could not be quoted directly, it was difficult to make the article lively. Struggling for a week, Reed sent off a draft to the White House, only to have it quickly rejected. A letter from Joe Tumulty, Wilson's secretary, suggested, "If you were to recast the article so as to leave out all . . . intimations of directly echoing what the President said and confine yourself to your own impressions received from the interview, I think it would be possible to authorize publication." Evidently devoid of any feeling for style, Tumulty said he should insert phrases like, "I got the impression, for example, that with regard to . . . he would be pretty certain to decide that, etc."[9] Gritting his teeth over such awkward circumlocution, Jack went back to work. By the time the piece was safe from the White House point of view, it was worthless as an article.

His disappointment was not too great. Provincetown was glorious in the summer, the sun glinting off the rippling bay, the nights warm and bright with stardust, the harbor calm with drying fishnets. In response to Reed's glowing reports, Bobby Rogers, Lee Simonson and Bobby Jones came by for a holiday, and there was plenty of drinking, eating and laughing. Sometimes they hiked a mile over the desolate, lonely white sand dunes to the ocean side of the Cape, swam in the sea and then cooked dinner on the beach, able to forget about Presidents, strikes, foreign affairs and revolution.

When his friends departed he launched into a frenzy of writing. The manuscript on Mexico finally complete, he composed a dedication to Copey: "As I wrote these impressions of Mexico I couldn't help but think that I never would have seen what I did see had it not been for your teaching me. . . . To listen to you is to learn how to see the hidden beauty of the visible world; . . . to be your friend is to try to be intellectually honest."[10] When the Ludlow article appeared, it was highly praised, and he was pleased that a bookstore in Denver had canceled a standing order of fifty *Metropolitans* as a protest against its alleged lies. He began to write free verse, completed a humorous dialect story about a bumbling sea captain named Grampus Bill, toyed with a one-act play and a theatrical masque, and once again sketched scenes for a novel about the magic Indian from the Northwest. Despite being "pretty broke," he turned down suggestions from Carl Hovey for articles on a variety of commercial topics. The only possibility to arouse his interest was that of traveling to Mexico City to greet Villa when—as was likely to happen soon—the rebel general captured it. From there he might continue to China to report a revolution just beginning.

The happy days at Provincetown were made complete by one more thing—his love for Mabel. Since his return there had been no more stormy scenes, no suicide attempts, no threats and recriminations, and he was filled with an emotion described in a letter from Denver: "You are so beautiful to me for just that soul of yours, and so alive. You are my life."[11] Now Jack expressed the love not in words, but with flesh against flesh on sweetly lingering summer nights. Yet he failed to see that the feeling was not wholly returned. The reasons were as complex as Mabel, a woman who would later drive two psychoanalysts to distraction and never find the lasting love she claimed to crave. Attracted by youth, vitality, energy and manliness, Mabel had simultaneously felt almost like a mother, often thinking he "was a child compared to myself."[12] Like any mother, she partially resented his growth and accomplishments, for if they made him more attractive as a man, they detracted from his dependence. No doubt Mabel had always exaggerated Jack's need for her anyway. Since Mexico it was increasingly obvious that he could stand on his own. A man who rode with Villa, won a national reputation and interviewed the President might still be a child, but it became more and more difficult to support such an idea.

While the mother in Mabel was increasingly threatened, the woman who believed love a struggle without quarter was also troubled. Retaliating for the Mexican venture, she had played around with other men, including painter Andrew Dasburg, a friend of Reed. Proud of the conquest, Mabel encouraged Marsden Hartley to write Reed describing a canvas by Dasburg which she had inspired. When this brought no response of jealousy, she wrote to him about Andrew's attractiveness, his angelic face and strength and the frosty light that glistened in his hair. In reply came a letter which ignored her comments and proclaimed: "I will write all our names across the sky in flame."[13] After Jack's return she resented the fact that "he was becoming more and more the Hero to everyone, especially to Women."[14] Once when she noticed an emancipated young lady looking at Reed with an obvious gleam of desire, Mabel was moved to write a nasty note warning her to keep away.

Suffering anxiety and fear about the relationship, Mabel that summer began taking unconscious steps to protect herself from pain. Outwardly affectionate as ever, she gave herself with a passion that kept Reed from realizing anything had changed. If she showed no anger—even over the presence of Boyd—it was not out of growing love, but just the reverse. Jack was able to understand the meaning of hysterics, but he was totally unprepared for a slow withdrawal of affection and did not sense that Mabel was beginning to withhold just that soul he claimed to love.

With little inkling of the change, Reed was in no way upset as Mabel prepared to take her son and Neith Boyce to the Villa Curonia for the second half of the summer. His own plans called for a long-delayed trip home to Portland in mid-July. After that—well, who knew what next fall would bring? Perhaps a trip to Mexico or China, or a contract for a book of Mexican ballads, or the time to get on with the novel he had been planning for years. Mabel would be back, and love would continue with Evenings, the theater, good food, writing, drinks with friends and more battles to help bring justice to America, Mexico and the world. Grandiose dreams, perhaps, but natural enough for a young man whose life was happy and complete.

In the summer of 1914 at Provincetown, Jack was tasting the full beauty of the world. Everything blended together now—love, art, career, self and life. Best of all, the beauty came from within; this piece of folk wisdom, dimly apprehended in the past, was obvious now. While stopping in Denver he had met a young female violinist who seemed too conventional to be a brilliant performer, and had delivered a lecture: "I told her if she could get a soul, she would be a real artist. But, she said, 'I don't see how one can get a soul without letting go all the ideals and standards of life one has set before oneself to hold one to the right.' There isn't any other way, I told her. There isn't any law you have to obey, nor any moral standard you have to accept, nor, in fact, anything outside of your own soul that you have to take any account of."[15] Since even extensive contact with Mabel had left Reed without a metaphysical bone in his body, the "soul" he meant was, like faith, "only another word for finding oneself."[16] Brimming with such faith now, having that long-sought soul, he felt free of any standards beyond those of his own beating heart.

12

Western Front

"It is a period of profound disillusionment, of bitter disappointment, for those of us who believed that the nations were coming of age—and that one day the United States of the World would allow the flowering of some wonderful ideas for the reconstruction of human society with which the earth was teeming like a field in spring. And here are the nations flying at each other's throats like dogs—and with as little reason. These military gentlemen present us with the sublime spectacle of every nation in Europe arming to defend itself against every other, of mutual panics, equivocations, spying and threats; and art, industry, commerce, individual liberty, life itself, taxed to maintain monstrous machines of death. . . . Indeed, this Militarism is something far stronger than we ever imagined it. It is no longer an expression of man's primeval impulse to combat; it is a science, and the conscript armies of Europe have impregnated every home with it. It is the one thing that the man of the street does not question. The tacit acceptance of the necessity for tremendous armaments by the tax-dodging bourgeoisie of Europe makes Militarism the *crowning fact of our time. This war seems to be the supreme expression of European civilization."*[1]

Shrouded by hopelessness in early October 1914, John Reed wrote these words of anger and despair. He had been in Europe for two months covering what was being called the "Great War," but this new assignment was bringing him no joy or fulfillment. Military action could not excite him unless it was part of a struggle aimed at social change. Battle and destruction could be justified only if the goal was a better society and more personal freedom, and if there was an opportunity for a man to test himself in the service of an ideal greater than self. The most immense war in history had none of these elements. Impersonal as science, it left little room for heroism. With no underlying ideal that Reed could accept, the conflict seemed worse than senseless as it rapidly destroyed those movements in thought, art and social life that had promised a new age of man.

Reed and his friends in Bohemia were, in a general way, pacifists, so the mere fact of war was disturbing enough; more dismal was the idea that this conflict was no aberration, but a natural "expression of European civilization." The countries of the Continent were considered the cradle of culture, not just for their ruins and history, but because in them had been born the most important modern movements in the arts, philosophy and social thought—Impressionism, Anarchism, Socialism, Naturalism, Cubism, Syndicalism—and the heroes at whose shrines Bohemians worshipped—Wagner, Marx, Freud, Nietzsche, Rolland, Wells, Dostoevsky, Shaw, Wilde, Baudelaire, Ibsen and Strauss. Europe was synonymous with culture, a place where artists and intellectuals were honored and esteemed. Seen through a golden filter, the Continent's poverty and backwardness appeared glamorous—unlike American farmers, European peasants were natural men, rooted deeply in the soil, while Europe's industrial slums teemed with color, song and life. Even social problems, strikes and turmoil were tinged with the romance of revolution, shadowed by lingering ghosts from the Paris Commune. A war in Europe was like a violent quarrel between parents; it left American intellectuals and artists feeling confused and homeless.

Sharing this romantic view of Europe, Reed reacted to the outbreak of war with less disbelief than did many Villagers. When news came of mobilization and the movement of vast armies across frontiers, most of his friends despaired. In Provincetown the summer colony gathered each evening at the small stationery store to buy the latest newspapers. Those who, like Hapgood, Boyd and Dell, combined political and artistic interests succumbed to nightly orgies of heavy drinking, endless talking and deep soul-searching as they wondered what good were ideas about art and society in a world gone berserk. Even the nonpolitical Harriet Monroe felt the world crumbling. Swept with a feeling of "blank amazement and bitter rebellion," she commented, "It was a sudden shattering of hope, a brutal denial of progress, a bloody anachronism in a civilization of peaceful industry. . . ."[2]

On a visit to Portland for the first time in two years, Reed was prepared for the news because Carl Hovey in late July had sent telegrams indicating that when war began, the *Metropolitan* wanted him there as its exclusive correspondent. Though treated in a manner commensurate with his recent fame at teas, luncheons and dinners, Jack was finding the town dull as ever. He escaped the stuffy atmosphere and dropped into the local IWW hall one evening to hear Emma Goldman lecture, then became friendly with Carl Walters, an artist who subscribed to the *Masses*. Accepting an invitation to address the University Club, he did not give the innocuous talk about life in far-off places that everyone expected. Instead Reed delivered an impassioned speech about exploitation and class war that annoyed the audience and led some to chalk him up as a rude young man, spoiled by life in New York and premature fame.

On the train East Jack met a clean-cut English university graduate with a neat mustache, expensive clothing and a reserved demeanor, on his way home to join the army. While the peaceful evening fields of mid-America flashed by the windows, the young man coolly explained the war: England was fighting to honor treaty obligations incurred by foreign policy, which was, unfortunately, "not in my line." Showing no sympathy for the French and no hatred for Germans, he was returning because "my people have always been army people." With no apparent doubts, he seemed the quintessence of the English ruling class, "one hundred and sixty pounds of bone and muscle and gentle blood, with the inside of his head like an Early Victorian drawing room, all knickknacks, hair-cloth furniture and drawn blinds." He would fight with the same spirit with which he "would wade through fire and blood to get a cold bath in the morning—because it was the thing to do."[3]

New York was unchanged. Streets, cafés, restaurants and theaters were crowded as ever, and only the extra editions of newspapers with huge headlines gave an indication of Europe's agony. Securing a $1500 advance for expenses from the *Metropolitan*, Jack was promised "the biggest price paid in the country" by the *World* for any exclusive stories he could get by the European censors in code.[4] In Washington he prevailed upon William Jennings Bryan to write a letter asking American diplomatic officials to extend him all "courtesies and assistance."[5] Returning to Manhattan, he was greeted by Fred Boyd, penniless and looking for a way to return to his native England. Reed paid for his passage, and while waiting to sail, the two went over the world situation many times. A Socialist to the core, Fred was not discouraged. Capitalist wars were to be expected, and he was returning to England to partake in the social upheaval that would follow. Even the capitulation of Continental Socialists to the nationalist fervor was not overly upsetting; this was a temporary aberration, and soon the workers' parties would return to class solidarity. Lamenting the killing, he nevertheless believed war was good because it would bring on the long-awaited revolution.

Impressed by this analysis, Reed was not personally comfortable hiding behind cold theory. He was upset by newspaper talk of vast American profits to be made off the war and worried by articles favoring the Allies and depicting the conflict as "Liberalism going forth to Holy War against Tyranny." A piece for the *Masses*, "The Traders' War," summed up a viewpoint that reflected Boyd's influence. Casting aside the Austro-Serbian dispute as "a mere bagatelle," Reed explained the general European war as basically commercial in origin. Germany, growing in industrial power and seeking markets, had been checked, contained and excluded from potential profits in Asia Minor and North Africa by the older colonial powers, France and England, for two decades. Abhorring Prussian militarism and the doctrine of "blood and iron" that stood "squarely in the path of democratic progress," he found that as bad as the Kaiser's "brutalizing ideals" was the "raw hypocrisy of his armed foes who shout for a Peace which their greed has rendered impossible." In this "falling out among commercial rivals," there was only one ray of possible light: "We, who are Socialists, must hope . . . that out of this horror of destruction will come far-reaching social changes." For America, the piece concluded, only one position was sensible: "This is not Our War."[6]

On his last night in the United States, Reed had dinner with Boyd and Eddy Hunt on the roof of the Astor Hotel, looking over Broadway until the early hours of the morning. All three were sailing the next day: Fred for England, Eddy to Holland as a representative of the *American Magazine* and Jack to Naples. Not yet in the war, Italy was expected to honor its membership in the Triple Alliance by entering on the side of Germany and Austria. Hoping to catch the first action on that front, he was being drawn there for other reasons. Mabel had sent her son home with Neith Boyce from the Villa Curonia and had then wired that she would keep Reed company while he covered the news. Time and distance had made her heart grow fonder, and she was awaiting him in Naples.

Aboard the Italian liner were 150 first- and cabin-class passengers, including members of the nobility from Italy, Germany and Austria, and a large number of military officers returning to join units in belligerent countries. Remarkably, these men who would soon be on opposite sides of battlefields were every companionable—sharing drinks and conversation while playing cards in the ship's lounges. Indeed, the interdependence of Europe was nowhere better shown; the Austrians and Italians read French novels; one German had lived most of his life in Paris and another was a student at Oxford; a Frenchman's wife had been born in Berlin; an Italian marquis had been graduated from the Sorbonne and had worked on a London newspaper. Seeing that the "amusements, education, the intellectual strength of every man on board, came, at least in part, from the very sources they were going, blindly, to destroy," Jack tried to ascertain their motives. Nowhere did he get a satisfactory answer. It all boiled down to a blind sort of patriotism expressed by the German officer who snapped, "You talk like a civilian. I am a soldier. To every man who wears a uniform, the man who wears a different uniform is an enemy. *Voilà tout!*"[7]

There was a serious cleavage on board, but not among the wealthy. Jammed into steerage were "three thousand miserable human beings," mostly Italian immigrants to America who, in a flush of patriotism, were on the way home to join the army. Their superiors, clad in evening dress, leaned on the rails of spacious first-class decks to look down on the masses below, stuck in the stench, heat and filth of the lower decks. Referring to them as "animals" and "vermin," men who would soon be their officers roared with amusement one evening when sailors cleared the crowds from the decks with hoses. Reed imagined he could hear "the grumbling threat of a hundred angry voices rising from the bowels of the ship," and wondered how long men who were treated like beasts by their leaders could remain patriotic. In fantasy the plight of the steerage passengers "pervaded the whole ship day and night—a symbol of the way the scent of the jumbled, stinking underworld is beginning to cling so ominously to the nostrils of power nowadays—a threat of awful things to come."

Wearing a long white ruffled dress and a flowery hat and carrying a lace parasol, Mabel was on the dock to greet Jack when he bounded down the gangplank, untidy, breathless and full of excitement. Naples was the perfect spot for a reunion, the blue of bay and sky and white of sun and city brightening the hotel room with colors of love. After taking one afternoon for a ride to Pompeii, they caught a night train for Rome.

Reed was impressed by the city's historical monuments, but the mood of the people was more interesting. Rome seethed with excitement—fresh newspapers were snapped up by café patrons, money seemed in short supply, regiments of soldiers marched through the streets, and in theaters bands played the "Marseillaise" as often as Italian anthems. In the Piazza of St. Peter, where tens of thousands awaited the election of a new Pope, there was more talk of war than of religion, and Reed had a "vision of one of the sombre and awful things of which this war is the sign—the end of the Christian era."[8]

When news came that German armies had sliced through Belgium and were sweeping toward Paris, Jack and Mabel took a train north on September 2. Annoyed that the large, organized Italian working class seemed unable to stifle a rising mood of patriotic militarism, and suffering simultaneously from dysentery and a bad summer cold, Reed retained enough sense of humor to describe how they were "pursued all the way to the frontier by the Amalgamated Association of Italian Guides, who had been brought to the most desperate extremities by the departure of American tourists. As [we] left one station, the Guides in that city telegraphed ahead so that at the next place [we] were greeted by a chorus of pleading voices . . . 'Would you like to see the city?' "[9]

Geneva was the gayest place in Europe, crowded and glittering like Monte Carlo at the height of the season, a city where it was "distinctly bad taste" to mention war. Here were gathered all the frivolous elements of Europe, refugees from France, Germany, Austria and England: "dowagers equipped with pearls and lorgnettes leaning back in smart automobiles, boulevardiers in gray spats and monocles, with flowers in their buttonholes and light canes raked carelessly over their shoulders, slope-shouldered young *civilisés* with touched-up cheeks and eyebrows, tall girls with fantastic figures, leading still more fantastic dogs, clipped in every pattern." At night, crowds strolled the lakeshore, sat in cafés and restaurants, thronged gambling clubs and filled theaters to see musical revues, while all the streets were patrolled by newly expatriated "exotic ladies" of the Parisian boulevards. In this atmosphere, war seemed a "remote . . . incredible thing." Only the shortage of money, the fact that everyone was living on credit, that well-dressed men wore dirty collars and elegant ladies had holes in their stockings, suggested that such life in neutral Switzerland was "the end of a phase of our civilization."[10]

With newspapers full of reports that the Germans were about to enter Paris, Mabel and Jack boarded what was said to be the last train to the French capital. At Cernadon, just across the border, they encountered ten third-class carriages which "rocked with singing and cheering" of young recruits off to training bases. Doors and windows of the cars were decorated with vines and the green branches of trees, and the sides were chalked with caricatures of Prussians and exultant slogans: "This train express for Berlin," or "This compartment reserved for the Prussian General Staff." After the troop cars were hitched behind, the train rolled across the rich French countryside through a gray afternoon darkening into rain. Every crossroad and station was full of pale-faced women, aged men and groups of children slowly waving handkerchiefs. Dinner at the Bourg station buffet was interrupted when a hospital train reeking with the "appalling stench of iodoform" slowly pulled up to the platform and hundreds of wounded men with arms, legs or foreheads swathed in bandages leaned out the windows begging for cigarettes.[11]

That night and the next day their journey was through a country where women seemed to have replaced men, harvesting in fields, driving carts, tending railroad gates. Often they passed military trains full of singing youngsters on the way to battle or silent ones returning from the front; then cobblestone barricades, gray guns along the tracks and regiments of men lounging beside highways marked the approach to the capital city. They reached Paris on a beautiful September morning, "one of those late summer, perfect days when the leaves are turning, there is a hint of autumn in the air, and the life of the city begins to move more swiftly." This time there was no such life. Leaving the station, they found a ghost town—long vistas of empty streets, endless shops with iron shutters down, the Grands Boulevards almost devoid of life, the famous cafés either closed or with only a few lonely patrons sitting on their terraces. On the Rue de la Paix not a soul was visible, and in the silence the hoofs of their cab horse echoed loudly on the cobblestones. Everywhere were displays of five flags—French, Belgian, English, Russian and Serbian; it seemed as if "the city had decked itself out for some vast rejoicing and then had sickened."

They took a small apartment on the Left Bank and began to explore the town, and found their first impression partly inaccurate. Large numbers of people had left the capital, and many of the luxurious hotels, restaurants and shops were closed, but residential streets were full of life, and in the Luxembourg Gardens a group of laughing children—some with black bands on their arms—were watching a puppet show. At night the change was greatest: cafés closed at eight, no theaters were open, the streets were deserted and "the great golden arcs of the boulevards, the graceful necklace of lamps that traced the curves of the river and the bridges, the white brilliance of the Champs Elysee—all were dark." White searchlight beams swept the sky for German airships, and in darkened streets ragged regiments of soldiers tramped from unknown posts toward others equally mysterious.

While Mabel languished in bed a good deal of the time, Reed moved around, meeting other journalists in cafés, trying to interview recalcitrant officials. The mood of the populace was disturbing; far from the calm stoicism that others had reported, Jack found apathy among the Parisians. While the government issued terse communiqués announcing that the "Allies continue their strategic retreat with great success," strangers asked one another, "When do you think *they* will enter the city?" with no tone of anger or resistance. As routed English and French troops straggled into town and rumors spread that the German army was only ten kilometers away, Reed determined to reach the front. Correspondents were forbidden to leave Paris, but with Robert Dunn of the New York *Evening Post* he made plans to foil French officialdom.[12]

Early on September 9, at the height of the crucial Battle of the Marne, the two Americans in a hired car driven by a chauffeur rode past barricades and troops of soldiers out into the countryside. Certified by a doctor to be suffering from angina pectoris, Dunn bore a police pass for travel to the south, and this got them by many sentry points. At the forest of Vincennes they turned north, hoping to find fighting, but the companies of soldiers marching the smooth roads looked like men on maneuvers. After a while the highways were empty and the tiny gray stone villages were shuttered and barred. Late in the morning they saw the first evidence of war, the dozen houses of Courteçan, sacked, looted and still burning, heaps of debris in the streets and groups of weeping peasant women who reported that the Germans had departed the night before.

For the rest of the day the car drove up and down narrow white, roads checkered with the shade of poplars. Refugees with household goods piled in mule-drawn carts were traveling in all directions, for nobody seemed to know where the front was. In Rozoy, over lunch in a small restaurant, they encountered three English journalists under arrest for being in a restricted area, but the officers detaining them did not bother Reed and Dunn. Late in the day they were in Crécy listening to friendly English Tommies unemotionally describe the retreat from Mons. When one private asked if the Russians were in Berlin, a corporal retorted sharply, "I tell you they haven't crossed the Pyrenees yet." Letting the car return to Paris, they spent a restless night in a hotel room listening to horsemen and trucks clatter beneath the window, learning from shouts of a motorcycle courier that the Second Army had crossed the Marne. moving the front more than fifteen miles north.

Since the action was too far away to reach on foot, Reed and

Dunn decided to approach British headquarters for permission to join a troop train. In a staff car with two lieutenants they drove to Coulommiers, where a provost marshal upbraided them for being in an area closed to journalists and made them promise not to leave town. During the afternoon they poked through delicate balconied houses smashed and looted by retreating Germans, crossed the ancient arched bridges over the Grand Morin and fraternized with British soldiers who were vainly demanding tea at the town's cafés. In the evening they ate a scanty dinner at the Mouton Blanc with four other journalists also under detention. The next morning they were turned over to French gendarmes, who filled out lengthy dossiers and put them aboard a train full of German prisoners. The following day they faced the prefect in Tours, who offered to free them in return for a written promise to keep out of the military zone in the future. An annoyed Jack demanded, "What if I refuse to swear?" and was told simply, "You will be obliged to remain in Tours until the end of the war." He signed the document.

Back in Paris things began to look bleak. Mabel was sinking into a strange mood of depression, and at night their lovemaking was tinged by melancholy as tears flowed from her eyes and dried against his cheek. During the day she moped around, refusing to see old friends. Wandering the streets, Reed felt more and more out of sorts. When it became apparent that the Allies had withstood the German onslaught along the Marne and that the city would not come under siege, it was easy to become cynical. Shops where placards had been posted saying, "The proprietor and all the clerks have joined the army," suddenly reopened and the owner and employees "shamelessly reappeared." Worse yet, Jack's ability to write effortlessly was gone. For days he labored over pieces for the *Metropolitan*, trying to capture the flavor of what he had seen, tearing up page after page, crossing out and rewriting and juggling scenes until they made little sense even to him. At the end of September he sent off a mass of material which he described in a cover letter to Hovey as "a sort of diary." Hoping it would not have to be printed, he confessed, "I have never done such awful work," and blamed this on the cold and diarrhea that had plagued him since Italy and the fact that "I haven't seen anything worth writing."[13]

Barred from the front, fed up with Mabel and himself, Jack thrashed around for a way out of the dilemma and decided to cross the Channel to London. Superficially, the English capital seemed less conscious of war than Paris—"The great, gray town still pours its roaring streams along the Strand and Oxford Street and Piccadilly; endless lines of omnibusses and taxicabs and carriages pass; in the morning the clerks go down to the

city in their carefully-brushed silk hats and thread-bare frock coats. . . .
At night the theaters and restaurants are going full blast, thronged with an
apparently inexhaustible supply of nice, young men in faultless evening
dress, and beautiful women. . . . The same ghastly ragged men rise up
out of the gutter to open your carriage door; the same bums slouch on
the benches of Hyde Park."[14] A few days of talks with a now gloomy
Fred Boyd and some personal observation gave a different picture—
fully as much as France, England was in the thrall of the military spirit.

Behind the bustle of the metropolis, the signs were everywhere;
thousands of proclamations plastered on walls and in store windows saying, "Your King and Country Need You"; khaki-clad officers swarming
through Piccadilly; territorials in olive drab, living in tents in Hyde Park;
women standing on the steps of the National Gallery handing out white
feathers to civilians; a truckload of clerks rolling toward a recruiting
station with a sign reading, "Harrod's Contribution to the Empire." Newspapers printed no opposition to war, and dissenting politicians were
being silenced. Rather than Parliament, the actual ruler of the land was
Lord Kitchener, who controlled the telephone, the telegraph and the
mails and censored the press. The idol of imperialism, he was "the cold,
the merciless, the efficient—the very Prussian ideal of a military man."

Observing the commercial classes and old aristocracy joining together
to whip up sentiment against Germany, Reed was not surprised—imperial England, an amalgam of greed and glory-seeking at the expense
of native peoples, was doing no more than a radical could expect. Yet,
"infinitely depressing" was the response of the people; more than half a
million had volunteered in the name of patriotism, "a humanly fine, stupid
instinct . . . the sacrifice for an ideal, the self-immolation for something
greater than self." Jack was able to understand sacrifice, but what was
admirable in Mexico seemed imbecilic here, where the ideal was so vague
it had no real meaning. Asked about causes, Englishmen answered they
were "fighting to destroy Prussian militarism" or "because Belgium was
invaded," excuses that even diplomats repeated with tongue in cheek.

The fact that the man in the street could offer his life for an empire
that both oppressed him and exploited others was one cause of Reed's
growing depression. It was even harder to face the notion that the war
had been embraced almost wholeheartedly by radicals and artists—
Socialists were talking about the need for exterminating Huns, lifelong
pacifists were making recruiting speeches, labor leaders were pledging
efforts toward victory, figures like H. G. Wells, Thomas Hardy and
G. K. Chesterton were invoking God and history in the struggle against
"Prussian despotism." In France and Italy it had been much the same—

a few voices raised in opposition amid a general capitulation of intellectuals, leftist leaders and common workingmen. In Paris Jack had heard soldiers who described themselves as Socialists say they were fighting to help free the Prussian working class. His retort that Germans similarly claimed to be fighting for Russian workers never dented the argument, and reluctantly he had to conclude that patriotism was stronger than class feeling.

Western Europe had become "a vast marsh of warlike feeling, of vengeance, spite, patriotism." Somehow the desire to kill was swallowing everything good about man, his intellect, dreams and capacity to love—"art, literature . . . amusement, family life, politics" were all being "checked and forgotten." The culture to which Reed belonged, from which he drew inspiration, had always been international in scope—a strange and wonderful mixture of painting, literature, free love, radicalism, social experimentation and revolution that had flowed freely back and forth across the Atlantic. Now he could say flatly, "Ideas are dead in Europe." Worse yet, in France, England and Italy reactionaries were "seizing this occasion for deliberately smashing" liberalism. Mixed up with proposals for exterminating Germany were suggestions for restricting suffrage and free speech and doing away with various social reforms. If this could happen on the Continent, was it not a portent of what might occur in America if war crossed the ocean?

In the blackest of moods, Reed sat down at the typewriter and poured his growing feelings of despair about the whole European situation into a bitter thirty-page denunciation of the iniquities and hypocrisy of the British Empire. England posed as a "champion of virtue," but it had in fact "crushed more human liberty and drenched the world in more rivers of blood" than any other country, and was as responsible as Germany for the current war. Good as it felt to vent anger this way, his pleasure was only temporary. Continually depressed, he turned to Mabel, but she was too full of her own misery, a gloomy mood that had less to do with the problems of the world than with Jack. By now it was clear she could never wholly possess him. He was a man who vibrated to external events, one who needed love but could not live for it alone. Knowing this before, Mabel had forgotten it during the trip to Italy, and relearning the lesson was a painful process of long, lonely hours in a hotel room. Once he had made her feel alive and vital, but now his presence seemed to push her into darkness. Obviously love was gone, but Mabel did not admit this to him. Deciding to return home, she forced Reed to swear his fidelity and eternal devotion. The words sounded hollow, and Mabel fretted that he appeared actually relieved to learn she was leaving.

Her departure freed Jack to indulge his own sorrow. With Fred Boyd's assistance, he drank his way to Dover and across the channel. In fog-shrouded Calais, French sailors led them to a combination café-whore-house, where they hired the services of flat-faced, chunky women in coarse negligees and then drank the night away with champagne while a band played the "Marseillaise" and a roomful of military men sang off-key. It was the best sort of therapy. When the same old opinions of the Kaiser, mixed with denunciations of war by men itching to kill Prussians, filtered through a thick alcoholic haze, they were transformed into humor. In the gray light of dawn they stumbled through the silent streets of the town, singing their way back to the hotel, free at last of morbid thoughts.

A journey several days later brought another perspective. With Boyd and Andrew Dasburg, Reed went out on a "crisp, golden after-noon" to the area between Esternay and Sézanne, site of fierce combat during the Battle of the Marne. All the towns of the region were decimated, and fields were covered with debris, pieces of machinery, torn bits of uniforms, rusting weapons. The yellow autumn countryside was blooming with crocuses, and peasants were once again calmly plowing in the fields. This provided a vision of life stronger than man's capacity to destroy: "For the plowing and sowing of the harvests, the swinging seasons—cold winter and the stirring of the blood of the world in March—love and death and the need of food and clothing will be the only reality of their life. As it has been from time immemorial, in spite of wave after wave of Hun and Visigoth and the devastation of forgotten wars. The fields shall heal themselves of their scars; but more patient than they, the people of this little village will do their will with the life impulse."[15]

The interlude ended abruptly when police arrested the three foreigners for being in a military zone and stamped their passports with a notice that would lead to two years' imprisonment if they were caught in a closed area again. Returning to Paris, Reed was still unable to write decently for either the *World* or the *Metropolitan*, and then his private life developed complications. In late October there came a wire from Mabel suggesting that the romance was at an end. Perhaps he had sensed this already, for though they exchanged a flurry of letters and cables in which he professed sorrow and confusion and she asserted there was no reason they could not go on as friends, Reed was simultaneously sliding into an affair with Freddie Lee, the wife of sculptor Arthur Lee, men-tioned in *The Day in Bohemia*. A close friend of Mabel, Freddie was currently recovering from diphtheria, and the Lees had accepted Reed's invitation to move from their bare, drafty studio to his comfortable apartment. In such close quarters something sparked between Jack and Freddie, and soon both were calling it love.

It was good to turn away from despair and war, to feel intimate emotion once again. The tangled nature of the affair only added spice. Arthur stormed out of the apartment, charging adultery, and there was some fear of violence from him. Jack cabled Mabel news of his new love, and she replied with an understanding letter. Then Freddie wrote to Mabel recalling her own doubt that "happiness between a man and woman was possible." Now she knew it was. Reed and she were drawn together by some "force vitale"; the "roundness" of his being somehow completed her—"It is the nearest I have ever been to the inward force of existence on earth." And Mabel—well, she was "better than a sister" for being so understanding.[16]

Occupied with nursing the still-weak Freddie and helping her get a divorce suit under way, Jack paid little attention to the war in November as the German threat receded from Paris. Late in the month a letter from Steffens arrived expressing approval of the affair: "All I wish is that it will be good, all good, forever." The warmth of this statement concealed a shade of impatience that for the first time crept into his mentor's words:

> You are up in the air now. It's good to be up in the air. It's beautiful to be in love. The emotional state of love is the most beautiful thing in the world. Of course it is. And the fact that it doesn't last has no power and no right to shadow the presence of it. Something else as good or even better may follow it. That is marriage. But neither you nor I nor anyone else can foresee whether the promise of the first stage is kept in the second. So there is nothing to be said as to it.

Comforting Reed over his problems with writing, Stef assured him, "It doesn't matter if you fail in this war; you are a success." On the other hand, there was no real reason for failure now. Scoffing at the idea there was nothing worth writing about in Europe, he gently chastised Jack for attempting political analysis like the article on England. Even from Mexico "your views . . . were not nearly so good as your descriptions and narrative." Besides, the United States was the "best point" from which to view the war as a whole—"New York gets the most news from the most places, and all the comments. And we have perspective, too, which you have not and cannot have." Certain Jack could still write well, his friend counseled: "Trust your eyes and ears again. . . . The things you see and hear in Paris and London and on the field would probably hold me spellbound with interest if you should sit down and tell them to me." Calling himself "eye-blind," Stef explained that he could only grasp events in "mind-sight," but Reed was gifted with the power of description: "You're not wise, Jack; not yet. But you certainly can see and you certainly can write."[17]

Unable to follow the advice, Reed did not answer Steffens directly, but thrashed out the problem in letters to Carl Hovey. Disappointed in Jack's work, the *Metropolitan* editor had managed to salvage two articles from a mass of material, but then he rejected the piece on England with a complaint about Reed's "evident inability to grasp this situation" as he had the Mexican. Reed admitted his reports were "horrible," and laid blame on the war itself. Because it was so "ghastly," such a "gray and unenthusiastic struggle," so devoid of any meaning for him, he found it impossible to write as he had in Mexico. The article on England might have been ill-tempered, but he thought it important to emphasize what all other correspondents were ignoring, that Great Britain was no innocent victim of Germany, but fully as much to blame for the war. What he really wished to write was more analysis, a series of articles on each country that would expose "the historical roots" of the conflict.[18] When Hovey countered this suggestion with a request that he make a trip home for consultation, Jack agreed to something his editor had been urging, a visit to the trenches.

Barred from the lines in France, Reed would have to seek battle elsewhere. This dovetailed nicely into plans he was making with Freddie Lee. By the first of December their love had led to a decision to marry; of German birth, she was anxious to visit her family with him. Jack now hinted to his editor that part of his writing problem had been the relationship with Mabel, "a burden that threatened to crush me for good." Now he felt "strong, well, energetic and able to see and hear, and at last *free* as I was in Mexico."[19] Grateful when Hovey had faith enough to wire $600 to help pay Freddie's expenses, Reed promised the *Metropolitan* something he had refused after Mexico, a two-year exclusive on everything he wrote. After expressing a positive hope that some good articles would emerge from Germany, he and Freddie in early December made a journey through Switzerland and on to Berlin.

The trip was neither fulfilling nor happy. In Paris, marriage had been a lovely, remote dream, but on the spot and faced with her family, the idea became simultaneously tangible and absurd. Their love dissolved into a series of angry scenes and bitter words that left him in the bars of Berlin, drinking heavily with other correspondents and criticizing German officialdom for not letting him go immediately to the front. While waiting for the government to arrange a tour, Reed attempted to make contact with German radicals. After some difficulties, he wangled an interview with Karl Liebknecht, one of the few Socialist delegates in the Reichstag who had voted against war funds in December. The meeting took place in a shabby Social Democratic district headquarters. In a dimly lit room, the Socialist leader showed dark circles of fatigue under the eyes, but his round face was gentle and he emanated a quiet strength. Asked about his hostility toward the war, Liebknecht stated simply: "There is no other attitude for a Social Democrat to take." Full of faith that the "international working class" was, despite temporary capitulation to pressure, opposed to the conflict, he serenely answered a question about world revolution: "To my mind nothing else can come out of the war."[20]

Liebknecht's calm optimism—belied by the current European situation—was nice to observe, but Reed was too depressed for the mood to be contagious. When in early January an officer from the German General Staff led a group of correspondents aboard a train for occupied Belgium, Reed tried to leave worries behind. Some of his companions were old friends like Robert Dunn and Ernest Poole, an aide on the Paterson Pageant, and at first the junket was gay. Treated almost like royalty—in part because United States Senator Albert Beveridge was along—the Americans were met by correct, smartly clad Prussian officers and from Belgium were driven into occupied France. They rode past former battlefields in open vehicles and argued good-naturedly over the prospects of a postwar world. Dunn foresaw a period of puritanism, self-denial, poverty and hard work, but Jack disagreed: "Socialism'll be in. Pie in the sky, champagne in thunder mugs for everyone."[21] Fed in the best restaurants and quartered in luxurious hotels, the reporters were jovial, and a giddy Reed sometimes converted his feelings about war into grotesque humor to entertain the company. Relating tales of sexual exploits, he blew the story of Arthur Lee's anger into a full-fledged drama in which an irate husband bearing a pistol chased him down Paris streets. But humor could turn to anger, and one night Jack became so drunk that he stormed into a wild tantrum of smashing lounge chairs before friends could calm him down.

Reed's contradictory moods in part reflected the confusing nature of conditions in occupied France. Closely watched by polite, sometimes friendly officers, the correspondents were taken from fully equipped army hospitals to reopened French schools, from major cities like Lille to tiny villages, from homey Bierstuben to an ornate palace for a dinner hosted by Crown Prince Rupprecht of Bavaria. Everywhere they saw bombed railroad stations, wrecked bridges, smokeless and shuttered factories, farmlands scarred with abandoned trenches, torn strands of barbed wire and "long, low mounds of earth that sometimes were the storage places of tons of beets, and sometimes graves—you couldn't tell which." There were also signs of both German efficiency and German determination to remain in control of this corner of France. Less than two months after major battles, reconstruction was under way. They saw newly equipped hospitals and electric plants, steel-and-concrete bridges transported from German factories, rebuilt lines of railroad track and torn highways being smoothed flat by steamrollers.[22]

One positive note was that here the French people showed a spirit lacking in Paris. The reporters touring in military cars were often taken for German bigwigs, and "as we rode about the country, misery and hatred darkened every face that watched our passing automobiles; and those who came last caught the curses that were hurled after us, 'Cochons! Boches!' " Delighted to find a streetwalker who was close to starvation because she refused to sleep with Germans, Reed was able to provide her with business that did not interfere with patriotism. Once in a tiny shop a stony-faced woman behind the counter broke into a glorious smile upon learning he was an American: "O monsieur. Tell me truly how goes it in Paris? Are they beaten? Do they think of us down there?" Such reactions provided a lift; it was "marvelous" to see the "faith and hope" of a people who refused to admit defeat despite the legions of foreign troops that ruled them.

More confusing were the Germans, a strange combination of childishness and efficiency, politeness and institutionalized cruelty. In beer halls Reed and Dunn were always warmly hosted by enlisted men, and Prince Rupprecht, after a formal dinner, chatted about his desire to travel in America after the war. Near Verdun they saw the Kaiser's headquarters, guards with flashing breastplates and spike helmets, princes and officers in beautiful uniforms, with swords, monocles and Iron Crosses —"This was a real empire in the Medieval sense. There was such a gallant pageantry in all these royalties, uniforms, decorations." Color and friendliness could not disguise the fact that this was a military machine that functioned "like clockwork," an army in which soldiers were absolutely submissive and obedient to superiors, a conquering host which was systematically exploiting the country because, as one officer explained, "France is rich." The result showed in Lille, where the Germans had confiscated all stores of food, fuel, clothing and precious materials like copper and rubber, and a once-rich population now verged on starvation.

Individual German soldiers showed no animosity toward the French, and officers often displayed generosity by throwing coins from automobiles to women and children in the streets. Sympathetic toward such "poor devils," they never reasoned beyond the concept: "This is war." Similar explanations came from enlisted men and officers, until Reed was tired of hearing the same litany from people whose humanity stopped short of the process of independent thinking. Full-blooded hatred might at least subjectively justify what was being done to France, but, like the Allies, the Germans showed blind obedience to the call of Kaiser and country: "We're in it. We're fighting for the Fatherland. It doesn't make any difference how or why we started. Every man, every mark, every idea is at the service of the Emperor."

Such attitudes fed Jack's anger, but he still hoped the situation might be different at the front. A brief visit to a quiet section of the long trench running from the North Sea to the Swiss border proved unsatisfactory. Expressing annoyance over being kept away from action, Reed and Dunn prevailed on Senator Beveridge to support their demand to observe the fighting. Approval came from the Second Bavarian Army Corps on January 11. After visiting a rest area in Comines, well equipped with showers, beds, beer halls and recreation facilities, the reporters were driven on a gray, cloudy afternoon out to the front just a few miles south of Ypres. Except for ambulances and military trucks, the countryside was deserted, "so thoroughly cleaned of anything but war that a peaceful civilization might never have flourished there." For days the sound of artillery had rolled faintly in the distance, and now, as they crossed land scarred with craters and the ruins of villages, the thunder of huge guns grew louder. A shell tore into a railroad embankment two hundred yards away as they dismounted and nervously waded through a soggy field into the lines.

Soldiers calmly went about their business manning the machines of war. Cigar-smoking artillerymen loaded howitzers in a leisurely manner, sighted and slammed the breech, covered ears while the gun roared, flame and gray haze belched from the muzzle and a shell screamed toward an unseen target. Nearby, a telephone operator in a dugout munched a veal sandwich and read a novel while repeating military reports and gossiping over the instrument. Darkness settled, and officers tried to discourage the Americans from going forward by repeating stories of casualties and deaths sustained in the sector. After wavering for a moment, their curiosity proved stronger than fear. As a black, misty rain began to fall, two soldiers led them up a gentle grade, past stone farm walls and through a shattered village. Conscious of "a droning in many keys, like the wind in telegraph wires," Jack suddenly realized they were under fire. Bullets slammed into a nearby fence, stinging pellets of mud splattered up from the road, and after that "the air was never quiet of whispering and whining and whistling steel."

A Bavarian colonel gave them dinner at his headquarters in an old, solid Flemish farmhouse. Serving as the dining room was a huge kitchen with a stone fireplace, beamed ceiling black with smoke and a jagged shellhole in one wall stuffed with rags. Food was plentiful: thick soup from the field kitchen, canned oxtails, cheese and bread, all complemented by white wine and Munich beer. Sitting in one corner, a soldier at a switchboard repeated messages aloud, but the genial colonel paid little attention and concentrated on entertaining guests with a series of military jokes. Messengers burst into the room with news from the trenches, and as their host kept opening beer bottles, the Americans heard enough reports of destruction in the lines to worry the bravest. When a lieutenant appeared to guide them to the front, only Reed and Dunn threw blanket rolls over shoulders, slipped bottles of liquor into pockets and followed him out into the "pelting, snapping, poisonously singing night."[23]

For the next few hours they experienced warfare in all its dullness, discomfort, boredom and sporadic danger. The rain never ceased, and they wallowed in mud that seemed to be alive, crawling up to their ankles, knees, thighs, waists, covering coats, sleeves and faces until they looked like creatures risen from the earth. For one short period they were dry, in a stone-vaulted wine cellar where they drank beer with a major who had toured the United States as a concert pianist and had a grand piano in the center of his underground headquarters. After that they were surrounded by slime; playing poker and drinking champagne in a tiny underground room where "moisture oozed slowly down the mud walls, and the air was heavy with the smell of the earth and with steam"; slogging along miles of soft, crooked trenches; tripping and pitching to the ground and being pulled along by friendly hands. In the front lines, silent men stood shoulder to shoulder, shielded by thin plates of steel pierced with loopholes for rifles: "Sodden with the drenching rain, their bodies crushing into the oozy mud, they stood thigh-deep in thick brown water and shot eight hours out of the twenty-four." Rockets from both armies soared aloft, lighting the battlefield with an eerie glow, allowing soldiers to fire at the heaped-up dirt parapets a hundred yards away without knowing if they ever hit the enemy. In the ashy light Reed and Dunn took turns peering through slits. Twenty yards away were the bodies of French soldiers who had fallen in the last assault, slowly burying themselves in earth "glistening like the slime of a sea bed."

An artillery duel began—"far away a mighty lightning split the night, and the roaring, accumulated thunder of a bursting big shell smote our ears and sent us reeling." In a quiet moment their guide took a Mauser from a rifleman and, half jokingly, handed it to Jack. Without thinking, Reed took the weapon, pushed it through a slit and pulled the trigger twice. A moment later Dunn did the same. Then artillery burst into action again, the ground shook and the violence of shrapnel drowned the rifle fire. Floundering back to a secondary trench, they took refuge in a small, steamy dugout. After that the night passed slowly, with cigarettes, beer and a strange interlude of listening over a telephone line to the major performing Chopin waltzes in his headquarters. In the pale morning light they walked beside a weary regiment returning to Comines for a three-day rest period. As they quietly crossed the open fields, sunk into their own feelings, a thousand replacement soldiers, washed, dried, fed, rested and singing a spirited military hymn, strode by. Three days from now these fresh troops, tired and caked with mud, would change places once again. It was an endless cycle, symbolizing the hopeless, recurrent muddle of the war.

In Berlin there was time to mull over what he had seen. Now Reed's last hope of finding meaning in the conflict was gone. The danger of the trenches had been enjoyable, the experience sharp and penetrating enough to provide material for his most lively article in five months of the Western Front. Yet excitement alone was not enough. His search was for action that implied values. In serving a smoothly running military machine the Germans were denying their humanity. Friendly as some of the soldiers had been, their camaraderie seemed one of soggy resignation, totally lacking in the fire and enthusiasm of La Tropa. As in France and England, here culture, learning and civilization were taking a back seat to the business of death.

Sobered by such thoughts in the calm of the German capital, Jack became gloomy, his mood deepened by the realization that his own life was in disarray. No longer did he enjoy the comfort of a love relationship. The affair with Freddie left a bitter aftertaste and a vague feeling that its reality had been only an attempt to find some meaning in an empty world. When a belated letter from Hutchins Hapgood tried to comfort him about the split with Mabel, he plunged into a drinking binge and then surfaced to realize that his love for her was far from dead. On January 16 he answered Hapgood: "I am coming home soon. Please don't mention it around, as I want to hide and think and work for a while. . . . I'm still all smashed up, but have recovered the faculty for getting drunk. Liberty's a damn sobering state."[24]

If freedom made Reed sober, so did the war—it was a kind of

sobriety he did not relish. For five months his only escape had been into love and liquor, and now love was absent and confusion a constant state of mind. In Europe his emotional life had been riding a wild roller-coaster where personal, professional and philosophic hopes and fears were completely jumbled. One thing was now clear: there was no more to be learned in the belligerent countries. It was time to go home, pull himself together and see what could be salvaged from the experience.

Basically, Reed believed there was no way in which the war could be justified. If Steffens and Hovey were correct that his political analysis was not good—and Reed suspected they were—there had been one assertion in Stef's November letter of advice that he could not swallow, the belief that distance provided insight and perspective, that "mind-sight" was more valid than experience, that New York was a better place to understand the war than France, Belgium or Germany. Without con-sciously saying so, he distrusted the power of the intellect to explain, understand, categorize, analyze and, ultimately, rationalize, thereby ignor-ing the evidence of the senses. This applied to Liebknecht as well as Steffens. Jack admired the German Socialist but believed his optimism unwarranted by the facts, based on an abstract theory. Negative about this "traders' war" from the outset, he had nonetheless tried to experience it from the participants' points of view. The result was disappointment, for the war contained "none of the spontaneity, none of the idealism of the Mexican revolution. It was a war of the workshops, and the trenches were factories turning out ruin—ruin of the spirit as well as of the body, the real and only death."[25] Steffens and Liebknecht might take comfort in a long view, but they both seemed to be whistling in the dark to keep up their own bravery.

Brooding and glum, drinking and smoking too much, Reed prepared to return to America. He knew that in August 1914 the world had turned a fateful corner and that things would never be the same again. His own sense of self had grown slowly, painfully, in a time of peace, in an atmos-phere of carefree experimentation in social life and the arts, in a time when even the word "revolution" had few ominous overtones of violence. All that was changing. America was still untouched, but enough of Bo-hemia's roots had been violated in Europe to make one fearful of what might happen at home. The world of 1915 was different, certainly worse than before the beginning of the war. The changes deeply affected Reed both personally and professionally, and the Western Front had taught him something about his limitations. Emotionally constricted by lack of sympathy for a cause, he was unable to depict battle as a glorious pageant, to cover death with the romantic glow that had lit his descriptions of Mexico. Moved toward analysis of the war's origins, he had found little audience for his angry, radical viewpoint. If all this meant that there was no more time to savor the fame won in the prewar period, Reed did not lament. Not one to live in the past, he knew life was always ahead, its pathways and opportunities unexpected. He hoped that at home he would be able to learn how his own talents could be useful in the new world of war.

13

New York

Pygmalion, Pygmalion, Pygmalion
A hillside meadow loved Pygmalion. . . .
And when he went away . . .
He left loveliness there;
Longing of the starved heart for a lover gone
When all is as before and yet how empty!
White moved his body, crushing the ferns in the valley,
And his happy singing died along far roads;
But love followed after him—flickered across his sleep,
Breathed pride into his walk, power into his hand,
Sweet restlessness into his quiet thought—
Till he who had needed life now needed more;
And so at last he came to the hills again.

Pygmalion, Pygmalion, Pygmalion—
He said in his pride, "Thou art wild, and without life!"
Never feeling the warm dispersed quiet of earth,
Or the slow stupendous heart-beat that hills have. . . .

He wrenched the shining rock from the meadow's breast,
And out of it shaped the lovely, almost-breathing
Form of his dream of his life of the world's women.
Slim and white was she, whimsical, full of caprice;
Bright sharp in sunlight, languid in shadow of cloud,
Pale in the dawn, and flushed at the end of day.
Staring, he felt of a sudden the quick, fierce urge
Of the will of the grass, and the rock, and the flowering tree;
Knew himself weak and unfulfilled without her—
Knew that he bore his own doom in his breast—
Slave of a stone, unmoving, cold to his touch,
Loving in a stone's way, loving but thrilling never. . . .

Hot moist hands on the glittering flanks, and eager
Hands following the chill hips, the icy breasts—
Lithe, radiant belly to swelling stone—
"Galatea!"—blast of whispering flame his throat—
"Galatea! Galatea!"—his entrails molten fire—
"Galatea! Galatea! Galatea!"—mouth to mouth. . . .

Rock is she still, and her heart is the hill's heart,
Full of all things beside him—full of wind and bees
And the long falling miles and miles of air.
Despair and gnawing are on him, and he knows her
Unattainable who is born of will and hill—
Far-bright as a plunging full-sailed ship that seems
Hull-down to be set immutable in sea. . . .[1]

In the spring of 1915 John Reed slipped into a frame of mind that resulted in a new rendering of an old myth. The turn to poetry was significant. For two years his poetic impulse had been wayward. Enticed away from the internal realm of emotion by people and world events, his creativity had been channeled into articles and deeds. Usually satisfying enough, such forms of expression could not always bear the full burden of feeling. In moments when confusion made reality elusive as a dream, he still needed poetry as an outlet. After 1914 Jack attempted little in this form, but every time he did complete a poem it was—unlike earlier works—one that wrestled with a problem that had penetrated to the marrow of his being.

Reed's relationship with Mabel was troubling him. She was elusive as ever, the continuing proof that love between men and women was always confusing and inscrutable. No Pygmalion creating love from the earth, he did feel strangely empty without her, and this need connected to some mysterious natural force. Her flaunted spirituality and mystical ties to rhythms of life underlying the temporal world had always seemed far-fetched and humorous, the fancies of an imaginative mind. But now Jack was less inclined to scoff, more willing to believe "her heart is the hill's heart" as he found her a "plunging full-sailed ship" on an ocean strangely out of reach.

On his return to America at the end of January, Reed's immediate worry was how to repair the relationship. Having abandoned the idea of hiding and working, he had been overwhelmed by feelings of love on the Atlantic crossing. Realistically, he knew the fling with Freddie stood in their way, as did Steffens' comment in one letter that Mabel desired Jack as a friend with no "sex love" between them. An ideal woman in his mind and heart, she seemed warm, sweet and motherly, a figure who would understand and forgive transgressions. Reed impulsively purchased two gold rings in New York, the prelude to an imagined marriage that would bind them together in stability. Full of plans for buying a piece of land and building a home, he tried to recapture his love.

He found her in a small house in the wooded hills above Croton, a town thirty miles up the Hudson from the city. Having withdrawn from any interest in activism or politics, she had mentally said goodbye to both the real and the symbolic Reed, "to the gay, bombastic, and lovable boy with his shining brow; to the Labor Movement, to Revolution, and to anarchy." She was in a spiritual mood and used Croton as a retreat from the "hot and harmful fevers of the world," attempting to draw life force and solace from the earth and plants and slow-changing seasons. Less annoyed by the affair with Freddie than worried that her own passion might once more make her dependent, Mabel was determined to "go on possessing myself."[2] Seeing Jack was an act of friendship and curiosity, but she had vowed never again to be his lover.

Their day in Croton was strained and lovely, peaceful and confusing. The stark winter hills, wind through naked trees and sheen of pale sunlight on the broad, distant river filled his bloodstream like a drug, making the war a nightmare dimly remembered from another life. Loafing along muddy roads recounting adventures, or sitting close together in the bright cottage, Jack found Mabel friendly but untouchable, while she was once more attracted to him: "Reed's boyish face, all curves and glowing with eagerness, the adorable high lights shining on his temples, his light hazel eyes, his humor, not quite vanished but peeping through . . . seemed . . . very dear and lovable." Flattered by the renewed ardor, she had to remind herself that, for all the "surface excitement," compared to the flow of nature "his outlook seemed thin and meager." With a conscious effort, she turned aside verbal advances and feigned indifference.[3]

Reed attempted to break her shell by awkwardly broaching the subject of marriage and producing the rings. Taking strength from his obvious need, Mabel refused so emphatically that a quarrel developed. While she kept repeating, "It's all finished for us," he hammered questions: "But *why?* What's *happened?* What has come between us?" Jack refused to take seriously the reply that "Nature" was the culprit, and certain she was punishing him for Freddie, he waited through a long dinner, expecting at any moment to seize Mabel and renew their physical love. Only when she pushed him out the door to stumble down Mount Airy Road toward the tiny Croton depot did Jack realize this true-life romance would not conform to the convention of a happy ending.

Lonely, Reed hung around the *Masses* office, the Liberal Club and Village bars. Good as it was to be home, he suffered a sense of dislocation. Prosperous, hurrying America seemed innocent and unreal. War was confined to magazines, newspapers and conversations, but, for all the words, none seemed to connect to his European experiences, and even in discussions with close friends the blood and death seemed remote. He was dismayed to find news of the conflict more often propaganda than fact, with atrocity stories making headlines and a few ominous voices pushing involvement on the side of the Allies. At the same time, the United States was impressively free. The Bohemian "Renaissance" was continuing, with manuscripts pouring into the *Masses* office and its monthly pages still brimming with insouciance. Unable to feel much elation, Jack could understand friends motivated by the knowledge that, despite war, life went on, and agree with the belief that if Europe was intent upon committing suicide, Americans had to keep culture alive.

His uneasiness paled before an apparent direct assault on his life-style and values made by an old friend, Walter Lippmann. One of the editors of the *New Republic*, a journal launched during Reed's absence, Lippmann had in December 1914 published an article there about Jack which was alternately affectionate, wry, insulting, amusing and a little cruel. In one sense, it was an answer to *The Day in Bohemia*, where Lippmann was depicted as brilliant, but dreadfully sober:

> His keen mind leaps like lightning to the True;
> His face is almost placid,— but his eye,—
> There is a vision born to prophecy! . . .
> Our all-unchallenged Chief! But . . . one
> Who builds a world, and leaves out all the fun,— . . .
> Who wants to make the human race, and me,
> March to a geometric Q.E.D.[4]

The response not only confirmed this picture, but implicitly drew a line separating radicals into two distinct groups, serious ones like Lippmann and frivolous ones like Reed.

The burden of "Legendary John Reed" was contained in the title— at twenty-seven Jack was a culture hero. Larger than life, lacking any firm, serious center, he spilled into one fashionable enthusiasm after another, summing up within himself the experiences and shifting interests of a generation. Admiring the triumphs at Harvard, Paterson and in Mexico, his love affairs and penchant for being arrested, the article's picture of his relationship to the *Masses* was humorous, but hardly complimentary:

> For a few weeks Reed tried to take *The Masses* view of life. He assumed all capitalists were fat, bald and unctuous, that reformers were cowardly and scheming, that all newspapers are corrupt. . . . He made an effort to believe that the working class is not composed of miners, plumbers and working men generally, but is a fine, statuesque giant who stands on a high hill facing the sun. . . . He talked with intelligent tolerance about dynamite and thought he saw an intimate connection between the cubists and the I.W.W. He even read a few pages of Bergson.

Such radicalism seems irresponsible, almost juvenile, and this was due to a central trait: "Reed has no detachment, and is proud of it." By throwing himself wholly into whatever caught his fancy, he had become a writer, a poet, a revolutionist and a lover, but no single role could hold him for long. Amusing and lovable as he might be, such a flighty person obviously was a danger to civilization, an "intractable" who would always find the "organized monotony and virtue" of any society "unbearable." This forced a serious social thinker to conclude: "You would have to destroy him to make him fit." Reed seemed an incurable perfectionist, and Lippmann essayed the idea that if one were establishing an ideal world, Jack would have to be the first person hung.[5]

Reed's reaction to his old friend's words was hardly surprising. He knew that his life had been scattered, ideas shifting, enthusiasms many and moods often frivolous. But this was not the whole story of his development. He held certain beliefs that had grown stronger until they were central to his character. The drive for personal freedom, excitement and recognition that had once made him so self-centered had slowly given way to the knowledge that his life was involved with other men, and a vision that his own liberation was connected to the freedom of people who were economically, politically or emotionally constricted by modern institutions. So palpable had this idea become on the Western Front that he had been unable to write well enough to sustain the reputation won in Mexico. A man playing at heroic reporter might easily have dashed off commercial articles, but an honest disgust with the meaninglessness of the conflict had prevented Reed from doing so. Ironically, Lippmann's article had appeared at a moment when Jack's commitment to an unpopular viewpoint was becoming deep.

The chasm between the two men was immense, with implications far beyond a personal quarrel. Different in temperament, Reed and Lippmann had always taken opposite approaches to the world. The key was "detachment." When Walter quite correctly pointed out that Jack was proud of having none, Reed would have agreed, but he would not have accepted the inference that this quality was a virtue. He distrusted "detachment" as much as Lippmann revered it, and these opposing attitudes were taking them on different courses. The intellectual Lippmann, after only a few months of working for the Socialist mayor of Schenectady, had withdrawn from practical action in favor of writing social analyses. Reed, the poet and adventurer, was slowly being pulled from art toward political commitment. Unlike Walter's reasoned actions, his moves never derived from theory, and his beliefs were no neat deduction from a set of principles. Reed's knowledge came from the heart; it was the intuition of a poetic temperament, the emotional insight that might sometimes lead to wayward paths, but ultimately returned to simple, straightforward truths, such as "This is not our war." In any conflict between the intellect and emotions, Reed let his feelings be the guide. Contrasting with the approach of men like Lippmann, he believed truth was something you did not reason your way to, but felt.

Jack was also suspicious of the source of the article. When helping to plan the magazine the year before, Walter had implied that the *New Republic* would be "socialistic" in policy, while the founder and chief editor, Herbert Croly—intellectual architect of Theodore Roosevelt's New Nationalism—continually referred to the publication as "radical." Yet, in practice its creed was a kind of nationalistic Progressivism, emphasizing the ability of intellectuals—such as the editors—to solve social problems. The first issues contained criticism of Woodrow Wilson's New Freedom, tolerance for labor unions and detailed analyses that proved the Socialist Party was no longer revolutionary; but on the question of the war, the magazine waffled. Advocating preparedness in case the country were forced into it, the editors refused to commit themselves on whether the United States should plan on entering or do everything to stay out of the conflict.

Not radical enough in policy, the *New Republic* was also uncongenial to Reed in its tone and underlying assumptions. Aloof, calm and

Olympian, its editors seemed removed from the world of factory and trench, picket line and caucus chamber, about which they wrote with such assurance. Knowing that for Lippmann such a stance was hardly novel, Jack found it positively insulting when it was adopted toward his life, and he was led to conclude that the editors were using intellect to avoid personal commitment. For Reed, radicalism was a matter which engaged the self, the body and the emotions as well as the mind. It was an attitude of feeling, color, pain and laughter more than sober, weighty analysis. By condemning passionate radicalism, Walter was only showing his own bloodlessness, his inability to understand that liberation came from the heart as well as the head.

A similar attitude pervaded the *New Republic*'s relationship to Bohemia. Opening its pages to new movements of expression, the magazine published the work of Amy Lowell, Robert Frost, Conrad Aiken, Van Wyck Brooks, Randolph Bourne and John Dos Passos, while Reed's old friend Lee Simonson defended artistic movements like Cubism and Futurism and ex-Harvard radical H. K. Moderwell praised the dissonant music of Arnold Schoenberg and treated jazz as a serious art form. This admirable policy hardly meant wholehearted endorsement of Bohemia. Cultural articles always appeared on back pages and political ones in front, underscoring an assumption that social concerns were more substantial than artistic ones. If he agreed with this view, Reed certainly objected to the *New Republic*'s editors making such a distinction. Not understanding that one could be a radical and yet full of fun, that life was to enjoy as well as understand, they missed the essence of radicalism, where questions of life-style, economics, art and politics were inextricably intertwined. By placing politics first, the *New Republic* showed itself no different from Progressives who viewed culture as icing on the social cake, and by insisting that social questions were primarily a matter of intellectual investigation the magazine cut itself off from the emotions that drove radical actions. Lippmann might think himself a "responsible" radical and make fun of wild enthusiasms, but in practice he was not radical at all.

At some other time Walter's article might have rolled off Reed's back, but he was depressed by the war and the impasse with Mabel, and his irritation turned to anger that filled a bitter letter. Rather than refuting charges, Jack took the offensive and accused his friend of being a sellout for having affiliated with a publication subsidized by Willard Straight, a banker-diplomat whose business connections included J. P. Morgan, and Kuhn, Loeb and Company. Lippmann replied with a scathing note that questioned Reed's staying power and announced that his own radicalism would be longer-lasting. Tacking the letter to the wall in a kind of showy revenge, Jack pointed it out to everyone as an example of Walter's friendship. A few weeks later they both made conciliatory gestures and reopened communication, but no real warmth ever returned to the relationship.*

Keeping occupied during this period of troubles was not difficult, for Reed was bursting with the desire to write. First he completed two long articles on Germany, then began to translate European experiences into fiction. For the *Metropolitan* he penned a tale about a timid French barber in Lille who slits the throat of his wife's lover—a German officer —in an attempt to start an uprising against the occupying army. Slick and sentimental, the story is saved from complete melodrama only by its ending—the town is living off German money and, gold being stronger than patriotism, the French people will not rise. More serious was "Daughter of the Revolution," a character sketch of a prostitute, obviously based on a real woman encountered by Jack and Fred Boyd one evening on the terrace of a Paris café. Marcelle, whose grandfather, father and brother have all been active leaders in radical labor movements, is both proud and ashamed of this heritage. Scorned by the family for her profession, she is depicted as someone who is also seeking liberty, if only the liberty to turn away from radicalism and indulge a longing for fancy clothes, jewelry, perfume and other luxuries. Like the Marxists in her family, a sober radical might condemn such a desire for possessions, but Reed found it understandable. He was displaying a faith that one person's liberty might be another's slavery and a belief that true liberation must be self-defined.

In mid-February Jack accepted an assignment from Hovey to cover a Philadelphia revival week led by Billy Sunday, the exponent of a two-fisted, hair-on-the-chest, slangy version of the Gospel. With George Bellows, who was to do the illustrations, he poked around the city for a couple of days trying to determine the effect of evangelism on a sophisticated, urban community. He interviewed clergymen, industrialists and labor leaders, and even finagled past a cordon of bodyguards to have a

---

* Evidence for the quarrel comes largely from outside sources, such as Luhan, *Movers and Shakers*, 298. Granville Hicks, in the introduction to *Ten Days That Shook the World* (New York: Signet, 1967), xii, says he has seen the Lippmann letter, now available only to Lippmann's biographer. In the JR Papers there is a note from Lippmann dated only "Sunday," which reads: "Dear Jack. You and I haven't any business quarrelling. You wrote hastily and hurt me. I answered hastily and hurt you. But it's all damn foolishness. Let's have lunch together some day this week. Yours, WL."

few words with the minister in private. Open, friendly and a trifle simple, Sunday impressively dominated audiences of twenty thousand in the wood-and-tarpaper revival hall with "fire and passion and enthusiasm." There might be contradictions between his words and his actions, between condemning luxury and accepting the hospitality of rich Philadelphians, between denouncing liquor and welcoming the endorsement of wealthy brewers, but somehow his faith transcended them. At the end of his sermon when multitudes of "hysterical women, children and men of all conditions and ages" poured to the front of the auditorium and the evangelist leaned down from the pulpit shouting, "Hallelujah," Jack was convinced Sunday was fully sincere.

Honesty was not the real issue. Depicting Sunday as likable enough despite the ballyhoo, Reed strove to place the revival in a social context. Important were the campaign committee members, "a compendium of Philadelphia's rich, respectable and socially great"—of forty-four names, twelve were captains of industry, twelve bankers and four corporation lawyers. One of them, Alba B. Johnson, president of Baldwin Locomotive Works, was a good symbol for all. Head of a company that underpaid employees and blacklisted union members, Johnson explained revivalism as necessary for a "moral awakening" to keep people's minds off material things: "You know the widespread Social Unrest is largely due to the workingman's envy. . . . Billy Sunday makes people look to the salvation of their own souls; and when a man is looking after his own soul's good, he forgets his selfish desire to become rich. Instead of agitating for a raise in wages, he turns and helps some poorer brother who's down and out."[6]

Like religious figures, writers could be used, and developments on the *Metropolitan* forced Reed to wonder about his position. A monthly largely devoted to fiction by such writers as Rudyard Kipling, Joseph Conrad, Arnold Bennett and Booth Tarkington, the magazine had embraced the cause of Socialism in 1912. Articles on political and economic questions by Frederic C. Howe, Bernard Shaw and Steffens began to fill its pages, while Lippmann and Socialist leader Morris Hillquit wrote monthly columns. So well had the radical tenor of Jack's reporting from Mexico and Colorado fitted into the format that he had disregarded suggestions that the magazine was less sincere about Socialism than about using the growing popularity of the movement to boost circulation. Certainly there was room for skepticism about the publication's commitment. Like the *New Republic*, the *Metropolitan* was underwritten by a millionaire, in this case, Harry Payne Whitney, married to a Vanderbilt and connected in business to the Guggenheim family.

By 1915 the magazine was backing away from radicalism. Editorially boasting that, despite its Socialism, advertising revenue was rising, it supported the most reformist elements within the Socialist Party. Happy over Bill Haywood's recall from the SP National Executive Committee, publisher H. J. Whigham wrote: "The Socialist Party of America has finally and definitely cut loose from the advocates of brute force, and has thereby taken its place as a great civilizing and constructive body. . . . Socialism . . . is becoming the main bulwark against war between class and class."[7] Lippmann and Hillquit still had columns, but the former no longer identified with Socialism, and the latter used editorial space to explain why the European Socialist parties which had capitulated to the war spirit had not really forsaken their long-range ideals. As if to counterbalance even this tepid radicalism, the *Metropolitan* in February 1915 added Theodore Roosevelt as a regular contributor.

His father's hero had come to symbolize almost everything John Reed hated. An advocate of preparedness, T.R. called for a large regular army and universal military training. This would not only make the country strong, but also "be of immense benefit to all our young men in civil life" by helping to "increase their efficiency in industry." Such a military force could also be used to police Mexico, another of Roosevelt's pet schemes. Attacking people who opposed intervention, dwelling on murder, rape and insults to the American flag, he chose Jack's hero as the symbol of barbarism: "To defend Villa as representing freedom and justice and democracy in the sense that the words are used in speaking of civilized nations is literally like defending an old-time Apache chief on the same grounds."[8]

Antipathy led to confrontation. Awestruck when first introduced to T.R. in 1911, Jack now relished meeting the ex-President in the *Metropolitan* offices. Because both were pugnacious and argumentative, the two men brought out the belligerent streak in each other. Often the clashes were good-natured enough. Once Roosevelt announced, "Villa is a murderer and a bigamist," leading Reed to retort, "Well, I believe in bigamy." Grabbing his hand, Roosevelt shot back gleefully, "I am glad, John Reed, to find that you believe in something." Knowing T.R. to be socially conventional, Jack enjoyed denouncing a sacred institution such as matrimony or the church and watching the older man turn red in the face and begin to bluster. Sometimes their exchanges turned bitter. Overhearing Roosevelt tell a group how he had ordered a soldier shot in Cuba, Reed broke in, "I always knew you were a murderer," and the result was angry words, rising voices and shaking fists until other editors pulled them apart.[9]

Journalism, like politics, makes strange bedfellows. In the *Masses*

Jack could answer the ex-President's proposal for a huge army by denouncing the "germ of blind obedience" military training instills, affirming that the end of preparedness is always war, and stating flatly: "They are talking now about building up an immense standing army to combat the Japs, or the Germans or the Mexicans. I, for one, refuse to join."[10] If this avoided the question of what his works were doing in the company of T.R.'s, the real answer was practical rather than philosophical. Paying a salary of $500 a month, the *Metropolitan*—however much it might be drifting to the right—gave Reed freedom and edited his writing hardly at all. In an ideal society he might work only for the *Masses*, but this was a world in which that publication could not pay a cent for contributions.

Since Jack was known as a foreign correspondent, Carl Hovey wanted him back in France. This became virtually impossible at the end of February when Robert Dunn, in the New York *Post*, published an account of the night in German trenches. Unlike Reed, who skipped the incident in his own article, Dunn described the way each had taken a rifle in hand: "Be it on our heads, we did it, both fired twice, turn and turn about, wicked, full-fledged franc-tireurs. . . . That Reed should have done so, with his scorn of force and soldiering, is sufficient, if sophistical, an excuse for me."[11] A mild furor followed, with denunciations of this violation of journalistic canons by such people as the president of Princeton, correspondent Richard Harding Davis and the assembled American reporters resident in Paris. After the semi-official *Le Temps* branded the reporters "assassins," the French government formally banned them from the country. Undaunted, Hovey suggested Reed visit French Ambassador Jusserand to straighten the matter out. In Washington the ambassador proved sympathetic and friendly and suggested that a letter from Teddy Roosevelt might soften the French government's attitude. With great reluctance, Reed approached his adversary. Roosevelt dictated the letter in his presence, made the appropriate request and ended with the sentence: "If I were Marshal Joffre and Reed fell into my hands, I should have him court-martialed and shot."[12]

Obviously barred from the Western Front, Jack seized Hovey's suggestion he go to the Balkans. He booked passage for late March, then made a long-delayed trip to Cambridge. For a year Professor Copeland had been urging him to come in letters that betrayed some ambivalence about his protégé. After receiving the first Mexican article, Copey had written, "It is good, and more than good," adding in a P.S., "You are a born writer—I discovered long ago. But I think you don't work hard enough at writing." Later he reacted to the dedication of *Insurgent Mexico* with the comment, "It is much more than I deserve." Asking for

a week's notice of any visit so that "we could meet and talk more satis-
factorily," he showed a fear that after exposure to the world Jack might
find him dull: "But perhaps you don't care whether we have a good
chance or a poor chance to talk."[13] Such worries were groundless, for
Reed still valued Copey's criticism, praise and friendship. He also delivered two lectures in the area. At the Tremont Temple in Boston he
vainly tried to convince an audience that Germans did not commit whole-
sale atrocities and that England was partly culpable in causing the war.
Speaking after a *Lampoon* dinner, he found most students pro-British.
Such attitudes boded ill for his hope that America would keep out of the
war.

Two weeks before he sailed Mabel reentered his life. Suddenly she was
there, professing love and leading him to the cool white bedroom of her
Fifth Avenue apartment. Mysterious as was her change of attitude, Jack
did not pry into its source, for he had dimly expected her return and was
not going to question the magic of emotional alchemy. Filled once more
by love, he could look hopefully at the future, and when Mabel consented
to wear the golden ring, his feelings were expressed in talk about marriage, plans for the home he would build and poetry that spoke of his
need for contact with the life rhythms that flowed through her.

But Reed still did not see Mabel whole and real: "He never reached
the core of me again as he once had." So confused were her own motives
that later she would create an elaborate fiction about the altruism of her
action, based on the idea she did it only to save him from a complete
breakdown.* In truth, despite her claims that "My spirit was safely
anchored deep in the natural universe and did not participate in the surface life of the flesh," Mabel was still a woman who took pleasure in the
body, and Reed had been one of the "movers and shakers" of her sexual
as well as emotional life. No doubt this was mixed with curiosity, nostalgia
and a highly volatile love. Later she admitted, "I liked Reed. I really liked
to see him happy," and happy he was during those last days in New York.
Parting was the sweetest kind of sorrow, and she remembered it as a
"long, passionate, more loving farewell than he had ever expressed when
I had really cared for him."[14]

Jack boarded the ocean liner with illustrator Boardman Robinson,
ignored the crowds on deck and went down to his cabin. Before the tug-
boats nosed the ship away from the dock and into the Hudson, he was

---

* Mabel's claim in her memoirs that Reed was breaking down (or suffering "brain
fever") is farfetched and unsupported by any other evidence. The trips to Philadelphia and Boston, the lectures, letters to friends and all the writing done in this period
(four long articles and two short stories) show a man functioning quite well.

working on "Pygmalion," a poem full of his wonder over the relationship with Mabel. Stuffing it only half completed into an envelope, he gave it to the pilot to mail and then finished a first draft on the uneventful voyage. The ship entered the Mediterranean on April 3 and ran afoul of England, "bully of the sea." At night a small British vessel pulled alongside and demanded to know the name and destination of the liner. Only after a signal from Gibraltar, a bright flash between sea and sky, were they allowed to continue, as "the moon came up over Africa full and round, and we sailed in a glittering sea."[15]

The next day a letter to his mother described Jack's state of mind:

> As I approach Italy, I feel really depressed. I have come to hate Europe. After this trip I want to stay in America about a year, and not have to return to Europe until I take you and Harry over here, after the war. But, of course, it will be different, and better, in the East. The Caucasus is something like Mexico, they say, and I'm sure I'll like the people. It will be great to get on a horse and ride over mountain passes where Genghis Khan invaded Europe. I find that I am a celebrated figure already, as all the people on board have read my WORKS. Am treated with amusing deference by all.[16]

Two months in America had not sweetened the fact of war, but the weeks had given him a sense of perspective, had allowed him to regain a psychological balance badly tilted by exposure to the Western Front. Negative as his feelings might be, the depressing conflict was fact, a basic condition of life tempered by the knowledge that eventually wars do end and modified by a renewed ability to experience the pleasantly warm sensation of fame. In eastern Europe, Reed would once more be a reporter plying his trade. At the same time he could allow his imagination to roam free and entertain the hope that unknown adventures awaited him in the Balkans, where he might recapture the triumphs of Mexico or be engulfed by the romantic spirit of an earlier, more colorful age.

The ability to face reality and simultaneously soar into fantasy indicated a new equilibrium, one which had been tested in the weeks at home. Most serious had been the rift with Mabel, and yet, as he found almost to his surprise, the absence of her love did not cause unbearable pain. Of course, it was good to have her back, and as his poetry showed, he was stronger, more complete, more in touch with the reality of earth and life when connected to her being. And yet he knew now he could live without her. If love could no longer turn him upside down, mundane problems like those with Lippmann, Roosevelt or the *Metropolitan* could be taken in stride. Having matured much in recent years, Jack had come to possess a strong stabilizing mechanism. No matter what shock awaited, no matter what happened in the outside world, he was still John Reed, a man with an admirable talent and a positive self-regard that might be momentarily shaken but could never be wholly taken away. As he had explained to Mabel before departing, somehow he now felt "immune from sin, sickness and death, as though nothing could ever hurt him again."[17]

14

Eastern Europe

Dear Cope:

Circumstances of mailing—convenience, neutrality and so forth, force me always to return to Roumania and the 'Paris of the Balkans,' though I detest the country and the people.

Imagine a small Paris in every essential respect—cafés, kiosks, pissoirs, an Academy occupied with producing a dictionary, Futurist painters and poets who are pederasts . . . politicians who are known by the mistresses they keep, craven newspapers, bawdy weeklies. . . .

Your true Roumanian boasts that there are more cocottes in Bucharest in proportion to the population than in any other two cities of the world. No one does anything but screw, drink and gabble. . . .

Officers in salmon-pink and baby-blue uniforms . . . sit at cafes sipping ices and eating tartlets all day long or drive up and down the Calea Victoriei in cabs, winking at the throngs of women. . . . There is a dinky Hohenzollern king, a dinky throne and court, a dinky aristocracy of fake Byzantine Emperor's spawn. Everybody is crooked. . . . It reeks with

*millionaires, grown rich by hogging the oil wells or by the absentee
ownership of vast lands where the peasants sweat out their lives for a
franc a day....*

*Their politics is as mean as anything about them. They persecute
the Jews with petty police tyranny; they sell the military secrets and the
Cabinet to Germany and the Entente ... and now, they are trying to sell
the lives of the peasant-soldiers to whichever side will pay the most cash
to the capitalist class.*

*If I ever saw a place ripe for revolution, this country is ripe. The
peasants are a very fine and poetic people, but they are cowed.*

I hate old Europe more every day. America's the place.[1]

Four months into the tour of eastern Europe in early August 1915, John
Reed was capable of turning annoyance and discomfort into humor.
Having seen far more atrocities, sickness, suffering and bloodshed than
on the Western Front, having suffered arrest, confinement, physical
pain and exposure to disease, he could still be buoyant and lighthearted.
The difference in tone and attitude from descriptions written in London
is striking; the same war, class-consciousness, exploitation and militarism
elicit a much less negative response. Despicable for aristocratic pretensions, decadence and police tyranny, the eastern countries at least allowed Reed to breathe easier and even enjoy himself. The war was
senseless as ever, but on a more human scale; there were no relentless
military machines, and if politicians sold armies, at least they were full
of good old-fashioned human greed as well as being captives of an abstract
nationalism. In many ways the individual still counted in eastern Europe—
perhaps he could not influence national policy, but at least the general
inefficiency of regimes allowed scope for cleverness and initiative.

Helping to make the trip enjoyable was the company of Boardman
Robinson—always called "Mike"—sent along to illustrate the articles.
Big, burly and bluff, his face dominated by bushy brows and a large red
beard, the fortyish artist was a longtime subscriber to the *Masses* who
shared Jack's radical views, delight in adventure and flexibility. The latter
quality was most necessary, for the journey proved totally different
from the one envisioned. On disembarking in Naples, the two men had
hopes of witnessing decisive events—Italy's entrance into the war, the
last stand of the Serbs, the fall of Constantinople, the march of Russian
armies to Berlin, the splendor of battles between Cossacks and Turks.
Instead, they witnessed virtually no military action, arriving everywhere
during lulls. This strange luck was not entirely bad. Feeling that war
flattened individuals, making men "become alike in the mad democracy

of battle," Reed found that in quiet moments he could learn more about traditions, environment and people.[2]

Disappointed to find Italy calm, the two men sailed from Brindisi for Greece. On the Aegean the spell of history was enveloping—here was the promontory of Sounion with Poseidon's crumbling temple drenched in white sunlight, and there, floating on the sea like blue clouds, were misty islands whose names—Euboea, Delos, Mykonos, Skyros—were redolent of long-vanished civilizations. The ship dropped anchor in the muddy port waters of Salonika, beneath a white city of crenellated walls, huge domes, towers and minarets, and they were surrounded by the sounds of a storybook world—"the cries of Arabian porters, the shouts of the bazaar, strange minor chants of sailors from the coasts of Asia Minor and the Black Sea as they hoisted their lateen sails on ships painted at the bows with eyes, whose shape was older than history; a *muezzin* calling the faithful to prayer; the braying of donkeys; pipes and drums playing squealing dance-music from some latticed house far up in the Turkish quarter. Swarms of rainbow-colored boats manned by swarthy, barefooted pirates jostled each other in a roar of shrill squabbling. . . ."

Ashore, they became "ecstatically interested" in the city, and Reed wrote to Hovey predicting "great stuff ahead."[3] Salonika was the point where East and West met, and its steep, narrow, tortuous streets held colonies of Serbs, Romanians, Turks, Greeks, Bulgars, Arabs and Jews who followed ancient customs and met to haggle noisily over business affairs in countless bazaars and cafés. This was ancient Thessalonika: "Here Alexander launched his fleets. She has been one of the free cities of the Roman Empire; a Byzantine metropolis second only to Constantinople, and the last stronghold of that romantic Latin Kingdom, where the broken wreck of the Crusaders clung desperately to the Levant they had won and lost. Huns and Slavs and Bulgars besieged her; Saracens and Franks stormed that crumbling yellow wall, massacred and looted in those twisting streets; Greeks, Albanians, Romans, Normans, Lombards, Venetians, Phoenicians, and Turks succeeded each other as her rulers, and St. Paul bored her with visits and epistles."[4]

The modern city was touched by war. Technically, Greece was neutral, but this seemed mere pretense. While German, Austrian, English and Turkish spies eavesdropped and plotted, Allied aid for Serbia— French, Russian and English artillery, ammunition and airplanes—openly arrived on freighters and was placed aboard trains which disappeared into the mountains to the north. American and English medical missions passed through on the way to combat epidemics in Serbia, while plague raged unchecked in the lower quarters of the town and pitiful funeral processions limped through the streets. Reed and Robinson drank *mastica* at outdoor cafés and bargained at stalls, wedged among crowds of Greek refugees from the Levant, Russian and Serbian officers in full-dress uniforms, Orthodox priests, veiled women, fishermen out of the *Arabian Nights*, bare-legged Arab porters, shopkeepers in fezzes, ragged newsboys, holy men in green turbans, dancing dervishes in flaring robes, farmers in cream-colored linens, dark women carrying immense jugs. Shouted at in "broad American" by shopkeepers, soldiers and vendors, they were often hosted for drinks by Greeks who had resided in the United States. Proud of their heritage, such men had come to serve the homeland in war, yet all planned to return to America. This attitude seemed very strange— men ready to die for a country but unwilling to live in it—and Jack again had to wonder over the strength of "that fierce irrational feeling called patriotism."[5]

The next stop was Serbia. With three hundred thousand fatalities from smallpox, diphtheria, cholera and typhus, it was nicknamed "The Country of Death." For protection the two Americans rubbed themselves from head to foot with camphorated oil, put kerosene on their hair and filled their pockets with mothballs. Eyes and lungs burning from the vapors, they were put aboard a train by an employee of Standard Oil, who sent them off lugubriously: "Do you want the remains shipped home, or shall we have you buried up there?" Crawling along the Vardar River, the train moved past the fertile tobacco fields and mulberry groves of Macedonia and crossed the frontier. In Serbia the people and land were very different—gaunt men with rifles lounging on station platforms, unkempt homes with crumbling roofs, rotting fields of cornstalks, quarantined villages where trees and buildings were splashed with chloride of lime and almost every door was draped in black.

For three weeks Reed and Robinson toured a land where destruction, disease, famine and death were commonplace and unremarkable. The hill-country wartime capital, Nish, was a city of mud with fetid open sewers and unspeakably filthy hotels and restaurants. Typhus had swept the region, leaving black flags flapping everywhere in the mountain breeze. Visiting a hospital, they found barracks where patients writhed in dirty blankets and the smell of decomposition was nauseating. Later they dined with the chief physician and his staff, filled themselves with local red wine and listened to young doctors first brag of how the Serbians had smashed the Austrian army, then complain that their English and French allies had not done the same to the Germans: "What they need there are a few Serbians to show them how to make war. We Serbians know that all that is needed is the willingness to die—and the war would soon be over. . . !"[6]

The old capital, Belgrade, in the shadow of Austrian guns invisible in the highlands across the Sava and Danube rivers, showed the grim effect of bombardments—huge holes gaped in the middle of downtown streets; roofs of houses cascaded onto sidewalks; sheds, stables, hotels, shops and office buildings were ripped by shrapnel; the royal palace was gutted and the university "a mass of yawning ruins." In muddy trenches along the Sava they talked with Serbian soldiers, men "unshaven, unwashed, clothed in rags," who jeered at the Austrians for not attacking and shouted happily when shots rippled across the water. Riding in a carriage, they turned from the front and went inland along roads that were little more than tracks between silent country villages. Many areas were lovely and fertile—long grass and wild flowers rioting on the hills, meadows bright with larkspur and buttercups, groves heavy and sweet with peach, apple and cherry blossoms, and silver marshes where graceful white storks solemnly fished. Nature's annual rebirth, the teeming forms of life, etched a sharp contrast with the world of men; across the landscape were scattered memorials to the casualties of war, little gravestone crosses of brightly colored stone and white ones painted on the fences of roadside houses.

Machva, the wealthiest area of the country, showed the results of two invasions. Houses were burned and looted, no men were to be seen, grass grew in town streets and the countryside was littered with debris, broken transport wagons, heaps of rusty rifles, parts of uniforms, caps, knapsacks and ammunition belts. In Shabatz, once a rich center, homes were a shambles: "The invaders had taken linen, pictures, children's playthings, furniture—and what was too heavy or cumbersome to move they had wrecked with axes. . . . In private libraries all the books lay scattered in filth on the floor, carefully ripped from their covers."[7] Beginning to hear of atrocities, Reed was at first skeptical. But, unlike the "unsupported rumors" of such events in Belgium and France, here the evidence could be scrutinized with his own eyes. In the prefecture were sworn affidavits from Yvremovatz reporting fifty people burned in a cellar; a photo from Lechnitza showing more than a hundred women and children chained together, heads struck off and lying in a separate heap; eyewitness accounts of forty-two village massacres. In Prnjavor he stood by a long, low pile of dirt while an aged peasant, in a flat voice, explained this was a mass grave for more than one hundred people who had been buried alive.

Such dreadful facts paled beside the single worst sight Jack encountered in the entire war. Led by a genial young captain, he and Mike rode on horseback one morning out of Losnitza and up into mountains where Austrian and Serbian armies had faced each other for fifty-four winter days in trenches twenty yards apart. The trails were steep and rugged, and as the horses labored upward through new spring brush, he enjoyed "the golden silence, heavy with the scent of the plum-trees and with humming bees." Dismounting when the hillside became almost sheer, they led the winded animals over ground strewn with military debris, past scarred trees, until they stood on the bare summit of Goutchevo Mountain. The view was spectacular, forty miles across the shining Drina River to the piled green mountains of Bosnia. But close at hand the scene was "ghastly." Between opposing lines of trenches were huge earth mounds from which protruded parts of ten thousand human beings—skulls with draggled hair, white arm bones with rotting flesh, bloody limbs sticking from worn army boots. Moving forward into a pervasive sick-sweet smell, "We walked on the dead, so thick were they —sometimes our feet sank through into pits of rotting flesh, crunching bones. Little holes opened suddenly, leading deep down and swarming with gray maggots. Most of the bodies were covered only with a film of earth, partly washed away by the rain—many were not buried at all."[8]

The romance of riding on horseback through Balkan mountains was marred by more than sights like Goutchevo. The jarring of rugged trails made Jack begin to feel sore in the lower back. Not one to betray weakness, he kept quiet until pain raced up his side and he was forced into groans. Putting off Robinson's first anxious questions, Reed eventually had to admit the trouble. When the sharpness became too severe, he dismounted and lay by the road until his body relaxed. The pain was only minor when they continued the journey by railroad, but the problem was not yet cured.

Neither illness nor war's most grisly aspects prevented Serbia from being an adventure. A country was people, and the spontaneity and ebullience of the inhabitants were reminiscent of Mexico. This judgment excluded the intellectuals assigned as guides by the government press office, men whose "European smartness, cynicism and modernism" seemed to cut them off from the peasant vitality that gave the country its character. All other Serbians Reed saw as a singing, dancing people who could laugh in the face of disaster. Every army regiment had two or three gypsies who played fiddle or bagpipes. On Sundays peasants all over the country donned colorful costumes and descended on village squares to dance some version of the kolo, a swift, wild step where men flung their legs high and leaped through individual variations as surrounding crowds clapped complex rhythms. Even Nish forgot its troubles in the feast of St. George, when women in bright dresses and men in clean linen romped into the nearby woods to gather flowers, returning to town to dance, sing and feast in the streets until long past dark.

Impressed by such life force, the Americans were won by Serbian hospitality. They were feasted and wined in many homes, and often made to feel like visiting royalty. Aching for tobacco in a remote town, they were assured "cigarettes are worth their weight in gold," then a shopkeeper unlocked a safe, handed each a package and said: "The charge is nothing. You are foreigners." When they entered the ruins of Shabatz, hungry after an exhausting night ride, the proprietress of a café emphatically told the guide there was nothing to eat. After hearing Reed's complaints in a foreign language, she suddenly brought forth some eggs saying they were not for sale: "But since the *gospodine* are strangers, we will *give* you some." The climax of such treatment came at the home of Gaia Matitch, the postmaster of Obrenovatz, who explained: "In Serbia it is the highest honor for a stranger to visit one's house." Here they were waited on hand and foot; children brought plates of apples, preserved plums and candied oranges; local soldiers pulled off their boots and poured water over their hands; and the host himself was ever present with a bottle of *rackia*. Before departing they drank glasses of sour native wine in toast to the host and hostess. Sorry they could not stay more than an afternoon, Matitch jumped up and shouted, "I now make you my *pobratim*—my blood-brother. It is the old Serbian ceremony." Jack glowed with pride: "One by one we linked elbows and drank thus, and then threw our arms about each other's necks and embraced loudly on both cheeks. The company roared and pounded on the table. It was done—and to this day we are *pobratim* with Gaia Matitch."[9]

This scene, like so many in Serbia, was reminiscent of Mexico, but colored by a subtle difference. One conversation with an artillery captain who had been a Socialist leader before the war underlined this. In a field near Obrenovatz, the officer led Jack along a line of trenches. A tall, broad man with a full beard and eyes quiet and direct, in four years of the military he had rarely spoken of politics. So much had the army become life that leaves to visit his family were boring, and it was a relief "when the time comes to return to my friends here, my work—my guns." Socialist beliefs now seemed a strange vision from another life; the idea of a just world an impossible, far-off dream. Only once did the soft voice fill with emotion as he gripped Reed's arm, turned to face him and said fiercely, "*I have lost my faith.*"[10]

Mulling over such experiences in Nish, Jack understood why ultimately Serbia did not feel like Mexico: here a dream of empire ran through the populace, corrupting its spirit. Too many children had been raised by mothers with the challenge "Hail, little avenger of Kossovo!" And though the fourteenth-century defeat had been avenged, the Turks driven out and the land free for almost a century, the desire for a greater

Serbia continued to grow, cutting across the map to include Slavs in Hungary, Croatia, Bosnia, Herzogovina and Montenegro who could be liberated only by force of arms. Much as he liked the Serbians, Reed could only despair that this "imperialistic impulse" would lead the country into "tremendous conflicts." Not against national tradition as such, he had no sympathy for ambitions that led to military ventures and negated hopes for a peaceful international order of men united against forces of social and economic oppression.

Chic and expensive Bucharest might look like the set of a comic opera, but during a stay there in the latter part of May, Jack was generally too sick to enjoy the show or investigate the pleasure of its "extravagant" women. After pain had flared again in Serbia, a doctor had diagnosed the back trouble as due to the lingering effects of syphilis. Protesting he had never been afflicted with the disease, Reed was met with scoffing tones: "Don't be absurd. Everybody's had syphilis," and when he persisted with denials, he was pushed out the door.[11] A Romanian doctor took the recurrent symptoms more seriously and, when X rays revealed gravel in the left kidney, confined him to a hospital. While a liquid diet and rest made the pains gradually subside, Jack worked in bed, completing articles on Greece and Serbia. He made two copies of each and shipped them off to the *Metropolitan* by different routes. Displeased with the first, he rationalized to Hovey, "I cannot write well away from home." Happily, Robinson's sketches were "magnificent," and Reed advised the editor to "cut the text rather than cut his pictures." A few days later he was "feeling lots better," both physically and about his third piece: "This is a damn fine article, one of the best I have ever written, and all new stuff. We are the first to make that trip and the first to see Goutchevo, etc. We've both worked like hell here and done nothing else. Hope you'll be satisfied."[12]

Mobilization and rumors of imminent war had drawn the two Americans to Romania, but after a couple of weeks it became obvious the country was remaining neutral. When news of an immense Russian retreat before an Austrian spring offensive in Galicia filtered into Bucharest, Jack was too itchy to heed the doctor's warning that roughing it might kill him. Undaunted by the Russian ambassador's claim he could issue no passes to visit the front, Reed and Robinson turned to the American legation. A helpful Foreign Service officer provided a letter on official stationery authorizing them to investigate the welfare of various Jewish-American citizens residing in Galicia and Bucovina. Because the accompanying list of names seemed short, Jack added those of several friends, including Walter Lippmann. Half expecting to be turned back, clad in corduroy knicker suits, with puttees and Stetson hats, and carrying only small cases, they took the train to Dorohoi, the northern terminus of the Romanian railway system. While trying to bargain for a coach to the border, they were accosted by the local chief of police, who first informed them the frontier was closed, then offered to help them cross it.

Russia had a special flavor, an indefinable presence that spread at twilight as a flat-bottomed scow carried them across the swollen spring waters of the Prut River. Adrift for a moment, they saw a dark shore rise and the giant figure of a soldier silhouetted against the dim red sky. Images from literature, scraps of conversations, snatches of melody, half-remembered folk tales—the whole Western image of a mysterious, splendid, savage, half-European, half-Oriental civilization flashed through Reed's mind; this was "Holy Russia—sombre, magnificent, immense, incoherent, unknown even to herself." First experiences validated the conceit. As a carriage rattled them through a starless night, a "chorus of deep voices swelled in a stern, slow song" and a meadow bright with campfires appeared. There squatted knots of flat-faced, swarthy men "with Chinese eyes and cheek-bones polished like teak, robed in long caftans and crowned with towering shaggy hats of fur." Turkomans, horseback soldiers from the steppes of Asia, they were remnants of "the boiling geyser that deluged Europe with the great Mongolian invasions. . . . The fathers of these warriors followed Ghenghis Khan and Tamerlane and Attila. Their cousins were Sultans in Constantinople, and sat upon the Dragon Throne in Peking."[13]

Captain Vladimir Madji, commandant of Novo Sielitza, received the two *Amerikantzy* with "gargantuan hospitality." At his combination home and military headquarters they mingled with an exuberant crowd of servants, hefty females and military men, conversing in an awkward mélange of German, French, Russian and English. Staff officers bustled back and forth with bundles of documents, but there seemed little system and not much worry even though the front was only twenty miles away. Talk of the military situation was frank to a point that might be considered treason elsewhere—yes, the army was "falling back like the devil" because of graft, disorganization and lack of supplies, but probably next year it would advance again. Such was the inevitable ebb and flow of war, which would last—said a captain with a grin—"so long as England gives money and the earth gives men." More important than battle was the camaraderie of the dinner table. First came sardines, smoked and raw herrings, caviar, sausage, shirred eggs and pickles, then huge platters of cornmeal polenta, pork and potatoes. All kinds of drinks were served—Cognac, Benedictine, kümmel, raspberry and plum brandies, Bessarabian wines—and liquor and conversation flowed freely until long past midnight, when a weary Reed and Robinson went off to bed leaving a boisterous table and their host murmuring, "To sleep is a ridiculous way to pass the night."[14]

The next afternoon an obliging General Baikov issued a pass for the correspondents to go north. With a dim-witted, grinning peasant driving a rickety wagon, they rolled along the Prut through fertile Bucovina while Russian artillery engaged in a desultory duel with unseen Austrian batteries. Afternoon found them in a battle-seared land where Slavonic crosses gave way to tall Catholic crucifixes, peasants spoke only Polish and soldiers swarmed over the hills, digging gigantic trenches and laying barbed-wire entanglements. At nightfall they reached Zalezchik. This once lovely town on the bank of the Dniester had been captured, burned and looted three times, and its population lived in terror. Amid ruins they found a few residents cringing before Russian soldiers and learned that most of the Jewish population—including the American citizens they sought—had been slaughtered by the Russians. Dining with the local commandant, Jack and Mike were told they could obtain a pass for the front only from General Lichisky, in Tarnopol. The cordial colonel then paid their fare, and put them aboard a third-class coach.

It took fourteen hours to cross forty miles of "the boundless Galician steppe, heavy with golden wheat." Tarnopol was a city of solid old structures whose streets swarmed with soldiers. Regiments tramped along with a heavy, rolling pace, singing chants "simple and tremendous as a Hebrew psalm." Booted, bearded peasants, giants with huge hands and broad chests, they wore brown blouses and had "strong, blank, incurious faces set westward toward unknown battles, for reasons incomprehensible to them."[15] Other soldiers were brightly clad: cavalry men in green trousers wearing broad sabers; Cossacks from the Urals with pointed, turned-up boots, long caftans and tall fur hats; members of unknown service branches with gold shoulder straps and breasts decorated with battle ribbons. Staff headquarters was thrown into confusion by the arrival of the Americans. No correspondent had ever been in the area, and by army edict none was allowed. After being questioned as possible German spies by subalterns, Reed and Robinson found General Lichisky sympathetic but powerless to issue a pass for the front. Generously he offered to let them stay in Tarnopol at army expense, but only Prince Bobrinski, governor-general of Galicia in Lvov, could give them the necessary permission.

Once more the train ambled through miles of wheatfields yellowing toward harvest. Everywhere was evidence of "utter disorganization"— battalions sidetracked without food while farther on in huge, empty dining sheds meals were spoiling, engines whistling impatiently for clear tracks, supply trains rushing in opposite directions, empty boxcars moving while half-armed regiments slouched on platforms awaiting transportation. How different it was from occupied France. There the "faultless German machine" ran like clockwork, while here "One had an impression of vast forces hurled carelessly here and there, of indifference on a grand scale, of gigantic waste."[16] In Lvov, the ancient royal Polish city with gloomy stone palaces, the confusion continued. Fighting through crowds of refugees, crippled soldiers and arguing civilians at the chancellery building, they ran afoul of a bureaucratic hierarchy of clerks who disappeared into offices and neglected to return. Initiative took them past suspicious sentries to the governor's headquarters. Greeted in English by a handsome young man who introduced himself as Prince Peter Troubetskoi, the governor's aide-de-camp, they immediately learned that reporters were not allowed in Lvov. To his question "How on earth did you manage to get here?" Reed produced quantities of passes. The prince sighed: "What's the use of regulations when Americans are about?" Of course, he wanted to help, but it was impossible. He was a civil official, and passes for the front had to come from the military. The best bet was Cholm, where General Ivanov, commander-in-chief of the southwestern front, would surely arrange matters.

Lvov is less than a hundred miles from Cholm, but the vagaries of the Russian railroad system condemned Mike and Jack to a three-hundred-mile, two-day trip through birch and pine forest, past wretched wooden villages and tiny stations where samovars steamed and heavy-faced peasants stared blankly at the world. Forced to change trains in Rovno, they spent several hours wandering through this typical Jewish town of the Pale. The streets were heaped with evil-smelling rubbish, clouds of bloated flies buzzed about, and before reeking, tiny shops stood greasy proprietors, bawling aloud to entice customers. In other Russian towns they had seen ghettos, but nowhere had Jews seemed so stooping and inbred as those confined here by institutionalized anti-Semitism. Faintly bearded boys with unhealthy faces, aged rabbis in long, dark coats, young girls prematurely aged, wrinkled women in slovenly wigs, all regarded visitors with deprecating, hateful stares. In casual conversation Reed had heard many Russians refer to Jews as "traitors," and in Zalezchik and Tarnopol he had gathered evidence of their slaughter by Cossacks. Seeing the conditions created by centuries of exclusion, he understood this lack of patriotism. Persecuted and despised, they had no reason to be loyal to Russia.

Cholm proved to be as jumbled, shabby and dilapidated as all Russian cities. In the dingy "best" hotel in town, the army arrived on the first morning in the shape of an officer with a shaven head who said they had been reported as German spies. At headquarters they produced the pass from Troubetskoi and explained their desire to visit the front. A genial English-speaking member of the staff nodded: "Very good. But we must first telegraph the Grand Duke—a mere formality. . . . We'll have an answer in two or three hours at the most."[17] That evening the bald officer bowed into their room, explained the Grand Duke had not yet answered, collected all their papers and asked them not to leave the hotel. When Cossacks began lounging in the hallways, it became apparent they were under detention. An angry note of protest to General Ivanov brought a colonel who explained that the case was grave: not only was Cholm forbidden to correspondents, but the fact it was Ivanov's headquarters was considered a military secret. Of course, Troubetskoi had sent them there, but his indiscretion did not justify theirs.

For two weeks Reed and Robinson were prisoners in a hotel room that measured four strides by five, under a slanting third-story roof. Large dormer windows opened onto a dirt courtyard and beyond were the patched tin roofs and busy cobbled streets of the ghetto. The June sun was warm. As heat increased, they stripped to undergarments, suffering from the stares of silent crowds that gathered below and the "inconceivable odors" that rose from the Jewish quarter and mingled with the smell of a foul toilet down the hall. With no books to read, they procured a pack of cards and played so much double-dummy bridge that ever after Jack would "shriek at the sight of a card." To pass the hours, Robinson drew designs for Reed's country house and sketched portraits of their guards. Reed wrote verses, planned novels, elaborated impossible plans of escape. Together they made speeches to the townspeople below, flirted with homely women, sang ribald songs, paced back and forth and spent hours composing insulting communications to the Czar, the Duma, the Grand Duke and General Ivanov. Even when the curiosity of the half-savage Cossacks, whose curved, jewel-encrusted, hiltless swords seemed so ominous, turned to a kind of childlike friendship, the dragging hours and days and the heat, stench and boredom made the ordeal "ghastly."[18]

The first day of captivity they were allowed to wire the American ambassador in Petrograd, but after that demands for communication were refused. Despairing that the message had disappeared "into the vast unknown" of the Russian communication system, Reed was surprised when on the eighth day a postman in a gaudy uniform bowed into the room with a telegram from the embassy: "You have been arrested because you entered the war zone without proper authority. The Foreign Office

notifies this embassy that you will be sent to Petrograd."[19] That was all.
For six more days nothing happened. Then, late one night, a lieutenant
came to free them. At headquarters all their papers were returned. Mixing
joviality with anger, Jack took the passport that had provided no protection and scribbled on the outside of it, "I am a German and Austrian spy.
I do it for money."[20] Still wishing to see the front, they learned that only
in Petrograd could permission be granted. When they asked for a pass
to protect them from arrest, the lieutenant said it was unnecessary, nobody
would bother them. Under prodding, he reluctantly made one out. It
came in handy. On the way to the capital they were picked up by military
police more than a dozen times.

In Petrograd, confusion over Reed's and Robinson's presence expanded to include American officialdom. Dressed in the now filthy
corduroy suits and wanting some "real comfort," they took a seven-dollar-
a-day room at the luxurious Astoria Hotel, where American Ambassador
George T. Marye also resided. At lunch, Jack rushed eagerly up to his
table and was greeted frostily. A precise little man with glasses, a white
mustache and a dry voice, Marye proclaimed, "My best advice is for
you to leave Russia immediately by the shortest route," and then poured
out his knowledge of the affair.[21] More than simply upset by reporters
arriving in Cholm, the military had become convinced that the list of Jews
from the Bucharest embassy proved Reed was in contact with subversive,
anti-Russian elements. They had been saved from court-martial and
possible execution only by a series of notes and telegrams between the
Petrograd embassy, the Russian Minister of Foreign Affairs, American
Secretary of State Robert Lansing and Carl Hovey. All this had provided
much work for embassy officials, and had left Reed and Robinson under
a cloud of suspicion. Marye himself, who knew of the German shooting
incident, appeared to believe that in some way or other they had been
up to no good purpose in traveling so close to the lines.

With any hope of reaching the front eliminated, the problem became
one of leaving. But Russia was a country where official approval was
needed for any move, and the American embassy's First Secretary was
nasty, snobbish, insulting and unhelpful. Openly suspicious of their activities, he ordered the two men to stay put in the hotel until the government
expelled them from the country, probably to Stockholm. When Reed
protested that he must go to Bucharest, the secretary waved them away.
Running into a surprised Marye the next day, Jack explained that the
secretary had told them not to leave. Uncertainly, the ambassador replied:
"Ah, did he? But I should like to see you out of the country, Mr. Reed—
your case is a great worry to me!"[22]

This professed concern did not translate itself into concrete action, or help produce a pass to let the two journalists depart. Touchy over the personal affronts, Reed raged about the negligence, cowardice and incompetence of embassy officials. He confronted Marye, demanded action and, when the ambassador wobbled, threatened to write an exposé for the *Metropolitan*. Still nothing happened. Robinson turned his own anger into a cartoon of Marye dressed in a comic half-military, half-diplomatic outfit, pointing to a sign above the embassy reading, "No Americans Need Apply." Having been born in Canada, he went to the British embassy, where a friendly First Secretary assured him the Russian government could not simply expel them to Stockholm. The diplomat offered to represent both men, sent an immediate note to the Foreign Office and promised that Ambassador George Buchanan would take the matter up at the highest level. Pleased to be helped by the firm diplomacy of the "Bully of the Seas," Jack let Marye know he felt "ashamed of my country."*

Two weeks later, after haunting embassies, pestering officials and always "expecting something and never even getting any hope," the two men were thoroughly demoralized. Realizing the stay could be lengthy, they shed the ragged suits, bought new outfits and managed a three-day trip to Moscow, where they savored the "barbaric" flavor of the old imperial center. Back in Petrograd, they moved into the less expensive Hotel d'Angleterre and began to explore the city. Built on a heroic scale, the capital was immense, with "façades of government buildings and barracks marching along as far as the eye can reach, broad streets, and mighty open places." Most impressive were the palaces along the Neva River, with their "fantastic cupolas and pinnacles." On warm summer evenings the streets, cafés, open-air theaters and amusement parks came alive with masses of people in "currents of shouting, laughing, singing humanity." Religion was omnipresent and on a vast scale. Churches were

---

* The phrase is from the draft of an angry note from JR to Marye, July 6, 1915, JR MSS; presumably another version of it was sent to the ambassador. Thoroughly outraged by his treatment at the embassy, Reed did not let the issue drop. Following several confrontations with Marye, he wrote an article entitled "No Americans Need Apply," sent it to the *Metropolitan* from Bucharest and insisted to Hovey in several letters that the piece must be run. On August 3 he told his editor, "It is very important to give him a jolt right away. He and his staff are spreading rotten rumors about me in Russia, and although none of the boys believe them, I want to express a pretty general opinion,—likewise to show the treatment American citizens are getting in some places abroad." The article must have been quite bad-tempered, for not only did the *Metropolitan* refuse to print it, but Reed did not include it in the full-length book *The War in Eastern Europe*, though here he did paint an unflattering portrait of Marye.

crowded day and night, and on a holiday, mobs in procession reverently followed icon-bearing priests. Exalted faces and moving chants showed the strength of a faith which to the common Russian was "a source of spiritual force, both a divine blessing on his undertakings and a mystical communion with God."[23]

Entree into the social side of Petrograd came through Negley Farson, an acquaintance from the Village. Now a representative of several munitions firms, Farson had been in the country almost a year, tangling with venal Russian officialdom. He was a fine storyteller and a well of information about the regime. From his tales, and those of other Western businessmen, the two reporters learned about the immense amount of graft in Russia. Payoffs were necessary to complete the most routine sales, but in some instances corruption reached truly giant proportions—battleships paid for and not built; seventeen million bags of flour, enough to fill thirty-one freight trains, vanished into thin air; contracted French artillery winding up in Brazil; millions of shells too large for Russian guns abandoned at the front and then used by Germany. Named in such stories were leading army officers and the highest nobility. The Czar himself was spared, but the court was known to be a center of intrigue where fortune tellers, quack doctors, the Czarina, the sinister monk Rasputin and reactionary advisers jostled for power and shielded the ruler from the realities of life.

Russian homes were delightful, something like perpetual salons, with relatives, friends and strangers flowing in and out all night long. Always a samovar was boiling, sideboards were heaped with food and liquor bottles while groups gathered to laugh, argue, tell stories and play cards. Conversations dealt with anything. People loved to talk about the state of their souls, or of sex, psychology, mysticism, literature, politics, art and the relationships between them all. Social questions interested Jack most, especially news of strikes and peasant uprisings never mentioned by the press. Talking to some intellectuals who claimed connection to underground parties, Reed found them more interested in words than deeds, in theory than action. After one long evening he told Farson, "It's not the real thing," and explained that a revolution would be led by professional radicals, not *dilettante revolutionnaires.*[24]

Government surveillance plagued the two Americans. Under a kind of "open arrest," they were constantly tailed by secret-service men, Charlie Chaplin types with patent-leather shoes, bowler hats and silver-headed canes. Making life miserable for the detectives became one source of amusement; sometimes they sat in the hotel room and lobbed empty bottles at the small group lingering beneath the window, or took a horse-drawn cab around a corner, leaped out and rushed off in opposite directions. Once they entered a weapons store and loudly asked the prices of machine guns, dynamite and rifles, and another time they managed to get behind a detective and then spent several hours following him. Soon they learned that what was sport for them could be very serious for Russian citizens. The country was ridden with police spies whose work often resulted in radicals, Jews, liberals and other "undesirables" being shipped to Siberia.

Tiring of Petrograd after three weeks, they bribed a police official to write an exit visa, left suddenly one evening, changed cabs several times and boarded a train for Bucharest. The next morning a policeman entered the compartment and calmly took them back to the capital, where a high police official read an order commanding them to leave for Vladivostok within twenty-four hours. There was only one hitch. A railroad schedule showed that no trains left for Vladivostok within that period of time. This meant nothing to the police, who insisted they had to leave anyway. Once more American officials refused to help, but the British ambassador went directly to the Foreign Office and made a protest. Two days later a decree freed them to depart for Romania. Worried that someone might change his mind, they caught the first train south. At the Vilna border station four soldiers searched their baggage inch by inch, ripped open the linings of clothing and wallets and confiscated all notes and sketches. The loss was "a small price to pay for getting free of the clumsy clutches of the Russian Army."[25]

At first it was pleasant enough to join the smart throngs at Bucharest's High-Life Hotel, the Jockey Club, the innumerable cabarets, café gardens and chic restaurants where rouged officers sat with heavily enameled mistresses to watch imitation French musical revues. Soon bored with the scene, Reed and Robinson stayed in their room at the Athénée Palace, working on articles about Russia. When letters brought rumors that America was moving toward involvement in the war, Jack was horrified: "I think I should go wild if we were mixed up in this awful mess. Every time I see a soldier, it seems to me, I feel more and more disgusted and outraged."[26] Fed up with traveling, both men wanted desperately to return home. But Hovey, dissatisfied that the *Metropolitan* had received no firsthand battle reports, kept demanding they continue looking for stories. Prodded and cajoled by his telegrams, they kept on the move from August to October in an attempt to find military action.

The Dardanelles, where the Turks were withstanding a British invasion, seemed a promising area. Because Robinson was barred by his

Canadian passport from making the journey, Reed had to travel alone. In late August he entered Constantinople and immediately succumbed to its spell. The yachts on the Golden Horn; dazzling alabaster mosques with huge domes and spiky minarets; Byzantine palaces; narrow streets jammed with prostitutes, thieves, cutthroats and vendors of obscene postcards; the crowds of veiled women, desert Arabs in turbans, Armenian porters, Muslim merchants and helmeted police; and the lingering ghosts of Mohammed the Conqueror and legendary sultans made the city the most varied, colorful spectacle he had ever seen. After complaining in his last letter from Bucharest of being "terribly sick of it all" and ready to come home immediately, Jack caught fire with the idea of a six-week trip to the Caucasus: "*No one* has been there, and it will be a story of desert and savage fighting that is unequalled in the world. And then what a chance to see the country and the people of the Turkish Empire!"[27] Reed bargained in the Grand Bazaar for amber, interviewed officials and an Ottoman prince, sampled opium and hashish, and wandered endlessly through the jumbled, active streets for two weeks before it became obvious that Turkish officials would not give him permission to visit any military front.

After a reunion in Bucharest, Reed and Robinson entered Bulgaria in September. The contrast with the overly sophisticated Romanians was apparent the moment they crossed the Danube. Border guards had the "simple, flat, frank faces of mountaineers," voices crackled with the "virility of Slavic speech" and it seemed a relief to be once again "in a real man's country." Sofia, the capital, a sober little town of "practical, ugly buildings and clean streets paved with brick," made him feel at home. Except for the occasional view of a mosque or Byzantine ruin, "It might be a bustling new city of the Pacific Northwest."[28] Like Serbia, Bulgaria was a country with few rich men and widely distributed peasant ownership. A major difference was that, untouched by war, the farming areas here were prosperous and content. But the Bulgars, however simple and guileless, were led by politicians who played the game of ambition, personal profit and national aspiration. In the middle of the month the country began to mobilize to join Germany and Austria against Serbia, and because of Mike's passport, the companions had to flee across the border to Nish.

This time Serbia did not welcome them. The first two articles in the *Metropolitan* had been badly received by government officials, and rumor had it that Jack and Mike would be expelled from the country as soon as the expected war with Bulgaria began. Exhausted, they left for Salonika. Six months of experience made Reed see Greece with less sympathetic eyes. No longer was Macedonia an enchanted land. The inhabitants, "stunted, unfriendly . . . without any flavor," seemed a scruffy mob of money-changers and sharp traders. And now corrupt government leaders were using references to Pericles and Alexander the Great to work the populace into an expansionist mood. Finally, in early October, they boarded a ship. The next morning they saw twelve transports full of British troops bound for Salonika, the advance guard of an Allied Expeditionary Force. About the same time Germany, Austria and Bulgaria were in the process of launching a combined offensive that would in two months wipe Serbia off the map.

Eastern Europe remained with Reed for several months as he transmitted his experiences into words. After seven long articles appeared in the *Metropolitan*, he added some extra material to round out a full volume; in April 1916 Scribner's published *The War in Eastern Europe*. Unlike the predecessor on Mexico, with its rearrangement of material for both personal and dramatic effect, the new book was a generally straightforward, chronological account. The amount of artistry used was no different from that in all Reed's reporting. Not "objective" in the normal journalistic sense, he had explained the method one day in Bucharest when Mike, looking over a chapter, complained, "But it didn't happen that way." In reply, Reed seized some of his companion's sketches and announced, "She didn't have a bundle as big as that," and "He didn't have a full beard." Retorting he was not interested in photographic accuracy, Robinson claimed to be giving a feeling, an impression. "Exactly," said Jack, "that is just what I am trying to do."[29]

Despite fine individual sections, the lack of overall dramatic shape makes *The War in Eastern Europe* less interesting than *Insurgent Mexico*. For all the evocative descriptions of lands and people, and the harrowing and humorous adventures of the narrator, it is a work that conforms to the contours of experience rather than art. The explanation for this is simple enough. Reed's time in Mexico had been a period when a sense of manhood emerged, when individual concern fused with a larger, meaningful cause, and when self and cause could be united through the medium of words. In the Balkans there was no such unity—no John Reed aching to test himself against death, no figure like Villa to personify a movement, no people whose viewpoint could be wholly embraced. There was only a good reporter doing a job under difficult conditions, sometimes allowing an active imagination to roam, but usually remaining planted on the stubborn ground of fact.*

* Ironically enough, *The War in Eastern Europe* received better reviews than *Insurgent Mexico*, and then sold much less well. Perhaps by 1916 reviewers were more

If it lacks dramatic impact, *The War in Eastern Europe* fairly crackles with the author's world-view. Peasants and workers are lionized, the overly sophisticated viewed with suspicion, politicians and the wealthy treated with contempt. Sometimes Reed's accuracy of observation conflicted with his preconceptions. Horrified at the "boundless territorial ambitions"—a recurrent phrase—of all the Balkan states, he would have liked to blame them solely on corrupt leaders. Yet honesty compelled him to report similar views often expressed by unlettered peasants. Much as Jack would have liked to wriggle out of this, it was impossible, and the work's pages leave the feeling that imperial ambitions have sunk deep into the hearts of the populace. Certainly this is a main reason that, for all the attraction of Serbs and Bulgars, Reed could never feel at one with them or wholly consider their cause his own.

Everywhere in eastern Europe the contrast between a romantic past and realistic present struck sharply, and all adventures were underscored by death, disease and war. Perhaps as in Mexico, revolution might be a way of turning this reality into something more meaningful, but the hope for upheaval was slender—Turkey was a sodden, dissolving empire; Romania was ripe, but the peasantry was beaten down; Greece was a country where sentimental patriotism overrode desire for change; Serbia and Bulgaria were egalitarian, but interested in expansion rather than reform. Only one country was exceptional—Russia, which managed to brew past, present and possible future in a vast cauldron bubbling with excitement. After suffering the idiocies of the military system and imprisonment in Cholm and while still being harassed in Petrograd, he could write, "Russia is all it is cracked up to be . . . an amazing and most interesting land."[30] Months later he attempted to encompass both the country and people:

"Russians seem to have a Greek feeling for the land, for the wide flat plains, the deep forests, the mighty rivers, the tremendous arch of

---

used to reading of atrocities, while the audience was more interested in the major struggle—from the United States point of view—on the Western Front. Or perhaps, since there was no focus on a radical figure like Villa, reviewers were not put off. The *Literary Digest*, LIII (September 23, 1916), 751, reported, "It may justly be said of this volume that no more admirable presentation in word and picture of one of the most terrible phases of the war has yet been attempted. It is history of grandiose and unprecedented character, actually caught upon the wing." The *Independent*, LXXXVI (June 5, 1916), 401, remarked, "It would be impossible in less than a chapter to do justice to the wealth of material gathered by John Reed. . . . The author presents a succession of swiftly-moving pictures, from which strong character sketches of all manner of strange people hang in the reader's mind."

sky . . . the churches incrusted with gold and jewels . . . for the cruel hardness of the northern winter, for the fierce love and the wild gayety, and the dreadful gloom, and the myths and legends which are Russia. . . .

"This vast chaotic agglomeration of barbarian races, brutalized and tyrannized over for centuries, with only the barest means of intercommunication, without consciousness of any one ideal, has developed a profound national unity of feeling and thought and an original civilization that spreads by its own power. Loose and easy and strong, it invades the life of the far-flung savage tribes of Asia; it crosses the frontiers into Rumania, Galicia, East Prussia—in spite of organized efforts to stop it. . . . It takes hold of the minds of men because it is the most comfortable, the most liberal way of life. Russian ideas are the most exhilarating, Russian thought the freest, Russian art the most exuberant; Russian food and drink are to me the best, and the Russians themselves are, perhaps, the most interesting human beings that exist.

"They have a sense of space and time which fits them. In America we are the possessors of a great empire—but we live as if this were a crowded island like England. . . . Our streets are narrow and our cities congested. We live in houses crushed up against one another, or in apartments, layer on layer; each family a little shut-in cell, self-centered and narrowly private. Russia is also a great empire; but there the people live as if they knew it were one. In Petrograd some streets are a quarter-mile broad and there are squares three-quarters of a mile across, and buildings whose façades run on uninterrupted for half a mile. Houses are always open; people are always visiting each other at all hours of the day and night. Food and tea and conversation flow interminably; every one acts just as he feels like acting, and says just what he wants to. There are no particular times for getting up or going to bed or eating dinner, and there is no conventional way of murdering a man, or of making love. To most people a Dostoevsky novel reads like the chronicle of an insane asylum; but that, I think, is because the Russians are not restrained by the traditions and conventions that rule the social conduct of the rest of the world."[31]

This description—one of many such—shows the extent to which John Reed was captivated by Russia, how much it fulfilled his image of what a great society should be: vast, primitive, powerful, variegated, exuberant, romantic, colorful and free; a kind of Greenwich Village spread across the face of a continent with a solid peasantry to give it flavor, a place where men could love, play, drink, talk and live outside all conventions that hampered self-expression and liberation. Of course, he well knew and explicitly described the elements working against this—

the police and military tyranny, the injustice, corruption and gross inefficiency of the Czarist regime, the anti-Semitism expressed even by liberal elements. Yet that could be changed, and he reported much about labor troubles, clandestine political movements and peasant uprisings. These, he hoped, showed hidden "mighty currents" of Russian life that might well alter its future. Unwilling to make any firm predictions, he left hanging a most important question: "Is there a powerful and destructive fire working in the bowels of Russia?"[32] Only time could provide an answer, but if such a conflagration were to break into the open, John Reed was already primed to help fan the flames.

15

Provincetown

Death comes like this, I know—
Snow-soft and gently cold;
Impalpable battalions of thin mist,
Light-quenching and sound-smothering and slow.

Slack as a wind-spilled sail
The spent world flaps in space—
Day's but a grayer night, and the old sun
Up the blind sky goes heavily and pale.

Out of all circumstance
I drift or seem to drift
In a vague vapor-world that clings and veils
Great trees arow like kneeling elephants.

How vast your voice is grown
That was so silver-soft;

Dim dies the candle-glory of your face—
Though we go hand in hand, I am alone.

Now love and all the warm
Pageant of livingness
Trouble my quiet like forgotten dreams
Of ancient thunder on the hills of storm.

Aforetime I have kissed
The feet of many gods;
But in this empty place there is no god
Save only I, a naked egotist.

How loud, how terribly
Aflame are lights and sounds!
And yet I know beyond the fog is naught
But lonely bells across gray wastes of sea . . .[1]

Never a man to worry much over mortality, John Reed in the summer of 1916 faced the idea long enough to compose this restrained, simple work of acceptance. Despite the subject, it was not a gloomy period. War was far from mind, obliterated by his passion for a new woman and by the activity of friends joining together into an artistic community amid the sea and sun of Cape Cod. An omen of death in such circumstances arose only because sweet days revealed the fullness of life that a happy man might lose. The poem mirrors something of Reed's self-concern in the year following the return from eastern Europe.

Exhausted from traveling, weakened by the recurrent kidney ailment, weary of patriotism and war and sick of world problems, he began tentatively to settle down in 1916. When inner voices said he was lonely, tired, in need of help, companionship or love, he was more likely to listen and less ready to dash off. As a journalist he had to travel anyway, and staying on top of issues was a matter of professional responsibility. This meant no sharp break in his pattern of behavior. Calls from friends or conscience could elicit stands on public questions, but the center of his life shifted imperceptibly toward the personal. For the first time Jack began to husband his resources, portion out energy and save strength to deal with private affairs.

The first problem involved Mabel. On leaving America, Reed had advised Hovey to forward all his letters to her, and often on the road he had taken time to scribble notes or cards. When no replies were forthcoming, he began to suspect what a letter from Hutchins Hapgood confirmed—Mabel had changed her mind again. It was July in Bucharest when a golden ring fell out of the envelope and he read Hutch's report that her "old feeling is dead." She was willing to accept Jack as "a very near friend," but feared that a relationship without sex would be impossible for someone of his temperament, and did not want him to return demanding "what she cannot give." Warning Reed it was no use to expect "that old feeling, that eternal illusion," Hapgood tried to soften the blow by making it impersonal: "If I know her at all, I know she cannot repeat an experience, a feeling, that is gone."[2]

Half expected, the news was more than a little upsetting. From five thousand miles away Mabel was less a flesh-and-blood woman than a symbol of home, comfort, security and love. In ten months they had spent only a few days together, and it was already a year since that summer when love, work and self had rolled into a moment of immortality. Not fully understanding his own feelings, Jack impatiently threw the ring into a canal, and then wrote an ambivalent answer. While he asked Hutch to find and destroy his collection of letters from Mabel, he also claimed to be ready for the kind of friendship now offered. Three months later this willingness had vanished, and he went to her directly.

Mabel was more than ready for him, her defenses shored by a new relationship with painter Maurice Sterne, whose rich, exotic, Jewish-European background made Reed seem plain as "bread and butter." When Jack arrived she retreated behind his words: "You have always said we must be free and lead our own lives. I don't see why we can't be friends."[3] Now living at Finney Farm, a large Croton estate, she offered him the third floor as a writing studio. He settled into a room overlooking orchards and hillsides warm with the colors of autumn, only to find Sterne living in a small cottage behind the main house. More than simply awkward, the situation was impossible. Mabel answered Jack's words of love with practical suggestions—he needed a place to work, she liked having him around and, no matter where he was, her relationship to Sterne would be the same. Such a matter-of-fact attitude made him realize at last that she no longer loved him, and he was able to leave. For many months the affair had been more nostalgia than reality, and the final break was so long overdue that it left few scars. A permanent part of him, Mabel would remain more as a sweet memory than a matter of regret.

Back in Manhattan, Reed had to deal with another kind of emotional tie, in this case familial. Ever since landing he had been deluged with letters of distress from Portland. Margaret mixed motherly advice with complaints about ailments and kept asking him to visit, while brother Harry was full of gloomy news about finances. Mailing ahead several hundred dollars of *Metropolitan* earnings, Reed took a train West at the beginning of December. Immediately he questioned the wisdom of the impulse, writing to Robinson's wife, Sally, "I have been here one day. It is awful beyond words. Mother is so kind, so loving, so absolutely hopeless in her point of view. It seems to me very wrong to have to undergo another long period of suspended animation after the seven months' one I've just gone through. I wish I were home!"[4]

A few days later his mind changed so rapidly and drastically that he dashed off his breathless note of explanation: "This is to say, chiefly, that I have fallen in love again, and that I think I've found her at last. No surety about it, of course. She doesn't want it. She's two years younger than I, wild and brave and straight, and graceful and lovely to look at. A lover of all adventure of spirit and mind, a realist with the most silver scorn of changelessness and fixity. Refuses to be bound, or to bound . . . has done advertising, made a success, quit it at the top of the wave; worked on a daily newspaper for five years, made a great success, and quit it because she outgrew it and wanted better. And in this spiritual vacuum, this unfertilized soil, she has grown (how, I can't imagine) into an artist, a rampant, joyous individualist, a poet and a revolutionary."[5]

Her name was Louise Bryant, and she was quite a few of the things Jack believed her to be. Physically, her charms were most evident—a slender body, dark hair, sparkling gray-green eyes, a facial expression alternately pert, questioning and devilish. Four years older than she told Reed and something less of a success than she admitted, Louise was flamboyant, reckless and wild, such behavior serving to mask her steely determination to make a name. As with Jack, the scorn of fixity had another side, a striking inability to remain quiet, and the refusal to be tied down was another way of saying that she had a great deal of trouble remaining faithful. So much like his own were her responses and dreams that loving Louise was like loving himself, wrapped up in a female form.

Because of an unwillingness to talk of it, Louise's background was always something of a mystery. Evidently her childhood was painful, for alternately she shunned all mention of parents or elaborated fantasies about ancestors touched with noble blood or great wealth. Some things are known—she was born in San Francisco in 1885, shortly before the death of her father, the journalist Hugh Mohan. After her mother married Sheridan Bryant, a railroad conductor, she spent her girlhood years in Wadsworth, Nevada. Escaping first by attending the state university at Reno, Louise then enrolled at the University of Oregon. On the Eugene campus an independent streak began to show—one of the first girls to wear lipstick openly, she acted in campus plays, took the lead in women's-suffrage demonstrations and made little attempt to conceal an affair with the scion of a prominent local family. After graduation and a brief stint as a schoolteacher, she went off to Portland to crash the newspaper game. Coveting a position on a daily such as the *Oregonian*, Louise had to settle for becoming social editor and fashion illustrator of the weekly *Spectator*, a journal devoted to the activities and interests of the city's elite. Financial security came shortly after her arrival in late 1909 when she eloped with Paul A. Trullinger, a handsome dentist and member of a wealthy pioneer family.

Louise was not one to settle quietly into marriage. Despite the lovely house her husband built in a smart, new section along the Willamette River, she maintained a separate studio in downtown Portland and continued to list herself in the city directory as an editor and artist. Trullinger was a liberal by local standards, but his cultural connections were too tepid to satisfy his wife, who began to search for excitement. The spirit of unrest, experimentation and innovation that gave birth to the new Greenwich Village had stirred urban areas all across the nation, and Louise soon found a circle of young people interested in both art and radicalism. After 1912 the *Masses*—which carried the satirical dialogues of the Bohemians' local dean, C. E. S. Wood—became their favorite magazine. Anxious to see her own writing there, but not yet accomplished enough, Louise sold so many subscriptions that Max Eastman in New York began to know her name. By 1915 her own poetry and sketches were going to the *Blast*, a San Francisco anarchist weekly edited by Alexander Berkman.

Long before they met, Louise was familiar enough with Reed's reputation to weave fantasies about this local rebel whose stage was the world. He seemed a heroic figure whose life bristled with excitement, a man "who wouldn't care what hour you went to bed or what hour you got up."[6] Learning he was due to pay a visit, she prevailed upon artist Carl Walters to introduce them, but Jack and Louise met by chance in a rainy Portland street on the very day of the scheduled introduction dinner. Big, brash and outgoing, his conversation redolent of far-off wars and avant-garde movements, he instantly fulfilled her version of the prince on horseback, only this hero was both friendly and accessible. Suffering from a bad cold, he allowed himself to be dragged off to Louise's studio for hot milk and honey and a look at her poetry. When they arrived at the Walters' together that night, it seemed to the artist and his wife that they were already in love.

John Reed, age 3.

Charles Jerome Reed.

Reed, age
approximately 18.

Strikers in
Paterson, New Jersey,
spring 1913.

Reed, around 1912, age 25.

Above left, Pancho Villa, early 1914.

Below left, Villa's irregulars, spring 1914.

Above, Villa's troops advance on Torreón, 1914.

Reed as a correspondent
during World War I, 1915.

Louise Bryant, Provincetown, 1916.

John Reed and Louise Bryant, Croton.

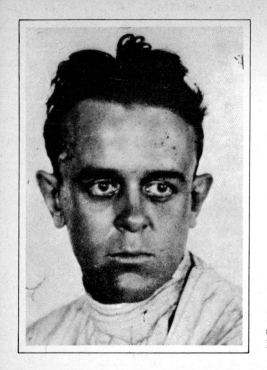

Reed's Finnish jail photo, 1920.

Reed's body lying in state
at the Labor Temple, Moscow, 1920.
Louise Bryant standing by coffin.

Loving rapidly was almost a pastime, yet in no other quick passion did Reed continue for years to maintain his original judgment: "I think she's the first person I ever loved without mental reservations,—without private criticisms I didn't dare voice. Such a vivid personality that I don't feel as if anything at all ought to be changed."[7] Ever after he would insist it was her unique qualities which captured him, but hints of a deep vulnerability emerged in the long, intimate hours in her studio. Needing to open himself and finding he could talk to Louise as to no woman before, Jack confessed weaknesses usually concealed. The portrait was not one the world knew. Lonesome for a long time, he felt weak, at the limit of "fighting strength," full of worry that another "combat" might somehow destroy him. All this was difficult for Louise to believe. Blinded by the image, she could not take such words seriously: "Wonderful man —I know there isn't another soul anywhere so free and so exquisite and so strong!"[8]

Two bright weeks together and he was on a train East. Letters followed, aching with her desire, full of vivid references to their love-making. Then, having told her husband and scandalized Portland, Louise was suddenly in New York, sharing 43 Washington Square South, a roomy apartment much like the site of *The Day in Bohemia*. She was a game partner for simple joys, walking through the different worlds of Manhattan, the Bowery, the Lower East Side, Chinatown and Yorkville, or riding the ferry to Staten Island. Through her eyes New York was renewed for him as they dined at the Brevoort or Polly's, danced at the Liberal Club, tipped steins at the Working Girls Home or the Golden Swan, argued politics and poetry with Eastman and Dell at the *Masses* office, or adjourned to Greenwich Avenue for a game of baseball in the street. Everywhere Louise's beauty, freshness and bravado made a hit, and Villagers found her a fitting companion for their Golden Boy. Only a few close friends were unimpressed. Some, like the Robinsons, thought her basically shallow and worried that she was a climber, willing to use Reed to advance her own career.

Early in February Jack had to go to Florida to interview William Jennings Bryan for *Collier's*. On the Palm Beach Limited he fell lonesome: "My little lover I become more gloomy and mournful to think I'm not going to sleep all over you in our scandalous and sinful voluptuous bed." Homesickness in letters alternated with complaints about Jim Crow cars and the cruelty of Southerners who threw "pennies and dimes and quarters to be scrambled for by the niggers, whenever we stop at a station. Lord how the white folks scream with laughter to see the coons fight each other. . . ."[9] Bryan was the same hefty, cordial, smiling figure

Reed had talked with in June 1914, right down to the statesman's cutaway. Six months earlier he had resigned as Secretary of State in a disagreement with President Wilson over the wording of notes to Germany
following the sinking of the *Lusitania*, and since then he had been on tour
lecturing against military preparedness. Reed could only approach his
folksy, religious style satirically, and the resulting article was a portrait
of a kindly but fatuous man, rooted in the farm-belt past, ignorant of
modern thought. Only as an afterthought did it concede, "Whatever else
is said, Bryan has always been on the side of democracy."[10]

Back in New York, issues had a way of impinging on private life.
The Village was being roiled by the kind of question that Bryan's old-
fashioned "democracy" could not comprehend—birth control. Perhaps
no issue was more divisive, more indicative of the split between Progressives and young radicals. Rooted in the old morality, their eyes focused
on national strength, Progressives—especially of the T.R. variety—
favored large families. For Villagers the issue was both personal and
social: here was a simple method of aiding poor workers burdened by
immense families. Currently Margaret Sanger was on trial for having
sent "lewd, lascivious and obscene matter"—information about birth
control—through the mails. A former Socialist who had subsumed all
social problems in that of family limitation, Margaret had been a friend
of Reed's since helping with the Paterson Pageant. Returning the favor,
Reed attended a fund-raising dinner at the Brevoort and wrote a vigorous
defense of her actions. The whole problem was one of class—rich
women already knew how to prevent conception, while the poor were
forced by moral and religious sanctions to keep on bearing children "so
that there may be a great hungry flood of unemployed to regulate the
labor market . . . [and] soldiers to fill the armies of the world."[11] By the
time Sanger was freed, Emma Goldman was facing trial for delivering a
lecture on the same subject. Again Reed wrote a protest and attended
support meetings, but Goldman went to jail for fifteen days.

From the national point of view, a more momentous issue arose in
March, when Pancho Villa's actions led to intervention in Mexico. Part
of the victorious coalition that had ousted Huerta in August 1914, the
ex-bandit had quarreled with Carranza, and following several military
defeats he was once more confined to Chihuahua in surly opposition.
After President Wilson gave Carranza de-facto recognition in October
1915 and embargoed arms to Villa, the angry general was moved to
revenge. On January 10, 1916, his men captured and killed seventeen
American engineers en route to reopening a mine in Chihuahua. The
uproar in the press was still in progress when, on March 9, four hundred

of Villa's raiders rode into the border town of Columbus, New Mexico, in broad daylight with guns blazing, leaving fifteen Americans dead. There could be only one result in an election year—Wilson would have to dispatch troops to capture Pancho Villa.

Reed's reputation as a journalist stemmed from the Mexican revolution, and his opinion on the subject was valued. Loyal to Villa, he saw no proof of the general's complicity in either the massacre or the raid, and was certain that both "hideous crimes" were due to "American interests in favor of Intervention."[12]* In interviews and articles Jack stressed that there was no cause for intervention, and he couched the argument in practical terms in the pages of the New York *American*. Contrary to popular belief, Mexicans were not lazy, comic figures but tough troops seasoned by years of warfare who were full of hatred for *gringos* because of exploitation by American companies. An arid land with extremes of climate and topography, northern Mexico favored native defenders: "For infantry harried by guerilla bands, hampered by insufficient railroad transportation, little water and no food in the country, I should think it would be an almost impossible task to find Francisco Villa."[13]

No arguments could stem the anger sweeping through press and Congress, and on March 16 six thousand troops led by General Pershing crossed the border. Much to Reed's delight, Villa proved elusive. On April 12 at Parral, 180 miles south of the Rio Grande, a group of civilian Villistas fired on a detachment of troops, and in the ensuing melee forty Mexicans and two Americans were killed. Jingoists on both sides clamored for full-scale war, but Jack urged a withdrawal rather than an advance. To friends he confided a willingness to join former comrades against the U.S. Army, but this was little more than idle talk born of the impotence of standing in opposition to outraged patriotism.

Mexico was a menace, but one that paled beside the potential danger of the United States becoming embroiled in Europe. That spring the war was everywhere. Like an ominous presence, it penetrated the Harvard Club as Reed described Balkan adventures to old grads, cut through the stone walls of Sing Sing, where he entertained inmates with humorous references to his own jail experiences, and hovered in the blue cigar

---

* The view that American big business was somehow connected to Villa's incursion into the U.S. was common in radical circles. The whole problem of the motives for Villa's antics in 1916 is complicated, and various theories have been advanced. One popular idea was that the general wished to bring on American intervention and then regain his power and popularity by opposing it. For a discussion of Villa's possible motives, see Clarence C. Clendenen, *The United States and Pancho Villa* (Port Washington, N.Y.: Kennikat Press, 1961), 240–6.

smoke of Madison Square Garden while he and George Bellows watched heavyweights Jess Willard and Frank Moran pummel each other for ten dull rounds. In December Reed had written an article for the New York *World* predicting that a stalemate on all fronts would lead to peace in 1916. The same month, after asking Congress to enact a huge program of national defense, the President had led a huge preparedness parade down Pennsylvania Avenue. Similar rallies were staged in other major cities, and the voices of military-minded leaders like Theodore Roosevelt and General Leonard Wood grew more strident in demands for a larger army. If pacifists, isolationists, radicals and pro-Germans stood against this mood, and if "I Didn't Raise My Boy to Be a Soldier" could become a hit song, there was little call for complacency. European experience had taught how quickly voices of opposition could change to cheers of support for columns of marching, uniformed men.

Frequently sought as a lecturer, Reed began to use the podium for denunciations of preparedness to such groups as the Columbia University Social Study Club, the Labor Forum and the Intercollegiate Socialist Society. For the *Masses*' "Preparedness Number," he wrote the lead article, a piece that began with ironic humor: "One safe rule to follow is, that nowadays when you hear people talking about 'patriotism,' keep your hand on your watch." This led to the central argument that certain interests were trying to frighten the country into "an heroic mood." The culprits were Roosevelt, with his Prussian ideas of national power, various military leaders, and, above all, the presidents of big corporations that stood to benefit from war orders. Quoting Congressional reports, Reed showed how the National Security League, the Navy League and other preparedness organizations were dominated by owners of the large steel, copper, nickel, shipbuilding, armor-plating and munitions companies, which in turn interlocked with Wall Street banking and investment concerns. Naming men like Hudson Maxim, J. P. Morgan, Jr., Henry C. Frick, T. Coleman du Pont, Elbert H. Garry, Frank A. Vanderlip and Jacob H. Schiff, he even included *Metropolitan* owner Harry P. Whitney. Beyond war contracts, such men foresaw a potential American empire, born of the surplus wealth squeezed from underpaid labor at home. From this the workingman had to learn a major lesson: "He will do well to realize that his enemy is not Germany, nor Japan; his enemy is that 2% of the United States who own 60% of the national wealth, that band of unscrupulous 'patriots' who have already robbed him of all he had, and are now planning to make a soldier out of him to defend their loot. We advocate that the workingman prepare to defend himself against that enemy. This is our Preparedness."[14]

Although he contributed occasional stories to the magazine, Reed no longer played a very active role on the *Masses*. He was rarely present at editorial conferences, and he even neglected to attend a series of crucial policy meetings in March and April that showed how war pressure was beginning to affect Bohemia. Open to all forms of radicalism, the magazine was split between editors who emphasized art and Bohemianism and those for whom Socialism took precedence. In response to the growing seriousness of the times, Max Eastman had begun to tack captions onto drawings to underline their social content. Annoyed by this, a group of protesting artists led by John Sloan started a movement to fire the editor for his "dictatorship" and attempts to enforce a "policy" on a publication committed to freedom. For the showdown, Reed, who was practical enough to know the *Masses* could not survive without Eastman's talents as a fund-raiser, gave his proxy to Floyd Dell to vote for Max. When Eastman won the test vote, several dissenting artists resigned from the publication.

His failure to attend the decisive meeting was one indication that in the spring of 1916 Reed was most concerned about personal matters. Confronting him were the difficult, interwoven problems of money, family, writing and health. Because of Harry's difficulties managing family affairs, which now included the need to support their mother and grandmother plus occasional aid for Uncle Ray, Jack toyed with the idea of bringing Margaret East. Learning the relationship with Louise was offensive to her, he abandoned this solution, but continued to send several hundred dollars to Portland every couple of months. The need for money meant commercial writing, the necessity of accepting assignments from *Collier's* or the *Metropolitan* just when recurrent and painful kidney attacks left him with less strength than ever before.* Weary of insoluble national problems, Reed was beginning to long for space and time to create only for himself.

By now there was no question that he was a first-rate correspondent. What other kind of artist he was, how much of a short-story writer or novelist, remained open, and at the age of twenty-eight there was growing pressure to find out. The experience in Russia had led Jack to read heavily among that country's classic novelists—Turgenev, Tolstoy and Dostoevsky. He had also secured an English copy of D. H. Lawrence's *The Rainbow* from Ben Huebsch, who wanted to publish it in America.

---

* Publication of *The War in Eastern Europe* in April 1916 did not help to ease financial pressure. A letter from Scribner's on September 11, 1916, informed Reed that only about 1000 had been sold in the U.S. and 500 abroad, and blamed Mexico and the election for the fact that war books in general were not selling.

This novel convinced him that, for all the cultural differences, English literature could be similarly profound: "This book is the life of our race, made beautiful yet true. It is the only book I know that dares to face the truth that human relationships have no God, that passion is human, not divine, or that divinity itself is a matter of the human soul."[15] Reed enthusiastically recommended publication, but knew his own fiction fell far short of such standards. Between the *Masses*, the *Metropolitan* and the *New Republic* he had published five stories since November; all were realistic slices of life, views from the outside that hardly differed from journalism, and none was an advance on work done before. Somehow certain emotions and states of being always eluded his imagination and prose. As in poetry, lack of technical proficiency fused with deficiency of insight to limit Reed's depiction of the human condition.

There was only one way to test his ability to grow as an artist—take time to really work at it. Bobby Rogers, whose own self-doubts on the same score were a constant plague while he taught English at MIT, had a knack of phrasing Jack's inner questions. Several times in early 1916 he urged a major work:

> We all know what you can do in the way of reporting. The Lord knows you can do it. . . . Why don't you . . . sweat out a novel or a whole of a long poem (even unpublishable) and give us a synthesis. Syntheses are the only thing that really count; all the splended snapshots in the world are snapshots after all. . . . You've had all the earth and the waters around the earth, not to mention New York, and I wish you'd begin to make a painting out of the photos.[16]

With some such goal, Jack and Louise decided to leave the city. The Village was too hectic to permit undisturbed work, and it also prevented them from spending enough time alone together. Their aim was a productive summer in the quiet of Provincetown, where he might capture the novel which had floated on the edge of consciousness for years.

Before they were fully settled, he was off on a three-week jaunt for the *Metropolitan* to help pay for the summer. Accompanied by cartoonist Art Young, he went to Chicago and St. Louis for the national political conventions, then to Detroit to interview Henry Ford. It was a hectic, sleepless, hopeful and disappointing trip. Basically, the Republican and Democratic conventions were a farce, for the nominations of Charles Evans Hughes and Wilson had been decided months before. Yet they were colorful, raucous and typically American, a veritable "national circus," with brass bands, swirling crowds, chanted slogans, loud songs, waving banners, ballyhoo, drunken delegates and oceans of oratorical bunk. Banging around Chicago wearing an open blue workshirt, and an expensive tweed suit with a red Socialist badge on the lapel, Reed ridiculed the proceedings, and his continual question "Are conventions necessary?" struck some staid reporters as provocative and hostile. But in St. Louis the poet Orrick Johns saw him as a jovial playboy, "a big, curly-haired kid" who over lunch at a fine hotel made everyone laugh with comments on the wild-eyed appearance of various delegates and imitations of their windy monologues.[17]

For a radical the important story was neither of the major conventions, but that of the Progressive Party, running simultaneously with the Republican meeting in Chicago. Once more the crusaders whose strenuous drive for social justice had gone under the Bull Moose banner in 1912 were gathered together. Enthusiastic men and women from cities and towns, villages, farms and ranches, they were fighters "who all their lives had given battle alone against frightful odds to right the wrongs of the sixty percent of the people . . . who own five percent of [the] wealth." From the platform of the Chicago Auditorium, Jack was tempted to sneer at their worship of T.R., hysterical singing of revival hymns and faith in purifying the political system, but he realized "that among those delegates lay the hope of this country's peaceful evolution." For them, Teddy was more than a man, "he was democracy—he was justice and fairness and the cause of the poor." What they ignored was that now Roosevelt was Preparedness and national might. When he refused the Progressive nomination and suggested, in an act bordering on contempt, that they choose the bleakly conservative Henry Cabot Lodge in his place, Progressivism as a faith seemed dead. Reed's comment on the performance was severe: "As for democracy, we can only hope that some day it will cease to put its trust in men."[18]

His own trust in men was hardly destroyed. Well before meeting Henry Ford, Jack was prepared to like the man whose name was synonymous with the auto industry. Ford was a fervent advocate of ending the war, and he had underwritten the famed Peace Ship voyage to Europe. Unlike most American industrialists, he believed in caring for employees, had been the first to pay a five-dollar daily wage and had instituted medical care, insurance and profit-sharing for his workers. In the smoky city sprawling along the Detroit River, the 276-acre factory which employed thirty-three thousand men and the "miraculous" moving line where an automobile was assembled in twenty-four minutes were equally impressive. Ford was alternately charming and cranky, a mixture of vision and narrow prejudice. Pushing a pet project, a new daily newspaper devoted to the antiwar movement, Reed at first saw only the idealist. Armed with a letter from attorney Amos Pinchot, he attempted to sell the million-dollar venture, but the canny industrialist was not in the market. Hope lingered on until midsummer, when he finally confessed to having overestimated Ford, who was, after all, "a very ignorant man."[19]

After the frantic hustle of Midwestern cities, Provincetown was blessedly silent. This onetime whaling port, three miles long and two streets wide, was populated by a mixture of native Yankees and immigrant Portuguese fishermen whose dark skins and bright clothing added a touch of the exotic to the sandy streets, board sidewalks and weathered clapboard houses. Increasingly popular as a summer retreat, the town in 1916 would be packed with Villagers, but Jack and Louise, among the first to set up housekeeping, were able to spend a few days alone in a white cottage fronting the bay. Three weeks of separation had given perspective, etching their need for each other. Without him, she had found life empty and "absurd," while to Reed distance had shown "in how many ways how much I love you."[20] Now life was as fine as the soft June days, and they glowed together, took long walks over the dunes, swam in the placid waters of the bay and talked happily to sleep each night.

Such a mood could not last. Neither was suited for total commitment, and disruptions came in many forms that summer. Conditions south of the Rio Grande reached a flash point on June 21, when a clash of Mexican and U.S. troops left twelve Americans dead. Calls for revenge in the press and Congress made full-scale war appear inevitable, and Reed was bombarded with offers to cover the action by editors appealing to both his vanity and his pocketbook. Comparing him to Richard Harding Davis in Cuba and claiming he was more fit for Mexico "than any man alive," the head of the Wheeler News Syndicate said flatly: "This war will be a vehicle on which you could ride to a position in the literature of the country." Carl Hovey was no less emphatic: "You have a chance to be the one correspondent with this war . . . it is too big a thing to miss."[21]*

At any time in the past his response would have been positive. But Jack was now able to look beyond career to more personal considerations, and he refused the offers. Still, he was not impervious to all distractions, and in the summer of 1916 Provincetown provided a grand one. Out of the colony of writers, artists and actors there emerged the Provincetown Players, which some critics believe gave birth to modern American drama. Three men were particularly instrumental in developing the Players: John Reed, Eugene O'Neill and George Cram Cook.

Cook was the most important. Novelist, critic, farmer, college in-

---

* F. V. Rank of the New York *American* sent telegrams on June 19 and 21 urging Reed in similar terms to go for his newspaper.

structor, "Jig"—large and prematurely gray—was haunted by a vision of ancient Greece that would eventually lead him to live and die among the shepherds of that country. His most recent enthusiasm was theater. Disgusted with the commercialism of Broadway, he took a dislike to the experimental Washington Square Players after they rejected *Suppressed Desires*, a one-acter he and his wife, Susan Glaspell, had written satirizing the superficial Freudianism rampant in the Village. In 1915, as a kind of lark, a group of summering friends had performed both that play and Neith Boyce's *Constancy*, a humorous work based on the romance between Jack and Mabel, at the Hapgoods' bayside cottage. Favorable responses made other acquaintances request a viewing, and Jig talked Mary Vorse into letting them use an old, weather-beaten fishhouse on her wharf as a theater for the subsequent performances.

But for Cook, the experiment might have ended there. Never able to consummate the plays and poetry stirring within, he seized on the new theater as a kind of mission. Jig thought in terms of human community, a dream city based on the image of Athens, which included a theater where writers, actors, designers would work together free from commercial demands. Staying after the summer visitors had departed, he produced a credo: "One man cannot produce drama. True drama is born only of one feeling animating all the members of a clan—a spirit shared by all and expressed by the few for the all."[22] In the spring of 1916, he was full of hopes for such a clan and bursting with energy enough to make others respond to his dream.

Long before Cook persuaded Reed, Jack's influence was already present. Three years earlier Jig had sat enthralled at the Paterson Pageant, which gave an insight into "what the theater might be."[23] Then in 1914 Reed had come home from Mexico raving about an ancient miracle play performed at a fiesta in El Oro in northern Durango. Handed down by word of mouth for generations, it was played to viewers who knew it by heart and participated fully in the tale of virtue triumphing over evil. Obviously such a work was an expression of a community's shared faith and morality, and Reed's words to this effect had become part of Cook.*

Throwing himself wholly into a theater project was natural enough for Jack. In a way, his life was theatrical. He talked loudly, gestured broadly, he was always brushing back tousled hair, hitching up pants and wearing odd combinations of clothes, and his enthusiasms, political stands, dashes about the globe and journalistic style might seem the mark of a man acting the heroic character on a world stage. If such actions were

* A description of the play can be found in "Los Pastores," the final chapter of *Insurgent Mexico*, 307-26.

unconscious, Reed did possess an overt interest in the stage that went back to the plays performed in his Portland attic, had continued in the many Harvard productions and had reached a climax at the Dutch Treat show and the pageant. His own writing in the genre had tapered off, but his interest remained strong. A much reworked *Enter Dibble* was now in the hands of an agent, the naturalistic one-act *Moondown* would soon be done by the Washington Square Players, and in the spring he had become involved with plans by a Committee on Labor Drama to produce inexpensive plays of interest to workingmen.

Led by Cook, in June the loose-knit troupe optimistically announced a season of four programs and began selling subscriptions for $2.50 a pair. When eighty-seven people had pledged support, the resulting capital of $217.50 was used to pay for electrical installations and lumber, then Jig and his friends renovated the fishhouse, installing lights, benches and a ten-by-twelve-foot stage. By July 1 what Hapgood termed "the play fever" was burning through Provincetown. Everyone was sawing, hammering, painting sets, rehearsing, directing, writing or criticizing manuscripts. The first bill, set for July 15, included a revival of *Suppressed Desires*, a new play by Neith Boyce and Reed's *Freedom*. Turned down by the Washington Square group the year before, it was a good-natured satire of the romantic temperament that found heroic stances and words more important than deeds. The second program, still one play short, included a work by Louise, which led to at least one complaint: "Just because someone is sleeping with somebody is no reason we should do her play."[24]

Like a character from the wings, at this point Eugene O'Neill entered. He was tall, slender, dark and good-looking, a famous actor's son, and he shared with Reed that drive to rub elbows with the tough lower-class elements of society. Stopping briefly at Yale and later Harvard, he had been to sea, bummed around Latin America and prospected for gold. He was a tormented figure whose self-destructiveness came out in monumental drinking bouts, and for a couple of years he had hung around the edges of the Village. More comfortable with petty criminals than with artists, O'Neill was a close friend of Terry Carlin, a Village anarchist who boasted that he had never done a single day's work. It was Terry who led Gene to the Cape. Intrigued by the new theater group but desirous of keeping a distance, the penniless O'Neill settled with Carlin into the wrecked hulk of a ship on the beach in nearby Truro.

In town to borrow money, Carlin let the group know his friend had a "trunk full" of plays, and then conveyed to Gene an invitation to hear them. The shy, nervous O'Neill turned up at the Cooks' with the script of *Bound East for Cardiff*, then paced in the next room while the actor Freddie Burt began to read it aloud. There was immediate recognition in the audience that here was a major talent, and when the reading was done, as Glaspell phrased it, "We knew what we were for."[25] For the opening of O'Neill's play on July 28, everything was perfect. It was a sea story and the sea was there, the high tide washing under the audience and spraying through holes in the floor, a fog shrouding the harbor just as the script demanded, and a mournful bell tolling faintly across the bay. When the curtain fell on the tale of a dying sailor lamenting the life on land he had never led, the wharf quite literally shook with applause.

The discovery of O'Neill made the season a success, but the contributions of people like Jack and Louise should not be obscured. She acted the lead role in a second of O'Neill's works, *Thirst*, while Reed penned a brief farce, took the role of Death in Louise's stylized morality play, *The Game*, and gave so much time to the company that by mid-August he complained, "Like a damned fool, I have been working so hard in the theater up here I am quite exhausted again. But I am going to take a lay-off now."[26] Firm words, they show only a capacity for self-deception. Happy and committed, he enjoyed the pressure, excitement and camaraderie of the close-knit community. Writing in the morning, sun on the beach, long refreshing swims, rehearsals and endless talk about theater—it was, in Glaspell's words, "a great summer. . . . Life was all of a piece, work not separated from play."[27]

Thriving on the atmosphere, Reed sent off invitations to friends. Soon the house was filled with guests—Fred Boyd, Marsden Hartley, Dave Carb and Bobby Rogers all stayed most of the season. The large front parlor became a social center, full of people day and night, and to get any time alone for writing, Jack was forced to rent another cottage. At mealtime there was always a crowd. Because Louise was hardly domestic, this posed a problem until Hippolyte Havel, annoyed at Paula Holliday for taking his free-love views seriously by entertaining a series of lovers, offered his services as cook. A master at the stove, Havel could never fully control the anger which underlay his beliefs, and his stormy temper kept mealtime lively. Contempt for radical theorizing once led him to shout at Reed, "You're nothing but a parlor socialist." The quick reply, "And you're a kitchen anarchist," labeled Havel for the summer.

Even with a separate place to write, Reed found that the long-planned novel remained elusive. If the energy that went into the theater prevented him from tackling such a lengthy form, something about the beauty of life on Cape Cod made poetry accessible, and he completed two mature, personal works, "Fog," the poem about death, and "A Dedication," which honored Max Eastman's radicalism. After the articles on Ford and the conventions, he could not rest, for new financial difficulties beset the family in Portland. Reed whipped out several potboilers, including a four-part serial for *Collier's* that featured financiers, crooks, anarchists, a brave hero and a beautiful heroine, and concluded, "They all lived happily ever after," and two labored dialect stories for the *Metropolitan.* When payment was slow in coming, he was forced to plead with Hovey, "For God's sake, Carl, please get that five hundred in the bank by next Monday. I am absolutely broke and if my family don't get that money by then, it will be a real calamity."[28] Continuing to write in this genre, he seemed to be working against his deepest literary impulses, and three further stories were so feeble that they could never find a market.

The lack of time for serious writing did not blight the summer. Warming to the reticent O'Neill, Reed insisted he and Carlin—now living in a shack across the road—take meals at the Reed house. He admired Gene's knockabout background, but was surprised to find his new friend cynical about the lower classes and their failure to revolt, yet full of detailed fantasies about revolution. Puzzled by the contradiction, Jack let it go—friendship was more important than politics. This was reaffirmed late in August when he backed Eddy Hunt's proposal for a memorial edition of Alan Seeger's works. A volunteer in the French Army, their former classmate had recently been killed on the Western Front.* Reed recalled Seeger's explicit dream of an "epic life" and felt that he had found it. Those early Village days, when Alan had haunted the apartment like a homeless ghost, specializing in lyric poetry and grand, romantic gestures, seemed far off and innocent. Once Seeger had knelt before his lady in Union Square and sworn in the name of love to resign his job for her. This was hardly a knight slaying a dragon, but Jack remembered it as a fine moment because "it was the only tribute he had to offer."[29]

---

* Seeger's development provides an interesting contrast to Reed's. Both began by thinking themselves poets, but Seeger was far more serious an artist, and also more deeply sunk into the role of poet (everyone always commented he "looked like a poet"). Boredom with middle-class life and a search for experience were common to both. Living in Paris at the outbreak of war, Seeger enlisted in the army in September 1914. Feeling no dislike for the Germans, his motive was that war would be the most intense experience of the century, and as a poet he could not afford to miss sharing its emotions. Seeger seems to have been, in short, what Lippmann and others thought John Reed was, a kind of mindless searcher for experience. But Reed's intelligence and social conscience saved him from sheer adventurism. Seeger's wartime experiences may be followed in his posthumous *Letters and Diary* (New York: Charles Scribner's Sons, 1917).

The news of Seeger helped trigger the mood that led to reflections on mortality. As he walked along the sandy roads of the Cape, Reed was distressed by the uneasy state of the world, the destructive actions of men that led to turmoil and violence. In the past he had always savored the role of writer and partisan and had enjoyed the battles. Now the insecurity of it all, the continually shifting nature of men and events broke through his armor of laughter, youth and strength. Seeking stability in the quiet of the Cape, he put a down payment on a damp, leaky cottage in Truro and hired a local carpenter to make it habitable for the next year.

Well before the end of summer, news of the Players reached the outside world when a vacationing Boston journalist wrote admiringly of them in the *Sunday Globe*. Among the pictures was one of Louise, with a capsule description full of the usual self-exaggeration: in this instance she had spent five years on the *Oregonian*. Jig Cook's resolve to take the group back to Manhattan was strengthened and Reed was a key supporter. On September 4 the Wharf Theatre was the scene of a formal business meeting, which opened discordantly when Hutch Hapgood shouted, "Organization is death." But the group elected Cook president and delegated a committee including Reed, Eastman and Burt to draw up a constitution. The next evening the document defined their common purpose: "To encourage the writing of American plays of real artistic, literary and dramatic—as opposed to Broadway—merit. That such plays be considered without reference to their commercial value, since this theater is not to be run for pecuniary profit. . . ."[30] Twenty-nine people, including Dave Carb and Bobby Rogers, were on the original roster, and when donations built the treasury to $320, Cook left for New York to find a theater.

Jack and Louise lingered in Provincetown in September. Most of their friends were gone now, and the chill evening air off the Atlantic hinted the coming of fall. They could still swim and hike to the cottage in Truro, sitting to gaze at the crumbling wharves where whalers had once unloaded their catches. It was a shaky period. Reed had never been so conscious of the moment, of wanting to stop the rolling days, to hold on to part of life. Never before had he felt nostalgia for his own experiences or shivered with the intimation of what might lie ahead. One of the reasons for the long vacation had been the need for rest, the hope of easing his kidney problem. But the summer had not been quiet, and there had been many moments of searing pain. What doctors had tentatively suggested the preceding spring could no longer be discounted. Going back to the city meant the possibility of a surgeon's knife.

On the first of October they returned to New York and immediately were in the midst of preparations for launching the Players. Cook had rented an old brownstone at 137 MacDougal, next door to the Liberal Club, and the first performances were less than a month away. Extensive renovations, quarrels with building inspectors, conferences, directors' meetings, rehearsals and attempts to sell subscriptions—all took as much time as each member was willing to give. Often at night the company met at the Reed apartment to thrash out problems. Decisions were theoretically democratic, but Jack could be a prima donna. Once he threatened to resign unless *Lima Beans* by Alfred Kreymborg was accepted for production, and the group bowed to his demand. They also adopted his suggested motto for the theater door: "Here Pegasus Was Hitched."

For George Cram Cook and some other members of the company, the Players was now the focus of life; for Reed it could be central only away from the city. In Manhattan many worlds and lives demanded his attention. The unfair harassing of a vagrant by a policeman could lead him to register a lengthy written complaint with the Police Commissioner; the shaky financial state of the *Masses* could inspire him to ask acquaintances to give money, arguing that if the magazine failed, "there's going to be no place where we can say our say";[31] the suppression of a strike of Standard Oil workers in Bayonne, New Jersey, could lead him to take an assignment from the New York *Tribune* and write such a blistering account that officials protested to the newspaper and demanded another reporter go over the same ground—this follow-up story confirmed his report of company and police brutality. The war once again concerned him. In the *Masses* Reed defended the militant pacifism of Bertrand Russell, which had led to a conviction for interference with English recruiting. Jingoes like T.R. might call pacifism cowardice, but Jack—who had seen millions ready to die in Europe—thought military heroism "the cheapest of all virtues," and emphasized that "it took more courage to do the thing [Russell] . . . did than to fight in the trenches." So many intellectuals—Wells, Anatole France, Gilbert Murray and Peter Kropotkin—had embraced nationalism that Russell's action was one of the few which could give hope "in these dark and darker days."[32]

In the fall of an election year the problem of war led inevitably to politics. With little real faith in the system, Reed still felt the necessity of acting the responsible citizen: "I'm not a believer in anything lasting coming out of purely political action; but I don't want this country to become a hell for the next four years." Since the Socialist candidate, Benson, was "too small to be spoken about with seriousness," and Republican Hughes hopelessly conservative, Wilson gained Reed's support almost by default. The President's campaign theme about keeping the country out of the war seemed promising, and his progressive domestic record was decent enough. Hardly ideal, Wilson would do "because the only real principles he has (few enough) are on our side."[33] In August, Reed—along with Steffens, Fred Howe, Hapgood, Cook and Glaspell—had joined a group of writers who were supporting the President. He signed an appeal asking Socialists not to waste votes on Benson, and then wrote a syndicated article backing Wilson. If this was almost a duty, there was real pleasure in helping Denver Judge Ben Lindsey, under heavy conservative attack for supporting the Ludlow miners and sailing on the Ford Peace Ship. Later the judge credited an article by Reed as a significant factor in a winning reelection campaign.

In October, Jack and Louise often escaped the city to stay in Croton at the home of Mike and Sally Robinson. Several Villagers owned weekend cottages there now, and when the old dream of living away from the rush of New York arose again, Louise backed the notion. Ambitious for him, worried over his tendency to "waste [himself] with Greenwich Villagers," she found Croton "quiet and peaceful and happy" and urged Jack on: "I think it will be so fine to do *work* out here, uninterrupted, and play in town. We can't put off real work year after year."[34] By the beginning of November he had put a down payment of $2000 on a small cottage with a large, fenced garden, and arranged a mortgage for the balance of $1750.*

It was odd that John Reed, normally rootless and free as the wind, should purchase two homes within a period of three months. But at that time his life was severely out of joint. Visits to doctors had confirmed the worst; an operation on the kidney had become imperative, and he was scheduled to enter Johns Hopkins Hospital in Baltimore on November 12. It seemed necessary to put affairs in order. Being practical rather than morbid, he had the Croton deed made out in Louise's name. Then, quite casually on the morning of November 9, the two of them journeyed to Peekskill and were married in the city hall. The ceremony meant little, but he wanted her to be a legal heir.

Beginnings and endings, suddenly they all ran together. A marriage, two houses—settling past issues and facing a future that might never arrive. The first week in November it was the same with the Provincetown Players. For five nights Jack acted in *The Game*. It was the group's debut and, with *Bound East for Cardiff*, the first appearance of an O'Neill

---

* The house he purchased was the one Mabel had previously rented, where she had pushed him out the door in February 1915. This was no doubt due to the small number of suitable houses in Croton rather than because of any unconscious desire for continuing closeness to her.

play in New York. No moment of greatness, perhaps, but a promising beginning. Yet for Reed it was an end. Five days after the final curtain he
entered the hospital, and if his future works would be performed by the
Players, after the operation he would never again be one of the group's
inner circle. For a time he had given himself wholly to the Players, but
any ambition to create great drama would not be fulfilled.

One other beginning and conclusion fused before he entered the
hospital. A collection of his poetry, entitled *Tamburlaine* and dedicated
to his mother, was accepted by publisher Frederick Bursch. Twenty-five
poems, including several from Harvard days, made up the volume, which
he described in a foreword written on November 1 as "a combination of
a First Book of Verse, and a collection of Juvenilia—such as is laboriously
dug up by the literary executors of celebrated bards after they are dead. I
prefer not to take any chances of that." The tone was lighthearted but the
meaning clear—this would be his last book of verse.

In the autumn of 1916, John Reed was putting his twenty-nine years
in order. As the poem "Fog" indicated, he could confront mortality
squarely. Confusion and distress came not from death, but life, from the
problem of trying to understand how changes in the self related to the
tumbling motion of the outside world. Overflowing with love for Louise
and the simple joys of nature rediscovered at Cape Cod and Croton, he was
forced to wonder how much of life was his own, and what he owed the
world. His most recent poem weighed his own situation as much as that of
Eastman, to whom it was dedicated, with a quite explicit message:

> There was a man, who, loving quiet beauty best,
> Yet could not rest
> For the harsh moaning of unhappy humankind,
> Fettered and blind—
> Too driven to know beauty and too hungry-tired
> To be inspired.
> From his high, windy-peaceful-hill, he stumbled down
> Into the town,
> With a child's eyes, clear bitterness and silver scorn
> Of the outworn
> And cruel mastery of life by senile death;
> And with his breath
> Fanned up the noble fires that smoulder in the breast
> Of the oppressed.

Like so many sensitive, artistic men torn between private and public
worlds, Reed could increasingly see that choices had to be made. The
dream of quiet beauty, "the high-souled bliss of poets in walled gardens,"

had grown in the heart of a weak and sickly child. Submerged through the years when the self was tested, it now surfaced once more when manhood was secure. For many years Jack had been cut off from his private imagination—now he could see it once again, begin to tap the hidden wells of inner self and write poetry and fiction more serious and profound than ever before. Yet the growth that freed his imagination entailed commitments that could not easily be ignored. As the poem concluded, the reward for stirring the oppressed would not be peace or quiet time for creativity, but something grander:

> A vision of new splendor in the human scheme—
> A god-like dream—
> And a new lilt of happy trumpets in the strange
> Clangor of Change![35]

Perhaps men are not wholly self-willed, but in the autumn of 1916 John Reed reached a peak of self-consciousness, recognizing fully that two worlds dwelt in him, and he in them. Whatever came after, he would choose his way knowing this. Unless life were wide enough to let him exist in both, any choice would involve a partial loss of self, an irreparable nostalgia for all the things which might have been.

16

Croton

"I am twenty-nine years old, and I know that this is the end of a part of my life, the end of youth. Sometimes it seems to be the end of the world's youth, too; certainly the Great War has done something to us all. But it is also the beginning of a new phase of life; and the world we live in is so full of swift change and color and meaning that I can hardly keep from imagining the splendid and terrible possibilities of the time to come. The last ten years I've gone up and down the earth drinking in experience, fighting and loving, seeing and hearing and tasting things. I've travelled all over Europe, and to the borders of the East, and down in Mexico, having adventures; seeing men killed and broken, victorious and laughing, men with visions and men with a sense of humor. I've watched civilization change and broaden and sweeten in my lifetime, and tried to help; and I've watched it wither and crumble in the red blast of war. . . . I'm not quite sick of seeing yet, but I will be—I know that. My future life will not be what it has been. And so I want to stop a minute, and look back, and get my bearings. . . ."[1]

In the spring of 1917 John Reed was for the first time impelled toward autobiography. It was a brief period when his mood coincided with that of the nation—both were similarly adrift. Decisions in Washington and Berlin about the rights of neutrals and the necessity for submarine warfare had already made American entrance into the World War a certainty, with only the time, place and exact circumstances to be determined. Sensing rather than knowing this, disturbed to find opportunities constricting, he found it important to understand his relationship to the dark, historical flood.

Typically more descriptive than analytical, the resulting essay, "Almost Thirty," relates the story of a fearful child struggling to become a man. Most of it deals with life through college—the years of childhood and adolescence at the Academy, Morristown and Harvard—while the last section chronicles early successes in New York, the raising of social consciousness at Paterson and the realization of personal and artistic self in Mexico. Everywhere the emphasis is on activity. From the teens on, "a furious energy drove me to all kinds of bodily and mental exercise, without any particular direction—except that I felt sure I was going to be a great poet and novelist. . . . I was increasingly active and restless, more ambitious of place and power . . . scattering myself in a hundred different directions; life became a beloved motion picture, thought about only in flashes, conceived as emotion and sensation." Now, verging on thirty, weakened by an operation and distressed by the war, he felt that things had changed: "Some of that old superabundant vitality is gone, and with it the all-sufficient joy of mere living. . . . Some things I think I have settled, but in other ways I am back where I started—a turmoil of imaginings. . . . "

If most of the memoir reads like a heroic tale, some parts reflect a new introspective mood. Jack now understood the recurrent pattern of ups and downs that explained past behavior and his current state of mind: "I must find myself again. Some men seem to get their direction early, to grow naturally and with little change to the thing they are to be. I have no idea what I shall do one month from now. Whenever I have tried to become some one thing, I have failed; it is only by drifting with the wind that I have found myself, and plunged joyously into a new role." This view of himself as a role-player was close to the criticism by Lippmann two years before. But Reed felt that underlying the actor was a core of integrity, a continuing openness to experience and a solid commitment to writing: "I have discovered that I am only happy when I'm working hard at something I like. I never stuck long at anything I didn't like, and now I couldn't if I wanted to; on the other hand, there are very few things

I don't get some fun out of, if only the novelty of the experience. . . . I love beauty and chance and change, but less now in the external world and more in my mind." With the war destroying beauty and providing fewer opportunities for meaningful action, it was a period of "waiting, waiting for it all to end, for life to resume so I can find my work."

Waiting, along with considerable pain, began in Johns Hopkins, where he was confined for a month. At first there was the agony of repeated cystoscopic examinations—"a whole crowd of strangers sticking their fingers up my insides." Following the removal of his left kidney on November 22, the pain was quite severe for two weeks, leaving him "bored, and tired and uncomfortable and lonely for my honey."[2] Dozens of get-well letters from friends and acquaintances were cheering, and two reconciliations helped make the stay more bearable. One was with Carl Binger, snubbed by Reed at Harvard, now a physician on the hospital staff. At first Carl's visits aroused feelings of shame, but when the incident remained unmentioned, Jack began to feel himself forgiven. The other contact was with Lippmann, who made a special trip to Baltimore. Deeply touched, Reed so much forgot the quarrel that in the autobiographical sketch he would give Walter almost single-handed credit for creating the "Harvard Renaissance."

Visits and letters, glances at page proofs for *Tamburlaine* and attempts to work on short stories—none of this could make up for the absence of Louise. On November 21 she had arrived and remained until the operation was successful. Back in New York to pack for the move to Croton, she wrote notes filled with affection—"one just aches for you when you are away and everyone else seems so stupid"—reports on how he was missed— "everyone here has been pouring love over you all day"—and complaints that in trying to keep her from being lonely, friends were dropping in with bottles of liquor at all hours of the day and night to party until the "terrible stale smell of booze [was] hanging about the room."[3] After casually mentioning some visits to a doctor, on December 7 Louise dropped a bombshell—she, too, might need an operation: "My whole left insides (ovaries, etc.) seem to be inflamed and infected. They think maybe I got it from your condition." A horrified Reed demanded to know the whole truth, threatened to come to New York on a stretcher if the answer was not satisfactory, and sounded both hurt and annoyed: "Oh, honey. When you were feeling so rotten why did you wait so long before going to see a doctor? That wasn't fair to me." Explaining that his condition was definitely not contagious, he worried over any operation: "It's awful to remove your ovaries, isn't it? Doesn't it make you incapable of having children and everything like that? I never heard of that being done to anybody but dogs, cats and horses."[4]

Surgery did not prove necessary for her, and by mid-December they were recuperating together in Croton. Country living suited both of them. Tired of Village faces and gossip, Louise had grown annoyed when she was not chosen by the Players for its governing committee. She also felt New York was too hectic for long, intimate talks—"the best way to keep close to each other and I want to be very close"—and believed it an "unpardonable pity" to waste energy on "Villagers" rather than on "real work."[5] Reed agreed. Growing slowly stronger, he found his longings for Manhattan were tempered by a sober realization: "In the city I have no time for much but sensation and experience; but now I want some time of quiet, and leisure for thought, so I can extract from the richness of my life something beautiful and strong." It was good to be close enough so that an hour's ride allowed him to "plunge again into the sea of people, the roaring and the lights—and then come back here to write of it, in the quiet hills, the sunshine and clean wind."

Their removal from the city was part of a strategic retreat being undertaken by many friends. The Village community always had a nosy side, with continual drop-in parties and social drinking making serious work difficult. Worse, as a result of press coverage, the Village had been "discovered." Over the years journalists had toured the area as if it were a foreign land, writing reports full of bemused condescension for the ways of the native people. In 1914 the *Dial* had portrayed the region as a kind of sanctuary from real life, a continuation of college days, complete with a football hero, Bill Haywood, a humor magazine, the *Masses,* and an errant playboy, Jack Reed. Two years later the *Literary Digest* was ironic and nasty in describing Liberal Club members as either crazy, Semitic or Bohemian, all evidently pejorative terms.[6] However negative in tone, such articles struck a responsive chord among growing numbers of young Americans who found the offbeat and unconventional attractive. Soon the Village began to respond to the desires and money of invading newcomers.

The first guidebook to Greenwich Village was published in 1917. Written by a nonresident, Anna Chapin, it was simultaneously sympathetic and patronizing. Residents were depicted not as immoral, but as youngsters who loved to flaunt "bizarre haircuts and unusual clothes" in an attempt to show "the prosaic outer world how different they are!"[7] Like children, they were clever, spontaneous, warm, artistic and irresponsible, but altogether lovable and harmless. Naming places to dine, like the Brevoort basement, Bertolotti's and Polly's, the book also recommended many new restaurants and tea rooms for their "Bohemian" atmosphere. Hidden in garrets and cellars, these were a response by enterprising residents to the commercial possibilities of artiness, and their origins were bespoken in costumed waitresses, tasteless decoration and arch names—the Will o' the Wisp, the Mad Hatter's, the Samovar, the Mousetrap, the Wigwam, the Crumperie, the Pollywogge, the Black Parrot and Aladdin Attic Tea Room. Also new on the scene were nightclubs like the Pirate's Den, with a door shaped like a coffin and waiters wearing cutlasses. Popping up everywhere were tiny shops selling paintings, batiks, sandals, jewelry, hand-made clothing and books of poetry at prices no real Villagers could afford. The ultimate in commercial ventures was Bruno's Garret, at 58 Washington Square South, where for twenty-five cents visitors could watch bearded men and smock-clad women read verse aloud, strum guitars, daub paint on canvas or just loll about, drinking and discussing art, sex or whatever else might outrage or titillate viewers.

Older residents both deplored such antics and helped foster them. Nobody resented commercialization more than Floyd Dell, who fled old hangouts as uptown crowds appeared and prices rose. These newcomers "stared, giggled and made loud remarks . . . they thought nothing of intruding themselves upon a private party, introducing themselves and asking to be shown about." After being accosted and asked, "Are you a merry Villager?" Dell resolved to avoid all tourist places. But soon there appeared a new kind of Villager, one who cadged drinks and meals and sold poor sketches or bad poetry to the unwary: "It was a bitter thing to have to look at these professionals, and realize that this was the sort of person oneself was supposed to be."[8] Unfortunately, his own actions contributed to the Village as "show-place." When the Liberal Club needed to raise money, Dell suggested the idea of a masquerade ball, the Pagan Rout. Openly appealing to outsiders through advertising, the annual event drew crowds of middle-class Americans into Webster Hall to watch artists and intellectuals, in outlandish and scanty costumes, dance to ragtime. This success only meant failure, for the tempo of tourism was increased.

Such commercialism was an annoyance, but hardly the major factor in Reed's own flight from the city. His travels had made him no more than a sometime Villager, and early in 1917 his eyes were once more focused abroad, this time on the Far East. Since the preceding autumn Jack had been planning a trip to cover revolutionary developments in China. The journey became a real possibility in January when doctors pronounced his recovery complete. While Louise received press credentials from the New York *Tribune*, the *Metropolitan* announced the forthcoming venture: "He will hold up the mirror to this mysterious and romantic country, and we shall see its teeming millions and the big forces at work there." Gathering introductory letters—including one from Secretary of State Robert Lansing—names of Harvard classmates now in the Orient, and lists of Japanese and Chinese Socialists, Reed made ready to sail in February, while Louise voiced their joint excitement: "China is going to be a splendid thing for both of us."[9]

Late in January the German ambassador to Washington informed the American government that after February 1 his country's submarines would sink all ships, belligerent and neutral, in a vast zone around the Allied countries. In response, Woodrow Wilson severed diplomatic relations with Germany. Despite his claim that "We are the sincere friends of the German people and earnestly desire to remain at peace with the Government which speaks for them," the path to war had been irrevocably paved. Two days later Carl Hovey canceled Reed's assignment, saying it was absurd to spend money on articles from China "until we can see more clearly ahead." Evidently hoping Reed might return to Europe, the editor asked, "Is there anything in connection with the new situation you can suggest we could do in place of it?"[10]

Given his feelings about the "mad-dogfight of Europe," there was nothing. Sensing that the tepid Socialism of the *Metropolitan* was giving way to patriotism, realizing his days on the magazine were numbered, Jack angrily personalized the problem by one day snapping at publisher H. J. Whigham, "You and I call ourselves friends, but we are not really friends because we don't believe in the same things, and the time will come when we won't speak to each other."[11] Even so, there was no sharp break with the magazine. After Art Young had been asked to tone down his radical column, Reed carefully worked on a profile of Samuel Gompers, attempting to praise organized labor while exposing the inadequacies of the longtime AFL president's reformist leadership. Cogent and insightful as similar pieces on Bryan, Ford and Sunday, it was rejected. In a time of growing crisis, respectable union leadership was a part of the national consensus.

While the advocates of peace began a last-ditch struggle against U.S. entry into the war, a gloomy Reed remained in Croton. He sympathized with the efforts of the American Union Against Militarism, the Women's Peace Party and new organizations like the Committee for Democratic Control—led by friends Amos Pinchot, Randolph Bourne and Max Eastman—but could not shake the feeling that such were in vain. They could stage rallies in the cities of America, flood editorial pages with letters and the halls of Congress with petitions, demand embargoes or referendums and even threaten general strikes—but it would make no difference. A tiny minority of the population, the Roosevelts, the Anglophiles, the superpatriots and warmongers were about to have their way. In the autobiographical sketch he made a solemn promise: "If the United

States, on any excuse, is forced by the flag-wavers, the munitions-makers, into that chaotic stupidity, I for one will not fight." Then, realizing the operation would keep him out of any military organization, Jack crossed out the sentence. His opposition would have to take other forms.

Before finding what they might be, there was a more immediate problem: money. The *Metropolitan* had paid $500 for each story or article, and his last piece had appeared in January. With medical bills, monthly installments on two mortgages and continuing family requests for assistance, it was a grim time to be without a market. A few unaccepted humorous or romantic works of fiction cried for rewriting, but he was hardly in the proper mood to tackle them. Increasingly out of phase with the editorial policies of major publications, Reed was also short of ideas. When the head of a news syndicate expressed interest in anything suitable, his mind went blank. Only the war was important, and nothing he wrote on that would be acceptable. Soon Reed was forced to extreme measures to raise cash. With great reluctance he pawned the gold watch that had belonged to C.J., then, in March, sold the Truro house. Taking over the mortgage, Margaret Sanger paid out his investment. For the price of $500, one gentle dream was a casualty of war.*

With the world closing in, Reed could not continue to bury his head. In early March a bill to arm merchant ships passed the House before being talked to death by a dozen Progressives in the Senate. The President denounced this "little group of willful men, representing no opinion but their own," and announced he was putting guns and naval crews on merchant ships anyway. On the eighteenth came news that three American vessels had been sunk in the Atlantic. While longtime preparedness groups issued calls for a declaration of war and neutralist sentiment slowly swung their way, Wilson called a special session of Congress for April 2 "to receive a communication concerning grave matters of national policy." Knowing this meant war and yet hoping for a last-minute miracle, pacifists and radicals poured into the national capital.

Face to face with this longtime fear, Jack needed to put his thoughts in order. The result was an article for the April *Masses*, a curious combination of irony, disgust and weary resignation. Beginning with derisive jabs—"the Boston Budget for Conveying Virgins Inland has grown

---

* Margaret Sanger, *Margaret Sanger: An Autobiography* (New York: W. W. Norton, 1938), 264, reports buying the house, and the JR MSS contain a bill of sale dated March 27, 1917. Yet three years later, when in a Finnish jail, Reed several times in letters asked Louise to keep up mortgage payments on the Truro house. It is possible his mind was wandering in jail (see Chapter 21) and that he really meant the payments on the Croton house.

enormously"—he shifted to sentences that smashed like trip-hammers: "War means an ugly mob-madness, crucifying the truth-tellers, choking the artists, sidetracking reforms, revolutions and the working of social forces. Already in America those citizens who oppose the entrance of their country into the European melee are called 'traitors,' and those who protest against the curtailing of our meagre rights of free speech are spoken of as 'dangerous lunatics.' . . . For many years this country is going to be a worse place for free men to live in." To explain why a President elected six months before on the slogan "He Kept Us Out of War" was now leading the country into it, Reed argued that neutrality had been no more than a sham. Continually winking at English violations, the United States had held Germany strictly accountable for the slightest misdeeds. The reason for this unequal treatment was simple. Using the same argument made in Congress by Progressive Senators like La Follette and Norris, he wrote, "We have shipped and are shipping vast quantities of war materials to the Allies; we have floated the Allied loans." Voters did not want war, but the stockbrokers, bankers and manufacturers did. In any showdown, their power would prevail. Speaking in the name of the common man, he closed with the phrase that was now an empty wish: "It is not our war."[12]

On the evening of April 2 Jack was in Washington. Unable to bring himself to use a Senate pass from Robert La Follette, he went instead to a meeting of antiwar elements. Before his turn to speak arrived, a man entered the hall, strode to the platform and announced that the President had called for war. Presiding officer David Starr Jordan followed with a statement that he was now prepared to support the nation, but Reed rose, stepped forward on the platform and shouted, "This is not my war, and I will not support it. This is not my war, and I will have nothing to do with it."[13] Remaining in Washington, he joined a group of liberals, radicals and peace-movement people testifying to the House Judiciary Committee against the censorship provisions of a proposed Espionage Act. A few days later he returned to Capitol Hill to argue against conscription. When he told the Committee on Military Affairs, "I do not believe in this war. . . . I would not serve in it," he was interrupted and denounced by two Representatives.[14] It was an ominous portent of things to come.

In New York the community of artists, intellectuals and radicals was thrown into disarray. The responses to American entry covered the entire spectrum of possibilities. Walter Lippmann and other editors of the *New Republic*, who had been edging toward intervention for months, argued that with liberal intellectuals and progressives helping direct the effort, a more sane world order would emerge from the conflict. On the other extreme, men like Van Wyck Brooks and James Oppenheim of the *Seven Arts* and Jig Cook practiced a kind of withdrawal, proclaiming the necessity of keeping art alive. Between these positions were those who had to balance belief against patriotism, idealism against practicality, the security of acquiescence against the cost of standing in opposition to national policy. For both men and organizations the choices were difficult and often unexpected. The militant IWW, resurgent among Western miners and lumberjacks, never took an official stand, while the milder Socialist Party immediately branded the declaration "a crime against the people of the United States" and pledged that "we will not willingly give a single life or a single dollar."[15] When the membership ratified this stand by a vote of ten to one, prominent leaders like Upton Sinclair, William E. Walling, Charles Edward Russell and Allan Benson deserted the party to support the national effort. Among the *Masses* crowd—generally antiwar—some differences emerged. Walling and Benson had occasionally written for the magazine, while another contributor, George Creel, became head of the government's Committee on Public Information. Anarchist George Bellows soon went from drawing antiwar cartoons to pro-victory posters, artist Horatio Winslow volunteered for officer's training and Floyd Dell, after facing trial for praising conscientious objectors, ultimately enlisted in the Army.

From Portland came word of Margaret's solid Americanism: "It gives me a shock when your father's son can say that he cares nothing for his country and his flag. . . . As things are now anyone . . . against his country is fighting for its enemy. . . . I do not want you to fight— heaven knows—for us, but I do *not* want you to fight against us—by word or pen—and I can't help saying that if you do . . . I shall be deeply ashamed. . . . I think you will find that most of your friends and sympathizers are of foreign birth; very few are real Americans."[16] Angrily Jack answered with a letter that left his mother in tears. An immediate reply from Harry, about to leave for officer's training, explained that things at home were difficult enough without him becoming touchy: "Be honest and admit one thing—there has never been a time when either mother or myself has not had the utmost respect for your views and opinions, even if we haven't always agreed."[17] Acknowledging this, a cooler Reed wrote a conciliatory note and sweetened it with a check for fifty dollars.

It was easier to reconcile differences with family than with society at large. Invisible yet palpable, the war brought gloom to a Bohemia already beginning to drown in commercialism. People seemed confused and touchy, discussions with friends turned into bitter quarrels and rationalizations for accommodation sounded on unexpected lips. Jack's worst fears were realized as vigilantes began to raid radical meetings and the government clamped down on dissent. The first week in June he attended a No-Conscription League meeting at Hunt's Point Palace to help protect Emma Goldman and Alexander Berkman from threatened disruptions. When servicemen began to bombard the stage with light bulbs, disrupt the talks with shouts and jeers and swarm forward, policemen looked the other way, yet outside the auditorium they did not hesitate to disperse a crowd of workers. Because of three similar meetings, Goldman and Berkman were arrested and charged, under provisions of the May 18 Draft Act, with having formed a "conspiracy to induce persons not to register." At the trial—with Reed as a defense witness—the prosecution emphasized radicalism more than specific antidraft actions and played on the patriotism of jurors. The verdict was never in doubt, and the two anarchists received maximum sentences of two years in prison and $10,000 fines.

Reed's freedom was also constricted as editors grew wary of reporters who opposed the war. A society which once had promised everything now withheld the means of making a living, unless he were prepared to compromise his beliefs. Jack did not waver, and finally at the end of May he was hired by the New York *Mail* to write a daily feature.* Less hysterically patriotic than most newspapers, the *Mail* provided some assignments, but also gave him a free hand in the choice of topics and allowed room for personal observation. Covering an execution at Sing Sing, Reed could argue that a killer's crime, the result of a robbery attempt, was hardly surprising "in a civilization in which money means privilege and freedom." In an article on the draft, he predicted that several thousand men in New York "will go to jail rather than register."[18] Twice in early June he wrote sardonic accounts of the Alley Festa, a week-long street carnival in MacDougal Alley, catering to members of the Social Register, with proceeds going to relief organizations in Allied countries:

> It was New York's last real laugh. Within a very few months now the casualty lists will be appearing. . . . Our streets will slowly fill with pale figures in uniform, leaning on Red Cross nurses; with men who have arms off, hands off, faces shot away, men hobbling on crutches, pieces of men.

* A syndicate secretly underwritten by German money had purchased the *Mail* the preceding year as part of a vain attempt to counteract the immense amount of pro-Ally propaganda in the United States. Reed certainly did not know this, and the paper itself was not pro-German but only somewhat less fervent in its patriotism than other dailies. See H. C. Peterson, *Propaganda for War: The Campaign Against American Neutrality* (Norman: University of Oklahoma Press, 1939), 139.

Then New York will not laugh any more. Europe has stopped laughing long ago. . . . These rich and ever comfortable people are the only people in New York who can still laugh—even now, before battle, before loss, in time of peace. The poor who moved restlessly up and down on the fringes of the spectacle could no longer laugh . . . the police couldn't laugh, the actors and actresses, the chauffeurs of all those splendid limousines, the conductors and motormen of the streetcars going past—all these had forgotten how to be gay. Life was too exhausting, too harsh. . . . If I were Weir Mitchell or somebody like that I should paint a picture of flaunting wealth and extravagance, with the submerged and groaning masses of mankind, driven to desperation, thrusting their fists up through the concrete floor of MacDougal Alley. But, alas, I cannot. There is no bloody fist. It is a Belshazzar's feast without the writing on the wall.[19]

Frustrated and depressed by external circumstances, Reed was driven more deeply into a private world, cleaving tightly to Louise. Because both were volatile, the relationship had often been stormy, with arguments common. Still, it appeared more solid than any previous love, solid enough to allow him to claim that with her close by, "I don't care what comes." As a refuge, love is always shaky. For the private, sensitive man who cares deeply for others, cherishes relationships, builds a life around closeness, it may possibly work, but for Jack it was out of character. Warm and often giving, he had never been particularly sensitive to the moods of others. So peripheral was love to his major concerns that it was mentioned only in the final few sentences of the autobiographical essay: "In my life as in most lives, I guess, love plays a tremendous part. I've had love affairs, passionate happiness, wretched maladjustments; hurt deeply and been deeply hurt." The offhand phrases showed an attitude that carried over to life. Louise might be "closer to me than anyone has ever been," but this did not prevent him from occasionally sleeping with other women. When she learned about one of these affairs, the result was an emotional explosion. Angry words, screams of pain, tears, shouts and black rage filled the cottage until a crashing door signaled her departure and drove home the irony that the chaos and disorder of the world were now a part of his personal life.

The situation was more complicated than Reed would ever know. Soon he learned that Louise had gone directly to Provincetown to stay with Eugene O'Neill. But he did not realize that since the preceding summer she had been having an affair with Gene, that her rage over Jack's transgression was in fact fed by her own burden of guilt. Even when he learned of her love, he probably was never confronted by the whole truth—that Louise had been attracted by Gene from the moment he first appeared; that she had made the advances, breaking down O'Neill's reticence by saying Jack's kidney condition rendered him impotent and that they lived together as brother and sister; that at Provincetown everyone in the Players knew she was slipping away to spend quiet hours alone on the dunes with Gene; that some of her tender poetry in the *Masses* reflected her love for O'Neill; that while Jack lay at Johns Hopkins worrying over her illness, she was sleeping with Gene both in town and at the Croton house.*

Given Village beliefs about sex, the messy situation was not unusual—it was easier to cast off the shackles of the old morality, and proclaim the idea of sexual freedom, than to live with its full consequences. Despite ideas about free love, young women rarely played with sex as lightly as men, and usually looked for marriage after a period of experimentation with bed partners. Meanwhile the most radical liaisons, those in which each person openly entertained other lovers, were often as disastrous and destructive as the old-fashioned marriages Bohemians scorned. Jack and Louise were now painfully learning that the new ideology dwelt alongside traditional emotional responses. Without theorizing about free love, they had casually lived it, and the result was a bumpy and downward spiral of anguish.

Reed puttered despondently in the garden for a week, then sent a telegram to Provincetown saying, "The fruit trees are in bloom," and this simple message brought Louise back.[20] Sometimes they could momentarily regain closeness, but too often the past hovered over them, and continual emotional storms made life together torture. To break the painful cycle, Louise seized on a suggestion that she go to Europe as a correspondent. Confused by feelings of sorrow, anger and relief, Reed helped her secure a job with the Wheeler News Syndicate and took her to the dock on Saturday, June 9. Perhaps time and space would solve a problem that words could not mend.

Back in a newly rented Village room, he found a short note: "Please believe me Jack—I'm going to try like the devil to pull myself together over there and come back able to act like a reasonable human being. I

---

* Doris Alexander, *The Tempering of Eugene O'Neill* (New York: Harcourt, Brace, 1962), 236, has even suggested that Louise's illness was in fact the need for an abortion since she was carrying O'Neill's child. The evidence is problematic and seems to be based partially on Reed's supposed impotence, alleged by Louise to Gene. Since that story is contradicted by Reed's affairs with other women, the real question would be how did she know the pregnancy was caused by Gene, not Jack? It might have been possible if kidney pain made Reed abstain from sexual relations for some period of time before the operation. There is no way of knowing if this is true.

know I'm probably all wrong about everything. I know the only reason I act so crazy is because it hurts so much. . . . I love you so much—it's a terrible thing to love as much as I do." Immediately he responded and assumed all the blame: "In this last awful business you were humanly right and I was wrong. I have always loved you my darling ever since I first met you—and I guess I always will. This is more than I've ever felt for anyone, honestly. I know that the one thing I cannot bear any more is consciously to hurt you, honey." He went out to Croton, but found the empty cottage "a terrible place," and at midnight caught a train back into town.[21] Unable to sleep, he walked through the streets until dawn.

In the next seven weeks, with "a kind of incurable bitterness running through my veins and a taste of ashes in my mouth," Reed would for the first time experience moments of not caring if he lived or died. The job, anticonscription meetings, writing for the *Masses*—none of these activities gave meaning to his existence or banished the ache of separation. Bored and listless, depressed and gloomy, sleepless, suffering from the muggy weather, avoiding friends to spend hours brooding in his room or escaping to Croton, he wrote letters to Louise filled with anguish and apologies: "I realize how disappointed and cruelly disillusioned you have been. You thought you were getting a hero—and you only got a vicious little person who is fast losing any spark he may have had." At rare moments he could believe pain was useful, for it helped self-education: "I am finding out things about myself, dearest, in all this loneliness; I have discovered, with a shock, how far I have fallen from the ardent young poet who wrote about Mexico." Somehow, he had "let himself go," and it was obvious now that "all this sex stuff is a symptom of that." The cure was not yet apparent, but the wish overwhelming: "Please, God, I intend to get back to poetry and sweetness, some way."[22]

Such words were brave and hopeful, but there was no easy road to happiness. Life had to be faced each day. Favoring a pet scheme of the *Mail*, an excess-profits tax, Jack went down to Washington to help lobby. At first the atmosphere proved tonic: "I don't suppose there is a place in the world so exciting as this city now, missions continually arriving, uniforms, decorations, swords, all sorts of pageants in Congress when the different ambassadors arrive and are received in the Senate." After a brief interview with President Wilson, he had the pleasure of rejecting three job offers, two from Washington newspapers and the third from George Creel, who wanted him for the censorship office. Speaking at several women's-suffrage meetings, he was pleased when Steffens breezed into town, fresh from a fact-finding tour of Russia for the administration. At first his mentor responded sympathetically to tales of marital woe: "I said I'd been a fool and a cad, and he just told me most people were at some time." But after a couple of dinners together, Stef seemed bored with the continual talk of personal problems and Reed was driven back into gloom. Gradually newspaper work became a "desperate grind," with endless political conversations and dull statistical research necessary to bolster the tax articles. Growing indifference led to mistakes: in one case he listed a Congressman dead six months as a supporter of the measure. When Washington palled, he again felt "restless, aimless and dis-satisfied."[23]

Returning to New York, he sometimes dropped in on old haunts, but when friends spoke of Louise, his own misery grew. Hag-ridden by the insoluble problems of sex, love and the future, Jack was kept together mentally by the daily job. Complaining about some assignments—"I'm . . . waiting for a damned actress . . . whom I've got to interview about her damned marriage to a damned prizefighter," he managed to enjoy others —trips to the after-hours saloons on the Hoboken waterfront, reports of gangland murders centering on control of the kosher meat industry, a brief crusade to convince the city to build a swimming pool for the poor in Central Park.

It was not until July 5 that the vagaries of wartime mail brought the first batch of letters from Louise, full of anguish deep as his own: "I just can't stand this *any longer*. It is *too* terrible and *too* utterly sense-less! You are desperately unhappy over there and I am absolutely despondent over here. The only thing I want to live at all for is to be with you—*if we can be happy* again. Otherwise—*I'm sick of the whole thing*. . . . Sometimes I'm physically sick—always I'm mentally sick. I just *can't* go on! . . . I'm so awfully alone and I can't bear it. I'd much, *much* rather be dead. I love you so much and you are all I have." Totally out of sympathy with the prevailing war spirit of France, she was sending back stories on the first American troops to reach the continent, but her heart was not in the work. Separation was good only if it renewed their love: "This just *had* to happen—not this particular little miserable mess but *something* to make us find each other. . . . I can never love anyone else. I want everything about you to be beautiful and fine. You are essentially so wonderful and big." Fearful that the full details of her own indiscre-tions might be revealed, Louise filled each letter with self-recrimination. Promising to be "a better mate . . . more kind and more understanding," she once offered herself as a sacrifice: "I never want to keep you away from where you want to be. I'm a fool, a damn fool—but please believe me dear, rather than interfere with your growth I'd gladly get out alto-gether."[24]

These confessions made Reed feel sick "with relief, and love and shame and all kinds of terrible emotions." Having promised to abstain from sex during her absence, he described an incident of refusing a young girl in Washington who wanted to make love: "I've been true all right." This triggered a mood of self-examination that brought forth the most self-revealing words he ever wrote: "I think perhaps there's something terribly wrong about me—that I may be a little crazy, for I had a desire once, just the other day. I can't tell you how awful, how wretched that made me feel—how I have looked into myself and tried to know why these things happen. I told you once, my darling, that this had all done something to me. It has, O it has. I am awfully tired a good deal of the time, lonely, and without much ambition or much incentive. I feel pretty dull and old. I don't know why all this is.

"But I know why it is that people run to vice when they feel loss—I know that—I can imagine it—I should do it.

"You see, my dearest lover, I was once a free person. I didn't depend on anything. I was as humanly independent as it is possible to be. Then along came women, and they set out deliberately, as they always instinctively do, to break that armor down, to make the artist a human being and dependent upon human beings. Well, they did it, and so now without a mate I am half a man, and sterile. (Now, honey, there is no use denying this. It is true I'm not regretful for it—I'd rather be human than artist.)

"I am under repression a good deal of the time late years. I dare not let myself go. I feel that I am always on the verge of something monstrous. This is not as bad as it seems, dear—it is just that no one I love has ever been able to let me express myself fully, freely, and trust that expression.

"I suppose you're right. I suppose it would wreck things to let nature take its course. I am perfectly convinced that that is so. And I am perfectly ready to admit that my nature is not to be trusted. . . . I've had four or five of these things that have worn you down. Still my darling, you've got to make up your mind to trust me to certain extent, or our life together will be a farce.

"In other words, you've got to recognize the fact that I'm defective (if that is it) or at any rate different, and though I won't do anything you ask me not to, you must accept a difference in my feelings and thoughts.

"It would be intolerable for both of us if you felt you had to direct and censor my thoughts, my actions, as you have in the past—as you did even in your letter telling me not to drink."[25]

The mood did not last, and two days later he was resentful over the need for self-control: "What does all this penance of mine prove? You know well that I, or anyone with a decent experience and knowledge of himself, can shut down on his temptations. All this absence, my darling, did not make me love you any better—it could not. I know, and have known, that you are my only lover. It was never necessary for you to go away in order to make me conscious of my love." A week later a cable announced her arrival in two weeks. Again he was contrite: "Don't blame yourself for anything between us. I am all to blame. I think I'm cured now—anyway I know there is nothing I would do to hurt you."[26] Her final letters showed a similar mood. Picking up on Jack's one comment that might refer to O'Neill—"It is not worth keeping going if you love somebody else better"—she flatly stated: "I *don't* love anyone else. I'm *dead sure* of that. I just love you." The blame for all their problems she fixed on the atmosphere of the Village—"it breaks most everyone." Her suffering had been deep, but just "A few days with my honey will make me feel so happy and peaceful."[27] The last letters of both were suffused with a desire to be alone together, removed from the complications of other people, but for Reed the fantasy could not overcome reality; in debt, partly from sending Louise abroad, and continually short of cash, he realized isolation and escape would be impossible.

The knowledge that Louise was returning seemed to end the need for introspection. Generally calmer, Reed's moods could still swing rapidly to inexplicable despair. The summer had been "terrible" and he predicted, "It is probably going to be hard still for a while; but when you are here I won't mind so much."[28] Stabbed less by personal guilt and feeling stronger for having kept the vow of fidelity, he was distressed over national issues. In June a letter from radical cartoonist Bob Minor had hailed his "remarkable achievements in two worlds—the world of the other people, where you have forced their respect, and the world of our people, where your self-respect has placed you."[29] Such praise was nice, but did not seem fully deserved. While others bore the brunt of antiwar activity, it was impossible to pretend that the *Mail* articles were more than token gestures of dissent. After covering the first day of the fashionable Saratoga racing meet in early August, Jack attended a three-day spiritualist encampment at Lily Dale and he found the participants happier and more good-natured than anyone else he knew. Reflection made the symbolism of otherworldliness and joy too overt to be ignored. Three days after returning, he wrote his final feature for the *Mail*.

To make up for trivial newspaper work, Reed devoted many hours to the *Masses*, contributing one major article and several short pieces each month. Hammering at the relationship between business profits and war, he was capable of attacking all segments of the social spectrum. He denounced Samuel Gompers for leading labor into support of the war, then went on to describe plans of the self-styled "First Fifty" to help the national effort by cutting down on the number of their residences, butlers and courses at meals: "It is a worthy program, and will doubtlessly be imitated on the lower East Side." The August issue featured "Militarism at Play," which began: "We always used to say certain things would happen in this country if militarism came. Militarism has come. They are happening." Then it described the systematic disruption of peace meetings by secret-service men and military personnel, the June incidents at Hunt's Point Palace and raids on Socialist district headquarters. The same issue reprinted part of an article from the New York *Tribune* in which a physician was quoted about the frequency of mental disease in the army. Reed's contribution was a simple headline: "Knit a Strait-Jacket for Your Soldier Boy."[30]

Many of the regular *Masses* subscribers never saw the August issue. On July 5 the magazine was informed that the Post Office Department had declared it "unmailable under the [Espionage] Act of June 15, 1917," on grounds that it was interfering with the conduct of the war. When the department refused to abide by its own rules and state what sections of the magazine had violated the law, Counsel Gilbert E. Roe persuaded Federal Judge Learned Hand in New York to grant an injunction against the Postmaster General on the grounds that there had been in fact no violation of the law. The Post Office then countered by having Circuit Judge C. M. Hough of Vermont issue an order staying execution of the injunction. The effect was simply that the August magazine was sold only on a few Manhattan newsstands.

Like the other editors, Reed was exasperated, and this mood pervaded every line of a September article which began: "In America the month just past has been the blackest month for free men our generation has known. With a sort of hideous apathy the country has acquiesced in a regime of judicial tyranny, bureaucratic suppression and industrial barbarism." The evidence was blunt and simple: the conviction of Berkman and Goldman; the suppression of eighteen radical periodicals, despite the defeat of censorship provisions of the Espionage Act; the wrecking of Boston's Socialist Party Headquarters by a mob of soldiers and sailors; the race riot in East St. Louis, where thirty blacks had been killed; the open terror practiced in Arizona by vigilantes against striking workmen and their families, packed aboard cattle cars and shipped off to the middle of the desert; the prosecution of anarchist Tom Mooney on highly tainted evidence for a Preparedness Day Parade bombing; the arrest of female-suffrage pickets outside the White House. It all added up to a simple moral: "In America law is merely the instrument for good or evil of the most powerful interests, and there are no Constitutional safeguards worth the powder to blow them to hell."[31]

Strong, fearless, indomitable—but, after all, words, only words in a small-circulation radical magazine that might not even reach its audience. With Louise coming home, he began to rise out of the sticky subjective morass to confront old questions made new again. On the one hand, writing; on the other, action—here was a problem that could never be settled. Early in the summer Floyd Dell's girlfriend had teased Jack that he was "a coward for not getting arrested." The accusation had nagged enough for him to mention it to Louise and say perhaps he should "raise hell and go to jail." Cautioning against this, she warned with the prescience of love: "You are too precious to waste your energy. . . . All of your best strength you'll need a little later for big, big things and it would be too terrible if you were out of the running by some rash deed when you are needed most—and you will be needed."[32]

This was faith, the faith of a selfish lover, and it connected to the faith of Bob Minor and that expressed in many conversations with acquaintances. Reed was a culture hero whom people emulated. Burdened by the obscure knowledge that he acted for others as well as himself, Jack was driven to survey his total relationship to the war. The resulting article was accepted by the *Seven Arts*. This was a most significant market. Begun in September 1916 by Waldo Frank, Van Wyck Brooks and James Oppenheim, and bankrolled by one wealthy patron, the magazine was in many ways the chief literary organ of the avant-garde, the essence and culmination of the prewar Village "Renaissance." A first-issue letter from Romain Rolland, living on the Continent, had set the tone by calling on Americans to keep art alive, and the editors accepted this as their mission. Leaving politics to the *New Republic* and a mixture of art and radicalism to the *Masses*, they ignored social questions to publish the latest work of Robert Frost, Carl Sandburg, Amy Lowell, Sherwood Anderson, Theodore Dreiser, John Dos Passos and Maxwell Bodenheim. By the summer of 1917 the enormous pressure of wartime society was forcing a slow change in policy. In June the magazine carried Randolph Bourne's "War and the Intellectuals," a sharp attack on the pragmatic-*New Republic*-Lippmann-John Dewey attitude that an American war supported by intellectuals was more noble, just and beneficial than an old-fashioned conflict. Bourne was at least a staff member; by accepting Reed's work, the editors were moving one step closer to commitment.

The tone and argument of "This Unpopular War" was calm and sober. Bringing together themes suggested for over two years, it showed a reflective author turning over wartime experiences with a kind of innocence, full of sorrowful wonder that a pleasant world had driven itself mad. Reed admitted having journeyed to Europe in 1914 already believing "the capitalistic ruling classes had cynically and with malice tricked their people into war." But experiences on many fronts had only confirmed this idea. Country after country had joined the war, without any government daring to ask the people for their compliance. Once it began, millions became involved, if only for emotional reasons of defense and revenge. Yet even they had no real interest in the outcome and were ready to lay down arms. Now it was America's turn. Here the common man had a natural inclination to neutrality. Caring little about abstract, commercial seagoing rights, he had reelected Wilson, the antiwar leader. Then, as in England, Bulgaria, Turkey, Romania, Russia, Italy or Germany, he was not consulted about the decision which would put a rifle in his hand. Soon American deaths might convince him it was important to struggle under the banner of "democracy." But what kind of democracy was it that went to war without asking "the consent of those who are to do the fighting"? The problem was more than political, for something was stronger than the will of elected officials—"Political power without economic power makes 'democracy' a hollow sham."[33]

By the late summer of 1917 John Reed had absorbed this kind of Marxist interpretation of the World War and social development; nothing else could explain the turbulence, suffering and chaos that edged the contours of life. Such ideas came partly from reading and partly from conversation with Village radicals. But abstract theory did not weigh very heavily with Reed. Knowledge always began with basic feelings, and experiences of the last three years had only reaffirmed those ideas to which he had been exposed. In the spring he had simultaneously expressed faith and doubt in the "inevitability" of class struggle and revolution: "I wish with all my heart that the proletariat would rise and take their rights—I don't see how else they will get them. Political relief is so slow to come, and year by year the opportunities for peaceful protest and lawful action are curtailed. But I am not sure any more that the working-class is capable of revolution, peaceful or otherwise; the workers are so divided and bitterly hostile to each other, so badly led, so blind to their class-interest."

Having seen radicals, intellectuals and antimilitarists respond to the call of patriotism in Europe and at home, he might have slipped into cynicism about the capacity of the common man or society to change.

But Reed was no cynic: "I cannot give up the idea that out of democracy will be born the new world—richer, braver, freer, more beautiful." Wanting to aid with the delivery, in the spring—when he was burdened with personal problems, weak from the operation—his future had been cloudy: "As for me, I don't know what I can do to help—I don't know yet. All I know is that my happiness is built on the misery of other people, that I eat because others go hungry, that I am clothed when other people go almost naked through the frozen cities in winter; and that fact poisons me, disturbs my serenity, makes me write propaganda when I would rather play."

Since he had written those words, some intimations of change had arisen on the international scene. In March a revolution had begun in Russia. At first more a middle-class than a proletarian affair, the upheaval had in succeeding months provided evidence that some radical parties in Russia were still active, pushing the country toward Socialism. From thousands of miles away and through the screens of wartime censorship it was impossible to know what was really happening, and Reed increasingly felt in the summer of 1917 that he must see developments there for himself. The reasons were both personal and professional. A writer whose reputation stemmed from one revolution, he sensed that he could be fulfilled in another. More important, Russia was full of the promise that the working class might seize control of a capitalist country and help put an end to the dismal war.

After mid-July Reed swam daily at the Harvard Club, and on weekends worked in the garden at Croton until his tanned body was so healthy he could boast to Louise, "You'll be surprised to see how strong I've got again."[34] In some obscure way, he was girding himself both to meet his lover and to partake of the "big things" she had foreseen. The long dark night of his soul, the lonely period of waiting was at an end. Once again he was eager to grapple with the problems of the world.

17

Petrograd

"If I were asked what I consider most characteristic of the Russian Revolution, I should say, the vast simplicity of its processes. Like Russian life as described by Tolstoy and Chekhov, like the course of Russian history itself, the Revolution seemed to be endowed with the patient inevitability of mounting sap in spring, of the tides of the sea. The French Revolution, in its causes and architecture, has always seemed to me essentially a human affair, the creature of intellect, theatrical; the Russian Revolution, on the other hand, is like a force of nature...."[1]

Four months after the Bolshevik Party took control of Russia and commenced a major experiment in social reorganization, John Reed began to assess what he had witnessed in Petrograd. These were hardly his first words about the revolution. From the moment of arriving in Russia in September 1917 until departing in February 1918, his views, opinions and observations had been jotted into notebooks and run through his portable typewriter. His accounts of meetings, speeches, proclamations, interviews, resolutions, troop movements, uprisings and skirmishes were written at a furious pace by a man who was going everywhere, trying to see, feel, understand, describe and explain the complex events of social transformation. Stuck temporarily in Christiania, Norway, in mid-March, he suddenly had time for a quieter look at the meaning of all his experience.

Writing for an audience assumed to be hostile to the atheism and collectivism of the Bolsheviks, Reed fell readily into images of simple, natural forces moving regardless of human will, then added enough history to show the October Revolution as the inevitable result of historical trends. The argument went like this: Basically democratic and communistic, the Russian masses had never responded to the liberal ideas of western Europe which had fascinated the intelligentsia and led to a century of abortive middle-class revolutionary movements. Passionate, volatile and superstitious, an oppressed, fatalistic people had gone their own slow way, occasionally bursting forth in spontaneous orgies of violence, burning manors, killing nobility, slaughtering priests. They had been kept partly in line by the force of the church, but the masses' deep spirituality had in recent years become increasingly secularized, subsumed into new spiritual forces like Socialism. While intellectual leaders theorized and tinkered with government after both the 1905 and February 1917 revolutions, the "race-mind" of the people was slowly moving toward a decision. It came in November. War, starvation, corruption, the total breakdown of social services—all these had paved the way for the Bolsheviks. Like the turning of a season, a vast change had burst over the country with "tempest and wind, and then . . . a rush of red blossoming." Leaders who temporized were "tossed aside," while Lenin and Trotsky survived by swimming on a mighty tide, "the crowd," the real "hero of the Russian Revolution."

The new social order could seem frightful. Terrified by the "spectacle of a whole people going its own wild path to its own ends," much of the domestic intelligentsia had retreated into opposition, while the rest of the world looked on uncomprehendingly. Moral outrage over Russian actions —the expropriation of private property, the cancellation of international debts and the refusal to continue in the war—was beside the point, because values were culture-bound: "It is difficult for the bourgeoisie—especially the foreign bourgeoisie—to understand the ideas that move the Russian masses. It is all very easy to say they have no sense of Patriotism, Duty, Honor; that they do not submit to Discipline or appreciate the Privileges of Democracy; that in short they are Incapable of Self-Government. But in Russia all these attributes of the bourgeois democratic state have been replaced by a new ideology. There *is* patriotism—but it is allegiance to the international brotherhood of the working class; there *is* duty, and men die cheerfully for it—but it is duty to the revolutionary cause; there *is* honor, but [it] is a new kind of honor, based on the dignity of human life and happiness rather than on what a fantastic aristocracy of blood or wealth has decreed is fitting for 'gentlemen'; there *is* discipline—revolutionary discipline . . . and the Russian masses are showing themselves not only capable of self-government, but of inventing a whole new form of civilization."

A convert's faith did not obscure the massive problems facing the regime: "Standing alone, as it does, the only live thing in the universe, there is a strong probability the Russian Revolution will not be able to defy the deadly enmity of the world." No matter. The poet's imagination could take flight, soar beyond what might happen in days to come and bend back to encompass the glorious moments a people had lived: "Whether it survive or perish, whether it be altered unrecognizably by the pressure of circumstances, it will have shown that dreams can come true." If such dreams largely belonged to the "toiling masses," there is no doubt Reed's own were deeply engaged, infusing words with a spirit of lyric energy, driving a body past weariness into the ecstasy of exhaustion, turning fear and doubt into joy. The revolution was a dream incarnate—touched by its spirit, man, poet, journalist soared into a realm of visionary transcendence.

For Reed—as for troubled Russia—this dream had been a long time coming. Ever since childhood, romance, adventure and pageantry had fired his imagination, helping to create a lifelong quest for meaning in the great deeds of men. Desire for heroism had fused with a growing social conscience until the two were indistinguishable. Overlapping images merged—the feats of classic literature, primitive Indians stalking through a frontier forest, a port with tall-masted ships and fragrant cargoes, the politics of a father whose penalty for honor was death, the jumble of Eastern metropolises and piled tenements, masses of dark immigrants, desert skies steepled with the sombreros of comrades, trench slime and mountains of bone and human flesh. In 1915 such visions had converged in Russia, a land where unconventionality was bright enough to shine through the ugliness of an oppressive regime. Listening hard for the rumble of change, Reed had then eagerly seized upon every sound of dissent as the potential birth cry of a new order.

Russia was a strange land for Americans, and he was far from the only one to project upon it images formed from personal desires. Among Bohemians a Russian cult had flourished, with figures like Nijinsky,

Chekhov, Stravinsky, Diaghilev and Dostoevsky worshipped not only for individual genius, but also for the way they expressed that mysterious force known as the Slavic soul. Believed to be the polar opposite of materialistic America, Russia was loved for her exoticism, passion and spirituality. Such a view was hardly shared by political thinkers, for whom the autocracy, pogroms and corruption of the Czarist regime were reprehensible. Yet these beliefs began to creep into the rhetoric of American leaders after the February 1917 revolution deposed the Czar and set up a Provisional Government which promised the advent of Western constitutionalism. Coming at an opportune moment, this upheaval made United States entry into the war easier, for now the world struggle seemed a clear-cut one between democracy and autocracy. Not only did newspapers and pro-war liberals argue this way, but in his war speech to Congress, Woodrow Wilson had rhapsodized in words that Reed might write a year later, claiming that autocracy "was not in fact Russian in origin, character, or purpose," the President saluted her as a country "always in fact democratic at heart, in all the vital habits of her thought, in all the intimate relationships of her people that spoke their natural instinct."

Reed's initial reactions to the February Revolution were temperate. Assessing it as the work of "liberal-minded provincial nobles, business men, professors, editors and army officers," he was fearful of exactly what American leaders desired, that the Provisional Government would strengthen the country and prolong the World War.[2] This opinion began to change as it became obvious that a second center of political power was in existence, the Councils of Workingmen's and Soldiers' Delegates, soon to be referred to by the Russian word "Soviets." When *The New York Times* labeled their members "extreme radicals and syndicalists, corresponding to the IWW agitators in this country," his interest was stirred, and in June, when Soviet agitation for a separate peace forced the resignation of two conservative ministers in the Provisional Government, Jack apologized for having misunderstood the revolution: "It was only the 'front' we saw . . . the real thing was the long-thwarted rise of the Russian masses . . . and the purpose of it is the establishment of a new human society upon earth." The engine for this would be the Soviets, "the real revolutionary heart of the New Russia."[3]

Steffens, back from Russia in late June, glowed with firsthand accounts of the Soviets as centers of democratic debate and decision-making, and even mentioned a disciplined party named "Bolshevik," whose aim was to carry the revolution further. These words registered, but did not penetrate an unfocused Jack until after Louise's decision to return home.

Landing the first week in August, she was swept up by a husband bursting with the desire to get to Russia. For her it was easy to connect with a press syndicate, but Reed—a year earlier one of the highest-paid correspondents in the country—could find no editor ready to hire an antiwar radical. The *Masses* and the Socialist daily, the New York *Call,* provided credentials, but neither had money for the trip. This problem was solved when Max Eastman and his friend Eugen Boissevain convinced a wealthy socialite to donate $2000 toward the journey.

Before obtaining a passport, Reed had to clear up the problem of military service. Requesting an appearance before the Croton draft board, he underwent a complete physical on August 14 and was pronounced in good health. The next day, after considering a report on the nephrectomy from Johns Hopkins, the board discharged him from military obligation. Then the Passport Office asked him in for special questioning. In response to a call from the Soviets, an international peace conference of Socialists was scheduled to assemble in Stockholm, and the State Department was denying passports to representatives of the American party. Unable to distinguish between radicals of various stripes, government officials insisted Reed take an oath swearing he would not represent the SP. He was interested in the meeting, but was neither a party member nor a delegate, so this was easy enough to do. His last article before sailing on the Danish ship *United States* was based on materials Louise had gathered overseas. Reporting war dissatisfaction in France and linking it to changes in Russia, he made a prediction: "Events grand and terrible are brewing in Europe, such as only the imagination of a revolutionary poet could have conceived."[4]

From New York they sailed to Halifax, where the ship was held for a week as English authorities searched for contraband. Worried that letters from American radicals to Socialists abroad might be confiscated, Jack concealed them under the carpet, and when a party of marines appeared, diverted them from the task of searching the cabin by sharing a bottle of whiskey. The trip was strangely joyous, the band playing continually and people dressing formally for dinner. Among the diverse group of passengers—Scandinavians, a group of college boys due to work in the Petrograd branch of an American bank, a large number of poor Jewish political exiles going home, American salesmen hoping to tap Russian markets—there was little talk of the war. Interest in the revolution was high, and of many opinions, the most unusual was held by a young Russian aristocrat: "The Russian people, they have the art instinct. They have done it grandly, magnificently. They have made what the French call the *grande geste.* . . . It is all I care for in life. The ballet, the opera, the grand extravagances of the rich—what are they beside this epic?"[5]

After debarking in Christiania, Norway, Jack and Louise boarded a jam-packed train for an uncomfortable eighteen-hour, overnight journey to Stockholm. There they learned the peace conference had been postponed. At the headquarters of the International Socialist Bureau they met Secretary General Camille Huysmans, whose thin, drawn face and wispy mustache drooped with weariness. Quietly, but firmly, he assured them that, despite the actions of the United States, France and Italy in preventing representatives from attending the meeting, it would soon be held. At least the lines were clearly drawn: "Only the governments prevent the Socialist Parties from sending their appointed delegates here. . . . Now it is at last the peoples who want peace, and the governments alone who want to continue the war."

Socialist headquarters was crowded with representatives from many Continental countries, all full of enthusiasm and hopeful plans for building "a new world." From Panin, a delegate of the Russian Workmen's and Soldiers' Council, Reed learned about the spontaneous origins of the Soviets in 1905 and their rebirth earlier in 1917; this was a tale "more dramatic and infinitely more inspiring than the history of the Romanoffs." Paul Axelrod, whose thick glasses and bushy beard made him every inch the "absent-minded German professor," was full of news about central European radical movements. Both men emphasized that the Russian revolution would soon move further in the direction of Socialism. This was happy news, for it meant, "There as in our own country, the greatest days are to come."[6]

Waiting for the Russian consulate to issue a visa, Jack and Louise explored Stockholm. The graceful city on canals, prosperous from war trade, was crowded and gay, a neutral meeting place for citizens of belligerent nations, a center for spies, conspirators and profiteers, a haven for secret conferences of eastern European nationalists. Mingling in cafés and restaurants with Turks and Russians, English and German diplomats, South Americans, Poles, Finns and Czechs, they heard many rumors about Russian events. On September 10, newspapers carried stories that Riga, in Latvia, had fallen to German armies. Worried the frontier might be closed, Reed asked Panin if the visa could be hurried. It could and was, and the same afternoon, "by the power of the Soviet," they boarded a train heading northward.[7] Sharing the car were an assortment of passengers—a tall, thin, silent general coming home from two years in England, several other officers, a gray-bearded anarchist returning from thirty-eight years' exile, half a dozen young Russian graduates of British aviation camps, an English general with three adjutants. The Swedish countryside was reminiscent of the Pacific Northwest, ranges of hills wooded with dark fir and pine, river rapids bearing logs, wooden houses and barns painted red, stony fields with shocks of barley stiffly tied to poles. At the port of Haparanda, just below the Arctic Circle, authorities searched the baggage and removed all foodstuffs. Then the travelers boarded a small boat and crossed a corner of the Baltic to Finland, whose gloomy iron waterfront sheds and neat church steeples gave little hint that this was part of a country where social change was under way.

Suddenly the revolution appeared. It was there in the uniforms of the Russian soldiers, imperial brass buttons torn away and red strips sewn on their coats, and in the casual behavior of men on duty, a sentry smoking and making no move to salute a superior, guards at the railroad station lounging in chairs, a squad of slovenly privates in the baggage room watching to see that officers took no bribes, refusing to give preferential treatment to the general. Placards on the waiting-room walls announced that two days earlier General Lavr Kornilov had begun a march on Petrograd to suppress the Provisional Government of Alexander Kerensky. Nobody knew what had happened since, and crowds roared in debate. Officers favorable to the idea of a strong man restoring "law and order" were contested by common soldiers. A few months earlier they had known little of politics, but now, their pockets stuffed with pamphlets, they talked about liberty and democracy and listened intently "with a pathetic eagerness to learn."

A Russian train carried Jack and Louise south across Finland, past wide fields and quiet towns of solid wooden houses. At every station startling rumors greeted them—Kornilov had captured Petrograd, Kerensky had been assassinated, the Bolsheviks had risen, the streets of the capital city were running with blood. Listening to the pro-Kornilov comments of upper-class passengers, Reed began to "dimly perceive that the Russian Revolution had become a class-struggle, *the* class-struggle." Preferring order to further change, the middle class which had helped overthrow the Czar was now behind the counterrevolution. Troubled by fantasies of Cossacks rampaging through Petrograd, Jack's thoughts hurried ahead, along with prayers for the revolution's safety.

The night was long and dark with heavy rain. At each stop the train was locked while privates with red armbands scrutinized papers, insolently staring at the high-ranking officers. The next day, beyond the port of Abo, the revolutionary soldiers were openly hostile. Little bands stalked beside the cars, staring through the windows and angrily muttering, "Bourgeoisie!" Their behavior spun Reed into the past: "I felt as must have felt some English traveller from Boulogne by coach to Paris, in 1793, when the Terror was on, stopping to change horses at a little post-house, while the fierce, hairy faces of the local Jacobin militia were thrust in at the window." At Viborg, terror became a reality. Crowds milled through the station discussing the day's events. When a commanding general refused an order to send troops to defend Petrograd against Kornilov, soldiers had burst into headquarters, dragged a number of officers into the streets and drowned them in a canal.

Even here, only seventy-five miles from Petrograd, reports of conditions in the capital were sensational and contradictory. Not knowing who held the city, some frightened passengers left the train, but Jack and Louise stayed aboard as it moved off behind a wood-burning engine belching showers of sparks. There was little to see until they rolled into the empty Finland Station in the early hours of the morning and managed to catch a ride with two soldiers in a staff car. On the way to their hotel, the city was quiet and dark. No buildings were burning, no Cossacks patrolled the streets, no blood ran in the gutters. The forces of General Kornilov, undermined by radical propaganda, had melted away. The revolution was still alive.

In the autumn of 1917 Petrograd was a feverish place where the tattered fabric of an outworn political and economic system was being rent by the birth throes of a new order. Winds blew off the Gulf of Finland, fogs rolled through twilight streets, rain fell from gray skies and mud was deep underfoot. The city was dark and cold, with fuel in short supply and electricity turned off from midnight until dawn. Food was scarce, the daily bread ration having fallen to a quarter of a pound, and in workers' districts long queues waited patiently to buy milk, sugar, meat and tobacco that were rarely available. In stark contrast, the theaters, opera and ballet houses were packed every night, galleries held exhibitions of avant-garde paintings, handsome young officers festooned with gold braid and elaborate swords lounged about the lobbies of hotels. And everywhere, talk was of the advancing German armies, the servant problem, the food problem and the problem of ruling an increasingly turbulent nation.

More than six months after the abdication of the Czar, the question of power lay unresolved, and two distinct centers of authority existed uneasily side by side. One was the Provisional Government, its legitimacy stemming from the last Duma (parliament), and the other was the Soviets, especially the strategic Petrograd Soviet and the national Central Committee of Soviets. These spontaneous organizations of workers, peasants and soldiers were Socialist in sympathy, with representatives of Mensheviks, Socialist Revolutionaries, Bolsheviks and several splinter groups. Commanding the confidence of industrial workers and the politically conscious rank-and-file of the armed forces, the Soviets' importance was heightened by the fact that Czarist police had been shattered in February, leaving the maintenance of order in urban areas largely in the hands of workers and soldiers.

In this situation the pressure of the masses was crucial. Traditional Socialist theory held that capitalism had to develop more fully before Russia could become a collective state, and, suspicious as they might be of "bourgeois" democrats, Soviet leaders were prepared to let the PG continue in power. Their constituents had other ideas. Fed up with high prices, short rations and unequal distribution of the land, workers and peasants burst into uprisings that left even radical Socialists running furiously to catch them. The spark was always the war. In June popular pressure forced the Foreign and War ministers to resign. Then an offensive in Galicia, begun largely to please the Allies, collapsed ignominiously, and the first week in July workers and soldiers took to the streets and rampaged through the capital, firing rifles, looting stores and homes and besieging the headquarters of the Soviet with angry demands that its leaders take control of the country. While Mensheviks and Socialist Revolutionaries vacillated, the Bolshevik Party associated itself with the demonstrations just in time to receive the blame as the disturbances were quelled.

The result of the July days was a further polarization papered over by an apparent compromise. When Prince Lvov, the Constitutional Democrat premier, resigned, Alexander Kerensky, a moderate Socialist, took his place. The new cabinet, with a majority of conservative Socialist ministers, won the qualified support of the Soviets on the condition it push more quickly for peace and social reform than its predecessors. Simultaneously the Kerensky government moved to destroy the Bolsheviks on the drummed-up charges that its leaders were German agents. Newspapers were suppressed and most of the party's top leaders jailed, with the significant exception of Lenin, who escaped to Finland. Such repression did not have the desired effect. In industrial centers across the nation the party continued to grow as the new cabinet proved unable to effectuate social change. When Kornilov rose with apparent middle-class backing, the Soviets came to Kerensky's aid, forming a Committee for Struggle with Counterrevolution. This group included Bolshevik representatives, who immediately pushed through approval of an armed workers' militia, the Red Guard. As the counterrevolution dissipated, more than ten thousand men, armed by the Bolsheviks and loyal to them, remained as the most reliable military force in the Russian capital.

Arriving in Petrograd just after Kornilov's failure, Jack and Louise checked into the Hotel d'Angleterre, where clerks recalled his escapades with Robinson of two years before. He immediately wrote Mike: "The old town has changed! Joy where there was gloom, and gloom where there was joy. There is so much dramatic to write that I don't know where to begin—but I'll have a tale to unfold. . . . For color and terror and grandeur this makes Mexico look pale."[8] If his knowledge of recent events was fragmentary, he quickly absorbed enough to report the current situation with considerable accuracy: "This revolution has now settled down to the class-struggle pure and simple, as predicted by the Marxians. The so-called 'bourgeois liberals,' Rodzianko, Lvov, Miliukov, *et al.*, have definitely aligned themselves with the capitalist elements. . . . The intellectuals and romantic revolutionists, except Gorky . . . are shocked at what revolution really is, and either gone over to the Cadets, or quit. The old-timers—most of them—like Kropotkin, Breshkovskaya, even Alladdin, are entirely out of sympathy with the present movement; their real concern was with a political revolution, and the political revolution has happened, and Russia is a republic, I believe, forever—but what is going on now is an economic revolution which they don't understand nor care for; the conquest of German kaiserdom now seems to them the most important thing in the world. Through the tempest of events tumbling over one another which is beating upon Russia, the Bolsheviki star steadily rises."[9]

Reed did not have to rely solely on his own meager Russian to gather information. In the wake of the February Revolution's amnesty, émigré radicals had come home from exile. Some he knew, like Bill Shatov, a member of the IWW. Others he met—Mikhail Yanishev of Detroit; V. Volodarsky of the American Socialist Party; Samuel Voskov, an organizer for the Carpenters' Union in New York; Boris Reinstein, a member of the Socialist Labor Party from Buffalo; Jake Peters from England. Anarchist or Socialist abroad, most identified with the Bolsheviks in Petrograd. They warmly welcomed Jack for his "exuberance, his love of life, his hilarious antics."[10] Only one, Alexander Gumberg of New York, was cool. Brother of a high Bolshevik, Gumberg was a kind of lone wolf, functioning in the shadowy role of intermediary between the innermost revolutionary circles and the American embassy crowd. Intellectual and know-it-all, he made mordant quips that piqued Reed, and quarrels between them were common.

Most important both as a friend and a source of information was a native-born American, Albert Rhys Williams. Four years older than Jack, educated at English and German universities, he was an ordained minister who had preached the social gospel and had supported Eugene V. Debs as early as 1908. Leaving a Boston church to become a correspondent in

Europe at the beginning of the war, Rhys had been in Russia for the New York *Post* since June. In America the two men had occasionally met, and Williams had been taken with Reed: "I liked him for the very qualities that his pettifogging critics considered his faults as well as for his accepted virtues. They were very engaging faults, if faults they were. . . . To the ham actor in him, to his ebullient pranks and antics and humor, I responded wholeheartedly."[11] Alienated from most other correspondents and members of the American colony, Rhys welcomed the kindred spirit.

In a very real sense, Williams and Reed were on the same trajectory. Each identified with radicalism at home and had been driven further left by the experience of war. Romantics and lovers of adventure with no profound understanding of Marxism, both were ready for the kind of revolution that meant real change, an end to war and a significant redistribution of political and economic power. After three months' observation of the Russian scene, Rhys was convinced that only the Bolshevik program—peace, no annexations, confiscation of estates and power transferred to the proletariat and peasantry—was capable of fulfilling the revolution. No joiner, he confided to Jack an interest in working with the Bolsheviks because "they want the sort of social justice you and I want. They want it more passionately than any other group here. They want it *now*."[12]

Reed did not have to be convinced—a lifelong admiration for men of action predisposed him toward the Bolsheviks. This left two troubling questions—would they be able to pull it off, implement the slogan "All Power to the Soviets" and complete the revolution, and would he personally be able to measure up, be ready to commit himself fully? Powerless to answer the first, he worried more about the second. In conversation his moods swung back and forth. Bantering with Rhys, he once laughingly asked, "Do you think we'll ever make the grade? Or are we tagged for life—the humanitarians, the dilettantes?" More somberly he could comment, "It's easy to be fired by things here. We'll wind up thinking we're great revolutionaries. And at home?" The question hung unanswered because Williams' thoughts were much the same. Knowing his own doubts, he could describe Reed's shifts from gaiety to self-recrimination as the result of "the natural wavering of a very human young American before he set himself a goal more difficult than any he had yet picked."[13]

Partisanship did not act as a blinder; it only made Reed more eager to discover what was going on. Along with Williams, often accompanied by Louise and Bessie Beatty, correspondent for the San Francisco *Bulletin*, he began to investigate the city's life. Among many rich and middle-class people there was a distinct longing for the good old days. At the apartment to which he and Louise moved to save money, the nightly conversation of the bourgeois landlords inevitably got around to a wish for the arrival of German armies to restore "law and order." One evening, over tea, caviar and gleaming sterling at the home of a rich merchant, an elegant company showed in a straw poll that it favored the Kaiser over the Bolsheviks by a vote of ten to one.

It was good to escape such people and cross the steel-gray Neva to the Viborg section, a crowded district of slums and tenements near armament factories and mills, where orators spoke nightly. From residents in such an area even overt hostility could give pleasure. Asked about his politics in broken Russian, a rough-clad worker could stare at Reed and Williams fixedly, contemptuously spit out a sunflower seed and growl, "This may be *your* war, but it's not mine. You are bourgeois and I am a worker." Amid such radical sentiment, partisanship became overt. On September 30 at the Cirque Moderne, a bare, gloomy amphitheater, Jack was on the platform while Bill Shatov led six thousand workers in a mass protest against American treatment of the imprisoned Emma Goldman and Alexander Berkman.* The principal resolution called on the United States government to end its Czarist-like repressions, then heartily saluted all "who in 'free' America fight for the social revolution."[14]

Reed's participation in this meeting threw the American embassy into an uproar. Ambassador David R. Francis, an ex-governor of Missouri whose tastes ran to cigars, whiskey and poker, had a distinct distaste for radicals. Soon he was "reliably informed" that Jack had been "cordially welcomed by Bolcheviks [*sic*] whom he apparently advised of his coming."[15] Annoyed at such sympathies, the ambassador was ready to believe a report that Reed had been responsible for a rumor that Berkman was about to be executed. Cabling Washington to learn the identity of Goldman and Berkman, the diplomat also arranged to find out more about the journalist. On the crowded Nevsky Prospekt an agent picked Jack's pocket, and a letter in his wallet from Camille Huysmans, secretary of the International Socialist Bureau, gave convincing proof he was a "suspicious character" who should be investigated.† One of the ambassador's hirelings soon filed

---

* All dates in this chapter are from the Gregorian calendar; the date according to the old-style Julian calendar then used in Russia was thirteen days earlier, which is why in Russia the revolution is called the October Revolution. Russia adopted the Gregorian calendar shortly after the Bolsheviks took power.

† In his letters to the Department of State and in his memoirs, the ambassador always maintained that Reed had lost his pocketbook, which was then delivered to the consulate. But Negley Farson, *Way of a Transgressor*, 286, maintains that Reed's pocket was picked, and this appears most likely; it seems too convenient that

a detailed report of a conversation, the contents of which show that Reed knew a secret investigator when he saw one. After revealing himself a Socialist and a devotee of "the Marx theory," he had expanded on the theme of how much foreign diplomats were interfering "with the internal politics of the country." This meant that when the Bolsheviks took control, "the very first thing they would do would be to kick out all the Embassies and all those connected with them."[16]

Having his wallet lifted, being tailed, hearing harsh words from U.S. diplomats—these were petty annoyances in portentous times. To see more of the country, Reed—along with Williams and Reinstein—made a five-day tour of the Latvian front in early October. Conditions in the Twelfth Army were turbulent as those in the capital. Decimated units had lost sixty percent of their personnel through casualties and desertion, and those who remained were ill-fed and poorly equipped. While German shrapnel burst over the fields, soldiers crowded around to ask about developments in Petrograd. In each regiment two sources of authority—the regular command staff and the Soldiers' Soviet—jostled one another in mutual contempt. By now the Soviet had the upper hand, but, committed to continuing the war, it was being outflanked by the rank-and-file. Over objections of both headquarters and the Soviet, a peace meeting was held behind the lines on Sunday afternoon. Under a bleak, wintry sky rumbling with heavy artillery, thousands of dun-colored soldiers listened to five hours of speeches denouncing the war, the Provisional Government, and the imperialism of the Allies. Impressed, Reed commented: "Surely never since history began has a fighting army held such a peace meeting in the midst of battle."[17]

In the capital the Provisional Government tottered toward oblivion. Rumored to be deathly sick, or given to hysterics, or addicted to drugs, or all three, Kerensky feverishly improvised with cabinets and coalitions in an attempt to hold power until the election of a Constituent Assembly in November. Late September had seen a Democratic Conference, with twelve hundred representatives from all parties and groups; this gave way to a smaller Council of the Republic in October. Both were stillborn. Far from the ornate halls of the Marinsky Palace, where the Council met, the Russian people were making decisions. Soldiers deserted trenches, peasants seized estates, workers took control of factories or went on strike and the Soviets swung further to the left. In September the Petrograd Soviet

---

a man whom Francis was spying upon and cabling America to find out more about should suddenly lose his wallet and have it then turn up in the hands of United States officials.

had for the first time elected a Bolshevik majority, and soon Moscow followed suit. Dozens of other Soviets across the country, from Siberia to the Urals, from the Donetz Basin to Finland, were bombarding the Central Committee with petitions demanding that it take control of the country, and the Baltic Fleet was calling for the removal of Kerensky.

Hovering on the edge of power, the Central Committee writhed with indecision. It had been elected at the First Congress of Soviets in July and was dominated by the Mensheviks and Socialist Revolutionaries, both committed to ending the war only on the basis of international agreement. Tacitly approving Kerensky's moves, aware of the leftward shift in factories and barracks, its members wished to ignore a promise to convene a Second Congress of Soviets. Pressure on the Central Committee came not only from insistent Bolsheviks, but from growing numbers of Socialist Revolutionaries, who broke with more conservative comrades, took the name Left Socialist Revolutionaries and began to share policies and strategy with the Bolsheviks. Finally the Committee capitulated, called for elections and set November 2 as the date for the new Congress.

While propaganda material poured from presses; party orators fanned out into factories, workshops, garrisons and front-line trenches; debates rang out in theaters, schoolhouses, clubs and barracks; and street corners became public tribunes, the fate of Russia revolved around the figure of one short, balding, deadly sober man—Vladimir Ilyitch Ulianov, known as Lenin. Ever since returning from Switzerland in April, the creator of Bolshevism had, over the objections of many close associates, been insisting Russia was ready for a socialist revolution. After the July Days he directed the party from Finland, and in late September he bombarded the Bolshevik Central Committee with letters calling for insurrection. On October 20 Lenin moved to an apartment in the Viborg district. Three days later twelve members of the party's Central Committee met in secrecy to hear their leader insist the time had come to make good the slogan "All Power to the Soviets." With only two negative votes, those of Grigory Zinoviev and Lev Kamenev, the group agreed. The resolution cited the Bolsheviks' growing strength, a supposed decision of Kerensky to surrender Petrograd to the Germans, and the danger of a rightest coup as reasons for making "armed insurrection . . . the order of the day."

During the last two weeks of October, debates and recriminations filled the party press, news of separatist national independence movements came in from the Ukraine, Poland and Finland, and rumors of an impending Bolshevik uprising swept through Petrograd. While moderate Socialists denounced the idea, Kerensky and other government officials issued warnings and foreign embassies cabled anxiously for instructions, an intoxicated, hopeful Reed wrote Mike Robinson: "It looks like a show-down soon."[18] Seizing one of Lenin's dramatic phrases—"History will not forgive us if we do not assume power now"—he enjoyed rolling it off his tongue as he roamed about the city, notebook in hand, a reporter covering the story of a lifetime.

Everywhere the class lines of battle were being sharply drawn. Stepan Georgevitch Lianozov, known as the Russian Rockefeller, explained in an interview that "revolution is a sickness" and predicted foreign powers would intervene to cure it.[19] At the Council of the Republic the gulf between left and right deepened hourly, tearing the SRs into two distinct parties. Leaders of the Right called for more stringent army discipline, while the Left sounded exactly like Bolsheviks in demanding an immediate withdrawal from the war. While a middle-class newspaper editor in the gallery of the Marinsky told Reed, "What Russia needs is a strong man," Kerensky from the dais thundered near-hysterical speeches, attacking Bolsheviks and defending his own policies before collapsing into tears. Granted an interview with the prime minister, Jack and Louise found him in the plush mahogany library of the Winter Palace. His gray, puffy face and deeply circled eyes emanated an aura of sickness, but Kerensky's mind was clear and he showed a firm grasp of national problems—the army would not fight because people were tired of war; the revolution was not merely "political" but also "economic," and this meant a "profound re-evaluation of classes"; above all, "the Revolution is not over—it is just beginning." Impressively charming, honest and sincere, Kerensky was wanting in one crucial aspect—he showed "no real fixity of purpose—as the leader of the Russian Revolution should have."[20]

Purpose lay elsewhere. At a meeting in the Obukhovsky Zavod arms factory it showed in the cries of a soldier, "I ask the American comrades to carry word to America that the Russians will never give up their revolution until they die"; it sounded quietly in the voice of the slender, scholarly Anatol Lunacharsky insisting the Soviets must take power; it rolled solemnly in the slow, implacable words of the Russian-American Petrovsky, "Now is the time for deeds, not words."[21] If purpose seemed to be wavering, Reed was ready to add a voice of encouragement. One night over tea and borscht at the Astoria Hotel, Sam Voskov, exhausted from speaking in factories and barracks, slipped into an unaccustomed mood of pessimism: "We are such a small handful. I often feel that ours are pipsqueak voices in a hurricane. You can't stop a hurricane." Clapping him on the shoulder, Jack cried out, "Then roar with it, *tovarisch!*"[22]

Hurrying back and forth between factories and the Marinsky, damp, huddled breadlines in Viborg and smart cafés on the Nevsky Prospekt,

Reed increasingly focused attention on Smolny Institute. Here, far from central Petrograd, in what had once been a finishing school for the daughters of nobility, was the center of opposition to the PG. The institute was now the improbable home of both the Petrograd Soviet and the Central Committee of the All-Russian Congress of Soviets. An elegant, pale yellow, three-story structure, Smolny in October crackled with excitement. Inside its dim, vaulted corridors, soldiers and workmen bent under the weight of huge bundles of newspapers and proclamations. In bare white rooms where delicate young ladies had once studied French, radical parties caucused, committees debated policies, men's voices grew shrill and loud in argument. Hanging around the hallways, Jack and Louise buttonholed leaders like Kamenev or friends like Shatov to catch both statements and evasions that gave glimpses of events behind the scenes. For meals they went to the wooden tables of the basement dining hall to share cabbage soup, piles of kasha and slabs of black bread with hordes of "hungry proletarians, wolfing their food, plotting, shouting rough jokes across the room." On October 30 they were ushered into a bare attic room to talk with Leon Trotsky, president of the Petrograd Soviet, next to Lenin the most influential of radical leaders. While downing a huge meal, he talked steadily for an hour, condemning the PG, worrying over counterrevolution, speaking of the Soviets as "the most perfect representatives of the people" and flatly predicting, "It is the *lutte finale*. . . . We will complete the work scarcely begun in March."[23]

In the first week of November the opening of the new Congress of Soviets was postponed five days. Municipal government seemed to have broken down and the morning papers were filled with accounts of robberies and murders. On gloomy evening streets, tides of people flowed slowly along, arguments flared on corners and mysterious individuals circulated anti-Semitic and anti-Bolshevik rumors. Armed guards now barred Smolny's doors and demanded passes. Upstairs in the great white hall, a former ballroom with delicate columns and crystal chandeliers, the Petrograd Soviet met in day-and-night sessions. Workers, soldiers, party leaders spoke at length, fell asleep on the floor, then rose to roar approval for calls to action. Downtown, luxurious gambling clubs functioned from dusk to dawn, the streets were thick with prostitutes, and cafés buzzed with talk of monarchist plots, German spies, schemes for smuggling black-market goods and the anticipated Bolshevik move.

When it came, it was like nothing anyone had foreseen. Revolution meant violence, pitched battles over barricades, machine guns roaring, armored cars in the streets, snipers on rooftops and blood running in the gutter. Hectic as were the preparations, feverish as were government leaders, the takeover was almost as quiet and orderly as a normal transfer of power, with only part of the population aware of what was happening before leaflets announced the news. Despite Kerensky's fulminations, virtually no troops stood with the PG other than a few companies of Junkers—officers-in-training—and a well-publicized but ineffectual women's Death Battalion. The Cossacks held aloof, the Petrograd Garrison declared for the Soviets, and on November 6–7, while people went to work, ate dinner in restaurants, attended the ballet, shopped in department stores and told stories to their children, one social order died and another was born.

Close to the centers of power, Jack, Louise and Rhys saw only parts of the diffuse action. On the night of Monday the fifth, after attending a movie, they went to Smolny. In room ten, on the third floor, the Military Revolutionary Committee sat in continuous session. A week old, formed to defend the city and wrest control from old-line officers in the Petrograd Garrison, it was staffed largely by Bolsheviks and was in charge of the insurrection. Late in the evening Jack learned from its eighteen-year-old chairman, a Left SR, that the crucial Peter-Paul Fortress, across the river from the Winter Palace, had declared for the Soviets. Then at three a.m., as they departed through a front door flanked by two machine guns, Bill Shatov clapped Reed on the shoulder, shouting, "We're off! Kerensky sent the *Junkers* to close down our papers. . . . But our troops went down and smashed the Government seals, and now we're sending detachments to seize the bourgeois newspaper offices!"[24]

Tuesday, November 6, was full of confused activity. Groups of soldiers with fixed bayonets patrolled streets, but nobody knew if they belonged to the PG or the Soviets. At the Marinsky, Jack watched Kerensky plead for extraordinary powers to stop the insurrection, but the Council ignored the request. Out at Smolny, the old Central Committee was holding a stormy final session. Trotsky mounted the tribune on a wave of roaring applause, his thin, pointed face full of malicious irony as he vigorously defended insurrection as "the right of all revolutionists." Even as he spoke, Red Guards and regular army units under the direction of the Military Revolutionary Committee were on the march, taking control of the railroad stations, Telegraph Agency, Telephone Exchange, State Bank, Central Post Office and other government buildings. When Reed learned this at about four in the morning, the realm of the PG had virtually shrunk to the Winter Palace.

By the time Jack and Louise rose the next day, Kerensky had fled the city and troops had dispersed the Council of the Republic. The noon cannon boomed from Peter-Paul as they noticed soldiers guarding the closed gates of the State Bank. "What side do you belong to, the Government?" asked Reed. With a wide grin, one of them answered, "No more Government, Glory to God!"[25] All entrances to the huge square in front of the Winter Palace were blocked by sentries, but, flashing American passports and shouting "Official business," they moved through the lines. Inside the gloomy palace, a young officer nervously pacing up and down in front of Kerensky's door told them the prime minister had left for the front. Wandering down dark, silent corridors, they came upon galleries converted into barracks, with soiled mattresses on the floor and young Junkers moving about in a stale atmosphere of tobacco smoke and unwashed bodies. Somewhere in the reaches of the palace the cabinet of the PG was in session, but the location of the meeting was a mystery.

The Americans departed in the late afternoon and found troops grumbling over a delay in orders to attack. Near Palace Square, streets were dark, but a few blocks away on the Nevsky, bright shopwindows and electric signs lit promenading crowds. Well-dressed people in fur coats shook fists at squads of soldiers posted on corners, and an occasional armored vehicle cruised the boulevard. Forgetting about tickets for the ballet, they caught a taxi to Smolny. The massive façade was ablaze with lights, in the courtyard automobiles and motorcycles raced engines, an enormous gray armored car lumbered through the gate, and huddled around bonfires were groups of Red Guards. Inside, crowds fought through hallways—workers in black blouses with rifles over their shoulders, soldiers in dirt-colored coats, Bolshevik leaders with harassed, anxious faces, holding fat portfolios. A four-day-long meeting of the Petrograd Soviet had just concluded. Not only had they missed Trotsky declaring, "The Provisional Government has ceased to exist," but also Lenin's first public appearance in four months and his announcement, "Now begins a new era in the history of Russia, and this third Russian Revolution must finally lead to the victory of Socialism."

The transfer of power basically complete, a last symbolic act remained to be played out—the capture of the Winter Palace. At ten forty, in a meeting hall crammed beyond capacity, the old Central Committee convened the Second Congress of Soviets. Balloting gave the Bolsheviks fourteen of twenty-five posts on the new presidium. As the new leaders—minus Lenin—ascended the platform, the noise of artillery penetrated the chamber. The cruiser *Aurora*, anchored in the Neva, was firing blank shells at the Winter Palace, and bolstered by sailors from the Kronstadt Base, troops surrounding it were making ready to move. While the shelling continued, the meeting hall exploded into bedlam. Mensheviks, Right SRs and members of the Jewish Bund arose to denounce the MRC and the Bolsheviks, demanding negotiations with the PG and an end to the attack. Shouting to be heard above masses surging up and down the aisles, they were interrupted by angry yells of "Kornilovist" and "Counterrevolutionary." Amid a tumult of cheers, curses, hoots and threats, fifty moderates stalked out while Trotsky in a voice laden with contempt roared, "Let them go! They are just so much refuse which will be swept into the garbage-heap of history!"

Jack, Louise, Beatty, Rhys and Gumberg also left. They collected MRC passes, then came out onto Smolny's steps and climbed shivering into the back of an open truck full of soldiers. While lurching toward the city's center, they tore open bundles of leaflets announcing the deposition of the PG and scattered them into the streets. The truck halted at a barricade near Palace Square, where a line of armed sailors confronted several hundred men and women—delegates who had left the Congress, ministers from the PG and members of the city administration, some accompanied by their wives. Waving credentials, they attempted to reach the Winter Palace, but the sailors refused to let them through. After some hot words about dying for the regime, the officials retired in silence. Revolutionaries were not the only ones interested in symbolic gestures.

Using the MRC passes, the five Americans went through the cordon, passing a three-inch field gun and several groups of soldiers near the dark square. They were just in time. After some shots whined through the blackness, a voice shouted, "It's all over. They have surrendered," and then they found themselves rushing forward amid masses of troops pouring out of surrounding streets and over half-built barricades toward the bright windows and open doors of the palace. Inside the maze of corridors, stairways, offices and galleries, near-chaos reigned as ragged soldiers and Red Guards, suddenly among fabulous riches, lost any semblance of discipline and degenerated into a mob. Men broke into packing cases, pulled out carpets, curtains, linen, porcelain plates and cut glass, while others seized statuettes, stripped bedchambers of blankets and spreads, and ripped leather upholstery from chairs. The Americans paused when a detachment of troops marched by, guarding a half-dozen sullen civilians, the cabinet of the PG, then pushed on until they reached the gold-and-malachite chamber where the ministers had been arrested. On the green baize table were sheets of paper covered with writing, the beginnings of hopeless proclamations and proposals half scratched out and tapering into aimless doodles, the last futile markings of a regime that had nothing more to say.

Soon the palace was quieter. Soldiers had been ordered out and sentries posted at each door to confiscate loot. In a far gallery Reed and his friends were surrounded by Red Guards, who contemptuously pushed aside their

papers and began to shout, "Looters, provocateurs!" before an officer
interceded to lead them from the building. Hailing a taxi, they arrived at
Smolny after three o'clock and found the building full of hollow-eyed,
dirty men. The meeting hall was still crowded with delegates. Soldiers
from front-line regiments rose to pledge solidarity with the Soviet, and
after five a.m. Nikolai Krylenko, staggering with fatigue, climbed to the
tribune to read a telegram from the Twelfth Army announcing that a
Military Revolutionary Committee had taken over command of the Northern Front. The hall rocked with emotion as delegates cheered, embraced,
wept and shouted. At six in the morning Jack, Louise and Rhys emerged
onto the steps, stretched aching limbs and breathed deeply until the air
cleared their heads. The locus of power had shifted, but the future was
still a question mark. In his mind's eye Reed could see "a faint unearthly
pallor stealing over the silent streets, dimming the watch-fires, the shadow
of a terrible dawn grey-rising over Russia."[26]

Thursday, November 8, was superficially quiet. Streetcars were running,
stores were open, citizens rose at the usual hour and went to work. But in
the cities of Russia, in Moscow, Helsinki, Kiev and Odessa, from the
Urals across Asia to far-off Vladivostok, battles between Soviets and PG
forces were raging. Closer at hand, while Bolshevik leaders in Smolny
struggled with the problems of organizing a government, revolution was
being followed by counterrevolution as night follows day. Coalescing
around the city Duma, the disgruntled political elements—Cadets, members of the local administration, the old Soviet Executive Committee, moderate Socialists, delegates to the Council of the Republic—were burying
old differences to organize a Committee for the Salvation of the Country
and the Revolution. And not far away from the capital, Kerensky was
visiting military installations, making contact with generals and rousing
Cossacks.

As with the revolution, attacks on the new regime were so diffuse
that Reed and his friends could only catch glimpses of them. Always on
the go, living and breathing the atmosphere of Smolny, the Duma, Viborg
and the front, they would taste the mood, flavor and texture of counter-
revolutionary events. Already a war of propaganda posters between the
Soviets and the Committee for Salvation had broken out. Rumors that the
Bolsheviks were German agents and that MRC troops had slaughtered men
and raped women in taking the Winter Palace filled the opposition press
and were being repeated at the Duma. At Smolny unshaven and filthy
Bolshevik leaders worked furiously. Government employees were on
strike, railroad unions were refusing to run trains, Cossacks were rumored

on the way, and this small party of men with little administrative experience was trying to grasp the reins of government. The chief of commerce confessed to Reed in a humorous panic that he knew nothing of business, and the head of finance, appointed because he had once worked in a bank, was scribbling figures on the back of an envelope. Hurrying out of the MRC office were commissars bound for the far corners of Russia to carry news, rouse support, fight for the regime however they could.

Victory depended upon a program as well as action, and the Bolsheviks moved swiftly to enact the promises which had gained them support. At eight forty in the evening the second session of the Congress convened. When the presidium entered, Reed caught a first glimpse of Lenin: "A short, stocky figure, with a big head set down in his shoulders, bald and bulging. Little eyes, a snubbish nose, wide, generous mouth, and heavy chin . . . dressed in shabby clothes, his trousers much too long for him." Unimpressive as a crowd idol, he seemed "a strange popular leader— a leader purely by virtue of intellect." Lenin rose to speak and gripped the lectern while long-rolling ovations filled the hall. His first words were direct: "We shall now proceed to construct the Socialist order!"[27] Again a long roar from the crowd, and then, with no gestures, no dramatics, he proceeded to business. Before the night was over, the Congress had unanimously endorsed a proclamation calling for immediate peace without indemnities or annexations and a decree abolishing landed estates and distributing property to the peasants. With the election of an all-Bolshevik Council of People's Commissars—as the ministers were to be called—and the new Central Committee of the Soviets—with 62 Bolsheviks out of 101 members—the Congress was dissolved. Going home in a streetcar at seven a.m., the tired delegates seemed more subdued than the night before, evidently wondering how long the regime could endure.

The question was answered in the next three days. While the MRC whipped together a defense force, a verbal battle racked the city as the Committee for Salvation attacked the promises of the Soviet. The crucial arenas were military, and Reed witnessed a decisive encounter among the armored-car troops in a vast, dim hall of the Imperial Riding School, where two thousand men gathered around their machines to hear speakers debate. After a final talk in which Krylenko cried, "Great Russia belongs to you. Will you give it back?" the vote went overwhelmingly in favor of the Soviets.[28] Imagining this action repeated in barracks, trenches, factories and villages, at union locals and aboard warships, Jack found the essence of the revolution—millions of men all over the country listening intently, trying to understand the issues and then deciding to support the new regime.

On Saturday, November 10, while the Soviets spun out decrees and weary leaders painfully joked, "Tomorrow maybe we'll get a sleep—a long one," Cossack troops under General Krasnov and acting in Kerensky's behalf moved on Tsarskoye Selo, a short train ride from the capital. Rumors swelled the seven hundred mounted troops to many thousands, and the question of whether the sixteen-thousand-man garrison at Tsarskoye would join them loomed ominously. From the steps of Smolny, Jack could see thousands of men and women carrying rifles, picks, spades and rolls of wire, heading towards the outskirts of the city. Denied passes, Reed, Williams and Gumberg talked their way into an automobile with Antonov-Ovseenko and Dibenko, two of the chief military commissars. The trip was typical of the time's confusion. When Dibenko, wearing a rakish astrakhan hat, complained he had not eaten in twenty-four hours, the driver stopped at a store to buy sausages and bread, but neither commissar had a kopek and Gumberg had to pay the bill. On the edge of town, the vehicle broke down and it was necessary to commandeer a passing taxi. Across the muddy fields of the gray plain, irregular bands of soldiers, Red Guards and workers dug haphazard trenches, brewed tea over open fires and awaited the Cossacks. Stopping to talk with one group, they were told everything was in readiness except for one slight problem: "We have no ammunition." Antonov replied confidently that there was plenty at Smolny and said, "I will give you an order." Fingering his pockets, he turned to ask the others, "Has anyone a piece of paper." Gumberg offered a sheet from a notebook. "A pencil, too, comrade," the commissar said, "I seem to have none."[29]*

On Sunday morning Petrograd awoke not to church bells but to bursts of rifle fire. Prodded by the Committee for Salvation, Junkers had during the night seized the Telephone Exchange, the Military Hotel and other strategic points. Reed raced around the city while single shots, volleys and the occasional thud of artillery sounded from different quarters. By nightfall Soviet troops had crushed the uprising, and the next day, while Reed went from the Duma to a secret meeting of the Committee for Salvation in a private apartment, the expected battle settled the fate of the city. Attempting to advance, Krasnov's cavalry ran into a stubborn wall of defenders and then fled before counterattacks. Just as the Junkers

---

* In all his writings, Reed concealed the fact that he was on this jaunt. In *Ten Days That Shook the World* (New York: Boni and Liveright, 1919), 182-3, he attributes the story to a friend. But Albert Rhys Williams, *Journey Into Revolution: Petrograd, 1917-1918* (Chicago: Quadrangle, 1969), 140-2, gives the full story, explaining Reed did not want the commissars to get into trouble for letting reporters come along.

had gained no support from the Petrograd masses, the Cossacks had been unable to win over the Tsarskoye garrison. By inaction and neutrality, the mass of citizens and soldiers proved to Jack not only that few people were willing to die for the PG, but also that to the masses only the Bolshevik program of peace, land and bread made any sense.

As a few snowflakes fluttered down on Tuesday morning, Reed encountered a grinning soldier in front of Smolny who cried, "Snow! Good for the health." Inside, heaps of dirty, mud-caked workers and soldiers filled the corridors, offices and eating halls, the "victorious proletarian army" sleeping away the weariness of battle. Reports from across the country indicated that local Soviets were taking control of cities and pledging fidelity to the Bolsheviks. Happily Jack jumped aboard an ambulance heading for the front. Victory over counterrevolution made the day glorious. The clouds lifted, a pale sun tinted the marshy fields and the vehicle raced by laughing men and women who shouted as they tramped homeward. At Tsarskoye there was the unreal sight of ragged proletarian heroes wandering through the delicate rooms of Catherine the Great's green palace. After another very bumpy ride in a truck full of sensitive contact bombs, Reed was grabbed by an illiterate group of Red Guards near the front. Contemptuous of "papers" issued in Petrograd, they casually led him to a wall and raised rifles. Responding to pleas, they stopped long enough to find someone who could read, then brought Jack to headquarters, where he was hugged, wined and dined as a representative of American Social Democracy. Somehow it all made sense, all fitted together, for to embrace the revolution was to be fearless and immortal in a very special way.

Five days later real snow came, so thick it was impossible to see more than ten feet ahead. Even before it fell, driving away the colds and rheumatism of rainy days, John Reed was in a buoyant mood. With the city secure, there was time now to assess the onrushing tide of events, time to sort out the hastily scribbled notes, the stacks of newspapers, the proclamations illegally torn from walls, time to savor the splendid moments, time to commit the great story to words. Having sent a brief cable to the *Call* announcing the advent of a workers' state, he was now ready for a long, hard look at the meaning of all the furious activity.

The events of those ten days would fill Reed's next three years. From his typewriter would flow hundreds of thousands of words about the origins and workings of Soviets, Kerensky and the Provisional Government, workers' control of factories, the state of the army, the character of the Russian people, Bolshevism, the personalities of Lenin, Trotsky, Lunacharsky and other leaders, the tangled web of foreign affairs, the meaning of counterrevolution, the implications of the revolution for the rest of the world. Because of roadblocks erected by the United States government, it would be more than a year before all his observations, research and artistry could be combined into a single work that would convey the importance, power and excitement of those November events, *Ten Days That Shook the World*. Yet long before that summation of his experience, in fact from the first articles written in Petrograd, Jack's words contained the deep feelings stirred in him by the revolution.

Passion fills all his pages on Russia because events there provided meaning, a way of organizing reality which he had sought for years. Once he had been content with personal fulfillment, with the fame that writing brought. A growing social awareness had changed his world-view, provided new heroes. He had seen brave Wobblies and Mexican revolutionaries, but their heroism had been in defeat, or in victories soon dissipated by stronger forces. Russia represented another chance, one on a vaster scale, and here social change was bolstered by theories which could account for and make sense of a mass of confusing phenomena, the shallow tastes of the middle class, the timidity of American publications, the commercialization of Bohemia, the lurch into World War, the oppression of workers in the United States and around the globe. Months earlier, he had longed for a rising of the proletariat, believing that only in that way could the world be set on a hopeful course. Ready for revolution, confidently predicting it would occur in Russia even before arriving there, he had seen his fondest hopes fulfilled. The workers had risen, and even though defeat remained a possibility, every nerve and muscle in Reed's body was betting that this time they would make it stick.

His first lengthy article in late November 1917 reeked with hope that "this proletarian government will last . . . in history, a pillar of fire for mankind forever."[30] This religious image of salvation wrought in secular terms gives a penetrating insight into what the revolution meant. Long ago he had embraced a new vision of human life, had tied his own hopes to an unbounded dream of freedom for all mankind. In Russia he found what he had sought. The revolution was an impossible dream grounded in reality, a series of airy palaces guarded by honest workers for the future of all mankind. Later would come doubts, friction, compromises —all the dreary, inevitable daily realities of life at any time, in any place. But for John Reed the meaning and vision of Petrograd in November 1917 touched the remainder of his days.

18

Christiania

Across the sea my country, my America
Girt with steel, hard-glittering with power,
As a champion, with great voice trumpeting
High words, "For Liberty . . . Democracy. . . ."

Deep within me something stirs, answers—
(My country, my America!)
As if alone in the high and empty night
She called me—my lost one, my first lover
I love no more, love no more, love no more . . .
The cloudy shadow of old tenderness,
Illusions of beautiful madness—many deaths
And easy immortality . . .[1]

Amidst the chaos of revolution there were moments when the mind turned homeward and the shadow of past and future fell across the present. Somehow, after witnessing Russian events, John Reed found it important to grapple with the meaning of America. Natural as it might be to contrast his homeland's democratic pretensions with the reality of its power politics, or to see it as a country loved no more, it was impossible to sustain this tone. The landscape, color and resonances of home lay too deep to be easily exorcised, and over the next three months, in Petrograd and then Norway, he worked on a poem that vibrated with a passion for the United States. Never completed, its three hundred lines stand as a testament to the refusal of the unconscious to accept the bonds of intellect or ideology.

The title, "America, 1918," was more a statement of intentions than a description of what emerged. Obviously modeled on Whitman, the work begins with an apparent attempt to swallow life whole:

> By my free boyhood in the wide West,
> The powerful sweet river, fish-wheels, log-rafts,
> Ships from behind the sunset, Lascar-manned,
> Chinatown, throbbing with mysterious gongs,
> The blue thunderous Pacific, blaring sunsets,
> Lost beaches, camp-fires, wail of hunting cougars . . .
> By the rolling range, and the flat sun-smitten desert,
> Night with coyotes yapping, domed with burst of stars . . .
> By miles of yellow wheat rippling in the Chinook,
> Orchards forever endless, deep in blooming,
> Green-golden orange groves and snow peaks looming over . . .
> By raw audacious cities sprung from nothing,
> Brawling and bragging in their careless youth . .
> I know thee, America!

Then follows a catalogue of sharply etched scenes—Astoria fishermen launching into foggy dawns, cowpunchers overlooking their herds, prospectors trudging through alkali deserts, forest rangers watching for fires, brakemen astride swaying freights, Indians squatting behind summer lodges, miners roaring in wooden barrooms, prostitutes and cardsharps crowding frontier camps. After a single stanza's nod to Harvard days, the work moves on to its main subject, setting the tone with one of the only three stanzas published during Reed's lifetime:

> By proud New York and its man-piled Matterhorns,
> The hard blue sky overhead and west wind blowing,
> Steam plumes waving from sun-glittering pinnacles,
> And deep streets shaking to the million river—

The remainder is celebratory, an evocation of the multiple, overlapping, swarming worlds of New York:

> Soaring Fifth Avenue, Peacock Street, Street of Banners,
> Ever-changing pageant of splendid courtesans . . .

Broadway, gashing the city like a lava stream,
Crowned with shower of sparks, as a beaten fire,
Blazing theaters, brazen restaurants . . .
The East Side, worlds within a world, chaos of nations,
Sink of the nomad races, last and wretchedest
Port of the westward Odyssey . . .
Old Greenwich Village, citadel of amateurs,
Battle-ground of all adolescent Utopias,
Half sham-Bohemia, dear to uptown slummers,
Half sanctuary to the outcast and dissatisfied . . .
Exotic Negro-town, upper Amsterdam Avenue,
And its black sensuous easily-happy people, shunned
     of men . . .

Through them all moves the poet, joyfully recalling his own escapades:

In dim Romanian wine-cellars I am not unwelcome . . .
In Grand Street coffee-rooms, haunts of Yiddish
     philosophers . . .
Fenian saloons, with prominent green flag . . .
Italian *ristorantes*, Chianti and spontaneous tenors,
Armenian kitchens hung with Oriental carpets from
     New Jersey . . .
German *bier-stuben*, painted with fat mottoes . . .
     French cafes, neat madame at the *caisse*,
Greek *kaffeinias*, chop-suey joints with contemptuous
     slant-eyed waiters . . .

Well do I know the Russian brass-shops on Allen Street,
The opium-stinking dens of the Cantonese lottery-men,
And where the Syrians sell their cool grey water
     jars . .
Bowery old-clothes men, stale sand-floored drinking
     room spotted with old spittle . . .
The blasted twilight under the hysterical thunder of
     East River bridges,
And South Street fragrant still with the spices of
     long-vanished clipper-ships . . .

I have watched the summer day come up from the top
     of a pier on the Williamsburgh Bridge.
I have slept in a basket of squid at the Fulton
     Street Market . . .
I have shot craps with gangsters in the Gas-House
     district . . .

I can tell you where to hire a gunman to croak a
    squealer,
And where young girls are bought and sold, and how
    to get coke on 125th Street . . .

The descriptions catalogue the city's harsh, raucous and plaintive sounds, its smells of sweetness and decay, its endless occupations, until finally in a spasm of hopelessness at ever completing such a task, the work crashes to a halt:

All professions, races, temperaments, philosophies,
All history, all possibilities, all romance,
America . . . the world . . . !

Strange as it may seem for revolution abroad to create such sharp visions of home, the poem itself provides some explanation. Recurring throughout are images of Manhattan as beloved, as dear and unforgettable "as the face of my mother," as familiar and ever new "as the body of my lover." Being away from such a city-mother-lover was to "burn in exile" with a desire that only a homecoming could fulfill. Beyond this the work does not explicitly go, but certainly its images suggest that reasons far deeper than words were pulling Reed back to the United States.

The ardor of the poem emerged from a man alive with a new faith, one continually renewed in the three months following the ten days. Immediately after Petrograd proved secure, Reed's attention was focused on the struggle between Soviets and the PG in Moscow. In mid-November there were rumors that Bolshevik artillery was destroying the Kremlin, and on the twentieth, armed with passes from Smolny, Jack and Louise joined a mob of soldiers aboard a train bound for the ancient capital. Checking out tales of destruction was one motivation, but there was another: "Moscow is real Russia, Russia as it was and will be; in Moscow we would get the true feeling of the Russian people about the Revolution."[2]

A twenty-four-hour ride through a wintry landscape ended at a deserted railroad station in the early twilight hours. For fifty roubles, twenty-five times the normal price, a horse-drawn sleigh carried them through shell-torn streets to the center of town. In hotels where candles had replaced electric lights, proprietors turned them away until the National provided a room on the top floor, overlooking the spires and domes of the nearby Kremlin, which flickered with the light of bonfires. After dinner beneath a portrait of Tolstoy in a vegetarian restaurant named "I Eat Nobody," they were drawn to Red Square, where the unreal domes of St. Basil's loomed against a sky thick with stars. Hundreds of men were digging with picks and shovels, piling up dirt and rock by the Kremlin wall. In broken German, a young student, his arm in a sling, explained this was the Brotherhood Grave for five hundred proletarians killed in Moscow fighting: "Here in this holy place, holiest of all Russia, we shall bury our most holy. Here where are the tombs of the Tsars, our Tsar—the People—shall sleep. . . ."[3]

Moscow's experience had been similar to Petrograd's. Because supporters of the Provisional Government had been better organized and the Soviets less disciplined, the fighting had been longer and bloodier. Despite rumors, the Kremlin in daylight showed little serious damage. Reed examined the old fortress closely and catalogued the destruction—some interior damage to the churches, a few façades shattered, the walls of one monastery crumbled, two gate towers smashed. What appeared minimal to him could seem massive to someone less enamored of revolution, and he noted one cost of the bombardment: "Angry priests. Angry bourgeois—artists, etc. Angry poor pious folks, crossing themselves as they look toward Kremlin, and muttering. Arguing angry groups on Red Square. This result of uprising a dangerous thing for the Bolsheviks."[4]

Such danger was obliterated by the fervor of the great proletarian funeral. On a bitterly cold morning the Reeds joined members of the Executive Committee in front of Soviet headquarters on Skoboliev Square. Beneath waving banners they marched in a growing procession down the Tverskaya, past boarded shops and darkened chapels, to Red Square. Standing on a dirt mound, they had a fine view of a moving pageant. Into the square poured thousands of people, with groups of workers shouldering coffins. Military bands blared the "Internationale" and a revolutionary funeral march, red banners with fiery slogans snapped in the wind, and companies of soldiers, squadrons of cavalry riding at salute and artillery units with cannon draped in black went solemnly past. Their hands and feet were frozen, but the Americans stood through many hours while the huge square filled, the procession continued and one by one the five hundred coffins were placed gently in the earth. At dusk, with the leafless trees by the Kremlin wall covered with the artificial blossoms of memorial wreaths, the crowd sang revolutionary melodies. No priest had dared attend the funeral, but Reed viewed it in religious terms: "I suddenly realized that the devout Russian people no longer needed priests to pray them into heaven. On earth they were building a kingdom more bright than any heaven had to offer."[5]

Back in Petrograd the Bolsheviks were trying to take control of the country. Government workers were on strike, ministry bureaucrats refused to turn over keys to safes, filing cabinets and archives, bank clerks denied combinations to vaults, railway unions ignored orders for trains, and the city was suffering shortages of food and fuel. Jack listened to the proclamation of decrees at Smolny, saw Red Guards arrest civil servants and seize trains, watched workmen force locks to enter darkened offices, and attended the first Revolutionary Tribunal, where Countess Sofia Panina, Kerensky's Minister of Welfare, was sentenced to imprisonment until she turned 93,000 roubles over to her Soviet successor. Tilting the balance toward the Bolsheviks was the vote of the Peasants' Congress to merge leadership with the Soviet Executive Committee. This was marked by another spectacle. Pouring out of their headquarters into a black night, a long procession of peasants with orange torches marched from central Petrograd to Smolny, where Soviet deputies came out to clasp them in ferocious hugs. In the white meeting hall Reed witnessed the triumphal joint session unanimously adopt a resolution voicing his own hope that the merger would assure "the victory of Socialism."[6]

To help bring that victory, he joined the newly founded Bureau of International Revolutionary Propaganda headed by Karl Radek. Part of the Foreign Office under Trotsky's direction, the bureau was housed in the former ministry building on the square facing the Winter Palace. Here the old and new regimes jostled uneasily side by side. Elderly door-men in formal blue uniforms obsequiously took the hats and coats of shabby workers, while frock-coated young bureaucrats ran errands for commissars wearing muddy boots and torn uniforms. System was non-existent: "Things are done, but why or how they are done is beyond me. The different departments are organized in the most slip-shod manner, overlapping in many places, more or less ignorant of each other's activities . . . and crippled by the inherent Russian penchant for tea and discussion. Hundreds of people writing laborious hundreds of documents by hand, which documents are thereupon carefully placed where nobody could possibly find them."[7]

Humorous about the surroundings, Jack was dead serious about the job. The Bolsheviks had come to power on a promise of ending the war, and they were already negotiating for a separate peace with Germany. Acting in the context of a belief that Socialism could not be attained in a single country, that the safety of the Russian regime was intimately tied to the spread of revolution, the Soviets were using the peace talks partly as a cover for fomenting revolt. This led to the work of the Propaganda Bureau. Under the direction of Boris Reinstein, the Socialist Labor Party member from Buffalo, Reed and Williams were putting together flyers, pamphlets, leaflets and newspapers aimed at German troops, urging them to overthrow the Kaiser and follow Russia's example toward Socialism.

The papers, featuring numerous pictures, bold headlines and simple phraseology, were turned out in editions of half a million and secretly distributed across enemy lines. So passionately did the Americans appeal for revolt that wishes took on a reality of their own, and ever after Jack would partially ascribe Germany's surrender in 1918 to unrest among troops stirred up by such publications.*

However serious the bureau's work, Reed was happy enough to let the old sense of adventure flourish with impossible schemes. When he learned that a band of prospectors were leaving for Siberia to dig gold, he talked of joining them. Hearing that most officials in the Ukraine were on strike, he burst into Rhys' room with the excited suggestion they leave immediately for Kharkov. Williams would become Commissar of Education and also take charge of church affairs. Claiming the commissarship of Art and Amusement for himself, Jack planned to "get up great pageants. Cover the city with flags and banners. And once, maybe twice a month have a gorgeous all night festival with fireworks, orchestras and plays in the squares and everybody participating."[8] He could hardly have been ignorant of the terrible conditions in the Ukraine, its rich fields blasted, its population starving, and this frivolous suggestion exposed his deep belief that singing, dancing, pageantry, the human joy of festivals were all important parts of revolution.

So were the wit and good humor with which Reed sparkled. Admiring Reinstein's dedication, he could not help bantering when his boss soberly emphasized the importance of studying Marx. At one meeting where Boris was introduced as "the representative of the great Socialist Labor Party," Jack quipped, "How many members does your party really have? Is it three and a half or four?"[9] This good spirit was broad enough to encompass his own increasingly difficult financial situation. The original money gone, Jack cabled several requests for funds to the

---

* The effect of the publications should not be discounted. German negotiators at Brest-Litovsk were much annoyed at the spread of Bolshevik propaganda, and a year later Major General Max Hoffmann told an American reporter, "Immediately after conquering those Bolsheviks we were conquered by them. Our victorious army on the Eastern Front became rotten with Bolshevism. We got to the point where we did not dare to transfer certain of our eastern divisions to the West." See John W. Wheeler-Bennett, *The Forgotten Peace: Brest-Litovsk, March 1918* (New York: William Morrow, 1939), 352. Hoffmann's *War Diaries and Other Papers* (London: Martin Secker, 1929), II, 232, says much the same thing. Though much of the propaganda was promoted by agitators and German Communists, the effect of the newspapers Reed helped edit must also have been important. For JR's account, see "How Soviet Russia Conquered Imperial Germany," *Liberator*, I (January 1919), 16–25.

Masses, but no replies came back. Since his salary at the bureau was barely enough to pay for lodgings, he was forced to mail articles rather than send them by wire, and he grumbled about a revolutionary magazine that could not even raise money for cables concerning the only revolution of its kind in history.

Temporarily Reed accepted a job working for Colonel Raymond Robins of the American Red Cross Mission. A Westerner who had made millions prospecting for Alaskan gold, Robins was a bulky, two-fisted out-doorsman, half preacher, half political reformer, who had financially supported the Bull Moose Party in 1912 and owed his current appointment to Teddy Roosevelt. He was as devout a capitalist as a Christian, but a man who refused to let either narrow self-interest or ideology act as blinders. Like others on the mission, his role had more to do with politics than medical aid, and since August he had been devoting considerable time and energy toward keeping Russia active in the war. With the Bolshevik takeover, he switched support from Kerensky to Lenin, going over Ambassador Francis' head to urge upon Washington recognition of the new regime. Bolshevism might be distasteful, but Robins was a realist: "At stake is not what we think they should do, but what they are going to do."[10]

Active and emotional, the colonel shared with Reed a brashness that put both of them at odds with the embassy crowd. They met often to share both food and insights, becoming close despite real differences in attitudes. Interested in keeping Russia friendly toward the United States, Robins hoped that eventually American business could profit by selling products to the Soviet government. One instrument to this end could be an official American daily newspaper in Petrograd which, at the same time, might agitate against a separate peace. He suggested that Jack both draw up a prospectus for the publication and sound out Soviet leaders about the need for American aid and investment. The offer made Reed uneasy. Wondering if the task were being offered as a kind of handout, he fretted that such a newspaper might mislead the masses. When his desperate need for cash overrode such worries, Jack eased his mind by insisting on a convenient fiction: he was not really working, but only doing a favor for a friend and accepting a loan that would be repaid. As he explained to Robins: "I wouldn't like to be put down by anybody as having served the interests of the United States or any other capitalist government, for I haven't—if I could help it."[11]

The job was simple. For the newspaper it was largely a technical matter of format, with information on type sizes and faces, makeup, staff, expenses for supplies and suggested contents. Even so, Reed salved his conscience by telling Rhys that, to avoid any misrepresentation, he had dummied a bold line under the masthead, "This paper is devoted to promoting the interests of American capital!"[12]* Searching out opinion on the possibility of American investment took longer, but in a few weeks he put together a suggestive four-page "Skeleton Report." Based on interviews with members of the Soviet Executive Committee, the paper made one thing clear: anyone dealing with Russia would have to realize it was a Socialist state which controlled all natural resources, factories, land and banks. The Bolsheviks might be suspicious of the United States, but they were realists. They needed foreign aid in everything from food to technical matters, and might be prepared to allow some capitalist investment within a restricted framework and for a limited period of time. Any policy of "real, material help to Russia would create a love for America in this country which it would be difficult to alter." Indicating a kind of aid United States officials would never think of, Reed ended on a note of irony: "We American Socialists are going to organize here shortly, and I think you could help America if you would cooperate with us."[13]

In the last month of 1917 the pressure of events eased. Especially interested in the problems and activities of women in the revolution, Louise had been pursuing stories on her own, and she and Jack had often been apart. Now they had more time for each other. Life was not easy. In their bare, unheated apartment they were always cold. At night they rolled to sleep wearing bulky overcoats, and meals were often no more than bowls of soup heated over an open fire built on the tile bathroom floor. Together in tranquil moments they began to wander through the city, savoring its changes. The massive palaces of nobles were now the homes of deserving workers; the parks once reserved for the imperial

---

* Reed's work in this matter has been the subject of some misunderstanding, particularly on the part of George Kennan, *Russia Leaves the War* (Princeton: Princeton University Press, 1956), 407–10. Here Kennan suggests Reed may in fact have been playing both sides, but Williams, *Journey into Revolution*, 225, straightens out the matter. The Raymond Robins papers contain a nine-page prospectus for a newspaper to be called the *Russische Tageblatt*, dated December 27, 1917. While this probably was based upon Reed's proposal, internal evidence makes it unlikely that he wrote it entirely. For one thing, the typing is much too neat to be Reed's, but, more important, the document contains some praise for Gumberg that Jack would never have been caught dead writing. The "Declaration" of intention for the newspaper contains a first sentence much like the one Williams says Reed dummied on a sample issue: "This newspaper is financed by American commercial and financial interests, in order to promote American business in Russia, and friendship and understanding between the two peoples."

family were now open to the humblest peasant; the Peter-Paul Fortress was now a prison for counterrevolutionaries rather than radicals. On Christmas they dropped by a service at the ornate Isaac Cathedral and found a scant hundred worshippers gathered in the cavernous interior, then joined Bessie Beatty and Williams for a turkey dinner hosted by Robins. As presents they exchanged poems. Louise's was a testament to the persistence of her original view of Jack:

> I want you to know that sometimes when I am thinking
> About you
> I have a lump in my throat
> And I am a little bit awed.
> You are the finest person I know
> On both sides of the world
> And it is a nice privilege to be your comrade.[14]

Like the Reeds, Petrograd for a few weeks around the turn of the year enjoyed a period of relaxation, a breathing space. At points across Russia, centers of counterrevolution were only beginning to coalesce. The opening peace talks at the Polish town of Brest-Litovsk concealed grandiose German designs on Russian territory, while news of strikes fired the hope that Central Europe was about to collapse into revolution. In Allied chancelleries plans for suppressing Bolshevism were muffled, and if no country had recognized the new regime, Woodrow Wilson's widely publicized Fourteen Points speech indicated this might be only a matter of time. Of course, there were problems of food and fuel, evidence of peasant unrest and plenty of open grumbling, but among men who had passed through the November days, faith and hope were much stronger than doubt. On New Year's Eve, at Left Socialist Revolutionary headquarters, Jack and Louise enjoyed a festive party where roast pig, meat pastry and stuffed cabbage, vodka and wine, and singing and dancing blotted out thoughts of revolution. When Markim, the Commissar of Posts and Telegraph, tried to make a serious speech, Commissar of Justice Kamkov instituted a mock trial that convicted his fellow official for mentioning politics and sentenced him to forfeit dessert.

In this atmosphere Reed's desire to return home grew strong. As early as mid-November he had begun to plan a departure in January, and now in spare moments he was jotting lines for "America, 1918." Wholly committed to Bolshevism, he was still a reporter with the story of a century waiting to be written. When news arrived that the *Masses* had been suppressed and Jack indicted along with four other editors, his resolve to depart was only strengthened. Bolshevik friends who were amused by this "bourgeois" decision to stand trial did not realize that the trial was as much an excuse for as a cause of the drive to depart.

Before he left, however, there were two important meetings to cover: the Constituent Assembly and the Third All-Russian Congress of Soviets. For Bolsheviks the CA was a most delicate matter. During Kerensky's time they had mercilessly criticized the PG for postponing the election of such a parliamentary body. After they seized power, such arguments came back to haunt them. Wanting to bury the idea, Lenin found himself in a minority on the Executive Committee. At the same time comrades wholly accepted his view that the Soviets, from which propertied classes were excluded, represented a higher form of democracy than any parliament. In allowing the CA to convene, the Bolsheviks were being more than a little cynical. If it approved of the current government, the CA would in effect begin delegating its power to another body; if it balked at doing so, it would be swiftly dissolved.

Programmed for disaster, the Constituent Assembly stumbled into being. Elections were from rolls so outdated they made no distinction between Left and Right SRs, and the results gave the Bolsheviks only twenty-five percent of the delegates. The moderate Socialist majority who gathered in the capital in January found themselves in an armed camp controlled by enemies. Middle-class supporters who demonstrated were dispersed by Red Guards, and an attempt on Lenin's life became an excuse for stern measures. When the Assembly convened late on the afternoon of January 18, the snow on the domed roof of the yellow, freshly painted Tauride Palace seemed festive, totally out of keeping with the companies of guards patrolling the area. In the press gallery just above the podium in the semicircular meeting hall, the Reeds and other reporters were crowded by suspicious, heavily armed soldiers. When a Swedish Socialist friend came by and announced, "It's going to be a real Wild West show—everyone seems to be carrying a gun," the Americans looked for suitable hiding places.

The actual meeting proved anticlimactic. For Reed the highlight came during an early break when Williams introduced him to Lenin. He had no chance to ask questions, for the short, bearded leader began to lecture on the importance of learning Russian, passionately reciting his own method of tackling foreign languages. Back in the press box, the Americans watched while moderate SRs elected a chairman. When a demand that the Assembly approve of Soviet rule was voted down, the Bolshevik delegates walked out. After that, speeches from the floor were interrupted by obnoxious hoots, jeers and hostile shouts until even Jack scratched a note about the "arrogant, silly behavior of Bolsheviks and

Gallery Crowd."[15] Hours of debate were cut off at five o'clock in the morning when soldiers with fixed bayonets dispersed the delegates. A few hours later the Soviet Executive Committee formally dissolved the CA, calling it a cover for "bourgeois counterrevolution."

Like all Soviet supporters, Reed was not disturbed. Admittedly a "most democratically elected governing body," the CA was an idea whose time had passed.[16] He saw territorial representation as irrelevant, a bourgeois invention. Industrial democracy, the democracy of the Soviets, was more flexible and representative, a new kind of government for a new age. Putting his beliefs into action, Jack carried a rifle and joined Red Guards patrolling in front of the Foreign Office on the day the Assembly was dismissed. Partly this was theater, a nose-thumbing gesture at the American diplomatic corps. But when no supporters of the CA rose up in its favor, either in Petrograd or anywhere else throughout the nation, it seemed final proof to him that the Russian people had moved beyond the idea of a Western parliament.

The Third Congress of Soviets was a celebration, more pageantry than politics. Less than three months after the Second Congress had set the stage for revolution, workers, soldiers and peasants were coming together to consider and ratify their leaders' policies. As part of the opening ceremony in the Tauride on January 23, a number of sympathetic foreigners addressed the eleven hundred delegates, many clad in regional costumes. In flowery phrases, Boris Reinstein introduced Reed as a fearless revolutionary returning home under threat of forty years' imprisonment for opposition to the imperialist war. Conscious that in the audience were men whose actions made the *Masses*' editors seem like a group of pranksters, Jack delivered a modest speech that began with a few words in Russian. Heartened by the victory of the proletariat, he promised to bring to workers in the United States—"a country of utter reaction"—news of everything that had happened in Russia, and he expected this to "call forth an answer from America's oppressed and exploited masses." With applause ringing in the hall, he sat down beside Williams and quietly commented, "We never got such a reception at home."[17]

Three days before the Congress opened, Louise had departed. Prepared to follow, Reed ran afoul of American officialdom. Well aware of his reputation as enfant terrible, he asked Robins to intervene with the "Stuffed Shirt"—Ambassador Francis—for a statement "that I am *not* the dangerous dynamiter and German spy that he has described me in official dispatches to his government—and mine."[18] In mid-January, Jack had wrangled with Consul Roger Tredwell over American suppression of free speech. The annoyed official called him unpatriotic and openly expressed regret there were no laws to keep him out of the United States. After issuing Reed a visa, Tredwell secretly warned the State Department that he might be "carrying papers."[19] When Washington requested further details, the embassy explained that Reed was on the payroll of the Bolsheviks and sent along a copy of his remarks to the Third Congress.

Cognizant of official hostility, Jack worried over the safety of his baggage. For months he had been collecting documents, posters, newspapers and pamphlets, and taking copious notes. Casting about for a way to protect them, he approached Trotsky with a request for status as a diplomatic courier. In an enigmatic act that may have been part spoof, the normally humorless leader said he would do better than that—he would appoint Reed as Soviet Consul to New York. It was just the kind of unprecedented gesture Reed loved. When he began to brag about it long before any announcement, sedate friends grew worried. Arno Dosch-Fleurot, correspondent for the New York *World*, argued that acceptance might lead to jail. Jack was not upset: "Perhaps it is the best thing I can do to advance the cause." Then he mischievously added: "When I am consul I suppose I shall have to marry people. I hate the marriage ceremony. I shall simply say to them: 'Proletarians of the world unite.' "[20]

The galling official notification—"Citizen John Reed has been appointed consul of the Russian Republic in New York"—reached the American embassy on January 29 in a note signed by Grigori Chicherin, Assistant Commissar for Foreign Affairs. An annoyed Ambassador Francis asked Robins to persuade the Soviets it was unwise. Having commented to Williams, "Jack already hears the salute of guns hailing his arrival. . . . It's just the thing to appeal to his sense of the romantic, but it won't help relations between the two countries," the colonel turned to Gumberg.[21] Armed with copies of the newspaper prospectus and the "Skeleton Report," Gumberg approached Lenin with the argument that his new consul was untrustworthy. Lenin, who was well acquainted with Gumberg, then asked Trotsky why he trusted a man like Reed who worked for the revolution one day and capitalism the next. In the tense period of the Brest-Litovsk negotiations the issue was minor, and Russia's leaders settled it swiftly and simply by withdrawing the appointment.

The affair hardly ended here. Knowing Reed would be suspicious about the source of the cancellation, Ambassador Francis tried to appear conciliatory. He dictated an official letter that asked passport officers to let Reed through without examining his documents, explaining they would be scrutinized at the American port of entry.* Armed with this

---

* The enmity of Francis for Reed now showed in various ways. Reed's passport was given a private code number which indicated he was a suspicious character,

and a note from Chicherin, Jack left Petrograd early in February. He was downcast about the consulship but at least took satisfaction in having accomplished the original purpose—for the moment, the papers were safe. Unfortunately, while he traveled slowly toward Stockholm and Christiania by rail and boat, a flurry of diplomatic activity served to undermine that safety. Now he was about to learn the cost not only of radicalism, but of a flamboyance which rubbed sober people the wrong way.

His nemesis could have been anyone at the embassy, but it seems most likely the role fell to Edgar Sisson, who had arrived in late November as the representative of the Committee on Public Information with the task of distributing propaganda favorable to America. Prim, furtive and staunchly anti-Bolshevik, Sisson was Reed's polar opposite. From the moment of their first meeting, the two men heartily disliked one another. Initial impressions were reinforced when Jack began openly to refer to Sisson as "the weasel," and deteriorated completely when the CPI official presumed to lecture on manners and canons of behavior. After Reed's patrol with the Red Guards on January 19, Sisson solemnly broached the subject of his "good family" and Harvard background, explaining like a schoolmaster that the Bolsheviks were only using him. When Sisson attempted to extract a promise that Reed would not address the Third Congress, Jack's reply was short, nasty and offensive. Highly affronted, Sisson probably then used his direct line through George Creel to the White House to even the score, and more.

Complaints and misinformation from Petrograd to Washington led to a game of diplomatic hide-and-seek. On February 12 a confidential report emanating from the London embassy pictured Reed as aiming to cause trouble in the United States and quite ready to create an "international incident" if arrested en route. Four days later the State Department issued word that Scandinavian missions should refuse to visa his passport. These instructions caught up with Jack in Christiania, Norway, where on the nineteenth, Consul George N. Ifft bluntly told him he could go neither forward nor backward. The consul was a zealous man who went far beyond instructions. Entrusted by Louise with two letters for her husband, he took it upon himself to forward them to Washington instead. Learning Reed had slipped a packet of mail to a passenger sailing for America on February 22, he somehow had it intercepted. This, too,

---

and in a report to Washington on February 6 the ambassador concluded, "As to the contents of his documents I am entirely unacquainted. I recommend that they be censored severely."

went off in a diplomatic pouch, along with several notes of advice that Reed would be safer in the United States, "where his activities can be controlled," than at large in Scandinavia, where he could pose as a martyr.[22]

Any such pose was far from his mind. Obviously stuck, Jack telegraphed the *Masses* about his predicament, asked that his mother and wife be informed, rented a room and settled down to write. On the twenty-fifth two cables were delivered through the consulate. The first, signed by Steffens and Louise, said only, "Don't return. Await instructions." The second, over Steffens' name, said Reed could render a "historical international service" if he convinced Lenin and Trotsky that President Wilson was sincere in his Russian policy. Basically, his old friend was concerned that the Soviets, after extended negotiations and further incursions, were about to accept a separate peace with Germany. This was feared by the Allies as an act that would free German troops for action on the Western Front. Close to White House circles, Steffens was referring to Wilson's vague promises of recognition and possible aid in return for keeping alive the Eastern Front. The terms imposed by Germany were disastrous, stripping Russia of immense territories and resources, but at this point the Soviets believed that anything was preferable to war. Not knowing the Council of Commissars had already voted to sign the treaty, Jack believed the idea ridiculous, but out of sentiment he passed it along through local Bolshevik sympathizers.

Suspended in time and space, Reed had no word from America for a month. He wrote an introduction for a book on the revolution, then began to outline chapters, and as his mind fixed on New York, he let memories pour forth in poetic lines. Low on money, he sold articles on Russia to local newspapers. Restless and increasingly angry, he composed a heated letter to the American minister, protesting against being illegally deprived of the right to return to his own country and demanding "that the United States Government reimburse me for my expenditures."[23] With it went an itemized account tinged with humor. Along with room, board and cables home were detailed analyses of weekly laundry and cleaners' bills.

Late in March there was a pleasant interlude when radical cartoonist Robert Minor stopped by on the way to Russia and delivered a message from Louise. His departure left Jack lonelier than before. Haunting the consulate, he could receive no answer as to when he might be allowed to leave, and thoughts of never being allowed back into the United States began to plague him. To ward off gloom, he worked furiously, but writing could not exorcise longings for home. Then in April the State Department changed its orders, and one morning the consul at last stamped his passport with a new visa.

The crossing on the S.S. *Bergensfjord* was rough, and halfway over he suffered a nasty attack of ptomaine, but nothing could dampen each day's sense of rising expectation. Early on the morning of April 28 he watched the dark towers of Manhattan emerge from the gray river mist. It was five years to the day since his arrest in Paterson. Almost half the time since he had spent abroad, witnessing war and revolution. Through all the steps that led from Paterson to Petrograd, one thing had remained constant—the magic pull of New York City. But as he smiled hello to home, Reed found himself answered by a frown. Four days earlier, Sisson, now returning to the U.S., had cabled from London precise suggestions to the State Department: seize Reed's papers, look them over slowly and, if possible, hold them for his, Sisson's, perusal. Despite Bolshevik sympathies, the journalist should not be feared, for "his role has probably been only that of a foolish tool."[24]

While other passengers were disembarking, Reed was accosted by two customs officers and an Army lieutenant. They confiscated all his papers, forced him to strip for a personal examination and held him for questioning. An interrogation lasting for hours covered everything from earlier journeys abroad to his connection with the *Masses*. Repeatedly the examiners returned to Russia and Bolshevism—who had paid for his trip, why had he been appointed consul, would he engage in revolutionary propaganda in the United States? His answers were generally blunt: "I am a Socialist and I am going to engage in Socialistic work within the law. If I do anything against the law I will take the consequences. I am in this country to write my book and I would rather do that than anything else in the world." Late in the afternoon when the interrogation ended, Jack made a formal statement for the record. Fearful the papers might be lost or destroyed, he emphasized they were invaluable for his work. This concern was answered in the bland tones of bureaucracy: "They are in proper hands, but it must be determined whether they contain anything contrary to the interests of the American government. [They] are to be submitted to the State Department. . . . Your interests will be looked after."[25]

The pall cast by the reception committee vanished on the dock in the warm arms of Louise. Riding in a cab, they held each other close. At the Brevoort basement crowds of friends shouted hello, then food and wine filled his body with warmth and touched his head with dizziness. Swelling, alive and full of laughter, Jack floated through a glorious evening much like those of long-past days when the Village and the

Masses and friends were young and innocent. For a single night it was possible to forget governments, revolutions and all the work that lay undone. He was home in America, home in New York, home in the center of all those scenes his poem so lovingly described. Tomorrow there would be time enough for the problems of today. Tomorrow there would be time enough to learn that writing about "America, 1918" was one thing, attempting to live in it distinctly another.

19

America

"My dear Steff—

"Your letter just reached me. I have been on the point of writing you many times, but did not know where to reach you. . . . I have heard stray accounts of your adventures. I think you must have been suffering a good deal—perhaps more than anybody. Wish I could have a good talk with you.

". . . I have been making many speeches about Russia, and tomorrow go to Chicago and Detroit to address meetings there. I started a big newspaper syndicate series, like Louise's, but the newspapers were afraid to touch them: some of them sent the stuff back after it was in type. Then Collier's took a story, put it in type, and sent it back. Oswald Villard told me he would be suppressed if he published John Reed!

"I have a contract with Macmillan to publish a book, but the State Department took away all my papers when I came home, and up to date has absolutely refused to return any of them. . . .

"I am therefore unable to write a word of the greatest story of my life, and one of the greatest in the world. I am blocked. Do you know any way to have my papers sent to me? If they don't come pretty soon it will be too late for my book—Macmillan's won't take it.

"I was arrested the other day in Philadelphia, trying to speak on the street, and am held for court in September on the charges of 'inciting to riot, inciting to assault and battery and inciting to seditious remarks.' . . .

"I feel sort of flat and stale. My kidney isn't well—I suppose that is why. Mother writes daily threatening to commit suicide if I continue to besmirch the family name. My brother is going to France next week. . . .

"Excuse the depression. I don't see why I chose this low, grey moment in which to write you. I felt pretty good this morning, and probably will tomorrow morning. . . ."[1]

Six weeks after returning, John Reed knew the worst. More than a year earlier he had predicted what would happen if the United States entered the World War, had spoken of mob-madness which would choke artists and crucify truth-tellers. Now government interference, police harassment, censorship, political trials and imputations of treason were a daily reality. The difficult problem was to keep up the spirits, to look beyond the trials of the moment to a better future.

In an answer from San Francisco, Steffens offered little hope. His own national speaking tour had been terminated by irate public officials in San Diego, to whom any hints of peace or any kind words about Soviet Russia sounded like sedition. Philosophically, Stef took refuge in believing that war hysteria was "normal and typical," in saying that "the public mind is sick." This led to a simple conclusion: "Jack you do wrong to buck this thing . . . it is wrong to try to tell the truth now. We must wait. You must wait. I know it's hard, but you can't carry conviction. You can't plant ideas. Only feelings exist, and the feelings are bewildered. I think it is undemocratic to try to do much now. Write, but don't publish."[2]

Reed could hardly accept such words: "I am not of your opinion that it is undemocratic to buck this thing. If there were not the ghost of a chance, if everybody were utterly for it, even then I don't see why it shouldn't be bucked. All movements have had somebody to start them, and, if necessary, go under for them. Not that I want particularly to go under—but—

"And you are wrong to think that this business is unanimous. There are many—oh so many—who crowd to my meetings—thousands; and they are with us. And it's growing, growing fast. . . . My people weep with joy to know that there is something like dreams-come-true in Russia. And moreover I have seen what is happening abroad. . . ."[3]

The difference between the two old friends was more than one of temperament. Certainly it was always difficult for Jack to be philosophical, but more important was the fact that while Steffens had been watching the home front, Reed had had a faith kindled in Russia, and that faith was being refired by the enthusiasm of radicals who hungrily flocked to hear lectures on the revolution. Feeling warm despite their differences, he invited Stef to share the Croton house. Friendship was more important than politics, and it was obvious that in coming days pacifists, liberals, radicals—all dissenters—would have to stand together against attacks and oppression. For Stef, for many friends, for Jack himself, the struggle to survive such adversity while retaining compassion, humor and the ability to work would be a severe test.

The conditions that provided the test can be described in terms of pathology—bitten by the dog of war, America had gone mad. The reasons were as complex as the result was simple. A historic anxiety over national identity, and long-running trends of nativism, individualism, capitalism and antiradicalism, issued in the demand for total conformity and one-hundred-percent Americanism. In practice, this meant intolerance of any deviation from the war effort, either by deed, word or the slightest shifting of the eyes at mention of the holy cause. Punishment for dissidence came at all levels of society. The federal Espionage Act of 1917, penalizing false statements obstructing the war effort, was supplemented by the 1918 Sedition Act, which made "disloyal" references to flag, government or the Constitution subject to a twenty-year sentence.* Under an act of 1798, enemy aliens were incarcerated and deported, while the Postmaster General withheld mailing privileges from publications that hampered the war effort. Such official instruments were supplemented by semilegal forms of social control. New patriotic societies boasted thousands of chapters, and one of them, the American Protective League, became a semiofficial auxiliary of the Justice Department, its 250,000 members each equipped with a badge and a fervor for reporting disloyal and seditious utterances. In many areas such investigative activities merged into terrorism. Groups of zealous patriots would beat, whip, stomp, thrash, kick, tar-and-feather or lynch people deemed disloyal. In a 1918 report to Congress, the Attorney General proudly stated, "Never in its history has this country been so thoroughly policed. . . ."[4]

Theoretically, this activity was directed against foreign agents plotting to subvert the war effort. When genuine spies proved elusive, hatred encompassed all things German, leading to such measures as bans on the teaching of German in school districts, boycotts of German music and

---

* Almost two thousand persons stood trial under the Espionage and Sedition acts.

the hounding of German-named performers from the stage. After sauer-kraut was renamed "liberty cabbage" and the nation was not yet wholly secure, patriots subjected countless alien residents and German-Americans to indignities and acts of vigilantism, and other victims were sought. These proved easy to find. Radicals had long been scapegoats in America, and now their opposition to the war provided a new excuse for old hostility. Because most Socialists stood by the party's declaration against the capitalist conflict, raids on SP headquarters across the nation by soldiers, sailors and outraged citizens became a popular sport, while party leaders stood trial for sedition. The IWW refused to honor the no-strike pledge of other labor organizations, an action that led to stoppages in copper mines, lumber regions and agricultural areas, reinforcing the long-held view of Wobblies as un-American. While state legislatures moved toward "criminal syndicalist" laws against organizations advocating violence, posses and armed bands of citizens drove Wobblies out of towns. In September 1917 the federal government abetted this mood by raiding every major IWW meeting hall in the nation, seizing all records and holding some three hundred leaders for trial.

Bohemia was less directly plagued by the hysteria. In little physical danger, its members were caught between two subtler kinds of violence: on one side the threat of censorship, on the other the increasingly pro-war atmosphere fostered by the media. Subject to a barrage of publicity emanating from the Committee on Public Information and disseminated by the press, many who had once opposed the war found it easier to go along with the national mood. Cooling friendships and growing personal animosity hurried institutional changes. By mid-1918 so important a center as the Liberal Club was disintegrating. With thirty members in the military service, its never robust financial condition became precarious. Giving up some rooms, canceling magazine subscriptions and firing the maid proved no more than temporary palliatives. In a society increasingly pressured by war, there was simply less need of an institutional meeting place for freewheeling discussions of art, life and revolution.

Living by the media, Bohemia began to die by them. Wartime society was little amused by Village antics, and large-circulation publications that had toyed with radicalism and provided markets for avant-garde works now backed away. As commercial markets shrank, war pressed in on the world of little magazines. Some remained lucky. The apolitical *Poetry* appeared as usual, while Margaret Anderson's *Little Review*, after labeling one blank page "The War," continued on its way. Others fell because an affluent middle class which paid the bills was growing less tolerant. The most severe casualty was the *Seven Arts*, which ceased in December 1917, fifteen months after heralding the advent of an American Renaissance. Unable to focus solely on cultural matters, the editors had printed Randolph Bourne's articles and Reed's "This Unpopular War," with the result that a nervous patron had withdrawn the subsidy that had kept the magazine afloat.

Wavering of support undermined some periodicals and government repression sank others. In the first year of conflict, seventy-five publications were proscribed by the Postmaster General. Most were radical, but, along with the Socialist Milwaukee *Leader* and New York *Call* and Tom Watson's Populist *Jeffersonian*, action was taken against national magazines. On one occasion *The Public* was barred from the mails for advocating higher taxation rather than loans as a means of raising revenue, while *Pearson's* met the same fate for referring to England in a discourteous manner. *The Nation* was denied mailing privileges in September 1918 for criticizing labor leader Sam Gompers, but this ban was lifted in four days through direct Presidential intervention. Even so, its influential editor, Oswald Garrison Villard, remained wary of publishing anything by Reed.

Despite some powerful connections, the *Masses* became another casualty. After barring the August 1917 issue from circulation, the Post Office revoked privileges for the September issue on the grounds that nonmailing in August meant the magazine was irregular in publication and therefore not "a newspaper or periodical within the meaning of the law." A federal judge termed the revocation—obviously due to the Postmaster's own action—"a rather poor joke," but nonetheless upheld it. Hardly amused, Max Eastman journeyed to Washington with newspaper magnate E. W. Scripps—a longtime backer—to see Postmaster General Burleson. Having once told Scripps that his chain of newspapers had been crucial in Wilson's 1916 reelection, Burleson proved friendly and effusive, assuring the publisher, "We love Max Eastman."[5] This emotion made no difference. Mailing privileges were not restored, and after struggling to distribute two more issues solely on newsstands, Eastman was forced to bury the *Masses*.

Continuing its peculiar brand of love, the administration then moved against five of the publication's editors with an indictment for conspiracy to obstruct the draft. While awaiting trial, Eastman was toying with the idea of resurrecting the *Masses* when Reed's first telegram from Petrograd arrived in mid-November. Once more Jack's words proved decisive in his friend's editing career. Realizing that priceless articles on the Bolshevik Revolution would follow, Max now found the idea of a new magazine irresistible. With his sister Crystal as copublisher and Floyd Dell as managing editor, he attracted all the old regulars and listed Reed as a contributing editor of the new *Liberator*. The format was much the same, but two differences separated the magazine from its predecessor: this was a personal rather than a cooperative venture, with the Eastmans controlling fifty-one percent of the stock; and, to ensure survival, Max decided to avoid bucking government authorities—"Some things we felt deeply must be left unspoken, on others we would have to temper our speech to the taste of the Postmaster General."[6]

Worried by the possibility of twenty years in prison, other editors lodged few objections. They continued the old *Masses* spirit and circulated invitations to editorial meetings which read, "Come to the conspiracy Tuesday night," but in cartoons and articles they were definitely softer on the war.[7] Their apparently conciliatory behavior, however, failed to mollify the government. While Reed was sailing home, Eastman, Dell, Art Young and business manager Merrill Rogers went on trial in one of the first major cases under the Espionage Act. The day before he landed, a jury, after nine days of testimony and forty-eight hours' deliberation, deadlocked ten to two in favor of conviction. After being discharged, the jury's majority members showed the temper of the times by complaining to the press about the "Socialist and pacifist" tendencies of the two recalcitrant jurors.[8]

The day after he arrived, Reed appeared for arraignment at the Federal Building accompanied by the *Masses'* counsel, Dudley Field Malone. He pleaded not guilty and was released on $2000 bail. Next on the agenda was the problem of his papers. Confident his connections could spring them loose, Jack made a trip to Washington. At the Russian division of the State Department he was promised a quick answer, but no word came. During May and June he sent off many letters and telegrams without getting action. Two friends in the State Department, Counselor Frank L. Polk and William Bullitt, were genuinely concerned, but despite their promises to expedite matters, nothing happened. As weeks passed, confidence edged into despair: "As long as I am accused of no crime in connection with the papers why aren't they given to me? . . . each day carries me further away from the time I knew in Russia, and makes my story less valuable." Bullitt agreed that the continued silence was "abominable" and promised to redouble his efforts.[9] But the summer slipped away without any action, an indication that Reed was quite likely being blocked at the highest levels of government.

The story in the publishing world was equally discouraging. Louise could syndicate a rather gushy series of articles, and newspapers could carry stories about Russia containing as much fancy as fact, but Reed placed only one short piece about the revolution in a commercial publication, the *Independent*, and this was hedged with a disclaimer of his "Socialist" views. Casting about for a means of making a living, he fell into a plan for a new magazine with Frank Harris, editor of *Pearson's*, whose anti-British views had caused his journal to be twice barred from the mails. Social criticism would have to be avoided, but Jack envisaged the publication as "the best expression of uncorrupted American artists" in all fields. Even confined to "works of the imagination," a strong-willed, original journal could have "a powerful effect upon the whole color and texture of the public mind."[10] Gathering Dell's support, Reed sought out friends like Sherwood Anderson, Randolph Bourne, James Oppenheim, Van Wyck Brooks and Carl Sandburg for contributions. Enough had replied positively to promise a solid beginning when plans fell through. In current conditions backers were wary of an expensive new venture in literature.

Despite failure, the experience had an educational side. Hustling for contributions, Jack gained an insight into the growing effect of war upon friends. The previous conjunction between artistic and political radicalism was beginning to reveal a latent split. This was most evident in the attitude of Marsden Hartley, a Provincetown houseguest in 1916. Living on the edge of starvation in New Mexico while attempting to paint, Hartley's answer to a request for contributions reeked with bitterness at editors, art dealers and a public that desired fashionable rather than serious works. Full of self-pity—"I want release from old-fashioned wearisome poverty . . . I am sick of asking to live," the artist showed no recognition of his connection to the rest of society. The war was no more than a personal affront, something which "lost me a fine chance to show in every city in Europe."[11]

Blocked from supporting himself by writing, Reed turned to the lecture platform. For a radical there was no regular circuit, no agent to package a neat tour of the provinces. During the summer of 1918 he spoke where and when he could, often in New York or nearby New Jersey industrial towns, occasionally in the Boston area, with two swings into the Midwest. Everywhere his message was the same as that he was hammering home in the pages of the *Liberator*. Attempting to stem the tide of anti-Bolshevik sentiment rolling through the commercial press, he argued that the Soviet government, based on "the universal will of the Russian masses," should be recognized by the United States.[12] Forced into the Treaty of Brest-Litovsk, Russian leaders were the very opposite of the German agents some people now accused them of being. In truth, their revolutionary doctrines were working to undermine the Kaiser. Not anarchists, not bomb-throwers and terrorists, the Bolsheviks were visionaries and prophets who were creating a democratic and just society. To oppose them, to aid their internal enemies or urge foreign intervention, was to give aid and comfort to those reactionary elements which had kept the Russian workers and peasantry in misery for centuries.*

The pay for lecturing was not high, but there were other compensations. Since the first issue in March, the highlight of the *Liberator* had been Reed's monthly article, widely quoted and reprinted in other radical outlets. Hailed in the *Call* both as "the greatest reporter in America" and as a Socialist with the most "intimate and reliable" knowledge of Russian events, he came before left-wing audiences as a hero, a man who had taken part in the revolution so long hoped for, a man who had experience to back his flat statement that "The masses of workers are capable not only of great dreams, but . . . have in them the power to make dreams come true."[13] Other radicals often shared the platform, but on leaflets, posters and the podium itself Reed was the star attraction. The meeting places were usually bare, seedy union halls or drab Socialist locals, and the audiences were largely working-class men and women with ill-fitting clothes who asked questions in heavy foreign accents. But for one who had been in the Cirque Moderne and Smolny, such people were the stuff of revolution. When he rose to begin addresses with the single word "Tovarischi," Jack was meeting audiences in a realm where dreams are engaged.

Words that brought cheers from radicals were bound to elicit a negative response in other quarters. At the Tremont Temple in Boston heckling by a group of Harvard students seemed evidence that radicalism in the student body was a thing of the past. On May 31, when officials in Philadelphia refused to issue a speaking permit, Reed stood on the street near the closed hall and began to address a crowd of one thousand. Grabbed by police, he was arraigned on a charge of inciting to riot and released on $5000 bail. Two weeks later in Detroit uniformed officers conspicuously lounged about his audience and afterward seized two hundred young men supposedly for nonpossession of draft cards. Cleveland proved the most ominous of cities. While Jack was trailed by two detectives,

---

* Growing anti-Bolshevism was based on the radical views of the Soviets and the widely circulated rumor that they were German agents who had signed the Treaty of Brest-Litovsk to free the Kaiser's troops to fight more fully against the Allies in the West. For the manner in which anti-German sentiment merged into anti-Bolshevism, see John Higham, *Strangers in the Land: Patterns of American Nativism, 1860–1925* (New York: Atheneum, 1970), 194–233, and Robert K. Murray, *Red Scare: A Study in National Hysteria* (Minneapolis: University of Minnesota Press, 1955).

others seized his baggage from a friend and confiscated his papers. Following the evening lecture twenty members of the American Protective League—"odious looking thugs"—swarmed around and began to mutter about treason. Reed was saved when agents of the Department of Justice interposed themselves, but then was forced to answer questions about his beliefs for almost an hour. He heard one officer boast about Cleveland's surveillance of radicals: "We know everything that's going on about everybody. . . . You can't eat your dinner in a restaurant, you can't go to the theater, you can't lay down to sleep, without we hear every word you utter."[14]

Alternately buoyed by enthusiastic audiences and enraged by the hostility of officials and "patriots," Reed found his sense of purpose stiffened on July 4, when he and Art Young met Eugene V. Debs. From the train rolling toward the Socialist leader's home in Terre Haute they saw trim villages with church spires, white farmhouses, muddy rivers, cornfields and soft hills with lazy cows, a fertile, steaming land that brought home the thought "*This* is the real America." Debs was fully a part of this region, a tall, shambling, homespun radical with roots in the Greenback Party and Populism, who for twenty years had made Socialism seem American as Thanksgiving. Now times had changed, and on a June speaking tour Debs had been indicted in Canton, Ohio, for violating the Espionage Act. In person he was to Reed a rare combination of courage and humanity. Rising from a sickbed, obviously in pain, Debs welcomed the two visitors with a radiance, affection and warmth that made him seem a child's version of Uncle Sam. Face glowing, voice intense, he described recent experiences—brushes with vigilantes and detectives, threats of reprisals in small towns, ill-concealed hostility from former local friends. He was able to understand that others might be terrorized into abandoning beliefs, although his own remained strong and secure: "Socialism's on the way. They can't stop it no matter what they do . . . you tell all the boys everywhere who are making the fight, Gene Debs says he's with you, all the way. . . ."[15]

A few days later in Chicago the mass trial of Wobblies provided further examples of patient courage. Jack's first love among radical organizations, the IWW was American to the core, a union of men in a lifelong battle against "a force which has limitless power, gives no quarter, and obeys none of the rules of civilized warfare."[16] One hundred and one Wobblies were in court for the first of a series of government prosecutions clearly aimed at destroying the union. After languishing in jail for seven months, each had been charged with over one hundred separate crimes, from sedition to conspiracy to sabotage. With almost no tangible evidence, the state's attorneys were indulging in an increasingly familiar tactic—through extensive quotation from publications, they were attempting to convict the Wobblies for their radical philosophy.

The defendants who filed into the dark, wood-paneled courtroom were a tough-looking group of "lumber jacks, harvest-hands, miners . . . who believe the wealth of the world belongs to him who creates it." On the bench was Judge Kenesaw Mountain Landis, "a wasted man with untidy white hair, an emaciated face in which two burning eyes are set like jewels, parchment skin split by a crack for a mouth." Formidable in appearance, Landis was reasonable enough in behavior, perhaps "the best of the old regime." Impatient with traditional formality, he sat in a business suit rather than robes and allowed spittoons to be placed about for the convenience of the prisoners. Such acts could not soften the basic confrontation, the fact that 101 men were on trial for believing in "One Big Union," that their only crime was preaching social revolution. Viewing the proceedings with eyes full of Russia, Jack found the defendants reminiscent of the Executive Committee of the Soviets, and for a moment his mind flashed with the sweet idea that this was a tribunal of American Bolsheviks trying the judge for counterrevolution.

In the middle of July, Reed and Louise moved out to Croton to be alone. For a time the garden, a "beautiful and ineffably quiet growing spot," was a refuge, and for hours he carefully planted seedlings, weeded, trimmed overgrown hedges, pruned fruit trees.[17] Valuable as therapy, gardening could not permanently down his mounting agitation. Confusion, pain and sorrow, coupled with impossible wishes that the world might be other than it was, made him moody. Some friends found him bright and cheerful, bursting with elation over the Russian experience, but others saw him as tense, somber and harsh. Eastman was especially worried that Reed seemed continually depressed and began to wonder if loss of gaiety was the price of revolution. One evening over dinner when Jack was characteristically haranguing about the state of the world, Max at least made him laugh with an angry exclamation: "The trouble with you is you're getting too damned adult!"[18]

Eastman's perception was true enough, but Reed's attitude in his presence was partly colored by a growing uneasiness over the *Liberator*. Debs and the Wobblies were standing firm, but he was supporting a publication that soft-pedaled opposition to war. Necessary as this might be for survival, it was cowardice, and yet without the magazine there would be no place to continue explaining the revolution. Deciding on a compromise in late July, he attempted to discuss it with Max, but his hurt friend refused to listen. In August, Reed wrote a letter that appeared in the next *Liberator*: "I've thought about it for a long time, and I make this decision not without emotion, remembering our long work together on *The Masses*. But I feel I must take my name off the editorial page. The reason is, I cannot in these times bring myself to share editorial responsibility for a magazine which exists upon the sufferance of Mr. Burleson. Of course this does not mean I want to stop contributing. . . ." Replying in print, Max expressed a "deep feeling of regret," but said the members of the editorial board believed it was their duty to the "social revolution" to keep the publication alive.[19] Two years earlier Reed had written a poem about Eastman's deep dedication to revolution; now they were on different paths, but in a note, and then in person, he expressed happiness that their friendship remained.

September was a month of trials, arrests and blatant government deception. It opened with bad news from Chicago. Two weeks before, after a single hour of deliberation, the jury had found the Wobblies guilty on a total of ten thousand counts. Now came news that Judge Landis had imposed drastic sentences, five to ten years for most defendants, twenty years for fifteen IWW leaders and fines totaling two million dollars. A few days later Haywood wrote Reed from the Cook County Jail: "The big game is over we never won a hand. The other fellow had the cut, shuffle and deal all the time, personally we didn't lose much just a part of our lives. . . . All in the world they had against us was morsels of fragmentary evidence, not enough to convict a ward heeling politician, but we were off our field, we will do better when we get organized and can tie into them on the Industrial ground."[20]

Troubles came closer to home in the middle of the month. On September 13 Reed made his first major speech since the release of news that Allied troops—French, English, Japanese and American—had landed both in Siberia and in northern Russia during August. Official explanations for this intervention cited the need to keep war materials from falling into German hands, the possibility of reconstituting the Eastern Front, the hope of aiding a large legion of Czechoslovakian troops who were attempting to leave Russia. To Jack its import was simpler: capitalism was out to crush Bolshevism. He bitterly denounced intervention to an audience of four thousand at Hunt's Point Palace, and the following morning he was arrested. Freed on $5000 bail, he returned for arraignment on the twenty-fourth, pleading innocent to charges of using "disloyal, scurrilous and abusive language about the Military and Naval Forces of the United States." The two quotes included in the indictment indicated how far the government could stretch the definition of sedition. One had

Reed saying, "This intervention that I am talking to you about is here not allowed to be spoken about in any other way than the Government wants it to be spoken about; but in every other country in the world . . . this intervention is characterized very boldly as an adventure of brigands."[21] The second was a reference to an editorial in the *Manchester Guardian* which blamed intervention on the desire of French bankers to recover foreign debts repudiated by the Soviet government.

Reed also faced another challenge. On September 15, under the aegis of the Committee on Public Information, newspapers began to print a series of documents secured by Edgar Sisson in Petrograd. Purporting to be copies of archival materials from Smolny, they depicted the Bolshevik leaders as agents of the German government. Such notions had been bruited in the press before. Now there seemed proof that without German money the Soviet regime would collapse. Because the documents had been in Washington since the spring, Jack guessed their release was meant to help justify intervention, and editorial exclamations over this new evidence of Soviet perfidy showed they were playing such a role. This led to a hastily written *Liberator* pamphlet. Explaining that many similar papers had been for sale the year before in Russia, he dissected both internal and external inconsistencies and flatly labeled them "mainly forgeries," a judgment later confirmed by careful historical scrutiny.[22]*

September closed in the Foley Square courthouse with the beginning of the second *Masses* trial. The charge was conspiracy to violate the Espionage Act, to interfere with recruiting and cause disloyalty in the armed forces. Each defendant, except for business manager Rogers, was cited for one specific work—Eastman for an editorial expressing admiration for conscientious objectors; Dell for commending the example of some English conscientious objectors; Young for a cartoon depicting a mad war dance of figures representing business, the press, politicians and clergymen to an orchestra led by a gleeful devil; and Reed for the article reprinted from the *Tribune* on mental disease among soldiers, over which he had placed the headline "Knit a Strait-Jacket for Your Soldier Boy." The intent of such works seemed so trivial that Jack entered the courtroom with a light heart, nudging Young with the question, "Well, Art, got your grip packed for prison?" Outside in City Hall Park a band was playing the national anthem and bonds were being sold for the Fourth Liberty Loan. Inside the dark room it was like a family reunion. Friends

---

* George F. Kennan, "The Sisson Documents," *Journal of Modern History*, XXVIII (June 1956), 130–54, has done a thorough examination of evidence to show the documents are largely forgeries.

from the Village and contributors to the *Masses* crowded the benches, noisily greeting the defendants. Louise was radiant and reassuring; Dell's current girlfriend, Edna St. Vincent Millay, declaimed a new sonnet; Louis Untermeyer stopped Reed to quote a recent example of abominable verse.

The menacing tones of the bailiff announcing Judge Martin Manton's entrance made the atmosphere more serious, and the selection of jurors proved unsettling. All the talesmen questioned seemed pro-war and anti-radical. One pompous gentleman who gave his business as "Wall Street" answered a defense attorney's question about socialism by saying, "I don't know what it is, but I'm opposed to it!" Keeping notes, Jack worried that anyone who profited from the war would be against them. One manufacturer seemed a poor selection because he looked "like an exploiter." Of another choice, he penned a simple "Son of a bitch."[23] By the end of the afternoon the reality of twenty years behind bars was hovering like an unpleasant ghost in the courtroom.

This specter was soon dispelled. Testimony and argument consumed five days, but early on it was apparent the prosecution was not doing well. The conspiracy charge was difficult to prove because the haphazard nature of *Masses* editorial meetings was attested by all witnesses. Even disruption of the military seemed highly questionable. Prosecutor Earl Barnes managed to produce a solitary military subscriber who argued that the *Masses* had been damaging to morale, but the defense easily destroyed his testimony:

Q. When you first began to read the Masses what was your rank in the army?
A. I was a lieutenant, sir.
Q. And what is your rank today?
A. I am a captain.

Confessing that all "isms" were a mystery to him, Judge Manton allowed a wide range of issues to be discussed, and the court took on the air of a college lecture hall. Dell, now in the Army, explained the philosophic basis of conscientious objection. Young spoke in favor of revolution—"the boys at Lexington and Concord did a good job"—and firmly maintained that a cartoon, like a painting, could not be explained beyond what it was. Asked by the court, "What have you got this Devil here for?" he answered, "Just patriotic reasons, Judge. You see, General Sherman said that war was hell, and how can you have hell without a devil?"[24] Eastman took the opportunity for an exposition of Socialism, its philosophy and history, including everything from praise of the American party's antiwar stand to a defense of Soviet Russia's recent actions. His eloquent three-hour summation, which left the courtroom in silence, moved Reed deeply: "Standing there, with the attitudes and attributes of intellectual eminence, young, good-looking, he was the typical champion of ideals—ideals which he made to seem the ideals of every real American."[25]

Taking the stand on October 3, Jack looked rumpled, boyish and a bit uneasy. His eyes were soft, his voice was high-pitched, his manner engagingly honest. This image was fortunate, for some of his answers were less than forthright. Asked to explain exactly what he had had in mind when writing the headline, he launched into a rambling half-hour account of experiences as a war correspondent. While he gazed at a window high in the wall above the jury box, his words brought far-flung battlefields into the silent room—Gómez Palacio, where corpses were piled like cordwood in the streets; Serbian towns, where hundreds of peasants chained together were burned in glowing heaps; Galicia, where the hacked bodies of Jews bespoke the work of Cossacks; Flanders, where German soldiers lived in waist-deep mud and men broke into fits of screaming madness. Back in the United States after witnessing such things, he had found frivolous, uninformed attitudes about war as "fashionable" that made him sick. The article was no more than an attempt to combat ignorance and misinformation, to "call attention to the fact that war was not what we thought it was."

These descriptions did not impress Judge Manton, who thought the issue was simple: had he intended the article to interfere with recruiting? The question was put directly, but Reed equivocated. It had never crossed his mind that people might be influenced against enlisting; he had only wanted them to "know the truth about the European war." Dissatisfied, Manton pressed further:

Q. You were opposed to the war?
A. I was opposed to our going in the war.
Q. Were you opposed to the war after going into it?
A. Yes, sir . . .
Q. Therefore, of course, you are opposed to obtaining the necessary military forces to prosecute the war?

Squirming in the chair, Reed hesitated. An affirmative answer might bring prison very close—defense attorneys had been clear on this point. It was so difficult not to tell the truth, and yet what purpose would be served by going to jail on such a trifling charge, dating from another life before the revolution? Once more he attempted to talk around the point, but the court cut him short: "Were you opposed to our obtaining the military forces?" Slowly, softly, Jack answered, "No." The judge then put it another way: "Didn't you think this article, in which you throw fear into the mothers and families of boys that might go to the front, was something in opposition to gathering military forces?" This time it was easier: "No, I did not."[26]

The rest was a breeze. After Reed parried some provocative questions about his belief in a proletarian war against capitalism—"Well, to tell you the truth, it is the only war that interests me"—the prosecutor attempted a moving summation, growing eloquent over a young friend killed in France: "Somewhere he lies dead, and he died for you and he died for me. He died for Max Eastman, he died for John Reed, for Floyd Dell, for Merrill Rogers. . . ." At this point Art Young, snoozing soundly on the defendants' table, woke up abruptly and asked in a stage whisper, "Didn't he die for me too?" and the room exploded into laughter. Charging the jury, Judge Manton emphasized that Americans still had a right to criticize the government so long as they did not intend to hinder recruiting or cause disobedience in the armed forces. Jurors met for a short time and took two ballots, both with similar results: seven for conviction, five opposed. Late on the afternoon of October 5 the *Masses* defendants were free.

Some friends viewed the outcome as a victory for free speech, and a sharp setback for government repression. But Reed did not agree. A few weeks before, Debs had been convicted in Cleveland and sentenced to ten years. In Chicago, the Wobblies had been devastated. Two weeks after the *Masses* trial, a group of young Russian-Americans were given stiff sedition sentences in the same courtroom where Eastman and associates had been freed. The different result for a similar offense was explained by a member of the DA's staff: "You are Americans. You *looked like* Americans. . . . You can't convict an American for sedition before a New York judge." Heritage, the luck of having an open-minded judge, a trial in New York, where patriotism was less hysterical—these had been the conditions of victory. Describing the trial for the *Liberator*, Reed paid due respect to the judge and jury, but went on to assert that "In the United States political offenses are dealt with more harshly than anywhere else in the world."[27] Comfort was to be taken only from the fact that punishment was a sure breeding ground for revolution.

In the weeks after the trial, rumors arose of an impending armistice. Receiving news from Europe that negotiations were already under way, Jack celebrated one evening with Dell and Edna Millay by riding back and forth half the night on the Staten Island Ferry. It was foggy and damp, with ships' horns lowing mournfully, just the atmosphere for poetry and good tales. Relaxed and happy, Reed began to recount his adventures, and as the tiny, beautiful, red-haired girl gazed up with eyes full of wonder, he grew expansive, his words full of life and heroism. As theatrical as Jack, Millay took him gently by the arm and, echoing Othello's words about Desdemona, murmured, "I love you for the dangers you have passed."[28]

The real armistice was an anticlimax. The guns fell silent on November 11, but the social structure of Europe teetered on the brink of disaster. Once-rich lands were stalked by famine; the empires of Austria-Hungary and Turkey splintered into warring nationalities; Germany, Bavaria and Budapest collapsed into revolution; and in Russia, counter-revolutionary armies marched and foreign intervention continued. For American radicals it was the best of times and the worst of times. Upheaval abroad and demobilization at home promised great changes, the smell of revolution was wafted across the Atlantic, and yet hysteria continued unabated. Now the targets were solely domestic dissenters, Socialists, anarchists or liberals who might have something good to say about the Soviet regime.

On Armistice Day, Socialists paraded up Fifth Avenue towards a Carnegie Hall meeting celebrating both peace and the German Revolution. Just beyond Thirty-fourth Street a group of soldiers and sailors in uniform waded into the procession, tearing down red flags, punching both men and women. Some newspapers praised the military men, and the mayor responded by forbidding displays of "anarchistic emblems" like the red flag. Two weeks later, a Madison Square Garden meeting on Tom Mooney's behalf was disrupted by men in uniform who pursued and beat some of those in attendance. On November 26, the Board of Aldermen passed an ordinance against displaying red or black flags, and the police commissioner began a campaign to convince all meeting hall owners to refuse rentals to radicals. That same night, outside a gathering of the Women's Internationalist League being addressed by Oswald Villard and a Republican Congressman, a mob of sailors and soldiers battled police, smashed windows and threatened lynching for anyone speaking sedition. The next day's *Tribune* described the "clear-headed, justifiable wrath which our men in uniform displayed," and pointed out that such a "Bolshevik" gathering "was designed to be provocative of disorder."[29] These events gave Reed more pain than surprise. For a year the press had dwelled on the Red Terror of Bolsheviks, much of it imaginary, while the supposed atrocities of native radicals like the IWW had been a longtime news staple. Reed thought it was now quite natural for them to hail the advent of a White Terror in America.

But Jack's mind was elsewhere. In September, Steffens' influence had led to Colonel House, the President's closest adviser, and suddenly, miraculously, one November day all of Reed's papers were returned. Macmillan had canceled the contract, and there was a good chance that nobody would dare "publish a friendly book about Russia," but this hardly mattered. For an entire year the work had been there, fermenting in his unconscious, haunting his dreams, disturbing his sleep at night, emerging in bits and pieces in *Liberator* articles. Adventurer, activist, revolutionary—perhaps he was all of these, too, but his sense of self, integrity, humanity even, were all tied up with that stream of words and images that had begun to flow in Portland twenty-five years before. Reed was a writer, and with the materials now at hand, he was ready to commit to paper a book that would be a monument both to the revolution and to his own identity.

Often in the past Reed had done his best work in a fury of activity; *Ten Days That Shook the World* was written in two months. He secretly rented the top floor of Paula Holliday's new restaurant, the Greenwich Village Inn, and, surrounded by piles of newspapers, pamphlets, placards, books and notes, a Russian dictionary close at hand, a cigarette always burning in an overflowing ashtray, he pounded the typewriter for days and nights on end. For months he had worried that the year-old story might be fading. Now he knew nothing had been lost. Some of the information came from articles already written, but for the most part he was telling the story anew. Words that captured the past freed him from the present. The walls fell away and he was back in Petrograd, hurrying through muddy streets, rubbing elbows with boisterous soldiers in the Smolny cafeteria, joshing with Williams, questioning Trotsky, listening to Lenin lay down programs with the iron logic of history. Gone from the mind were American courtrooms and police, the lies of newspapers, the questions of prosecutors, the depression of indecision. One morning when he stumbled out for a cup of coffee, he encountered Eastman in the middle of Sheridan Square. Max was startled by his friend's appearance, "gaunt, unshaven, greasy-skinned, a stark sleepless half crazy look on his slightly potatolike face," and he listened raptly to Jack rattle on about his work, transfixed by the look of "unqualified, concentrated joy in his mad eyes." Like all men in the grip of some strange destiny, Reed "was doing what he was made to do."[30]

Eastman was correct. A sensitive writer, Reed had proved in Mexico that reporting could be raised to an art, and his whole life seems to have been a special preparation for describing the Russian revolution. His pages crackle with more vitality, drama and power than can be found in any other accounts by eyewitnesses or historians. Compared to his past work, the book on Russia is a major stride forward. For all the brilliant descriptions and set pieces, *Insurgent Mexico* is disjointed, a series of episodes held together by the theme of a young man finding himself amid the violence of agrarian revolution, while *The War in Eastern Europe* has little focus or tension, sustaining interest only through the sharp eyes of the narrator. *Ten Days That Shook the World* is far different. If there is still an "I" relating the action, this narrator is in the background, no more than a camera recording history that dwarfs the story of any individual or group of men.

The structure of the book is that of drama.* Three historical-background chapters stand as a prologue; two are a first act in which the people rise; three describe the counterrevolutionary offensive; two more form a final act in which the people emerge triumphant, while a two-chapter epilogue forms a slow denouement, summarizing subsequent events. Underlying the story is an epic theme, the avenging of historic injustice by a trial of arms, the rising of the oppressed and underprivileged to regain power and freedom. The hero is mass man rather than the individual, the epic seen from below rather than above. Standing tradition on its head in this way, Reed was only following a writer's instinct toward a new kind of truth. Living at that point when the mass was entering history with a vengeance, he fixed an image of the crowd as hero for a new age.

Structure and theme keep *Ten Days That Shook the World* focused and tight, providing a driving power. With descriptions toned down, with far fewer consciously poetic flights than in earlier books, Reed keeps the eye centered on concrete places and events—Petrograd with its meeting halls and shabby factories, Smolny and the languid flow of crowds in the streets, idle conversation in cafés and grandiloquent speeches of ministers, proclamations tacked on walls and newspapers fresh with rumors. The work is heavily documented, but the lengthy texts of decrees and speeches become more than idle words to skim. Realizing the feeling inherent in the events, the eloquence of men speaking their hearts in moments of passion and crisis, the author lets their own words create drama and excitement. In this way the vacillating moods, the doubts, hesitation, debates, confusion, anger, betrayal, surprise, purpose and hostility of a revolutionary city are conveyed. Broadening the scope, brief references to decrees, articles, resolutions and actions from the rest of Russia give a sense of the tides of history beating against Smolny, the Marinsky, the

---

* The insightful theory that the structure of a dramatic play underlies the book was first voiced by John Howard Lawson in the introduction to the edition issued by International Publishers, 1967.

Winter Palace, and place Petrograd in a context of anguish and triumph of workers, soldiers and Soviets. The capital city is a test case, a model of struggle that drastically changed the course of a nation. By implication it is also a model for other countries and for all mankind.

Ten Days That Shook the World is a distillation, a summation of Reed's feeling about the revolution and its importance. Being that, it is streaked with bias. Good examples are its attitudes toward the middle classes, moderate Socialists and intellectuals. For years the bourgeoisie had seemed amusing to Bohemians for bad taste and money-grubbing; in Russia the bourgeois were the enemy, the backers of counterrevolution, people who sold out liberalism to embrace reaction—when Reed uses the word it is always pejorative. Moderate Socialists, those who had embraced the World War, were contemptible because in a revolutionary situation they were unable to live with the consequences of their ideas. Toward intellectuals Jack had been ambivalent for years. Here his own definition of manhood was involved, leading to disdain for the effete, those to whom theory was all, those whose heads seemed severed from their bodies and guts. This resulted in many unflattering portraits of the anti-Bolshevik Russian intelligentsia and a hearty admiration for the Lenins and Trotskys, men who were both intellectuals and activists, who could turn theory into reality.

In writing *Ten Days That Shook the World*, John Reed was working at the limit of his artistic capacities. For years he had believed himself a poet, but only recently, in a few brief works, had he been free and brave enough to bare those inner regions of pain that forge a bond of images between people. The Russian revolution allowed him to do the same on a broad canvas. A movement rooted in objective conditions that simultaneously oppressed people's bodies and stunted their imaginations, it was much more than a series of external events. The fullness of the revolution could be encompassed only by a writer sensitive to its emotional basis and overtones, and Reed was such a man. Because he shared the commitment and vision of the participants, he was able to capture the emotions that people pour into waking dreams. Inaccurate in details, biased in point of view, *Ten Days That Shook the World* conveys the kind of truth that is beyond fact, that creates fact. More than history, it is poetry, the poetry of revolution.

20

Chicago

"In response to anxious queries from our capitalist acquaintances as to the danger of a Bolshevik Revolution in the United States within the next two weeks, we wish to settle the question once for all.

"The American working class is politically and economically the most uneducated working class in the world. It believes what it reads in the capitalist press. It believes that the wage-system is ordained by God. It believes that Charley Schwab is a great man, because he can make money. It believes that Samuel Gompers and the American Federation of Labor will protect it as much as it can be protected. It believes that under our system of Government the Millennium is possible. When the Democrats are in power, it believes the promises of the Republicans, and vice versa. It believes that Labor Laws mean what they say. It is prejudiced against Socialism. . . ."[1]

Being enraptured with the idea of revolution did not prevent John Reed from seeing the world with enough detachment to depict the ironic gulf between what could be and what was. On the lecture platform, in *Liberator* articles, during the intense weeks of writing *Ten Days That Shook the World*, he could lose himself in a Bolshevik past and future. Yet simultaneously, in the winter of 1918–19, he could fix a level gaze on the American scene and humorously show that any revolution dependent upon the working class was hardly around the corner in the United States.

The problem was more than academic. Pragmatists in action, Bolshevik leaders believed that Socialism could never succeed in Russia alone, that a world or at least a European revolution would be their only salvation. Many actions in the months following November 1917 were based on such a premise. The publication of the Allies' secret treaties, the international appeals for proletarian support, the Propaganda Bureau for spreading Bolshevism among the troops of the Central Powers, the dispatch of agents and agitators to nearby countries—all these were attempts to hasten revolution. Even the peace of Brest-Litovsk had been based partly upon the idea that whatever was conceded at the conference table would soon be nullified by a Socialist takeover in Germany.

Aware of the importance Bolsheviks placed upon international support, Reed looked toward revolution in America as a solution for many old problems. The concept was a promise of a libertarian advance on social, cultural, economic and political fronts all at once. Russia had given it a particular form that convinced Jack the working class would be the motive force of any such historic change. This made the American situation especially discouraging. A captive of the national ideology, that brew of individualism, gullibility, greed and the comforting belief that one's son could become President, the working class in the United States was hardly a fertile ground for radical activity.

The Socialist Party itself exhibited barely more revolutionary potential. To Reed it seemed made up of petty bourgeois "for the most part occupied in electing Aldermen and Assemblymen to office, where they turn into time-serving politicians, and in explaining that Socialism does not mean Free Love." It was true the party could "swing a million votes," but this was only because it presented Socialism as a species of "Jeffersonian Democracy." The result was that "fully a third of the Socialist votes in normal times are . . . cast by middle-class persons who think Karl Marx wrote a good Anti-Trust law." Divorced from the "great mass of the working class," it would remain a weak competitor of progressive movements until it connected itself to the strength of the proletariat.[2]

Given such a situation, one might wonder how useful was a Socialist Party. Here the Russian experience was crucial. The SP should be, as

Lenin said, the "vanguard of the working class; it must not allow itself to be halted by the lack of education of the mass average, but it must lead the masses." In the United States this meant finding out the workers' grievances, and then explaining them in terms of the way capitalist society necessarily functioned. To conservative workers the party should expose the sham of political democracy, making them think economically rather than politically, showing that, no matter who elected them, representatives always served the interests of big business. To the few revolutionaries disgusted with politics—like members of the IWW—the SP should demonstrate the educational value of political action. By preaching "Socialism, straight Socialism, revolutionary Socialism, international Socialism," and by setting the problems of labor within a total world picture, the party could "make the workers want more—make them want the whole Revolution."[3]

These arguments, published in midwinter 1918–19, reflected not only Reed's views, but a growing movement within Socialist ranks. As an analysis of the party they were both cogent and more than a little unfair; this made them part of a new mood, too. The American SP was in the midst of an internal struggle that was upsetting world Socialism. Under pressure of the Russian revolution, every party was being torn by arguments over the tactics of taking power. Dividing lines in Europe were especially sharp—on one side the conservative majority Socialists who had supported war efforts; on the other, the small radical factions who had refused the lure of nationalism. While the former were ready to participate in parliamentary governments, the latter called for revolution.

The situation in the United States was not quite the same. A split between left and right had divided the party ever since its founding in 1901, with differing attitudes toward labor unions, the use of violence and—as some electoral success was achieved—how a Socialist should act when in office. Despite quarrels, the prewar SP was a diverse, flourishing organization. Claiming hundreds of officeholders, it supported three hundred publications with a circulation of two million. In distinct contrast to Europe, the American party was united against the war. After United States entry a few well-known intellectuals bolted, but virtually the entire membership remained true to internationalism. This brought on the wrath of both government and vigilantes. While leaders were prosecuted, publications suppressed and meetings raided, the SP prospered as well as suffered for its principles. Fifteen hundred of five thousand locals—mostly in small Middle and Far West communities—were wiped out during war years, but membership among immigrant industrial workers and Socialist votes in local elections increased.

What repression could not accomplish, the Russian revolution managed with ease. The Bolshevik example became the most divisive issue ever encountered, and debates over its meaning tore the American SP to shreds. Past struggles and personality conflicts were involved, but the basic issue was how to bring Socialism to the United States. Russia showed that a tiny party—there were only eleven thousand Bolsheviks at the beginning of 1917—could make a revolution, and from half a world away the myriad factors that brought success were obscured. What seemed clear was that the Bolsheviks were the most uncompromising, the most determined, the most revolutionary of all the Russian parties. Moderate Socialists might talk revolution, but Bolsheviks acted. Parliamentarism could seem flabby, soft, suspect. For many radical party members the issue in late 1918 surfaced in a desire to take the party away from the leaders and set it on a truly revolutionary course.

The militancy of the new Left Wing and the prospect of American Bolshevism helped to draw John Reed into SP affairs. Scornful of the party for a long time, his revolutionary ideal had been the Wobblies, but now Russia provided a new model. The Bolsheviks were a political party whose success indicated to Reed that the IWW's antipolitical, syndicalist stance was shortsighted. Industrial militancy was a must, but so was the guiding hand of a well-organized party. Eventually the Socialist parliament would be an industrial parliament, but the transformation from the political to the industrial system had to be expressed in political action which served both to educate workers and to help protect the working class during the struggle for power.

Reed had an enormous personal influence on radical Socialists. In party hangouts like the offices of the Russian-language daily *Novy Mir* and the James Connolly Socialist Club on 29th Street, he crowded the room with the enthusiasm of revolutionary Petrograd, helping to convert listeners. His own full commitment came slowly. Arrests, trials, hearings and official harassment tied him up for months, but, more important, his character stood between Reed and party work. Genuinely close to the workers' movement, he was at heart an individualist who might submerge himself for days or weeks, but was wary of doing so permanently. Uncomfortable in organizations, uninterested in political infighting, he was not a party man. Temperamentally his home was the freewheeling atmosphere of the IWW or Greenwich Village. His slow edging toward involvement suggests that the rebel poet understood the price an organizer would have to pay.

The first step was easy. A few weeks after returning from Russia he joined a branch of the New York Socialist Party. So happy were members to have the best-known interpreter of the Russian revolution among them that he was immediately asked to become a candidate for Congress. He declined, however, and followed party matters from afar while speech-making, writing and trials absorbed him through the summer months and into fall. Temporarily free in mid-October, he appeared at a few meetings for Scott Nearing, Socialist candidate for Congress in New York's Fourteenth District. In November he accepted a position as contributing editor to the *Revolutionary Age*. Published in Boston and edited by Louis Fraina, it was the first organ of the Left Wing movement within the SP, the first rallying point for those who wished to capture the party for Bolshevism.

By mid-January 1919, *Ten Days* was in the editorial offices of Boni and Liveright, a year-old firm spun off from the prewar Village scene. After Reed finished his manuscript, he gravitated toward political action. Despite the end of warfare and the opening of the Versailles Peace Conference, Allied troops were still occupying Russian soil—their presence could now be seen only as a means of aiding counterrevolution. Lenin's "A Letter to American Workingmen" was smuggled into the U.S. at the turn of the year and published with Reed's aid. Less a plea for help than a defiant cry, "Invincible is the Proletarian Revolution," it, too, was a challenge to greater activity. So were the actions of a moderate Socialist government in Germany. Having taken power when the Kaiser abdicated, this regime did not hesitate to call on the army to crush a workers' rising led by the Left Socialist Spartacists. The assassinations of Rosa Luxemburg and Karl Liebknecht with government connivance proved to Jack that moderate Socialists were allies of the middle class.

A series of meetings in New York resulted in a formal organization for the Left Wing, for which Reed helped to draft a manifesto. At an all-day convention on February 15 he was elected a member of the fifteen-man City Committee, and he accepted a nomination from the Left Wing for the post of International Delegate. To help promote the faction's program, another publication seemed necessary, and Jack became editor of a weekly, the New York *Communist*, which began to appear in April.

Left Wingers were spurred by the belief that a revolutionary situation was at hand. Reed did not agree. He refused to speak in terms of a timetable, but occasionally voiced a hope that within a few years—perhaps five—a true American revolutionary movement would be in existence. Sometimes in the spring of 1919 the pace of events made upheaval seem closer. In Europe strikes and severe unrest racked victors and vanquished alike. Governments teetered in Italy and Austria, while in March Hungary was declared a Soviet Republic and the Spartacists rose once more in Berlin. The next month Bavaria announced independence under a new government of Soviets, while French sailors in the Black Sea mutinied rather than aid counterrevolution in Russia.

The specter of Bolshevism haunting Europe frightened the Great Powers at Versailles and floated across the Atlantic. Free of a wartime no-strike pledge, American labor began a series of strikes that would number thirty-six hundred in a single year and involve more than four million workers. Some appeared extraordinarily radical. Under direction of an IWW-influenced Labor Council, a Seattle shipyard walkout became the first general strike in America. At Lawrence, Massachusetts, thirty thousand textile workers walked out, shutting every mill in town. Striking copper miners in Butte were directed by a Workers', Soldiers' and Sailors' Council, while unions in Portland, Oregon, joined together in a Soviet whose aim was "to strike the final blow against the capitalist class."⁴ For a brief few weeks it seemed that labor was spontaneously bringing the country to the brink of revolution.

Superpatriots were enraged. The National Civic Federation, the American Defense Society and the National Security League—all promoters of a wartime drive for hundred-percent Americanism—now joined employer groups like the National Association of Manufacturers in an all-out propaganda attack on "Bolshevism," construed broadly enough to include the doctrine of the closed shop. The Judiciary Subcommittee of the Senate switched its investigation from German propaganda to Bolshevism. Under the chairmanship of Lee S. Overman, members acted more like reporters seeking exposés than investigators looking for facts. Directing attention to Russia, the Senators listened to a series of witnesses almost wholly opposed to the Soviet regime: ministers, college professors, YMCA workers, businessmen, Russian refugees, bank employees from Petrograd and embassy officials, including Ambassador Francis. The most hair-raising and farfetched tales of Communist horror were treated as hard fact: the Red Army was composed mainly of criminals; the revolution had been conducted largely by New York Jews; all white-collar workers and educated men were being killed; Bolshevik leaders were immoral beasts who not only specialized in rape, but had both nationalized women and established free-love bureaus—and the nation's newspapers fed the public all these lurid tales of Soviet sex and brutality.

Horrified that such ideas could go unchallenged, Louise, Jack and Rhys Williams wired the committee demanding they be permitted to testify. Already they had been named as among the chief Bolshevik propagandists in the United States, and their request was granted. From the moment Louise took the stand on the afternoon of February 20, it was obvious the group hoped to expose agents of Lenin's government. The Senators, more interested in discrediting than listening to her, were alternately hostile and patronizing. Testy and combative, she was ready for them, and the result was a five-hour verbal struggle. Questioned at first about her belief in the sanctity of the oath, Louise exploded, "It seems to me as if I were being tried for witchcraft."[5] The atmosphere never much improved. While the Senators fired questions about her marriages, beliefs and political activities and tried to imply she had been a Bolshevik courier, she kept returning to the subject of the Revolution in an attempt to refute rumors about violence and cruelty.

Reed moved to the witness table the next afternoon. He impressed one hostile reporter as "a fine figure of a man . . . ideal physically as a football captain," with broad shoulders, a smiling face, "a swagger in his gait, a suggestion of a chip on his shoulder, the glint of steel" in his eyes.[6] Having watched the Senators berate Louise, he was well prepared for the committee's behavior. Many topics raised were obviously designed to make him sound disreputable, or a Bolshevik agent, or both—the rifle-firing incident in German trenches, an alleged violation of a 1917 oath saying he would not attend the Stockholm Peace Conference, his appointment as consul, work in the Propaganda Bureau, indictments in America. Patiently answering questions, Jack refused to be bogged down in side issues and insisted on relating the background and development of the revolution. He was so eloquent, so full of facts, quotations and statistics about the Soviets, workers' control of factories, food distribution, nationalization of land, press laws and the suppression of crime, that for long periods the Senators silently listened.

Eventually the questions focused on a specific point—did he advocate a similar revolution for America? Reed's answer was blunt: "I have always advocated a Revolution in the United States." Shocked by such frankness, a member put the question again, and Reed qualified, "Revolution does not necessarily mean a revolution by force. By revolution I mean profound social change. I do not know how it is to be attained." A Senator asked, "Do you not know, Mr. Reed, that the use of the word 'revolution' in the ordinary meaning carries the idea of force, arms, and conflict?" Jack answered: "Well, as a matter of fact, unfortunately, all these profound social changes have been accompanied by force. There is not one that has not." Further questions attempted to win an admission that he actually favored force, but Reed maintained that the overthrow of capitalism might occur peacefully. The point was that Socialism would come only when "the mass of people is ready for it." Here he was adamant: "I just want to state that anybody who advocates the overthrow of the majority by the minority is nothing but a criminal, because it means an abortive lot of bloodshed without any object at all, killing for no purpose." This was consistent with his impressions of

Russia: the Bolsheviks were a small party that had enacted the will of the majority of workers and peasants, and the proof was that opposition came only from the "minority" middle and upper classes.

In following days, friends like Williams, Bessie Beatty and Raymond Robins gave further details of Russian conditions. This minor victory for enlightenment—the shreds of information that crept into the press—were tempered by the minimal impact on the committee, which wrote a report concluding that Bolshevism was the greatest danger facing America and recommending stringent legislation to combat the menace. Subject to a number of sharp editorial attacks—including one entitled "One Man Who Needs the Rope"—Reed could at first ignore them because, in general, things were going well.[7] In January the government dropped its case against the *Masses*, the next month he won acquittal on the Philadelphia "inciting to riot" charge, and a few weeks later the Hunt's Point Palace indictment was quashed. Annoyed that a radical could go unpunished, a *New York Times* editorial compared Reed unfavorably to past revolutionaries and intimated that he expected to "share in the profits" of Bolshevism.[8] Stung, he answered with a blistering letter which the *Times* refused to print: "The business of spreading what you call 'Bolshevik propaganda' is not very lucrative. . . . There is no money in speaking to working class audiences, or writing in working class papers, which are the only audiences and papers open to any advocacy of the truth about Soviet Russia. . . . All persons who work for an unselfish purpose for little or nothing are incomprehensible to persons who never work for nothing, and who can be hired to work for anything."[9]

Angry words came from pain, and pain came from the difficulties of being a revolutionary in America in 1919. One source was the problem of money, and here Socialist beliefs provided little comfort. Never much interested in luxury, Jack and Louise could somehow get by on odd bits of income, the $25 to $50 for a speech, the small sums Eastman doled out for *Liberator* works, the $75 she received for an occasional article. Of course, it was annoying to have a bank cancel his account because it was so often overdrawn, or to be suspended from the Harvard Club for owing $34. But the deeper wound came from home, where money was tied up with memories of his father's unfailing generosity and the pull of family responsibility could not be denied.

Margaret Reed was currently living with her mother in the Multnomah Hotel, and her letters were full of complaints about physical ailments, insomnia and fears she would have to live in "drab boarding houses" the rest of her life. Sometimes when Jack sent checks she returned them on the grounds that he was short of money, too. Evidently annoyed at being dependent, she was adept at turning hostility outward:

"I can't seem to get up any very wild enthusiasm about having a pension under *soviet* rule!"[10] Such sentiments both hurt and angered Reed, and their correspondence was splashed with hostility, recriminations and reconciliations. Harry, now out of the service, was married and about to become a father. After some trouble finding work—"people don't give a damn if you were in the army or not"—he was just beginning a job with an investment company when sickness put Mrs. Green into a hospital and Margaret moved to her own apartment.[11] Knowing he must help, Jack was haunted by C.J.'s wish that his son would never become a debtor. In the desperate days of 1917 he had pawned his father's gold watch. The $500 advance from Boni and Liveright had brought it back, but now, for the second time, it went off to a broker.

Money worries unsettled his private life. For months speaking trips had taken him away from home. Now, with her syndicated articles gathered into a book, *Six Months in Red Russia*, it was Louise's turn to help support them with a tour. Departing in mid-March, she was gone more than a month, journeying as far as the Pacific Northwest and California on a hectic, exciting, exhausting jaunt, with large, enthusiastic crowds applauding her news of Russia and calls for an end to intervention. Wary of their hometown—"It gives me cold shivers to think of even *being* in Portland"—she found it a pushover. Reporters were sympathetic and referred to her as a "celebrity," the auditorium was packed, and at dinner Harry and Margaret were pleasant, warm and proud: "I seem to stand high with the family at the present moment. . . . So much for the return of the prodigal daughter."[12]

At Croton, Jack read her letters on chill spring days. Digging in the garden, reading deeply in history, writing diligently to earn $300 for a syndicated Press Forum debate on "Bolshevism—Promise or Peril?" or visiting Manhattan for Socialist meetings—none of these activities cured his loneliness. Along with details of gatherings and receptions, Louise expressed similar feelings. In her letters, politics mixed perilously with love:

> Dearest lover . . . White stars hang from a cold sky. I have read the news about Hungary—the *Great News*! I look out of my windows at the stars and the winds of spring fan my hot face. It is wonderful—all this my lover, all this new awakening—all over the earth; and this *other awakening*. I can hear the feet of that great army across the world. It will lull me to sleep—All my love to you.[13]

Reed's replies showed there was more to life than Socialism. News of party activities often took a back seat to private plans. In several letters he went on about a growing desire to purchase a dog and gave detailed instructions on where she should go in San Francisco to find Chinese textiles for new curtains.

Committed to the Left Wing, Reed still withheld some of himself, admitting once to Eastman, "You know, this class struggle plays hell with your poetry!"[14] The relationship between art and radicalism was an old problem which no amount of analysis could solve. Late one cold night on a street in the Village he encountered Sherwood Anderson, and for an hour the two discussed artists and revolution—should writers be observers, or did they give and gain more by throwing themselves into the fight? Jack could see both sides of the issue; neither way was wrong, but somehow he felt drawn towards action. Yet one curious statement left Anderson with the impression that if Reed knew for certain he was a poet, knew he "really had the stuff, he would chuck the radicalism."[15]

Any such self-doubt about writing was momentary, but Reed did sometimes pause over the problem of associates. Radical politics was drawing him away from old friends and into new circles. Ties with Copeland had been severed during the war because of the professor's patriotism. College chums like Hallowell, Rogers and Hunt had slowly drifted away, and Croton neighbors like the Robinsons and *Masses* associates like Dell and Eastman were friendly, but dwelt increasingly in separate worlds. The strongest bond was with Steffens; this made it the most painful to sever. His longing to see Stef had developed increasingly into annoyance at the older man's continued ability to remain aloof in a world where lines were being sharply drawn. When finally they met by accident under a New York street lamp one night, Steffens' joyous greeting was answered by stiffness and ill-concealed anger: "Why don't you join us? We are trying to do what you used to talk and write about."[16]

Many of his new colleagues were a different breed. The *Masses* crowd had been an elite—middle-class, native-born, college-educated, worldly and talented men, as much interested in Freud as in Marx, in Dostoevsky as in Debs. The leaders of the New York Left Wing were narrower, more provincial and younger than Reed. Immigrants or the sons of immigrants—and mainly Russian Jews—they had largely grown up in poverty and had seen little of the world. Some were graduates of CCNY, others were self-educated; virtually all had been active Socialists for years and enjoyed both theological disputations over Marxist texts and the self-enhancement that came with party leadership. Radical politics was their world, and in accepting Jack they were interested in only one part of the man.

Another part, the artist, reemerged in March when the *Liberator* carried "The Peace That Passeth Understanding," a fantasy play satirizing the proceedings at Versailles. Set in a room with a clock fifty years slow, it details the shenanigans of the Big Five leaders holding an "open conference" behind closed doors. Tossing out Serbian and Belgian delegates protesting their involvement—"That was *war*! This is *peace*!"—to make the room "Safe for Democracy," the men get down to business. A master of persuasion, President Wilson adeptly shows his colleagues how the idealistic Fourteen Points can easily be interpreted to allow them to carve up the postwar world. The principle is the same as in domestic politics: "At home we think nothing of putting fifteen hundred people in jail for their opinions, and calling it free speech. . . ." While Lloyd George and Baron Makino of Japan gleefully roll dice for Germany's Pacific colonies—"Pair o' nines! . . . What's this for? The Caroline Islands?"—the President composes a press statement celebrating his own "moral victory." Just as it is delivered, news of revolution in Western countries arrives, and the five depart hastily through the window for Russia, the only stable government left in the world.[17]

Late in March the Provincetown Players performed the work for a week, and viewing it on the twenty-fifth, Reed was pleased with the amusement of the audience. Most of his current writing was in a far different vein. In the *Liberator* there was still color to his prose; drama in an obituary for Liebknecht that imaginatively reconstructed his death at the hands of military men; humor in a definition of Bolshevism for the benefit of the Justice Department: "It is not Anarchism, it is not Vegetarianism, it has no connection with Free Love or the *New Republic*. . . ."[18] But his articles for the Left Wing press, the *Revolutionary Age*, or his own New York *Communist*, were sober, straightforward, expository, full of quotations from Marx, whose works he was now reading. Analyzing the needs of the SP, giving advice to workers on how to prepare for taking over factories, explaining the antiradicalism of America, Reed controlled romantic impulses and weighted words with a scientific approach to social life.

Jack had bought revolution intuitively—now he was involved in justifying it intellectually. The search for enlightenment led not only to Marx and his disciples, but back to the roots of American civilization. In a lengthy attempt to prove "Why Political Democracy Must Go" that sprawled over seven issues of the *Communist*, he drew on the "new history" of Charles Beard and James B. McMaster to show that the supposedly democratic government of the United States "was designed by its founders to protect the rich against the poor, property against the necessities of life and liberty, and the monopolistic minority against the majority." Despite various reforms, the system had remained basically the same, a surface democracy where real power lay in the hands of economic interests untouched by votes. Tracing the course of American radical movements, he explained their continued impotence as due to "the disastrous effect of . . . ideology upon the growth of class-consciousness." If workers believed in the goals and values of the system, they would not be moved to change it. It was the task of radicals to show that "Political Democracy is a fake."[19]

Exactly because ideology was so strong, "democracy" was a difficult word to banish. It was all very well to assert that Socialism was the best government because it based "aspiration to freedom on scientific fact," but that did not answer the question. Occasionally Reed would argue that the system of Soviets, delegates who could be instantly recalled, was basically a "more democratic" arrangement than any Western legislature. Elsewhere, he came to grips with the phrase publicized by Bolsheviks, "Dictatorship of the Proletariat." Knowing it sounded harsh to American ears, he justified it as one of the "fearful birth pangs" of the Socialist commonwealth. Because the propertied classes could buy their own protection, such a dictatorship was necessary to break their strength. When capitalism was eliminated by confiscation of property and abolition of private ownership, when the war between classes was completely won —not in a single country, but all over the world—dictatorship would cease "and democracy will follow, based upon equality and the liberty of the individual." Then society would harbor no exploitation or misery, create no prostitution or wars. With education, leisure and culture for all, artists would be "honored and supported . . . the products of their genius . . . the property of the whole world."[20]

While such writing clarified matters in Reed's mind, *Ten Days That Shook the World* brought increased fame. It was published in March and was well reviewed not only in radical journals but also by conservative newspapers like the Los Angeles *Times*, Philadelphia *Public Ledger* and New York *American*. Greeted as "prophetic" and "illuminating," a "handbook of reference" for future revolutions, a work that "cannot be ignored by friends or enemies" of the Bolsheviks, it sold five thousand copies in the first three months.[21]* More gratifying than sales were the accolades of

---

* Reviews in publications unfavorable to the Bolsheviks generally recognized *Ten Days* as the most effective, accurate account of its subject. Realizing it was an openly partisan work—as Reed boldly stated in the preface—some reviewers followed the tack of Harold Stearns in the *Dial*, XLVI (March 22, 1919), 301-5, in saying that admitted partisanship was a better stance toward such controversial events than a hidden bias which masked as "objectivity." Full of praise, Stearns saw it as "not only the record of a great event, but a kind of handbook of reference for the future,"

fellow radicals. Emma Goldman, in the Missouri State penitentiary, became totally absorbed in its pages: "I felt myself transferred to Russia, caught by her fierce storm, swept along by its momentum. . . ." Among the many Wobblies in Leavenworth it was avidly read, discussed and referred to as the "Minutes of the Revolution." From that prison came personal letters asking for copies or thanking Reed for writing "so graphically" that iron bars fell away and men could experience an event they had so long dreamed.[22]

Louise returned in mid-April. Weary from the trip, she let Jack fuss over her for a few days, until he came down with influenza and she had to play nurse. Lying on a bed in the living room while she chopped wood, cooked, walked to the village for supplies, rubbed him with alcohol to keep the fever down, Reed enjoyed the attention and was well enough to give directions through the window as to where a new tree should be planted. These were good days, full of long hours alone together before a cheery fireplace. The tour had eased finances, and Louise's visit had brightened his mother's life. Full of praise for her daughter-in-law, Margaret was now reading *Ten Days*. Her judgment, "It is great," was warming to her thirty-one-year-old son.[23]

As Jack recuperated, his indecision over politics was dissipated by events. Sweeping the Socialist Party elections, the Left Wing captured twelve of fifteen Executive Committee seats and four of five International Delegate positions, including one for Reed. On April 21 a New York City group issued a call for a National Left Wing Conference in June. Proselytizing in the weekly *Communist*, Jack became a target for Right Wing hostility. A new rival, the *Socialist*, recalled his support for Wilson in 1916, alternately ridiculed his political views and accused him of plagiarizing other Socialist writers, then had harsher words for the "unsavory" techniques and actions of his associates. Letting others carry on polemics, Reed struck back in a characteristic way. Copying the format, type and style, he and some friends produced a satirical issue of the *Socialist* that included a denunciation of John Reed. It was distributed through regular channels and sold several hundred copies before the

---

because the Russian revolution would obviously not be the last of the century. Many reviews spent much space paraphrasing Reed's story, attempting to give a straightforward account of events which had generally been confused in the American press. The *New Republic*, XIX (May 31, 1919), 158–9, took this approach and said the work was "unsurpassed for the period it covers, and seems likely to remain so for some time to come. It is a thorough and painstaking résumé." With a similar approach, the *Nation*, CVIII (May 3, 1919), 699, termed it a "detailed and illuminating chronicle."

fakery was discovered. In the next issue the *Socialist* stuffily termed the affair "a depressing new chapter in the . . . history of this country," and bitterness between the factions increased.[24]

On May Day, labor demonstrations across the nation turned into battles involving police, military men and radicals, with the latter bearing the brunt of violence. In Boston, Socialist headquarters was demolished and 116 radicals were arrested; in New York the Russian People's House and offices of the *Call* were raided by soldiers and civilians; in Cleveland a workers' parade was broken up with a tank, SP offices were wrecked, one man was killed and 106 were arrested. The daily press ignored the fact that "patriotic" citizens had touched off the violence and spoke of the disorders as a "dress rehearsal" for revolution. This serious external harassment was less destructive than internal developments. Frightened by the challenge of young Leftists, the SP National Executive Committee, meeting on May 24, invalidated the spring elections and began to purge itself of locals affiliated with the Left. Like a surgeon cutting rotten limbs, the party lopped off entire state organizations—Michigan, Massachusetts, Ohio—then went on to many city locals. The job was thorough and devastating. In January 1919 the party had reached the second-highest membership in its history, almost 110,000. After the Executive Committee finished its work, fewer than 40,000 were still affiliated with the SP.

When the National Left Wing Conference convened in Manhattan on June 21, anger in the party over the high-handed action was matched by public fury against all radicals. Early in the month a series of mysterious explosions at the homes of legislators, police officials, judges and industrialists in eight cities had brought new calls for the suppression of "anarchism." On the very day of the conference, investigators working with the recently appointed New York State Committee on Seditious Activities swept down on the offices of the Left Wing, the IWW and the Socialist Rand School, seizing literature and mailing lists. Overseas, the Bavarian Soviet had been crushed and in Hungary the revolutionary government was barely hanging on against White Guard attacks. It was a time for unity among radicals, but SP factions utilized most of their energy quarreling with one another.

Impressive in attendance—ninety-four delegates from twenty states representing a potential membership of seventy thousand—the Left Wing conference was splintered by intense factionalism. Probably half of those thrown out of the SP belonged to foreign-language federations—Russian, Hungarian, Polish, Lettish—made up of urban immigrant workers whose knowledge of English was almost nonexistent. In March a First

Congress of the new Communist International had met in Moscow and called for Leftists to engage in a "merciless fight" against Right Wingers who had supported the war. Nobody now in the American SP fitted the description, but this did not stop the language federations from using such tactics anyway. Bolshevism meant extremism and no compromise, and they came to the conference determined to set up a Communist organization immediately.

As a first experience in radical political infighting, the meeting was illuminating for Reed. He had not hesitated to bend history and unjustly accuse the Right of giving only "lip-service" to the antiwar St. Louis Declaration. Justifying the Left organization, he used the example of the Bolshevik split of the Russian Social Democratic Party in 1902, and he demanded uncompromising adherence to the principle of "Dictatorship of the Proletariat."[25] Yet when the language federations, led by the Russians, proposed the organization of a Communist Party, Jack voted with the majority whose objective was still "the capturing of the Socialist Party for revolutionary Socialism." One third of the delegates denounced this as opportunism, and stalked out of the convention.

Since the differences in program between what was now a majority Left Wing and a minority Left Wing were negligible, the quarrel may be difficult to understand. Reed's group expected to attend a convention of the SP in Chicago on August 30 and there revalidate the original spring election and take over the party. Failing that, they were committed to forming a new party. So the split really occurred over the issue of waiting ten weeks. Behind a break on such thin grounds was a quality theoretically absent from the gathering: nationalism. Contemptuous of American workers, foreigners—above all, Russians—felt a direct kinship with the Bolsheviks and hastened to follow what they thought was their example. It was more important for a revolutionary party to be small, disciplined and politically pure than to win adherents. The majority hoped that by staying in the party they could win support of some wavering elements in various sympathetic locals, especially in the West. Jack was one of many unwilling to see the party cut off from a potential broad base of American workingmen who had previously joined the IWW.

With the foreign federations gone, the conference continued for four days, approving a lengthy manifesto based on the idea that capitalism was in its death throes, electing a governing council of nine, combining the *Communist* with the *Revolutionary Age* and plotting strategy for capturing the Chicago convention. Reed was named to a Committee of Labor and helped draft a report calling for revolutionary industrial unionism, the organization of shop committees and workers' councils like those which had taken control of Russian industries in 1917. To help educate workers toward such action, a new periodical, *Voice of Labor*, was proposed, and he was chosen editor. Its policy was hammered out in a series of discussions in which Jack emphasized the need to make it interesting as well as useful. This could be done by focusing on the actual experience of the American workingman, describing and analyzing the history and conditions of the United States that led to his current personal plight.

By the time the seceding group had issued a call for a September convention in Chicago to organize a Communist Party, Reed was on holiday. Louise dragged him to Truro in July because "He is not well and has no idea of how to take a vacation near New York. Here he cannot even hear the rumblings of battle."[26] The Cape was warm with memories and summer sun. Ignoring the crowds in Provincetown, Jack and Louise spent slow, restful days on lonely dunes, and long hours making love. Sharply aware of incompleteness apart, they planned a future together, spoke of a rambling old-fashioned home, the novels each would write. These bright dreams were fragile, evanescent. One evening Susan Glaspell and Jig Cook hiked over for a visit and found Reed softer than his revolutionary image. "I wish I could stay here," he told them. Asked why he didn't, Jack's face clouded, and he answered quietly, "I've promised too many people."[27]

Behind the scenes the National Left Wing Council had been negotiating with the seceding foreign-language groups and on July 28 suddenly joined them in supporting the call for a Communist convention. Shocked at the betrayal, Reed hurried to Manhattan and joined such leaders as Benjamin Gitlow and Jim Larkin in taking the case to the rank-and-file. This meant daily talks, arguments and confrontation with men who had recently been comrades. At one acrimonious debate before the Bronx local, Jay Lovestone ignored issues to accuse Jack of being a "so-called proletarian who lives on a sumptuous estate in Westchester."[28] Disgusted when the vote went against his position and Lovestone offered a handshake of conciliation, Reed told him to go to hell and walked out.

Jack resigned from the *Revolutionary Age* because it supported the National Council and spent sticky August days at the Connolly Club, where his group was headquartered. Deep in a study of Socialism, he began to enjoy the wrangles over Marxist theory that seemed the staple conversation, but most of his energy went into preparing the first issue of the *Voice of Labor*. In contrast to the unpleasant aspects of party strife, the working class was something clean. One close associate, Eadmonn MacAlpine, noticed that, unlike many other middle-class radicals, Reed

"did not go down to the working class . . . he was with it and of it."[29]
The revolution was by and for them after all, and his vision of a Communist Party was one which reached out to the proletariat: "We've got
to have a movement with guts, whose members will hoof it over the
country and concentrate wherever they are needed. We must build a
disciplined movement but not one dominated by politicians."[30]

At the end of the month the leaders of radicalism in America
descended on Chicago for a showdown. The atmosphere was tense, with
serious issues sometimes lapsing into farce. Early on the morning of
August 30, Reed led some eighty delegates into the second-floor auditorium
of Machinists' Hall, where the SP convention was about to begin. Julius
Gerber, in charge of credentials, ordered them out and, when Jack refused to budge, tried to move him forcibly. Shoving gave way to punches,
and in a moment Reed was holding the smaller man at arm's length while
the latter flailed away at the air. The scuffle was ended by Chicago police,
called in to clear all irregular delegates from the hall. Regrouping in
another room downstairs, the expelled Socialists decided to hold a convention of their own.

In a billiard room on the first floor of the same building, eighty-two
delegates from twenty-one states opened proceedings by jubilantly singing the "Internationale" and raucously cheering Debs, the IWW and
other class-war prisoners. The new group had already lost any reason
for existence since the Left Wing split had been over the advisability of
trying to capture the SP convention. But the wounds inflicted by two
months of vitriolic denunciations in the foreign-language press and exacerbated by the Left Wing Council's stab in the back were not easily
healed, and Reed was one of many speakers to argue vehemently against
immediate unity. Proposals for a joint convention were voted down. As
a compromise, a committee was appointed to conduct talks with the
Communist Party.

The time for understanding was past. Negotiations between the two
groups got nowhere because Reed, Benjamin Gitlow and Alfred Wagenknecht and their CP counterparts, Louis Fraina and Charles Ruthenberg,
were all basically unwilling to make meaningful compromises. As this
became apparent, Reed's group moved to the IWW hall, proclaimed
themselves the Communist Labor Party and proceeded to create their
own organization. Appointed chairman of the program committee, Jack
was instrumental in drawing up a platform that led to a stormy floor
debate. One opponent was Louis B. Boudin, whose 1907 book, *The
Theoretical System of Karl Marx*, had won a worldwide reputation
among Socialists. Objecting to the phrase "conquest of political power,"
he laughed at Reed's attempt to defend it by quoting Marx. In danger of

losing the debate, a fuming Jack left the room, returned with a copy of the *Communist Manifesto* and pointed to the exact words. While the multilingual Boudin sputtered, "It's a very poor translation," his position was voted down, and he strode out of the meeting hall and the CLP.[31]

This departure did not end opposition to the platform's revolutionary tenor. Basic to it was the concept of Dictatorship of the Proletariat, which entailed training the working class for a seizure of power. Praising the IWW as the model for industrial unionism, the report endorsed political action only to the extent that CLP candidates, or elected officials, would spend their time exposing the sham of political democracy. Most important was the unconditional pledge of loyalty to the new Third International. Unreconciled delegates fought against the extremist thrust of the document, but eventually it was adopted by a vote of 46 to 22. Despite this opposition, Reed wired Louise, "Wonderful convention. Everything going fine."[32]

Politics could be tedious, and one afternoon Jack deserted the hall to walk with Sherwood Anderson in a park, discussing the state of modern poetry. Elected to the important post of International Delegate* at the final session, he hurried home and bragged to everyone, "We've got it—a real American working-class . . . party, at last!"[33] Privately it was hard to be so elated. Since the Communist Party had adopted a virtually identical platform, two groups were now vying for the same constituency. For Reed this meant endless, tedious meetings and talks with members of the Socialist locals, attempting to convince the dubious that the CLP's version of Communism was closest to that of the Bolsheviks. Despite his reputation, the struggle was discouraging. Popular and convincing with American workers, Jack was in a movement where most members were foreign-born and barely able to speak English. Within a few weeks it was obvious that with the rival CP very strong in the former Socialist foreign-language federations, the CLP would remain the smaller party. Reed's group had more support in former Western strongholds of Socialism like Washington, Missouri, Colorado, Oregon and Kansas, and more native Americans in leadership positions, but by the end of September it was difficult to be happy about the response of workers to either Communist organization. Of seventy thousand preconvention Left Wing adherents, no more than thirty-five thousand affiliated with either of the new parties, and only about one-third of these joined the CLP.

Looking back over six months of intense activity, Reed could be con-

---

* This was an important position because the International Delegate would handle negotiations with the new Communist International, to which all Communist parties hoped to be admitted. Alfred Wagenknecht was chosen as second International Delegate and also as Executive Secretary of the CLP.

tent with having helped significantly in the birth of American Bolshevism. Trying to understand why two parties had emerged, he carefully separated the foreign-language workers—necessary for a revolutionary movement—from their leaders, an autocratic bunch who tried to segregate followers from American comrades. In creating a party along Russian lines, the leaders had made "no attempt to adapt it to the psychology of the American working class." Knowing nothing and caring less about natives, they exhibited a shortsighted chauvinism, for no revolution in the United States could be built with a group in which "not a single man . . . can speak in the simple language [and] be understood by the workers of this country." The reason for dual organizations ultimately was human nature, the "ambitions" of certain people who wished to go down in history as having been founders of a Communist Party.[34]

John Reed could recognize the trait of ambition in others. Since his own longings for immortality had nothing to do with politics, he found it easy to scorn this method of trying to gain entry into the history books. His own drive for recognition well taken care of by the reception of *Ten Days That Shook the World*, Reed could generally approach politics more selflessly than most men. Of course he could still become angry, stubborn, demanding and opinionated when dealing with radicals who saw the road to revolution in a manner contrary to his own view. But in calm moments Jack did not much care for the way he was forced to act in the political arena. At those times the idea of a quieter life, close to loved ones, dominated his consciousness. He could only hope that soon there would be time for love and poetry, walks along country roads, spring birdsongs, blooming trees, sunsets aching with the beauty of death in life. Now there was the narrower, drabber, angrier, necessary world of organizing to live through. The last six months had taught him an important lesson: necessary as politics might be, it could not wholly fulfill his needs. It was sobering to learn that creating a revolutionary political party was a much less satisfying task than creating a revolution.

21

Russia

"*I was clinging to a ladder in a sort of iron shaft down in the bowels of the ship. It was black dark, stifling. Just above my head was a brass plate leading to the deck. The hot air from below, rising against this—it was bitter cold outside—made the metal 'sweat': great drops of foul water dripped on my head, down my back.*

"*Feet passed to and fro across the brass plate, and I could hear men talking, coughing. Below me lights flickered across the mouth of the shaft, as the Finnish police and customs officers searched the corners of the ship.*

"*The ship had docked at four o'clock. At eight, in the silence below, somebody hissed. I clambered down, and following the spurt of a match, found my clothes in a corner. Beyond a little iron door a voice kept nervously whispering, 'Quick! Christ's sake, quick!' Feet came stumbling down from above. I flattened myself in a corner. The unknown stumbled past me.*

"*A hand took mine, and we fled through the night of the ship,* mounted a ladder, a companion-way, and emerged on deck, in the bright glare of arc-lights. The sharp cold hit me like a blow. Here it was full winter—snow on roofs, snow and ice on the ground. We were alongside a dock. Two gigantic steam-cranes were already dipping into the forward hold. Longshoremen were steadying immense packing-cases as they lifted, heaving together with shouts. What was in these packing-cases? Parts of tanks, as I had been told, to be sent against Petrograd with the Finnish Army? Perhaps. This was White Finland, the land of broken Revolution, the country of the Bourgeois Terror.

"On deck were men in uniform, with gold-braided caps, and half a dozen grey-coated police, with revolvers strapped to their belts. A few loungers, dressed like workmen, stood about. I knew that two men were to meet me; as soon as I left the boat they would start to walk away, and I was to follow.

"My guide dragged me forward toward the gangway. At the head of this stood two of the ship's officers, at the bottom a policeman. We retreated and dived down the companion-way leading to the forecastle. Hurrying, we came onto the cargo-deck, where the men were rigging the tackle of the great cranes, a place of shouting and confusion. There lay the cargo-gangway, at its foot a group of customs officials.

"'Now! Go!' whispered the man with me, and gave me a tremendous shove between the shoulders. I stumbled forward, elbowed my way between the customs officials as if I were on business of importance, and without looking around, walked out on the dock. Right in front of me a policeman looked at me with doubt and suspicion, but before he could make up his mind I was past. Two of the loafers detached themselves from the side of a warehouse and began to walk away up the dark street. I followed.

"Overhead the sky was glittering with stars, and streets and roofs sparkled with biting frost. Away off, up on a height, a great building blazed with lights—the prison, thronged with political prisoners. The streets near the waterfront were dark, but as we approached the center of the little town there were street-lights, an occasional café, a factory with the night-shift working. Where the railroad crossed the street, sentries with bayonetted rifles went to and fro. A barracks—soldiers in a lighted room, equipped for service, trench-helmets and gas-masks. Police everywhere, mounted and on foot, with conspicuous revolvers . . ."[1]

In this fragment from November 1919 John Reed is fully a character in a kind of adventure sought since childhood. Fact and fiction, life and art, history and poetry—often over the years he had ignored or transcended the kinds of distinction by which most men nail reality to a cross. He celebrated his own adventures in first-person reports and short stories, but Reed's narrator was always separated from world-shaking events by a thin but significant screen. Often in danger, followed by secret agents, slapped in prison, a target of bullets or violence, he was a partisan of causes not fully his own. Much as Reed might sympathize, empathize or propagandize, strikes, wars, uprisings or revolutions were out there, processes initiated by the needs, hopes and actions of some group to which he did not belong.

Now things were different. His active commitment to the Left Wing Socialists and the Communist Labor Party led across a shadowy line into a new reality where there was less time for literary activity. Begun in a Finnish hiding place, the description of jumping ship in Abo was never completed. Similar in style to works written before, it was underlined by a new kind of motivation. After September 1919, Jack undertook adventures not with an eye on publishers, editors or potential readers, but for a political party and a cause that was his own. Danger was everywhere, because a Communist was a marked man, an enemy to most governments in the world.

The change was not made without regrets. Long past that period of life when there was excess energy to burn, Reed hoped to do his duty and still save time for private life, for Louise and poetry and a second book on the Revolution entitled *From Kornilov to Brest-Litovsk*. Late in September 1919 it was apparent that such ideas would have to be postponed. Within the world of American Communism the founding conventions had created more problems than they had solved. Survival for both the CP and CLP seemed to depend upon recognition by the Communist International. Certain the Comintern would allow only one American party to affiliate, each dispatched a representative to Moscow. For the CLP the choice was obvious. Of all American radicals, Jack knew the leading Bolsheviks best, and he could not refuse the assignment.

The decision caused an uproar at home. Never as fully dedicated to revolution as her husband, Louise was furious at the idea of another separation. This anger was fueled by the stresses and strains of the relationship that had resulted from the ambition and desire of each. Ever since she had left Russia earlier in 1918, there had been long stretches of separation, periods that had revived the old pattern of wandering loyalties. On returning to the United States, Louise had attempted to contact Eugene O'Neill, but the playwright had refused to see her. Knowing herself untrustworthy, she entertained similar worries about her husband. Such suspicions were confirmed once in 1919 when she returned to

Croton to find Jack romping about the house with a naked female. Fleeing hysterically to Sally Robinson, Louise was soon reconciled, but a scar
remained. Now ready to interpret his mission in most personal terms,
she threatened and hurled accusations that he cared more for other
women and abstract ideas than for her. Emotionally battered, full of
doubts anyway, Reed stood his ground. True, he was not always faithful,
but neither was she, and that had nothing to do with his assignment.
Much as he wanted to remain at home, some things in life could not be
controlled, some commitments could not be ignored. Solemnly he swore
love and promised that this would be the final separation. He would
hurry the trip, make the report to Moscow and return immediately.
Three months, three short months, and he would be home. After that,
their life together would come before anything else, no matter what the
outside demands.

As departure time drew near, hostility gave way to anxiety. The trip
was dangerous, for to reach Russia it would be necessary to pass through
regions torn by civil war, and Louise was little comforted by Jack's air
of confidence. Clad in old workclothes, carrying forged seaman's papers
bearing the name "Jim Gormley," he was already a half-stranger on the
early-morning dock as he prepared to join the crew of a Scandinavian
freighter. Surrounded by a few close friends, Reed appeared gay and
alive, full of jokes about life's ironies. This trip, his eleventh crossing,
resembled the first. As in cattle-boat days, he could not afford to go as a
passenger. Gliding over the differences, the one less kidney and the weight
of hard years, he ignored the shadow in Louise's eyes, embraced her,
heaved a bundle over his shoulder and mounted the gangplank.

The crossing was slow, the work as a stoker tiring enough to keep
him from brooding over the world behind and ahead. In Bergen he went
on shore pass. Left Wing Socialists took him to Christiania, where a
week-long stop brought disquieting news from Russia. In the civil war,
things were not going well for the Red Army. From the Baltic the White
armies of General N. N. Yudenitch were approaching Petrograd, while
the forces of General A. I. Denikin, pushing up from the south, were
within 250 miles of Moscow. Faced with worrisome news of a White
terror raging through eastern Europe and spilling into Scandinavia, Reed
sent a long letter to Louise by courier. It was resigned in tone, its words
a close mixture of the personal and public, with political news broken by
repeated professions of longing. Admitting the trip was no lark, "but
more or less a grim business," Jack managed to find some cause for satisfaction: "I am the big cheese in these parts. . . . The *Voice of Labor* is
greatly admired here. . . . I was never in better health and am doing

well. . . . Inform mother I am well. Back before Christmas, I hope."
Underlining his need and future hopes was the flat statement, "From now
on it seems to me we must never be separated."[2]

Reed's movements were controlled by an underground railway of
Bolshevik sympathizers. On the night of October 22 he was led over the
Swedish border, and after a few days in Stockholm was smuggled
aboard a ship crossing the Baltic. At the port of Abo there was a mix-up.
The men followed from the dock turned out not to be his contacts, and
for several hours he was a fugitive with no papers and no knowledge of
Finnish, dodging the authorities in the strange town. Finally he located
the right people and was passed onward until a twelve-hour journey in
an unheated vehicle through a blizzard left him frozen to the bone in the
house of a friendly radical near Helsinki. Here the news was both good
and bad. Defeated before Petrograd, the forces of Yudenitch were melt-
ing away, while the Red Army had taken the offensive against Denikin.
But raids by Finnish police had smashed the local Bolshevik organization,
making any move impossible. Jack was comfortable enough in hiding, but
his boundless impatience showed in a November 9 letter: "I . . . fret and
fume at my delay, and spend the time thinking about my honey and
wanting her. It is awful. I can go neither forward nor back. . . . Am very
well and happy and still expect to be with you before Christmas. If this
hadn't happened I should now be in headquarters, and almost ready to
start back. . . . I do nothing but long for my honey. Other people don't
matter at all."[3]

After two restless weeks Reed was finally allowed to move, traveling
by sleigh, then on foot across a subarctic landscape. Somewhere amid
frozen fields and birch forests Finland became Russia. Welcomed by the
hugs of soldiers with the friendly red star sewn to their uniforms, Jack
was impressed by glimpses of the new army—well-equipped troops dug
into camouflaged positions. He enjoyed the familiar chaotic bustle of
railroad stations, the overcrowded trains, the forests and ramshackle
weathered buildings of the countryside. Petrograd was splendid as ever,
but it was no longer the capital. In the spring of 1918, Soviet leaders
had removed the government to Moscow, and he hurried there without
delay.

The Executive Committee of the Communist International accepted
his report on the American situation and plea for recognition of the
CLP, and promised to study the situation. Realizing no quick decision
would be made, Jack could not immediately return home. But he was glad
to linger at the center of revolution. Curious about the texture and feel,
the sights and sounds of daily life in this "new state of civilization," he

refused a special apartment and food allowance offered to distinguished guests and found a room in the dark wooden house of a textile worker. His simple lodging had a low ceiling, small windows, a kerosene lamp and a small iron stove. It was an appropriate base for exploring the progress of the regime.

Russia had undergone many changes since Reed's departure two years before, though it was still a country of contradictions and extremism, order and chaos, kindness and brutality, heroism and cowardice, oppression and freedom. Some major differences were the result of counterrevolution, foreign invasion and blockade, which had turned a relatively bloodless change of regime into a tumultuous, sanguinary civil war. Armies led by White generals had marched in from the Caucasus, the Ukraine, the Baltic and Siberia, threatening to engulf the center. Foreign expeditionary forces had landed in the Crimea, at Archangel and at Vladivostok in ill-coordinated support of counterrevolution. Growing nationalism of ancient ethnic groups had added to the division of the old empire. The Bolsheviks had also been plagued by the defection of internal allies such as the Social Revolutionaries and opposed by segments of the peasantry. Resorting to traditional methods, leaders of the regime had conscripted a huge Red Army to defend Russian territory and created a secret police force, the Cheka, to suppress internal enemies. In late 1919 the attempt to create Socialism was proceeding, its survival inextricably linked with these two instruments of state power.

The results of continuing internal turmoil were evident everywhere. Bad as conditions had been before the revolution, in the winter of 1919–20 they were far worse, with poverty supplemented by famine and raging epidemic.* In Moscow the season was especially cruel. Food rations were meager and some days black bread was unavailable. With the coal-producing regions of the Don and the oil fields of the Caucasus in White hands, wood in short supply and power problematic, suffering was widespread: "In some houses there was no heat at all the whole winter. People froze to death in their rooms. The electric light was intermittent—for several weeks in Moscow there were no street lights whatever—and the street cars . . . stopped running altogether."[4] As a minor consolation, there was equality in some kinds of misery. Within the Kremlin, Reed saw a top official, Foreign Minister Chicherin, laboring over papers in an icy office, bundled in coat and fur hat, his hands stiff with cold.

Despite such conditions, few leaders despaired. In mid-December the White threat was receding as the Red Army drove forward on all

---

* Russian deaths from famine, disease and battle are estimated at four million in 1919 and five million in 1920.

fronts, and Bolsheviks were full of hopes for an end to the fighting. This was emphasized on the fifteenth when Jack caught Leon Trotsky for an interview. Wearing a splendid military uniform, the Commissar of War and builder of the Red Army looked heavier than before, but the humorless manner and cold voice were familiar. Voluble as ever, Trotsky brushed aside questions on the current military situation and dwelt at length on plans for peace. His aim was to transform the army into a compulsory labor force that would speed reconstruction all over the land. Asked if men would go willingly, he emphasized discipline and dedication and said, "We shall make it an especially attractive life for unpleasant jobs and places."[5]

Reed admired Trotsky, but he preferred the company of Lenin. After he delivered a report on America and presented a copy of *Ten Days That Shook The World*, Jack was invited back for several late-night conversations. The chief commissar was relaxed, genial and animated, at once friendly and a little frightening. In his spartan Kremlin apartment, Lenin liked to hitch his chair forward until their knees touched. Giving the impression of intense interest, he drew Reed out about American developments, wanted to know his reactions to Russia and in a fatherly manner warned him to care for his health. Delighted to learn the Bolshevik chief had taken time to read the book, Jack was highly flattered when Lenin agreed to write an introduction for future editions. It read in part: "Unreservedly do I recommend it to the workers of the world. Here is a book which I should like to see published in millions of copies and translated into all languages. It gives a truthful and most vivid exposition of the events so significant to the comprehension of what really is the Proletarian Revolution. . . ."

Interested in artistic matters, Reed sought out Lunacharsky, the poet in charge of cultural development, who detailed programs for new schools and told of struggles to save art treasures that some revolutionary leaders wished to sell. He was impressed by examples of avant-garde graphics on posters and found the meeting places of Moscow's Bohemia, met the explosive Vladimir Mayakovsky and talked with a group of revolutionary Futurists who were surprised to find an American interested in art. At the other end of the spectrum was P. O. Pasternak, an elderly painter, who was pleasant despite his conservative views: "Doesn't participate in politics. Old-fashioned, submerged in himself, a real artist." Visiting at a Prolet Cult center housed in the confiscated mansion of a businessman, Jack found artists working in all media and teaching classes for workers in the evening. The object was to break down artificial separations between the arts and people. Pleased with the idea—familiar enough to any longtime Greenwich Village resident—Reed declined to make qualitative judgments: "Sculpture, paintings and engravings *very interesting*. Character all their own. Proletarian."[6]

Moscow was hardly Russia, and soon he was ranging far from the capital, visiting factory towns and collective farms, villages and peasant communes, journeying as far east as the frozen Volga. Transportation was at best problematic. Trains ran late and often not at all. On one occasion Reed sat for two days in the waiting room of a railroad station with broken windows and a slick coating of ice upon the floor, while the bodies of dead soldiers were piled like cordwood on the platform and heaps of men, tossing and muttering in the delirium of typhus, covered the benches and tables. Finally he caught an empty military train and shared a boxcar with a few peasants and soldiers. To keep warm they built a fire on the floor, and except for the smoke were comfortable until the bottom of the car burned out. Much better than trains were the many rides in the horse-drawn sleighs of friendly peasants. Bundled in furs, he enjoyed the crisp beauty of the plains, bright with snow and slashed by dark belts of forest, the solid rivers quilted with tracks and speckled with fishing holes. At night such rides were mysterious and evocative. Villages flickered out of the dark, the tang of wood fires sweetened the air and it was easy for war and revolution to be flooded out by visions of mythic riders on the frozen steppes.

People were a country, and, as so many times in the past, Reed felt at home among the most primitive of Russians. Welcomed everywhere, he was asked to share meager rations with the traditional phrase, "May it give you health." There was misery, disease and endless struggle in the land, and yet strength, endurance and hope existed, too. People talked openly, complained and rationalized, damned the government and praised it. Experiences were varied and contradictory, painful and happy. He went to textile factories where underfed workers collapsed over looms, visited communes in which peasants lived largely on seeds, saw new dispensaries where doctors had no medicines or drugs, heard a young girl lament that she lacked a marriage trousseau, listened to an aged peasant curse the Bolsheviks for requisitioning his horse, toured villages decimated by typhus and influenza, was pained by the sight of children with the mottled skin of pellagra, entered onion-domed churches that now housed classrooms, learned in one village that all religious leaders had been jailed, then in another watched a priest in splendid robes lead a dark funeral procession across a stark winter landscape.

Everywhere governmental problems and mistakes were closely intertwined with accomplishments. Men spoke quietly of Cheka terror and of personal reprisals carried out in the name of justice. Disgruntled middle-class technicians worried over the inefficiency and the disobedience of the lower classes, while peasants denounced food requisitions and the draft. Some policies were overtly disastrous. To prevent profiteering, food distribution was centralized and townspeople were forbidden to deal directly with farmers. Yet in certain areas government machinery simply could not provide food, and to avoid starvation, factory workers were forced to sneak into rural areas at night to purchase provisions. At Serpukov, a manufacturing center, Reed addressed a meeting of factory shop-committee delegates. Weary from long workdays, the ragged men gathered in the large hall of a former nobles' club, dimly lit by a smoky kerosene lantern. His ritual greetings from American workers brought them alive to answer with the kind of emotion that had rocked Smolny in the great November days. Passionate speeches gave way to fiery resolutions and a hoarse, fervent rendition of the "Internationale," reinforcing what Reed already believed—that among the most class-conscious elements the spirit of revolution had not been dimmed.

His jaunts about the country, meetings with Bolshevik leaders, long talks with foreign Communists and a desultory passion for a young Russian girl kept Jack too busy for sustained writing. Upon request he completed two articles for the official organ of the Comintern, one on the revolutionary situation in America, the other on the IWW. He was too absorbed in experiencing Socialism to analyze it deeply, and mostly confined his comments to scribbled notes. In these he never mentioned the Soviet Constitution of 1918 or voiced thoughts about the actual functioning of government. It was easy to justify the fact that power was exercised at the top by the Council of Commissars, rather than by the Soviets where it theoretically resided. In a time of counterrevolution the Dictatorship of the Proletariat was a necessity. Only later would a workers' democracy be able to function.

More serious potentially was the opposition voiced by peasants to conscription, food requisitioning and hints of collectivization. Created by industrial workers, the revolution had been endorsed by the peasantry of a primarily rural country only because of land distribution. Jack saw the peasant as petty bourgeois in mentality, a man who wanted a farm and a free market. Far removed from the ferment of great towns and usually illiterate, he understood neither Communism nor the ultimate aims of the revolution. Agitation and education would change his viewpoint, but since now there was little energy for such work, "the peasant must be made to fight, so that the Revolution and his own future happiness may not be lost." Noting that despite all the grumbling there was little rural resistance to the draft, Reed expected military service, with its emphasis on education and propaganda, to work great changes until each peasant "will return to his village a revolutionist and a propagandist."[7]

Unlike some foreign visitors, Reed was little concerned about the terror associated with the Cheka. Such an attitude did not spring from any blood lust, but was due to his understanding of the organization's origins and role. The Cheka grew in response to genuine plots against the government, including assassination attempts on Lenin and abortive Socialist Revolutionary uprisings. Once under way, the secret police acted like all such organizations in parlous times, zealously discovering plots where none existed, acting as prosecutor, judge and jury against many people in the name of revolutionary justice. The Council of Commissars tried to curb its powers, but all Russian revolutionaries, anarchists and SRs as well as Bolsheviks, approved of terror in theory. For Jack it was a matter not of theory but of practice. Describing the Cheka as a "vast net-work of half-detective, half-revolutionary vengeance organizations all over Russia," he believed it acted against "clearly proven" traitors only after adequate hearings, and fully expected its powers to give way to regular tribunals as counterrevolution subsided. Noting "7 months ago about 6,000 men shot," he explained it with the flat comment, "This is war."[8]

The existence of terror in the United States was closer to Reed's concerns than its counterpart in Russia. After his departure, antiradicalism reached new levels. Fed by the social dislocation of demobilization, widespread strikes, radical pronouncements and wildcat bombings, hysteria peaked in late 1919 and early 1920. From the Moscow newspapers Reed did not learn all the details, but the general outlines were clear. November raids in twelve cities by operatives of Attorney General A. Mitchell Palmer and simultaneous actions by state and local officials resulted in the arrest of close to a thousand radicals. Under the Alien Act of 1918, trials were not necessary for suspect foreigners, and in late December 249 of them were placed under guard aboard the S.S. *Buford*, an old transport vessel, for deportation from New York to Finland. Two weeks later Palmer's men led a series of more extensive raids and rounded up over four thousand suspects in thirty-three cities, including many unpolitical people as well as numerous radicals. In New York, Reed's associates in the Left Wing SP movement were indicted, while on January 21 in Illinois he himself was named along with thirty-seven other CLP leaders on a charge of criminal anarchy, which carried a maximum penalty of five years in jail.

Facing trial and likely imprisonment, Jack prepared to leave Russia in early February. By now his mission was accomplished, for the Comintern had rendered a decision, suggesting a convention to merge both American parties. Given current conditions, holding such a meeting would be difficult, but Reed was satisfied. With no direct word from America for months, he sensed that his own fear for Louise's welfare must be surpassed by her concern for him. But in an effort to help the revolution, he carried 102 diamonds worth more than $14,000, as well as $1500 in a variety of currencies. Hardly a fortune, it was all the Comintern leaders wished to spare to help foster Communism in America.

The first leg of the journey ended at the Astoria Hotel in Petrograd. Learning that Emma Goldman, just off the *Buford*, was there, Jack burst into her room "like a sudden ray of light." Over a steaming cup of coffee, brewed from beans carried across the ocean, they celebrated a reunion. Emma brought word that Louise was fine, and then elaborated the story of government repression at home, while Reed described the revolution coming true in the land of her birth. An anarchist suspicious of state power, she demanded to know about the Cheka, and proved dissatisfied with his defense of its activity. Reminded of all the old Russian revolutionists who had broken with the Bolsheviks, Jack blurted, "You are a little confused by the Revolution in action because you have dealt with it only in theory."[9]

Leaving Petrograd late in February prepared for trouble, Reed sported a large, dark mustache, and his normally unruly hair was slick with grease and brushed smoothly back. He wore a long coat and a fur hat, and carried no valise or change of clothing, but secreted on his body were the diamonds and currency, and under his arm was a package containing notebooks, autographed photos of various Bolshevik leaders, Lenin's introduction to his book, some Communist writings in manuscript and others on film, and more than fifty letters from *Buford* deportees. He still carried seaman's papers with the name Jim Gormley, and also bore several forged documents—a passport with the name "Samuel Arnold," a letter from the Committee on Public Information identifying Arnold as an authorized representative and a letter from the ambassador in Paris asking diplomatic officials to expedite the transport of Arnold and his baggage across all international borders.

Despite such precautions, two attempts to reach home ended in failure. The first route was through Latvia, where clashes between White and Red soldiers made it impossible to reach the coast. After a few days back in Petrograd, Reed went farther north, crossed into Finland during a snowstorm and reached the home in Helsinki where he had hidden in November. In Abo he was sneaked aboard a freighter on March 13 and hidden in the engine room. Just before the ship was to sail, two customs officials on a routine inspection found a hat and a package in the corner of the coal hold, and summoned police. Without a struggle, Jack emerged from the bunker, his face black as his despair.

Intensively questioned by the police, Reed at first maintained he was Jim Gormley. When the diamonds, currency, false documents, photos and radical articles rendered this story untenable, he admitted his real name and background, but refused to say anything about contacts with the Finnish Communist underground. A brief report of the arrest reached American newspapers in mid-March, but when he went on trial, reporters were not present and local United States diplomats refused to appear on his behalf. At a series of closed hearings of the Abo Municipal Court Jack faced counts of smuggling currency and diamonds. More serious accusations of treason were hinted at during the proceedings. A letter from state police in Helsinki on March 19 alleged he had "participated in communist undertakings in our country, being in secret contact with the enemy of our State—Soviet Russia—for agitation purposes."[10] The Ministry of the Interior flatly instructed Abo authorities that he was to remain imprisoned no matter what the verdict.

Unconcerned over the smuggling case, Reed worried about the potential charge of treason. To publicize his whereabouts he somehow leaked a story to the press that John Reed had been executed in Finland. The news was printed in America on April 9, forcing the State Department to look into the matter. On the fifteenth an announcement from Washington confirmed he was alive. Both frantic and relieved, Louise bombarded American officials with requests for aid and urged influential friends to intercede. There were responses from many who no longer had much use for Reed's politics; Carl Hovey, Jane Addams and Fred Howe all tried to pressure the government, while one acquaintance managed to interest Bernard Baruch in the case.

Reed knew nothing of all this until after a verdict of guilty was rendered on April 26, the sentence being a $300 fine and confiscation of the jewels. Three days later he was for the first time permitted to communicate with America. Cabling Louise and following with a letter, he soon received replies. Less lonely and worried, his problem was far from over. Through Aino Malmberg, a Finnish woman helpful to radicals, and also via the jail grapevine came all sorts of unnerving, contradictory rumors—soon he would be shipped to a detention camp, negotiations were going on between the United States and Finland for his release, he was being kept in jail at the request of United States officials. All appeared plausible because, despite elaborate legal structures, he knew that "It is impossible to say what a bourgeois government cannot do."[11]

Whatever the backstage maneuverings, and despite occasional letters from Louise, prison life was dreary. He was allowed to walk in the yard each day and to visit a dentist for some major work, and he received reading matter from Mrs. Malmberg. But no amount of decent behavior could alter the basic situation—Reed was a political prisoner, held in solitary confinement in a tiny cell, forced to wear one dank set of clothes day and night, living on meager rations of bread and dry, salted fish. Hoping to keep healthy, he gave up cigarettes and attempted to exercise regularly. But as weeks gave way to months the limited diet took a toll, leaving him increasingly weak and sickly.

Jack's mental state deteriorated along with his physical condition, undermining his conceit that it would be possible to endure jail indefinitely. He did not want to worry Louise, and claimed in his letters to her that things were "cheerful enough." Other comments, however, revealed less happy states of mind: "The thought of you drags at me sometimes until my imagination plays tricks, and I almost go crazy."[12] As weeks slowly passed, he grew "more and more nervous" and his resolve not to complain eroded. A letter begun on May 30 stated that the Finnish government had announced he would be turned loose, yet here he was, still confined, "spending most of my time worrying about my honey and longing for her." Two days later all optimism was gone: "Still no word. It seems to me as if I shall never get out. The worst is to keep expecting release day after day. My mind is getting dull." On June 2 he scrawled, "It is dreadful to wait so, day after day—and after three months, too. I have nothing to read, nothing to do. I can only sleep about five hours, and so am awake, penned in a little cage, for nineteen hours a day. This is my thirteenth week."

One obvious means of combating depression was closed, for aside from a few sheets for letters, authorities refused him writing paper. He drifted into a fantasy world, floating into a past more real than the thick gray walls. Confinement and solitude edged him toward the philosophic, allowed him to see beyond revolution to sheer experience, which carried the burden of its own meaning. He was his own past, and meaning lay in what he had done and whom he had touched. Out of memories and love for home, family and friends, the face of his father shone forth. Focusing on the one tangible object C.J. had bequeathed, the gold watch now in a New York pawnshop, Reed in a kind of rising panic felt he must repossess it, and every letter beseeched Louise to redeem the timepiece. When he finally managed to hide a few sheets of paper, he began to scratch notes for both an autobiographical novel and a romance. But weariness and a tired and dulling mind prevented him from getting very far. And then, one day when hope had reached a desperate ebb, he was suddenly released.

Gaunt and sallow, his clothes in shreds, Reed walked into the sunlight the first week in June. After months of longing for America, he knew a westward journey now was impossible. Warnings from Louise about the intolerable political climate were not enough to stop him, but the United States government was definitely not interested in welcoming home another radical. In May he had applied to Chargé d'Affaires Alexander Magruder for a passport, but it had been denied. This was just as well. Three months in solitary confinement had left him in no shape to face another trial or spend more time in jail.

Jack caught a steamer in Helsinki after the government of Estonia had approved his passage to Russia. On June 7 he cabled Louise from Revel, "Temporarily returning headquarters. Come if possible," and then boarded a slow-moving train. Reaching Petrograd, he collapsed into bed at the Hotel International. Emma Goldman found him there, alone and ill, limbs swollen, body covered with a rash and gums discolored with scurvy. As she nursed Reed, Emma was struck by his strength of will. She was on the road to disillusionment with Bolshevism and sharply at odds with his politics, but she could not help loving the "big, generous spirit" of the man.[13]

Reed was strong enough to leave the room in a few days to enjoy the lovely weather that put Petrograd in a holiday mood. The parks were crowded and thousands strolled along the newly paved Nevsky Prospekt, renamed October 25th Prospekt. From quays small pleasure boats carried passengers past the regilded spire of the Peter-Paul Fortress up the Neva to Smolny, and on islands at the mouth of the river vacationing workers walked in gardens and slept in bedrooms at the villas of nobility. Twenty miles away, Tsarskoye Selo, where Reed had gone one dark night to investigate Kerensky's advance, had been renamed Dietskoy Selo, Children's Village, and tens of thousands of well-fed, happy youngsters were there on vacation. Their generous treatment was a good omen: "This is a country for children. . . . In every city, in every village, the children have their own public dining rooms, where the food is better, and there is more of it, than for grown-ups. . . . The children pay nothing for their food; they are clothed free of charge by the cities. . . . The immense, gorgeous State theaters [are] crowded with children from orchestra to gallery."[14]

Reed went to Moscow in June and found the same air of ease and pleasure. For the first time in years the capital was like any other great summer city, flowers blazing in public gardens, outdoor theaters going day and night, shirt-sleeved crowds lolling beneath trees, vendors selling glasses of tea and coffee, tourists from the country gazing at historic monuments and wandering through the fully restored walls, towers and churches of the Kremlin. The Red Army was involved in a struggle with invading Polish forces in the Ukraine, but it was apparent this was the last gasp of intervention. Meanwhile the blockade was weakening and neighboring countries were beginning to adjust to permanence of the Soviet state. Moved to write an article for the *Liberator*, Jack described the joy and beauty of Moscow and Petrograd, then became cautious: "This does not mean that all is well with Soviet Russia, that the people do not hunger, that there is not misery and disease and desperate, endless struggle." But if difficulties were not fully over, the long, dark night was nearing a close and Socialism would endure: "In spite of all that has happened, the Revolution lives, burns with a steady flame, licks at the dry inflammable framework of European capitalist society."[15]

Wavering between an intense desire for home and the knowledge that serious trouble awaited him there, Jack knew he needed Louise. Three times in June couriers carried messages out of the country to her. Each promised a quick reunion without mentioning a definite location. With the first on the sixteenth went $100 and advice that she not leave yet: "Trust me and try to hang on until I send. Everything is going to be all right. . . . I do so long to see you again." A week later he promised something even better: "We shall not be separated another winter. . . . I can say no more now, except that I love you and want you all the time." The third missive, on a sheet of notebook paper, indicated that perhaps he was planning to return: "If you haven't arranged to leave America, don't do so. You will soon know why. . . . If you'll just hold out my dearest, we'll soon be together all right and safe."[16]

Before making any final decision about the future, Reed was looking forward to the Second Congress of the Communist International, scheduled for mid-July. This, the Third International, was the Bolshevik answer to the Second, the worldwide organization which had lost much of its credibility when the Socialist parties had embraced the war. A First Congress in March 1919, when Russia was shut off from the world by civil war and intervention, had been sparsely attended; most of the fifty-one foreign delegates had been émigrés with little knowledge of current affairs in their native lands. The result was more a propaganda show than a serious attempt to create an organization of revolutionary parties. A platform for Russian leaders like Grigory Zinoviev, head of the Executive Committee, to denounce moderate Socialists and fulminate about imminent world revolution, the meeting had chiefly affected radical movements, hastening splits like that in the American Socialist Party and bringing forth Communist groups like the CP and CLP. The important business of adopting a constitution, setting criteria for membership and mapping strategy had been put off. This meant the Second Congress would be the first in which world radical leaders would seriously plan revolution.

Helping to organize the Congress, Reed took a room in the Dielovoy Dvor, a hotel near the Kremlin set aside for delegates. Tough, hardy and dedicated, they seemed a remarkable group, "real proletarians . . . actual workmen-fighters-strikers, barricade defenders. . . ." Their journeys to Russia were "the most thrilling tales ever told." Like Jack, they had come illegally, without passports, hiding on ships, hiking across deserts and mountains, dodging police and hostile military forces, suffering arrest, seeing comrades captured and shot. Their varying backgrounds and origins reflected the widespread opposition to capitalism—German Spartacists, Spanish syndicalists, Hungarian Soviet leaders, British shop stewards, Dutch transport workers, Hindu, Korean, Chinese and Persian insurrectionists, Irish Sinn Feiners and Argentine Socialists. Not all were sold on Communism, not all accepted the idea of the Dictatorship of the Proletariat or the need for political parties; but they were all "brothers in revolution, . . . the best fighters of the working class . . . comrades that were willing to die for the overthrow of capitalism."[17]

Proud to be among them, Reed acted as a self-appointed welcoming committee, seeking out newcomers and showing them about Moscow. Conscious that many delegates were skeptical of Bolshevism, Jack tried to win them over. He was a good salesman. One American anarchosyndicalist, O. W. Penney from the Middle West, was so swept up by the warmth of his "sparkling, smiling, sympathetic" eyes that he did not mind when Reed immediately referred to his cherished beliefs as "absurdo-stupidism."[18] Before long he had been converted by Jack's arguments. Individual conversions were important, but institutional changes could have even more effect upon the future. Remembering his own miseducation, its irrelevance to modern life, Reed was happy to join the conversations of a group of European delegates concerned with schooling. Just before the Congress, they issued a call for a separate conference devoted to a new system of education that would combine scientific theory and manual labor in experimental schools for workers and young people.

For symbolic reasons a preliminary session of the Congress was held in Petrograd. The one hundred sixty-nine delegates from thirty-seven countries were transported in special trains and greeted by seventy thou-

sand cheering people in front of the Winter Palace, then honored with
a parade that Jack found impressive: "Tremendous masses flowed like
a clashing sea through the broad streets, almost overwhelming with their
enthusiastic affection the delegates as they marched from the Tauride
Palace to the Fields of Martyrs of the Revolution, protected on both
sides by long lines of workers holding hands, forming a living chain."[19]
In the evening on the riverfront steps of the old Stock Exchange more
than five thousand costumed performers depicted the history of revolution
from the Paris Commune to Petrograd, 1917, while flag-decked cruisers of
the Red Fleet saluted with cannon shots. After one session at the Tauride,
the delegates returned to Moscow and more demonstrations. The largest
was in Red Square, a procession of three hundred thousand people while
airplanes and dirigibles soared over the Kremlin walls.

Inspired and exalted by the collective emotion generated in such
demonstrations, Reed was brought back to earth by the workings of
the Congress. When the first regular session opened in the great Vladimir
Throne Room of the Kremlin's Imperial Palace, a serious political fight
was brewing. Seated there was a most impressive body of men, "the
revolutionists who fill the eye of the working masses of the world."
But many of these confident, ebullient men would soon disappoint Reed.
Believing the Congress a meeting of equals, he respected the Russians as
men who had made a revolution, but did not view them as infallible.
When during the next two weeks Bolsheviks would assert themselves in
debate, foreigners who knew more on particular issues would often
capitulate to their reputations rather than their arguments. This behavior
would shake Jack's faith both in fellow revolutionaries and in Soviet
leadership.

The basic problem grew out of Lenin's reassessment of the world
situation. By early 1920 the revolutionary wave was ebbing; the spontaneous ferment that had produced strikes across Europe and given birth to
short-lived Soviet regimes in Bavaria and Hungary was over, leaving
capitalism and parliamentarism intact. Having believed revolution could
only be international, Bolshevik leaders began to confront the idea of
Socialism in one country. Because Marxist theories provided no guidelines,
Lenin produced *Left Wing Communism: An Infantile Disorder*, which
essentially set policy for the Congress. Its model for the Third International was the Bolshevik Party, with absolute control resting at the top,
in this case with the Executive Committee in Moscow. Most important
was the retreat from the idea of imminent revolution. Lenin implicitly
criticized policies laid down at the First Congress, denouncing two
main errors of the "ultra" Left—the refusal to participate in "bourgeois

parliaments" and the unwillingness to work in "reactionary trade unions." Like anyone else, Communists had to learn to both "compromise" and "maneuver."

Having read Lenin's pamphlet before the opening session, Reed was in a quandary. Basically he had no objection to the Comintern as a centralized "General Staff of World Revolution" that shaped policy for parties all over the globe, and he could even accept the need for parliamentary activity. But at trade unions he drew the line. After years of loathing and denouncing the AFL, he had no intention of working with it, or even trying to capture it for Communism, no matter what anybody decided.* Convinced that Lenin did not understand the hopelessly reactionary structure of Gompers' union, hoping to advocate the little-understood idea of industrial unionism as exemplified by the IWW, Reed was prepared to take on any and all Bolsheviks. Perhaps he even sensed the greater problem: already within the Comintern it was impossible to override the Russians. Though willing to debate and listen to criticism, Soviet leaders were determined to set policy for the entire revolutionary world, and were ready to use their power and prestige to prevail.

The battle began early and lasted all through the Congress. Prior to the first working session Jack had gathered support not only from other Americans—the two CP delegates and two fellow CLP representatives—but also from some English industrial unionists, IWW adherents and various Continental syndicalists. As soon as proceedings opened on the twenty-third, he made two requests in the name of twenty-nine comrades—that the trade-union question be considered first, and that English be made one of the official languages. Both motions were quickly defeated, and Zinoviev then launched into an opening report on the role of Communist parties in the proletarian revolution. Anticipating trouble, the Comintern chief went out of his way to answer the objections of Reed

---

* Like many radicals, Reed had long been critical of the AFL. Disliking the elitism of such a craft organization, he was annoyed that over the years the AFL leadership, personified by its perennial president, Samuel Gompers, refused to show solidarity with radical unions. Distaste turned to hatred during the war years, when Gompers adopted a posture of cooperation with the federal government and pledged labor to a no-strike policy. After 1917 Gompers denounced Bolshevism as strongly as any big businessman and squelched the small radical movement within his organization. Reed had often poked fun at Gompers in the *Masses*, and before departing for Russia in 1919 he covered the annual meeting in the *Liberator* under the title "The Convention of the Dead," pointing out that "there was little to differentiate the assembly from the annual convention of the National Association of Car Manufacturers, which was meeting at the same time in another hall." See the *Liberator*, I (August 1919), 12–20.

and his allies, stating flatly that nobody should "deny the role of trade-unions in the process of social revolutions."[20]

Undaunted by the setback, Reed continued to agitate. Five commissions were set up to report on major issues, and he was appointed to two of them—National Minorities and the Colonial Question, and Trade Union Activities. Discussion in the former centered on the question of to what extent Communists should support bourgeois independence movements. This problem touched him so little that sometimes he missed parts of working sessions. Cast as an expert on American Negroes, he did his best on an unfamiliar topic and found a way simultaneously to advance his ideas on unions. Addressing the assembly on July 26, he was full of statistics on America's exploitation of its largest minority, then in passing noted that many trade unions helped exacerbate their problems by refusing to admit Negroes.

The major struggle occurred at meetings of the Trade Union Commission, chaired by Comintern Secretary Karl Radek, whose sharp wit was not enough to silence Jack. Arguing that Europeans did not understand how American trade unions restrained members from revolutionary activity, he claimed the only thing to do was smash them and build industrial unions in their place. As the Russians on the commission remained immovable and foreigners slowly swung their way, Reed grew desperate. After meetings he was awake late every night, collaring delegates, debating, arguing, demanding they not give way on such a fundamental issue. He lobbied so effectively that Radek was driven to accuse him of sabotaging the group's work. Reed typed an appeal to Lenin: "I object to Radek's assertion that we have tried to sabotage the work of the Commission. . . . That sort of remark takes the place of argument with Comrade Radek, because, knowing very little about Trade Unionism, he naturally has no attitude on the question. This is the real explanation." Looking it over, he tried to improve the wording, inserted a phrase about Radek's "curious tactics," and crossed out the assertion that he knew nothing about unionism.[21] Then, realizing that Lenin himself had begun the trade-union line, he put the note away without delivering it.

Within the commission the vote went against Reed by the lopsided margin of 57 to 8. Still he refused to give up. At the general debate on the evening of August 3, talk was cut short by a resolution stating that the question of unions had been overly discussed in committee. The next evening Jack and four other delegates, including Louis Fraina of the CP, raised the issue in the context of a debate on the Comintern Constitution by introducing a series of amendments. From the podium Zinoviev squelched this insurgency with an angry speech. On August 5

Radek took the floor to deliver the official report, which carried a specific supplement stating that "the revolutionary proletariat considers the position of our American comrades absolutely incorrect." Despite strong pleas for unanimity, Reed once more raised a voice in opposition. Wrathful and impatient, Zinoviev asserted that his position might lead to the collapse of the International and the Communist movement. But Jack refused to back down. When the final vote overwhelmed his position, there was still one small consolation—Radek's report was one of the few not accepted unanimously.

Despite the setbacks, Reed was open-minded enough to judge the Congress a success, for many wavering delegates had moved into Communist ranks. The Comintern had adopted twenty-one conditions for admission that effectively excluded "opportunist" radicals like the American Socialist Party and had created a "centralized and disciplined body of revolutionists" to whom "millions of workers all over the world" would look for leadership.[22] Reaffirming the earlier decision, the Congress had ensured continuity for the American Communist movement by ordering the splintered parties to unite on a single program, and provided that Jack's own views would continue to be heard by naming him the American representative on the Executive Committee of the Communist International (ECCI). Reed was pleased at the honor and in good spirits for the closing session at the Moscow Opera House, where international delegates, Russian Communists and the general public cheered orations by Trotsky, Radek and Zinoviev, roared together through the "Internationale" and applauded an impromptu finale of Italians singing revolutionary songs. As the audience surged through the aisles, Jack put into action a long-cherished plan, when he and two comrades grabbed Lenin and swung him up on their shoulders. No fan of American football, the Bolshevik leader shouted protests, and when that did no good, began to kick violently at the men below until, laughing and happy, they lowered him to earth.

When the Executive Committee began meeting to scrutinize applications for admission to the Comintern, a stubborn Reed once more brought up the labor question. Defeated again, he sent home an article for an official Communist publication that was adamant: it had been foolish to reverse the original Comintern policy of destroying the AFL, and he promised that "At the next Congress, these theses must be altered."[23] After two hectic weeks of political infighting, Jack was drained by the continuing struggle within the ECCI. Increasingly he was critical of the leadership—Radek, who used sarcasm to sidestep worrisome issues, and Zinoviev, a flabby bureaucrat with a penchant for intrigue and tyranny. Together at the Congress they had steamrollered the opposition, maneuvering, cajoling and threatening behind the scenes to stifle the revolt on the union issue. Reed expected openness and fair decisions, and he was appalled when such tactics continued in meetings of the Executive Committee. Sometimes Zinoviev contemptuously refused to answer questions or peremptorily silenced opponents. Annoyed by a series of unwarranted gibes, a hardly subtle indication that his status was slipping, Jack's growing frustration one day exploded into a rage that ended with his resignation. Hurling the worst insult possible, Zinoviev denounced such factionalism as "petty bourgeois."[24] Reed withdrew the resignation, but the emotional wound continued to fester.

Brooding, he tried to understand how personalities were overlapping with organization in a most unsettling way. The Bolshevik Party and Comintern gave Zinoviev the power he was now misusing. Believing in the organization, Jack was inclined to fix blame upon the man. If it came down to faith in the revolution, that was firm, and yet doubts left him confused. Exhausted, moody, low in spirits, he shared his concerns with Angelica Balabanova, Radek's predecessor as Comintern secretary, whose own troubles with Zinoviev had been legion. In a kind of camaraderie of depression they comforted each other. Neither had ever supposed that a revolution would be free of mistakes, but both were idealistic enough to be intensely frustrated by their inability to prevent a man like Zinoviev from running things in an arrogant, autocratic way.

A letter that arrived in mid-August announced that Louise was on the way. This news emphasized an inner struggle over how to arrange going home without giving the impression he was escaping defeats, and without losing his effective voice in the Comintern. He immediately sent word that she should remain outside the country, but knowing the message might not get through, began arranging a trip to meet her in Petrograd. The following days brought further letters until on August 25 there came a climax of sharp joy and disappointment. Within a few hours of receiving a message from Stockholm saying she was coming via Murmansk, Reed learned that when Louise arrived, he would be far off in Baku, attending a meeting of the Peoples of the East.

A spinoff of the Second Congress, the Baku conference grew from the notion that colonialism was capitalism's weakest link. Knowing the World War had ripened the Middle and Far East, the Communists hoped to take leadership of the burgeoning national struggles for liberation. Jack approved the idea, but did not personally want to take part. Weary, hoping Louise would somehow lift his confusion and doubt, he tried to beg off, but Zinoviev insisted it was necessary for ECCI members from imperialist countries to attend. Seeing no way out, Reed asked permission to wait a few days and make the trip with her, but this too was denied. Civil war still sputtered in the Caucasus and the journey would be made in a special armored train. All he could do was type a letter full of apologies and instructions. Responding to a call of duty, he left no doubt where his real feelings belonged—"I am so disappointed not to be able to meet you . . . telegraph me the minute you are in Russia, so that I may hurry back . . . I am longing to see my honey more than I can tell. It seems years. . . ."[25]

Reed's lifelong openness to experience allowed the difficult trip to become an adventure. A long ride through the fertile Volga plains led to the dusty south and then Baku, on the shores of the Caspian Sea, an old Tatar city reeking with sights and smells of the Orient. The conclave was out of a storybook. Almost two thousand men of the East—dark-skinned Turks and Persians, nomadic Arabs and Armenians, Oriental Russians from towns with magic names like Samarkand, Tashkent and Bokhara, and a scattering of Hindus and Chinese—wandered through shaded bazaars, talked over tea in a dozen languages, joined in the rites of various religions and met together in halls draped with splendid rugs and glistening banners. Wearing a collarless, striped shirt and baggy trousers, Jack moved among comrades in fezzes and skullcaps, flowing robes and tunics, some with sabers or pistols hanging from colorful sashes. He communicated with sign language and in half a dozen broken tongues, seeking their life stories, finding it wondrous that faith in revolution had spread so far, and began to dream of mounting a horse and following new friends over mountain ranges and across deserts in the footsteps of Alexander, Tamerlane and Genghis Khan.

As in Moscow, the congress itself brought him back to earth. Managed by Zinoviev with the assistance of Radek and Bela Kun, head of the short-lived Hungarian Soviet regime, its thrust was not Marxist but anti-imperialist. The Comintern chiefs played on the most primitive emotions, and worked delegates into a fury of anti-Western resentment. The climax was Zinoviev's plea for eight hundred million Asians to declare a "real holy war" and to re-create "the spirit of struggle which once animated the peoples of the East when they marched against Europe under the leadership of their great conquerors." He was answered by the audience roaring to its feet, brandishing rifles and swords and screaming revenge against the infidels. However dramatic, however effective as theater, the moment seemed misleading and wrongheaded. Holy war was not proletarian revolution, and to obscure the difference was to mislead the masses. When Jack's own turn to speak came, he was less powerful but considerably more precise. After a half-hour catalogue of America's iniquities against Filipinos, Cubans, Mexicans and workers at home, he concluded, "There is but one road to freedom. Unite with the Russian workers and peasants who overthrew their capitalists and whose Red Army conquered foreign imperialists. Follow the Red Star of the Communist International."[26]

After ten days of meetings, the return journey seemed interminable, for Louise had already wired from Moscow. Reed's companions were drunk, ebullient and boisterous, but his discontent with Comintern leadership prevented him from sharing this mood. Annoyed with the demagoguery, half-truths perpetrated in the name of revolution, phony calls for holy war, he once again mulled the implications and found himself viewing a boundless, frightening world of question marks.* Analysis settled nothing, faith in ultimate goals helped to calm doubts, and action provided a diversion from worries. An attack on the train by horseback bandits was fought off by a Red Army squad. When cavalry rode in pursuit, Jack boarded a peasant wagon mounted with a machine gun and bounced over hills, full of memories of Mexico and La Tropa.

On the morning of September 15 he ran into Louise's room at the Dielovoy Dvor, and the reunion went from noisy ecstasy to the calm of love once more fulfilled. Emptier, fuller and more complete, at once tired, happy and full of potentialities, Reed shared a verse scribbled during a time of despair in the Finnish prison:

> Thinking and dreaming
> Day and night and day
> Yet cannot think one bitter thought away—
> That we have lost each other
> You and I. . . .[27]

Never wanting to feel that way again, clasping Louise close, he poured

---

* One of the perennial points of controversy about John Reed concerns the extent of his "disillusionment" with Bolshevism-Communism in the summer and fall of 1920. It is useless to assess the evidence here, since Theodore Draper in *The Roots of American Communism* (New York: Viking Press, 1957), 282–93, has done a splendid and thorough job of analyzing the available historical testimony. Concurring with his conclusion that Reed never "renounced" Communism, I do take some issue with his statement, "Reed was probably as disillusioned as it was possible to be and still remain in the movement." Having been driven to Bolshevism by world events and his own needs and goals, Reed had embraced it as a philosophy that allowed him to make sense of his experience, and he would not have abandoned it easily. While it is difficult to think of Reed in future years defending Stalin, whom he hardly knew, against Trotsky, whom he admired, or remaining permanently within the narrow, contentious sect that the American Communist Party would become, it certainly would have taken much more than some disagreements with individuals like Zinoviev to turn him onto a different path.

out intimacies to weld them together, mixing his innermost thoughts on public and private matters. Jack confessed to the casual affair with the Russian girl, swore such things would not continue, then haltingly explained the nagging doubts and confusions over Comintern actions. To rebuild their lives one thing above all was necessary—at the first opportunity they must leave Russia for home.

For all Reed's intensity, Louise was shocked to find him greatly changed, "older and sadder and grown strangely gentle and aesthetic [sic]."[28] Clothes in rags, complexion sallow and flesh loose like that of an older man, he seemed to live in the community of suffering that was the Russian people, their hardships showing fully on his gaunt body. This made her stifle any reciprocal impulse toward confession. Feeling abandoned when he had departed for Russia a year before, Louise had turned to other men for comfort. History circled in strange ways, for in the spring and summer she had lived in Woodstock with Andrew Dasburg, the painter to whom Mabel Dodge had turned when Reed was off in Mexico. Torn by Jack's letters, she had secured credentials from the Hearst press and left America in early August, bursting with guilt. She explained to Andrew in a letter from the ship that the journey served two functions. Success as a correspondent would further her career so that never again would she be "stranded and ill" as she had been the previous winter. More important was keeping Reed from coming home. The reason for this was simple: "If J comes he will only go to prison and that will be horrible. Always to know he is there—more dependent than ever—it would destroy us—you can see that. It would destroy all three."[29]

Never especially open about her own affairs, Louise understood this was not the moment for honesty. Something about Jack—the sufferings undergone, the obvious effect of prison, the pain and confusion that showed in his eyes—made her feel closer to him than ever before. For years she had been jealous of his writing talent and fame. Now such feelings were gone. On their first meeting in Portland, he had admitted to inadequacies and fears that Louise had never believed. Now his frailty, humanity, even weakness made her both protective and afraid. She suggested that perhaps going home was not a good idea until he was much stronger, because prison might kill him. He answered her with a strange look and soft, firm words: "My dear little Honey, I would do anything I could for you, but don't ask me to be a coward."[30]

The following days were full of love. Jack introduced Louise to friends both old and new—Balabanova, Turkey's Enver Pasha, Bela Kun and Bolshevik leaders like Trotsky and Kamenev, and secured her an interview with Lenin, the first given to an American journalist in six months. Together they wandered through Moscow, attended the ballet and opera, visited museums and art galleries, walked on embankments of the river and under the white birch trees of parks, speaking tirelessly of how life would soon be. Confessing himself ready to leave the most active tasks of organizing to other hands, Jack foresaw some limited work helping to unite American Communists. But mainly he was consumed by a desire to write, to finish the story of the revolution with a second volume and then launch into the novel that had been gestating in his unconscious for so many years.

Louise brought to mind green memories of home, and Reed planned a long vacation in Portland with his family. A recent letter from Margaret, showed Reed she not only understood, but fully supported him. Responding to some of his self-criticism, his mother wrote, "What you say about feeling selfish makes me feel badly, dear. Don't ever feel like that. You are doing what you think is right—that is all any of us can do in this world, and if we don't do it, we're all wrong. Except in fear for your personal safety, the rest is all right in my eyes, if you feel it is."[31]

Certain that if Margaret had reached this point, C.J. would have approved wholeheartedly of his life's work, Jack was especially disappointed that Louise had not secured the gold watch. Sending a letter to a friend in New York, he asked that the timepiece be redeemed. Then thoughts of father and family brought forth a long-latent desire. As if needing another hedge against mortality, a connection to life stronger than words on paper, he spoke seriously about having a child, no matter what the future. To his great joy, Louise agreed.

Ten days after his return from Baku, Jack began to feel ill. Stricken with dizziness and sharp headaches, he took to bed with a high temperature. A doctor pronounced the illness influenza, but after five days, as the symptoms grew steadily worse, Reed was moved to the Marinsky Hospital. Further examinations led to a diagnosis of typhus, the dread spotted fever he had seen so often during the war, and though more doctors arrived, worried over him and consulted, there was little they could do. Talking her way into the hospital room, Louise sat beside him while friends scoured the city for medicine. Since the blockade, medical supplies were scarce and nothing could be found. It became apparent that, as in previous battles, he would be forced to fight with little more than courage. But the toll of hard years, the kidney operation, the months in solitary, the battles in the Comintern had sapped his reserves.

Soon it was difficult to swallow, and slowly his body began to waste away. Pain was constant, rolling up in waves as fever raged and ebbed, and he desperately gripped Louise's hand and tried to smile. Sometimes he drifted into a foggy world of hallucinations, but there were periods of remission when his mind was clear and he asked questions about the progress of the Red Army. Friends dropped by to visit, bringing political news. Skimming a stenographic report of the Second Congress and seeing that his speeches had been garbled in translation, he asked Louis Fraina to straighten out their meaning before publication. Whatever happened, it was necessary that his position in the world Communist movement be clear.

Halfway into delirium again, he found poems and stories swarming through his brain. Sharing them with Louise, he spoke of dangerous adventures they would brave together, explained that the water he drank was full of little songs, or suddenly recalled with great clarity incidents from the past: "You know how it is when you go to Venice. You ask people—Is this Venice?—just for the pleasure of hearing the reply." Ten days after he entered the hospital came the searing pain of a stroke. One side was now paralyzed, and he was unable to utter a word. Silently, for five days more, while Louise prayed to a God neither of them believed in and peasant nurses slipped off to a chapel to burn candles, Jack seemed to struggle with fate. Cut off from words, those human symbols which had defined his being and carried him to the kind of life dreamed of as a youngster, he lived wholly within the soundless reaches of the mind. Like young Will in the early story, he had scorned the flower of contentment in favor of the rock of wealth, fame, beauty and victory. Tasting each, he had known their opposites, too, and the days of his years had been full and swift as any good adventure story or lovely dream. Knowing this did not make it easy to let go, but perhaps gave comfort and even a sense of fulfillment until that moment in the early hours of October 17 when the heart stopped beating, the cold body grew still and nothing became all.

22

Ever-Victorious

"The last of this ancient dynasty was . . . called the 'Ever-Victorious,' who was never defeated in battle. . . ."—The Great Book of Sarpedon

"*When at last they got secret word the battle was surely lost, they took the old King and rode down the west.*

"*It was night. Faint and thunderous, the rumor of combat came over the plain. The great camp, yet unsuspecting, flashed with jovial flame on steel, where for miles deep choruses ran counter to bursts of warrior-laughter. Here were dancing girls, courtesans and slaves, the toll of conquered peoples; and there jewels heaped up, and bolts of rich fabric, plundered in proud cities.*

"*His majesty . . . the Invincible, the Ever-Victorious, lay rigid in his brazen pavilion, robed in cloth-of-silver so heavy that he could not have moved, even if he were not paralyzed these many years. He could no longer speak; only his eyes lived. His aged body was cold and shrunken.*

"*The Captain came clanking into the heavy-splendid place, and without looking at the King, plucked him up and tossed him on his shoulder, and strode out. All in black armor the Ten were waiting, holding their black horses by the bridle, with the Captain's horse and a horse for the King. They lifted up the withered, brittle thing and spread its legs across the saddle. . . .*

"*Mounting all together, they spurred into the street of tents; and, as the light struck them, dropped their visors, upon which was writ in gold the unspeakable Word. Men screamed, and with clashing armor cast themselves on their faces, at the passing of the Ten. Along the way ahead ran tidings of their coming, and they rode in chill silence, with waves of sound before and after rolling. Without challenge they passed out into the plain, westward, and galloped.*

"*High hung the hollow ringing shield of heaven, embossed with stars. The steady wind, unhindered for a thousand miles of plain, brought down the smell of bloody sweat from the battle, roaring off to the north with a sound of trees in storm. A lurid pallor shot up the sky there. The Ten lifted their visors and sniffed the taint of slaughter.*

"*They laid a course by the young moon's arc. Behind, the clamoring camp drew down to nothing, and the battle fell away over the shoulder of the world. . . . They pressed on, hour after hour, and the flat country flowed under their horses' pounding hooves, while the wide horizons stood still and torrents of stars poured down the sky. . . .*"[1]

The last story was like one of the first, a tale from a mythic realm where victory and defeat, life and death are surrounded by pageantry. First outlined in the Finnish jail cell, it seems a strange foreshadowing of John Reed's own end. Like any ancient or mythical kingdom, Soviet Russia knew how to honor heroes. From the hospital bed he was borne on the shoulders of Russian workers to the Temple of Labor. For a week his body lay on a dais in a dim hall brightened by wreaths of garish metallic flowers and colorful revolutionary posters, while soldiers of the Red Army stood guard and visitors filed past in homage. On Saturday, October 23— one day after what would have been his thirty-third birthday—a military band playing a funeral march led a solemn procession through Moscow's streets to Red Square and halted at the grassy bank before the Kremlin wall. It was a gloomy afternoon, the gray autumn sky damp with bursts of rain and sleet. Fluttering over the open grave, above the mass of spectators, was a red banner with golden letters proclaiming, "The leaders die, but the cause lives on." Speeches by officials who had known him— Nikolai Bukharin, Alexandra Kollantai and Boris Reinstein—echoed the sentiment, and when the voices finally stopped, red flags were dipped, rifles fired in salute and the coffin was lowered into the earth. Close to the Brotherhood Grave where he had seen five hundred Russians buried three years before, in front of the walled brick citadel built by the rulers of Muscovy, Reed lay beside the remains of ancient kings and martyrs of the revolution.

It was a conclusion he would have appreciated, the kind of ending toward which his days seem to have been aimed, a fit resting place for a man whose last work of fiction indicated that he had never wholly abandoned boyhood dreams of an epic life. Reed had been that unusual kind of man whose needs, energies and talents are strong enough to carry adolescent fantasies into adult reality. An urban industrial era, the early twentieth century might limit opportunities for romance, but did not totally eliminate them, and though once he had proclaimed that reality surpassed poetic invention, this meant a very special kind of reality, one far different from that which most men accept. Unerringly Reed had always steered to just those activities where the scope for the individual seemed greatest: walking alone about Europe, pursuing the self-exploration of the artist, experimenting in Bohemia with unconventional life-styles, becoming a foreign correspondent, embracing the causes of embattled radicals and revolutionaries.

The impulse to transcend everyday life can capture men in any age, but the form, content and context of such a quest are provided by history. In Reed's case, an affluent society of loosening social bonds at first provided opportunities and rewards for his kind of self-expression, then labor turbulence, war, revolution and repression began to define the contours of reality. This was the subject of the notes for an autobiographical novel also sketched in jail, the story of a young journalist who becomes famous in pre-war New York, then suffers professional boycott and social ostracism for opposing American involvement in the war. Like the paralyzed king who, despite impending defeat, will be named in legendary chronicles destined to awe men across succeeding ages, the journalist would be remembered for his connection to historic events, for identifying with those special heroes of the modern world, the "real revolutionists . . . men who go the limit."[2]

Sick and delirious in his prison cell, Reed used writing as a way of giving meaning to both the painful present and the days of all his years. If the notion of worldly immortality was on his mind, there was also the desire to understand his own place in history. The story was named "The Ever-Victorious," and the novel, *The Tides of Men*, and both titles were significant. Despite pain and imprisonment, he could both believe himself the ever-victorious and understand that his life had been pulled by those tides. Somehow, early, carefree Greenwich Village days were inextricably, if obscurely, connected to the great problems that followed them. The social forces which had created a society in which his powers could bring fame and fulfillment had also created an America so unstable that reactions to war would destroy the culture that had sustained Reed. What society could give it could take away. Why this had happened he did not fully understand. Marxism provided a possible explanation, but ultimately he could not retreat into a theory, and was less interested in society than in the individual. The child who had found meaning in the great deeds of men remained alive. No matter what the era, the value of life came in meeting those tests which challenged integrity. Manhood was a matter of acting in accord with an inner code, of committing oneself fully and accepting the consequences; for this reason, even in defeat one could be ever-victorious.

Such a view brought him to jail and then carried beyond it, through the months of 1920 when weakness, pain and politics left little time for contemplation. Ironically, it was not the basic revolutionary struggle which took Reed on the final trip to Russia. The journey had resulted from the squabbles of ambitious men, too concerned with their own role in history and with marginal doctrinal differences to unite American Bolshevism under a single banner. Death by typhus was a far cry from clean destruction by the sword of a knight or the bullet of a counter-revolutionary, and it showed that pettiness as well as heroism could pave the road to the grave.

The final, even the logical cost of an epic life, death could easily be encompassed by Reed's scheme of values. But he was less prepared to understand other costs that had plagued him while alive. Seeking external experience had always meant cutting off some of the things he wished to be, ignoring both inner voices that cried out for expression and the soft, insistent tones of love. Never had he allowed himself time for the poetry and novels that seemed so important, and often he had let abstract commitments blind him to the needs of those most dear. The result was anguish over the creative works that remained unwritten and long periods of suffering from the agonies of love abused. Dimly recognizing that such problems were self-inflicted, he accepted such frustration as a normal part of life and never fully faced the pain he caused for others. Perhaps it made no difference. If he had known in advance that the cost of external strivings would be a loss of intimacy and of a certain kind of creativity, no doubt he would have paid the price and behaved the same. Ultimately there was a kind of selfishness in Reed, one based on the notion it was more important to shake the world than to care for others or oneself.

After the man died, the legend lived. The "Golden Boy" of Greenwich Village, the "Playboy of the Revolution," had given his life for a cause, and the giving seemed to friends and admirers more important than the cause. Few acquaintances followed him into the Communist movement, but this was hardly surprising, for not many had wholly followed his actions when he was alive. Often termed reckless, foolish, naïve, self-destructive or immature, Reed was also called fearless. Perhaps all such words amount to the same thing. Certainly some quality they describe allowed him always to take at least one step beyond where most men dare to tread, to live out the fantasies of others, to give substance to inchoate impulses and desires of contemporaries. That is, after all, what made him a culture hero—that is the basis of legend.

The meaning of a legend is given by those who recount it, not the one who lived it. Reed the hero was the creation of his generation of artists, intellectuals and radicals. Coming to maturity in the hopeful years before the First World War, such people were in theory and life attempting to smash the value systems of the nineteenth century, and Reed was one of their natural leaders. Believing themselves in the midst of a renaissance, his friends optimistically proclaimed a revolution on the way, one in art, politics and social life that would free society from the hand of the past and usher in a new age of self-fulfillment. They were convinced that artistic vision and intellect could jointly shape society, but their optimism was shattered by war and revolution and the onslaught of irrational forces that have ever since haunted the world. Life which had begun as a grand lark, a glorious experiment, became a series of challenges. Some equivocated, backed away and altered beliefs to avoid uncomfortable confrontations. Despite doubts, hesitations and desires to escape, Reed faced it all, lived it all, and ultimately refused to compromise. Alongside the laughing playboy, adventurer, lover and poet grew the image of the committed radical, then death enshrined the revolutionary. This final view has helped to confine the legend of Reed to narrow circles. America may grudgingly immortalize some artists who have led lives of commitment and passion, but—except for the homage paid the generation of 1776—it has never been a country to forgive or admire its revolutionaries.

John Reed certainly was a revolutionary, but this term must include more than political and economic notions and encompass ideas beyond those embodied in Soviet Russia. Never content with prepackaged reality, he always had to see, feel and learn for himself. Such an attitude might foster a tendency to be quarrelsome, self-righteous and stubborn, but it was also a source of strength, of a vision rarely blinded by truths accepted on mere authority. His days unfolded like a series of attempts to test the limits of self-expression, and his questioning of traditional views on morality, art, politics and social life naturally moved toward revolution. The dreams of a new society held by Wobblies and Villistas, then carried into practice by the Bolsheviks, were full of passion and seemed to promise worlds where life was a performance acted on a grand scale. Adopting the rhetoric and dreams of each group in turn, he experienced the colorful days of upheaval as the reality of a social order to come. When nagging doubts of what technology or bureaucracy would do to such regimes surfaced—as they did in Mexico and Russia—he barely acknowledged them. But surely his basic stance, the playing out of his deepest motivations and desires, indicated that any rigid system would ultimately have earned his scorn.

The revolutionary impulse in John Reed was deeply rooted in premises he never clearly articulated. Central to his notion of revolution was the belief that society—any social order—should be prevented from locking men into rigid forms of consciousness, into values that remain unquestioned. From this perspective the drives toward poetry and revolution have much in common. Poetry is a way of seeing the world afresh, of creating a vision of truth which other men can share. Revolution is an attempt to carry vision to the barricades, to create a new kind of social truth. Both are extensions of the idea that life can somehow be greater and more meaningful than the routine daily existence that most men know.

The impulse to experience, question and discover carried Reed through realms of ideas and to many sites of physical struggle, turned him into a critic of American culture and then an opponent of capitalism. Experience at home and war abroad convinced him that what at first had seemed a crass, tasteless civilization was in fact an unjust, even a deadly social order, and so he came to oppose it as strongly and openly as he opposed prudery in art and behavior, as single-mindedly as he would have opposed any social system that constricted and stunted development. The demand that life be large and intense for himself eventually stretched out to include the lives of other men, of all humankind. Such a vision was simple, grandiose and perhaps impossible, but the worlds where Little Will could leave home to become a hero, and where a weak, sickly lad named John Reed could become an international figure, were ones where the impossible could come true. Far from the western sea, far from Portland, were great arenas where men battled against the domination of old beliefs, old systems, old realities, and faced an angry destiny. Such struggles are never-ending and always available for those who seek them, the poets, the visionaries, the romantics. John Reed was one of them, one of those rare individuals who see beyond things as they are, act upon dreams of what they may become, and are willing to clothe their vision with all the frail power of mortal flesh.

Notes

The following are sources of direct quotations in the body of this work. For additional material or more general background on the period, see Bibliography. Throughout, John Reed is abbreviated as "JR." Frequently cited manuscript collections are abbreviated as follows:

JR MSS   John Reed Papers, Houghton Library, Harvard University

Hicks MSS   Granville Hicks Papers, George Arents Research Library, Syracuse University

Morristown Archives   Archives of the Morristown School, Morristown, New Jersey

Reed Family MSS   Papers of John Reed family, now in possession of John Reed, Chevy Chase, Maryland

Gold Archive   Lee Gold Archive, Institute of Marxism-Leninism, Moscow, U.S.S.R.

Steffens MSS   Lincoln Steffens Papers, Columbia University Library

1 THE LEGEND

1 Walter Lippmann, "Legendary John Reed," *New Republic*, I (December 26, 1914), 15–16.

2 Floyd Dell, "John Reed: Revolutionist," New York *Call*, October 31, 1920 (Sunday Magazine), 5.

3 Lincoln Steffens, "John Reed," *Freeman*, II (November 3, 1920), 181.

4 Robert Hallowell, "John Reed," *New Republic*, XXIV (November 17, 1920), 298–9.

5 Edwin Justus Mayer, *A Preface to Life* (New York: Boni and Live-right, 1923), 95.

6 Max Eastman, "Contribution to an Apotheosis," in *Heroes I Have Known* (New York: Simon and Schuster, 1942), 213.

7 Louis Untermeyer, *Bygones* (New York: Harcourt, Brace and World, 1965), 32–3.

2 PORTLAND

1 John Reed, "The Winged Stone," *Harvard Monthly*, XLVII (April 1909), 77–8.

2 H. W. Scott, ed., *History of Portland, Oregon* (Syracuse, N.Y.: D. Mason, 1890), 451.

3 *Ibid.*, 453.

4 "Almost Thirty," unpublished, JR MSS. A somewhat edited version appeared in *New Republic*, LXXXVI (April 15, 1936), 267–70. Many of Reed's childhood memories used in this chapter are from this work, his only attempt at autobiography. All subsequent unfootnoted quotations in this chapter are from this essay.

5 T. B. Merry, "Henry D. Green," *Oregonian*, April 12, 1885, 3.

6 *Ibid.*

7 "Death Takes Pioneer in Portland's Social Life," *Oregonian*, October 31, 1926, 20.

8 Quoted in Louise Bryant, unpublished autobiographical sketch, Hicks MSS.

9 C. J. Reed to Francis Woodman, March 1906, Morristown Archives.

10 Untitled, unpublished essay on the Chinese in Portland, JR MSS.

11 Charlotte Green to Louise Bryant, December 31, 1920, JR MSS.

12 *Oregonian*, November 17, 1895, 2.

13 *Seventh Annual Circular, Portland Academy* (Portland, 1895).

14 Hugh Hardman to Granville Hicks, February 17, 1935, Hicks MSS.

15 Alice Strong to Granville Hicks, February 17, 1935, Hicks MSS.

16 "The Best Camping Experience," unpublished, JR MSS.

3 MORRISTOWN

1 JR, "The Winged Stone," 78–80.

2 "Almost Thirty." All subsequent unfootnoted quotations in this chapter are from this essay.

3 *Morristonian* clipping, date unknown, Reed Family MSS.

4 Frank Damrosch to Granville Hicks, January 26, 1935, Hicks MSS.

5 Arthur P. Butler to John Stuart, October 17, 1934, Hicks MSS.

6 Francis Woodman to Granville Hicks, October 29, 1934, Hicks MSS.

7 C. J. Reed to Francis Woodman, n.d. and September 18, 1906, Morristown Archives.

8 *Ibid.*, December 16, 1904, and February 25, 1906, Morristown Archives.

9 *Ibid.*, n.d., Morristown Archives.

10 George Allen to Granville Hicks, April 27, 1935, Hicks MSS.

11 *Morristonian*, date unknown, Reed Family MSS.

12 Quoted in Steffens, "John Reed," 181.

13 "A Dedication," *Morristonian*, VIII (June 1906), 14.

14 "Sonnet to a Daisy (Apologies to Milton)," *ibid.* (January 1906), page unknown. Because the Morristown School does not have a complete file of the *Morristonian*,

the pages of some JR contributions remain a mystery. These works can be seen in clippings in the Reed Family MSS.

15 "Lines to Tennyson," *ibid.* (June 1906), 9.

16 "Twilight," *ibid.* (December 1905), 9–10.

17 "The Storm at Midnight," *ibid.*, VII (April 1905), page unknown.

18 "Atlantis," *ibid.* (May 1905), pages unknown.

19 "The Transformation," *ibid.*, VIII (December 1905), 4–6.

4 HARVARD

1 JR, "The Red Hand," *Harvard Monthly*, XLVI (April 1908), 72–5.

2 C. J. Reed to Francis Woodman, September 18, 1906, Morristown Archives.

3 Hallowell, "John Reed," 298–9.

4 "Almost Thirty." All subsequent unfootnoted quotations in this chapter are from this essay.

5 George W. Martin to Granville Hicks, November 28, 1934, Hicks MSS.

6 C. J. Reed to Lincoln Steffens, April 19, 1908, Steffens MSS.

7 "The Harvard Renaissance," unpublished, 9–10. This 73-page essay was written by Reed in the spring of 1912 for the *American Magazine*. For the reasons it was not accepted, see Chapter VI.

8 Quoted in Granville Hicks, *John Reed: The Making of a Revolutionary* (New York: Macmillan, 1936), 30.

9 *Harvard Lampoon*, LIV (October 28, 1907), 72.

10 *Ibid.* (January 22, 1908), frontispiece.

11 *Ibid.*, LV (March 4, 1908), 41.

12 "The Harvard Renaissance," 3, 4.

13 Simonson quoted in *ibid.*, 5–7. Reed quotations from same pages.

14 *Ibid.*, 8–9.

15 Quoted in *ibid.*, 12–13.

16 Quoted in *ibid.*, 45.

17 Quoted in *ibid.*, 2.

18 JR to Edward Hunt, June 4, 1909, JR MSS.

19 *Harvard Crimson*, April 27, 1935, quoted in J. Donald Adams, *Copey of Harvard* (Boston: Houghton Mifflin, 1960), 172.

20 All quotations about Copey from JR, "Charles Townsend Copeland," *American Magazine*, LXXIII (November 1911), 64–5.

21 "L'Aurore—To Amy Stone," unpublished, January 8, 1909, JR MSS.

22 Harold Stearns, "Confessions of a Harvard Man," *Forum*, LI (January 1914), 75.

23 JR to Francis Woodman, March 14, 1909, Morristown Archives.

24 JR to Robert Hallowell, April 20, 1909, JR MSS.

25 JR to Woodman, May 6, 1909, Morristown Archives.

26 Byron S. Hurlbut to Woodman, May 11, 1909, Morristown Archives.

27 "Daily Bulletin #7," unpublished, JR MSS.

28 Frances Nelson Carroll to the author, n.d., 1971.

29 JR to Frances Nelson, August 2, August 7 and September 2, 1909, letters in the possession of Frances Nelson Carroll, Portland, Oregon.

30 Ibid., August 7, 1909.

31 Quotation from a story that grew out of a similar walking trip made the year before. See JR, "From Clatsop to Nekarney," Harvard Monthly, XLVI (December 12, 1908), 110–13.

32 JR to Hallowell, August 26, 1909, JR MSS.

33 JR to Frances Nelson, September 18, 1909, in the possession of Frances Nelson Carroll.

34 Quoted in William F. Avery to John Stuart, September 8, 1935, Hicks MSS.

35 JR, "By the Way," Lampoon, LVIII (December 7, 1909), 146; "Editorial," Monthly, XLIX (January 1910), 177; "Editorial," Lampoon, LVIII (November 5, 1909), 72; "Editorial," Lampoon, LVIII (October 20, 1909), 46–7.

36 Monthly, L (March 1910), 36–7.

37 Lampoon, LVIII (December 7, 1909), 145.

38 "The Charge of the Political Brigade," unpublished, JR MSS.

39 Diana's Debut (Cambridge: privately printed, 1910).

40 Quoted in Hicks, John Reed, 50.

41 "The Novel of Romance and Honor During the Eighteenth Century," unpublished, JR MSS; "The Sea Gull," Harvard Advocate, LXXXVI (October 16, 1908), 29; "Coyote Song," Monthly, XLVII (October 1908), 40–1.

42 "L'Aurore—To Amy Stone."

43 Along with "The Red Hand" and "The Winged Stone," both already cited, see the following: "In England's Need," Monthly, XLIX (January and February 1910), 161–70, 191–9; "The Singing Gates," Monthly, XLVII (February 1909), 247–50; "Bacchanal," Monthly, XLIV (June 1907), 210–12; "The Pharaoh," Monthly, XLVII (January 1909), 156–60; "The Lady of the Lake," unpublished, and "Story About Kubac," unpublished fragment, both JR MSS.

44 JR, "The Lure of the Life Disperse," unpublished, JR MSS.

45 "Editorial," Lampoon, LVII (March 18, 1919), 40–1; "By the Way," ibid. (June 24, 1909), 12–14.

5 EUROPE

1 JR to Alan Gregg, November 23, 1910, JR MSS.

2 Ibid.

3. Ibid.

4 JR to Lincoln Steffens, July 3, 1910, JR MSS.

5 All quotations about the cattle-boat trip are from an untitled, unpublished essay in JR MSS. A fictionalized version of the voyage, written in collaboration with Julian Street and entitled "Overboard," ap-

peared in the *Saturday Evening Post*, CLXXXIV (October 28, 1911), 15 ff.

6 JR to Bob Hallowell, July 2, 1910, JR MSS.

7 JR to C. J. Reed, August 3, 1910, Reed Family MSS.

8 JR to Harry Reed, July 29, and C. J. Reed, August 3, 1910, Reed Family MSS.

9 JR to C. J. Reed, August 15, 1910, Reed Family MSS.

10 JR to Joseph Fels, August 17, 1910, JR MSS.

11 JR to Margaret Reed, August 21, 1910, Reed Family MSS.

12 All Grez quotes from JR to C. J. Reed, n.d., Reed Family MSS.

13 All Spain quotes from "A Dash into Spain," a 54-page unpublished essay in JR MSS.

14 JR to Bob Hallowell, September 1910, JR MSS.

15 JR to Alan Gregg, November 6, Eddy Hunt, October 21, and Bob Hallowell, September 30, 1910, all JR MSS.

16 JR to Bob Hallowell, September 30, 1910, JR MSS.

17 JR to Margaret Reed, October 9, 1910, Reed Family MSS.

18 JR, "Letter from Paris," *Boston Advertiser*, March 13, 1911.

19 JR to Harry Reed, October 15, 1910, JR MSS.

20 JR to Alan Gregg, November 23, 1910, JR MSS.

21 *Ibid.*

22 *Ibid.*, and November 28, 1910, JR MSS.

23 JR to Harry Reed, October 15, 1910, JR MSS.

24 JR to Margaret Reed, October 14, 1910, Reed Family MSS.

25 JR to Margaret Reed, January 8, 9 and 10–11, and C. J. Reed, January 9, 1911, all Reed Family MSS.

26 JR to C. J. Reed, January 12, 1911, Reed Family MSS.

27 *Ibid.*, January 23, 1911, Reed Family MSS.

28 *Ibid.*, January 12, 1911, Reed Family MSS.

29 Quoted in Hicks, *John Reed*, 63.

6 MANHATTAN

1 "Almost Thirty." All subsequent unfootnoted quotations in the chapter are from this essay.

2 C. J. Reed to Steffens, March 21, 1911, Steffens MSS.

3 Quoted in Steffens, "John Reed," 181.

4 JR to Waldo Peirce, February 24, 1911, JR MSS.

5 JR to Steffens, February 23, 1911, Steffens MSS.

6 JR to Eddy Hunt, July 27, 1911, JR MSS.

7 Ida Tarbell interview with Gran-ville Hicks, October 31, 1934, Hicks MSS.

8 "The Quick Lunch," unpublished essay, JR MSS.

9 "Immigrants," *Collier's*, XLVII (May 20, 1911), 10.

10 JR to Waldo Peirce, July 17, 1911, JR MSS.

11 C. J. Reed to JR, July 10, 1911, JR MSS.

12 JR to Waldo Peirce, July 17, 1911, JR MSS.

13 JR, *The Day in Bohemia* (New York: printed for the author,

1913), 16. Descriptive quotes in the following three paragraphs are from the same work.

14 Steffens to JR, June 14, 1912, JR MSS.

15 "Essay," unpublished fragment, JR MSS.

16 JR to Waldo Peirce, July 17, 1911, JR MSS.

17 Charles T. Copeland to JR, May 6 and October 18, 1911, and February 21, 1912, all JR MSS.

18 Robert Benchley to JR, February 3, 1912, JR MSS.

19 Margaret Reed to JR, n.d., JR MSS.

20 C. J. Reed to JR, March 2, 1912, JR MSS.

21 Carl Chadwick to JR, n.d., JR MSS.

22 Thomas Beer, "Playboy," *American Mercury* XXXII (June 1934), 180–1.

23 JR to Eddy Hunt, July 20, 1911, and February 29, 1912, JR MSS.

24 *American Magazine*, LXXV (February 1913), frontispiece. Reprinted in *The Day in Bohemia*, 34, and in *Tamburlaine* (Riverside, Conn.: Frederick C. Bursch, 1917), 16.

25 "The Foundations of a Sky-Scraper," *American Magazine*, LXXIII (October 1911), 735. Reprinted in *Tamburlaine*, 17.

26 "Sangar," *Poetry*, I (December 1912), 71–4. Reprinted in *Tamburlaine*, 11–13, and printed as a separate booklet (Riverside, Conn.: Frederick C. Bursch, 1913).

27 Gilman Hall to JR, June 12, 1912, JR MSS.

28 "Back to the Land," unpublished story, JR MSS.

29 JR to Bob Hallowell, March 19, 1912, JR MSS.

30 JR to Eddy Hunt, February 29, 1912, JR MSS.

31 *Ibid.*, April 1, 1912, JR MSS.

32 *Ibid.*, May 29, 1912, JR MSS.

33 "Art for Art's Sake," May 1912, JR MSS.

34 JR to Eddy Hunt, July 12, 1912, and to Bob Hallowell, July 15, 1912, both JR MSS.

35 *Ibid.*

36 JR to Robert Andrews, October 17, 1912, JR MSS.

37 Quotation from an earlier letter, Margaret Reed to JR, May 16, 1911, JR MSS. The sentiment was continual for her.

38 *International*, V (January 1912), 28.

39 "Article on New York," October 1912, JR MSS.

40 "Essays," unpublished fragment, JR MSS.

41 JR to Harriet Monroe, September 11, 1912, in *Poetry*, XVII (January 1921), 209.

42 JR to Robert Andrews, October 17, 1912, JR MSS.

7 GREENWICH VILLAGE

1 Untitled manifesto, JR MSS.

2 Malcolm Cowley, *Exile's Return* (New York: Viking Press, 1951), 55.

3 Quoted in Albert Parry, *Garrets and Pretenders* (New York: Dover, 1966), 26.

4 Quoted in Joseph Freeman, *An American Testament* (New York: Farrar and Rinehart, 1936), 266.

5 Cowley, *Exile's Return*, 47.

6 "The Dinner Guests of Big Time," *American Magazine*, LXXV (December 1912), 101–4.

7 William Rose Benét to JR, November 8, 1912, JR MSS.

8 Harriet Monroe to JR, September 28, 1912, JR MSS.

9 JR to Percy MacKaye, December 21, 1912, JR MSS.

10 Steffens to JR, October 27, 1912, JR MSS.

11 Max Eastman, *Enjoyment of Living* (New York: Harper and Brothers, 1948), 406.

12 Art Young, *Art Young: His Life and Times* (New York: Sheridan House, 1939), 276.

13 Eastman, *Enjoyment of Living*, 398–9.

14 *Ibid.*, 406–7.

15 *Ibid.*, and Max Eastman to JR, December 2, 1912, JR, MSS.

16 Eastman, *Enjoyment of Living*, 420–1.

17 Louis Untermeyer, *From Another World* (New York: Harcourt, Brace, 1939), 57–61.

18 Art Young, *On My Way* (New York: Liveright, 1928), 278.

19 Untermeyer, *From Another World*, 58, and *Bygones*, 33.

20 Young, *On My Way*, 281.

21 "Almost Thirty."

22 Quotations from Barbara Rose, *American Art Since 1900* (New York: Frederick A. Praeger, 1967), 67–77.

23 "Article Against Uplift," unpublished; letter to the New York *Times*, January 27 (1913?); and unpublished fragments, all JR MSS.

24 Julian Street to JR, February 21, 1913, JR MSS.

25 "Century, Scribner's and Harper's," "Outlook" and "The Freedom of the Press," all from *Everymagazine, An Immorality Play* (New York: privately printed, 1913).

26 JR to Eddy Hunt, March 10, 1913, and to Sam McCoy, April 17, 1913, both JR MSS.

27 Sara Teasdale to JR, March 20, 1913, JR MSS.

8 PATERSON

1 JR, "A Taste of Justice," *Masses*, IV (April 1913), 8. Reprinted in Floyd Dell, ed., *Daughter of the Revolution* (New York: Vanguard Press, 1927), and William L. O'Neill, *Echoes of Revolt: The Masses, 1911–1917* (Chicago: Quadrangle, 1966).

2 "War in Paterson," *Masses*, IV (June 1913), 14, 16–17. Reprinted in O'Neill, *Echoes of Revolt*, and John Stuart, ed., *The Education of John Reed* (New York: International, 1955). Quotations about Paterson strike without footnotes are from the same article.

3 New York *Evening Sun*, April 28, 1913. New York *Times*, April 29, 1913, has an accurate report of the arrest and trial.

4 JR to Eddy Hunt, n.d. There are several such notes, all undated, in the JR MSS.

5 *Ibid.*, and Harry Kemp, "To Jack Reed," JR MSS.

6 Eddy Hunt to JR, n.d., and JR to Hunt, n.d., both JR MSS.

7 Robert Rogers to Eddy Hunt, n.d., JR MSS.

8 "War in Paterson." A further view

of his jail experience can be found in "Sheriff Radcliffe's Hotel," *Metropolitan*, XXXVIII (September 1913), 14–16, 59–60.

9 "Almost Thirty." Subsequent unfootnoted quotations in the chapter are from this essay.

10 Quotations all from two unsigned letters of June 9 and 12, 1913, in JR MSS. Internal evidence indicates Eddy Hunt as the probable author. They are lengthy documents describing in detail the workings and problems of the pageant committee and the difficulties of staging.

11 Quoted in New York *Times*, June 8, 1913.

12 Quoted in Mabel Dodge Luhan, *Movers and Shakers* (New York: Harcourt, Brace, 1936), 205–10.

13 Hutchins Hapgood, *A Victorian in the Modern World* (New York: Harcourt, Brace, 1939), 351.

14 New York *Times*, June 9, 1913.

15 Elizabeth Gurley Flynn, *I Speak My Own Piece* (New York: Masses and Mainstream, 1955), 156. See also her speech, "The Truth About the Paterson Strike," in Joyce Kornbluh, ed., *Rebel Voices: An I.W.W. Anthology* (Ann Arbor, Mich.: University of Michigan Press, 1964), 212.

16 H. K. Moderwell and Sam Eliot to JR, July 14, 1913, JR MSS. Emphasis added.

17 JR to Margaret Reed, June 18, 1913, Reed Family MSS.

18 *Ibid.*

19 "War in Paterson."

9 23 FIFTH AVENUE

1 "Story About Celia," unpublished fragment, JR MSS.

2 Fragment of a play, quoted in Luhan, *Movers and Shakers*, 224.

3 Hapgood, *A Victorian in the Modern World*, 351.

4 Luhan, *Movers and Shakers*, 36.

5 *The Autobiography of Lincoln Steffens* (New York: Harcourt, Brace, 1931), 655.

6 Luhan, *Movers and Shakers*, 92; Carl Van Vechten, *Peter Whiffle* (New York: Alfred A. Knopf, 1922), 124.

7 Hapgood, *A Victorian in the Modern World*, 349.

8 Luhan, *Movers and Shakers*, 215–16.

9 JR to Margaret Reed, June 18, 1913, Reed Family MSS.

10 JR to Eddy Hunt, June 27, 1913, JR MSS.

11 *Ibid.*, and JR to Fred Bursch, June 27, 1913, JR MSS.

12 Luhan, *Movers and Shakers*, 212–13.

13 Quoted in *ibid.*, 215. A slightly different version was printed in the *Masses*, VIII (May 1916), 10, reprinted in *Tamburlaine*, 21, and appears in O'Neill, ed., *Echoes of Revolt*, 88.

14 Luhan, *Movers and Shakers*, 215–16.

15 *Ibid.*, 216–17.

16 Gertrude Stein, *The Autobiography of Alice B. Toklas* (New York: Random House, 1960), 134–5.

17 JR to Margaret Reed, July 12, 1913, Reed Family MSS.

18 JR to Eddy Hunt, July 20, 1913, JR MSS.

19 JR to Margaret Reed, August 1,

1913, Reed Family MSS.

20 JR to Eddy Hunt, n.d., JR MSS.

21 Muriel Draper, *Music at Midnight* (New York: Harper and Brothers, 1929), 121, 123.

22 JR to Eddy Hunt, July 20, 1913, JR MSS.

23 JR to Eddy Hunt, n.d., to Bob Hallowell, August 14, 1913, both JR MSS; and to Margaret Reed, August 1, 1913, Reed Family MSS.

24 Quoted in Luhan, *Movers and Shakers*, 218.

25 *Ibid.*, 217–18.

26 *Ibid.*, 219.

27 Quoted in *ibid.*, 227–8.

28 JR to Albert J. Nock, August 25, 1913, JR MSS.

29 Luhan, *Movers and Shakers*, 229.

30 Mayer, *A Preface to Life*, 95.

31 Floyd Dell, *Homecoming: An Autobiography* (New York: Farrar and Rinehart, 1933), 247.

32 Lawrence Langner, *The Magic Curtain* (New York: E. P. Dutton, 1951), 69.

33 Luhan, *Movers and Shakers*, 234.

34 *Ibid.*, 232.

35 *Ibid.*, 233–4.

36 *Ibid.*, 242.

37 Quoted in Hapgood, *A Victorian in the Modern World*, 353.

38 Quoted in Luhan, *Movers and Shakers*, 242.

39 Bobby Rogers to JR, June 13, 1913, JR MSS.

40 Lincoln Steffens to JR, November 23 and 25, 1913, JR MSS.

10 MEXICO

1 JR, *Insurgent Mexico* (New York: D. Appleton., 1914), 35–6.

2 Luhan, *Movers and Shakers*, 246.

3 JR to Eddy Hunt, December 16, 1913, JR MSS.

4 "El Paso," unpublished article, JR MSS.

5 This and all following quotations about Presidio and Ojinaga from *Insurgent Mexico*, 1–9. Entitled "Endymion, or On the Border," this chapter appeared in the *Masses*, IX (December 1916), 5, 6, 8, and in Dell, ed., *Daughter of the Revolution*, 51–63.

6 "Almost Thirty."

7 JR, "With Villa in Mexico," *Metropolitan*, XXXIX (February 1914), 72. This is not an article, but a publication of two personal Reed letters of December 21 and 26, 1913, probably written to Hunt.

8 *Ibid.*

9 Quotations about Villa from JR, "Mexican Notebook," JR MSS. Much of the material in these jumbled, often chaotic notes entered the pages of *Insurgent Mexico*, sometimes with little change in phrasing.

10 *Insurgent Mexico*, 122.

11 *Ibid.*, 131–3.

12 *Ibid.*, 146.

13 "Mexican Notebook."

14 JR, "Mac—American," *Masses*, V (April 1914), 8–9. Reprinted in Dell, ed., *Daughter of the Revolution*, 41–50.

15 *Insurgent Mexico*, 152–3.

16 *Ibid.*, 153, 160, and "Mexican Notebook."

17 "Mexican Notebook."

18 The period with La Tropa is covered in *Insurgent Mexico*, 13–111; all quotations on the next few pages are taken from that section

unless otherwise designated.

19 "Almost Thirty."

20 *Ibid.*

21 "El Paso"; JR to Carl Hovey, February 10, 1914, Gold Archive.

22 *Ibid.*

23 Both telegrams JR MSS.

24 JR to Carl Hovey, February 17, 1914, Gold Archive.

25 *Ibid.*

26 JR to Carl Hovey, February 10, 1914, Gold Archive.

27 "In Short," unpublished article, JR MSS; "What About Mexico?," *Masses*, V (June 1914), 11, 14; *Insurgent Mexico*, 40.

28 *Insurgent Mexico*, 263–79; New York *World*, March 4, 1914, 1–2.

29 *Insurgent Mexico*, 190. The assault on Torreón covers 175–261.

30 Walter Lippmann to JR, March 25, 1914, JR MSS.

31 *Ibid.*, and Dave Carb to JR, March 21, 1914, JR MSS.

32 Lippmann, "Legendary John Reed," 15.

33 "Mexican Notebook."

34 "Almost Thirty."

11 LUDLOW

1 Quoted in Luhan, *Movers and Shakers*, 280–2.

2 *Ibid.*, 257.

3 Quoted in Hicks, *John Reed*, 142.

4 Jane Addams to Louise Bryant, July 27, 1932, JR MSS.

5 JR, "Bryan on the Ocklawaha," unpublished article, JR MSS. A later version of this article appeared as "Bryan on Tour," *Collier's*, LVII (May 20, 1916), 11–12, 40–1, 44–7, but this version excluded the scenes of Reed's first meeting with Bryan in his Washington home.

6 Quotations here and in following two paragraphs from "Presidential Interview," unpublished article, JR MSS, unless otherwise noted.

7 JR to Upton Sinclair, June 18, 1914, Upton Sinclair Papers, Lilly Library, Indiana University.

8 Woodrow Wilson to JR, June 17, 1914, JR MSS.

9 Joseph Tumulty to JR, June 29, 1914, JR MSS.

10 *Insurgent Mexico*, dedication.

11 Quoted in Luhan, *Movers and Shakers*, 261.

12 *Ibid.*, 263.

13 Quoted in *ibid.*, 256.

14 *Ibid.*, 261.

15 Quoted in *ibid.*, 259–60.

16 "Almost Thirty."

12 WESTERN FRONT

1 "Rule Britannia," unpublished article, JR MSS. The quotation is from an early version of the article, evidently a false start that Reed discarded in the final draft, also unpublished.

2 Harriet Monroe, *A Poet's Life* (New York: Macmillan, 1938), 341.

3 "The Englishman: A War Correspondent's Wondering Observation," *Metropolitan*, XL (October 1914), 39–40. Reprinted in Dell, ed., *Daughter of the Revolution*.

4 JR to Carl Hovey, August 15, 1914, Gold Archive.

5 William Jennings Bryan to United

States Diplomatic and Consular Officers in Europe, August 12, 1914, JR MSS.

6 JR, "The Traders' War," *Masses*, V (September 1914), 16–17.

7 Quotations in this and following two paragraphs from JR, "The Approach to War," *Metropolitan*, XLI (November 1914), 15–16, 65–9.

8 Untitled, unpublished article, datelined Paris, September 18, JR MSS.

9 *Ibid.*

10 *Ibid.*, and JR, "With the Allies," *Metropolitan*, XLI (December 1914), 14–16.

11 Untitled, unpublished article, datelined Paris, September 18, and JR, "With the Allies." Quotations in succeeding four paragraphs also taken from these sources.

12 Untitled, unpublished article, datelined Paris, September 22, JR MSS.

13 JR to Carl Hovey, September 25, 1914, JR MSS. The confused mass of material remains in the JR MSS as the two articles datelined Paris, September 18 and 22.

14 Quotations in this and succeeding five paragraphs from "Rule Britannia." See also "Notes on the War,"

Masses, VI (November 1914), 14.

15 "With the Allies," 14.

16 Quoted in Luhan, *Movers and Shakers*, 299.

17 Lincoln Steffens to JR, November 19, 1914, JR MSS.

18 JR to Carl Hovey, October 11 and November 15, 1914, Gold Archive.

19 *Ibid.*, December 1 and December 4, 1914, Gold Archive.

20 JR, "Karl Liebknecht's Words," *Revolutionary Age*, I (February 1, 1919).

21 Quoted in Robert Dunn, *World Alive* (New York: Crown, 1956), 214.

22 Quotations here and in the remainder of the chapter, unless otherwise noted, are from JR, "German France," *Metropolitan*, XLI (March 1915), 13–14, 81–2, and "In the German Trenches," *ibid.* (April 1915), 7–10, 70–1.

23 Robert Dunn, *Five Fronts* (New York: Dodd, Mead, 1915), 186.

24 Quoted in Hutchins Hapgood to Max Eastman, January 14, 1942, Max Eastman Papers, Lilly Library, Indiana University.

25 "Almost Thirty."

13 NEW YORK

1 Quoted in Luhan, *Movers and Shakers*, 358, 384–5. Reprinted in *Tamburlaine*, 18–20.

2 Luhan, *Movers and Shakers*, 303.

3 *Ibid.*, 356.

4 *The Day in Bohemia*, 42.

5 Lippmann, "Legendary John Reed," 15–16.

6 "Back of Billy Sunday," *Metropolitan*, XLII (May 1915), 9–12, 63–6.

7 Quoted in Hicks, *John Reed*, 177.

8 *Ibid.*, 178.

9 Quoted in *ibid.*, 178–9. See also William Hard to Granville Hicks, n.d., and Boardman Robinson to John Stuart, n.d., both in Hicks MSS.

10 "The Worst Thing in Europe," *Masses*, VII (March 1915), 17–18. Reprinted in O'Neill, ed., *Echoes of Revolt*, 259.

11 New York *Post*, February 27, 1915.

12 Quoted in Boardman Robinson to John Stuart, n.d., Hicks MSS. Robinson was present at the encounters with Jusserand and Roosevelt.

13 Charles T. Copeland to JR, April 28, 1914, and February 7, 1915, both in JR MSS.

14 Luhan, *Movers and Shakers*, 357.

15 JR to Margaret Reed, April 4, 1915, Reed Family MSS.

16 *Ibid.*

17 Quoted in Luhan, *Movers and Shakers*, 385.

14 EASTERN EUROPE

1 JR to Charles T. Copeland, August 8, 1915, quoted in Adams, *Copey of Harvard*, 212–14.

2 JR, *The War in Eastern Europe* (New York: Charles Scribner's Sons, 1916), ix.

3 JR to Carl Hovey, April 14, 1915, Gold Archive.

4 *The War in Eastern Europe*, 7–8.

5 *Ibid.*, 15.

6 *Ibid.*, 49.

7 *Ibid.*, 83.

8 *Ibid.*, 98. Another description of Goutchevo by Reed appeared as one of several articles by journalists under the general heading "The Most Tragic Incident I Saw in the War," New York *World*, April 22, 1917 (Sunday Section), 1.

9 *Ibid.*, 81–3.

10 JR, "The World Well Lost," *Masses*, VIII (February 1916), 5–6. Reprinted in Dell, ed., *Daughter of the Revolution*, 23–8.

11 Quoted in Louise Bryant, unpublished autobiographical sketch, Hicks MSS.

12 JR to Carl Hovey, May 17 and 22, 1915, Gold Archive; and May 24, 1915, quoted in Luhan, *Movers and Shakers*, 380.

13 *The War in Eastern Europe*, 111–13.

14 *Ibid.*, 117, 120.

15 *Ibid.*, 150.

16 *Ibid.*, 159.

17 *Ibid.*, 177.

18 JR to Carl Hovey, July 4, 1915, Gold Archive. A typewritten copy of this originally handwritten letter is in the JR MSS.

19 Quoted in *The War in Eastern Europe*, 196.

20 Quoted in Luhan, *Movers and Shakers*, 385.

21 *The War in Eastern Europe*, 198.

22 JR to Carl Hovey, July 4, 1915, Gold Archive.

23 *The War in Eastern Europe*, 241.

24 Quoted in Negley Farson, *Way of a Transgressor* (New York: Literary Guild, 1936), 186.

25 *The War in Eastern Europe*, 205.

26 JR to Sally Robinson, August 1, 1915, Gold Archive.

27 JR to Carl Hovey, August 16 and 25, 1915, Gold Archive.

28 *The War in Eastern Europe*, 310–11.

29 Quoted in Hicks, *John Reed*, 197–8.

30 JR to Fred Bursch, June 14, 1915, JR MSS.

31 *The War in Eastern Europe*, 208–11.

32 *Ibid.*, 232.

15 PROVINCETOWN

1 JR, "Fog," *Scribner's*, LXVI (August 1919), 228. Reprinted in the *Liberator*, III (December 1920), 4, and Stuart, ed., *The Education of John Reed*, 222.

2 Quoted in Luhan, *Movers and Shakers*, 383.

3 *Ibid.*, 418.

4 JR to Sally Robinson, December 5, 1915, JR MSS.

5 *Ibid.*, December 18, 1915, JR MSS.

6 Louise Bryant, unpublished autobiographical sketch, Hicks MSS.

7 JR to Sally Robinson, December 18, 1915, JR MSS.

8 JR to Louise Bryant, June 5, 1917; Louise Bryant to JR, June 23, 1917, and December 29, 1915, all JR MSS.

9 JR to Louise Bryant, February 10 and 16, 1916, JR MSS.

10 JR, "Bryan on Tour," *Collier's*, LVII (May 20, 1916), 47.

11 JR, untitled, unpublished article, JR MSS.

12 "The Legendary Villa," *Masses*, IX (May 1917), 32.

13 New York *American*, March 13, 1916. See the same newspaper, April 16, 1916, for a similar article.

14 "At the Throat of the Republic," *Masses*, VIII (July 1916), 7–8, 10–12, 24.

15 JR to Ben Huebsch, quoted in *Memoir of Ben Huebsch*, The Oral History Collection of Columbia University, 316–21.

16 Robert Rogers to JR, January 11, 1916, JR MSS. See also letter of February 15, 1916, for similar sentiments.

17 Orrick Johns, *Time of Our Lives: The Story of My Father and Myself* (New York: Stackpole Sons, 1937), 236.

18 JR, "Roosevelt Sold Them Out," *Masses*, VIII (August 1916), 19–20, 26. Reprinted in O'Neill, ed., *Echoes of Revolt*, 138–9, and Stuart, ed., *The Education of John Reed*, 159–65.

19 JR to Amos Pinchot, July 14, 1916, Amos Pinchot Papers, Library of Congress (hereafter referred to as Pinchot MSS).

20 Louise Bryant to JR, June 8, 1916; JR to Louise Bryant, June 18, 1916, both JR MSS.

21 John N. Wheeler to JR, June 26, 1916, and Carl Hovey to JR, June 28, 1916, both JR MSS.

22 Quoted in Susan Glaspell, *The Road to the Temple* (New York: Frederick A. Stokes, 1927), 252.

23 *Ibid.*, 250.

24 Quotation from Louis Sheaffer, *O'Neill: Son and Playwright* (Boston: Little, Brown, 1968), 346.

25 *The Road to the Temple*, 254.

26 JR to Amos Pinchot, August 9, 1916, Pinchot MSS.

27 *The Road to the Temple*, 256.

28 JR to Carl Hovey, September 7, 1916, Gold Archive.

29 JR to Eddy Hunt, August 25, 1916, JR MSS.

30 Quoted in Sheaffer, *O'Neill*, 358–9.

31 JR to Amos Pinchot, September 22, 1916, Pinchot MSS.

32 JR, "An Heroic Pacifist," *Masses*, IX (November 1916), 10.

33 JR to Socialist Party, October 13, 1916, Socialist Party Collection, Duke University Library.

34 Louise Bryant to JR, December 9, 1916, JR MSS.

35 "A Dedication: To Max Eastman," *Tamburlaine*, 14.

16 CROTON

1 "Almost Thirty." All subsequent unfootnoted quotations in this chapter are from the same essay.

2 JR to Louise Bryant, November 13 and 29, 1916, both JR MSS.

3 Louise Bryant to JR; three notes written Thanksgiving Day, Sunday a.m., and n.d., all JR MSS.

4 JR to Louise Bryant, Sunday a.m. (December 1916), JR MSS.

5 Louise Bryant to JR, December 2 and 9, 1916, both JR MSS.

6 "Greenwich Village," *Dial*, LVII (October 1, 1914), 239–41; "Disillusioned by Bohemia," *Literary Digest*, LIII (September 16, 1916), 688–93.

7 Anna Alice Chapin, *Greenwich Village* (New York: Dodd, Mead, 1917), 211–13.

8 Dell, *Homecoming*, 324.

9 Louise Bryant to JR, December 9, 1916, JR MSS.

10 Carl Hovey to JR, February 5, 1917, JR MSS.

11 Quoted in Julian Street, "A Soviet Saint: The Story of John Reed," *Saturday Evening Post*, CCIII (September 13, 1930), 8–9, 65–8.

12 "Whose War?" *Masses*, IX (April 1917), 11–12.

13 Quoted in Hicks, *John Reed*, 233.

14 United States House of Representatives, Committee on Military Affairs, *Hearings on Volunteer and Conscription System*, 65th Cong., 1st Sess., April 7–17, 1917 (Washington: Government Printing Office, 1917), 31–3.

15 Quoted in James Weinstein, *The Decline of Socialism in America 1912–1925* (New York: Vintage Books, 1969), 125.

16 Margaret Reed to JR, April 5, 1917, JR MSS.

17 Harry Reed to JR, Tuesday, n.d. (1916), JR MSS.

18 New York *Mail*, May 25 and June 1, 1917.

19 *Ibid.*, June 13, 1917. See also issue of June 7.

20 Quoted in Louise Bryant, autobiographical essay, Hicks MSS.

21 Louise Bryant to JR, June 9, 1917, and JR to Louise Bryant, June 11, 1917, both JR MSS.

22 JR to Louise Bryant, July 10 and 15, 1917, both JR MSS.

23 *Ibid.*, June 25 and July 4, 1917, JR MSS.

24 Louise Bryant to JR, July, n.d., 2, 5, and June 24, 1917, all JR MSS.

25 JR to Louise Bryant, July 5, 1917, JR MSS.

26 *Ibid.*, July 7 and 18, 1917, both JR MSS.

27 Louise Bryant to JR, July 17, 1917, JR MSS.

28 JR to Louise Bryant, July 15, 1917, JR MSS.

29 Robert Minor to JR, May 31, 1917, JR MSS.

30 "Self-Denial Among the Upper Classes," *Masses*, IX (July 1917), 29; "Militarism at Play," *ibid.* (August 1917), 18–19.

31 "One Solid Month of Liberty," *ibid.* (September 1917), 5–6.

32 Louise Bryant to JR, July 4, 1917, JR MSS.

33 "This Unpopular War," *Seven Arts*, I (August 1917), 397–408.

Reprinted in Stuart, ed., *The Education of John Reed*, 166–74.

34 JR to Louise Bryant, July 18, 1917, JR MSS.

17 PETROGRAD

1 JR, "Introduction," unpublished, dated Christiania, March 18, 1918, JR MSS. This is a first attempt to begin a book on the revolution; none of the material included appeared in *Ten Days That Shook the World* (New York: Boni and Liveright, 1919), written almost a year later. Quotations in the succeeding four paragraphs from the same source.

2 "Fall of the Russian Bastille," New York *Tribune*, March 25, 1917.

3 "The Russian Peace," *Masses*, IX (July 1917), 35; "Too Much Democracy," *ibid.* (June 1917), 21.

4 "News from France," *ibid.* (October 1917), 5–6, 8.

5 "A Letter from John Reed," *ibid.*, X (November–December 1917), 14–15.

6 "Scandinavia in Wartime," unpublished article dated September 7, 1917, JR MSS.

7 "Red Russia—Entrance," unpublished article, JR MSS. Quotations in the next two paragraphs from the same source.

8 JR to Boardman Robinson, September 17, 1917, JR MSS.

9 JR to Sally (Robinson?), September 17, 1917, JR MSS.

10 Albert Rhys Williams, *Journey into Revolution: Petrograd, 1917–1918* (Chicago: Quadrangle, 1969), 53.

11 *Ibid.*, 36.

12 *Ibid.*, 35.

13 *Ibid.*, 41–2.

14 Quoted in David R. Francis, *Russia from the American Embassy* (New York: Charles Scribner's Sons, 1921), 166.

15 David R. Francis to the Secretary of State, October 1, 1917, David R. Francis Papers, Missouri Historical Society, St. Louis, Missouri.

16 Quoted in Francis, *Russia from the American Embassy*, 169.

17 "A Visit to the Russian Army," *Liberator*, I (May 1918), 28–34.

18 JR to Boardman Robinson, October 16, 1917, JR MSS.

19 Quoted in *Ten Days That Shook the World*, 7.

20 "Red Russia—Kerensky," *Liberator*, I (April 1918), 18–19.

21 Quoted in *Ten Days That Shook the World*, 29–30.

22 Quoted in Williams, *Journey into Revolution*, 59.

23 Quoted in *Ten Days That Shook the World*, 51.

24 *Ibid.*, 62.

25 *Ibid.*, 74.

26 *Ibid.*, 111.

27 *Ibid.*, 125–6.

28 *Ibid.*, 162.

29 *Ibid.*, 182–3.

30 "Red Russia—The Triumph of the Bolsheviki," *Liberator*, I (March 1918), 14–21.

18 CHRISTIANIA

1 "America, 1918," *New Masses*,
XVII (October 15, 1935), 17–20.
The original version remains in the
JR MSS; it is almost identical with
the published one. Quotations
in the next few paragraphs are
from the same work.

2 *Ten Days That Shook the World*,
246.

3 *Ibid.*, 255.

4 "Russian Notebooks," unpublished
fragments of the small notebooks
he carried in Russia, JR MSS.

5 *Ten Days That Shook the World*,
259.

6 *Ibid.*, 313.

7 JR, "Foreign Affairs," *Liberator*, I
(June 1918), 28.

8 Albert Rhys Williams to Granville
Hicks, n.d., Hicks MSS.

9 Quoted in Williams, *Journey into
Revolution*, 223.

10 *Ibid.*, 204.

11 JR to Raymond Robins, January
11, 1918, Raymond Robins Papers,
State Historical Society of Wisconsin, Madison, Wisconsin (hereafter referred to as Robins MSS).

12 Quoted in Williams, *Journey into
Revolution*, 224.

13 "Skeleton Report," unpublished,
JR MSS. Another copy is in
Robins MSS.

14 Untitled, unpublished poem, dated
"Christmas," JR MSS.

15 "Russian Notebooks," JR MSS.

16 "The Constituent Assembly in
Russia," *Revolutionary Age*, I
(November 11, 1918), 6–7.

17 Quotations from *Izvestia*, January
11 (old style), 1918. Translations

of the speech appear in Edgar
Sisson, *One Hundred Red Days*
(New Haven: Yale University
Press, 1931), 257–8, and in David
R. Francis MSS.

18 JR to Raymond Robins, January
11, 1918, Robins MSS.

19 Handwritten note signed JBW in
State Department files, labeled
"Important." Department of State,
Records of the Foreign Service
Posts, United States Embassy,
Russia, 1918, File 800, National
Archives.

20 Quoted in Arno Dosch-Fleurot,
"World Man Tells of Reed in
Russia," New York *World*, October 19, 1920, 8. In his later autobiographical work, *Through War to
Revolution* (London: John Lane,
1931), 194, Dosch-Fleurot gave the
quote slightly differently, but the
sense was the same.

21 Quoted in Williams, *Journey into
Revolution*, 220–1.

22 George N. Ifft to the Secretary of
State, February 20, 1918; Depart-
ment of State (Record Group 59),
File 360d. 1121 R25/9, National
Archives.

23 JR to American Minister to Norway, March 24, 1918, Department
of State (Record Group 59), File
360d. 1121 R25/13, National
Archives.

24 Edgar Sisson to George Creel,
April 24, 1918, Department of State
(Record Group 59), File 360d.
1121 R25/20, National Archives.

25 Transcript of the examination for-
warded by Assistant Secretary of

the Treasury Department to Secretary of State, May 9, 1918, Department of State (Record Group 59), File 360d. 1121 R25/22, National Archives.

19 AMERICA

1 JR to Lincoln Steffens, June 9, 1918, Steffens MSS.

2 Lincoln Steffens to JR, June 17, 1918, JR MSS.

3 JR to Lincoln Steffens, June 29, 1918, Steffens MSS.

4 Quoted in John Higham, *Strangers in the Land: Patterns of American Nativism, 1860–1925* (New York: Atheneum, 1970), 212.

5 Max Eastman, *Love and Revolution* (New York: Random House, 1964), 61–3. The case is more fully covered in Zechariah Chafee, Jr., *Freedom of Speech* (New York: Harcourt, Brace, 1920), 46–56.

6 Eastman, *Love and Revolution*, 70.

7 Quoted in Young, *Art Young*, 330–1.

8 Quoted in Morris Hillquit, *Loose Leaves from a Busy Life* (New York: Macmillan, 1934), 222–3.

9 JR to William F. Sands, June 4, 1918; William Bullitt to JR, July 22, 1918, both JR MSS.

10 Unpublished, undated memorandum, JR MSS.

11 Marsden Hartley to JR, n.d., JR MSS.

12 "Recognize Russia," *Liberator*, I (July 1918), 18–20.

13 *New York Call*, May 2, 1918: "A Message to Our Readers from John Reed," *Liberator*, I (June 1918), 25–6.

14 JR to the New York *Call*, July 18, 1918, unpublished letter, Hicks MSS.

15 "With Gene Debs on the Fourth," *Liberator*, I (September 1918), 7–9. Reprinted in Stuart, ed., *The Education of John Reed*, 186–90.

16 "The Social Revolution in Court," *ibid.*, 20–8. Quotations in the following paragraph are from the same article.

17 JR to Lincoln Steffens, June 29, 1918, Steffens MSS.

18 Eastman, *Heroes I Have Known*, 221.

19 Both letters in the *Liberator*, I (September 1918), 34.

20 William D. Haywood to JR, September 1, 1918, JR MSS.

21 *USA vs. John Reed*, United States District Court, Southern District of New York, Criminal Docket 15–11.

22 *The Sisson Documents* (New York: Liberator Publishing Company, 1918), 1.

23 Unpublished notes, JR MSS.

24 Quotations from Charles Recht, unpublished autobiography, Hicks MSS. Recht was one of the defense attorneys.

25 "About the Second Masses Trial," *Liberator*, I (December 1918), 36–8.

26 Transcript of Testimony of John Reed, *USA vs. The Masses Publishing Company, et al.*, October 3, 1918, United States District Court, Southern District of New York, Hicks MSS.

27 "About the Second Masses Trial."

28 Quoted in Dell, *Homecoming*, 328.

29 "The White Terror in New York," galley proofs of an article for the *Liberator* that never appeared, JR MSS; and JR, "A White New Year," *Revolutionary Age*, I (January 4, 1919), 8.

30 Eastman, *Heroes I Have Known*, 223-4.

20 CHICAGO

1 "Bolshevism in America," *Revolutionary Age*, I (December 18, 1918), 3.

2 *Ibid.*, and "A New Appeal," *Revolutionary Age*, I (January 18, 1919), 8.

3 *Ibid.*

4 Quoted in Theodore Draper, *The Roots of American Communism* (New York: Viking Press, 1957), 139.

5 United States Senate, *Brewing and Liquor Interests and German and Bolshevik Propaganda: Report and Hearings of the Subcommittee on the Judiciary*, 66th Cong., 1st Sess. (Washington: Government Printing Office, 1919). Testimony by Louise Bryant, 465-561, and John Reed, 561-601. All quotations in next two paragraphs from the same source unless otherwise noted.

6 Stanley Frost, "John Reed—Revolution as a Sport," New York *Tribune*, March 27, 1919.

7 "One Man Who Needs the Rope," Jacksonville *Times-Union*, February 24, 1919, clipping in JR MSS.

8 New York *Times*, April 7, 1919.

9 Refused by the *Times*, the letter appeared as "On Bolshevism, Russian and American," *Revolutionary Age*, I (April 12, 1919), 6.

10 Margaret Reed to JR, March 11, 1919, JR MSS.

11 Harry Reed to JR, April 21, 1919, JR MSS.

12 Louise Bryant to JR, March 31 and April 4, 1919, JR MSS.

13 *Ibid.*, March 24, 1919, JR MSS.

14 Quoted in Eastman, *Heroes I Have Known*, 223.

15 Sherwood Anderson to E. H. Risley, in Howard Mumford Jones and Walter B. Rideout, eds., *The Letters of Sherwood Anderson* (Boston: Little, Brown, 1953), 395.

16 Lincoln Steffens, "A Letter About Jack Reed," *New Republic*, LXXXVII (May 20, 1936), 50. Reprinted in *Lincoln Steffens Speaking* (New York: Harcourt, Brace, 1938), 307-10.

17 "The Peace That Passeth Understanding," *Liberator*, I (March 1919), 25-31.

18 "Great Bolshevik Conspiracy," *Liberator*, I (February 1919), 32.

19 "Why Political Democracy Must Go," New York *Communist*, I (June 14, 1919), 4. The series appeared in weekly issues between May 8 and June 14, 1919.

20 "Aspects of the Russian Revolution," *Revolutionary Age*, II (July 12, 1919), 8-10. The last quotation in the paragraph is from the final section of an outline for the article in the JR MSS; evidently it was to have been part of a series discontinued when JR quit the publication's staff.

21 Quotations from reviews in the *Dial*, XLVI (March 22, 1919),

301–3, *New Republic*, XIX (May 31, 1919), 158–9, and the *Nation*, CVIII (May 2, 1919), 699.

22 Emma Goldman, *Living My Life* (New York: Alfred A. Knopf, 1931), II, 684; Ben H. Fletcher to JR, May 10, 1919, JR MSS.

23 Margaret Reed to JR, May 20, 1919, JR MSS.

24 The fake issue of the *Socialist* was dated May 17, 1919; the next issue of the real *Socialist* appeared on June 4, 1919.

25 "Article on Left Wing," unpublished, summer 1919, JR MSS.

26 Louise Bryant to editor of *Soviet Russia*, July 19, 1919, JR MSS.

27 Quoted in Glaspell, *The Road to the Temple*, 302.

28 Quoted in Benjamin Gitlow *The Whole of Their Lives* (New York: Charles Scribner's Sons, 1948), 27.

29 Eadmonn MacAlpine to Granville Hicks, December 26, 1934, Hicks MSS.

30 Quoted in Gitlow, *The Whole of Their Lives*, 24.

31 Quoted in Draper, *The Roots of American Communism*, 180.

32 JR to Louise Bryant, September 2, 1919, JR MSS.

33 Quoted in Flynn, *I Speak My Own Piece*, 271.

34 JR, "Communism in America," *Workers' Dreadnought*, VI (October 4, 1919), 3.

21 RUSSIA

1 Unpublished, incomplete story, dated November 3, 1919, JR MSS.

2 JR to Louise Bryant, October 21, 1919, JR MSS.

3 *Ibid.*, November 10, 1919, JR MSS.

4 "Soviet Russia Now—I," *Liberator*, III (December 1920), 9–12.

5 JR, "Russian Notebooks." As with those from 1917, fragments of his notebooks from 1919–20 remain in the JR MSS.

6 *Ibid.*

7 "Soviet Russia Now—II," *Liberator*, IV (January 1921), 14–17.

8 "Russian Notebooks," JR MSS.

9 Goldman, *Living My Life*, 739–40, and *My Disillusionment in Russia* (New York: Doubleday, Page, 1923), 15–16.

10 Quoted in "Copy of the minutes of the proceedings of the Abo Municipal Court, Second Section," an enclosure to Dispatch No. 22, July 2, 1920, from Chargé d'Affaires in Helsingfors to the Secretary of State in Washington. Department of State (Record Group 59), File 360d. 1121 R25/58, National Archives.

11 JR to Louise Bryant, May 13, 1920, JR MSS.

12 *Ibid.*, May 3, 1920.

13 Emma Goldman, *My Further Disillusionment in Russia* (New York: Doubleday, Page, 1924), 24.

14 "Soviet Russia Now—I."

15 "Soviet Russia Now—II."

16 JR to Louise Bryant, June 16, 23 and 29, 1920, JR MSS.

17 JR, "The World Congress of the Communist International," *Communist*, X. A typescript copy of this article, difficult to obtain in the original, is in the Hicks MSS.

18 O. W. Penney, "John Reed—One of Us," manuscript enclosed in a

letter from Penney to Granville Hicks, October 23, 1935, Hicks MSS.

19 "World Congress of the Communist International." Quotation in next paragraph is from the same source.

20 *The Second Congress of the Communist International: As Reported and Interpreted by the Official Newspapers of Soviet Russia* (Washington: Government Printing Office, 1920), 34.

21 Undated, unsigned note in JR MSS.

22 JR, "World Congress of the Communist International."

23 *Ibid.*

24 Lewis Corey to Granville Hicks, December 30, 1935, Hicks MSS.

25 JR to Louise Bryant, August 26, 1920, JR MSS.

26 Handwritten speech, JR MSS.

27 Quoted in Louise Bryant, "Last Days with John Reed," *Liberator*, IV (February 1921), 11–12.

28 *Ibid.*

29 Louise Bryant to Andrew Dasburg, August 5 (1920), Andrew Dasburg Papers, George Arents Research Library, Syracuse University.

30 Bryant, "Last Days with John Reed."

31 Margaret Reed to JR, June 16 (1920), JR MSS.

22 EVER-VICTORIOUS

1 "The Ever-Victorious," unpublished fragment, JR MSS.

2 "The Tides of Men," unpublished notes, JR MSS.

Bibliography

Since the preceding notes largely identify direct quotations, this section may serve as a guide to further sources for the life of John Reed. Because there already exist two bibliographies of his own writings (see below), I will not give a complete guide to his published work. Here I include those manuscript and printed sources which were most important to me. The sections on each chapter are not intended to be exhaustive lists of works about historical events or periods. Rather I include only writings which seem most relevant to my own interpretations.

MANUSCRIPT COLLECTIONS

The *John Reed Papers* at the Houghton Library, Harvard University, comprise some thirty boxes of material, much of it originally collected by his widow, Louise Bryant. Included are not only his personal papers, books, unpublished manuscripts, notebooks, scrapbooks, galley proofs, memorabilia and letters to him, but also many items given to Bryant by Reed's friends for a book about him that she was planning to write. Less extensive but equally important are the *Granville Hicks Papers* at the George Arents Research Library, Syracuse University. This collection includes material that Hicks collected for his biography of Reed in the mid-1930s. Along with many original manuscripts and documents are hundreds of letters from people who had known Reed (a few are addressed to John Stuart, who was originally working on a biography also, but then turned his information over to Hicks and was listed as an assistant) and notes from a number of interviews with his friends. Also in the collection is Louise Bryant's rambling autobiographical memoir of her life before and with Reed; written shortly before her death, it is the product of a wandering mind, alternately insightful and full of flights of fantasy. The *Reed Family Papers*, now in the possession of John Reed (a nephew) of Chevy Chase, Maryland, is another crucial source. Along with letters to members of the family are clippings, photos and pages torn from various publications that carry Reed's marginal comments. Some of them were evidently used by Hicks, then returned to Margaret Reed.

The following important sources were never tapped by Hicks: The *Archives of the Morristown School*, Morristown, New Jersey, contain a large number of letters from C. J. Reed to the headmaster; these provide excellent insight into John Reed as a teenager and into the relationship between father and son. The *Lee Gold Archive* at the Institute of Marxism-Leninism, Moscow, U.S.S.R., includes approximately one hundred pages (some twenty-five letters) from Reed to Carl Hovey, editor of the *Metropolitan*. Largely written on three trips abroad—Mexico in 1914, western Europe in 1914 and eastern Europe in 1915—they contain much personal news and are significant for showing his attitudes toward war, revolution and journalism. The *David R. Francis Papers*, Missouri Historical Society, St. Louis, Missouri, are a good source for the negative reactions of Ambassador Francis and other American embassy personnel to Reed's involvement in the Russian revolution. They are supplemented by official State Department records now on deposit in the National Archives. Most pertinent are Records of the Foreign Service Posts, United States Embassy, Russia, 1918 (File 800), and Record Group 59, File 360d. 1121 R25/1-60; the latter also includes documents concerning Reed's first trip to Russia in 1915. (Unfortunately, official documents about his journey to Mexico in 1914 were among those destroyed with Congressional approval.)

Other collections which contain a number of items include the following: *Lincoln Steffens Papers*, Columbia University Library; *Max Eastman Papers* and *Upton Sinclair Papers*, both at Lilly Library, University of Indiana; *Amos Pinchot Papers*, Library of Congress; *Raymond Robins Papers*, State Historical Society of Wisconsin; *Edward M. House Papers*, Sterling Memorial Library, Yale University; *Hutchins Hapgood Papers* and *Alfred Stieglitz Papers*, both in the Beinecke Rare Book and Manuscript Library, Yale University; *Socialist Party Collection*, Duke University Library. The *Andrew Dasburg Papers*, George Arents Research Library, Syracuse University, has letters from Louise Bryant to Dasburg that give insight into her relations with both Dasburg and Reed. The *Oral History Collection* of Columbia University has a number of references to Reed; most important are those in the Ben Huebsch memoir. The *Mabel Dodge Luhan Papers*, Beinecke Library, Yale University, have a few postcards from Reed (she burned virtually all his letters to her), but these are currently not available. The *Walter Lippmann Papers*, at the same library, are now being used by his biographer, Ronald Steele, who was kind enough to share some information with me. There are a few references to Reed in the *Floyd Dell Papers*, Newberry Library, Chicago. Mr. Ronald Preissman of Beverly Hills, California, showed me his small collection of Reed letters, and Mrs. Frances Nelson Carroll of Portland, Oregon, generously let me see the personal letters Reed had written to her in 1909–10.

BIBLIOGRAPHIES AND BOOKS

Granville Hicks, *John Reed: The Making of a Revolutionary* (New York: Macmillan, 1936), contains a good bibliography. The section on Reed's own writings is virtually complete, but there is no guide to manuscript sources (other than the JR MSS) and the section on works about Reed is obviously dated. Wholly devoted to bibliography is I. M. Levidova, *Dzhon Rid: Bibliograficheskiy Ukazatel* (Moscow: Izdatelstvo Kniga, 1967). Ignoring manuscript materials, this book not only updates Hicks in English, but provides an extensive guide to Russian sources, pulling together articles from a wide variety of periodicals and regional newspapers. Unfortunately, my sampling of these Russian sources proves them to be, for the most part, trivial. Many are newspaper articles that may report one or two facts about Reed's movements in Russia, perhaps from an interview with someone who met him, but are largely devoted to warm praise of an American who came to aid the Soviet Union in troubled times. The few that were useful are listed below in the sections on Chapters 18 and 21.

The Hicks biography is a good one, its main shortcoming being a tendency to overemphasize the political side of a man who was not primarily a political creature. Much less satisfactory is Richard O'Connor and Dale L. Walker, *The Lost Revolutionary: A Biography of John Reed* (New York: Harcourt, Brace & World, 1967), which exhibits slipshod research and the Cold War mentality of the authors, who are obviously embarrassed by Reed's genuine radical commitments. Barbara Gelb's recent *So Short a Time: A Biography of John Reed and Louise Bryant* (New York: W. W. Norton, 1973) concentrates on the years 1915–20. Chatty and uncritical, it is dreadfully weak on the historical background, ignores many manuscript sources, and is marred by factual errors. Russian books on Reed are generally brief and seem based on secondary materials; none, to the best of my knowledge, has even used the materials in the Lee Gold Archive at the Institute of Marxism-Leninism in Moscow. They include I. Kramov, *Dzhon Rid* (Moscow: Groslitizdat, 1962), T. K. Gladkov, *Dzhon Rid* (Moscow: Molodaia guarditsya, 1962) and B. A. Gilenson, *On videl rozhdenie Novovo Mira* (Moscow: Politscheskaia literatura, 1962). The most important work in Russian is Abel Startsev, *Russkie bloknoty Dzhona Rida* (Moscow: Ogonek, 1968), an exhaustive attempt to track down the source of all the obscure references in the fragmentary Russian notebooks in the JR MSS.

INTERVIEWS AND LETTERS

Few acquaintances of Reed were still alive at the time this book was being prepared, and not all of those I could track down would consent to be interviewed. Fortunately, the Hicks MSS contained notes from interviews with people who knew Reed, and letters from many others, and Hicks himself talked with me for an afternoon. Carl Binger of Cambridge, Massachusetts, and Andrew Dasburg of Taos, New Mexico, both spent time with me during 1970 and answered all questions put to them. Mrs. Lesley Miller of Gearhart, Oregon, and Mrs. Frances Nelson Carroll of Portland, Oregon, both shared memories of the young Reed with me in letters. Mrs. Pauline Reed, his sister-in-law, who never met Reed, told me many family stories in a series of interviews in her Pasadena home.

2 PORTLAND

Because he was reluctant to write about his childhood, the unpublished autobiographical sketch "Almost Thirty" is the chief source for Reed's early years. Notes for novels made at various times during his life usually give a similar portrait of a lonely, introspective young man at odds with his fellows. Much early poetry and the later work "America, 1918'" are full of sharp pictures of frontier Oregon. Only fragments of a couple of letters and the essay "Best Camping Experience," JR MSS, remain of early writings.

Most informative of the letters Hicks received from Reed's Portland acquaintances were those of Alice Strong. A couple of notes from Harry Reed to his father, Reed Family MSS, tell of Jack's doings. In her unpublished memoir Louise Bryant gives a glamorous, inaccurate sketch of his upbringing. A note from Dr. F. J. Chipman, still in the Morristown Archives, explains his kidney problem in detail.

Background on Portland and sketches of leading citizens such as the Greens and Reed are available in H. W. Scott, ed., *History of Portland, Oregon* (Syracuse: D. Mason, 1890) and Joseph Gaston, *Portland, Oregon, Its History and Builders* (Chicago: S. J. Clark Publishing Co., 1911), 3 vols. Useful are the *Oregonian* obituaries of family members. The probated will of Henry D. Green, in the Multnomah County Court House, gives an insight into his extensive financial holdings. The *Oregonian*, November 16, 1895, carries a lengthy article on Hal Green's suicide. Family movements in homes and jobs can be traced in the appropriate annual volumes of the *Portland Directory*. Knowledge of the curriculum and faculty of the Portland Academy comes from the yearly *Bulletin*. Arlington Club information comes from the *Portland Blue Book* (Portland: Blue Book Co., 1895), and *Officers, Members, Articles of Incorporation, By-Laws and Rules of the Arlington Club of Portland, Oregon, 1910–1911* (Portland, n.p., n.d.), supplemented by *The Arlington Club and the Men Who Built It* (Portland: Arlington Club, 1968). The best insight into C. J. Reed comes from letters written to the headmaster, now in the Morristown Archives.

3 MORRISTOWN

"Almost Thirty" is a good source for how Reed later viewed his Morristown experience. The monthly *Morristonian* gives insight into the school year; besides carrying literary works, it covered sports and other activities. Also useful is the *Salmagundi*, the school annual. The Morristown Archives contain not only these publications but also a file on Reed that includes an important collection of letters from C.J. to Headmaster Woodman, academic grade records and miscellaneous notes and items.

Important letters from classmates and teachers at Morristown in Hicks MSS include ones from Woodman, teacher Arthur P. Butler and students Frank Damrosch, John Kennard and George Allen.

No full history of the Oregon timber frauds has been written. The subject is barely mentioned in Elmo R. Richardson, *The Politics of Conservation: Crusades and Controversies, 1897–1913* (Berkeley and Los Angeles: University of California Press, 1962), 19, 55; and in James Penick, Jr., *Progressive Politics and Conservation: The Ballinger-Pinchot Affair* (Chicago: University of Chicago Press, 1968), 22, 89–91. The conviction of United States Senator Mitchell is treated in "Senator Mitchell and the Oregon Land Frauds, 1905," *Pacific Historical Review*, XXI (August 1952), 255–61. A good contemporary account is Lincoln Steffens, "The Taming of the West," *American Magazine*, LXIV (October 1907), 585–602. Also useful is Frederick B. Stevenson, "The Land-Grabbers," *Harper's Weekly*, LI (June 24, 1905), 898–901, 919–20. Most sensational is S. A. D. Puter, *Looters of the Public Domain* (Portland: Portland Printing House, 1907), a detailed account of the frauds by one of the chief looters, written while he was serving time in jail. I have followed the fraud cases through the pages of the *Oregonian*.

C. J. Reed's role is mentioned in the works by Steffens and Puter. The latter, who made it his business to know bad things about everyone, terms Reed a man "whose official record is without a blemish" (p. 285). For his original appointment, see the *Oregonian*, May 14, 1905. John Reed always exaggerated his father's importance in the cases, and both he and Steffens wrote as if all Oregonians except C.J. opposed Heney and the prosecutions. This is not so. The *Oregonian*, the official voice of the establishment, praised Heney in an editorial as late as March 20, 1907.

4 HARVARD

Along with "Almost Thirty," Reed's unpublished essay "The Harvard Renaissance" is crucial for understanding the undergraduate ferment. Reed works appear in the *Lampoon*, the *Monthly*, the *Advocate* and the *Illustrated*. Especially useful were dozens of pages in the Reed Family MSS torn from the *Lampoon* on which he circled numerous short articles and jokes that carry no byline. The JR MSS contain a wealth of letters from and to friends, lists of courses, grades and activities, programs from banquets and other miscellany, plus many unpublished, sometimes incomplete stories, songs, poems and sketches. Most important is "The Lure of the Life Disperse," his only attempt to evaluate the meaning of college life. Letters to Frances Nelson were lent to the author by Frances Nelson Carroll. For the relationship with Copeland, see JR, "Charles Townsend Copeland," *American Magazine*, LXIII (November 1911), 64-6, and J. Donald Adams, *Copey of Harvard* (Boston: Houghton Mifflin, 1960).

Fellow students are another good source. See Walter Lippmann, "Legendary John Reed," *New Republic*, I (December 26, 1914), 15-16; Robert Hallowell, "John Reed," *New Republic*, XXIV (November 17, 1920), 298-9; Edward Eyre Hunt, "Prophets of Rebellion," *Outlook*, CXXXIX (March 18, 1925), 411-15, reprinted as "Stelligeri—A Footnote on Democracy," in *Essays in Memory of Barrett Wendell* (Cambridge: Harvard University Press, 1926), 311-16. Harold E. Stearns, two years behind JR, described the 1910 political upheavals in *The Street I Know* (New York: Lee Furman, 1935), and gives a good insight into Harvard life in "Confessions of a Harvard Man," *Forum*, L (December 1913), 819-26, and LI (January 1914), 69-81. Important letters from classmates include those of W. T. Pickering, William F. Avery, George W. Martin, Wheeler Sammons and Paul Lieder, all Hicks MSS. Carl Binger, in a personal interview in March 1970, told the author of his relationship with JR. Fred Lockley, "Impressions and Observations of the Journal Man," Portland *Journal*, March 11, 1929, tells something of JR on summer trips home. Later works include Elmer H. Bernard, "Storm Boy," *Harvard Graduate's Magazine*, XLII (March 1934), 236-41, an innaccurate panegyric; Herbert Shapiro, "Steffens, Lippmann, and Reed," *Pacific Northwest Quarterly*, LXII (October 1971), 142-50; and Edwin Bingham, "Oregon's Romantic Rebels: John Reed and C. E. S. Wood, *Pacific Northwest Quarterly*, L (July 1959), 77-90. See also Lincoln Steffens, *Autobiography* (New York: Harcourt, Brace, 1931), 653. A splendid picture of Harvard during Reed's time is Van Wyck Brooks, "Harvard and American Life," *Contemporary Review*, XCIV (1908), 610-18.

Much can be learned from Samuel Eliot Morison, ed., *The Development of Harvard University: Since the Inauguration of President Eliot, 1869-1929* (Cambridge: Harvard University Press, 1930) and Hugh Hawkins, *Between Harvard and America: The Educational Leadership of Charles W. Eliot* (New York: Oxford University Press, 1972). Rollo W. Brown, *Harvard Yard in the Golden Age* (New York: A. A. Wyne, 1948) is an affectionate memoir about the faculty and includes a chapter on Copeland. Edward E. Slosson, *Great American Universities* (New York: Macmillan, 1910) contains a section on Harvard. Frederick Rudolph, *The American College and University* (New York: Alfred A. Knopf, 1962) and Laurence R. Veysey, *The Emergence of the American University* (Chicago: University of Chicago Press, 1965) both are good at placing the university in a context of political and social movements like Progressivism. Calvin B. T. Lee, *The Campus Scene, 1900-1970* (New York: David McKay, 1970), gives a breezy view of undergraduate life-style.

5 EUROPE

The JR MSS contain a wealth of letters and cards to friends, unpublished essays and photos and mementoes of the sojourn. Flashes of Europe appear in a variety of partial manuscripts; the only complete story to emerge is "Showing Mrs. Van," *Smart Set* (December 1913), 123–6. Insight into relations with women is given in a letter from Kate Carew, Hicks MSS.

6 MANHATTAN

"Almost Thirty" provides important memories of Reed's first years in New York, but the crucial contemporary evidence—aside from published writings—is to be found in the JR MSS. Here are not only a vast number of literary fragments, unpublished works, letters to and from friends and family, but also an important scrapbook containing rejection slips, social invitations, ticket stubs and programs from plays, athletic contests, art shows and operas. Some marked issues of *American Magazine*, with marginal comments by JR, are in the Reed Family MSS.

Letters from JR and C. J. Reed to Steffens are in his papers at Columbia University; his *Autobiography*, 653–4, describes life at 42 Washington Square. Laudatory obituaries of C.J. are in the *Oregonian* and the Portland *Journal* on the appropriate days; his will remains in the Multnomah County Court House. Glimpses of days on the *American Magazine* can be found in Ida Tarbell, *All in the Day's Work* (New York: Macmillan, 1939), 258–67. Notes from an interview with her and another with Frank Shay, owner of a Greenwich Village bookshop, are in the Hicks MSS.

7 GREENWICH VILLAGE

In the JR MSS his shifting moods and desires can be followed through letters, especially those to and from friends, and in many unpublished fragments.

There is no reliable and comprehensive work on the development of American Bohemia or Greenwich Village. The best is still Albert Parry, *Garrets and Pretenders: A History of Bohemianism in America* (New York: Dover, 1960), originally published in 1933, a book marred by the occasionally sneering attitudes of the author, a reformed Bohemian. Allen Churchill, *The Improper Bohemians* (New York: E. P. Dutton, 1959), is chatty and anecdotal as it covers 1910–30, while Emily Hahn, *Romantic Rebels* (Boston: Houghton Mifflin, 1967), is an almost worthless "informal history" with some egregious factual mistakes. The chapter "American Bohemianism" in Gilman M. Ostrander, *American Civilization in the First Machine Age: 1890–1940* (New York: Harper and Row, 1972), is an insightful brief survey. Van Wyck Brooks, *The Confident Years: 1885–1915* (New York: E. P. Dutton, 1952) touches the literary Bohemian scene of which he was a part. Ralph I. Bartholomew, *Green-*

wich Village (New York: Champion Monographs, 1920) gives a chatty insider's view, and so does Clement Wood, "The Story of Greenwich Village," *Haldeman-Julius Quarterly*, V (October 1926), 169–85. Charles Hanson Towne, *This New York of Mine* (New York: Cosmopolitan Books, 1931) is a superficial view of "fashionable" literary life from the 1880s on, useful only for showing the vast differences between earlier Bohemians and those of Reed's era.

Scholars have done some important studies of artistic and intellectual life in the pre-World War I period. The best is Henry May, *The End of American Innocence* (New York: Alfred A. Knopf, 1959). Early chapters in Daniel Aaron, *Writers on the Left* (New York: Harcourt, Brace and World, 1961) are especially good on this period, as are those in James Gilbert Burkhart, *Writers and Partisans: A History of Literary Radicalism in America* (New York: John Wiley and Sons, 1968), and Frederick T. Hoffman *et al.*, *The Little Magazine* (Princeton: Princeton University Press, 1946). Several chapters from Robert Spiller *et al.*, eds., *Literary History of the United States* (New York: Macmillan, 1948), especially "The Discovery of Bohemia," 1065–79, "Creating an Audience," 1119–35, and "The 'New' Poetry," 1171–96, are useful as background. Dale Kramer, *The Chicago Renaissance* (New York: Appleton-Century, 1966) covers literary life in that Midwestern center, and Milton W. Brown, *American Painting, from the Armory Show to the Depression* (Princeton: Princeton University, 1955) is a brief survey. A useful specialized study is June Socken, "Now Let Us Begin: Feminism in Greenwich Village, 1910–1920" (Northwestern University: Unpublished Ph.D. dissertation, 1967).

Firsthand accounts are the best way of understanding the excitement of Village life before the war. Floyd Dell, *Love in Greenwich Village* (New York: George H. Doran, 1926) is a series of short stories that tell much about changing manners and morals, and Bruce St. John, ed., *John Sloan's New York Scene* contains selections from the artist's diaries, notes and correspondence from 1906 to 1913. Biographies of writers and artists are legion; among autobiographies, the following were most useful in this study: Floyd Dell, *Homecoming: An Autobiography* (New York: Farrar and Rinehart, 1933); Max Eastman, *Enjoyment of Living* (New York: Harper and Brothers, 1948) and *Love and Revolution* (New York: Random House, 1964); Joseph Freeman, *An American Testament* (New York: Farrar and Rinehart, 1936); Susan Glaspell, *The Road to the Temple* (New York: Frederick A. Stokes, 1927); Hutchins Hapgood, *A Victorian in the Modern World* (New York: Harcourt, Brace, 1939); Orrick Johns, *Time of Our Lives: The Story of My Father and Myself* (New York: Stackpole Sons, 1937); Alfred Kreymborg, *Troubadour: An Autobiography* (New York: Sagamore Press, 1957); Edwin Justus Mayer, *A Preface to Life* (New York: Boni and Liveright, 1923); Harriet Monroe, *A Poet's Life* (New York: Macmillan, 1938); James Oppenheim, *The Mystic Warrior* (New York: Alfred A. Knopf, 1921); Margaret Sanger, *Margaret Sanger: An Autobiography* (New York: W. W. Norton, 1938); Harold E. Stearns, *The Street I Know;* Louis Untermeyer, *Bygones* (New York: Harcourt, Brace and World,

1962) and *From Another World* (New York: Harcourt, Brace, 1939); Art Young, *Art Young: His Life and Times* (New York: Sheridan House, 1939) and *On My Way* (New York: Horace Liveright, 1928). Almost all the works above mention the *Masses*. Parry, *Garrets and Pretenders*, devotes a chapter to it and Hoffman, *The Little Magazine*, part of one. The magazine's flavor may be savored in William L. O'Neill, ed., *Echoes of Revolt: The Masses, 1911–1917* (Chicago: Quadrangle, 1966). Richard Fitzgerald, *Art and Politics: Cartoonists of the Masses and Liberator* (Westport, Conn.: Greenwood Press, 1973) is a useful survey of five major cartoonists.

8 PATERSON

The best study of the IWW, a splendid work that supersedes all earlier ones, is Melvin Dubofsky, *We Shall Be All: A History of the Industrial Workers of the World* (Chicago: Quadrangle, 1969). Information on the strike and the pageant can be found in the following autobiographies: Eastman, *Enjoyment of Living*; Elizabeth Gurley Flynn, *I Speak My Own Piece* (New York: Masses and Mainstream, 1955); Hutchins Hapgood, *A Victorian in the Modern World*; William D. Haywood, *Bill Haywood's Book* (New York: International Publishers, 1929); Harry Kemp, *More Miles* (a heavily autobiographical novel where Reed appears as "Halton Mann"); Mabel Dodge Luhan, *Movers and Shakers* (New York: Harcourt, Brace, 1936); Ernest Poole, *The Bridge: My Own Story* (New York: Macmillan, 1940); Upton Sinclair, *American Outpost: A Book of Reminiscences* (New York: Farrar and Rinehart, 1932) and *The Brass Check* (Long Beach, Calif.: Published by the author, 1928); Mary Heaton Vorse, *A Footnote to Folly* (New York: Farrar and Rinehart, 1935).

Joyce Kornbluh, ed., *Rebel Voices: An I.W.W. Anthology* (Ann Arbor: University of Michigan Press, 1964) is an excellent source book which contains a chapter on Paterson, including outside reports, articles by participants and the program of the pageant. Originals of the latter are rare; edited by Fred Boyd, one of Haywood's lieutenants, a copy of it remains in the Reed Family MSS. Boyd's memoir is in the Hicks MSS. For the Executive Committee financial report, see Luhan, *Movers and Shakers*, 210–12, or the New York *Times*, June 25, 1913. A chapter from Carlo Tresca's unpublished autobiography, "How I Met John Reed," is in the Hicks MSS. The *Outlook* (June 21, 1913), 352–3, is a typical contemporary account of the pageant, balancing admiration for the performance against distaste for the IWW.

9 23 FIFTH AVENUE

Aside from letters to friends in JR MSS and those to his mother in the Reed Family MSS, the best source for this period is Mabel Dodge Luhan's *Movers and Shakers*. Dedicated to Reed, it makes him the central figure in this third volume of her "Intimate Memories." Though the portrait is hardly disinterested,

Mabel gives good insight—sometimes in spite of herself—into their passionate, complex relationship.

Mentioned in all studies of Greenwich Village, the salon is especially well depicted in Steffens, *Autobiography*, and Hapgood, *A Victorian in the Modern World*. Carl Van Vechten's *Peter Whiffle* (New York: Alfred A. Knopf, 1922) gives a thinly disguised, fictionalized account of Mabel as "Edith Dale," and is especially good on both the salon and the Villa Curonia. Muriel Draper, *Music at Midnight* (New York: Harper and Brothers, 1929) is picturesque on the summer of 1913 at the villa. An undated clipping in the JR MSS from the newspaper *Il nuovo giornale* relates the story of the Socialist congress and his appearance there.

Development of Bohemia can be followed in the scholarly works and autobiographies mentioned in the bibliography of Chapter VII. A useful study of the Liberal Club is Keith N. Richwine, "The Liberal Club: Bohemia and the Resurgence in Greenwich Village" (University of Pennsylvania: Unpublished Ph.D. dissertation, 1968).

10 MEXICO

The best of Reed's writing on Mexico, the articles in the *Metropolitan*, form the bulk of *Insurgent Mexico* (New York: D. Appleton, 1914), which has been reprinted by several publishers in recent years. The most important pieces left out are "With Villa in Mexico," *Metropolitan*, XXXIX (February 1914), 72, and "Mac—American," *Masses*, V (April 1914), 8–9, reprinted in Floyd Dell, ed., *Daughter of the Revolution* (New York: Vanguard Press, 1927). Articles in the New York *World* include a portrait of Villa on March 1, 1914, an interview with Carranza on March 4, and five articles essentially about the fall of Torreón, on March 25, 29 and 31 and April 1 and 4, 1914. The unpublished "Mexican Notebooks," JR MSS, while sometimes hasty and confused, show the sharpness of his daily observations, and supplement his published work. His anaylsis of the whole revolutionary situation is "What About Mexico?" *Masses*, V (June 1914), 11, 14.

An interesting view of JR in Mexico is Gregory Mason, "Reed, Villa and the Village," *Outlook*, CXL (May 6, 1925), 1, 3. Of many books on the Mexican revolution, three deal with U.S.-Mexican relations. The most helpful was Clarence C. Clendenen, *The United States and Pancho Villa* (Port Washington, N.Y.: Kennikat Press, 1961), which provides much about the general as well as the international problems surrounding him. Focusing more narrowly on diplomacy is Edward P. Haleys, *Revolution and Intervention: The Diplomacy of Taft and Wilson with Mexico, 1910–1917* (Cambridge: Massachusetts Institute of Technology Press, 1970). Covering the whole historical scope is Howard F. Cline, *The United States and Mexico* (Cambridge: Harvard University Press, 1963 revised). Also helpful are the following: Victor Alba, *The Mexicans: The Making of a Nation* (New York: Frederick A. Praeger, 1967);

R. E. Quirk, *The Mexican Revolution* (Bloomington: University of Indiana Press, 1960); Frank Tannenbaum, *Mexico: The Struggle for Peace and Bread* (New York: Alfred A. Knopf, 1950).

11 LUDLOW

"The Colorado War" appeared in the *Metropolitan*, XL (July 1914), and was reprinted in John Stuart, ed., *The Education of John Reed* (New York: International, 1955), 88–120. Knowledge of the stay in Provincetown comes not only from Mabel Dodge Luhan's *Movers and Shakers*, but also correspondence between JR and both Hunt and Carl Hovey, all in JR MSS, which also include letters from Robert Dunn about the proposed expedition to Kamchatka.

Many labor histories cover Ludlow, but by far the most succinct, incisive account is Howard Zinn's "The Ludlow Massacre," in *The Politics of History* (Boston: Beacon Press, 1969), 79–101. George Creel, *Rebel at Large: Recollections of Fifty Crowded Years* (New York: G. P. Putnam's Sons, 1947), 126–32, gives some local Colorado reactions to the massacre. Further developments in Mexico can be followed in the sources listed for Chapter 10.

12 WESTERN FRONT

Luhan's *Movers and Shakers* and Hapgood's *A Victorian in the Modern World* are both essential as background. Robert Dunn's book on the war, *Five Fronts* (New York: Dodd, Mead, 1915), tells much about escapades with Reed, and his autobiography, *World Alive* (New York: Crown, 1956) adds more information. An article by Dunn in the New York *Evening Post*, February 27, 1915, describes firing from the German trench; it became the source of a controversy over that incident. Ernest Poole, *The Bridge*, mentions JR in Germany. In an interview with Hicks he gave more details, and one with John Kelley described Reed's visit to Portland in the summer of 1914. Andrew Dasburg shared his memories of the trip to Sézanne with the author. The unpublished Boyd manuscript (see Chapter 8) describes JR on the eve of leaving for Europe and England. Arno Dosch-Fleurot, *Through War to Revolution* (London: John Lane, 1931) gives a view of Paris at the time of the Battle of the Marne. Arthur Marwick, *The Deluge: British Society and the First World War* (Boston: Little, Brown, 1965) is good on London in the early days of the war and confirms JR's observations. Karl Liebknecht's role in German Socialism is mentioned in Merle Fainsod, *International Socialism and the World War* (Cambridge: Harvard University Press, 1935).

13 NEW YORK

Luhan, *Movers and Shakers* is the only direct source on their on-again-off-again affair, but it must be used with care (see footnote, p. 212). Villagers' feelings about the war can be sampled in Dell, *Homecoming*, 292–3, and Glaspell, *The Road to the Temple*, 267.

An excellent study of the beginning of the *New Republic* is Charles Forcey, *The Crossroads of Liberalism: Croly, Weyl, Lippmann and the Progressive Era* (New York: Oxford University Press, 1961). Also good is the chapter on "The *New Republic* and the War" in Christopher Lasch, *The New Radicalism in America* (New York: Vintage Books, 1967). Dunn, *World Alive*, 221, mentions the trench-shooting controversy. Reed's lecture in Boston was advertised in the Boston *Herald*, March 3 and 4, and covered there on March 6, 1915. Important undated letters from William Hard and Boardman Robinson are in the Hicks MSS.

14 EASTERN EUROPE

All Reed's articles from the *Metropolitan* appeared unchanged in *The War in Eastern Europe* (New York: Charles Scribner's Sons, 1916), which also incorporated additional material. (An edition three years later by the same publisher dropped several chapters.) JR MSS includes postcards from Russia to Fred and Anne Bursch and Robert Hallowell, and long letters to Carl Hovey from Bucharest and Petrograd, as well as credentials for Reed issued by the American legation in Bucharest, authorizing him to investigate the welfare of American citizens in Galicia and Bukovina. Department of State (Record Group 59) File 360d. 1121/R25, the National Archives, includes a series of diplomatic letters from the American and British embassies in Petrograd to the Minister of Foreign Affairs, all concerning the arrest of Reed and Robinson in Cholm.

Boardman Robinson left a brief note of the jaunt to Moscow; titled "A Memory," it appeared in the *Liberator*, IV (February 1921), 17. More informative is an undated letter from him in the Hicks MSS. Albert Christ-Janer, *Boardman Robinson* (Chicago: University of Chicago Press, 1946) contains a section on the trip, including some letters by Robinson. Negley Farson, *Way of a Transgressor* (New York: Literary Guild, 1936) gives a good view by an outsider of the stay in Petrograd, but George T. Marye, *Nearing the End in Imperial Russia* (Philadelphia: Dorrance, 1929) adds little, though it does confirm Reed's idea that the ambassador knew little about what was really occurring in Russia. The background given in Michael T. Florinsky, *The End of the Russian Empire* (New Haven: Yale University Press, 1931), which chronicles the incompetence and demoralization in Russia, serves to underline the perceptiveness of Reed's account.

15 PROVINCETOWN

Luhan, *Movers and Shakers* is important for the end of their affair. William Greene, now working on a book about Louise Bryant, generously shared with me his extensive research into her background. An undated letter from Boardman Robinson in the Hicks MSS gives a somewhat negative view of Louise.

The birth-control controversy may be followed in Sanger, *Margaret Sanger* and in Emily Taft Douglas, *Margaret Sanger: Pioneer of the Future* (New York: Holt, Rinehart and Winston, 1970). Emma Goldman's involvement may be found in Richard Drinnon, *Rebel in Paradise* (Chicago: University of Chicago Press, 1961), 168–9. The reemergence of Villa as a national issue can be seen in Cline, *The United States and Mexico* and Clendenen, *The United States and Pancho Villa*. An unpublished piece on the Willard-Moran boxing match is in JR MSS. Reed's article predicting an end to the war appeared in the New York *World*, December 26, 1915.

The quarrel over control of the *Masses* is from Dell, *Homecoming*, 251–2; Untermeyer, *From Another World*, 62–3; Eastman, *Enjoyment of Living*, 548–55; "New Masses for Old," *Modern Monthly*, VIII (June 1934), 297–8; and a letter to the editors of the *Masses*, March 27, 1916, in the Amos Pinchot MSS. The five short stories Reed published between November 1915 and May 1916 are: "The Rights of Small Nations," *New Republic*, V (November 27, 1915), 94–6; "The World Well Lost," *Masses*, VIII (February 1916), 5–6; "The Capitalist," *ibid.* (April 1916), 5–6; "Broadway Night," *ibid.* (May 1916), 19–20; "The Head of the Family," *Metropolitan*, XLIV (May 1916). The visit with Ford resulted in two articles, "Industry's Miracle Maker," *Metropolitan*, XLV (October 1916), 10–12, 64–8, and "Why They Hate Ford," *Masses*, VIII (October 1916), 11–12. The convention trip produced "The National Circus," *Metropolitan*, XLV (September 1916), 12–14, 62–4. Other views of Reed on that trip from Young, *Art Young*, 305–7; Johns, *Time of Our Lives*, 236; and Julian Street, "A Soviet Saint: The Story of John Reed," *Saturday Evening Post*, CCIII (September 13, 1930), 8–9, 65 ff.

Mary Heaton Vorse, *Time and Town: A Provincetown Chronicle* (New York: Dial Press, 1942) explains the development of the town as a summering spot. Basic for the Provincetown Players is Helen Deutsch and Stella Hanau, *The Provincetown: A Story of the Theater* (New York: Farrar and Rinehart, 1931), but the best inside picture is certainly Glaspell, *The Road to the Temple*. All memoirs by participants like Eastman, Hapgood and Dell add something. Books on O'Neill naturally describe the Players; see Arthur and Barbara Gelb, *O'Neill* (New York: Harper and Row, 1960); Doris Alexander, *The Tempering of Eugene O'Neill* (New York: Harcourt, Brace, 1962); and Louis Sheaffer, *O'Neill: Son and Playwright* (Boston: Little, Brown, 1968). Elizabeth McCausland, *Marsden Hartley* (Minneapolis: University of Minnesota Press, 1952) adds a little. Reed's play *Freedom* was published in *The Provincetown Plays, Second Series* (New York: Frank Shay, 1916). The serial "Dynamite" appeared in *Collier's*, LVII (August 26 and September 2, 9, 16, 1916), and the two commercial stories were "The Last Clinch," *Metropolitan*, XLV (November 1916), 23–5, 41 ff., and "The Buccaneer's Grandson," *ibid.*, XLVI (January 1917), 24–6, 59ff. Three similarly commercial, unpublished works remain in JR MSS.

Reed's first exposé of the strike in Bayonne was "A City of Violence," New York *Tribune*, October 29, 1916; this was followed by "Industrial Violence in Bayonne," *Metropolitan*, XLVI (January 1917), 12–13, 63 ff. Creel, *Rebel at Large*, 153, mentions organizing the writers for Wilson, and Reed's October letter supporting the President is in the Socialist Party collection at Duke University.

16 CROTON

The unpublished profile of Gompers is in the JR MSS.

Increasing commercialization of the Village can be seen in autobiographies of residents and also Parry, *Garrets and Pretenders*, and Churchill, *The Improper Bohemians*. Of early articles discovering the Village, perhaps "Greenwich Village," *Dial*, LVII (October 1, 1914), 239–41, and "Disillusioned by Bohemia," *Literary Digest*, LIII (September 16, 1916), 688–93, are the best. Anna Alice Chapin, *Greenwich Village* (New York: Dodd, Mead, 1917) is only the first of many guidebooks. The second was Egmont Arens, *The Little Book of Greenwich Village* (New York: Published by the author, 1918), which mentions Jack Reed among the "Who's Who" of Bohemia. Chapin's book is reviewed by Dell in the *Liberator*, I (May 1918), 40–1; the article gives an old-time (four years) resident's view of the invasion by uptowners; this theme is carried further in his autobiography, *Homecoming*.

Arguments by Progressive Senators against the war are summarized in John Milton Cooper, *The Vanity of Power: American Isolationism and the First World War, 1914–1917* (Westport, Conn.: Greenwood Press, 1969). An appreciative view of La Follette's fight against the Armed Ship Bill is in JR, "A Friend at Court," *Masses*, IX (May 1917), 10–11. Reed's testimony to Congressional committees can be found in *Espionage and Interference with Neutrality: Hearings Before the Committee on the Judiciary*, House of Representatives, 65th Cong., 1st Sess. (Washington: Government Printing Office, 1917), 64–5, and *Volunteer and Conscription System, Hearings Before the Committee on Military Affairs*, House of Representatives, 65th Cong., 1st Sess. (Washington: Government Printing Office, 1917), 31–3.

The background of Allied propaganda in the United States is surveyed in H. C. Peterson, *Propaganda for War: The Campaign Against American Neutrality* (Norman: University of Oklahoma Press, 1939). The origins of censorship, the Espionage Act, the Sedition Act and the Committee on Public Information are treated in the following: James R. Mock and Arthur Larson, *Words That Won the War: The Story of the Committee on Public Information, 1917–1919* (Princeton: Princeton University Press, 1939); James R. Mock, *Censorship, 1917* (Princeton: Princeton University Press, 1941); and Creel, *Rebel at Large*. Zechariah Chafee, Jr., *Freedom of Speech* (New York: Harcourt Brace, 1920) contains a section on the *Masses'* problem with the post office. Morris Hillquit, in *Loose Leaves from a Busy Life* (New York: Macmillan, 1934), tells of being a defense attorney in some early cases under the Espionage Act. The conviction of Emma Goldman and Alexander Berkman is treated in Drinnon, *Rebel in Paradise* and Emma Goldman, *Living My Life* (New York: Alfred A. Knopf, 1931).

All the biographies of O'Neill treat the affair between Gene and Louise. Alexander, *The Tempering of Eugene O'Neill* is the only one to suggest pregnancy with Gene's child as the source of her illness in late 1916. Much of the original insight for all these works comes from Agnes Boulton, *Part of a Long Story* (New York: Doubleday, 1958); having married O'Neill in 1917, she was given firsthand (though distorted) information on the affair. The difficulties of living with the free-love ethic is shown in many autobiographies. Dell's story "A Piece of Slat," *Love in Greenwich Village*, 203–35, gives a good portrait of the problem in fictional form. The origins of the *Seven Arts* is treated in James Oppenheim, "The Story of the Seven Arts," *American Mercury*, XX (June 1930), 156–64.

Boardman Robinson in an undated letter and Eric Parson in a similar missive, both in Hicks MSS, describe Reed in this period. Dr. Carl Binger gave the author his memories of Reed at Johns Hopkins.

17 PETROGRAD

This chapter is as dependent upon unpublished material as on that which appeared in print. Because the *Masses* was suppressed, many of Reed's articles from the period never appeared, and the structure of his main work, *Ten Days That Shook the World* (New York: Boni and Liveright, 1919), precluded using the information they contained. Such articles in the JR MSS include "Across the War World," which covers the boat trip to Norway; "Scandinavia in Wartime," principally about Sweden; "Red Russia—Entrance," a description of the trip from Stockholm to Petrograd. Also in the JR MSS are parts of several small notebooks and a number of fragments written and typed on various kinds of paper, all obviously notes made while watching events or typed in the evening. A long "Introduction," written in Christiania in March 1918, was obviously intended as the first chapter of his proposed book; never used, it is valuable for Reed's attempt to put the revolution in historical perspective. The papers also include a letter from Johns Hopkins to his draft board, reports of the physical given by Army medical examiners, and a letter from the board excusing him from military service. Two Reed articles on the revolution appeared in the Socialist New York *Call*. The first, datelined November 13, was held up by censors and not published until November 22 under a seven-column banner, "John Reed Cables the *Call* News of the Bolshevik Revolt." The second, on December 26, was headlined, "Bourgeoisie Forced Bolshevik Uprising, John Reed Says." An earlier article from Stockholm, "World Sick of War, Socialists Tell U.S.," appeared in the *Call* on September 9, 1917.

Accounts by other eyewitnesses that supplement Reed's include Louise

Bryant, *Six Red Months in Russia* (New York: George H. Doran, 1918); Bessie Beatty, *The Red Heart of Russia* (New York: Century, 1918); Albert Rhys Williams, *Through the Russian Revolution* (London: Labour Publishing Co., 1923). Williams' later work, published posthumously and edited by his wife, Lucita, *Journey into Revolution: Petrograd, 1917–1918* (Chicago: Quadrangle, 1969), is an illuminating volume; its freshness is due to the fact that it was written from notes and diaries of the time. More than any other account it is important for understanding Reed. Farson, *Way of a Transgressor* adds to the picture, and Eastman, *Love and Revolution* tells how money was raised for the journey. David R. Francis, *Russia from the American Embassy* (New York: Charles Scribner's Sons, 1921) is good not only for showing how Reed was viewed with suspicion in official circles, but also for the shortsighted anti-Bolshevism of American officials. It is supplemented with material from the David R. Francis collection at the Missouri State Historical Society, which includes a number of official letters between Washington and Petrograd asking that Reed be watched and investigated.

For a general narrative approach to the Revolution, see William Henry Chamberlain, *The Russian Revolution, 1917–1921* (New York: Macmillan, 1935), 2 vols. More analytical is Edward Hallett Carr, *The Bolshevik Revolution, 1917–1923* (New York: Macmillan, 1950), vol. 1. Fainsod, *International Socialism and the World War* is good on the Stockholm Conference; Alexander Rabinowitz, *Prelude to Revolution: The Petrograd Bolsheviks and the July 1917 Uprising* (Bloomington: University of Indiana Press, 1968), excellent on the Bolsheviks during the summer of 1917; Richard Luckett, *The White Generals: An Account of the White Movement and the Russian Civil War* (New York: Viking Press, 1971), a good corrective to oversimplified approaches to the Whites, especially the Kornilov movement; Robert D. Warth, *The Allies and the Russian Revolution: From the Fall of the Monarchy to the Peace of Brest-Litovsk* (Durham, N.C.: Duke University Press, 1954), useful if pedestrian. The Ten Days period is carefully reconstructed in Robert V. Daniels, *Red October: The Bolshevik Revolution of 1917* (New York: Charles Scribner's Sons, 1967). Lee E. Lowenfish, *American Radicals and Soviet Russia, 1917–1940* (University of Wisconsin: Unpublished Ph.D. dissertation, 1968) is a readable chronicle that includes a chapter on the attitudes of eyewitnesses of the revolution. Abel Startsev, *Russkie bloknoty Dzhona Rida* is helpful.

18 CHRISTIANIA

Sources here are the same as those for the preceding chapter. The JR MSS contain notes from Ambassador Francis and Chicherin to help expedite his papers and the telegrams from Steffens. The Raymond Robins MSS at the Wisconsin State Historical Society contain the prospectus for a newspaper entitled *Russische Tageblatt* which was in part Reed's work (see footnote p. 310), and also some letters from JR.

The National Archives contain considerable material pertaining to Reed's activities. Much of this is in Records of the Foreign Service Posts of the Department of State, United States Embassy, Russia 1918: File 800 (Reed, John—Appointment by People's Commissariat as Consul to New York). Included here are notes by embassy counselors, letters back and forth between Petrograd and Washington, and then between Christiania and Washington. Also in the National Archives is the transcription of Reed's interrogation by two customs officials and one military officer. The David R. Francis MSS also contain some material on this period.

Edgar Sisson gives his side of the disagreement with Reed in *One Hundred Red Days* (New Haven: Yale University Press, 1931). Arno Dosch-Fleurot, "World Man Tells of Reed in Russia," New York *World*, October 19, 1920, 8, adds some facts, as does Elizabeth Drabkina, "I Knew John Reed," *New World Review*, XXXVI (Fall-Winter 1968), 17–23, and "Dozlednyaya rech Dzhona Rida," *Novii Mir* (No. 8, 1960), 279–80. William Hard, *Raymond Robins' Own Story* (New York: Harper and Brothers, 1920) is as much hagiography as biography, but useful. George F. Kennan, *Russia Leaves the War* (Princeton: Princeton University Press, 1956), while mistaken about some of Reed's activities, is a splendid picture of the workings of American diplomacy. The chapter entitled "John Reed and the Russian Revolution" in Max Eastman, *Heroes I Have Known* (New York: Simon and Schuster, 1942), 201–37, goes into the affair of Gumberg obtaining Reed's papers to bring to Lenin, but differs from the version told here. Eastman suffered from not having had a look at the State Department documents which show that Robins was involved in this cancellation, a fact later confirmed by Williams in the posthumous volume. Another version of the same chapter appeared in *Modern Monthly*, X (December 1936), 14–21; essentially it is a review of Hicks' volume. John W. Wheeler-Bennett, *The Forgotten Peace: Brest-Litovsk, March 1918* (New York: William Morrow, 1939), is a detailed study of its subject.

19 AMERICA

A memorandum for the new literary magazine is in the JR MSS. The Edward M. House Papers at Yale University contain letters from JR from September 1918 and a long memorandum explaining his problems since returning to the United States. The Hicks MSS contain his testimony during the Philadelphia trial. Indictments and other information on the *Masses* trial and the sedition arrest in September 1918 may be found in the dockets of the Federal District Court, Southern District of New York; the former is Criminal Docket 10–327 and the latter 15–11. Many handbills, flyers and programs from JR's speaking tours remain in his papers. The one article on Russia he was able to place in a commercial publication was "The Case for the Bolsheviki," *Independent*, XCV (July 13, 1918), 55, 72; he also managed to get a letter to the editor into the *Public*, XXI (October 19, 1918), 1312–13.

Reed's Midwestern swing is seen through Art Young's eyes in *On My Way*, 111–12. The *Masses* trial and other events of this period are detailed in Eastman, *Love and Revolution*; Young, *Art Young*; Untermeyer, *From Another World*; Dell, *Homecoming*; Hillquit, *Loose Leaves from a Busy Life*; Benjamin Gitlow, *I Confess: The Truth About American Communism* (New York: E. P. Dutton, 1940); and Charles Recht, unpublished autobiography, in the Hicks MSS. Chafee, *Freedom of Speech* also has a section on the trial.

Problems encountered by people opposing the war can be seen in H. C. Peterson and Gilbert C. Fite, *Opponents of War, 1917–1918* (Madison: University of Wisconsin Press, 1957). The beginnings of what would later become the Red Scare are covered in many works. The best for a long perspective is John Higham, *Strangers in the Land: Patterns of American Nativism, 1860–1925* (New York: Atheneum, 1970). An analytical approach is taken in Stanley Coben, "A Study in Nativism: The American Red Scare of 1919–1920," *Political Science Quarterly*, LXXIX (March 1964), 52–75. Oswald Garrison Villard, *Fighting Years: Memoirs of a Liberal Editor* (New York: Harcourt, Brace, 1939) gives a firsthand account of the *Nation's* brief suppression. Robert K. Murray, *Red Scare: A Study in National Hysteria* (Minneapolis: University of Minnesota Press, 1955) covers the national scene; Julian F. Jaffe, *Crusade Against Radicalism: New York During the Red Scare, 1914–1924* (Port Washington, N.Y.: Kennikat Press, 1972) is a detailed study of one state; William Preston, Jr., *Aliens and Dissenters: Federal Suppression of Radicals, 1903–1933* (Cambridge: Harvard University Press, 1963), focuses largely on the IWW. For the general story of the IWW trial, see Dubofsky, *Industrial Workers of the World*.

20 CHICAGO

JR MSS contain many letters from this period concerning the Left Wing and organizing efforts within the SP, people running for office and intraparty strife; also there is a long, unpublished "Article on the Left Wing," written in the summer of 1919, an incomplete prospectus for a publication to be called "Struggle" (probably this became the *Voice of Labor*), transcribed notes from some Left Wing discussions on what such a paper should contain, and the full outline for "Aspects of the Russian Revolution" (only part of which appeared in print), which shows JR concerned with how the revolution would improve all of society, including the lot of artists and intellectuals. A series of letters between JR and Upton Sinclair show how fair he could be in debate; they appeared as articles entitled "John Reed vs. Maxim Gorky" and "John Reed on the Bolsheviki" in *Upton Sinclair's*, I (August and December 1918).

Various memoirs are good for this period: Louise Bryant's unpublished autobiography; Young, *On My Way*; Eastman, *Love and Revolution*. Reed's impact on fellow radicals can be seen in James P. Cannon, *The First Ten Years of American Communism* (New York: Lyle Stuart, 1962), part history, part autobiography; Benjamin Gitlow, *The Whole of Their Lives* (New York: Charles Scribner's Sons, 1948) and *I Confess*, both of which must be used with care, for Gitlow was a longtime "professional" ex-Communist. George Ashkenaze, "How John Reed Brought the Good News to U.S.," *Worker*, December 9, 1962, 5, shows him in the office of *Novy Mir*, and Emmett Larkin, *James Larkin, 1867–1947* (Cambridge: Massachusetts Institute of Technology Press, 1962) is a solid biography that shows JR's enormous influence on the radical Irish leader. Pyotr Travin, "How Lenin's Letter Was Delivered," in Daniel Mason and Jessica Smith, eds., *Lenin's Impact on the United States* (New York: New World Review Publications, 1970), 118–20, explains his role in the translation and publication of Lenin's "Letter to American Working Men."

For the Red Scare, see titles listed in Chapter 19; Murray's *Red Scare* is the most informative. The small Left Wing publications like *Revolutionary Age* and New York *Communist* are good for following party organization, but some splendid scholarly achievements make the task even easier. Theodore Draper, *The Roots of American Communism* (New York: Viking Press, 1957) is excellent at sorting out the labyrinth of factions, and James Weinstein, *The Decline of Socialism in America, 1912–1925* (New York: Vintage Books, 1969) shows how the party splintered. Also useful is Irving Howe and Lewis Coser, *The American Communist Party* (New York: Frederick A. Praeger, 1962).

21 RUSSIA

The notes for the novel "The Tides of Men" and a short story, "The Ever-Victorious," the Russian notebooks, a copy of the Theses for International Proletarian Education and a letter from Louise Bryant to Margaret Reed, October 20, 1920, which describes their last days together, are all in JR MSS. The Hicks MSS contain an important letter of December 20, 1935, from Lewis Corey (pseudonym for Louis Fraina), who was with Reed in Moscow in the last days.

Works by others who knew JR in the final months include the following: Angelica Balabanoff, *My Life as a Rebel* (New York: Harper and Brothers, 1938) and "John Reed's Last Days," *Modern Monthly*, X (January 1937), 3–6; Emma Goldman, *My Disillusionment in Russia* (New York: Doubleday, Page, 1923) and *My Further Disillusionment in Russia* (New York: Doubleday, Page, 1924); Manuel Gomez, "From Mexico to Moscow," *Survey: Journal of East European and Russian Studies* (October 1964), 33–47; Marguerite Harrison, *Marooned in Moscow* (New York: George H. Doran, 1921) and *There's Always Tomorrow* (New York: Farrar and Rinehart, 1935); Manabendra Nath Roy, *Memoirs* (Bombay: Allied Publishers, 1964); Clare Sheridan, *Mayfair to Moscow* (New York: Boni and Liveright, 1921). One other work, Jacob H. Rubin, *I Live to Tell* (Indianapolis: Bobbs-Merrill, 1934), is so flawed with factual mistakes about Reed's doings, so implausible in its quotes (Emma Goldman promising to be a "good little girl" if let back into the United States), so certain that Reed was totally disillusioned with Bolshevism and so hostile to Communism, that it must be used with great suspicion and care. Other accounts are "John Reed Died Big Figure in Russia: Buried in Kremlin," New York *World*, August 11, 1921, and a letter of January 15, 1935, from his host in hiding in Finland, Hella Wuolojoki, Hicks MSS.

A number of Russian sources shed light on Reed's last year in the Soviet Union. Along with Startsev, *Russkie bloknoty Dzhona Rida*, the following are useful: S. Pavolova, "Dzhon Rid—pevets revoluutsi," *Sovetskiye profsoyuzi*, No. 16 (1963), 40–1; Yu. Grivov, "Razbuzheniya pecniya," *Sovetska Rossiya* (November 5, 1964); Z. Zlatopolski, "Dva Dnya Dzhonom Ridom," *Sovetskaya Latviya*, February 20, 1963. While these are basically memoirs of individuals who met Reed during his travels around Russia, two other sources contain official documents. E. Raidmaa, "On cyvazal sebya tselikom s russkoi revolyutsii. Neicvsestnaya stranitsa o prebivanii Dzhnoaa Rida v. Estonii," *Sovetskaya Estoniya*, February 7, 1960, includes documents from archives on how Reed arranged passage through Estonia in the spring of 1920. *Inostrannya literatura*, No. 11 (1957) contains some brief extracts from Lenin's diaries and letters that pertain to Reed.

For the Communist International and the Baku Conference, see Franz Borkenau, *World Communism: A History of the Communist International* (New York: W. W. Norton, 1939); Michael T. Florinsky, *World Revolution and the U.S.S.R.* (New York: Macmillan, 1933); and Gunter Nollau, *International Communism and World Revolution: History and Methods* (New York: Frederick A. Praeger, 1961).

22 EVER-VICTORIOUS

Details of JR funeral from Goldman, *My Further Disillusionment*; Sheridan, *Mayfair to Moscow*; Alexander Berkman, *The Bolshevik Myth* (New York: Boni and Liveright, 1925); and Bryant, "Last Days with John Reed."

Index

A NOTE ABOUT THE AUTHOR

Robert A. Rosenstone is professor of history at California Institute of Technology. Born in Montreal, he received his B.A. from the University of California, Los Angeles, in 1957 and his Ph.D. in history from that institution in 1965. He worked for the Los Angeles *Examiner* and the Los Angeles *Times*, and taught history at the University of Oregon. The recipient of both a Fulbright and a National Endowment for the Humanities grant, Mr. Rosenstone is also the author of *Crusade of the Left: The Lincoln Battalion in the Spanish Civil War* (1969) and the editor of *Seasons of Rebellion: Protest and Radicalism in Recent America* (1973). *Romantic Revolutionary: A Biography of John Reed* (1975) won a Commonwealth Club of California Silver Medal Award, and was included in the "America Through American Eyes" exhibition at the Moscow Book Fair.

VINTAGE BIOGRAPHY AND AUTOBIOGRAPHY

VINTAGE BELLES—LETTRES

VINTAGE CRITICISM: LITERATURE, MUSIC, AND ART

VINTAGE FICTION, POETRY, AND PLAYS